Poetry for Students

National Advisory Board

Susan Allison: Head Librarian, Lewiston High School, Lewiston, Maine. Standards Committee Chairperson for Maine School Library (MASL) Programs. Board member, Julia Adams Morse Memorial Library, Greene, Maine. Advisor to Lewiston Public Library Planning Process.

Jennifer Hood: Young Adult/Reference Librarian, Cumberland Public Library, Cumberland, Rhode Island. Certified teacher, Rhode Island. Member of the New England Library Association, Rhode Island Library Association, and the Rhode Island Educational Media Association.

Ann Kearney: Head Librarian and Media Specialist, Christopher Columbus High School, Miami, Florida, 1982–2002. Thirty-two years as Librarian in various educational institutions ranging from grade schools through graduate programs. Library positions at Miami-Dade Community College, the University of Miami's Medical School Library, and Carrollton School in Coconut Grove, Florida. B.A. from University of Detroit, 1967 (magna cum laude); M.L.S., University of Missouri–Columbia, 1974. Volunteer Project Leader for a school in rural Jamaica; volunteer with Adult Literacy programs.

Laurie St. Laurent: Head of Adult and Children's Services, East Lansing Public Library, East Lansing, Michigan, 1994–. M.L.S. from Western Michigan University. Chair of Michigan Library Association's 1998 Michigan Summer Reading Program; Chair of the Children's Services Division in 2000–2001; and Vice-President of the Association in 2002–2003. Board member of several regional early childhood literacy organizations and member of the Library of Michigan Youth Services Advisory Committee.

Heidi Stohs: Instructor in Language Arts, grades 10–12, Solomon High School, Solomon, Kansas. Received B.S. from Kansas State University; M.A. from Fort Hays State University.

Poetry for Students

Presenting Analysis, Context, and Criticism on Commonly Studied Poetry

Volume 19

David Galens, Project Editor

Foreword by David Kelly

THOMSON
GALE

ST. PHILIP'S COLLEGE LIBRARY

Detroit • New York • San Diego • San Francisco • Cleveland • New Haven, Conn. • Waterville, Maine • London • Munich

THOMSON GALE

Poetry for Students, Volume 19

Project Editor
David Galens

Editorial
Anne Marie Hacht, Julie Keppen, Ira Mark Milne, Pam Revitzer, Kathy Sauer, Timothy J. Sisler, Jennifer Smith, Carol Ullmann

Research
Tracie Richardson

Permissions
Shalice Shah-Caldwell

Manufacturing
Stacy Melson

Imaging and Multimedia
Dean Dauphinais, Leitha Etheridge-Sims, Lezlie Light, Daniel W. Newell

Product Design
Pamela A. E. Galbreath

© 2004 by Gale. Gale is an imprint of Gale, Inc., a division of Thomson Learning Inc.

Gale and Design® and Thomson Learning™ are trademarks used herein under license.

For more information, contact
Gale
27500 Drake Rd.
Farmington Hills, MI 48331–3535
Or you can visit our Internet site at
http://www.gale.com

ALL RIGHTS RESERVED
No part of this work covered by the copyright hereon may be reproduced or used in any form or by any means—graphic, electronic, or mechanical, including photocopying, recording, taping, Web distribution, or information storage retrieval systems—without the written permission of the publisher.

For permission to use material from this product, submit your request via Web at http://www.gale-edit.com/permissions, or you may download our Permissions Request form and submit your request by fax or mail to:

Permissions Department
Gale, Inc.
27500 Drake Rd.
Farmington Hills, MI 48331-3535
Permissions Hotline:
248-699-8006 or 800-877-4253, ext. 8006
Fax: 248-699-8074 or 800-762-4058

Since this page cannot legibly accommodate all copyright notices, the acknowledgments constitute an extension of the copyright notice.

While every effort has been made to ensure the reliability of the information presented in this publication, The Gale Group, Inc. does not guarantee the accuracy of the data contained herein. The Gale Group, Inc. accepts no payment for listing; and inclusion in the publication of any organization, agency, institution, publication, service, or individual does not imply endorsement of the editors or publisher. Errors brought to the attention of the publisher and verified to the satisfaction of the publisher will be corrected in future editions.

ISBN 0-7876-6958-X
ISSN 1094-7019

Printed in the United States of America
10 9 8 7 6 5 4 3 2

Table of Contents

Guest Foreword
"Just a Few Lines on a Page"
by David J. Kelly ix

Introduction xi

Literary Chronology xv

Acknowledgments xvii

Contributors xix

And What If I Spoke of Despair
(by Ellen Bass) 1
   Author Biography 1
   Poem Text 2
   Poem Summary 2
   Themes 4
   Style 5
   Historical Context 6
   Critical Overview 7
   Criticism 7
   Further Reading 12

The Boy
(by Marilyn Hacker) 13
   Author Biography 13
   Poem Text 14
   Poem Summary 15
   Themes 16
   Style 17
   Historical Context 17
   Critical Overview 18
   Criticism 18
   Further Reading 26

Table of Contents

Childhood
(by Rainer Maria Rilke) 28
- Author Biography 28
- Poem Text 29
- Poem Summary 30
- Themes 30
- Style 32
- Historical Context 32
- Critical Overview 33
- Criticism 33
- Further Reading 53

The Cinnamon Peeler
(by Michael Ondaatje) 54
- Author Biography 55
- Poem Summary 55
- Themes 58
- Style 58
- Historical Context 59
- Critical Overview 60
- Criticism 61
- Further Reading 76

The City Limits
(by A. R. Ammons) 77
- Author Biography 78
- Poem Text 78
- Poem Summary 79
- Themes 80
- Style 81
- Historical Context 82
- Critical Overview 83
- Criticism 84
- Further Reading 93

His Speed and Strength
(by Alicia Ostriker) 95
- Author Biography 96
- Poem Text 96
- Poem Summary 96
- Themes 99
- Style 100
- Historical Context 100
- Critical Overview 101
- Criticism 102
- Further Reading 111

Ithaka
(by C. P. Cavafy) 113
- Author Biography 113
- Poem Text 114
- Poem Summary 114
- Themes 115
- Style 117
- Historical Context 117
- Critical Overview 119
- Criticism 119
- Further Reading 128

Once Again I Prove the Theory of Relativity
(by Sandra Cisneros) 129
- Author Biography 129
- Poem Summary 130
- Themes 131
- Style 133
- Historical Context 133
- Critical Overview 134
- Criticism 134
- Further Reading 152

On Location in the Loire Valley
(by Diane Ackerman) 153
- Author Biography 153
- Poem Summary 154
- Themes 156
- Style 157
- Historical Context 158
- Critical Overview 158
- Criticism 159
- Further Reading 170

Ordinary Words
(by Ruth Stone) 172
- Author Biography 172
- Poem Summary 173
- Themes 174
- Style 175
- Historical Context 175
- Critical Overview 176
- Criticism 176
- Further Reading 185

Perfect Light
(by Ted Hughes) 186
- Author Biography 187
- Poem Text 187
- Poem Summary 187
- Themes 189
- Style 190
- Historical Context 190
- Critical Overview 191
- Criticism 192
- Further Reading 204

Proem
(by Alfred, Lord Tennyson) 205
- Author Biography 206

Poem Summary 206	Critical Overview 256
Themes 208	Criticism 257
Style 209	Further Reading 262
Historical Context 210	
Critical Overview 211	
Criticism 212	
Further Reading 236	

Seven Seeds
(by Jill Bialosky) 237
    Author Biography 238
    Poem Summary 238
    Themes 240
    Style 241
    Historical Context 242
    Critical Overview 243
    Criticism 243
    Further Reading 248

Social Life
(by Tony Hoagland) 250
    Author Biography 250
    Poem Text 251
    Poem Summary 252
    Themes 254
    Style 255
    Historical Context 255

somewhere i have never travelled,gladly beyond
(by e. e. cummings) 264
    Author Biography 265
    Poem Text 265
    Poem Summary 266
    Themes 267
    Style 269
    Historical Context 269
    Critical Overview 270
    Criticism 271
    Further Reading 282

True Night
(by Gary Snyder) 283
    Author Biography 283
    Poem Summary 284
    Themes 285
    Style 286
    Historical Context 287
    Critical Overview 288
    Criticism 289
    Further Reading 310

Glossary 311

Cumulative Author/Title Index 331

Cumulative Nationality/Ethnicity Index 339

Subject/Theme Index 345

Cumulative Index of First Lines 351

Cumulative Index of Last Lines 357

Just a Few Lines on a Page

I have often thought that poets have the easiest job in the world. A poem, after all, is just a few lines on a page, usually not even extending margin to margin—how long would that take to write, about five minutes? Maybe ten at the most, if you wanted it to rhyme or have a repeating meter. Why, I could start in the morning and produce a book of poetry by dinnertime. But we all know that it isn't that easy. Anyone can come up with enough words, but the poet's job is about writing the *right* ones. The right words will change lives, making people see the world somewhat differently than they saw it just a few minutes earlier. The right words can make a reader who relies on the dictionary for meanings take a greater responsibility for his or her own personal understanding. A poem that is put on the page correctly can bear any amount of analysis, probing, defining, explaining, and interrogating, and something about it will still feel new the next time you read it.

It would be fine with me if I could talk about poetry without using the word "magical," because that word is overused these days to imply "a really good time," often with a certain sweetness about it, and a lot of poetry is neither of these. But if you stop and think about magic—whether it brings to mind sorcery, witchcraft, or bunnies pulled from top hats—it always seems to involve stretching reality to produce a result greater than the sum of its parts and pulling unexpected results out of thin air. This book provides ample cases where a few simple words conjure up whole worlds. We do not actually travel to different times and different cultures, but the poems get into our minds, they find what little we know about the places they are talking about, and then they make that little bit blossom into a bouquet of someone else's life. Poets make us think we are following simple, specific events, but then they leave ideas in our heads that cannot be found on the printed page. Abracadabra.

Sometimes when you finish a poem it doesn't feel as if it has left any supernatural effect on you, like it did not have any more to say beyond the actual words that it used. This happens to everybody, but most often to inexperienced readers: regardless of what is often said about young people's infinite capacity to be amazed, you have to understand what usually does happen, and what could have happened instead, if you are going to be moved by what someone has accomplished. In those cases in which you finish a poem with a "So what?" attitude, the information provided in *Poetry for Students* comes in handy. Readers can feel assured that the poems included here actually are potent magic, not just because a few (or a hundred or ten thousand) professors of literature say they are: they're significant because they can withstand close inspection and still amaze the very same people who have just finished taking them apart and seeing how they work. Turn them inside out, and they will still be able to come alive, again and again. *Poetry for Students* gives readers of any age good practice in feeling the ways poems relate to both the reality of the time and place the poet lived in and the reality of our emotions. Practice is just another word for being a student. The information given here helps you understand the way to read poetry; what to look for, what to expect.

With all of this in mind, I really don't think I would actually like to have a poet's job at all. There are too many skills involved, including precision, honesty, taste, courage, linguistics, passion, compassion, and the ability to keep all sorts of people entertained at once. And that is just what they do with one hand, while the other hand pulls some sort of trick that most of us will never fully understand. I can't even pack all that I need for a weekend into one suitcase, so what would be my chances of stuffing so much life into a few lines? With all that *Poetry for Students* tells us about each poem, I am impressed that any poet can finish three or four poems a year. Read the inside stories of these poems, and you won't be able to approach any poem in the same way you did before.

David J. Kelly
College of Lake County

Introduction

Purpose of the Book

The purpose of *Poetry for Students* (*PfS*) is to provide readers with a guide to understanding, enjoying, and studying poems by giving them easy access to information about the work. Part of Gale's "For Students" Literature line, *PfS* is specifically designed to meet the curricular needs of high school and undergraduate college students and their teachers, as well as the interests of general readers and researchers considering specific poems. While each volume contains entries on "classic" poems frequently studied in classrooms, there are also entries containing hard-to-find information on contemporary poems, including works by multicultural, international, and women poets.

The information covered in each entry includes an introduction to the poem and the poem's author; the actual poem text (if possible); a poem summary, to help readers unravel and understand the meaning of the poem; analysis of important themes in the poem; and an explanation of important literary techniques and movements as they are demonstrated in the poem.

In addition to this material, which helps the readers analyze the poem itself, students are also provided with important information on the literary and historical background informing each work. This includes a historical context essay, a box comparing the time or place the poem was written to modern Western culture, a critical overview essay, and excerpts from critical essays on the poem. A unique feature of *PfS* is a specially commissioned critical essay on each poem, targeted toward the student reader.

To further aid the student in studying and enjoying each poem, information on media adaptations is provided (if available), as well as reading suggestions for works of fiction and nonfiction on similar themes and topics. Classroom aids include ideas for research papers and lists of critical sources that provide additional material on the poem.

Selection Criteria

The titles for each volume of *PfS* were selected by surveying numerous sources on teaching literature and analyzing course curricula for various school districts. Some of the sources surveyed included: literature anthologies; *Reading Lists for College-Bound Students: The Books Most Recommended by America's Top Colleges*; textbooks on teaching the poem; a College Board survey of poems commonly studied in high schools; and a National Council of Teachers of English (NCTE) survey of poems commonly studied in high schools.

Input was also solicited from our advisory board, as well as educators from various areas. From these discussions, it was determined that each volume should have a mix of "classic" poems (those works commonly taught in literature classes) and contemporary poems for which information is often hard to find. Because of the interest in expanding the canon of literature, an emphasis was also placed on including works by international, multicultural, and women poets. Our advisory board members—educational professionals—helped pare down the list for each volume. If a work was not selected for the present volume, it was often noted as a possibility for a future volume. As always, the editor welcomes suggestions for titles to be included in future volumes.

How Each Entry Is Organized

Each entry, or chapter, in *PfS* focuses on one poem. Each entry heading lists the full name of the poem, the author's name, and the date of the poem's publication. The following elements are contained in each entry:

- **Introduction:** a brief overview of the poem which provides information about its first appearance, its literary standing, any controversies surrounding the work, and major conflicts or themes within the work.

- **Author Biography:** this section includes basic facts about the poet's life, and focuses on events and times in the author's life that inspired the poem in question.

- **Poem Text:** when permission has been granted, the poem is reprinted, allowing for quick reference when reading the explication of the following section.

- **Poem Summary:** a description of the major events in the poem. Summaries are broken down with subheads that indicate the lines being discussed.

- **Themes:** a thorough overview of how the major topics, themes, and issues are addressed within the poem. Each theme discussed appears in a separate subhead and is easily accessed through the boldface entries in the Subject/Theme Index.

- **Style:** this section addresses important style elements of the poem, such as form, meter, and rhyme scheme; important literary devices used, such as imagery, foreshadowing, and symbolism; and, if applicable, genres to which the work might have belonged, such as Gothicism or Romanticism. Literary terms are explained within the entry, but can also be found in the Glossary.

- **Historical Context:** this section outlines the social, political, and cultural climate *in which the author lived and the poem was created*. This section may include descriptions of related historical events, pertinent aspects of daily life in the culture, and the artistic and literary sensibilities of the time in which the work was written. If the poem is a historical work, information regarding the time in which the poem is set is also included. Each section is broken down with helpful subheads.

- **Critical Overview:** this section provides background on the critical reputation of the poem, including bannings or any other public controversies surrounding the work. For older works, this section includes a history of how the poem was first received and how perceptions of it may have changed over the years; for more recent poems, direct quotes from early reviews may also be included.

- **Criticism:** an essay commissioned by *PfS* which specifically deals with the poem and is written specifically for the student audience, as well as excerpts from previously published criticism on the work (if available).

- **Sources:** an alphabetical list of critical material used in compiling the entry, with full bibliographical information.

- **Further Reading:** an alphabetical list of other critical sources which may prove useful for the student. It includes full bibliographical information and a brief annotation.

In addition, each entry contains the following highlighted sections, set apart from the main text as sidebars:

- **Media Adaptations:** if available, a list of audio recordings as well as any film or television adaptations of the poem, including source information.

- **Topics for Further Study:** a list of potential study questions or research topics dealing with the poem. This section includes questions related to other disciplines the student may be studying, such as American history, world history, science, math, government, business, geography, economics, psychology, etc.

- **Compare and Contrast:** an "at-a-glance" comparison of the cultural and historical differences between the author's time and culture and late twentieth century or early twenty-first century Western culture. This box includes pertinent parallels between the major scientific, political, and cultural movements of the time or place the poem was written, the time or place the poem was set (if a historical work), and modern Western culture. Works written after 1990 may not have this box.

- **What Do I Read Next?**: a list of works that might complement the featured poem or serve as a contrast to it. This includes works by the same author and others, works of fiction and nonfiction, and works from various genres, cultures, and eras.

Other Features

PfS includes "Just a Few Lines on a Page," a foreword by David J. Kelly, an adjunct professor of English, College of Lake County, Illinois. This essay provides a straightforward, unpretentious explanation of why poetry should be marveled at and how *Poetry for Students* can help teachers show students how to enrich their own reading experiences.

A Cumulative Author/Title Index lists the authors and titles covered in each volume of the *PfS* series.

A Cumulative Nationality/Ethnicity Index breaks down the authors and titles covered in each volume of the *PfS* series by nationality and ethnicity.

A Subject/Theme Index, specific to each volume, provides easy reference for users who may be studying a particular subject or theme rather than a single work. Significant subjects from events to broad themes are included, and the entries pointing to the specific theme discussions in each entry are indicated in **boldface**.

A Cumulative Index of First Lines (beginning in Vol. 10) provides easy reference for users who may be familiar with the first line of a poem but may not remember the actual title.

A Cumulative Index of Last Lines (beginning in Vol. 10) provides easy reference for users who may be familiar with the last line of a poem but may not remember the actual title.

Each entry may include illustrations, including a photo of the author and other graphics related to the poem.

Citing *Poetry for Students*

When writing papers, students who quote directly from any volume of *Poetry for Students* may use the following general forms. These examples are based on MLA style; teachers may request that students adhere to a different style, so the following examples may be adapted as needed.

When citing text from *PfS* that is not attributed to a particular author (i.e., the Themes, Style, Historical Context sections, etc.), the following format should be used in the bibliography section:

"Angle of Geese." *Poetry for Students.* Eds. Marie Napierkowski and Mary Ruby. Vol. 2. Detroit: Gale, 1998. 5–7.

When quoting the specially commissioned essay from *PfS* (usually the first piece under the "Criticism" subhead), the following format should be used:

Velie, Alan. Critical Essay on "Angle of Geese." *Poetry for Students.* Eds. Marie Napierkowski and Mary Ruby. Vol. 2. Detroit: Gale, 1998. 7–10.

When quoting a journal or newspaper essay that is reprinted in a volume of *PfS,* the following form may be used:

Luscher, Robert M. "An Emersonian Context of Dickinson's 'The Soul Selects Her Own Society.'" *ESQ: A Journal of American Renaissance* Vol. 30, No. 2 (Second Quarter, 1984), 111–16; excerpted and reprinted in *Poetry for Students*, Vol. 1, eds. Marie Napierkowski and Mary Ruby (Detroit: Gale, 1998), pp. 266–69.

When quoting material reprinted from a book that appears in a volume of *PfS,* the following form may be used:

Mootry, Maria K. "'Tell It Slant': Disguise and Discovery as Revisionist Poetic Discourse in 'The Bean Eaters,'" in *A Life Distilled: Gwendolyn Brooks, Her Poetry and Fiction*. Edited by Maria K. Mootry and Gary Smith. University of Illinois Press, 1987. 177–80, 191; excerpted and reprinted in *Poetry for Students*, Vol. 2, eds. Marie Napierkowski and Mary Ruby (Detroit: Gale, 1998), pp. 22–24.

We Welcome Your Suggestions

The editor of *Poetry for Students* welcomes your comments and ideas. Readers who wish to suggest poems to appear in future volumes, or who have other suggestions, are cordially invited to contact the editor. You may contact the editor via E-mail at: ***ForStudentsEditors@gale.com.*** Or write to the editor at:

Editor, *Poetry for Students*
The Gale Group
27500 Drake Rd.
Farmington Hills, MI 48331–3535

Literary Chronology

1809 Alfred Tennyson is born August 6 in Somersby, Lincolnshire, England.

1850 Alfred, Lord Tennyson's "Proem" is published.

1863 Constantine Peter Cavafy is born on April 17 in Alexandria, Egypt.

1875 Rainer Maria Rilke is born December 4 in Prague, Austria.

1892 Alfred Tennyson dies on October 6 in England.

1894 e. e. cummings is born October 14 in Cambridge, Massachusetts.

1902 Rainer Maria Rilke's "Childhood" is published.

1911 C. P. Cavafy's "Ithaka" is published.

1915 Ruth Stone is born June 8 in Roanoke, Virginia.

1926 Rainer Maria Rilke dies on December 29 in Montreaux, Switzerland, of leukemia.

1926 A. R. Ammons is born on February 18 near Whiteville, North Carolina.

1930 Ted Hughes is born August 17 in Mytholmroyd in West Yorkshire, England.

1930 Gary Snyder is born on May 8 in San Francisco, California.

1931 e. e. cummings's "somewhere i have never travelled,gladly beyond" is published.

1933 Constantine Peter Cavafy dies on April 29 of cancer of the larynx.

1937 Alicia Ostriker is born on November 11 in Brooklyn, New York.

1942 Marilyn Hacker is born on November 27 in Bronx, New York.

1943 Michael Ondaatje is born on September 12 in Colombo, Ceylon (now Sri Lanka).

1947 Ellen Bass is born on June 16 in Philadelphia, Pennsylvania.

1948 Diane Ackerman is born on October 7 in Waukegan, Illinois.

1953 Tony Hoagland is born on November 19 in Fort Bragg, North Carolina.

1954 Sandra Cisneros is born on December 20 in Chicago, Illinois.

1957 Jill Bialosky is born in Cleveland, Ohio.

1962 e. e. cummings dies on September 3.

1971 A. R. Ammons's "The City Limits" is published.

1980 Alicia Ostriker's "His Speed and Strength" is published.

1983 Gary Snyder's "True Night" is published.

1984 Michael Ondaatje's "The Cinnamon Peeler" is published.

1994 Sandra Cisneros's "Once Again I Prove the Theory of Relativity" is published.

1998 Diane Ackerman's "On Location in the Loire Valley" is published.

1998 Ted Hughes dies on October 28 in Devon, England, of cancer.

1998 Ted Hughes's "Perfect Light" is published.

1999 Ruth Stone's "Ordinary Words" is published.

1999 Tony Hoagland's "Social Life" is published.

1999 Marilyn Hacker's "The Boy" is published.

2001 Ellen Bass's "And What If I Spoke of Despair" is published.

2001 Jill Bialosky's "Seven Seeds" is published.

2001 A. R. Ammons dies on February 25 in Ithaca, New York.

Acknowledgments

The editors wish to thank the copyright holders of the excerpted criticism included in this volume and the permissions managers of many book and magazine publishing companies for assisting us in securing reproduction rights. We are also grateful to the staffs of the Detroit Public Library, the Library of Congress, the University of Detroit Mercy Library, Wayne State University Purdy/Kresge Library Complex, and the University of Michigan Libraries for making their resources available to us. Following is a list of the copyright holders who have granted us permission to reproduce material in this volume of *Poetry for Students (PfS)*. Every effort has been made to trace copyright, but if omissions have been made, please let us know.

COPYRIGHTED MATERIALS IN *PfS*, VOLUME 19, WERE REPRODUCED FROM THE FOLLOWING PERIODICALS:

Americas Review, v. xviii, Spring, 1990. Arte Publico Press 1990 University of Houston. Reproduced by permission.—*Dalhousie Review*, v. 51, Summer, 1971 for "Tennyson's In Memoriam as Love Poetry," by Joanne P. Zuckermann. Reproduced by permission of the publisher and the author.—*Journal of Modern Literature*, Summer, 2000. Copyright 2000 Indiana University Press. Reproduced by permission.—*Ploughshares*, v. 25, Spring 1999 for "Social Life," by Tony Hoagland. Copyright 1999 by Tony Hoagland. Reproduced by permission of the author.—*Poetry*, v. 173, December, 1998 for "I Praise My Destroyer," by John Taylor. © 1998 by the Modern Poetry Association. Reproduced by permission of the Editor of Poetry and the author.—*Prairie Schooner*, v. 75, Fall, 2001. © 2001 by University of Nebraska Press. Reproduced from Prairie Schooner by permission of the University of Nebraska Press.—*Raritan: A Quarterly Review*, v. 21, Winter, 2002. Copyright © 2002 by *Raritan: A Quarterly Review*. Reproduced by permission.—*Southern Humanities Review*, v. 7, Spring, 1973. Copyright 1973 by Auburn University. Reproduced by permission.—*The Virginia Quarterly Review*, v. 62, Autumn, 1986. Copyright, 1986, by The Virginia Quarterly Review, The University of Virginia. Reproduced by permission of the publisher.

COPYRIGHTED MATERIALS IN *PfS*, VOLUME 19, WERE REPRODUCED FROM THE FOLLOWING BOOKS:

Ammons, A. R. From *Briefings: Poems Small and Easy*. W.W. Norton & Company, Inc. Copyright © 1971 by A. R. Ammons. Reproduced by permission.—Bass, Ellen. From *Mules of Love*. BOA Editions, Ltd., 2002. Copyright © 2002 by Ellen Bass. All rights reserved. Reproduced by permission.—Bradley, A.C. From A Commentary on Tennyson's in Memoriam. Archon Books, 1966. Reproduced by permission.—Capri-Karka, C. From *Love and Symbolic Journey in the Poetry of Cavafy, Eliot, and Seferis*. Pella Publishing Company, 1982. Copyright © 1982 by Carmen Karka. All rights reserved. Reproduced by permission.—Cavafy, C.P. From *C.P. Cavafy: Collected Poems*.

Acknowledgments

Edited by George Savidis. Translated by Edmund Keeley and Philip Sherrard. Princeton University Press, 1975. Translation © 1975 Edmund Keeley and Philip Sherrard. All rights reserved. Reproduced by permission of Princeton University Press.—Hacker, Marilyn. From *Squares and Courtyards*. W.W. Norton & Co., 2000. Copyright © 2000 by Marilyn Hacker. All rights reserved. Reproduced by permission.—Ostriker, Alicia. From *The Little Space*. University of Pittsburgh Press, 1998. Copyright © 1998, Alicia Suskin Ostriker. Reproduced by permission.—Rilke, Rainer Maria. From *Selected Poems of Rainer Maria Rilke*. Harper & Row, Publishers, 1979. Copyright © 1981 by Robert Bly. All rights reserved. Reproduced by permission of HarperCollins Publishers.—Tennyson, Alfred. From *In Memoriam, Maud and Other Poems*. J. M. Dent & Sons Limited, 1974. Reproduced by permission.

PHOTOGRAPHS AND ILLUSTRATIONS APPEARING IN *PfS*, VOLUME 19, WERE RECEIVED FROM THE FOLLOWING SOURCES:

Ackerman, Diane, photograph by Toshi Otsuki. © 1996 The Hearst Corporation. Reproduced by permission.—Ammons, A.R., E. Annie Proulx, New York City, 1993, photograph by Ron Frenm. AP/Wide World Photos. Reproduced by permission.—Bass, Ellen looking at camera, photograph by Joan Bobkoff. Joan Bobkoff Photography. Reproduced by permission.—Chambord, Chateau, built by Henry II, photograph by Adam Wooliftt. Corbis. Reproduced by permission.—Cisneros, Sandra, 1991, photograph by Dana Tynan. AP/Wide World Photos. Reproduced by permission.—Cummings, E. E. (wearing a dark coat, looking at camera), photograph. The Library of Congress.—Fountain of Persephone in front of the town hall in Pozan, Poland, photograph by Ludovic Maisant. Corbis. Reproduced by permission.—Hacker, Marilyn, 1975, photograph. AP/Wide World Photos. Reproduced by permission.—Hoagland, Tony, photograph by Dorothy Alexander. Reproduced by permission.—Hughes, Ted and wife Carol, 1984, photograph. AP/Wide World Photos. Reproduced by permission.—Lord Tennyson, Alfred, photograph. AP/Wide World Photos. Reproduced by permission.—Ostriker, Alicia, photograph by J. P. Ostriker. Reproduced by permission of Alicia Ostriker.—Rilke, Rainer Maria, photograph. Corbis-Bettmann. Reproduced by permission.—Snyder, Gary, photograph. AP/Wide World Photos. Reproduced by permission.—Stone, Ruth, as she receives the 2002 National Book Award for poetry, photograph Mark Lennihan. AP/Wide World Photos. Reproduced by permission.—Odyssey Sirens, photograph. Mary Evans Picture Library. Reproduced by permission.—Ondaatje, Michael, photograph by Thomas Victor. Reproduced by permission of the Harriet M. Spurlin on behalf of the Estate of Thomas Victor.

Contributors

Bryan Aubrey: Aubrey holds a Ph.D. in English and has published many articles on twentieth century literature. Entries on *Ithaka, Once Again I Prove the Theory of Relativity, On Location in the Loire Valley*, and *True Night*. Original essays on *And What If I Spoke of Despair, Ithaka, Once Again I Prove the Theory of Relativity, On Location in the Loire Valley, somewhere i have never travelled,gladly beyond*, and *True Night*.

Adrian Blevins: Blevins has published essays and poems in many magazines, journals, and anthologies and teaches writing at Roanoke College. Original essay on *Social Life*.

Tamara Fernando: Fernando is a Seattle-based editor. Original essay on *The Cinnamon Peeler*.

Joyce Hart: Hart is a published writer who focuses on literary themes. Original essay on *His Speed and Strength*.

Pamela Steed Hill: Hill is the author of a poetry collection, has published widely in literary journals, and is an editor for a university publications department. Entries on *Perfect Light* and *Social Life*. Original essays on *Perfect Light* and *Social Life*.

Catherine Dybiec Holm: Holm is a freelance writer with speculative fiction and nonfiction publications. Original essay on *The Boy*.

David Kelly: Kelly is a creative writing and literature instructor at two colleges in Illinois. Entries on *The City Limits* and *Proem*. Original essays on *The City Limits* and *Proem*.

Daniel Moran: Moran is a teacher of English and American literature. Original essay on *Perfect Light*.

Frank Pool: Pool is a published poet and reviewer and teaches advanced placement and international baccalaureate English. Original essay on *Childhood*.

Ryan D. Poquette: Poquette has a bachelor's degree in English and specializes in writing about literature. Entries on *And What If I Spoke of Despair, The Cinnamon Peeler, His Speed and Strength*, and *somewhere i have never travelled, gladly beyond*. Original essays on *And What If I Spoke of Despair, The Cinnamon Peeler, His Speed and Strength, On Location in the Loire Valley, Seven Seeds*, and *somewhere i have never travelled,gladly beyond*.

Chris Semansky: Semansky's essays and reviews appear regularly in journals and newspapers. Entries on *The Boy, Childhood*, and *Ordinary Words*. Original essays on *The Boy, Childhood*, and *Ordinary Words*.

Daniel Toronto: Toronto is an editor at the Pennsylvania State University Press. Original essay on *The Cinnamon Peeler*.

Scott Trudell: Trudell is a freelance writer with a bachelor's degree in English literature. Entry on *Seven Seeds*. Original essay on *Seven Seeds*.

Mark White: White is a Seattle-based publisher, editor, and teacher. Original essay on *The City Limits*.

And What If I Spoke of Despair

Ellen Bass
2001

Ellen Bass's "And What If I Spoke of Despair" was first published in the *Missouri Review* in 2001, although it experienced a wider distribution with its 2002 publication in Bass's latest poetry collection, *Mules of Love*. Bass's poem discusses her despair over the actions of modern humans, including the destruction of the environment and genetic engineering, two factors that make her lose hope in the sanctity of humanity as a whole. In her poem, Bass cautions her readers to do their part to fight these issues. Bass wrote her poem at a time when environmentalism and genetic engineering were both hot topics in the media, often leading to polarized debates. Unlike most of Bass's nonfiction works, like *The Courage to Heal: A Guide for Women Survivors of Child Sexual Abuse* (1988), this poem does not deal with the issue of child abuse. The poem does, however, address negative issues, like much of Bass's poetry and nonfiction. A current copy of the poem can be found in *Mules of Love*, which was published by BOA Editions, Ltd., as part of the American Poets Continuum Series, in 2002.

Author Biography

Bass was born on June 16, 1947, in Philadelphia, Pennsylvania. Bass attended Goucher College, where she graduated magna cum laude in 1968 with her bachelor's degree. She pursued a master's degree at Boston University and graduated in 1970.

Ellen Bass

From 1970–1974, Bass worked as an administrator at Project Place, a social service center in Boston. Bass has been teaching Writing About Our Lives workshops since 1974 in Santa Cruz, California. She also teaches nationally and internationally at writing conferences and universities.

In the early 1970s, Bass also began publishing her own and others' poetry. In 1973, she coedited (with Florence Howe) a collection of poems entitled *No More Masks: An Anthology of Poems by Women*. This collection included selections of Bass's own poetry, but she soon began to publish her own volumes, beginning with *I'm Not Your Laughing Daughter*, which was also published in 1973. Her other poetry collections include *Of Separateness and Merging* (1977), *For Earthly Survival* (1980), *Our Stunning Harvest: Poems* (1985) and *Mules of Love* (2002), which includes, "And What If I Spoke of Despair," a poem that was chosen for the 2002 Editor's Prize from the *Missouri Review*.

Bass is most known for her nonfiction works, such as *The Courage to Heal: A Guide for Women Survivors of Child Sexual Abuse* (1988) and *Beginning to Heal: A First Book for Survivors of Child Sexual Abuse* (1993), both of which she wrote with Laura Davis. These books, and others like it, have helped countless survivors come to terms with their painful pasts and move on with their lives.

Poem Text

And what if I spoke of despair—who doesn't
feel it? Who doesn't know the way it seizes,
leaving us limp, deafened by the slosh
of our own blood, rushing
through the narrow, personal   5
channels of grief. It's beauty
that brings it on, calls it out from the wings
for one more song. Rain
pooled on a fallen oak leaf, reflecting
the pale cloudy sky, dark canopy   10
of foliage not yet fallen. Or the red moon
in September, so large you have to pull over
at the top of Bayona and stare, like a photo
of a lover in his uniform, not yet gone;
or your own self, as a child,   15
on that day your family stayed
at the sea, watching the sun drift down,
lazy as a beach ball, and you fell asleep with sand
in the crack of your smooth behind.
That's when you can't deny it. Water. Air.   20
They're still here, like a mother's palms,
sweeping hair off our brow, her scent
swirling around us. But now your own
car is pumping poison, delivering its fair
share of destruction. We've created a salmon   25
with the red, white, and blue shining on one side.
Frog genes spliced into tomatoes—as if
the tomato hasn't been humiliated enough.
I heard a man argue that genetic
engineering was more dangerous   30
than a nuclear bomb. Should I be thankful
he was alarmed by one threat, or worried
he'd gotten used to the other? Maybe I can't
offer you any more than you can offer me—
but what if I stopped on the trail, with shreds   35
of manzanita bark lying in russet scrolls
and yellow bay leaves, little lanterns
in the dim afternoon, and cradled despair
in my arms, the way I held my own babies
after they'd fallen asleep, when there was no   40
reason to hold them, only
I didn't want to put them down.

Poem Summary

Lines 1–6

"And What If I Spoke of Despair" begins with the titular question: "And what if I spoke of despair—who doesn't / feel it?" Immediately, readers are engaged, because the poet is implying that everybody, including her readers, feels despair. In the second through sixth lines, she uses a long sentence to go into more detail about the physical effects of despair on people. The poet uses the phrase "Who doesn't know the way it seizes," to underscore her belief that everybody feels despair at some point or another. Likewise, by noting the blood sloshing through "our" veins, she attributes the rush of blood—the physical side effect of an increased heart rate, one of the side effects of many powerful emotions such as fear or despair—to the community at large. At the same time, the poet is careful to note that, while everybody feels despair, there is no comfort in this fact; grief is still very much a "personal" experience. Having defined her belief that despair effects everybody, although in individual ways, the poet now hooks the reader with a very odd statement that starts in the last half of line six and continues through until line eight.

Lines 7–11

The statement, "It's beauty / that brings it on, calls it out from the wings / for one more song," seems out of place. Bass is deliberately trying to disorient her readers. In the previous lines, she has introduced the idea of despair and grief, so one might expect that the rest of the poem is going to be a dark poem, filled with negative images. Bass takes the exact opposite approach, however. She says that the beauty of nature brings on her personal despair. She notes a very pastoral, natural image, "Rain / pooled on a fallen oak leaf." The pooled rain creates a mirror, in which the poet can see a reflection of a cloudy sky, an image that implies an uncertain future. At this point, Bass still has not explained why these beautiful images of nature make her grieve.

Lines 12–19

Over the next few lines, Bass continues this trend of providing a natural image, yet does not explain why this brings her pain. She talks about "the red moon / in September," which is so massive and awe-inspiring that people feel compelled to stop their cars and get out and look at it. Following this image, at the end of line thirteen and into the next line, Bass switches gears somewhat, with the phrase: "like a photo / of a lover in his uniform, not yet gone." The reader starts to get an indication of why natural images are bringing the poet grief. The hypothetical photo of the soldier in uniform, and the observation that he is "not yet gone," implies that someday he will be. Military service can be a dangerous job, and the poet is noting that even though the lover is alive in her hypothetical photo, he may someday live on only in the photo. In the same way, the poet is implying that someday natural phenomena might only be as alive as the images in a photo.

Although the poet is giving some indication that she is worried over the future life of nature, she has not yet explained why exactly she is concerned. At the beginning of line fifteen, the poet once again turns the discussion from the global, general images of nature, to the specific life of the reader. She says "or your own self, as a child," encouraging each reader to remember back to his or her own childhood. The poet draws on an image that many of her readers will identify with, a family day on the beach. The scene she draws is one of peace and innocence, of a child falling asleep in the sun, without a care in the world.

Lines 20–25

At the beginning of line twenty, however, the poet brings the reader back from this happy memory into the present. It is at this point that the poet confronts the reader directly, "That's when you can't deny it." The poet talks about the fact that elements like water and air are still in existence, and equates these natural elements with a mother's nurturing, which she expresses in simple images: "sweeping hair off our brow, her scent / swirling around us." This underscores the family image that she already used of a child at the beach. Up until now, Bass has combined beautiful images of nature with an increasing sense of doom but has not explained why people should be concerned. In the middle of line twenty-three, however, the poet notes that the child, humanity, is destroying its mother, nature. Ultimately, humanity's pollution, such as the kind created by automobiles, could destroy Mother Nature's ability to nurture. Bass holds all humanity responsible, including the readers: "But now your own / car is pumping poison, delivering its fair / share of destruction." In the middle of line twenty-five, the poet begins to discuss genetic engineering, another factor that she says is destroying nature.

Lines 26–28

She starts by talking about a salmon that has been genetically engineered "with the red, white, and blue shining on one side." The colors refer to the colors of the American flag. Bass is noting the fact that when countries begin genetic engineering, they take ownership of nature and could start literally modifying natural organisms like fish to display a symbol of ownership, in this case the American flag. While Bass feels this is bad enough, in line twenty-seven, Bass notes that genetic engineering sometimes crosses even more profound natural boundaries, such as the boundary between plant and animal—as in the case of "Frog genes spliced into tomatoes." Bass sees this as an affront to the tomato, which she says has been "humiliated enough." Readers might wonder what Bass means by this statement. Most likely, the poet is referring to various genetic experiments on tomatoes that took place around the turn of the twenty-first century, when Bass wrote the poem.

Lines 29–33

In line twenty-nine, Bass uses the idea of genetic engineering to segue into the threat of nuclear war: "I heard a man argue that genetic / engineering was more dangerous / than a nuclear bomb." Through another question, presumably directed at the reader, Bass wonders about the implications of this argument: "Should I be thankful / he was alarmed by one threat, or worried / he'd gotten used to the other?" Bass is noting the fact that the threat of nuclear warfare, while still a threat, has been around for six decades, since the end of World War II ushered in the atomic age. This has given many people time to get used to it. The widespread discussion and use of genetic engineering, however, is relatively new. So for many it can be perceived as more of a threat, because people are not used to it yet. Bass's question also implies, in a subtle way, that if genetic engineering is allowed to continue, perhaps someday people will get used to this, too. At the end of line thirty-three, Bass shifts gears one last time.

Lines 34–42

For these remaining nine lines, Bass acknowledges that she has reason to lose hope that these issues will be resolved: "Maybe I can't / offer you any more than you can offer me." In other words, Bass is saying that she does not have any solutions to offer the reader, and the reader most likely does not have any solutions to offer her. Yet, Bass is defiant and refuses to just sit and do nothing. Her way of coping with the problems addressed in the poem is to confront her despair directly. In this final, extended image, the poet stands in a very natural setting, "on the trail, with shreds / of manzanita bark lying in russet scrolls / and yellow bay leaves." In this setting, the poet embraces despair as she has her own children. Just as she sometimes held her children even when it was unnecessary to hold them, the poet acknowledges that embracing despair is an unnecessary act because it probably will not change anything.

Themes

Despair

As the title indicates, the poet is mainly discussing despair, which is a profound and total loss of hope. In the beginning of the poem, Bass describes the physical effects of despair, the sudden rush of blood through a person's veins when they begin to feel this powerful emotion, the way that despair "seizes, / leaving us limp." Following this introduction, Bass gives readers several examples that explain why she is losing hope. She cites several natural items, such as rain, sky, leaves, and sand, drawing the reader into the natural world. She also talks about lost loved ones, or at least the potential for lost loved ones, by invoking a hypothetical "photo / of a lover in his uniform, not yet gone." This draws the reader into the human world. Throughout the poem, Bass warms her readers up to both of these worlds, invoking ideas with which most readers can identify, such as a family day at the beach, where "you fell asleep with sand / in the crack of your smooth behind." Bass speaks about the natural and human worlds in ways that imply they may not exist, at least in their present forms, someday. Over the course of the poem, Bass reveals that her despair is generated from the fact that the purity of nature and the sanctity of humanity, two things in which she believes deeply, are being compromised in various ways.

Environmental Destruction

The first major way that nature is being destroyed is through pollution. The example she cites is air pollution: "But now your own / car is pumping poison, delivering its fair / share of destruction." Air pollution results from the release of certain chemicals into the air. One of the most common is the release of carbon monoxide, which is a by-product from the use of internal combustion engines found in many vehicles. This is a form of pollution that many people, including Bass's readers, help to create. Air pollution is not the only environmentally destructive thing that humanity creates, but it is the only one mentioned in the poem. This is intentional on Bass's part. Generally speaking, poets aim to utilize as little space as possible to convey their meaning to the reader. Each word has a purpose, and extraneous words or lines are ruthlessly cut, so that the poem can be tightly constructed and have the most impact. Bass realizes that discussions of environmental destruction are generally not limited to one issue, such as air pollution. Like the Earth's ecosystem, many aspects of environmentalism are interconnected, and it is difficult to discuss one environmental issue without getting into other related issues. Bass could have filled this section of her poem with several examples of environmental destruction to get her point across. Yet, this is unnecessary, because most of her audience will understand that air pollution from cars is not the only issue that threatens to destroy the environment.

Genetic Engineering

Genetic engineering, on the other hand, is relatively new, so Bass feels compelled to give more than one example. Although some of Bass's audience may be familiar with the various genetic experiments that are being performed these days, they might not realize the extent to which genetics is being used to modify animals and plants. For this reason, Bass gives one example of each. The first example, a "salmon / with the red, white, and blue shining on one side," demonstrates the sometimes ludicrous applications that humans have for science. Genetic engineering gives humanity the power to change nature any way it wants, in theory at least, and Bass notes that this power is being used in frivolous ways—such as creating signs of ownership like the American flag.

In her second example, which addresses genetically modified food, Bass paints a Frankenstein-like picture of weird experiments involving mismatched parts—in this case "Frog genes spliced into tomatoes." Nature would never create this combination, and Bass is saying that since humanity is doing this, it is threatening the purity of both nature and humanity. Although the poem only directly addresses the genetic engineering of fish and tomatoes, the unspoken fear is that this tampering might eventually lead to tampering with or cloning of human genes. This is why Bass cites one man's argument that genetic engineering is "more dangerous / than a nuclear bomb." While a nuclear bomb can kill an immense number of people, it has only the power to destroy. Some people believe this is secondary to the effects of genetic engineering, which can change humanity itself at the genetic level.

Topics for Further Study

- Read through magazines, newspapers, or other media sources to research the major issues in the debate over human cloning. Plot the pros and cons of these issues on a board, citing at least one media source for each pro and con.

- Imagine that it is a time in the future and you are the world's first human clone. Write a short journal entry that describes what your life is like on a typical day. Be creative and try to incorporate situations that only a human clone would face.

- Research the pros and cons of genetically modified foods. Pick one major associated issue (ethical, political, medical, etc.) and use that issue to write and deliver a speech that explains why you are either for or against genetically modified foods. Use whatever support you can find to make your case and provide supplementary photos, charts, or other graphics, if possible.

- Research the state of environmentalism today and compare it to the state of environmentalism in the late 1980s, in the period following the Exxon *Valdez* oil spill. Research and discuss the effectiveness of environmentally motivated efforts such as recycling and paperwork reduction.

- Research the various processes that are required to create nuclear weapons and other weapons of mass destruction, as well as which countries have the most of these weapons. Create a board that lists all of these weapons. For each one, include a capsule description of the weapon and list the five countries who possess the largest amounts of these weapons.

Style

Imagery

One of the reasons that Bass's poem works so well is her use of powerful imagery that is both positive and negative. The poem begins with a negative image of the effects of despair that cause many to be deafened "by the slosh / of our own blood." The imagery soon turns positive, however, when Bass says "It's beauty" that evokes her despair. At this cue, Bass switches gears and gives the reader several positive images of natural and human beauty. Bass paints natural pictures such as "Rain / pooled on a fallen oak leaf," a sublime September moon, and even the image of her readers in childhood, frolicking at the beach, unaware of anything bad. Because the poet goes to such great lengths to show the good things about nature and humanity, these images give the poem more impact when it turns dark. The images ultimately work as an emotional hook to grab the reader, because the poet's argument, revealed over time through the poem, is that these pretty pictures might not exist in the future if current trends in environmental destruction and genetic engineering continue. At the end of the poem, these two image systems, negative and positive, combine in one final, powerful image of the poet embracing her despair even as she stands among the source of it—the beautiful nature that she fears will someday be destroyed or altered beyond recognition.

Personification

Besides imagery, Bass also relies on personification to explain the depths of her despair. Personification is a technique by which the poet ascribes human qualities to nonhuman objects or ideas. When she first introduces the beautiful nature that she is afraid of losing, Bass talks about it as if it is alive in the human sense: "It's beauty / that brings it on, calls it out from the wings / for one more song." Beauty is an intangible concept. It has no physical form, so it cannot actually call out. In the poet's world, however, beauty becomes a living thing, calling out despair, which in turn sings its mournful song. This is another use of personification, since despair is also an intangible concept that could not literally sing in the real world.

Bass uses other examples of personification in the poem, such as the "humiliated" tomato. The most notable use of personification, however, is the depiction of nature as a human mother. People use the term Mother Nature frequently, as a respectful way of referring to the natural world that has supported humankind since its inception. In this poem, however, Bass is giving Mother Nature actual, mother-like qualities, once again in the human sense. The water and air that the poet references act like a nurturing human mother, "sweeping hair off our brow." Bass's purpose for this soon becomes clear. By making nature a living, human-like thing, the effect is stronger when the poet talks about humanity killing it. Humans destroy plants, animals, and other agents of nature on a routine basis, and many do not notice. The loss of human life, however, is more likely to elicit an emotional response. Because of this, when Bass talks about humanity's "mother" being poisoned by air pollution, it seems like even more of a tragedy.

Historical Context

Environmentalism

Although environmentalism had existed in one form or another for centuries, environmental consciousness as we know it today did not happen until the late 1980s and early 1990s, thanks in large part to a number of high-profile environmental incidents. In 1985, French government agents sank the *Rainbow Warrior*, the flagship of the nonviolent, environmental pressure group, Greenpeace, in Auckland Harbor, New Zealand. The same year, British meteorologists confirmed their earlier suspicion that humans' use of certain chemicals had created a hole in Earth's ozone layer over Antarctica. The 1989 Exxon *Valdez* oil tanker spill, however, was the incident that really galvanized the public. On March 24, the tanker crashed into an underwater reef, dumping more than ten million gallons of oil into the pristine waters of Alaska's Prince William Sound. Shortly after this accident, the media began to cover all environmental issues, including pollution, deforestation, acid rain, the widespread use of landfills and incinerators, overpopulation, and wildlife extinction. This trend continued off and on throughout the 1990s, sparking an interest in recycling and other ecologically friendly methods that many consumers tried. Although environmentalism was still active by the time Bass wrote her poem in 2001, the world was beginning to turn its attention to more pressing issues, the most prominent being the new war against terrorism.

Genetically Modified Food

The 1997 announcement of the birth of Dolly the sheep, the first adult mammal clone, sparked a wealth of debates about cloning, as well as genetic engineering in general. By the time Bass wrote her poem, one of the most heated debates was about the use of genetic engineering to modify foods. A massive protest movement began in Great Britain and spread to the rest of Europe and the United States at the turn of the twenty-first century. Proponents of genetically modified (GM) foods claimed that crops could be made that were resistant to attacks by insects. They also stated that they could genetically engineer crops that included vaccines, which could in turn help fight diseases like hepatitis B. Opponents claimed that scientists were tampering too much with nature and that researchers could not possibly predict all of the potential consequences of such measures. Many people were also concerned about the commercialization of engineered crops. Large firms in the United States bought up many varieties of seeds, and some speculated that in the future the world's crops could be owned by a few companies who would determine the fate of much of the world's food supply.

Despite the controversy, scientists continued to study and implement new genetic methods. In 2001, researchers at Cornell University identified a gene in tomato plants that helps to determine the size of the tomato fruit. This landmark discovery caused some to speculate that crops in the future might be engineered to larger, previously unattainable sizes. Proponents of genetically modified foods say that larger fruits could be used to help wipe out starvation on a global level, since each fruit could feed more people.

Critical Overview

One searches in vain for criticism on Bass's "And What If I Spoke of Despair" or any of her poetry, for that matter. The most likely reason for this is that Bass is known mostly for her self-help books designed to help childhood survivors of sexual abuse, the most famous of which is *The Courage to Heal* (1988). Bass has also written *Free Your Mind: The Book for Gay, Lesbian and Bisexual Youth* (1996), a book designed to guide gay, lesbian, and bisexual youth through sexual-identity issues. "And What If I Spoke of Despair," while different in theme than most of Bass's other works, still deals with negative issues—the destruction of the environment and genetic engineering, as opposed to child abuse.

Criticism

Ryan D. Poquette

Poquette has a bachelor's degree in English and specializes in writing about literature. In the following essay, Poquette discusses Bass's use of opposites, symbolism, and metaphor in her poem.

Throughout history, poets have often written elegies—mournful, sorrowful poetry that expresses despair over something that is gone, generally something that was once living and is now dead. In most cases, the poet writes about a person or group of people that have passed away. Bass's

> *While many poets have talked about the positive aspects of childhood, in this poem childhood, like the beauty of nature, is a negative thing because it indicates something positive that is gone."*

poem is slightly different. Her elegy mourns the loss of nature itself, which is being altered by human intervention through processes such as environmental destruction and genetic engineering. Since her poem is mourning the loss of something, it does not differ in a basic sense from any other elegy. Bass's poem does have one huge difference, however. Her poem is an elegy for something that is not yet dead. As she is writing her poem, nature is still alive. Bass's point is that it will not be alive, or at least will not be alive in the same form, if current human interventions continue in the future. Bass uses several techniques to convince her readers to mourn the loss of something that is not yet gone, including juxtaposition of opposites and the use of symbolism and metaphor.

Bass's poem employs several techniques to give it a powerful effect. The first of these, and the technique that gives the poem its overall structure, is the juxtaposition of opposites. Throughout the poem, Bass bounces back and forth from positive to negative images and ideas, beginning with the overall negative idea of despair itself. Despair is a monumental feeling that affects everybody, as Bass notes when she says "who doesn't / feel it?" While despair affects everybody, it also does so in ways that are unique to each person. Although each person feels the same rushing of blood that is the physical side effect of powerful emotions like despair, Bass says that this blood rushes "through the narrow, personal / channels of grief." This image of personal grief only lasts for the first six lines.

At this point, Bass juxtaposes the negative image of despair with the positive image of beauty: "It's beauty / that brings it on, calls it out from the wings / for one more song." Here, Bass identifies several positive images of nature, such as rain, which pools "on a fallen oak leaf." She also reflects on the image of a beautiful September moon. Yet, even in the midst of these positive images, she carries the thread of negativity. For example, while the rain on the leaf is beautiful, it also reflects "the pale cloudy sky." The cloudy sky implies an uncertain future; it might rain again or it might not. Images like this draw on both the positive and negative feelings that the poet is trying to convey. Bass also uses this juxtaposition technique in her discussion of the September moon, which she says people are drawn to stare at, "like a photo / of a lover in his uniform, not yet gone." While the image of the beautiful red moon is inherently positive, the photo of the soldier has negative implications, namely of the possibility of the soldier's death. People who sign up for or are drafted into military service recognize that there is always the chance they might not return from fighting. By using a photo of a loved one in uniform, an inherently positive image, and juxtaposing this image with the possibility of the soldier's death, Bass once again carries the thread of negativity, albeit in a subtle sense.

This juxtaposition continues throughout the poem in several ways. Bass juxtaposes a pleasant image of a happy childhood day at the beach "on that day your family stayed / at the sea, watching the sun drift down" with the direct address to the reader: "That's when you can't deny it." This abrupt switch from a dream-like memory to an accusation-style directive produces a negative feeling in the reader, which only continues as the poem juxtaposes a living Mother Earth with the human-produced poisons that are killing her, salmon that have been genetically enhanced to display signs of ownership, and tomatoes that have been crossed with frogs.

In addition to juxtaposing these images and ideas, Bass also chooses her words very carefully, in many cases selecting words and phrases that have symbolic meanings. A symbol is a physical object, action, or gesture that also represents an abstract concept, without losing its original identity. Symbols appear in literature in one of two ways. They can be local symbols, meaning that their symbolism is only relevant within a specific literary work. They can also be universal symbols, meaning that their symbolism is based on traditional associations that are widely recognized, regardless of context. The poem relies on the latter type. Early in the poem, Bass uses the image of blood rushing through a person's veins to indicate the physical effects of despair, as noted above. There is a second purpose, however. Blood is a universal symbol that is often used to denote violence. Many of the negative images that Bass goes on to describe in the poem—such as the air pollution—imply violence, at least indirectly. The pollution is destructive, and is killing Mother Earth, just as a "nuclear bomb" has drastic and violent effects on the Earth. Even genetic engineering is considered dangerous because it disrupts the natural order of things. All of these are human inventions. Humans in general are often described as destructive animals, so Bass's use of the blood symbol is an effective, if subtle, way to underscore the theme of human-induced destruction.

Other potent symbols in the poem include childhood. Children, and childhood in general, is often a symbol for innocence, since most children are not aware of, nor understand, the various negative aspects of humanity. The example that Bass uses of the child at the beach underscores this idea of the innocence of childhood: "watching the sun drift down, / lazy as a beach ball, and you fell asleep with sand / in the crack of your smooth behind." The image is one of peace. The child does not have a care in the world and so can drift off to sleep with no worries. Even the use of the word "smooth" denotes the difference between children, whose smooth skin is a universal sign of youth, and adults, who become more wrinkled and haggard over time.

This symbol is ultimately not positive. While many poets have talked about the positive aspects of childhood, in this poem childhood, like the beauty of nature, is a negative thing because it indicates something positive that is gone. Bass's readers are no longer children. They can no longer simply fall asleep on a beach without a care in the world; they must face the negative issues of humanity. Likewise, Mother Nature is changing. The various forms of pollution will have an effect on her, changing her appearance just as time marks the smooth skin of a baby with wrinkles. Unlike the human process of aging, however, the destruction of the Earth's environment is not natural and could be prevented.

It is this realization that leads to the most powerful image in the poem. She "cradled despair / in my arms, the way I held my own babies." A metaphor is a technique where the poet gives an object a secondary meaning that does not normally belong to it. Bass does not literally mean that despair is one of her children, a situation that is physically impossible in the real world. Metaphorically speaking, however, and within the context of the poem, Bass does embrace her despair like she would one of her babies. The idea of cradling a negative emotion like despair is strange and sets up a compelling image for readers. This is especially true, since cradling is a protective gesture, and is generally considered a positive thing. As Bass notes, this maternal, protective instinct is hard to shut off sometimes. She remembers back to the time when she "held my own babies / after they'd fallen asleep, when there was no / reason to hold them." Despite the fact that the gesture was unnecessary, Bass notes that she "didn't want to put them down." Likewise, Bass feels the same way about her despair.

This idea, ultimately, leads to Bass's main point. She recognizes that there is probably nothing she, or any one person, can do to reverse the trends of environmental destruction, genetic engineering, and other human factors that are destroying nature and humanity as she knows it. Yet, she refuses to let her despair go and move on with her life. Holding on to these powerful emotions is the lesser of two negative choices. For the poet, it is better to mourn the future loss of nature and humanity, even if her suffering has no effect on a global scale, than to put her emotions aside and perhaps become as barren as life itself may be in the future.

Source: Ryan D. Poquette, Critical Essay on "And What If I Spoke of Despair," in *Poetry for Students*, Gale, 2003.

Bryan Aubrey

Aubrey holds a Ph.D. in English and has published many articles on twentieth-century literature. In this essay, Aubrey discusses the poet's protest against genetic engineering.

Bass's "And What If I Spoke of Despair" is a poem of passive protest. The poet sets appreciation of nature and her memories of childhood innocence against the ugly fact of environmental degradation caused by human activities. The despair the speaker feels is because she apparently sees no way of preventing or reversing the threat to the human environment. Instead of pursuing action to remedy the situation, the speaker concludes by turning her mind in on itself, examining the feeling of despair and musing over what attitude to adopt to it.

The poem mentions two man-made disruptions of the beauty of nature that the poet sees in phenomena, such as rain gathered on a fallen oak leaf or a full moon in September. The first is the pollution caused by the gasoline-powered automobile, "pumping poison, delivering its fair / share of destruction." The pollution caused by automobiles is due to the carbon dioxide they emit, which is one

> *The idea that living organisms can be patented by profit-driven private corporations is disturbing to many people. How can life be 'owned' in this way, they argue."*

of the chief causes of the phenomenon of global warming. Although the causes of global warming have long been known, the world community has still to take effective measures to combat it. Bass brings the problem home to the reader in a personal way by saying it is "your own car" that is doing the poisoning (by which she means herself, but the reader feels the jab too). In other words, the polluting is not something that is being done to people against their will or unbeknownst to them by some large corporation that can be conveniently demonized; ordinary citizens are doing it themselves.

The pollution caused by the automobile is a well-known fact. Less well known is the second target of the poet, to which Bass devotes much more space. This is the genetic engineering (GE) of food crops, fish, and animals that has become widespread since the mid-1990s.

Genetic engineering is the process by which scientists, using what are called recombinant DNA techniques, alter the genes of an organism. Genes carry the information that specifies the structures of an organism. When genes are individually manipulated, it is possible to cross the species barrier and create organisms that are not found in nature. The ostensible purpose is to make the food more useful or convenient for humans. For example, in genetic engineering, genes from arctic flounder, which give the flounder its "antifreeze" qualities, are spliced into a tomato so that the tomato is able to withstand cold temperatures and avoid frost damage.

Being forced to accommodate the genes of a fish was not the first indignity to be suffered by the "humiliated" tomato of the poem. The tomato was also the first food to be genetically engineered and sold to consumers. This was in the form of the Flavr

What Do I Read Next?

- Over the past two decades, Bass's *The Courage to Heal: A Guide for Women Survivors of Child Sexual Abuse* (1988), written with Laura Davis, has become one of the standard self-help works for abuse survivors.

- Bass's first nonfiction book is a collection of writings by women survivors of abuse: *I Never Told Anyone: Writings by Women Survivors of Child Sexual Abuse* (co-edited with Louise Thornton).

- The end of the world, by man-made or natural disasters, has been a favorite topic of science fiction writers for the last century. In *Bangs and Whimpers: Stories about the End of the World* (1999), editor James Frenkel collects nineteen apocalyptic tales by noted authors, including Isaac Asimov, Arthur C. Clarke, Connie Willis, and Robert Heinlein.

- Aldous Huxley's *Brave New World* (1932) is a nightmarish vision of what could happen in the future if politics and genetic technology supersede humanity. Huxley's novel depicts a futuristic, "ideal" world where there is no sickness, disease, or war. However, to achieve this ideal, people are mass-produced in test tubes and social classes are created through genetic manipulations that predetermine a person's intelligence and body type.

- Henry David Thoreau's *Walden; or, Life in the Woods* (1854), which is a collection of essays, chronicles Thoreau's attempts to get away from human civilization by living on his own in the woods. Today, the book is generally known by the shorter name of *Walden*.

Savr tomato, made by Calgene, that had been engineered to stay firm for longer, thus acquiring a longer shelf life. The Food and Drug Administration (FDA) approved it for sale in 1994. The Flavr Savr tomato was a commercial failure, however, since consumers resisted the idea of a genetically engineered product. It was withdrawn from the market in 1996.

Critics of genetic engineering claim that foods produced by use of recombinant DNA techniques may not be safe and may also damage the environment. A case in point, as highlighted in the poem, is that of salmon. By the use of foreign growth hormone genes, select salmon have been genetically engineered to grow to market size in half the time it takes normal salmon. Some ecologists fear that such salmon (which have not yet been approved by the FDA for human consumption) will escape from fish farms and mix with the wild salmon population. The ecological effects this might produce are unknown. A study at Purdue University concluded that genetically engineered salmon could eradicate natural populations of wild fish. This is because the genetically engineered male salmon would be larger at sexual maturity and would thereby attract more mates, and so would quickly spread the genetically engineered characteristics to wild populations.

The attempt to create GE salmon has already had unwanted effects. According to a report by the Associated Press in 2000 (referred to in Cummins and Lilleston's *Genetically Engineered Food*), one company in New Zealand decided to discontinue its interest in GE salmon because of fear of where the technology could lead. Some of the salmon had deformed heads and other abnormalities.

Bearing in mind this and other concerns about the ecological effects, still untested and unknown, that GE organisms may have, the immense ramifications of genetic engineering can be readily understood. As Suzanne Wuerthele (quoted in Cummins and Lilleston), a toxicologist with the Environmental Protection Agency, said in 2000, "This is probably one of the most technologically powerful developments the world has ever seen. It's the biological equivalent of splitting the atom." This explains Bass's comments in the poem that she heard a man say that genetic engineering is "more dangerous / than a nuclear bomb."

What drives the recent explosion of genetically engineered products, advocates say, is a desire to grow better food and to solve the world's food problem. Opponents say it is really about over-enthusiastic scientific experimentation allied with the desire for corporate profits. The salmon in the poem is red, white, and blue—not literally, but because it has been patented in the United States by the company that developed it. Virtually all genetically engineered foods, even though the companies that create them are often multinational, have been granted U.S. patents. A patent gives the owner the exclusive right to an invention and any profit that accrues from it. Patents on living organisms have been allowed since a U.S. Supreme Court decision in 1980. The patenting of a product, whether animal, plant, or seed, allows the companies concerned to reap a speedy return on the massive investments they put into the development of genetically engineered organisms.

The idea that living organisms can be patented by profit-driven private corporations is disturbing to many people. How can life be "owned" in this way, they argue. Add to this the fear that genetic engineering is in any case a violation of the integrity of nature, and the impulse that drives "And What If I Spoke of Despair" becomes clear. Nature is no longer nature as it came fresh from God's hands, with inviolable barriers placed between species, but a man-made jumble, created out of partial, highly fallible scientific knowledge that could cause irreversible damage to the fragile, interdependent ecosphere that humans share with all other life. Once a genetically engineered organism is released into the environment, for good or ill, it can never be recalled.

So, the speaker in Bass's poem feels despair, and she feels it, the poem hints, not just for herself but also for the young, who must live with the legacy of the previous generation's mistakes. The images of childhood innocence—children playing in the sand, babies sleeping in the arms of their mother—add poignancy to the poet's belief that nature, which has sustained humanity throughout its existence as a species, has now become the victim of the humans it nourishes. It is as if the child has turned on the mother and forgotten its filial obligations. This analogy is suggested by the recurring tender images of human mother and child. These serve as an ironic commentary on the ruptured relationship between Mother Nature and her human children, which has been violated by the carelessness and selfishness of the child.

The speaker's despair at humanity's arrogance and foolishness is not, many would say, surprising. She is not the first and will not be the last to feel that way. What is perhaps surprising is her unusually passive, contemplative reaction to the ills she depicts. Many people who feel the way she appears to feel take courage from action. They actively oppose what they believe is wrong and encourage others to do so as well. The poet's attitude is quite different. She ceases, it seems, to think further about what Mother Nature suffers at the hands of her children and returns to an exploration of the feeling of despair with which the poem began. Rather than examining the reasons why despair has appeared in her life, she contemplates the feeling as an object in itself. She seems to be weighing different ways of dealing with this emotion, exploring what it really might be and what possibilities lie within it. The emphasis has shifted from the outer world, with its hopeless rash of insoluble problems, to the inner world, full of mysterious possibilities. The speaker wonders what would happen if she were to embrace the feeling of despair as if it were something to be loved and cherished. She imagines a situation in which, surrounded by examples of nature's own beauty, she might "cradle" despair. This at first seems a curiously passive way to end a poem that has expressed such a keen awareness of social and environmental problems. One might perhaps call it a fatalistic or pessimistic attitude. It is as if, renouncing all hope, a condemned prisoner has attained a state of calm: nothing can be done, so the inevitable fate must be embraced.

It may also be much more than this. The last eight lines of the poem hint at the speaker's readiness to explore a counterintuitive method of dealing with a negative, strength-sapping emotion such as despair. Rather than fighting against it, which is the normal human instinct, the poet suggests accepting it. Perhaps the belief that informs the poet at this point is that to fight against an emotion only has the effect of making it stronger; to accept it lessens its grip. Embracing despair rather than running from it therefore offers, paradoxically, a way beyond it. At least this is what the speaker seems to envision, although she does not actually take the proposed step. Her thought remains at the stage of "what if"—an approach contemplated but not yet taken. She clearly hopes, at some level of her being, that like a fairy tale in which the feared monster turns into a charming prince, the emotion she experiences as despair may turn out to be, once known and welcomed, no more substantial than a cloud that temporarily hides the sun. For there is no doubt that this poem that begins in despair ends with a startling image of serenity and happiness.

Source: Bryan Aubrey, Critical Essay on "And What If I Spoke of Despair," in *Poetry for Students*, Gale, 2003.

Sources

Bass, Ellen, "And What If I Spoke of Despair," in *Mules of Love*, BOA Editions, 2002, pp. 78–79.

Cummins, Ronnie, and Benn Lilleston, *Genetically Engineered Food: A Self-Defense Guide for Consumers*, Marlowe, 2000, pp. 17, 59.

Steinberg, Mark L., and Sharon D. Cosloy, *The Facts on File Dictionary of Biotechnology and Genetic Engineering*, rev. ed., Checkmark Books, 2001.

Yoon, C. K., "Altered Salmon Leading Way to Dinner Plates, but Rules Lag," in the *New York Times*, May 1, 2000, p. A1.

Further Reading

McGee, Glenn, ed., *The Human Cloning Debate*, 3d ed., Berkeley Hills Books, 2002.

> First published after the 1997 cloning of the sheep Dolly, this updated collection of essays outlines the major ethical issues involved in human cloning. It also gives a comprehensive overview, in layperson's terms, of the science involved in cloning.

Nader, Ralph, and Martin Teitel, *Genetically Engineered Food: Changing the Nature of Nature*, 2d ed., Inner Traditions International, 2001.

> Nader, a well-known environmentalist and Green Party political candidate, and Teitel give a thorough overview of how food is genetically engineered. The authors also examine the potential ethical and environmental consequences of genetically engineered food.

Schor, Juliet, and Betsy Taylor, eds., *Sustainable Planet: Solutions for the Twenty-First Century*, Beacon Press, 2003.

> Schor and Taylor, both involved administratively with the Center for a New American Dream (CNAD), compile sixteen essays from a variety of environmental commentators. The mission of CNAD is to protect the environment, enhance the quality of life, and promote social justice. Each essay offers suggestions for how to achieve this goal.

Stock, Gregory, *Redesigning Humans: Our Inevitable Genetic Future*, Houghton Mifflin, 2002.

> Stock is the director of the Program of Medicine, Technology and Society for the School of Medicine at the University of California, Los Angeles. In this book, Stock discusses his belief that the same genetic engineering that is being used to redesign natural foods like tomatoes will also be used to redesign humans at the genetic level.

The Boy

Marilyn Hacker
1999

Marilyn Hacker's poem "The Boy" first appeared in the *Breadloaf Anthology of Contemporary American Poetry* in 1999 and is the opening poem in her 2000 collection, *Squares and Courtyards*. Written in eight rhyming stanzas, the poem explores the roles of gender, race, and writing in shaping identity. Hacker is known for her new formalist meditations on history, womanhood, and the "stuff" of everyday life. This poem addresses all three. As the narrator imagines herself as a boy completing a school assignment, the poet muses on the boy's life, his way of looking at the world, his relationship to gender, and his own identity as a Jew. Part fantasy, part character study, "The Boy" investigates the fluidity of human identity, pokes at the boundaries that separate one person's life from another's, and interrogates the ways in which human beings are called on to be one thing or another.

Hacker wrote the poem in response to a book review by Robyn Selman in the *Village Voice* of poem collections by Rafael Campo and Rachel Weztsteon. In the review, Selman describes the position of the young male poet as someone who sits at a window and looks out at the world and the position of the young female poet as someone who examines the room in which she sits—the room of the self.

Author Biography

Editor, translator, and teacher, Marilyn Hacker is also one of the most sophisticated poets writing in

Marilyn Hacker

America today. Known for the acuteness of her observations as well as her formal inventiveness, Hacker creates tight, elaborate poems that have the quality of sculpture. Hacker's poems stand out for their craft and intelligence.

Hacker was born November 27, 1942, to business consultant Albert Abraham Hacker and teacher Hilda Rosengarten Hacker, both Jewish immigrants. She grew up in the Bronx, graduating from the Bronx School of Science and enrolling in New York University at the age of fifteen. In 1961, she married novelist Samuel R. Delany. From 1969 to 1971, they edited *Quark: A Quarterly of Speculative Fiction*. This was the first of many editorial positions she would hold. Hacker graduated from New York University in 1964. In 1974, she and Delaney separated.

Hacker's first collection of poems, *Presentation Piece*, published in 1974, was a Lamont Poetry Selection and won the National Book Award in 1975. Critics lauded her deft handling of complicated subject matter and the original manner in which she interwove personal and political themes. With her next book, *Separations* (1976), Hacker established herself as a master of traditional forms, such as the sestina, villanelle, and pantoum, and as one of the best younger American poets alive. Living openly as a lesbian since the late 1970s, Hacker has also made her poetry the place in which she explores questions of identity, particularly how the self is fashioned through discourses of sexuality, gender, class, and ethnicity.

In addition to the National Book Award, Hacker has received a number of other awards for her poetry including a New York Poetry Center Discovery Award in 1973, the Jenny McKean Moore Fellowship, 1976–1977, and fellowships from the Guggenheim Foundation, 1980–1981, the National Endowment for the Arts, 1985, and the Ingram Merrill Foundation, 1985. She has also won a Lambda Literary Award and the Lenore Marshall Award from the *Nation* and the Academy of American Poets for *Winter Numbers* in 1995. In 1996, Hacker won The Poet's Prize for *Selected Poems*. Hacker has two books due to be published in 2003: *She Says*, a translated collection of Venus Khoury-Ghata's poems in a bilingual edition, and Hacker's own collection, *Desesperanto: Poems 1999–2002*. "The Boy" appears in Hacker's *Squares and Courtyards* (2000).

In addition to the praise she receives for her writing, Hacker is also highly respected for her work with literary magazines, having served as editor for *Little Magazine*, *13th Moon*, *Kenyon Review*, and a special issue of *Ploughshares*. Hacker has also directed the masters program in English Literature and creative writing at City College of New York.

Poem Text

Is it the boy in me who's looking out
the window, while someone across the street
mends a pillowcase, clouds shift, the gutter spout
pours rain, someone else lights a cigarette?

(Because he flinched, because he didn't whirl   5
around, face them, because he didn't hurl
the challenge back—*"Fascists?"*—not
    "Faggots"—*"Swine!"*
he briefly wonders—if he were a girl . . .)
He writes a line. He crosses out a line.   10

I'll never be man, but there's a boy
crossing out words: the rain, the linen-mender,
are all the homework he will do today.
The absence and the privilege of gender

confound in him, soprano, clumsy, frail.   15
Not neuter—neutral human, and unmarked,
the younger brother in the fairy tale
except, boys shouted *"Jew!"* across the park

at him when he was coming home from school.
The book that he just read, about the war,   20

the partisans, is less a terrible
and thrilling story, more a warning, more

a code, and he must puzzle out the code.
He has short hair, a red sweatshirt. They know
something about him—that he should be proud   25
of? That's shameful if its shows?

That got you killed in 1942.
In his story, do the partisans
have sons? Have grandparents? Is he a Jew
more than he is a boy, who'll be a man   30

someday? Someone who'll never be a man
looks out the window at the rain he thought
might stop. He reads the sentence he began.
He writes down something that he crosses out.

Poem Summary

Stanza 1

In the first stanza of "The Boy," the narrator questions who it is looking out the window. "The boy in me" suggests another identity, or way of seeing, of which the narrator is becoming aware. The gender of the narrator is not clear at this point. What is clear is the assumption that one's gender influences the way that one sees the world, the things to which one pays attention.

Stanza 2

In this stanza, the narrator continues questioning the gender of the boy inside her, wondering if he would have responded differently to his taunters "if he were a girl." The last line alerts readers to the fact that the narrator is in the process of composing a piece of writing, possibly a school exercise on a fairy tale or book about World War II.

Stanza 3

The poem becomes more transparently self-reflexive in this stanza. That is, the boy mentioned in the opening stanza is now the one crossing out words in the second. The "homework" he is doing includes writing the words, "the rain, the linen-mender," which refer to the images in the first stanza. The last sentence runs over into the next stanza and explicitly states what the previous stanzas have illustrated: the boy's dawning awareness of what it means to be a boy. "The absence ... of gender" refers to the way that the young boy is not aware of himself as a boy, and "the privilege of gender" refers to the ways in which boys, as opposed to girls, often do not have to think of themselves *as* boys but are nonetheless socially rewarded for simply being male.

Media Adaptations

- Caedmon released an audiocassette titled *Poetry & Voice of Marilyn Hacker* (1984) with Hacker reading a selection of her poems.

Stanza 4

The speaker continues attempting to describe the character of the boy inside her, who resembles someone on the edge of puberty. That he is "unmarked" does not mean that he is "neutered," or without sexuality, but rather that he feels himself in the moment sexually undefined, ungendered. He experiences a moment of self-awareness when the boys in the park taunt him, calling him "Jew!"

Stanza 5

In this stanza, the speaker describes the book the boy in her (who is making observations and writing a story) read about World War II. "Partisans" refer to the organized resistance to Nazi occupation. The speaker makes the point that the story of the war contains a warning, but the nature of the warning is unclear. It is a "code" to the young boy, who is just learning what it means to be a boy and a Jew.

Stanza 6

This stanza describes the boy's appearance. "They" refers to the Nazis, and the "thing" they know is that the boy is Jewish.

Stanza 7

In asking if the partisans have sons or grandparents in "his story," the speaker is speculating about the story the boy (who is an alter ego of the speaker) is writing. The speaker wonders which identity, Jewish or male, is stronger.

Stanza 8

This stanza returns to the image of the boy looking out the window in the first stanza. The person "who'll never be a man" is the speaker speaking *as the poet* (i.e., Marilyn Hacker), referring to herself as a boy and in the third person. The boy's

Topics for Further Study

- As a class, construct a time line of events concerning the plight of Jews in Europe in 1942 and post it in class. Could something like the Holocaust ever happen again? Discuss your answers as a class.

- In groups, collect ads from the personals section of your local newspaper or from an online site such as Yahoo. Analyze the language men use to describe themselves and what they want in a partner. Then, analyze the language women use to describe themselves and what they want in a partner. Make a chart outlining the similarities and differences in both self-representation and representation of the desired partner. What does your analysis tell you about how men and women see themselves? What gender stereotypes do the ads illustrate?

- List five descriptive phrases you would like a member of the opposite sex to use to describe you and then list five descriptive phrases you would like a member of the same sex to use to describe you. To what degree is what you would like to hear from a member of your own sex similar or different from what you would like to hear from a member of the opposite sex? What do these similarities and differences say about how you view yourself as a man or a woman? Discuss as a class.

- Make a list of all the times when you are most aware that you are a man or a woman and all the times when you are least aware. What do these lists tell you about the idea of gender as a category of identity? Discuss in groups.

- Compare the image of the schoolgirl gazing out the window in Hacker's poem "Squares and Courtyards" with the image of the boy in "The Boy." Discuss similarities and differences and what these depictions say about the importance of the image of the child in Hacker's poetry.

---

last act in the poem is crossing something out that he just wrote.

Themes

Chaos and Order

Puberty is a chaotic time, full of powerful and new emotions, bodily changes, and self-reflection. "The Boy" describes someone in the midst of such changes, which include a budding awareness of the boy's sexuality and cultural identity. The boy, however, is also *in* someone else, who is similarly questioning *her* identity, testing the limits of her own self-reflection. The "twinning" of these two personas creates a challenging poem for readers, especially beginning poetry readers, to comprehend. One device that helps readers is the order of the poem—the regular meter and consistent rhyme scheme. The form of the poem helps shape and contain the whorl of changing pronouns, the movement between imagined selves, and offers readers a way to consider their own relationship to the outside world and to their own identities.

Writing

Hacker demonstrates the power of writing to do more than simply record the details of the physical world; she uses it as a tool to investigate the social construction of gender and ethnicity. Social constructionism is a school of thought that claims categories such as gender (masculine/feminine) and sexuality (hetero/homo) stem from cultural influences and not from essential features of a person's biology or psychology. By assuming the character of a young boy just coming into knowledge of what it means to be a boy and Jewish, Hacker also assumes how the boy sees and interprets his environment. She tempers her description of his appearance ("He has short hair, a red sweatshirt") with speculation about his history ("In his story, do the partisans / have sons? Have grandparents?"), underscoring his future as *possibility* rather than destiny. The shifting pronouns in the poem and the boy's constant revision of his writing highlight the speaker's identification with the boy's way of knowing and seeing and emphasizes the fluidity of gender roles. Social constructionism is heavily influenced by anthropological cultural relativism, and its roots can be found in the thinking of postmodernists such as Julia Kristeva, Jacques Derrida, and Michel Foucault.

Gender

Hacker wrote her poem at the end of the twentieth century when human identity is a question to be explored rather than a problem to be solved. Traditional categories of identity such as race and gender are no longer as stable as they once appeared to be. In America, sex-change operations are increasingly common, more states recognize same-sex unions, and scientists argue that at root there is no real distinction among the races. University programs in gender studies, which draw on feminist scholarship but also study masculinity in historically specific ways, are gaining in popularity, and many of the assumptions that people once had about the psychological and biological roots of gender are being challenged and disproved. The boy in the speaker is both a product of the speaker's imagination and a reflection of a part of herself that she is exercising. The melding of the speaker's and the boy's identity in the last stanza illustrates the mysterious nature of gender.

Style

Rhyme

With the exception of the second stanza, "The Boy" is composed of quatrains rhyming ABAB written in iambic pentameter. The second stanza is rhymed AABAB. Some of the rhymes are "true" rhymes, meaning there is an identical sound of an accented vowel in two or more words (e.g., "gender / linen-mender"), and some of the rhymes are half-rhymes, meaning the consonants in the terminal syllables rhyme, as in "cigarette / street." Iambic pentameter quatrains rhyming ABAB are sometimes called "elegiac" quatrains, after Thomas Gray's "Elegy Written in a Country Churchyard." Writing in a traditional rhymed verse form is not common for contemporary American poets, the bulk of whom write in a conversational, free-verse style. Hacker is one of the very few living American poets who is noted for writing in traditional forms.

Characterization

Characterization refers to the ways in which poets and writers develop characters. Techniques include describing characters' physical appearance, the way they behave and talk, and how they think. Hacker creates the character of the boy largely through describing his thought processes and through melding those thought processes with those of the narrator. The physical description of the boy, "He has short hair, a red sweatshirt," is minimal but, along with the way he responds to others who taunt him and how he begins to ponder his own cultural and ethnic heritage, it contributes to creating an image of a boy just coming into knowledge about himself and his place in history and the world.

Historical Context

End of the Twentieth Century

Hacker wrote "The Boy" in the spring of 1999, when Israel and the Palestinian Authority were still engaged in the Oslo peace talks with the United States acting as facilitator. The talks ended in the summer of 2000 with the sides unable to agree on a framework for peace. In September, Knesset member and Likud party leader Ariel Sharon visited the Temple Mount in Jerusalem, home of the al-Aqsa Mosque and the third holiest site in Islam. Muslims believe Temple Mount is where the prophet Muhammad ascended to heaven. It is also a holy place for Jews, who believe it is where Abraham prepared to sacrifice his son, Isaac. Sharon's visit provoked massive protests by Palestinians, who considered Sharon's visit a desecration of the site. The ensuing violent demonstrations by Palestinians became known as the "al-Aqsa intifada." The uprising has developed into the worst period of violence in Israel's history, with the exception of periods of warfare with neighboring Arab countries. Hundreds of Palestinians and Israelis have been killed since 2000 in Palestinian suicide bombings, border clashes, and Israeli missile attacks on suspected terrorists. Four months after his visit, Sharon was elected Prime Minister, roundly defeating incumbent Ehud Barak.

Partly as a result of the media's coverage of Israel's policy towards Palestinians, anti-Semitic attitudes in the United States persist. Anti-Semitic incidents have increased in the United States in the last decade, as attacks against Jews and Jewish institutions were up 11 percent in the first five months of 2002, compared with the same period in 2001, according to a nationwide survey by the Anti-Defamation League, "Anti-Semitism in America 2002." The survey also found that 17 percent of Americans held "hardcore" anti-Semitic views. The findings indicate a reversal of a ten-year decline in anti-Semitism and raise concerns that "an undercurrent of Jewish hatred persists in America."

1942

Although "The Boy" has a contemporary setting, the speaker mentions 1942, when being a Jew in certain parts of Europe could get one killed. Although the Nazis had been deporting Jews from Germany and Bohemia since 1939, it was not until 1941 that they began building death camps, developing gassing techniques, and organizing the evacuation system that was to take European Jews to their deaths. Under the orders of Adolph Eichmann, Chief of the Jewish Office of the Gestapo charged with implementing the "Final Solution," hundreds of thousands of Jews from all over Europe were forcibly brought to camps in places such as Sobibor, a small town a few miles from Poland's eastern border. Between April 1942 and October 1943, approximately 250,000 Jews were gassed to death there. All told, more than six million Jews were slaughtered in Nazi death camps during World War II.

Critical Overview

Squares and Courtyards has garnered considerable praise in the short time that it has been in publication. Reviewing the collection for *The Progressive*, Matthew Rothschild writes, "Elegant in form, casual and observational in style, these poems wrap themselves around large themes: death, friendship, parents' and children, Nazism, sex, nature, empire." Although the poems address emotionally heavy subjects, they are not anchored there. "What is redemptive here," Rothschild says, "is Hacker's devotion to words, friends, food, and nature." Ray Olson is similarly admiring in his review for *Booklist*. Olson zeroes in on Hacker's concern with death in the poems, claiming that the collection "is a book of midlife" that midlife poetry readers will especially appreciate. Olson lauds Hacker's keen skills of observation, noting, "how she and her peers react to the crises death imposes on them." In her review for *Prairie Schooner*, Esther Cameron also notes the prevalence of death in Hacker's poems, writing, "[The] collection is written under the aspect of transiency." Cameron points out the intensely personal nature of the poems, how their subjects come straight from Hacker's own experience battling breast cancer, losing friends to AIDS, and remembering victims of the Holocaust. "The poet both fights and celebrates the flux, Cameron writes, "as if from a deep understanding that life and death cannot be separated."

Criticism

Chris Semansky

Semansky's essays and reviews appear regularly in journals and newspapers. In this essay, Semansky considers ideas of identity in Hacker's poem.

Human beings are not "essentially" female or male in any kind of set manner. Rather they become aware of their gendered identity in specific situations, when they are called upon to behave or think in a particular way, or when certain words position them as male or female. Hacker's poem explores the territory of gender and self-recognition, as its narrator inhabits one gender, then another, in response to the words and worlds in which she finds herself.

It seems natural to categorize people according to their sex, and one commonly hears statements describing certain kinds of behavior as "male" or "female." Indeed, conventional feminism is rooted in the notion that all women share something that sets them apart from men. It is this "something" that sanctions much feminist political activity and helps to create the notion that gender is a fixed, rather than a constructed, category. In her essay, "Sexual Difference and the Problem of Essentialism," theorist Elizabeth Grosz sums up this "something," which she calls essentialism, as follows:

> Essentialism . . . refers to the attribution of a fixed essence to women. . . . Essentialism entails the belief that those characteristics defined as women's essence are shared in common by all women at all times. . . . Essentialism thus refers to the existence of fixed characteristics, given attributes, and ahistorical functions.

"The Boy" attempts to debunk the notion that human beings have an essentially masculine or feminine essence, by showing how the narrator changes in relation to the circumstances and discourses in which she finds herself. She not only responds to the world, but, as a writer, she is actively engaged in creating that world through her words and her imagination. She writes her poem "as if" a boy, living inside the head of a boy who, himself, is only intermittently aware of his "boyness." Gender, then, in Hacker's poem, is more an act of the imagination than it is a fixed point of identity waiting to be accessed.

The idea of gender as something that floats rather than something that is fixed is obvious in the first line of the poem, when the narrator asks, "Is it the boy in me who's looking out / the window ... ?" If the boy is *in* the narrator, what does this say about the narrator's identity? It is unclear and that is the point. Certainty itself, in relation to human identity, is a fantasy, a vestige of a fading order that imposes categories on people to better understand and control them.

In the next stanza, the narrator continues with the process of self-interrogation, this time proposing a "what if" scenario for the "boy inside." What if, the boy thinks, he were a girl, because he did not have the guts to face his accusers who hurled epithets at him? This kind of reasoning is based upon gender stereotypes: a real man would defend himself and challenge his accusers; only a "girl" would turn away from them. The boy is struggling not only to understand his own behavior but also to write, penning a line and then crossing it out. In the very next stanza, the poem moves out of the mental space of the boy and into that of the narrator.

Hacker's exploration of the space of gender takes place in her imagination and in her writing, which are indistinguishable. A writer's imagination is necessarily in her writing; where else could it be? That is why the "boy inside" the narrator is the persona the poet inhabits. This is where the poem becomes tricky. A persona is a kind of mask the writer uses to speak through. Say, for example, you put on a mask of George W. Bush and then give a speech to the American people about terrorism. You would be inhabiting (or trying to) his identity to do this; you would be speaking *as if* you were George Bush, using his intonations, vocabulary, describing the world the way you believe George Bush sees it, etc. In some ways, writers *always* use a persona, even when they are writing autobiographically.

"The Boy" resonates more loudly if readers also know that Hacker is both lesbian and Jewish, as these identities inflect the others she tries on in the course of the poem. In a panel discussion hosted by the Poetry Society of America and later transcribed as the online essay, "Poetry Criticism: Po-

> "Hacker's exploration of the space of gender takes place in her imagination and in her writing, which are indistinguishable."

etry and Politics," Hacker says this about other intersections in the poem:

> "The Boy" began as a mental conversation with a poet-critic friend, who, in an essay, posited the stance of the young woman poet as "examining the room she's sitting in" where the young male poet is looking out the window ... The "boy in me" who was indeed looking out the window as he/I wrote, responded to her essay. But, although the questions of Jewish identity as inflecting masculinity become central to the poem, as the old saw goes, "I didn't know he was Jewish"—at least, not until I was well into writing it.

Hacker emphasizes the differences between how a male poet might look at the world and how a female poet might. Hacker's friend presents male poets as concerned with the world outside of them, the physical world. This is what the first stanza describes—things seen from a window. In claiming that a young woman poet is prone to "examining the room she's sitting in," the friend suggests not only that women's attention is drawn to their immediate vicinity but also that they are more inner-directed, more apt to use their bodies and emotions, their images of themselves as subjects for their poems. The "room she's sitting in" is the room of the self. These are stereotypes, of course, of certain kinds of gendered thinking, but they are stereotypes that Hacker fruitfully explores to craft her poem. The poem is surprising because Hacker herself was surprised when writing it, as she notes above. This is a common occurrence for writers, as characters often take on a life of their own once put down on paper. In an email to the author dated January 11, 2003, Hacker details how she came to the first images of the poem:

> "The Boy" was written in my flat in ... Paris, where my worktable faces a window with a vis à vis, beyond which the lives of the people living opposite, framed by door-sized windows, go on more or less before my eyes, as mine does before theirs. A schoolchild doing homework in one of those flats would

face me as I'd face him or her. But there is no such child; it was I who watched the elderly widow (I think she's a widow) with the enormous rubber plant in her front room sitting at the window hemming a pillowcase that day, while her young neighbor-on-the-landing leaned out the window with a lit cigarette, watching the street.

Hacker's willingness to imagine herself as other than what she is demonstrates a quality of imagination rare in today's poets, who often become stuck on one way of seeing. At root, "The Boy" is as much about the relationship between personal risk and poetic capital as it is about the slippery ground of subjectivity. In fashioning a poem that takes readers through the poet's process of self-discovery, Hacker shows how readers, as well as writers, participate in constructing (and reconstructing) conventions of personhood.

Personhood, memory, and the language of becoming are subjects Hacker frequently addresses in *Squares and Courtyards*, and the image of a child at the window contemplating the world appears again, in the last stanza of the title poem, this time as a young girl.

> Not knowing what to thank or whom to bless,
> the schoolgirl at the window, whom I'm not,
> hums cadences it soothes her to repeat
> which open into other languages
> in which she'll piece together sentences
> while I imagine her across the street.

Hacker is both the schoolboy and the schoolgirl, and is neither. Her capacity to write herself in and out of the world of others is her poetic gift, one she uses to share with readers the shape of her life, the shape of experience itself.

Source: Chris Semansky, Critical Essay on "The Boy," in *Poetry for Students*, Gale, 2003.

Catherine Dybiec Holm

Holm is a freelance writer with speculative fiction and nonfiction publications. In this essay, Holm notes the rich combination of narrative usage, allusion, word play, and mechanics that Hacker uses to drive home the subject matter of this poem.

Hacker, a lesbian, feminist, and Jewish poet, has no doubt experienced in her lifetime the ostracism that comes from being a minority or expressing a minority viewpoint on a number of fronts. In Hacker's powerful and heartrending poem "The Boy," the poet uses poetry-specific mechanics as well as narrative craft to hammer home the pain of being different and being apart from the majority. What is most amazing about this poem is the poet's ability to touch upon gender confusion, bigotry, racism, and anti-Semitism in such a small amount of space. The reader is hit with these issues on a number of simultaneous fronts.

To begin with, the identity and gender of the narrator in "The Boy" is murky, at best. Two different interpretations work in the poem's favor, even though the outcomes suggest slightly different issues. It does not matter. In both cases, the narrator is struggling with his or her sense of being different from the mainstream world and trying to nail down an identity.

The understood interpretation of the poem assumes a female narrator. If the reader decides that this is a poem about a lesbian woman, then it makes sense. But, the reader must work for this conclusion, amidst the confusion of the narrator and Hacker's clever mechanics. This is a poem that takes some thought to unravel.

The first stanza, then, might be interpreted as a lesbian narrator, acknowledging the "maleness" within herself. Even as early as this first line, one is given the sense of separateness and division. The male part of the narrator is "within" and "looking out."

Hacker further accentuates the narrator's separateness from the rest of the world in the first stanza. Across the street, others are engaging in innocuous, non-risky, everyday behaviors. Depending on how deeply one searches for subtleties in this poem, the word "shift" might also be seen as significant. This narrator seems to be walking a shifting line of gender identity, as a woman with the essence of a boy inside of her. The entire first stanza ends with a question mark, making the narrator's shifting gender identity much more interesting than if she had started out by saying "It is the boy in me." What part of this character is looking out the window, the male or the female essence?

The second stanza completely turns the tables. Here, the narrator refers to herself as the boy and actually recalls a painful incident of discrimination. Perhaps the most intriguing line in this stanza is the fourth line: "he briefly wonders—if he were a girl." The confusion of the narrator has been expressed. She refers to herself as "he" and wonders, "if he were a girl." If the boy were a girl, would the discrimination happen less often? Another way to say this might be if the narrator has less of that "boy" inside herself, would the discrimination occur less? Maybe the purpose of that fourth line is simply to show readers the truly wild experience of gender confusion. This character is neither boy nor girl, yet is both. Symbolically, the fifth line of the second stanza is another powerful remark about gender confusion. He creates something. He takes it away. It is the ultimate in transformation or destruction—bringing something into being and then erasing it.

The third stanza of "The Boy" shifts back into first person point of view, as at the beginning of the poem. The first line in this stanza ("I'll never be a man, but there's a boy") tells us that the narrator cannot be a man, yet she acknowledges the undisputed male presence within herself. "Crossing out words" in the second line refers back to the original mention of writing and crossing out lines. On a deeper level, the word "crossing" alludes to crossing boundaries, or existing in such a way as this narrator does. Regarding these activities as "homework" is as close as the narrator can get to participating in day-to-day activities like linen-mending, and Hacker states it baldly in the fourth line of this stanza ("The absence and the privilege of gender"). In other words, those with clearly defined gender identities have the "privilege" of a well-ordered world and mundane, usual happenings. The narrator is a person with an "absence of gender," a stunning concept in itself and made even more stunning by the stark economy of words that a poem demands.

Hacker continues to dig deeper into this concept; the narrator is not "neuter," but a "neutral human." The "fairy tale" is never identified, but the phrase is a thinly veiled reference to a derogatory remark aimed at a homosexual ("fairy"). Then, as if this were not enough, the narrator is insulted for his heritage and taunted by boys who shout "Jew!"

In the seventh stanza, "His story" is an intentional word play on "history" ("In his story, do the partisans / have sons?") The word "partisan" could be taken to allude to two situations that both affect this narrator: those who stood for one ideal during World War II, or those who hold strong, unmovable beliefs in the narrator's present-day life. "Partisan" implies a strong belief or focus on one identifiable system, whereas this narrator, because of who she or he is, lives life in a shifting understanding of gender identity, which does not necessarily follow previously established rules. The narrator is struggling to get to the crux of his identity ("Is he a Jew / more than he is a boy, who'll be a man / someday?") Both are sources of discrimination, but which define the narrator more?

The last stanza seems to return to the beginning of the poem (the narrator is looking out the window), but now the more distant third person

> "Perhaps what Hacker is saying is that it does not matter whether the narrator is male or female. The narrator simply is and is struggling to understand an identity that shifts and encompasses more than the commonplace world might be ready to understand."

point of view finishes off the poem. Again, the narrator demonstrates indecision (by writing something, then crossing it out), but, more importantly, the narrator shows deconstruction. The sentence ends with the word "out," an allusion to coming out as a gay or lesbian person in society. Truly, this narrator is a completely deconstructed person who asks, throughout the poem, How do I consider myself? Am I boy? Am I Jew? What am I? None of the usual rules of gender apply; this is the crux of the message of "The Boy."

A different, but no less effective, interpretation of this poem might assume that the narrator is a self-acknowledged homosexual male. Reading the poem this way still gives the reader the layers of complexity that are so prevalent in this poem. The "boy in me" can be taken to represent the narrator's inner essence, the part of him that will always be male even though society will never consider him a "man." When the narrator briefly wonders "if he were a girl," the phrase takes on a new meaning coming from a gay male narrator. If he were a girl, would he be teased in such a manner? He carries that essence of femininity inside him, just as surely as the female narrator (if interpreted in that way) carries "a boy" inside of her.

Perhaps what Hacker is saying is that it does not matter whether the narrator is male or female. The narrator simply is and is struggling to understand an identity that shifts and encompasses more than the commonplace world might be ready to understand. By presenting readers with an ambiguous narrator, Hacker effectively shows them what it is like to live with a shifting self-identity that fits no accepted rules.

Hacker plays with form and meter in "The Boy" though it is difficult to say whether the patterns presented are significant in the context of this poem. Most stanzas have an ABAB pattern, meaning that the ending syllables of the first and third lines of the stanza sound similar to each other, as do those in the second and fourth lines. The exception to this pattern is the second stanza, which has five lines and an AABAB pattern. This is also the stanza that first throws readers into new territory; one starts to realize that there is a lot more going on here than the original picture of a character looking out the window. Perhaps this deviation from pattern, and the addition of an extra line in this stanza, are meant to jar us as much as does the meaning of the text.

Similarly, with no discernible pattern, Hacker alternates lines of iambic pentameter with lines that vary from this pattern. The first two lines of the poem are in iambic pentameter. The third line of the poem is also iambic pentameter, with an extra unstressed syllable at the end of the line. The third stanza's second line starts out with an initial inversion of iambic pentameter, and then goes into iambic pentameter with another feminine ending. Two lines down, the line that ends with "gender" also ends with a feminine ending (the extra unstressed syllable), perhaps an intended irony for the reader to unearth. These inversions and variations on iambic pentameter may work to keep readers from getting too comfortable or grounded as they read the poem.

In a *Ploughshares* interview, Hacker is described as gloriously defying "all attempts at easy categorization." A *Publishers Weekly* review praises the poet's "strength of will with an evenness of tone" and claims that Hacker is "at her strongest when most stark and direct." Surely, "The Boy" is all these things, which is entirely appropriate given its subject matter: shocking, skillfully rendered, and not easily pinned down.

Source: Catherine Dybiec Holm, Critical Essay on "The Boy," in *Poetry for Students*, Gale, 2003.

Esther Cameron

In the following review, Cameron discusses the themes of transience found in Hacker's collection Squares and Courtyards.

Marilyn Hacker's ninth collection is written under the aspect of transiency. Reflected in the poems are the realities of a breast cancer diagnosis, mastectomy, chemotherapy, a body no longer whole, the fear of recurrence, the waking up to the "scandal" of death; also the illnesses and deaths of relatives, friends, acquaintances, strangers: other sufferers from cancer in the poet's circle, the victims of AIDS and drugs cared for by her lover, the poet's daughter's best friend in a car crash, the poet's grandmother in a pedestrian accident long ago, the victims of the Holocaust and World War II, a vital elderly friend, a revered older poet (Muriel Rukeyser), a homeless man whose funeral is described. Geographical transiency also pervades the book: the poet lives half in New York, half in Paris, and at one point settled in Ohio, only to be abruptly uprooted after starting a garden. The poem that relates this event, "Tentative Gardening," also laments the brevity of the connection with Nadine who had supervised the planting: "and I wonder where and from whom I'll learn to / put in a garden." Friends fade out in the transcontinental shuffle; strangers (like the schoolgirls in "Rue de Belleyme") appear as vivid images, give rise to equally vivid speculations about their lives, and move offscreen again. One of the central poems—"Again in the River"—shows the poet sitting beside the Seine; the book might have had for a motto Heraclitus's "All things are in flux."

The poet both fights and celebrates the flux, as if from a deep understanding that life and death cannot be separated. One strategy against the flux is, of course, form: "I will put Chaos into fourteen lines / And keep him there," as Millay wrote. Hacker is one of the masters of form of the age, and once again she proves her dexterity with the sonnet, the crown of sonnets, terza rima, sapphics. All the poems in the book are rhymed, except for a set of haiku, but the rhymes are so discreetly worked into the text that one can fail to notice them. A particular pleasure is the way exact and off-rhymes are blended without awkwardness, as in the final sonnet of "Taking Leave of Zenka," where the rhymes are: wound/ interred/ bird/ around/ beyond/ blurred/ shirred/ friend/ son/ floor/ rudiments/more/ France/afternoon. The meter, with varying degrees of rigidity, manages to be equally unobtrusive. The closing of the formal circle comes each time as a victory over the dissolving stream.

Another strategy for chaos control is the sharp focus on the particular: "as if dailiness forestalled change." There is a constant invocation of "innocent objects": "a tin plate, a basement / door, a spade, barbed wire, a ring of keys," cherries in an outdoor market (six varieties), a dog's coat, "spiced pumpkin soup," "Tissue-wrapped clementines /

from Morocco," the sci-fi paperback a homeless man is reading. By fixing the names of these objects in the sound-texture (always rich and bristling) of the verse, the poet reaffirms the fact of her existence, and the existence of her friends and fellow-sufferers and all the displaced, here and now and again in that ghostly semblance of permanence that the text gives ("Persistently, on paper, we exist").

But of course objects like a spade and barbed wire are not innocent. Neither are the cherries, as it turns out (they lead to birds, then to the yellow bird whistle, which the poet's grandmother had just bought for her at the moment of that long-ago fatal accident). Objects have associations that take one elsewhere in space and time, and the movement of the poem as a whole often seems to be determined by free association, by the stream of consciousness. Thus in the title poem, "Squares and Courtyards" (which received Prairie Schooner's Strousse Award in 1998) the poet is at first standing in the Place du Marche Sainte-Catherine, eating a baguette. She sees (or imagines?) a schoolgirl chewing on a pencil at a window. She thinks back to her own childhood, the courtyard of the house in New York where she grew up. By a train of association involving discussions of Holocaust news, ashes, chain smokers, she is drawn back to a sidewalk cafe on the Place du Marche Sainte-Catherine, where people are smoking and discussing personal and political events "as if events were ours to rearrange / with words[. .]." Then back to her own childhood, her early experience with languages and language: "I pressed my face into the dog's warm fur / whose heat and smell I learned by heart, while she / receded into words I found for her." Then into a meditation about how words replace things, give an illusion of summing them up, create expectations that reality declines to fulfill, and yet themselves represent a reality that can be lost, as in the case of the grandmother ("It's all the words she said to me I miss"). Then come questions about the languages of the poet's parents and grandparents. Finally the poet (who seemed to be alone at the beginning of the poem) appears to be speaking with a "she" (a friend? a daughter? a double?) who "walks home / across the Place du Marche Ste-Catherine." Once in her own room, this figure will "scribble down" the "cognates, questions, and parentheses" and become the imagined figure of "the schoolgirl at the window, whom I'm not." The poem's movement implies that the poet is only one vessel, so to speak, for a stream of language, consciousness, thought, which will pass through her to others. The final figure of the schoolgirl in the window is perhaps the reader, who will try in her own way to realize the aspirations that were the poet's: "thinking: she can, if anybody could."

> *The poet both fights and celebrates the flux, as if from a deep understanding that life and death cannot be separated. One strategy against the flux is, of course, form. . . ."*

This conclusion is of course not reassuring. What is in store for the schoolgirl: "Is there a yellow star sewn on her dress"? Moreover, the schoolgirl may not even exist; the conversation between the poet and the schoolgirl is only imagined. In "Again, the River" the poet will ask: "Who do we write books for—our friends? our daughters?," thus questioning (as many have recently) the existence of poetry's audience; and the question takes on a further edge from the reminder in "Squares and Courtyards" that a poet's kith and kin are under no obligation to find her words helpful or meaningful. And while the figure at the window may still dream, the poet has found out that she will "get old (or not) and die"—and also, by implication, that she "can" not, because no one "could."

So the poem becomes a repeated grasping after what slips away, and the book as a whole becomes an assemblage of images that at times seem less woven together than retained in juxtaposition on account of accidental collisions that marked the reporting self (like that terrible childhood accident that surfaces toward the end of the book, as if it were a kind of explanation for everything). No abstract meaning could subsume these details; that would go against the poet's fierce assertion of the unrepeatable uniqueness of each instant, each object, each person, as against the great void of nothingness and death. There is an anti-hierarchical insistence in the individual portraits of street people, which a structure of symbol, myth, archetype would only gloss over. But as a result, form too comes to seem permeable. The "squares and courtyards" of the poems, like the past and present

What Do I Read Next?

- Hacker has developed a reputation as a lesbian activist sympathetic to the plight of oppressed minorities. Dorothy Allison, who has also written about lesbianism, published *Bastard out of Carolina* in 1992. This autobiographical novel tells the story of Ruth Anne Boatwright ("Bone"), who was raised in a family of poor Southern whites and molested by her violent stepfather.

- Hacker's *Selected Poems, 1965–1990* (1995) contains selections from from five of her previous volumes and contains much of her best work, including some of her best-known sonnets, sestinas, and villanelles.

- Hacker's first collection of poems, *Presentation Piece* (1974), was a Lamont Poetry Selection and won the National Book Award in 1975. It remains one of her most accomplished volumes to date.

- Sheep Meadow Press published a bilingual edition of *Long Gone Sun* (2000), which is a collection of poems written by French poet Claire Malroux and translated by Hacker. This collectioin is about Malroux's childhood and her father's life in the French Resistance.

- Hacker edited the Spring 1996 issue of *Ploughshares*, which focuses on literary, gender, and racial diversity in contemporary American poetry.

moment, are not closed-off spaces but just eddies in the flow, nodes in the network. The traditional sonnet starts something and then finishes it, stands there as a Gestalt with a clear outline within which the details are balanced and interconnected. But in a sonnet like "And Bill and I imagined lives in France," the details contained within the form can seem like strangers who happen to be ascending or descending in the same elevator, each one more closely related to things outside the elevator (to analogous objects or moments in the book as a whole) than to the other passengers. But that is, we see, the form of contemporary life. Finally the work comes to seem like a single poem, a sign that Hacker has achieved, despite all the apparent fragmentation, a texture in which the details are, finally, at home. The associative flow dissolves the contour of individual poems, as it dissolves the poet's sense of being wholly at any point in spacetime; but it also connects the different points in space-time, pulls them together and makes them part of the Now: "Every- / place / is Here and is Today," as Paul Celan wrote in *The No-One's-Rose*.

Here and there a passage raises different questions. "Broceliande" harks back to an early interest in mythmaking and magic that is largely submerged here: "Yes, there is a vault in the ruined castle. / Yes, there is a woman waking beside the / gleaming sword she drew from the stone of childhood." But this ironic compliance with a request for symbolism is soon deflated altogether: "Sometimes she inhabits the spiring cities / architects project out of science fiction / dreams, but she illuminates them with different / voyages, visions: // with tomato plants, with the cat who answers / when he's called, with music-hall lyrics, work-scarred hands on a steering wheel, the jeweled secret / name of a lover." Again we are told that there are no great symbols, only the things that have meant most to one person and what those things tell us about that person, as a lover and activist. At the same time, the mythical world that has been invoked imbues these particular particulars with a slight magical aura: is the cat a familiar, is the jeweled secret name a charm? One thinks here of the powerful "Rune of the Finland Woman" in *Assumptions* (1985), or that early, splendid sestina, "An Alexandrite Pendant for My Mother," which didn't even make it into *Selected Poems 1965–1990*. One wonders if myth could return to poetic universe. Myth is after all an organizing device, a source of power; don't the dispossessed need it too?

Related questions start up when one reads the following:

> However well I speak, I have an accent
> tagging my origins: that Teflon fist,
> that hog wallow of investment
> that hegemonic televangelist's
> zeal to dumb the world down to its virulent
> cartoon contours, with the world's consent:
> your heads of state, in cowboy suits,
> will lick our leader's lizard boots.
> My link to that imperial vulgarity
> is a diasporic accident[.]

Suddenly, amid this scanning of a memory inflected by history, comes a statement that engages with the world polemically. In the Miltonic salvo of the fifth and sixth lines (one could imagine them as the closing couplet in a traditional sonnet), we are reminded that there is presently more at work than time and chance happening to all things: there is something actively at work against the nuanced world Hacker so lovingly invokes. The traditional poem, by coming to a sharp point, can supply the reader with ammunition (such as that couplet); its formal consistency has at certain times even helped readers to acquire consistency, to get their backs up and come together and offer a real resistance. (Example: Barrett Browning's "The Cry of the Children," which may have been of some use to the cause of labor reform.) Is then the decentered poetics of this book a poetics of resistance, or is it more a way of tentative survival while "waiting for the axe to fall," as "A Colleague" briefly suggests? Is an active resistance, over and above the acts of charity and generosity and loyalty which this book celebrates, still conceivable? Could the poet's wit and mythmaking skills be pitted more directly against the Dark Tower? But such questions indicate that the book's circle is not a closed one. Reading *Squares and Courtyards*, one has a sense of sharing in a struggle of life with death; and one puts it down fervently hoping that Hacker may live to one hundred and twenty.

Source: Esther Cameron, Review of *Squares and Courtyards*, in *Prairie Schooner*, Vol. 75, No. 3, Fall 2001, p. 186.

Jane Augustine

In the following essay, Augustine examines the themes running through the body of Hacker's work.

From the beginning of Marilyn Hacker's career her poems have established a unique counterpoint between classical rhyming forms—sestina, sonnet, villanelle—and blunt declarative sentences to display the deranged obsessiveness of contemporary minds. Her hard-edged language in the 1970s is darkly jewel-encrusted, redolent of a devastated inner world of difficult loving, tangled sexuality, and convoluted relationships. Semiprecious gems—onyx, amethyst, alexandrite—express the hardness, mystery, and richness of experience. Lured by the foreign and strange, Hacker invents "imaginary translations," playing with exotic locales and overblown emotions. Tours de force, these poems lead into her central concern, the elucidation of her own intense passions, whether sexual, moral, or political.

Love is the premier passion that runs as a continuing strand from the earlier to the later work. Because the poem sequence "Separations," from the volume of this title, is written in sonnet form, it deemphasizes obsession and becomes a graceful, almost Shakespearean delineation of the aspects of love, which always springs up lively and ubiquitous despite the poet's difficulties. But love arouses thoughts of death, as in the opening poem of *Presentation Piece* (1974), in which she speaks to "the skull of the beloved" as a brooding nobleman in a Jacobean play addresses the skull of his dead mistress. "The Navigators" foreshadows the heartbroken elegy "Geographer" in *Separations* (1976), a poem that unites in formal, sestina-like word repetition her continuing themes of death, cities, gems, language, and painful but persisting love.

As a descriptive phrase, "persisting love" grossly understates the obsession with a young lover that besieges Hacker for a year in *Love, Death, and the Changing of the Seasons* (1986). This "verse novel," as she calls it, is a book-length sonnet sequence that emphasizes physical love almost exclusively as the poet waits in various situations to be united with Rachel, called Ray. The poems perform in explicit, masculinized language a *Kama-Sutra* of fantasized ways of making love. When Ray breaks off the affair, the poet plunges into the utter bleakness, without perspective, of the coda's final poems. But the poems clarify an underlying motif: her lust arose from the foredoomed but irresistible wish to be young again. By 1990, in *Going Back to the River*, Hacker is on a more even keel, enjoying good food, drink, and the landscapes of two continents and appreciating quotidian objects. All is not pleasure, however, and the unassimilable horrors of wartime experience and the persecution of the Jews in France are evoked in "Days of 1944: Three Friends." Thus reminded of her Jewishness, Hacker meditates further on her ethnic background and her parents' lives in the title poem of the volume, as the rivers she goes back to—Thames, Hudson, Seine—are seen not as destinations but as reminders of the flux and uncertainties of experience.

In a sense, however, by the time Hacker wrote *Winter Numbers* (1994) flux had become a way of life. (She has homes in both New York and Paris.) Here the incorporation of French words renders her forms more supple and varied while also enriching the poems' sense of place. Her internationalism lessens the pain of change, making it a modus vivendi, a respite from narrow American prejudices. But her consciousness of painful change escalates as personal losses through AIDS and cancer assail her. Death is the ultimate change that everyone fears. The word "numbers" in the book's title has multiple associations: with the metrics of

> "Tours de force, these poems lead into her central concern, the elucidation of her own intense passions, whether sexual, moral, or political."

poetry, with mileage, with dates and time periods, the length of time, for instance, between the diagnosis of an illness and surgery or death. In the book's last section, "Cancer Winter," meditation on her own uncertain fate after breast cancer is enlarged to include history and the fates of those dead in the Holocaust.

Hacker's delight in French culture and language led to her 1996 volume, *Edge*, translations of the poems of Claire Malroux, who is herself a translator of H. D., Derek Walcott, and other modern writers into French. The French poet's themes align with the American's: a consciousness of aging, "prescience of death," and effort to connect this tangible world in its quirky sounds and flavors with the eternal world. These preoccupations—particularly a sharp and tender sense of mortality—also pervade Hacker's 2000 collection, *Squares and Courtyards*. Her favored form is the sonnet sequence, although she also likes the terse, imagistic three-line stanza characteristic of William Carlos Williams. In one section, "Paragraphs from a Daybook," she employs an interesting 15–line stanza invented by the poet Hayden Carruth, to whom the volume is dedicated. Close to a book-length unified narrative, it interweaves elegiac recording of deaths—youthful, accidental, elderly, inevitable—with direct notation of survivors' lives. The settings shuttle between two continents, as Hacker herself does. Her travels provide a metaphor for the passage between life and death:

> New passport stamps mark
> the week of my, Ellen's and Zenka's border
> crossings, unplotted flight-paths toward the dark

Haunted by death-consciousness, this work thematically builds on her earlier books. She has continued her commitment to make poetic intercession for women, blacks, homosexuals, Jews, whoever is ill and suffering. Her skilled use of form to serve candid observation, the ability to register ephemeral beauty, the strength to face loss and death for herself, for everyone—those powers infuse Hacker's poems and serve as markers of their profundity and accomplishment. Her long career continues to enrich the high tradition of English lyric.

Source: Jane Augustine, "Hacker, Marilyn," in *Contemporary Poets*, 7th ed., edited by Thomas Riggs, St. James Press, 2001, pp. 465–66.

Sources

"Anti-Semitism in America 2002: Highlights from a May 2002 Survey Conducted by the Marttila Communications Group and SWR Worldwide for the Anti-Defamation League, Including Poll Results from 1992 and 1998," http://www.adl.org/anti_semitism/2002/as_survey.pdf (last accessed July 7, 2003).

Cameron, Esther, Review of *Squares and Courtyards*, in *Prairie Schooner*, Vol. 75, Issue 3, Fall 2001, p. 186.

Campo, Rafael, "About Marilyn Hacker, A Profile," in *Ploughshares*, Spring 1996.

Grosz, Elizabeth, "Sexual Difference and the Problem of Essentialism," in *The Essential Difference*, edited by Naomi Schor and Elizabeth Weed, Indiana University Press, 1994, p. 84.

Hacker, Marilyn, "The Boy," in *Squares and Courtyards*, W. W. Norton, 2000, pp. 13–14.

———, "Squares and Courtyards," in *Squares and Courtyards*, W. W. Norton, 2000, p. 44.

Olson, Ray, Review of *Squares and Courtyards*, in *Booklist*, January 1, 2000, p. 864.

Review of "The Boy," in *Publishers Weekly*, Vol. 245, No. 24, June 15, 1998, p. 50.

Rothschild, Matthew, Review of *Squares and Courtyards*, in the *Progressive*, Vol. 65, Issue 1, January 2001, p. 42.

Sherry, James, et al., "Poetry Criticism: Poetry and Politics," Poetry Society of America: http://www.poetrysociety.org/journal/offpage/poetry_politics.html (last accessed January 12, 2003).

Further Reading

D'Emilio, John, and Estelle B. Freedman, *Intimate Matters: A History of Sexuality in America*, Harper, 1988.
  This study provides a comprehensive account of sexual attitudes, conflicts, practices, and legislation in American history and also aims to debunk notions that today's sexual behavior is more liberated than in the past.

Frank, Anne, *The Diary of a Young Girl: The Definitive Edition*, edited by Miriam Pressler, Bantam Books, 1997.

Originally published in 1947, this classic book is the account of a young Jewish girl living in hiding from the Nazis in Amsterdam. Frank and her family were later discovered and sent to concentration camps. Frank died at Bergen-Belsen, Germany, in 1945.

Fuss, Diana, *Essentially Speaking: Feminism, Nature & Difference*, Routledge, 1989.

Fuss analyzes essentialism in this groundbreaking study, taking apart its assumptions one by one.

Gamble, Sarah, ed., *The Routledge Companion to Feminism and Postfeminism*, Routledge, 2001.

In this text, Garber offers more than a dozen chapters and more than 400 A-Z dictionary entries on topics such as the history of feminism, postfeminism, men in feminism, feminism and new technologies, and feminism and philosophy.

Garber, Linda, *Identity Poetics*, Columbia University Press, 2001.

Garber, an associate professor in the department of English and the Program for the Study of Women and Gender at Santa Clara University, calls for recognition of the role of lesbian poets as theorists of lesbian identity and activism.

Riley, Denise, *Am I That Name?: Feminism and the Category of "Women" in History*, University of Minnesota Press, 1989.

Riley explores how the socially constructed category of women has shifted through history.

Childhood

Rainer Maria Rilke

1902

Rainer Maria Rilke's "Childhood" is included in his collection *Das Buch der Bilder*, first published in 1902. Various writers have translated the volume as "The Book of Images" or "The Book of Pictures." The poem can also be found in Robert Bly's collection of translations, *Selected Poems of Rainer Maria Rilke*. *The Book of Images* was published just after *The Book of Hours* and just before *New Poems* and marks a shift in Rilke's poetic development toward more imagistic, slightly less sentimental verse. Written in thirty-three lines of rhymed iambic pentameter verse and fit into four irregular stanzas, "Childhood" addresses loneliness and the passage of time, typical subjects for Rilke, who spent his life attempting to describe the effects of time's onslaught. Rilke wrote a number of poems about childhood, including "Duration of Childhood" and "The Child." All of these poems express feelings of wonder and bafflement and grapple with the puzzle of human existence. Childhood was a difficult time for Rilke. He was an effeminate and fragile child, and not at all cut out for the military schools to which his father sent him. Many of the images of childhood in his poems are dramatizations of his own memories.

Author Biography

Born December 4, 1875, in Prague, Austria, Rene Karl Wilhelm Johann Josef Maria Rilke was the only child of Josef Rilke, a minor railway official, and Sophie Entz Rilke. In 1897, Rilke changed his name to Rainer Maria Rilke. By most accounts, he had an unhappy childhood, raised by parents who were mired in an unhappy marriage. Rilke was educated at military boarding schools and, later, studied philosophy for a short time at Prague's Charles-Ferdinand University. His real education, however, came after he left Prague. In Munich, he socialized with the city's literati, published two poetry collections, and staged a few of his plays. In Venice, he met Lou Andreas-Salome, an intellectual more than a decade older than Rilke, who had a strong influence on many of Europe's writers and artists, including Freidrich Nietzsche. Andreas-Salome became Rilke's lover for a short time, accompanied him on his travels throughout Europe and Russia, and had a lasting influence on his thinking and work.

Raised Roman Catholic, Rilke was obsessed with religious questions, though he eschewed conventional religious thinking. He believed the human condition was essentially that of aloneness and that human beings could access God the most when they were alone. Because his early poems attempted to describe the contours of his own consciousness, they were often abstract and largely unsuccessful. However, once Rilke began studying the visual arts and learning the ways in which painters created effects, his poetry changed. The first book that began showing these changes was *Das Buch der Bilder* (The Book of Images) published in 1902. In poems such as "Childhood," Rilke uses finely honed language and focused similes to depict universal experiences.

Ril ke's style changed even more after serving as secretary to sculptor Auguste Rodin in Paris from 1905–1906. In place of the often abstract and sentimental verse he had been writing, he began writing poems that described concrete subjects in symbolic yet detailed terms, and his poems took on a more chiseled, tightly structured quality. He called these compositions "thing poems" and published a collection of them titled *New Poems* (1907). Following the publication of *New Poems*, Rilke began an itinerant existence over the next seven years, traveling to more than fifty different places, including North Africa, Paris, Egypt, Berlin, Spain (Toledo), and Duino (between Venice and Triest), where, as the guest of Princess Marie Tour en Taxis, he began writing what became *The Duino Elegies* (1923), the best-known and most celebrated of his works.

Rainer Maria Rilke

In addition to *The Duino Elegies*, Rilke's most popular and enduring works include *The Book of Hours* (1905), *Sonnets to Orpheus* (1923), the novel *The Notebooks of Malte Laurids Brigge* (1930), and *Letters to a Young Poet* (1929), a collection of advice in the form of letters. After a lifetime spent battling various ailments, Rilke died of leukemia on December 29, 1926, in Montreaux, Switzerland.

Poem Text

Time in school drags along with so much worry,
and waiting, things so dumb and stupid.
Oh loneliness, oh heavy lumpish time ...
Free at last: lights and colors and noises;
water leaps out of fountains into the air,   5
and the world is so huge in the woody places.
And moving through it in your short clothes,
and you don't walk the way the others do—
Such marvelous time, such time passing on,
such loneliness.   10

How strange to see into it all from far away:
men and women, there's a man, one more woman;
children's bright colors make them stand out;
and here a house and now and then a dog
and terror all at once replaced by total trust—   15
What crazy mourning, what dream, what heaviness,
what deepness without end.

Media Adaptations

- *Rilke: Selected Poems* (1998) is an audiocassette published by Audio Literature. It features Stephen Mitchell reading Rilke's poems.
- ParaTheatrical ReSearch produced *Requiem for a Friend* (1991), a VideoPoem/Docudrama by Antero Alli, based on the Stephen Mitchell translation of a Rilke poem.

And playing: a hoop, and a bat, and a ball,
in some green place as the light fades away.
And not noticing, you brush against a grownup,   20
rushing blindly around in tag, half-crazed,
but when the light fades you go with small
puppety steps home, your hand firmly held—
Such oceanic vision that is fading,
such a constant worry, such weight.   25

Sometimes also kneeling for hours on end
with a tiny sailboat at a grayish pond,
all forgotten because sails more beautiful
than yours go on crossing the circles;
and one had to think always about the pale   30
narrow face looking up as it sank down—
Oh, childhood, what was us going away,
going where? Where?

Poem Summary

Stanza 1

"Childhood" begins with the speaker addressing a child who is in school, describing the child's feelings of boredom, loneliness, and alienation from other children. Adopting the language of a typical school boy's view of the world, the speaker says, "Time in school drags along with so much worry / and waiting, things so dumb and stupid." The speaker contrasts this negative representation of school with the joy the child feels after school. When school lets out, the boy is free, the world now expansive and inviting. These feelings are illustrated in the images of leaping fountains and mysterious "woody places." However, even in his newfound freedom, the boy still feels odd, different from others. This difference is illustrated in the image of him walking oddly.

Stanza 2

In this stanza, the speaker foregrounds his point of view as someone looking back on childhood. He compares the "terror" of childhood with the "trust" of adulthood, as evoked in the images of men and women, a house and a dog, and both marvels at and grieves the change. Even though the poem is written from a third-person point of view and attempts to characterize the child's changing view of the world, the narrator is clearly present and makes his feelings known.

Stanza 3

The poem returns to images of childhood, this time to the boy playing at dusk, "as the light fades away." The "green place" is a descriptive metaphor for a park or a lawn. As dusk settles, an adult—most likely a parent—grabs the hand of the boy and leads him away. The "oceanic vision that is fading" can refer to both the boy's disappointment at having to stop playing, and the speaker's sense of loss and pain in remembering his boyhood. The progression of the events in this stanza are typical of the events of a child's day.

Stanza 4

In this last stanza, the speaker compares fading childhood to the sailboat the child is playing with that sinks. The imagery here is dreamlike, underscoring the confusion of a child's mind and the place of memory itself. The "sails more beautiful / than yours" suggests people more beautiful and lives more beautiful than the child's and the narrator's. The "pale / narrow face" is the face of the child himself, and his puzzling about the future is also the speaker's mourning about the past. The poem ends with the child wondering where childhood will lead him.

Themes

Art

Rilke studied art history and was a lifelong lover of the visual arts, writing essays on sculptors and impressionist painters, living at a colony for painters, and even marrying a sculptor. In *The Book of Images*, he tried to create the verbal equivalent to a gallery full of paintings. In "Childhood," he uses imagery in much the same way as painters do. For example, he uses successive images of the child

Topics For Further Study

- Rilke is a poet of memory and often seems obsessed with his personal past, especially his childhood. Describe at least two powerfully emotional incidents from your childhood in which one or both of your parents played a part. Use as much detail as possible. Then, ask your parents to describe the incidents. How does your memory of events differ from theirs? Write a short essay accounting for the difference.

- In groups, brainstorm a list of adjectives and images you believe represent your experience as a child and then compose a poem using as many of these words as possible. Take turns reading the poem aloud to the class.

- In groups, translate Rilke's poem literally, word for word, and then compare your translation with Bly's translation. Discuss the choices Bly made and the reasons why he might have made them. What does this exercise tell you about the practice of translating poetry?

- As a class, use a Venn diagram to compare and contrast childhood and adulthood. Note the differences that most surprise you and discuss them as a class.

- Rilke wrote "Childhood" after spending time at the artist colony at Worpswede, and some critics claim he uses words the way painters use paint. In groups, compose a visual representation of Rilke's poem using paint, crayons, markers, images from magazines, and any other appropriate materials. Present your compositions to the class, explaining the choices you made. Post the work in the classroom, gallery style.

- Rilke was very self-conscious, both in his poetry and in his interactions with others. Practice seeing as Rilke did by sitting still for a half hour and concentrating on one object. In writing, describe both that object and the emotions you experienced looking at it. Read the description to your class and have classmates ask you questions about your description, with the goal of helping them to experience it more powerfully.

---

being anxious, then happy, and then mournful to illustrate the rapid emotional changes that occur in childhood. In the foreground are the child's experiences, and in the background is the speaker's commentary on those experiences. Just as a painter uses the technique of chiaroscuro to produce the illusion of depth, Rilke uses images of light and darkness to evoke emotional volatility and psychological depth.

Memory

For Rilke, memory is a tool used to unlock the mystery of human existence. The speaker alternates between describing the child's reactions to his surroundings with making statements commenting on those reactions. At the end of the third stanza, after describing the child playing and then being led home by an adult, the speaker writes, "Such oceanic vision that is fading, / such a constant worry, such weight." Statements such as these describe the state of mind of the adult speaker as much as they describe the state of mind of the child. The child is a younger version of Rilke himself, and by describing the child's confusion and feelings of alienation Rilke is, in fact, describing his own ongoing experiences of the same. In this way, he presents the relentless demands of memory as an affliction that the poet must exorcise *and* exercise.

Isolation

Although the child dreads the prison-like atmosphere of school and celebrates his freedom when the school days end by playing tag with others, he feels alone and is aware of how different he is from other children. This condition of otherness is a theme that runs throughout Rilke's poem and one he links to loneliness. Rilke evokes the feeling of loneliness both in imagery and statement. For example, in the second stanza, the adult speaker reflects on the child's being suddenly thrown into the adult world, lamenting, "What crazy mourning, what dream, what heaviness, / what deepness without end." In the last stanza, the boy, playing with a sailboat, worries about other boats that are better than his and contemplates the meaning of his life while gazing into a pond.

Style

Impressionism

Rilke describes emotions in this poem impressionistically. Impressionism seeks to depict scenes or characters by using concrete details to evoke subjective and sensory impressions, rather than to accurately depict an objective reality. For example, Rilke refers to the experience of the child's unbearable waiting for the school day to end as "lumpish time," and the place where he plays after school ends as "some green place." Writers who helped popularize impressionistic writing include Thomas Mann, Virginia Woolf, and James Joyce.

Juxtaposition

By using contrasting images and emotions, Rilke underscores the torment and fear that come with childhood. In one stanza, the child is lonely, bored, and anxious, but, in the next, he is full of light and life. In one stanza, he is terrified by the world he sees and then comforted by the sight of adults, a house, and a dog. Juxtaposing these emotions allows Rilke to get at the heart of his experience as a child and to show how the experience remains fresh in the adult speaker's mind.

Sound

Rilke uses a variety of sonic techniques to create his impressionistic effects. He uses alliteration in phrases such as "Dumpfen dingen" ("things so dumb and stupid") and "Welt so weit" ("world . . . so huge") to emphasize the imagery, and he uses assonance in phrases such as "kleinen steifen" ("small / puppety") and "O Traum, o Grauen" ("what dream, what heaviness") to focus the reader's attention on the emotion packed in the images.

Historical Context

Early Twentieth Century

In 1900, Rilke, disgusted by the industrialization of Europe's cities and the waning of communal life, traveled to Russia for the second time, with his friend Lou Andreas-Salome. There, he met writer Leo Tolstoy and attended numerous Russian religious services that, in their rituals and passion, instilled in Rilke a sense of the divine in humanity. Rilke was especially taken by the Russian peasants' conception of God, whom they saw not only in one another but also in everyday objects and even animals. Upon returning to Europe, Rilke joined an artists' colony in Worpswede, near Bremen, Germany, where he met his future wife, sculptor Clara Westhoff, and painter Paula Becker, who became a very close friend. At Worpswede, Rilke, already a student of art history, participated in discussions of art and philosophy and solidified his devotion to writing and his sense of himself as an artist. In his poems during this period, he attempted to use "painterly" techniques.

In 1902, when *The Book of Images*, which includes "Childhood," was published, Rilke traveled to Paris, commissioned to write a monograph about the sculptor Auguste Rodin. He was chosen to write the monograph because of his relationship to Westhoff, who was a student of Rodin's. Rodin had established a reputation as one of Europe's greatest artists, revolutionizing sculpture and modernizing it. In 1900, Rodin held a retrospective of his life's work at the Universal Exposition in Paris. In addition to Rodin's work, the Exposition, which was visited by more than fifty million people, featured the work of many artists associated with Art Nouveau, which was fast becoming the dominant style for urban architects and designers. Art Nouveau championed a return to nature and to the rural traditions of arts and crafts and rejected the academic and cerebral. Rodin's work habits and his emphasis on the materiality of his art greatly influenced Rilke, who began to rely more on discipline than inspiration for his writing, and who began crafting poems as tightly structured linguistic objects that drew attention to the words themselves as much as what they signified.

In European intellectual circles during this time, people increasingly discussed the theories of Sigmund Freud, who had published *The Interpretation of Dreams* in 1899 and *The Psychopathology of Everyday Life* in 1901. Freud's explanation of dreams—where they come from, and how they work—made the concept of the unconscious subject matter for thinkers and artists throughout the twentieth century and influenced Rilke's own thinking about his childhood. In treating his patients, Freud noted that the topic of childhood seduction came up regularly. It was the repression of the individual's

Compare & Contrast

- **1900–1910:** In 1900, Freud publishes *The Interpretation of Dreams*, which attempts to explain phenomena such as sexuality and abnormal desires.

  Today: Freud remains popular, though many of his theories have been discredited.

- **1900–1910:** The December 1900 issue of the *Ladies' Home Journal* predicts that exercise will become compulsory in schools and that by the year 2000 those who cannot walk ten miles a day will be considered weaklings.

  Today: Obesity is a major health problem in both Western Europe and the Untied States, as people eat more and exercise less.

- **1900–1910:** German philosopher Friedrich Nietzsche, who proclaimed "God is dead" and whose ideas influenced Hitler, dies.

  Today: Nietzsche's ideas continue to influence philosophers and social theorists throughout the world.

---

childhood desires—a son for his mother, a daughter for her father—that developed into neurotic symptoms in adulthood, Freud argued. Childhood was also the subject of the bestselling children's book of all time, *The Tale of Peter Rabbit*, authored by Beatrix Potter and published in 1902.

Rilke struggled financially during this time and restlessly traveled throughout Europe, to Worpswede, Italy, Scandinavia, Germany, and back to Paris, searching for a place that could accommodate both his need to write and his desire for authenticity in human interactions.

Critical Overview

Although "Childhood" is a frequently anthologized Rilke poem because of its accessibility and subject matter, very little criticism has been written on it or *The Book of Images*. Edward Snow, who has translated the volume in its entirety, claims in his introduction that this is because of the collection's "scattered, hybrid quality, which makes generalizing about it so difficult." The collection itself appeared twice, once in 1902 and again in 1906, in a much-expanded version. Although Snow notes that many of the poems are rough and do not live up to Rilke's later work, he claims, "In the most brilliant of the poems in *The Book of Images* . . . Rilke is uncannily confident from the first."

Writing on Rilke in *European Writers*, James Rolleston points out the significance of the collection in Rilke's development as an artist, noting that it "illuminates the continuity of Rilke's maturing process." Critic Frank Wood agrees. In his study of Rilke's poetry, *Rainer Maria Rilke: The Ring of Forms*, Wood claims the collection marks a transitional phase in Rilke's poetry. Comparing *The Book of Images* to *The Book of Hours*, written around the same time, Wood says, "[*The Book of Images*] contains some . . . really superb poems. . . . we are at least aware that a poet, and not a stylized monk, is speaking."

Criticism

Chris Semansky

Semansky's essays and reviews appear regularly in journals and newspapers. In this essay, Semansky considers the tone of Rilke's poem and its relation to his other poems on childhood.

Rilke was obsessed with loss, with the presence of death in life. His writing is invariably dark, sad, elegiac. Elegies are laments written for the dead. However, Rilke's mourning was not limited to the dead. As someone who paid minute attention to the nuances of his own feelings, perceptions, and changes, Rilke also mourned the loss(es) of his

> "As an impressionistic representation of his own childhood, the poem captures the complexities of growing up Rilke."

previous selves. "Childhood" is representative in tone and theme of Rilke's poetry, as it laments both childhood and the passing of childhood.

It is impossible not to associate Rilke with the child in the poem. Rilke's own troubled childhood was fodder for so much of his writing. He insisted that it was only by being alone that one could truly be an artist, and Rilke made a life out of being alone. Like the child in the poem, who is engulfed in tortuously slow "lumpish time," waiting for his liberation from school, Rilke seemed to live waiting for his own death, chronicling the road to his impending demise. Time is the stuff that the poet swam in, the measuring stick he used to gauge his relationship to death, thus the speaker's repeated evocation of time throughout the poem.

It is normal for children to be attuned to time while in school. Their days are structured in periods, and the school day begins and ends at a certain hour. Enduring those hours, however, is often difficult, especially if the child already feels out of place in school, which Rilke did. In this sense, the time of childhood for Rilke stands in for the span of one's entire life, which has to be endured, witnessed daily. It is this witnessing of the body's inability to stop time's passing that causes the speaker to cry out, "Such marvelous time, such time passing on, / such loneliness." Time is "marvelous" because it is that which changes people and, without it, existence would be impossible. In this sense, the poet celebrates the passage of time, as he also mourns it.

Rilke is a different kind of witness. His vision goes deep into a thing, a moment, a memory, until he is able to distill its essence and characterize it in all of its complexities and intricacies. His style is so unique that critics often refer to a certain kind of lyric poem as "Rilkean," which means that it is often relentlessly self-conscious and that its insights are usually psychological. Knowing himself required constant witnessing to his past, and by choosing to represent his childhood in densely pictorial terms, Rilke is able to illustrate not only the jumble of conflicting emotions he experienced as a child but the continuing jumble of conflicting emotions he experienced as an adult. He evokes the sense of distance by repeatedly drawing attention to the difference between the child's inner and outer worlds—the frustration and anxiety he endures while in school and the joy he feels when out in the garden playing tag. The distance between the world of the adult speaker and the world of the child parallels the distance between the inner and outer worlds the child experiences.

As an impressionistic representation of his own childhood, the poem captures the complexities of growing up Rilke. The poet often described his childhood in less than flattering terms, noting that his mother sheltered him from others and so deferred his socialization and that his parents held each other in icy regard and eventually separated during his childhood. As an only child in Prague—a city rife with tensions between Czechs and Germans—Rilke was already an outsider. School simply increased his sense of alienation from others. In his biography of the poet, *Rilke: A Life*, Wolfgang Leppmann argues that for Rilke, coming to terms with his childhood was "one of the driving forces behind his literary production."

The drive to understand his childhood led Rilke to write numerous poems on the subject, and not surprisingly these poems sometimes reference one another. For example, a poem from his collection *New Poems*, also titled "Childhood," seems to directly address Rilke's attempt in *The Book of Images* to name the experience of childhood:

> It would be good to give much thought, before
> you try to find words for something so lost,
> for those long childhood afternoons you knew
> that vanished so completely—and why?

Just as Rilke addresses his childhood self in the earlier poem, so too he addresses a later incarnation of his self in this poem, creating a kind of poetic feedback loop that, potentially, can go on forever, or at least until he dies. Rilke stands out in modern poetry as a writer who elevated the self to an almost divine status and who took the darker side of his emotional life as the primary subject for his poems.

Rilke's obsession with the self and its permutations through time is in large part a result of his feeling of homelessness. A lifetime wanderer, he would spend a year in one place, a week in another, a month here or there. When he was not renting a cheap room in a run-down section of a city such as Paris, he would stay with wealthy patrons, often women. Place for Rilke was an interior space, populated by memories and a powerful desire to know himself. Geographically unmoored, Rilke sought stability in his dedication to his art.

Sometimes Rilke's excessive enthusiasm for self-knowledge intrudes into his poems, diluting their imagistic power. This happens in the "Childhood" of *The Book of Images*, where the narrator comments on the child's perceptions. By doing this, he makes explicit the speaker's presence and point of view toward the child. A more successful, though less anthologized, poem from *The Book of Images*, also on the subject of childhood, is "From a Childhood." In this much shorter poem, Rilke stays true to his desire to create a verbal snapshot of an event.

> The darkness was a richness in the room
> where the boy sat, hidden, by himself.
> And when the mother entered, as in a dream,
> a thin glass trembled on the silent shelf.
> She felt as if the room had betrayed her, but
> she kissed her boy and murmured: Are you here?
> Then both glanced shyly at the dark clavier,
> for often in the evening she would sing
> a song in which the child was strangely caught.
>
> He sat so quietly, his gaze bent low
> upon her hands, weighed down with heavy rings,
> moving along the white keys as men go
> heavily through the deep drifts of snow.

In this poem, there is no editorializing speaker punctuating the description. The images themselves tell readers everything they need to know about the relationship between the child and his mother. The last image of the poem, in which the boy plays with his sailboat and gazes into the pond, evokes a reality beyond that which one normally sees. Such an image is used to fuse the experience of the poet's inner self with his outer world. Poets rely on association and intuition, rather than rational thought processes to evoke meaning and emotion. The surrealists refined the use of the deep image, and it gained popularity again in the 1960s in the poetry of Robert Bly, Mark Strand, W. S. Merwin, Galway Kinnell, and William Stafford. Not surprisingly, most of these poets have translated Rilke, "updating" his work for the late twentieth-century sensibility.

Source: Chris Semansky, Critical Essay on "Childhood," in *Poetry for Students*, Gale, 2003.

Frank Pool

Pool is a published poet and reviewer and teaches advanced placement and international baccalaureate English. In this essay, Pool compares Rilke to impressionist painters and discusses problems of poetry in translation.

Rilke's poem "Childhood" appears in a collection that can be translated in English as *The Book of Images*, or, in an alternative translation, as *The Book of Pictures*. This collection was published twice, first in 1902 and later in an expanded version in 1906. As Edward Snow writes in his translation of Rilke's *The Book of Images*, the poems in this volume "tend to epitomize what it means to characterize... a mood, a stance, a cadence, a quality of voice, a way of looking" as typical of the poet. This poem is one of many images in the book; it is an image of childhood, looked upon from the perspective adulthood. It is a reflection in later life on powerful emotions from the poet's childhood and is similar to the work of such romantic poets as William Wordsworth. "Childhood" is a period piece about Rilke's childhood, and it participates in the impressionist movement that Rilke, under the influence of Parisian art and the sculptor Rodin, took part in during this time.

The impressionists were a group of artists in France and Germany near the end of the nineteenth century. The movement derives its name from the artistic movement founded by Monet with his painting called "Impression: Sunrise." With the advent of photography, artistic realism seemed to have been superseded by technology. The impressionists created an art in which light and colors dominated the canvas. Lines between forms were less distinct than before and, in fact, took on a blurry kind of existence. With respect to writers, impressionism made itself felt partly as poets began to explore the sensuality and eroticism of the unconscious. They also used words charged with sensory impressions, something Robert Bly in his translation of "Childhood" expresses in English as "lights and colors and noises; / water leaps out of fountains into the air, / and the world is so huge in the woody places."

A major key to understanding the intent of the poem lies in the German word *bild*, which means not only a literal picture, portrait, or visual representation but also an image as metaphor that points beyond itself. Snow says, "*bilder* in this sense can populate the visual realm with traces, invisible connections, imaginings, remembrances, intimations of things lost or unrealized, waiting to be recalled or brought (back) to life." It is as an image of a lost childhood, dually and simultaneously typical and unique, that this poem appears.

> "'Childhood' is a period piece about Rilke's childhood, and it participates in the impressionist movement that Rilke, under the influence of Parisian art and the sculptor Rodin, took part in during this time."

The poem begins with a confusion of opposites, with the first three lines expressing the boredom and *ennui* that even good students sometimes feel about school. Then, there is a sudden shift, and there is action, colors, noises, and the blooming, buzzing eruption and enlargement of the world that a child leaving the classroom and going out to play experiences.

Rilke alternates between narration and meditation in each stanza. He presents impressions of color and light, much as an impressionist painter might. Such lines as "children's bright colors make them stand out" and "in some green place as the light fades away" suggest the verbal equivalent of a painting. Yet, Rilke concludes each stanza, in a sort of parallel structure, with meditation on the images. Bly's translation works to be colloquial in modern English, but it neglects some of the explicit parallelism of the German, a parallelism that is caught in other translations.

Ultimately, a serious student of poetry in translation must make some effort to see what the poem must say either in the original or by comparing various translations to see what each of them seems to capture and how the translations diverge. With Rilke, the comparison is relatively easy because there are many translations of his work. Why do different translators continue to visit and revisit Rilke? As William H. Gass says in his book *Reading Rilke: Reflections on the Problems of Translation*, many translators have

> ... blunted their skills against his obdurate, complex, and compacted poems, poems displaying an orator's theatrical power, while remaining as suited to a chamber and its music as a harpsichord: made of plucked tough sounds, yet as rapid and light and fragile as fountain water.

In looking at the Bly translation and comparing it to the original, one fact stands out: Rilke's poem rhymes, and Bly's translation does not. Some translators of Rilke try to preserve the rhyme. Leishman produces rhymed translation, while Snow does not. Bly, in his *Selected Poems of Rainer Maria Rilke*, thoughtfully provides the German original on facing pages, as does Snow in his translation of *The Book of Images*. Looking at the German, even if one does not fully understand the language, can help one see the structures and repetitions in the original with which any translator must struggle.

In the original German, the poem's unification is enhanced by use of the interjection "O" plus a noun, repeated several times at the end of each of the four stanzas. The reader is forced to look at these nouns to see how they apply to the general theme of childhood. These combinations have positive, negative, or neutral connotations. For example, "Such marvelous time, such time passing on, / such loneliness" presents an immediate contrast at the end of the first stanza. In general, these parallel structures tend toward a sense of melancholy and gravity. Such words as "loneliness," "heaviness," "deepness," "worry," and "weight" express the poet's meditations on the images of childhood. It turns out that the meditations are much more somber than the images are. Perhaps Rilke reflects on childhood in tranquility, but he does not do so without anxiety.

In Bly's translation, he replaces the word "O," a word conspicuously absent in current American usage, with a variety of terms, such as "such," and "what" and, in both the first and last stanza, the less-elevated "oh." Bly's alterations of Rilke's original use of the "O" forms syntactical structures that are more pleasing to the contemporary ear, yet the parallelism that is evident in the original, as well as in Leishman's and Snow's translations, gets weakened in Bly's. Different readers may have diverse responses to Bly's translation; some readers enjoy Rilke's mastery of rhyme and structure, whereas others may find it too different from modern poetry to enjoy.

Rilke wrote in his *Letters to a Young Poet*,

> ... even if you were in a prison whose walls allowed none of the sounds of the world to reach your senses, would you not still have always your childhood, that precious, royal richness, that treasure house of memories? Turn your attention there.

In this poem, it is not immediately clear whether childhood is a happy time period for Rilke.

There are certainly idyllic moments in this poem. The sudden release of a child from school, the joys of parks and games of tag, and dogs and sailboats all seem to be perfect images of an idealized childhood. Indeed, these images seem to be metaphors for a safe, orderly, self-satisfied life. Yet Rilke is far from satisfied. Childhood recedes from him, eternally and inexorably. His last two lines say (in Bly's translation) "oh childhood, what was us going away / going where? Where?" Snow translates the same conclusion as "O childhood, O likeness gliding off / To where? To where?" In this instance, it seems that Snow has the better of it, in that his translation catches the sense of the German *entgleitende*, etymologically related to the English "glide," as well as *vergleiche*, which means "simile," "likeness," or "comparison." One must remember that this is a book of images, which are themselves metaphors. This likeness, which remains unnamed, is the ineffable mysteriousness of existence that the poet senses in meditating on his own childhood.

Rilke begins as something of an impressionist, but he puts his own distance and anxieties into this poem. Kathleen L. Komar, writing in the *Germanic Review* says "Renunciation and absence... take on a positive creative value for Rilke." It is to the constantly gliding-away past that he turns his attention in "Childhood." Like much of Rilke's work, this is a poem of depth and serious intent. It appeals because of its language, because of its formal structure. Unfortunately, Bly's translation cannot convey these elements. It is only through comparison with other translations that one can see the linguistic richness of the poem. In addition to the linguistic wealth, there is a universality in this poem. Far from being sentimental and conventional, it utilizes images of a fairly typical late nineteenth-century, middle-class childhood to convey something of the depth of the poet's perception. Many people find their childhood escaping them, and yet they cannot let them go. Such a duality, a desire to fix fluid memories in place is characteristic of a life of spirit and mind and perception. Rilke's poem evokes the creative spirit that many people have. It is through such poems that Rilke has gained an enduring reputation.

Source: Frank Pool, Critical Essay on "Childhood," in *Poetry for Students*, Gale, 2003.

George C. Schoolfield

In the following essay, Schoolfield discusses Rilke's personal history and how it affected his writing.

Rainer Maria Rilke is one of the major poets of twentieth-century literature. In the collections with which his early verse culminates, *Das Buch der Bilder* (The Book of Pictures, 1902; enlarged, 1906) and *Das Stunden-Buch enthaltend die drei Bücher: Vom mönchischen Leben: Von der Pilgerschaft: Von der Armuth und vom Tode* (1905; translated as *The Book of Hours; Comprising the Three Books: of the Monastic Life, of Pilgrimage, of Poverty and Death*, 1961), he appears as a creator or discoverer of legends—his own and history's—and, particularly in the latter work, as a special brand of mystic. With the poems of his middle years, *Neue Gedichte* (1907–1908; translated as *New Poems*, 1964), he is an expert instructor in the art of "seeing" as well as a guide through Europe's cultural sites just before the onslaught of general war and, subsequently, mass tourism. Because of statements in *Duineser Elegien* (1923; translated as *Elegies from the Castle of Duino*, 1931) and *Die Sonette an Orpheus* (1923; translated as *Sonnets to Orpheus*, 1936) on the limitations and possibilities of the human condition, he has become something of a teacher and consoler to readers aware of the fragility and the potential of man. Long the prey of cultists and often obscure exegetes and regarded as the bearer of a "message" or "messages," he has more recently been seen as a brilliant verse tactician whose visions may be more original in their manner of perception than in their philosophical core. His novel *Die Aufzeichnungen des Malte Laurids Brigge* (1910; translated as *The Notebook of Malte Laurids Brigge*, 1930) was initially received as a belated product of European decadence or as an autobiographical document (neither opinion is wholly off the mark); later it was identified as a striking example of the "crisis of subjectivity and its influences on the traditional possibilities of narration," in Judith Ryan's formulation. Of all Rilke's works, the large body of stories he wrote has received the least attention; as a mature artist he himself grew condescending when he occasionally mentioned them in his letters—in striking contrast to *Die Aufzeichnungen des Malte Laurids Brigge*, which he continued to praise and explicate until his death. These tales and sketches, some seventy of them, fall into the beginning of his career, before the changes that took place in his life and production in the years from 1902 to 1905.

Rilke's attitudes toward Prague, where he was born René Karl Wilhelm Johann Josef Maria Rilke on 4 December 1875, were mixed, as were those toward his parents. His father, Josef, was a former warrant officer in the Austrian army who at the time of Rilke's birth was a railroad official—a job perhaps owed to the influence of Josef's well-to-do elder brother, Jaroslav. His mother, Sophie (Phia) Entz Rilke, homely and socially ambitious, was the daughter of a perfume manufacturer. Rilke was their only child; a daughter, born before him, had survived only a few days. The parents were divorced before Rilke's childhood was past. The epistolary evidence indicates that Rilke was devoted to his father, who was simple, gregarious, and a lady's man, but saw rather little of him, and that he nearly detested his mother; yet it was the latter who encouraged his literary ambitions. The complexity of his feelings for his mother may be indicated in his early verse and stories by the appearance of a dream mother, lovely and even desirable; his reaction to Phia's bigoted Roman Catholicism, the faith in which he was reared, is reflected both in the ambiguous allusions to a Roman Catholic world in his early verse and *Das Marien-Leben* (1913; translated as *The Life of the Virgin Mary*, 1921) and in his much-proclaimed dislike of Christianity. Rilke's snobbery, which led him to cling obstinately to a family saga of age-old nobility, was encouraged by the genealogical researches of his uncle Jaroslav and by his mother's pretensions and prejudices; Phia Rilke was distinguished by her sense of extraordinary refinement and by her contempt for Jews and Czech speakers. Both the Rilkes and the Entzes were "Prague Germans," aware that they were up against an ever more aggressive Slavic majority in a city where German speakers were confronted, as the century wore on, by the rapid weakening of their social and political position.

At ten, after an elementary education, much interrupted by real or fancied illness, with the Piarist Brothers, Rilke was sent to the military school at Sankt Pölten in Lower Austria; save for summer vacations he remained there until 1890, when he was transferred to the military upper school at Mährisch-Weißkirchen in Moravia. The abrupt change from the cosseted existence at home to regimented boarding-school life cannot have been pleasant, even though his teachers encouraged him to read his poems aloud to his fellow students. As a young man Rilke planned to free himself from "jenes böse und bange Jahrfünf" (that evil and frightened half-decade) by writing a military-school novel, and in a letter of 1920 he made an extremely harsh reply to Major General von Sedlakowitz, his German teacher at Sankt Pölten, who had written to congratulate him on his fame: "Als ich in besonneneren Jahren . . . Dostojewskis Memoiren aus einem Toten-Hause zuerst in die Hände bekam, da wollte es mir scheinen, daßich in alle Schrecknisse und Verzweifelungen des Bagno seit meinem zehnen Jahre eingelassen gewesen sei" (When, in years of greater reflection . . . I first got hold of Dostoyevski's *Memoirs from the House of the Dead*, it seemed to me that I had been exposed to all the terrors and despairs of the prison camp from my tenth year on). After not quite a full year at the second school, from which he emerged, he told Sedlakowitz, "ein Erschöpfter, körperlich und geistig Mißbrauchter" (exhausted, abused in body and soul), he was discharged for reasons of health and went back to Prague—only to show off by wearing his cadet's uniform and bragging about a future return to the colors. His uncle Jaroslav then sent him to a commercial academy at Linz, an experience about which he later wrote that investigations were pointless, since he had not been himself at the time. Recent research indicates that he was a would-be bon vivant who persuaded a children's nurse to run away with him to a hotel in Vienna.

In 1892 Jaroslav agreed to finance private instruction leading to the qualifying examination at Prague's German Charles-Ferdinand University, so that one day Rilke could take over his uncle's law firm. Not that Jaroslav was at all confident about the boy's future: "Renés Phantasie ist ein Erbteil seiner Mutter und durch ihren Einfluß, von Hause aus krankhaft angeregt, durch unsystematisches Lesen allerhand Bücher überheizt—[ist] seine Eitelkeit durch vorzeitiges Lob erregt" (René's imagination is an inheritance from his mother, abnormally excited through her influence from the very beginning, overheated by the unsystematic reading of all sorts of books—his vanity has been aroused by premature praise). Tutorial instruction was congenial to Rilke's temperament; by 1895 he was ready to matriculate. He was already avidly seeking an audience—his unbearably sentimental first book, *Leben und Lieder: Bilder und Tagebuchblätter* (Life and Songs), had come out in 1894, dedicated to Valerie David-Rhonfeld, the niece of the Czech poet Julius Zeyer (Valerie had financed the book's publication). The twenty-one artificially simple poems of *Wegwarten* (Wild Chicory) appeared in January 1896. At the end of the summer of 1896 he moved to Munich, ostensibly for art history studies but with an eye to the cultural and publishing opportunities afforded by the Bavarian capital, which was then Berlin's equal as an artistic center. By this time he had considerably better proof of his lyric talent to display: *Larenopfer* (Offering to the Lares, 1896), with its tributes to Prague, was followed by *Traumgekrönt: Neue*

Gedichte (Crowned with Dreams, 1897), containing some turgid but striking erotic poems, and he was already a busy contributor to popular journals.

Some of Rilke's Munich acquaintanceships were plainly meant to further his career—for example, that with the dramatist Max Halbe. (Rilke's naturalistic drama *Im Frühfrost: Ein Stück Dämmerung. Drei Vorgänge* [1897; translated as *Early Frost* in *Nine Plays*, 1979] was produced in Prague in July 1897 with the young Max Reinhardt in the role of the weak father.) Others were more important: the novelist Jakob Wassermann introduced him to the Danish author whose works became his vade mecum, Jens Peter Jacobsen. Another young friend, Nathan Sulzberger from New York, provided him with a second major object of cultural devotion: in March 1897, at Sulzberger's invitation, he visited Venice for the first time. He spent an April vacation on Lake Constance with "the mad countess," Franziska zu Reventlow, who was pregnant with another man's child; and in May 1897 he met Lou Andreas-Salomé, fifteen years his senior, the author and former friend of Nietzsche, and the wife (in name only, it would seem) of the Iranian scholar Friedrich Carl Andreas. The summer Lou and Rilke spent at Wolfratshausen in the Bavarian Alps wrought remarkable changes in him: he altered his name from René to Rainer, his handwriting became firmer and clearer, and he gathered his passionate love poetry to Lou into the manuscript collection "Dir zur Feier" (In Celebration of You), which, at her request, he did not publish. (The title, transmuted into *Mir zur Feier: Gedichte* [In Celebration of Me], was used for a book of verse in 1899.) Some of these poems, estimated to have been about one hundred in number, were subsumed into published collections; others survived only in manuscript; others were destroyed. How long Lou and Rainer remained lovers is not known, but Rilke followed her and her husband to Berlin in the autumn of 1897.

The Prussian capital remained Rilke's home until the new century. His stay there was interrupted by trips that were to be of major importance for his poetic development: a springtime journey to Italy in 1898 (his verse play *Die weiße Fürstin* [published in *Mir zur Feier: Gedichte*; translated as *The White Princess* in *Nine Plays*, 1979] grew out of a stay at Viareggio); an excursion to Russia from April to June 1899 in the company of the Andreases; and a second and much more carefully prepared Russian trip from May to August 1900, again with Lou but without her husband. Rilke—who had learned Russian easily and quickly on the

> *"Long the prey of cultists and often obscure exegetes and regarded as the bearer of a 'message' or 'messages,' he has more recently been seen as a brilliant verse tactician whose visions may be more original in their manner of perception than in their philosophical core."*

basis of his school training in Czech—visited the peasant poet Spiridon Drozhzhin and had an uncomfortable interview with Leo Tolstoy at his estate, Yasnaya Polyana. The Russian experience under the tutelage of Lou, a native of Saint Petersburg, provided him with new poetic material: following a fad of the time, he professed a mystic love for the great land in the east; he read its literature carefully and used Russian themes in the poems in *Das Buch der Bilder* and *Das Stunden-Buch enthaltend die drei Bücher: Vom mönchischen Leben: Von der Pilgerschaft: Von der Armuth und vom Tode*, in his tales, and in *Die Aufzeichnungen des Malte Laurids Brigge*. During a late-summer stay with the artist Heinrich Vogeler in the artists' colony at Worpswede, near Bremen, after his return from Russia, he wore a Russian peasant's blouse and a large Greek cross. In Worpswede, thus attired, he met the painter and sculptress Paula Becker and the sculptress Clara Westhoff. Rejected by Paula, he turned his affection to her statuesque friend. On 28 April 1901 Rilke and Clara were married.

The affair with Lou had been broken off, but their years together had been enormously productive for Rilke. Some of the poems in *Advent* (1898) are from the Wolfratshausen summer; Rilke came to regard *Mir zur Feier: Gedichte* as the first of his "admissible" books; his career as a dramatist had been encouraged by the publication of *Ohne Gegenwart: Drama in zwei Akten* (1898; translated as *Not Present* in *Nine Plays,* 1979), with its Maeterlinckian suggestions of ineffable fears, but it concluded disastrously with *Das tägliche Leben: Drama in zwei Akten* (1902; translated as *Everyday Life* in *Nine Plays*, 1979), a play written in 1900 about a painter caught between two loves. Produced at the Residenz Theater in Berlin in December 1901, it was greeted with laughter: Rilke resolved never to try the stage again.

The writing of stories had occupied much of Rilke's time: a first collection, *Am Leben hin: Novellen und Skizzen* (Along Life's Course), had appeared in 1898. The book contains eleven tales, six of which can be identified as having been finished at Wolfratshausen during the summer with Lou. Some of the tales suffer from the mawkishness that beset Rilke during his early years, whether he was writing poems, plays, or narratives. In "Greise" (Old Men) a little girl brings a flower to her grandfather as he sits on a park bench. Other old men watch; one of them, Pepi, spits contemptuously as his companion, Christoph, picks up some stray blossoms from the street and carries them back to the poorhouse. Yet Pepi puts a glass of water on the windowsill of their room, waiting in the darkest corner for Christoph to place the scruffy bouquet in it. In "Das Christkind" (The Christ Child) a little girl, mistreated by her stepmother, takes the money her father has slipped to her as a Christmas gift, buys some paper ornaments, and adorns a young fir tree with them; then she lies down in the forest to die, imagining that she is in her mother's lap. Here Rilke ventures into a maudlin realm long since cultivated by certain nineteenth-century masters; in fact, he identifies one of them: in Elisabeth's dying dreams, "Die Mutter [war] schön, wie die Fee im Märchen von Andersen" (The mother [was] beautiful, like the fairy in the tale of Andersen). In "Weißes Glück" (White Happiness) a tubercular girl tells her sad life story to another traveler, a man hoping for erotic adventure at a railroad station in the middle of the night. A blind girl has a beautiful voice but will live out her life unloved in "Die Stimme" (The Voice). Gypsies fight over a girl, and the stronger, Král, slays the boyish flute player in "Kismet."

With such stories, save for his awareness of language and a certain psychological refinement, Rilke does not rise much above the level of, say, another popular writer from Prague, Ossip Schubin (pseudonym of Aloisia Kirschner, 1854–1934). Yet there are flashes of a brilliant satiric gift in the depiction of a moribund Prague-German family in "Das Familienfest" (The Family Festival) and "Sterbetag" (Death Day), and evidence of a keen insight into human relations in "Das Geheimnis" (The Secret), about the romantic dreams of two old maids, and "Die Flucht" (The Flight), about a schoolboy's plans for an escapade with a young girl and his failure—not hers—to carry through with them. In "Alle in Einer" (All in One Woman) Rilke shows a penchant for the shocking and the horrible which he shared with other Prague writers such as Gustav Meyrink and Paul Leppin: tormented by passion, a lame woodcarver makes one image after another of the same girl, until he ends by hacking at his own hands. The concluding story, "Einig" (United), has autobiographical tones: a son with artistic ambitions has returned home ill to his pious mother. It is spoiled by a contrived happy ending—each learns that the other has been sending money to the family's estranged father—but it offers a nice specimen for students of the Ibsen craze in Germany around the turn of the century: like Oswald in Henrik Ibsen's *Ghosts* (1881), Gerhard says that he is a "wurmfaule Frucht" (worm-eaten fruit), recalling Oswald's famous description of himself as "vermoulu," and claims that his illness has been bestowed upon him by his father.

Zwei Prager Geschichten (Two Prague Stories, 1899) was composed at Berlin-Schmargendorf in 1897–1898. The foreword says: "Dieses Buch ist lauter Vergangenheit. Heimat und Kindheit—beide längst fern—sind sein Hintergrund" (This book is nothing but the past. Homeland and childhood—both far removed, long since—are its background). The two lengthy stories, however, have little to do with the Prague Rilke had known; rather, they take place in Czech milieus and are expressions of Rilke's brief flaring-up of interest in Czech nationalism (other evidence is to be found in *Larenopfer*). No doubt Rilke was also aware of the interest of German publishers and their public in Prague's semi-exotic world: Karl Hans Strobl (1877–1946), for example, launched his long career as a popular author by writing about the city and the tensions between its language groups. "König Bohusch" (King Bohusch) uses Prague's Czech-speaking artistic circles as a contrasting background for two outsiders who are far more energetic and tormented than the ineffectual aesthetes, actors, and dandies of the city's cafés: the student Rezek, detesting both German speakers and the Austrian government, organizes a terrorist band; Bohusch, a hunchback, loves his "Mütterchen" (little mother), Prague, and dreams of an affair with the prostitute Frantischka. Familiar with the city's nooks and crannies, the self-important

Bohusch shows Rezek a hiding place for the latter's group; simultaneously, he falls into fantasies of his own power. The police capture all the plotters save Rezek, who kills the poor, addled Bohusch because he suspects him of betraying the gang to the authorities. In fact, it was Frantischka who did so; her high-minded sister, Carla, is a member of Rezek's group. Based on actual events in the Prague of Rilke's youth, the story is an attempt to provide a dispassionate view of what, for Rilke, was an alien world, however close at hand.

More loosely constructed, "Die Geschwister" (The Siblings) looks sympathetically at a Czech family that has moved to the capital from the countryside. The son, Zdenko, is at the university; the mother does washing for the arrogant German speakers, Colonel and Mrs. Meering von Meerhelm, the depiction of whom may be the most convincing part of the story. Zdenko takes up with the radical circles around Rezek, who is carried over from "König Bohusch," but dies of illness before he can be forced to participate in their activities. The daughter, Louisa, has aroused the interest of Rezek but falls in love with Ernst Land, a young Bohemian-German who rents the late Zdenko's room and stays on after the death of Louisa's mother. By the end it is plain that the Czech and the German, the representatives of two hostile camps, will marry. The simple plot is drawn out by allusions to Bohemia's history, especially to the legends surrounding Julius Caesar, the vicious illegitimate son of Rudolf II who was said to have driven a girl to her death as he attempted to rape her during a masked ball at Krummau Castle. Rilke describes the Daliborka, the "hunger tower" on the Hradčany, later to serve as the setting for the love and conspiratorial scenes in Gustav Meyrink's *Walpurgisnacht* (1917). These tidbits are not just window dressing but are used by Rilke in an attempt at psychological portraiture. Louisa mingles the tale of Julius Caesar with her impressions of Rezek: "Und sie konnte ihm nicht wehren, daß er auch in ihre Träume wuchs und endlich eines wurde mit dem dunklen Prinzen des alten Maskentraumes und nun für sie nicht mehr Rezek sondern Julius Cäsar hieß" (And she could not prevent him from entering into her dreams and finally becoming one with the dark prince of the old dream of the masked ball, and now for her he was no longer Rezek but Julius Caesar). When Zdenko, Rezek, and Louisa visit the Daliborka, the obsessive thought returns, and she imagines herself naked, fleeing before the advances of Julius Caesar. Her rescue from these fantasies by the calm presence of Land may indicate that Rilke naively thought his Czech compatriots could be saved from the destructive allure of a Rezek by good-natured German liberalism.

Plainly, Rilke is fascinated by sexuality; but he often shies away from addressing it directly. (One of the most linguistically tortuous and emotionally tormented poems in the whole of his work is "Das Bett" [The Bed] in *Neue Gedichte*.) It is surprising that in the title tale of his third story collection, *Die Letzten* (The Last, 1902), written in 1898–1899 under Lou's aegis, he can be as frank as he is in discussing a taboo theme: mother-son incest. (*Die Letzten* was the first of Rilke's books to be published by the Dane Axel Juncker, who shared, Rilke believed, his own interest in the physical makeup of books: a "quiet" text merited "quiet" and elegant printing and binding.) The first story, "Im Gespräch" (In Conversation), records the talk of a group of artists in the salon of the Princess Helena Pavlovna at Venice. The speakers each have roles to play: the German painter is clumsy and loud, the gentleman from Vienna (a city Rilke, from provincial Prague, especially disliked) speaks with empty elegance, the Frenchman Count Saint-Quentin is still and polite, and the Pole Kasimir is the mouthpiece for Rilke's theories of artistic creation: "'Kunst ist Kindheit nämlich. Kunst heißt, nicht wissen, daß die Welt schon *ist*, und eine machen. Nicht zerstören, was man vorfindet, sondern einfach nichts Fertiges finden'" ("Art is childhood, you see. Art means not knowing that the world already *is*, and making [one]. Not destroying what one finds but rather simply not finding something finished"). Turning to the princess, Kasimir quotes her: "'Man muß, sagen Sie, dort muß man anfangen, wo Gott abließ, wo er müde wurde'" ("One must, you say, one must begin there where God left off, where He became tired"). At the end, having almost found a kindred soul, the Pole leaves, "wie einer der nicht wiederkommen wird an einen lieben Ort" (like someone who will not return to a beloved place).

A sensitive man is the central figure in the next story, "Der Liebende" (The Lover). The fragile Ernst Bang (his last name may allude to the adjective *bang* [anxious, afraid] or the Danish writer Herman Bang, whose works Rilke deeply admired) talks with his friend, the vigorous Hermann Holzer. Like Král in "Kismet," Holzer shuts out the light with his "schwarzen Rücken" (black silhouette; in Král's case it was "breite schwere Schultern" [broad, heavy shoulders]). Bang is in love with Helene, whom Holzer is going to marry; after many pauses (Rilke was captivated by Maeterlinck's use of silences onstage), Bang summons the courage to tell Holzer that the latter will destroy Helene with his clumsy affection: "'Nimm mir's nicht übel, Hermann, aber . . . du . . . zerbrichst . . . sie. . . .' Pause" ("Don't take it amiss, Hermann, but . . . you . . . will shatter her . . ." Pause). The difficult conversation drifts along; affable and even respectful, Holzer asks what Bang thinks he should do. "'Sprich, die ganze Kultur steht hinter dir, bedenke'" ("Speak up—remember, the whole culture stands behind you"). The struggle may be not so much between two lovers of the same woman as between the subtle heir to an ancient tradition and the bluff bearer of contemporary strength: Holzer is a peasant's son and has his father's qualities— "Sowas Grades, Eichenes" (something straightforward, oaken). The juxtaposition of the two types is a common one in the fin de siècle, with its sense of the ending of an old Europe and the beginning of a less nuanced world. Helene enters, learns of the conversation, and weeps; taking her on his lap, Holzer tries to console her as she turns pale. The melodrama is obvious: she will stay with Holzer, but both she and Ernst know how sad her fate will be. Rilke's sympathy, however, is not wholly on the side of Bang and Helene; regarding himself as the spokesman of beleaguered refinement, he still looks with some admiration and envy at what is young and fresh and vigorous.

As Rezek turns up both in "König Bohusch" and "Die Geschwister," so an apparent relative of Hermann Holzer appears as the third person in the title story, "Die Letzten." Marie Holzer's grandfather was a peasant; more self-aware than Hermann, she has a sense of being "jünger in der Kultur" (younger in culture) than the members of the impoverished noble family to which she has become attached. She is engaged to Harald Malcorn, whom she met at a gathering of social reformers where he was the impassioned speaker. Now she and Harald's mother await his return from another speaking engagement amid the Malcorns' "Dinge" (things—a word to which Rilke attaches much significance), the great age of which Marie respects and yet cannot quite comprehend. Almost maternally concerned for little Frau Malcorn's well-being, Marie nonetheless senses a rival in the widow, and their competition for Harald comes to the surface in a long stichomythia. Returning home exhausted and ill, Harald decides to abandon his agitator's calling: he breaks with Marie and places himself in his mother's care.

In the story's second part the convalescent Harald and his mother talk of going to an uncle's estate, Skal; but the plan is dropped, in part because of a family curse: the death of a family member has always been presaged by the appearance of a "dame blanche," Frau Walpurga, at the castles the family once owned, and most frequently at Skal. Harald tells his mother about his misty notions of becoming an artist; after recalling circumstances that point to Frau Malcorn's having had a lover long ago and to his own role as a childish and unwitting surrogate for the lover, and after recalling his reaction to his father ("Er hatte einen dichten weißen Bart. Er war alt'" ["He had a heavy white beard. He was old"]), Harald entices his mother into adorning herself like a bride: together they will celebrate a festival of beauty. Frau Malcorn reappears in a white dress, and Harald collapses; hitherto the room has been illuminated only by moonlight, but now someone lights a light, and the reader sees a terrifying tableau: "Harald sitzt entstellt in den Kissen, den Kopf noch vorgestreckt, mit herabhängenden Händen. Und vor ihm steht Frau Malcorn, welk, in Atlas, mit Handschuhen. Und sie sehen sich mit fremdem Entsetzen in die toten Augen" (Harald sits distorted in his cushions, his head still stretched forward, with his hands hanging down. And Frau Malcorn stands before him, withered, in satin, with her gloves. And they gaze into one another's dead eyes with strange horror).

"Die Letzten" is a grotesque and fascinating melange of themes: the "last of the line," unable to create the art that might have been born of his sensitivity; the mother who is led into a fatal attempt to recover her lost youth; the well-meaning outsider, "healthier" than the inhabitants of the old world to which she is drawn. The literary echoes are many: Ibsen's *Ghosts*, Maeterlinck (the numerous pauses, the subtle anxiety), Jacobsen (Frau Malcorn's *nom d'amour* is Edel, reminiscent of Edele Lyhne, the aunt of whom the adolescent Niels Lyhne becomes enamored in the novel *Niels Lyhne* [1880; translated, 1919]), the Gothic tale. What were Rilke's intentions with the story, which comes dangerously close to unintentional comedy with its "white lady" and its family curse? Did he mean to write a *conte cruel* to vie with the most exaggerated specimens of contemporary decadent literature? The decadent apparatus is plainly on display: the ancient family, incestuous eroticism, a shocking close. Did he intend to plumb the depths of an erotic mother-son relationship of whose existence he was aware in his own case (the psychiatrist Erich Simenauer thinks so) and then mix these personal problems with his theories on the creation of art? Does the story (as Egon Schwarz believes) show the young Rilke's swerve away from the social concerns with which he had flirted to the aesthetic vision of life he subsequently and adamantly maintained? "Die Letzten" is one of Rilke's most tantalizing works, a bizarre conclusion to his early fiction.

In the years between the start of his career in Prague and his removal from Berlin-Schmargendorf and the ambience of Lou in February 1901, Rilke wrote some thirty other tales and sketches: some of these appeared in journals; others were never printed during his lifetime. Exaggerated and often banal effects are common: in a painful specimen of naturalism, "Die Näherin" (The Seamstress, first published in volume 4 of Rilke's *Sämtliche Werke* [Collected Works] in 1961), the narrator is seduced by a lonely and physically unattractive woman; in the lachrymose "Die goldene Kiste" (The Golden Chest, 1895) little Willy admires a golden chest in an undertaker's window, and his dying words express his desire to be laid to rest in it; a beautiful girl is the victim of brain damage in "Eine Tote" (A Dead Girl, 1896); a wife kills herself so that her husband can devote himself fully to his art in "Ihr Opfer" (Her Sacrifice, 1896); a tubercular girl is used and then forgotten, after her death, by a robust male in "Heiliger Frühling" (Holy Spring, 1897); the young bride of a jovial and hearty older man falls in love with her husband's willowy and melancholy son in "Das Lachen des Pán Mráz" (The Laughter of Pán Mráz, 1899); the story of the masked ball at Krummau Castle from "Die Geschwister" is retold in "Masken" (Masks, 1898); a mother loves her son too well in "Leise Begleitung" (Soft Accompaniment, 1898) and vicariously experiences his disappointment in a love affair with a girl of his own age as she sits beside her unfeeling husband. There are stunted figures: the emotionally frigid man searching for an "event" in "Das Ereignis" (The Event, published in *Todtentänze: Zwielicht-Skizzen aus unseren Tagen* [Dances of Death, 1896]); the doctrinaire Nietzschean in "Der Apostel" (The Apostle, 1896); the dreamy would-be artist in "Wladimir, der Wolkenmaler" (Wladimir the Cloud-Painter, 1899)—in "Die Letzten," Harald planned to paint clouds, a subject quickly transmuted into his mother, clad in her white dress. Attempts are made at comedy: in "Teufelsspuk" (Devilment, 1899) the new owners of the estate of Gross-Rohozec are terrified by what they think is the castle ghost, but it is merely the former owner, a nobleman, who—slightly intoxicated—has groped his way back to his family's previous possessions. The story might seem to have anti-Semitic overtones, since the buyers of the castle are Jewish and Rilke implies that they are somehow ennobled by their midnight contact with nobility. "Teufelsspuk" was printed in the Munich journal *Simplicissimus* and intended for inclusion in a new volume of novellas Rilke outlined for the publisher Bonz in the summer of 1899; nothing came of the project.

Some of Rilke's best tales are autobiographical. One of the stories unpublished during his lifetime is "Pierre Dumont" (first published in Carl Sieber's biography *René Rilke*, 1932), about a boy parting from his mother at the military school's gate. Another is *Ewald Tragy* (written, 1898; published, 1929; translated, 1958), a long story in two parts about a watershed in the life of a young man. The first half consists of the cruel yet somehow affectionate depiction of his last dinner with the members of his Prague family (made up mainly of desiccated oldsters and eccentrics) and his difficult relation with his father, the bestower of uncomprehending love; in the second, Ewald moves away to the loneliness and freedom of Munich. "Die Turnstunde" (The Exercise Hour), published in *Die Zukunft* in 1902, pays painfully accurate attention to the petty obscenities and large emotional deformations of adolescence. Little Krix tells Jerome, Rilke's alter ego, that he has beheld the body of Gruber, a boy who had died during gymnastics: "'Ich hab ihn gesehen,' flüstert er atemlos und preßt Jeromes Arm und ein Lachen ist innen in ihm und rüttelt ihn hin und her. Er kann kaum weiter: 'Ganz nackt ist er und eingefallen und ganz lang. Und an den Fußsohlen ist er versiegelt. . . .' Und dann kichert er, spitz und kitzlich, kichert und beißt sich in den Ärmel Jeromes hinein" ("I have seen him," he whispers breathlessly and presses Jerome's arm and a laughter is within him and shakes him back and forth. He can scarcely continue: "He's all naked and collapsed and very long. And there are wax seals on the soles of his feet. . . ." And then he giggles, in a sharp, tickling way, giggles and bites into Jerome's sleeve).

"Die Turnstunde" was written only four days before Rilke essayed another descent into physical and psychological horror in "Frau Blahas Magd" (Frau Blaha's Maid); like "Die Turnstunde," it was first set down in Rilke's diary in the autumn of 1899 at Berlin-Schmargendorf, but it remained in manuscript. An early Rilke biographer, Eliza M. Butler, called it a "truly ghastly tale," while a more sympathetic commentator, Wolfgang Leppmann, has characterized it as "one of the most impressive short stories we have from his hand." Annuschka, a simple-minded country girl leading a wretched life as kitchen help in Prague, gives birth to a child, throttles it with her apron, and puts the corpse away at the bottom of her trunk. Then she buys a puppet theater she has seen in a toy-store window: "Jetzt hatte Annuschka etwas für das Alleinsein" (Now Annuschka had something for her loneliness). Neighbor children cluster around the theater; Annuschka tells them she also has a very large doll. They want to see it, but when she comes back "mit dem großen Blauen" (with the large blue thing) they become frightened and run away. Annuschka wrecks her theater, and "als die Küche schon ganz dunkel war, ging sie herum und spaltete allen Puppen die Köpfe, auch der großen blauen" (when the kitchen was quite dark, she went around and split the heads of all the puppets, and of the large blue one too). Annuschka has found refuge in an imaginary world; then, at the intrusion of reality, she destroys it. More successfully than in "King Bohusch," Rilke demonstrates what he imagines goes on in a limited or disturbed mind.

Other stories from the diary seem almost compulsively to seek after gruesome effects: the title character in "Der Grabgärtner" (The Grave-Gardener) transforms a cemetery into a garden in full bloom; he has come from the outside world to take the place of the old gravedigger, who has died. During an outbreak of the plague the townspeople, believing that the stranger has caused the epidemic, try to murder him; they succeed in slaying Gita, the mayor's daughter, whom the gravedigger loves. He kills the leader of the mob and goes off into the night, "Man weiß nicht, wohin" (One knows not whither). The story's emphasis is not on the beauty and order the gravedigger has brought to the realm of death, but on mass hysteria and mass horror; Rilke was probably trying to emulate Jacobsen's story "Pesten i Bergamo" (The Plague in Bergamo, 1881; translated as "Death in Bergamo," 1971). Philippe Jullian has called attention to the popularity in late-nineteenth-century art of what may be called necrophiliac scenes, with a superabundance of beautiful dead or dying bodies, as in Jean Delville's *Les Trésors de Sathan* (The Treasures of Satan, 1895) and Aristide Sartorio's *Diana d'Efeso e gli schiavi* (Diana of Ephesus and the Slaves, 1899): "eroticism and death have been blended with great skill." In the Rilke story, revised and published as "Der Totengräber" (The Gravedigger) in *Österreichisches Novellenbuch* (1903), the same public taste is fully met: "Der Wagen ist über und über mit Leichen beladen. Und der rote Pippo hat Genossen gefunden, die ihm helfen. Und sie greifen blind und gierig hinein in den Überfluß und zerren einen heraus, der sich zu wehren scheint.... Der Fremde schafft ruhig weiter. Bis ihm der Körper eines jungen Mädchens, nackt und blutig, mit mißhandeltem Haar, vor die Füße fällt" (The wagon is laden with corpses, pile upon pile. And the red-haired Pippo has found comrades who help him. And they reach blindly and greedily into this abundance, and pull out someone who seems to fend them off.... The stranger keeps calmly at his work. Until the body of a young girl, naked and bloody, with ill-treated hair, falls at his feet).

In the same autumn of 1899—as Rilke claimed, "in einer stürmischen Herbstnacht" (in a stormy autumn night)—he composed the initial version of the work that, in his lifetime, would make his name familiar to a broad public. It was called "Aus einer Chronik—der Cornet (1664)" (From a Chronicle—the Cornet [1664]); a revision made in Sweden in 1904 became "Die Weise von Liebe und Tod des Cornets Otto Rilke" (The Lay of the Love and Death of the Cornet Otto Rilke) and was published the same year in August Sauer's Prague journal *Deutsche Arbeit*. The final version, with the hero's name changed to Christoph, was published by Juncker in 1906; in 1912 it was the introductory number in Anton Kippenberg's series of inexpensive but handsome little books, "Die Inselbücherei," and made its way into thousands of romantically inclined hearts. In twenty-six brief poems in prose (reduced from twenty-nine in the first version and twenty-eight in the second) it gives an account of the last days of a noble officer from Saxony, eighteen years old, during an Austrian campaign against the Turks in western Hungary. Rilke had found a reference to this supposed ancestor in the genealogical materials assembled by his uncle Jaroslav; when he sent the manuscript of "Aus einer Chronik—der Cornet (1664)" to Clara Westhoff, he told her that it was "eine Dichtung... die einen Vorfahren mit Glanz umgiebt. Lesen Sie sie an einem Ihrer schönen Abende im weißen Kleid" (a poetic work that surrounds a forebear with splendor. Read it, on one of your beautiful evenings, in your white dress). The boy rides over the dusty plain; makes friends with a French marquis; sits by the campfire; observes the rough life of the bivouac; is presented to the commander, Johann von Sporck (of whom a portrait had hung in the military school at Sankt Pölten); and frees a girl tied nude to a tree—she seems to laugh when her bonds are cut, and the boy is horrified: "Und er sitzt schon zu Ross / und jagt in die Nacht. Blutige

Schnüre fest in der Faust" (And he is already mounted on his steed / and gallops into the night. Bloody cords held tight in his grip). The cornet writes to his mother; sees his first dead man, a peasant; and senses that the enemy is near. The company comes to a castle, and the officers are feted—another of Rilke's festivals of beauty. Dressed in white silk (reminiscent of the dress uniform worn by Austrian officers in Viennese operettas), the virgin youth meets the lady of the castle, and shortly, "nackt wie ein Heiliger. Hell und schlank" (naked as a saint. Bright and slim), he spends a night of love with her. "Er fragt nicht: 'Dein Gemahl?' Sie fragt nicht: 'Dein Namen?' . . . Sie werden sich hundert neue Namen geben. . . ." (He does not ask: "Your husband?" She does not ask: "Your name?" . . . They will give one another a hundred new names. . .). The Turks attack, and the troop rides out to meet them; the cornet, whose task is to bear the flag, is not present. But he appears in the nick of time, finds the banner—"auf seinen Armen trägt er die Fahne wie eine weiße, bewußtlose Frau" (he carries the flag in his arms, like a woman, white and unconscious)—and gallops into the midst of the foes; "die sechzehn runden Säbel, die auf ihn zuspringen, Strahl um Strahl, sind ein Fest. / Eine lachende Wasserkunst" (the sixteen curved sabers that leap at him, beam upon beam, are a festival. / A laughing fountain). The next spring, a courier brings the news of his death to his mother. That the tiny book captured a large readership is quite understandable: the impelling rhythms of its prose, the colorful settings, the theatrically simple situations, the amalgamation of eroticism and early heroic death were irresistible. That Rilke's view of war was hopelessly false, and a throwback to the worst extravagances of romanticism, is another matter.

A second book that also found a devoted audience, *Vom lieben Gott und Anderes: An Große für Kinder erzählt* (Concerning Dear God and Other Matters), had also gotten under way in the busy autumn of 1899. These playfully "pious" tales were quickly delivered to the Insel publishing house, administered by Schuster and Loeffler in Berlin, and appeared just in time for the Christmas trade of 1900; a new edition, *Geschichten vom lieben Gott* (translated as *Stories of God*, 1932), came out in 1904, with a dedication to the Swedish feminist and pedagogical writer Ellen Key. The stories have held a prominent place among the "standard" items by the young Rilke, but the Rilke scholar Eudo C. Mason dismissed them as a reproduction of "much of the religious doctrine of *Das Stunden-Buch enthaltend die drei Bücher: Vom mönchischen Leben: Von der Pilgerschaft: Von der Armuth und vom Tode* in prose, in the form of whimsical little tales told to children by a lame cobbler." Professor Mason's statement might be refined to say that the stories reproduce in particular the message of the first part of *Das Stunden-Buch enthaltend die drei Bücher: Vom mönchischen Leben: Von der Pilgerschaft: Von der Armuth und vom Tode*, "Das Buch von mönchischen Leben" (The Book of Monkish Life), which Rilke also wrote in the early autumn of 1899. God is in a state of becoming, perceived by artists and repeatedly created in their works, or God is the mystery from which art emanates: "Du Dunkelheit, aus der ich stamme" (You darkness, out of which I come), as *Das Stunden-Buch enthaltend die drei Bücher: Vom mönchischen Leben: Von der Pilgerschaft: Von der Armuth und vom Tode* proclaims. Mason's indifference toward *Geschichten vom lieben Gott* is evidenced by his unwonted inaccuracy; the tales are told to several listeners—a neighbor lady, a visiting stranger, a priggish male schoolteacher, District Commissioner Baum, and an artistically inclined young man, as well as the lame cobbler Ewald.

Oddly, the gentle book delights in making fun of the establishment; amid the often sugary trappings and language a sense of rebellion can be detected. In the first tale, "Das Märchen von den Händen Gottes" (The Tale of the Hands of God), the Lord's hands let humankind loose from heaven before the Maker has had a chance to inspect His work; in "Der fremde Mann" (The Strange Man) God's right hand, long since out of favor with God, is cut off by Saint Paul and sent to earth in human form; in "Warum der liebe Gott will, daß es arme Leute gibt" (Why Dear God Wants There to Be Poor People) the shocked schoolteacher is informed that the poor are closest to the truth and so are like artists. (In *Das Stunden-Buch enthaltend die drei Bücher: Vom mönchischen Leben: Von der Pilgerschaft: Von der Armuth und vom Tod* Rilke coined the phrase that has garnered him some scorn from socially aware readers: "Denn Armuth ist ein großer Glanz aus Innen" [For poverty is a great shining from within].) The pompous Baum, with his bourgeois view of a "romantic" Venice, is told in "Eine Szene aus dem Ghetto von Venedig" (A Scene from the Venetian Ghetto) about the precarious lot of the Jews in that splendid city, and about the vision of one of them, old Melchisedech, whose daughter has just had a child by a Christian. The narrator wonders what Melchisedech has seen: "'Hat er das Meer gesehen oder Gott, den Ewigen, in seiner Glorie?'" ("Has he beheld the sea or God, the Eternal Being, in His glory?"), to which Baum confidently replies: "'Das Meer wahrscheinlich ... es *ist* ja auch ein Eindruck'" ("The sea, probably ... after all, *that's* an impression too"). As these examples show, the tales suffer from excessive archness; in "Wie der Fingerhut dazu kam, der liebe Gott zu sein" (How the Thimble Came To Be Dear God), the all too clear message is that God is to be found in the least significant of objects—as obvious a point as that made in "Ein Verein aus einem dringenden Bedürfnis heraus" (A Club Created To Meet a Pressing Need), a long-winded formulaic narrative directed against artistic organizations.

The best of the stories are the three devoted to Russian themes, "Wie der Verrat nach Russland kam" (How Treachery Came to Russia), "Wie der alte Timofei singend starb" (How Old Timofei Died Singing), and "Das Lied von der Gerechtigkeit" (The Song of Justice). They are all told to the receptive Ewald and illustrate that Russia is a land that borders on God, a land of true reverence. The opportunity of making a thrust at dry scholarly authority is not allowed to slip by: the tales are based on *byliny* and *skazki*, epic folk songs and folktales long hidden away by learned men. According to the narrator, the tales have died out among the Russian people, and it seems to be his intention to bring them to life again. The first of the trio tells how a simple peasant demands from the czar not gold but truth and integrity (one more example of the poverty—and poverty of spirit in the biblical sense—that Rilke so admired); the second hopes for a continuation of the ancient line of folksingers and their songs, "darin die Worte wie Ikone sind und gar nicht zu vergleichen mit den gewöhnlichen Worten" (in which the words are like icons and not at all to be compared with ordinary words), even though such a continuation requires the singer to abandon his wife and child; the third is an historical tale from western Russia, in which a blind singer inspires his listeners to throw off the yoke of the Polish lords and the greed of the Jews.

There are also three tales from Italy: the Venetian ghetto story; a tribute to Michelangelo, "Von Einem, der die Steine belauscht" (Concerning Someone Who Eavesdropped on Stones); and another legend on the nature of true poverty, "Der Bettler und das stolze Fräulein" (The Beggar and the Proud Maiden), in which a Florentine noble disguises himself as a beggar and asks the prideful Beatrice to let him kiss the dusty hem of her garment. She is afraid of the strange beggar, but gives him a sack of gold. The experience transforms him: he remains in his beggar's rags, gives away all his possessions, and goes off barefoot into the countryside. Hearing the story, the teacher concludes that it is a tale of how a profligate becomes an eccentric tramp; the narrator rejoins that he has become a saint; and when the children hear the tale, they assert, "zum Ärger des Herrn Lehrer, auch in *ihr* käme der liebe Gott vor" (to the annoyance of the teacher, that dear God appeared in *this* story too). Like "Der Bettler und das stolze Fräulein," "Ein Märchen vom Tode" (A Tale about Death), with its glorification of "der alten schönen Gebärde des breiten Gebetes" (the beautiful old gesture of broad prayer), offers an example of the author's belief in the efficacy of a great or brave gesture that transforms its maker. Having begun with a double prologue set in heaven—the two tales about the hands of God—the collection harks back at its end to Rilke's more realistic stories with "Eine Geschichte, dem Dunkel erzählt" (A Story Told to the Darkness). Klara Söllner defies society's norms by divorcing her husband, a state official, and embarking on an affair with an artist; she rears their love child by herself. The narrator, twitting a narrow-minded public one last time, claims that nothing in the tale is unfit for children's ears; in fact, it reflects the scandalous independence of Rilke's friend, Franziska zu Reventlow.

Klara generously encourages her lover to leave her in pursuit of his art; Rilke himself was settling down to a life of considerably less freedom than he had known before. The young couple took up residence in Westerwede, near Worpswede; Rilke did reviews for a Bremen newspaper and larger periodicals and prepared *Die Letzten* and *Das Buch der Bilder* for publication. On 12 December 1901, their only child, Ruth (named after the heroine of a novel by Lou), was born. Home life could not long appeal to Rilke, and he began to conceive new plans. As a result of his Jacobsen enthusiasm, further readings of the Nordic works that were phenomenally popular in Germany at the time, and his association with Juncker, his interest in the north grew. Spending a month in the early summer of 1902 at Castle Haseldorf in Holstein as a guest of the poetaster Prince Emil von Schönaich-Carolath, he found in the archives sources that had to do with the great Danish-German Reventlow family: "Diese Wochen hier haben doch ihren Sinn, auch wenn sie nur im Lesen einiger Bücher bestehen" (These weeks here have their meaning after all, even though they consist only of the reading of some books). Simultaneously, he wrote a review of the Swedish reformer Ellen Key's *Barnets arhundrade* (1900; translated into German as *Das Jahrhundert des Kindes*, 1902; translated into English as *The Century of the Child*, 1909), with its recommendation for greater openness in the education of children; the review led to a correspondence with Key and, in time, to an invitation to the north.

But Rilke's immediate plan, the composition of a book about Auguste Rodin, led him to Paris in August 1902. The autumn weeks in the metropolis were difficult for him and formed the basis for several episodes in *Die Aufzeichnungen des Malte Laurids Brigge*; leaving Ruth in her parents' care, Clara also traveled to Paris to study with Rodin, but maintained a residence separate from her husband's so that each would have greater freedom. Rilke's production at the time was varied: he had completed his book on the Worpswede painters and the north German landscape in which they worked before he set out for Haseldorf; the Rodin book was written in Paris during November and December 1902 and was published in 1903; the second part of *Das Stunden-Buch enthaltend die drei Bücher: Vom mönchischen Leben: Von der Pilgerschaft: Von der Armuth und vom Tode*, "Das Buch von der Pilgerschaft" (The Book of Pilgrimage), had been completed at Westerwede in 1901; and in Paris he wrote verses that would be included in the augmented edition of *Das Buch der Bilder*, as well as "Der Panther" (The Panther), destined to become one of his best-known poems and the earliest of the items included in *Neue Gedichte*. A springtime trip to Viareggio in 1903 gave him the third part of *Das Stunden-Buch enthaltend die drei Bücher: Vom mönchischen Leben: Von der Pilgerschaft: Von der Armuth und vom Tode*, the upsetting mixture of eroticism and thoughts about death called "Das Buch von der Armuth und vom Tode" (The Book of Poverty and Death).

After a summer in Germany, the Rilkes set out in September 1903 for Rome; the poet's reaction to the city was one of discomfort. He found himself yearning for the north, and he sent pathetic letters to Key about the failure of the Roman winter and spring to be "real." In February 1904 Rilke made the first sketches for a novel about a young Dane in Paris: "An einem Herbstabende eines dieser letzten Jahre besuchte Malte Laurids Brigge, ziemlich unerwartet, einen von den wenigen Bekannten, die er in Paris besaß" (On an autumn evening of one of these last years Malte Laurids Brigge, rather unexpectedly, visited one of the few acquaintances he had in Paris). Malte tells his listener of a dinner interrupted by a ghostly apparition, an experience he had had when he was twelve or thirteen during a visit to his maternal grandfather's estate, Urnekloster, in the company of his father. The story would become one of the Danish episodes in the novel.

By the most skillful sort of hinting, Rilke arranged a Scandinavian stay from June to December 1904 to collect material for the book. The trip was spent largely with the artist and writer Ernst Norlind and Norlind's fiancée at a chateau, Borgeby, in south Sweden, and then at the home of an industrialist, James Gibson, at Jonsered near Gothenburg. The Gibsons were friends of Key, and a Sunday at the farmhouse of Key's brother, Mac Key (like the Gibsons, the family was of Scottish origin), in late November 1904 inspired another episode in *Die Aufzeichnungen des Malte Laurids Brigge*, the visit to the manor house of the Schulins, the center of which has been burned out. There, young Malte learns about fear. For a while Rilke toyed with the idea of preparing monographs on Jacobsen and on the Danish painter Vilhelm Hammershøj, but dropped both projects. He had learned to read Danish but could not speak it, and Copenhagen, which had initially charmed him as he passed through it, had come to seem ominous to him. He left Denmark on 8 December 1904 and never returned to the north; meeting a young Danish woman, Inga Junghanns, in Munich during the war, he rejoiced to think that the book about Malte would be returned to its "original language" in her translation. But Paris remained his true home, if so peripatetic a soul as Rilke may be said to have had a home.

In many ways 1905 marked a turning point in Rilke's career, just as the liaison with Lou had been the turning point in his personal development. Anton Kippenberg took over the Insel firm; in Kippenberg, Rilke discovered a skillful and usually generous manager of his literary fortunes and personal finances. His employment as Rodin's secretary began in September; it would end abruptly, in a dreadful scene, in May 1906. He made his first public appearances in Germany, reading from his works with a fire that was in contrast to his frail figure and exquisitely gloved hands. And, in part through the agency of the Rhenish banker Karl von der Heydt, he began to make the acquaintance of the noble ladies who would offer him so much solace and so many refuges. The relationship with Clara, whom he had to "keep at bay," in Miss Butler's malicious phrase, grew ever more tenuous, and Rilke developed the talent for swift wooing that would make the Princess Marie von Thurn und Taxis (happily married and, save intellectually, not one of his conquests) tell him that Don Juan was an innocent babe in comparison to him. Clara and Ruth briefly joined him on a trip to Belgium, sponsored by von der Heydt, late in the summer of 1906, but he much preferred to travel alone. Perhaps the first of his extramarital romances was with the Venetian Mimi Romanelli, whom he met at the pension of her brother in the autumn of 1907. He was the guest of Frau Alice Faehndrich at the Villa Discopoli on Capri in the winter and spring of 1906–1907 and again in the winter and spring of 1908; there he was surrounded by admiring ladies, among them the young and beautiful Countess Manon zu Solms-Laubach, for whom he wrote the poem "Migliera" (published in volume 2 of his *Sämtliche Werke*, 1956). With Frau Faehndrich, before her death in 1908, he translated Elizabeth Barrett Browning's *Sonnets from the Portuguese* (1850). Some of the poems from the Capri days found their way into *Neue Gedichte*; the first part, dedicated to the von der Heydts, appeared in 1907, the second, dedicated "À mon grand ami Auguste Rodin," in 1908. The quarrel with the master had been patched up; Rilke remained grateful to Rodin for having taught him the doctrine of work: "Il faut travailler toujours, rien que travailler" (One must work always, nothing but work).

Capri was not the main growing ground for the *Neue Gedichte*; that was Paris, to which Rilke became more attached the more he was able to transform its beauties and horrors into literature. An apartment at the Hôtel Biron in the Rue de Varenne became Rilke's pied-à-terre in August 1908; Rodin liked the Louis-Quatorze mansion so much that he immediately moved his own Parisian studio there. In 1910, on a trip to Leipzig during which he stayed in the tower room of the Kippenbergs' home, Rilke looked after the final stages of *Die Aufzeichnungen des Malte Laurids Brigge*. The production of the slender book emptied him, he liked to declare, and no other major work came from his hand during the next twelve years, although the production of this so-called barren period includes some of his best verse.

Die Aufzeichnungen des Malte Laurids Brigge consists of seventy-one entries divided into two parts, with a break after entry thirty-nine. It has often been conjectured that the model for Malte was the Norwegian poet Sigbjørn Obstfelder (1866–1900), a devotee of Jacobsen who had lived for some time in Paris; his fragmentary novel *En prests dagbok* (1900; translated into German as *Tagebuch eines Priesters*, 1901; translated into English as *A Priest's Diary*, 1987), and a collection of his other prose, which Rilke reviewed in 1904, had come out in German translation. Much about Obstfelder does not fit, however, the picture of Malte in Rilke's novel: Obstfelder was of modest parentage, an engineer by calling, and had lived and had a nervous breakdown in the American Middle West; the aristocratic Malte—the last of his line—is fetched rather from Rilke's reading of Bang and his own musings about himself and his fancied background. The age of Rilke in February 1904, when the first sketches were made, is that of Malte as he looks back on his life as a man of letters: "Ich bin achtundzwanzig, und es ist so gut wie nichts geschehen. Wiederholen wir: ich habe eine Studie über Carpaccio geschrieben, die schlecht ist, ein Drama, das 'Ehe' heißt und etwas Falsches mit zweideutigen Mitteln beweisen will, und Verse. Ach, aber mit Versen ist so wenig getan, wenn man sie früh schreibt" (I am twenty-eight, and as good as nothing has happened. Let's repeat: I have written a study about Carpaccio, which is poor, a drama, called "Marriage," that tries to prove something false with ambiguous means, and verses. Oh, but how little is accomplished with verses when one writes them early in life). Rilke appears to have imagined that Malte was emotionally destroyed by the Parisian experience; he says in a letter of May 1906, after having heard the "inappropriate" laughter of a French audience at a performance of Ibsen's *Wild Duck*: "Und wieder begriff ich Malte Laurids Brigge und sein Nordischsein und sein Zugrundegehen an Paris. Wie sah und empfand und erlitt er es" (And once more I understood Malte Laurids Brigge and his Nordicness and his destruction by Paris. How he saw and felt and suffered it). Malte is undergoing a severe crisis: entry number twenty describes his visit to the Salpetrière Hospital, apparently for electrotherapy. (That Rilke sometimes feared that he would go insane is indicated by the "last will and testament" he sent to Nanny Wunderly-Volkart on 27 October 1925.)

The substance of the first part of *Die Aufzeichnungen des Malte Laurids Brigge*, on the one hand, is Malte's awareness of Paris: of "die Existenz des Entsetzlichen in jedem Bestandteil der Luft" (the existence of the horrible in every particle of the air)—the factory-like dying in the city's hospitals, the terrible street noises, the sordidness exposed on every side, coupled with the joy he feels while visiting an antiquarian bookseller's booth by the Seine, reading the poetry of Francis Jammes in the Bibliothéque Nationale, or viewing the tapestry "La dame à la licorne" in the Musée de Cluny. But intermingled with Parisian episodes are memories of his childhood in Denmark—a childhood of dramatic and terrifying scenes: the death of his paternal grandfather at Ulsgaard; ghost stories connected with Urnekloster, the maternal seat; hallucinations, such as a hand emerging from the wall, that he had while recovering from fever; his tender "Maman," his reserved father, and his maternal aunt Abelone, whom he loves in some never clearly defined way. He wishes he could show her the tapestries in the Parisian museum: "Ich bilde mir ein, du bist da" (I imagine that you are here). The kernel of the Parisian sections is Rilke's own observations, which he often put down in letters; save for quotations from Baudelaire's *Spleen de Paris* and the Book of Job, the Parisian material draws little on literary sources. The Danish components are more mixed, with strong echoes of the description of Danish estate life in the novels of Bang and Jacobsen and of Rilke's own childhood. Upon its appearance *Die Aufzeichnungen des Malte Laurids Brigge* was often treated by critics as another novel about the "decadent hero"—the scion of the old family, disheartened, quiveringly sensitive, and suffering from an inability to act, yet admiring those beings—such as a man with Saint Vitus' dance trying to sustain his dignity by a tremendous act of will—who are undefeated. The book is also one of the several works of German fiction from the time that display a strong "Nordic" side.

The second and more difficult part of the novel again employs the main figures from the Danish past: Maman reappears, appreciating the careful work of anonymous lace-makers; young Malte visits the neighboring estate of the Schulins (based on the Key farm); birthdays are celebrated. A mature Malte returns to Copenhagen ("Ulsgaard war nicht mehr in unserm Besitz" [Ulsgaard was no longer in our possession]); witnesses the perforation of his dead father's heart lest he be buried alive; and ponders the death of Denmark's great baroque king, Christian IV, an account of which his father kept in his wallet. Among the Scandinavian figures, Abelone is the most important: taking dictation from her aged father, Count Brahe, for whom the past is part of the present, and introducing young Malte to one of the great "loving women," Bettina Brentano, who outdid Goethe, Malte claims, in the sheer strength of her emotion. Memories of Abelone come to Malte when he hears a Danish woman sing about "besitzlose Liebe" (possessionless love) and its splendors in a Venetian salon: "'weil ich dich niemals anhielt, halt ich dich fest'" ("since I never detained you, I hold you fast"); other salutes to splendid women—the Portuguese nun Heloise,

What Do I Read Next?

- Rilke's *Letters to a Young Poet* (1929) remains one of his most popular works. In it, Rilke dispenses advice on art, love, life, and how to be a poet in ten intensely emotional letters to a former student of one of his own teachers.

- *Ahead of All Parting: The Selected Poetry and Prose of Rainer Maria Rilke* (1995), translated by Stephen Mitchell and released by Modern Library, provides a good introduction to Rilke's work.

- *The Notebooks of Malte Laurids Brigge* (1910) is Rilke's only novel. Malte Laurids Brigge is a Danish nobleman and poet living in Paris, who is obsessed with death, his family, and the city.

- Rilke has been a major influence on contemporary poets, such as Mark Strand. Strand's *Selected Poems* was released in 1990.

Louise Labé, Sappho, and others—who know that "mit der Vereinigung nichts gemeint sein kann als ein Zuwachs an Einsamkeit" (with union nothing can be meant save an increase in loneliness) prepare for this last quasi-appearance by Abelone. Thus far it is relatively easy to follow Rilke's arguments on love; save in the artistry of the presentation, not much difference exists between the selfless Klara Söllner of the last story of *Geschichten vom lieben Gott* and the singer of the song in Venice. It is harder to grasp, however, what Rilke means when he speaks of Abelone's yearning to take everything that was transitive out of her love, to make it objectless loving, "absolutely, in complete loneliness," in Eudo C. Mason's words.

The horrors of Paris are still with the diarist: Malte—"Ich lerne sehen" (I am learning to see) is the way he describes his most imperative task—cannot shut his eyes to a girl who stands "mit ihrem dürren, verkümmerten Stück" (with her stunted, withered stump) of an arm or to a blind newspaper vendor. The fear of death is still overriding, not only in the story of the post-mortem operation on

Malte's father but even in the comical tale of Nikolaj Kusmitsch, Malte's neighbor in Petersburg, who, realizing how much time he had in his account (he assumed he would live another fifty years or so), resolved to use it sparingly. The Kusmitsch tale leads into stories about a mother who comes to console her disturbed son and about the rebelliousness of objects, followed by glosses on the dangers of loneliness and an intense and horrifying rehearsal of the temptations of Saint Anthony.

Other narratives are baffling, especially the stories recalled from the little green book Malte owned as a boy about the end of the false Dmitri, Grischa Otrepjow; the death of Charles the Bold of Burgundy; the mad Charles VI of France; John XXII, the Avignon pope; and the terrible fourteenth century, "Die Zeit, in der der Kuss zweier, die sich versöhnten, nur das Zeichen für die Mörder war, die herumstanden" (The time in which the kiss of reconciliation between two men was merely the signal for the murderers standing nearby). This awful reflection comes to Malte after he has remembered a trauma of his childhood, a time of similar insecurity, in which he thought himself pursued by another of those large and threatening male figures, like Král and Holzer of the early stories. Perhaps the historical exempla are meant to illustrate Rilke's thoughts on the human will, a will that is variously jeopardized or fails: just before the pistol shot that ends Grischa Otrepjow's life, the pretender experiences "noch einmal Wille und Macht . . . alles zu sein" (once more the will and power . . . to be everything). The will also sustains Eleonora Duse, to whom tribute is paid after a sideswipe at contemporary theater, but here the artist's will has made her overrun—magnificently and frighteningly—the limits of the art in which she must perform. Much of the second part of *Die Aufzeichnungen des Malte Laurids Brigge* could be presented as a statement, as oblique as the first part's is direct, on the strange heroism of the exceptional human who exceeds, or attempts to exceed, his own limitations, forever standing alone. The original ending of the novel, criticizing Tolstoy, who had abandoned his art and was beset by fears of death ("Es war kein Zimmer in diesem Haus, in dem er sich nicht gefürchtet hatte, zu sterben" [There was no room in this house in which he had not feared he would die]), was supplanted by the story of the Prodigal Son, retold as "die Legende dessen . . . der nicht geliebt werden wollte" (the legend of him . . . who did not wish to be loved)—a representation, as Joseph-François Angelloz thought, of Rilke's long search for the freedom that would enable him to apply his artistic will to the fullest. The final lines are cryptic: "Er war jetzt furchtbar schwer zu lieben, und er fühlte, daß nur Einer dazu imstande sei. Der aber wollte noch nicht" (He was now terribly difficult to love, and he felt that there was only One who was capable of it. He, however, did not yet want to). Mason suggests that this is a "hyperbolic way" of implying that there is no plane, "human or superhuman," on which the problem of love can be solved for one who, like the Prodigal Son, is "governed by a daemonic dread of his sacrosanct, isolated selfhood being encroached upon through the love of any other human being."

Die Aufzeichnungen des Malte Laurids Brigge is at once a profoundly satisfying and unsatisfying book. It presents in unforgettable language the tribulations of a sensitive being in an overwhelmingly beautiful and ugly world—the omnipresence of fear; the search for small joys ("Was so ein kleiner Mond alles vermag" [How much such a little moon can do]); the residual terrors of childhood, never to be overcome; the problems of loving; the profits and torments of being alone. Formally, the novel seems less daunting than it did to readers of the past; Rilke advertises his intention of writing a nonlinear novel: "Daß man erzählte, wirklich erzählte, das muß vor meiner Zeit gewesen sein" (That people told stories, really told stories, that must have been before my time). Just the same, in many episodes—the banquet at Urnekloster, the death of the chamberlain Brigge, the visit to the Schulins, the death of Charles of Burgundy—Rilke proved himself a master of the short story, in which he had served such a long apprenticeship. As Wolfgang Leppmann points out, the reader can become "frustrated": he is asked to know the obscure historical facts Rilke had stored away in the corners of his mind or culled directly from other texts; he may find some of the doctrines advanced (for example, intransitive love) hard to grasp, let alone embrace. What may be overlooked, in grappling with *Die Aufzeichnungen des Malte Laurids Brigge*, is that it is, after all, a feigned diary and also incomplete: Rilke told Lou Andreas-Salomé that he had ended it out of exhaustion. Furthermore, it is a personal document: Rilke made fun of Ellen Key for having identified Malte with him, yet she was by no means inaccurate in her naiveté. In Paris for his last visit, he would write to Nanny Wunderly-Volkart: "Je m'effraie comme, autrefois, Malte s'est effrayé. . . ." (I am terrified, as, formerly, Malte was terrified . . .). In his letters, he could never let Malte go.

The post-*Malte* time was marked by flurries of frantic travel: to North Africa in the autumn of 1910; to Egypt in the spring of the next year with the mysterious Jenny Oltersdorf, about whom Rilke remained forever close-mouthed; to Castle Duino, near Trieste, a holding of the Thurn und Taxis clan, in 1911–1912 (here the "angel" of the *Duineser Elegien* is supposed to have spoken to him, inspiring the work that would not be complete until 1922); to Venice again, to spend much of the remainder of 1912–1913; to Spain in the winter of 1912–1913; and, in the summer of 1913, to Göttingen for a visit with Lou Andreas-Salomé. He spent October 1913 to late February 1914 in Paris and was in Munich when World War I broke out in August 1914. (The singer of the deeds of the cornet greeted the conflict with enthusiastic verse he soon regretted.) If the itinerary of these years is long, so is the list of feminine friends: the motherly and excitable Marie von Thurn und Taxis; the haughty Helene von Nostitz; the vivacious Sidonie Nádherný von Borutin, whom Rilke dissuaded from marrying the satirist Karl Kraus. On the passionate side, there was the simple Parisienne Marthe Hennebert, for a time Rilke's "ward"; and the pianist Magda von Hattingberg, or "Benvenuta," for both of whom he pondered a divorce from Clara. He could not do without the blue-blooded friends or the ones who became objects of his desire—such as the "douce perturbatrice," the phrase he bestowed on Marthe in one of the French poems he wrote more and more frequently.

The war years kept him far away from his Parisian books and papers, some of which were irretrievably lost, others saved through the good offices of his friend André Gide, whose *Le Retour de l'enfant prodigue* he had translated into German in 1913–1914. His principal residence was Munich, and his principal companion for a while was the painter Lulu Albert-Lasard. A rising tide of mainly erotic poetry in 1915 was interrupted by a draft call to the Austrian army at Christmas. He spent a wretched few weeks in basic training and was saved by powerful friends, including Princess Marie, who effected his transfer to the dull safety of the War Archive and comfortable quarters in Hietzing's Park-Hotel. Rilke continued to complain about his enforced residence in detestable Vienna and was released from service in June. The rest of the war went by in a kind of convalescence—mostly in Munich, but the summer of 1917 included a stay on an estate in Westphalia, and the autumn of the same year a stay in Berlin. There he saw both Walther Rathenau and Marianne Mitford (née Friedländer-Fuld), whose exceptionally wealthy family owned an estate in the vicinity of the capital: she received one of the first copies of his 1918 translation of the sonnets of the Lyonnaise poetess of the Renaissance, Louise Labé, whom he had ranked among the great lovers in *Die Aufzeichnungen des Malte Laurids Brigge*. Back in Munich, he lived first at the Hotel Continental and then in an apartment in the artists' quarter of Schwabing; observing the "Munich revolution," vaguely sympathizing with Kurt Eisner's idealistic socialism, and giving shelter for a night to the fugitive author Ernst Toller, Rilke was briefly suspected of leftist sympathies by the victorious "White" forces that took over the city on 1 May 1919. At the same time, he enjoyed the innocent attentions of Elya Maria Nevar, a young actress, and the less innocent ones of the would-be femme fatale Claire Studer ("Liliane"), shortly to become the mistress and then the wife of the expressionist poet and editor Iwan Goll.

Casting about for a refuge from postwar Germany's turbulence, Rilke was invited to undertake a reading tour in Switzerland. Once he had made fun of Switzerland and its scenic "Übertreibungen" (exaggerations), its "anspruchsvolle" (pretentious) lakes and mountains; now he was glad to cross the border. Some of his Swiss sanctuaries were much less satisfactory than he had hoped: at Schönenberg, near Basel, a summer home of the Burckhardt family, where he lived from March until May 1920, he liked neither the house's grounds nor its feeble stoves; at Castle Berg am Irchel, near Zurich, placed at his disposal by a Colonel Ziegler for the winter of 1920–1921, he was bothered by children at play and the noise of a sawmill—but at Berg there also appeared to him, he said, the phantom who dictated the double cycle of poems *Aus dem Nachlaß des Grafen C. W.* (1950; translated as *From the Remains of Count C. W.*, 1952). He quickly found new friends; the most important was "Nike," Nanny Wunderly-Volkart, the witty and self-controlled wife of the industrialist Hans Wunderly. Through her Rilke discovered and had rented for him a little tower at Muzot, near Sierre, in the canton of Valais; there—as literary histories never tire of repeating—he finished the *Duineser Elegien* and received the "additional gift" of *Die Sonette an Orpheus: Geschrieben als ein Grab-Mal für Wera Ouckama Knoop* in February 1922. (It is plain, though, that he knew the storm of inspiration was coming: he had some difficulty in persuading the great love of the first Swiss years, "Merline," or

Baladine Klossowska, that he needed to be alone, cared for only by his competent housekeeper, Frida Baumgartner.)

Rilke announced the completion of his task with justifiable pride; the afterglow of accomplishment permeates his letters during the remainder of 1922. A sense of aging also came over him, however: his daughter married, and in 1923 he became a grandfather. (The birth of Ruth herself, he had told a friend years before, had given him a similar sense of "l'immense tristesse de ma propre futilité" [the immense sadness of my own futility].) His health declined: he spent time at a half-resort, half-hospital at Schöneck on the Lake of Lucerne, and then repeatedly at the sanatorium of Valmont above the Lake of Geneva. Rilke had always had a weakness for the restful weeks at a sanatorium or spa—for the sake of his nerves, he liked to say—and they brought useful and interesting contacts: in 1905 at the sanatorium "Weisser Hirsch" near Dresden he had met Countess Luise Schwerin, who had put him in touch with the von der Heydt and Faehndrich circles. Nevertheless, he had become hesitant about the efficacy of physicians in dealing with his ills, real or fancied, and regarded sleep as the great cure-all. The year 1924 opened and closed with stays at Valmont. From January to August 1925 he had his final sojourn in Paris—he was lionized during his stay there, but perhaps the most sincere of his many admirers was the Alsatian Maurice Betz, who was at work on a translation of *Die Aufzeichnungen des Malte Laurids Brigge*. By December he was back at Valmont, staying until May 1926. His last works were his translations of Paul Valéry's poetry and prose and three small volumes of his own French verse. Carl J. Burckhardt, a Swiss diplomat who possessed a keen eye for Rilke's weaknesses, recalled that Rilke did not understand how reserved and even condescending Valéry was toward the "German" poet who late in his career tried his hand at French. Rilke appears to have sought Valéry's company, chatting with him a last time in September 1926 at Anthy on the French side of Lake Geneva. A special issue of *Les Cahiers du Mois*, "Reconnaissance à Rilke," edited by the faithful Betz, had appeared at Paris in the summer of 1926—its opening a restrained salute from Valéry's own hand.

Also in September 1926 the critic Edmond Jaloux introduced Rilke to Nimet Eloui Bey, an Egyptian beauty of Circassian background. When Rilke was still viewed as the devoted and sensitive admirer of women but not an erotic adventurer, Jaloux's account of this "last friendship" seemed the perfect finale for the poet's romantic life; gathering white roses for her, Rilke pricked his hand, and the injury became infected, a harbinger of the final onslaught of his illness. It is now known that the Egyptian was but one of the women and girls who surrounded and attracted him almost to the end: the eighteen-year-old Austrian Erika Mitterer, who carried on a correspondence in poems with him from 1924 to 1926; the Russian poetess Marina Tsvetayeva, who wanted to visit and consume him; the pretty Lalli Horstmann, a friend of Marianne Mitford; the Dutch singer Beppy Veder; and the actress Elisabeth Bergner were among the many. What may be more significant about the "last friendship" with Nimet Eloui Bey, though, is that she wanted to meet the author of *Die Aufzeichnungen des Malte Laurids Brigge*, which she had just read in Betz's translation—the book of his that lay closest to his own heart.

Source: George C. Schoolfield, "Rainer Maria Rilke," in *Dictionary of Literary Biography*, Vol. 81, *Austrian Fiction Writers, 1875–1913*, edited by James Hardin and Donald G. Daviau, Gale Research, 1989, pp. 244–71.

Sources

Gass, William H., *Reading Rilke: Reflections on the Problems of Translation*, Basic Books, 1999, p. 32.

Komar, Kathleen L., "The Mediating Muse: Of Men, Women, and the Feminine in the Work of Rainer Maria Rilke," in the *Germanic Review*, Vol. LXIV, No. 3, Summer 1989, pp. 129–33.

Leppman, Wolfgang, *Rilke: A Life*, Fromm, 1984, p. 16.

Rilke, Rainer Maria, "Childhood," in *New Poems*, translated by Edward Snow, North Point Press, 1984, p. 89.

———, "Childhood," in *Rilke: Poems*, translated by J. B. Leishman, Alfred A. Knopf, 1996, p. 16.

———, "Childhood," in *Selected Poems of Rainer Maria Rilke*, translated by Robert Bly, Harper & Row, 1989, pp. 72–75.

———, "From a Childhood," in *Selected Poems*, translated by C. F. MacIntyre, University of California Press, 1968, pp. 28–29.

———, *Letters to a Young Poet*, translated by Reginald Snell, Alfred A. Knopf, 1996, p. 217.

Rolleston, James, "Rainer Maria Rilke," in *European Writers*, Vol. 9, Charles Scribner's Sons, 1989, pp. 767–95.

Snow, Edward, "Introduction," in *The Book of Images*, by Rainer Maria Rilke, translated by Edward Snow, North Point Press, 1991, pp. ix–xii, 41.

Wood, Frank, *Rainer Maria Rilke: The Ring of Forms*, Octagon Press, 1970, p. 64.

Further Reading

Baron, Frank, Ernst S. Dick, and Warren R. Mauer, eds., *Rilke: The Alchemy of Alienation*, Regents Press of Kansas, 1980.

> This anthology contains English-language essays by Rilke scholars such as Stephen Spender, Lev Kopelev, Walter H. Sokel, Andras Sandor, and Erich Simenauer. It is a useful resource for students already familiar with Rilke's work.

Freedman, Ralph, *Life of a Poet: A Biography of Rainer Maria Rilke*, Farrar, Straus, & Giroux, 1995.

> Freedman's biography is a detailed accounting of Rilke's life with special attention paid to his many love affairs.

Gass, William, *Reading Rilke: Reflections on the Problems of Translation*, Knopf, 1999.

> Postmodernist Gass provides an idiosyncratic reading of *The Duino Elegies* while exploring some of the thornier issues of translation.

Sword, Helen, *Engendering Inspiration: Visionary Strategies in Rilke, Lawrence, and H. D.*, University of Michigan Press, 1995.

> Sword explores the early twentieth-century poetic visions of Rilke, D. H. Lawrence, and H. D. (Hilda Doolittle).

The Cinnamon Peeler

Michael Ondaatje

1982

Michael Ondaatje first published "The Cinnamon Peeler" in 1982 as part of his book *Running in the Family*. "The Cinnamon Peeler" appeared later in Ondaatje's collection *Secular Love*. As most critics note, this collection was influenced heavily by events in Ondaatje's life, namely his 1979 separation from his wife, Kim Jones, and his subsequent affair with another woman, Linda Spalding. The book is arranged into four different sections, which collectively detail the pain of Ondaatje's breakup and his path through despair to newfound love. "The Cinnamon Peeler" is located in the fourth and final section, "Skin Boat," and is one of the poems that glorifies love. In the poem, the speaker gives a very sensual description of his wife and their courtship, using the exotic qualities of cinnamon, especially its potent scent, to underscore his love and desire. Ondaatje's use of cinnamon, a plant found in his native Sri Lanka, indicates his desire to focus on his former homeland. Ondaatje, who has been a Canadian citizen since he was a teenager, often includes discussions of Sri Lanka in his works. Although critics responded favorably to the poems in *Secular Love*, this response pales in comparison to the critical and popular response that Ondaatje received for his third novel, *The English Patient* (1992), which was adapted into a blockbuster film in 1996. A copy of the poem can be found in *The Cinnamon Peeler: Selected Poems*, which was published in paperback by Vintage International in 1997.

Author Biography

Michael Ondaatje was born on September 12, 1943, in Colombo, Ceylon (now Sri Lanka). After his parents separated in 1948, Ondaatje's mother took him and two siblings to England, where Ondaatje attended Dulwich College. He was not satisfied with his British education and immigrated to Canada in 1962, at the age of 19, where he lived with his brother in Quebec. He attended Bishop's University in Lennoxville from 1962 to 1964, where he began to study English literature and write his first works. During this time, he met Kim Jones, wife of poet D. D. Jones, who some say was Ondaatje's mentor. Kim left her husband and four children in 1964 to marry Ondaatje, and the couple had two children together. The same year, he transferred to the University of Toronto, where he graduated with his bachelor's degree in 1965. He pursued his master's degree from Queen's University and graduated from there in 1967.

Also in 1967, Ondaatje began teaching at the University of Western Ontario and published his first book, *The Dainty Monsters*, a poetry collection. It was not until the publication of his third book, *The Collected Works of Billy the Kid* (1970), that Ondaatje received widespread recognition. The unique book combined poetry, prose, drawings, and other selections to bring the legendary American outlaw to life. The book won a Canadian Governor General's Award, an award that Ondaatje has won several times since. Ondaatje continued to impress critics with his poetry, publishing several collections over the next two decades, including *Rat Jelly* (1973) and *Secular Love* (1984). The latter was written during the period following Ondaatje's 1979 separation from Jones, when Ondaatje started living with Linda Spalding. The collection includes the poem "The Cinnamon Peeler."

Up until the early 1990s, Ondaatje was primarily regarded as a poet, although critics also gave him good marks for his two novels: *Coming through Slaughter* (1976) and *In the Skin of a Lion* (1987). In 1992, however, Ondaatje received worldwide recognition for his third novel, *The English Patient*, which was adapted as a blockbuster film in 1996. Since then, Ondaatje has been associated primarily with this book. His other works include a collection of poetry entitled *Handwriting* (1998) and a novel entitled *Anil's Ghost* (2000). Ondaatje has also served as a professor at York University's Glendon College in Toronto, Ontario, Canada.

Michael Ondaatje

Poem Summary

Stanza 1

"The Cinnamon Peeler" sets up a hypothetical situation right from the first line: "If I were a cinnamon peeler." Right away, readers can determine that the speaker is not a cinnamon peeler, but that the poem will discuss what might happen if he was. In the last three lines of the stanza, the poem takes on erotic overtones, as the speaker notes, "I would ride your bed / and leave the yellow bark dust / on your pillow." The verb "ride" is inherently innocent, but when it is combined with the word "bed," it becomes very sexual in nature. It is clear that the speaker is writing a sexual poem to his lover. The "yellow bark dust" that the speaker refers to is the dust that a cinnamon peeler has on his body after harvesting the spice, which comes from the bark of a specific type of evergreen tree that is Sri Lankan in origin. By talking about leaving the bark dust on his lover's pillow, the speaker sets up a graphic image of the couple making love and the man leaving evidence of his presence by the work-related cinnamon dust that falls onto the bed in the process.

Stanza 2

The poem gets increasingly erotic in the first line of the second stanza, as the speaker describes,

Media Adaptations

- Ondaatje's novel *Anil's Ghost* was adapted as an unabridged audiocassette and audio CD in 2000, both available from Bantam Books and both with Alan Cumming as reader.

- Ondaatje's novel *The English Patient* was adapted as a feature film in 1996 by Miramax Films. Written and directed by Anthony Minghella, the film starred Ralph Fiennes, Juliette Binoche, Willem Dafoe, Kristin Scott Thomas, and Colin Firth. It is available on both DVD and VHS from Miramax Home Entertainment.

- *The English Patient* was also adapted as an abridged audiocassette in 1993 by Random House. This audiobook is read by Michael York.

---

in detail, which areas of the woman's body would smell of cinnamon dust. In addition to referencing the woman's anatomy, the speaker also notes how the cinnamon smell would mark the woman as his wife even when she left the house. To further emphasize the power of this scent, the speaker gives an extended example of blind people stumbling from the potency of the odor. The speaker uses two images of water to indicate that the woman could not wash away the scent.

Whether the woman gets slightly wet from the light stream of water that falls from a rain gutter or thoroughly drenched from the torrential downpour of a monsoon, the scent of the man's profession, which also serves as a symbol of his love and desire, will stick to the woman. A symbol is a physical object, action, or gesture that also represents an abstract concept, without losing its original identity. Symbols appear in literature in one of two ways. They can be local symbols, meaning that their symbolism is only relevant within a specific literary work. They can also be universal symbols, meaning that their symbolism is based on traditional associations that are widely recognized, regardless of context. The poem relies on the former type. While the speaker starts out discussing the potent scent of cinnamon, it becomes clear through his erotic descriptions that within the context of the poem, cinnamon is a symbol for sexual desire.

Stanza 3

In the third stanza, the poem gets even more erotic. Whereas the second stanza talked about the woman's "breasts and shoulders," now the speaker is moving lower on the woman's body, indicating more body parts that his cinnamon scent would inhabit. The speaker mentions the woman's thigh. A woman's upper thigh has inherent erotic overtones. The use of the words "smooth pasture" increases the eroticism of the speaker's statement, because it highlights the smooth texture of the woman's skin. Smooth skin is another anatomical aspect that is used to indicate eroticism. In the third line, the speaker gives one of the most graphic descriptions in the poem: "neighbour to your hair." Although hair could normally mean the hair on a person's head, the fact that the speaker is talking about hair near the woman's upper thigh identifies it as the woman's pubic hair.

This reference is blatantly sexual, but the speaker only lingers here for a moment, before traveling on to the next body part, the woman's back. While not as blatantly sexual as a woman's pubic hair, a woman's back is still inherently sensuous, as is his last anatomical description of the woman's ankle. Although America's emphasis on sexual freedom has taken away the power and mystery of a woman's ankle, in some cultures, where women are expected to wear more clothes, the sight of even an ankle can be a very sensuous experience. The speaker sums up all of his descriptions in the last two lines of the stanza: "You will be known among strangers / as the cinnamon peeler's wife." In other words, the cinnamon peeler's scent, the symbol of his sexual desire and the marital connection that he shares with this woman, has marked this woman so much that even strangers will recognize the woman as the cinnamon peeler's wife.

Stanza 4

At this point, the poem switches gears. Up until now, it has functioned on a hypothetical level, as this married couple engages in a game of role-playing. Now it switches to a description of the couple's actual past. As he notes in the first line of the poem, the speaker is not a cinnamon peeler. The speaker's love for his wife, however, is as strong as the love that this hypothetical cinnamon peeler has for his wife. In fact, the poet uses the hypothetical example of the cinnamon peeler for a reason. He wants to emphasize his desire to his wife in a symbolic sense, as if it is literally a scent that can be noticed by others. As the poem shifts in this stanza, the reader can see why the speaker goes to all this trouble. The speaker is remembering back to a time before he and his wife were married, when they were dating. He was afraid to look at his beloved, because he did not want to betray his feelings for her. Even more importantly, the speaker says he could never touch his beloved. If he were to do this, it would be like the cinnamon peeler who touches his wife and leaves evidence of his desire, in the form of cinnamon dust. The speaker would not necessarily leave physical evidence of his desire such as dust by touching his beloved. Yet, as he notes in the next line, others, especially his beloved's family, would be able to literally smell his desire for her.

Because the mark of his desire is so potent, the speaker must take further steps to hide the scent of this desire, even beyond not looking at or touching his beloved. The narrator says that he must hide the potent scent of his desire by masking it behind other potent scents.

Stanza 5

In the fifth stanza, the speaker switches gears again. Up until now, he has spoken about the hypothetical cinnamon peeler and his wife making love, and he has described how he was unable to even look or touch his beloved while they were dating, for fear of betraying his desire. Now, however, he talks about his own experience making love to his beloved while they were dating. The speaker remembers a day during their marriage when he and his beloved went swimming together. The poet notes that when they were both immersed in the water together, "you could hold me and be blind of smell." In other words, when the couple were trying to hide their desire from her family during their courtship, it was difficult to hide its potency. In addition, they were both focused on it because their desire is a forbidden thing, which makes it that much harder to resist. In this private swim together as a married couple, however, they could be "blind of smell" because they had no reason to hide their desire anymore. They were fulfilling their desire, which takes away its smell, at least temporarily. This idea sets up the rest of the poem.

Stanza 6

This line leads into the sixth stanza, which starts out with a statement from the speaker's beloved. When one reads the first line of this stanza, it might seem as if the woman is saying that the speaker has literally made love to other women. One can interpret the poem this way. Yet, the speaker's choice of a "grass cutter" and "lime burner" is significant, and suggests a different interpretation. Both of these professions, unlike the profession of cinnamon peeler, involve working with natural substances that have little or no scent. While the scent of fresh-cut grass is unmistakable, it does not have the potency of freshly peeled cinnamon bark. Lime, on the other hand, contrasts even more sharply with cinnamon. Lime is inherently an odorless substance, and the lime burner, who obtains lime from limestone by burning off the carbon dioxide, therefore does not carry the scent of his profession with him to other places.

Because of these choices, it does not seem as if the speaker's beloved is accusing him of sleeping with other women. Instead, it seems as if she is creating a hypothetical situation of her own, to counter her husband's hypothetical cinnamon-peeler situation. She is imagining what it would be like for her lover to be with these other women, who do not carry the scent of their husband's profession, as she would in the hypothetical situation where she is the cinnamon peeler's wife. In the last part of the stanza, the speaker's beloved smells her arms, which no longer carry the scent of their desire.

Stanzas 7–8

The seventh stanza is very short, only two words long: "and knew." Though it is short, it is a powerful stanza. In its short space, it implies that the woman is having a revelation, which is explained in the next stanza. The speaker's wife is continuing both hypothetical situations, saying that it is no good to be without a scent, as a lime burner's daughter is. She would rather be marked with the scent of her husband's desire. To be otherwise, would be like she was "not spoken to in the act of love" or as if she was "wounded without the pleasure of a scar." The first idea suggests that the lack of strong desire between a couple is the equivalent of mechanical lovemaking without communication. The second idea is more visceral, once again using anatomical associations, although this time the speaker is talking about a wound, which most people would consider an inherently bad thing. Yet, within the context of the poem, even a wound can be a pleasurable experience if it leaves a mark, as the cinnamon peeler leaves a mark on his wife.

Stanza 9

The final stanza wraps up both hypothetical situations. The speaker's wife presents her body to her

Topics for Further Study

- Research the history of cinnamon as it relates to the international spice trade. Try to find one story, from any point in history, involving the importance of cinnamon in government or culture. Describe how you would direct this story as a modern-day film.

- Research the profession of cinnamon peeler in Sri Lanka. Write a modern-day job description for this position, including salary, expected duties, hours, etc.

- Research dating rituals in modern-day Sri Lanka and compare them to dating rituals described in the poem. Imagine that you are a Sri Lankan teenager and write a journal entry that describes a day in your courtship, using your research to support your ideas.

- Choose an important person from any point in Sri Lanka's history and write a short biography about this person.

---

husband, and the poem once again focuses on a part of the woman's anatomy, her belly. The speaker's wife closes the poem by going along with the role-playing game that her husband set up in the beginning. She acknowledges herself as his wife and tells her husband: "Smell me." In other words, as the speaker has demonstrated repeatedly throughout the poem, smell and scent are synonymous with desire in the speaker's mind and in this couple's experience. So when the speaker's wife asks him to smell her, she is asking him to desire her. This married couple is rekindling their passion for each other, by drawing on past memories and using a role-playing game where he becomes a cinnamon peeler, and she becomes the cinnamon peeler's wife.

Themes

Love

It is apparent from the beginning that this is a love poem from the speaker to his beloved. The use of the word "your" in the second line, especially within its sexual context indicates that the speaker is addressing his poem to a woman. This form of direct address is common in love poetry. As the poem continues, readers can see that the speaker is creating a hypothetical situation, a type of role-playing game in which he and his wife are such passionate lovers that their desire leaves a scent that others can notice. In addition to discussing this passionate scent, the poem also explores the path of love itself, from their courtship to their current marital relationship. The speaker discusses the time period during which they were dating. In this time of newfound love, their passion is so strong that they have to be careful around the woman's family members, for fear that they will betray their true emotions.

Sexual Desire

While the poem is a love poem, it is also specifically about the speaker's sexual desire for his wife and their desire for each other. From the first sexual reference in the beginning of the poem, where the hypothetical cinnamon peeler leaves evidence of his desire on his wife's pillow in the form of cinnamon dust, the poem gets increasingly more erotic. The strength of the speaker's desire is expressed in several ways, most notably as a scent that can be noticed by the "blind" and even by "strangers."

The Power of Scent

Unfortunately, the speaker notes that when they were dating this scent could also be sensed by the woman's mother and brothers. Smell is a powerful sense, which is used in the context of the poem to reveal hidden feelings and intentions. To keep these feelings hidden, the speaker had to mask his intentions behind even more powerful scents, including saffron and honey. In addition to revealing hidden feelings, the poem also indicates that scent evokes strong feelings and memories. Although the poem starts out as a hypothetical situation, the speaker's discussion of the cinnamon peeler, and the power of the cinnamon scent—a symbol of this man's desire—causes the speaker to think back on his own memories of the desire that he felt for his wife during their courtship.

Style

Setting

The poem takes place in Sri Lanka, a fact that can be determined by the author's background—he is a native of Sri Lanka—and by the importance of cinnamon in the poem, not to mention the reference to the cinnamon-peeler profession. Cinnamon is native to Sri Lanka, and a cinnamon peeler is a type of Sri Lankan agricultural harvester who cuts down the evergreen tree that produces cinnamon. The cinnamon peeler harvests the spice from the bark of this tree, in the process often getting the "yellow bark dust" on his hands. The poem contains other clues that indicate a Sri Lankan setting, including a discussion of "markets." Many Asian countries, such as Sri Lanka, conduct business in rural markets, especially when it comes to the sale of agricultural products such as cinnamon. Likewise, the poem's reference to a "monsoon" indicates that the poem takes place in one of the Asian tropical countries that experience these torrential downpours. The setting is very important to the poem, not just because of the use of the cinnamon peeler but also because Sri Lanka—and the spice trade—have often been associated with the exotic. As a result, its setting gives the poem a more exotic feel.

Imagery

The poem also relies on both direct and subtle imagery to underscore its focus on love and sexual desire. Direct imagery includes the many references to the anatomy of the speaker's wife. The speaker talks about her "breasts and shoulders," the "smooth pasture" of her "upper thigh," and other aspects of his wife's anatomy throughout the poem. This imagery is as potent as the scents that the speaker is trying to describe, and it is clear that his intent is to underscore the strength of his sexual desire. The poem also includes blatant imagery in the references to making love, as in the first stanza when the speaker notes "I would ride your bed," or in the fifth stanza, when he notes "I touched you in water / and our bodies remained free." There is little left to the imagination for the reader, who understands that the speaker is describing sexual experiences with his wife.

Yet, the poem also relies on more subtle forms of imagery, such as the images that the speaker uses to describe how hard it would be for his wife to lose the scent of her desire. This scent is so strong that the woman could not wash it away. Other subtle images include the steps that the speaker must take to hide this desire, which include burying his hands "in saffron."

Tense

The speaker switches verb tenses throughout the poem, which helps the reader understand what parts of the poem are hypothetical and what parts belong in the couple's actual past. In the first stanza, the speaker says "If I were a cinnamon peeler," and the use of the word "were" indicates that this is a hypothetical situation. Likewise, over the next few stanzas, the speaker continues using verb tenses that underscore the hypothetical quality of the situation. For example, in the second stanza, he notes that parts of his wife's anatomy "would" reek and that even though she "might" try to wash away the scent of his desire, she could not.

In the fourth stanza, however, the discussion switches from a hypothetical situation to the couple's actual past. This fact can be determined by the specific context of the word "could." The word "could" on its own can be used in a hypothetical situation, as it is in the second stanza, where the speaker notes that if his wife was the cinnamon peeler's wife, she "could" not walk down the street unnoticed. The use of the word "could" in the fourth stanza is different, however, thanks to the next line, "before marriage," which qualifies the statement and places it within a specific time in the past. The speaker also uses past tenses that are more direct, such as the first two lines in the fifth stanza.

Historical Context

Conflict and Transition in Sri Lanka

While Ondaatje focuses on the potency of his desire in "The Cinnamon Peeler," a poem that is set in Sri Lanka, the actual situation in the country was not ideal in the mid-1980s. During this time period, Sri Lanka was undergoing a period of political unrest, as various ethnic groups vied for power. The United National Party (UNP), a coalition of nationalist and communal parties, had come to power in the late 1970s, the latest of many times that this party had been in power. Yet, the authority and sovereignty of this government was constantly challenged by various radical groups, most notably the Tamils, who set up bases in jungle areas of Sri Lanka as well as in certain parts of Tamil Nadu—an Indian state. Although the UNP-led Sri Lankan government attempted to suppress these rebellions, it was not necessary. The common people, many of whom were Sinhalese, formed into mobs and attacked the Tamils themselves. As a result, many Tamil groups fled to Tamil Nadu.

The Spice Trade in Sri Lanka

Even while all of this fighting was taking place, Sri Lanka (formerly Ceylon) continued to

Compare & Contrast

- **1980s:** The Sri Lankan government faces a rebellion from the Tamil minority, although this rebellion is largely suppressed by certain groups of the Sri Lankan people.

  Today: Following the assassination of the Sri Lankan president in 1993, the premier is appointed acting president. The Sri Lankan army continues to battle the Tamil rebels.

- **1980s:** Sri Lanka tries to shore up its faltering economy by developing offshore banking and insurance industries.

  Today: Despite its efforts to strengthen its economy through foreign trade and investments, Sri Lanka is still dependent on foreign aid.

- **1980s:** Sri Lanka's economy is primarily agricultural, although textiles and garments become the biggest export product.

  Today: Although Sri Lanka's agricultural products—including cinnamon, tea, rubber, and coconut—continue to be in demand, textiles and garments are still the biggest export product.

---

play a huge part in the spice trade. Sri Lanka has been synonymous with the Eastern spice trade for thousands of years, and the island of Ceylon has been a central trading point for spices during this time period. In fact, the spice that Ondaatje focuses on in his poem, cinnamon, is a spice that is native to Sri Lanka. It comes from *Cinnamomum zeylanicum*, a form of evergreen tree that belongs to the laurel family. Cinnamon has always had exotic associations, and has been used in various cultures for spiritual rites and even witchcraft. In the modern world, it is used mainly as a flavoring, especially in baked goods. Its oil is also used in liqueur, perfume, and even drugs. Yet, despite the widespread use of cinnamon worldwide, its importance as a Sri Lankan export—and in fact the importance of other Sri Lankan agricultural products, such as tea and rubber—declined by the mid-1980s, when Ondaatje was writing "The Cinnamon Peeler." While these products were still being exported, they were no longer the number one export, a designation that was held by textiles and garments.

Critical Overview

Ondaatje's *Secular Love* has not received as much attention as his other works, most notably his 1992 novel, *The English Patient*, which became a critical and popular success, especially after it was adapted into a Hollywood film in 1996. Nevertheless, some critics have commented on *Secular Love*, and a handful have also commented specifically on "The Cinnamon Peeler." The overwhelming majority of critics discuss *Secular Love* in relation to the author's life, most notably the marriage breakup and new relationship that Ondaatje experienced while he was writing the poetry collection. Ann Mandel states in her entry on Ondaatje for *Dictionary of Literary Biography* that "In *Secular Love* ... the pain of the marriage breakup and the sensual and emotional growth of new love make their way into the poems." In fact, as Lucille King-Edwards notes in *Books in Canada*, this autobiographical focus was not evident in his earlier works. King-Edwards writes "Until *Running in the Family* and now *Secular Love*, the passion that Ondaatje has put into his poems and novels has been projected onto characters from the myths of his imagination."

In *Secular Love*, this autobiographical focus is apparent even from the book's structure, which is another of the elements upon which most critics focus. Sam Solecki, in his article in the *Canadian Forum*, notes the four sections of the book that chronicle "the break-up of a marriage and a way of life, the poet's own near breakdown and finally, after what one section calls 'Rock Bottom,' his recovery and return through the love of another woman." In this structure, "The Cinnamon Peeler" falls within the fourth and final section, "Skin Boat," which Solecki calls the "affirmative, celebratory section."

As for "The Cinnamon Peeler" itself, critics have interpreted the poem in different ways. In his article in the *Times Literary Supplement*, Michael Hulse notes that the poem shares the same "constant theme" as much of Ondaatje's other work. Hulse writes that "Above all, the breakthrough into communication is found instinctually in sexual harmony." On the other hand, reviewers such as Douglas Barbour, in his entry on Ondaatje for *Twayne's World Authors Series Online*, note the comedic aspects of the poem. Barbour states that the poem contains a "subtle comedy of marriage," which, when placed within the overall context of *Secular Love*, transforms it "into part of the personal discourse of confession this book sometimes admits to being."

Criticism

Ryan D. Poquette

Poquette has a bachelor's degree in English and specializes in writing about literature. In the following essay, Poquette discusses Ondaatje's use of structure to add to the poem's sexual overtones.

When one first reads Ondaatje's "The Cinnamon Peeler," it is clear that the poem is about sex, specifically, the speaker's sexual desire for his wife, which he rekindles through a role-playing game. In this game, the speaker poses a hypothetical situation where he is a cinnamon peeler and his wife is therefore marked physically by the scent of his profession. This cinnamon scent, indeed, scent in general, takes on very sexual overtones as the poem progresses. In fact, the poem needs no help from any additional poetic techniques to underscore its sexual theme. Yet, Ondaatje deliberately constructs his poem in ways that heighten its sexual overtones.

Poets are some of the most particular writers in all of literature. Since they are working with a much smaller canvas, space is at a premium, and so every word must count. In addition, poets often structure their poems in specific ways to achieve a desired effect. This structure can take place on the macro level, as in the way that the poet organizes stanzas and gives the poem its overall structure. It can also take place on the micro level, as in the way that the poet breaks certain lines so that they achieve maximum impact. In "The Cinnamon Peeler," Ondaatje relies on both of these techniques.

From a structural standpoint, Ondaatje takes his readers through two time periods, a hypothetical future and an actual past. The first, the hypothetical future, consists of stanzas one through three. In these three stanzas, beginning with the setup line "If I were a cinnamon peeler," Ondaatje creates an extended example of how his desire would literally coat his wife like a spice, if he were a cinnamon peeler. Throughout this example, Ondaatje increases the eroticism of the poem with each successive stanza, moving from general to specific details, as if he is building up his desire over the course of this opening section. In the first stanza, he briefly mentions a lovemaking session, "I would ride your bed," which some readers might think is risqué. Yet, this direct approach is not nearly as sensuous as the little details that Ondaatje adds in successive lines and stanzas. The first of these details, "the yellow bark dust / on your pillow," paints a very potent image of the cinnamon peeler and his wife after making love, during which he has literally left the sign of his profession on his wife's pillow.

The second stanza gets more specific, and focuses on the wife's travels outside of the home, where the evidence of their lovemaking—and of her husband's desire—would be clear. In this stanza, Ondaatje moves from the sterile image of the pillow, an inanimate object, to a brief discussion of her anatomy, her "breasts and shoulders." Although, since she is walking "through markets," one assumes that these parts of her anatomy are covered. That does not mean that the stanza is without eroticism. Ondaatje sets up a potent image in this stanza of a desire so strong that its scent can make blind people "stumble certain of whom they approached" and which cannot be washed away, even by the downpour of a "monsoon."

The third stanza takes readers back to the bedroom, but this time the woman's clothes are off, and the poet is describing various parts of his wife's anatomy, starting with her "upper thigh," which he calls a "smooth pasture," a description that heightens its erotic effect. He notes that this smooth pasture is "neighbour to your hair," a reference to the woman's pubic hair, and then discusses her "back" and "ankle." At the end of this anatomical inventory, the poet notes that even "among strangers," she will be known as "the cinnamon peeler's wife."

At the end of these first three stanzas, readers can see that Ondaatje is exploring sexual desire in

> "Although the speaker is talking about bathing in the sense of getting wet from 'rain gutters' or a 'monsoon,' the word 'bathe' sets up an image of a woman taking a bath, an act that commonly has erotic associations."

depth, and is using his poem's structure to heighten this effect. In the second half of the poem, Ondaatje switches gears from the hypothetical future to the actual past of the couple in the poem. Although these last six stanzas are not nearly as salacious as the first three in the poem, they do continue to underscore the eroticism of the poem, once again through their use of specific details. For example, in the fourth stanza, the speaker notes that the scent of his desire during their courtship was so strong that he needed to mask it behind scents that were even stronger, such as "saffron" and "smoking tar," for fear that her "keen nosed mother" would discover this desire.

This trend continues into the remaining five stanzas, which are all organized around a moment in the couple's past when they were swimming together after they were married. Readers can tell that it is, in fact, after they were married by a clue that Ondaatje provides at the end of the fourth stanza. Here, Ondaatje includes an ellipsis, a form of punctuation that generally implies something has been removed. In poetry, this punctuation mark is often used to indicate the passage of time. So, in the first three stanzas, the poet was talking about a hypothetical future; in the fourth stanza, he flashes back briefly to the past to examine an intense memory of his desire for his wife during their courtship; and, in the last five stanzas, Ondaatje flashes forward again, this time to a lovemaking session that the couple has while swimming together. In this concluding section of the poem, Ondaatje has his characters, the speaker and his wife, reconnect with the desire that they have felt in the past. These stanzas wrap up the poem by connecting with the first stanza in which the speaker is role-playing as if he were a cinnamon peeler. In the final stanza, the speaker's wife comes full circle in this role-playing game, telling her husband that she is "the cinnamon / peeler's wife. Smell me." In this short statement, the wife is indicating her willingness to play along with the role-playing game and rekindle their desire.

Besides this overall structure, Ondaatje also works in smaller structural ways to increase the sexual overtones of the poem, namely in his use of line breaks. Ondaatje uses these line breaks to increase the emphasis on certain statements. For example, in the second line of the first stanza, he notes "I would ride your bed." By ending the line here, the poet emphasizes this act, giving it more impact on its own, than if he was to tack on the next line "and leave the yellow bark dust." The statement given the most emphasis in the poem is the two-word stanza, "and knew." Ondaatje separates this part of the poem from the rest to heighten the sense of revelation that the woman has over the necessity of their desire.

In some cases, Ondaatje's emphasis also leads the reader to think that the poet is talking about something else. The most notable example of this technique is in the third stanza. In the first two lines of this stanza, the speaker has been describing his wife's upper thigh, which he says is "neighbour to your hair," a direct reference to his wife's pubic hair. Since he has, thus far, been moving around his wife's body as he describes her anatomy, the lines directly after this, "or the crease," seem calculated on Ondaatje's part. It seems as if he wants his readers to think, at least for a moment, that the crease he is referring to is his wife's vagina. Since he breaks this line abruptly after the word "crease," it makes it seem like this word is meant to stand on its own. Yet, Ondaatje only lingers on this concept for a minute before further explaining that the crease he is referring to is the crease "that cuts your back." Still, this playful line break suggests something much more and is in line with the other techniques that Ondaatje has used in the poem to increase its eroticism. Another example takes place in the sixth line of the second stanza, where he notes "though you might bathe." Although the speaker is talking about bathing in the sense of getting wet from "rain gutters" or a "monsoon," the word "bathe" sets up an image of a woman taking a bath, an act that commonly has erotic associations.

In the end, Ondaatje does everything he can to make the most erotic poem possible. On the surface, one can point to blatant examples of lovemaking and female anatomy. Yet, it is in the subtle structural details that Ondaatje's true art, and his ability to spice up an already erotic poem, makes itself known. Ultimately, this technique becomes as potent as the cinnamon spice that Ondaatje uses to indicate the strength of his speaker's desire.

Source: Ryan D. Poquette, Critical Essay on "The Cinnamon Peeler," in *Poetry for Students*, Gale, 2003.

Daniel Toronto

Toronto is an editor at the Pennsylvania State University Press. In this essay, Toronto discusses how cultural context affects the reading of Ondaatje's poem.

Ondaatje's "The Cinnamon Peeler" is a powerfully aesthetic portrayal of erotic love in which the transfer of scent, in this case that of a particularly potent spice, becomes a public and private declaration of union. The surface of the poem can hardly be scratched, however, before running into the signs of a clearly male-dominated society, with women being defined in terms of the males in their lives. The cinnamon peeler's wife is an obvious example, but there is also the lime burner's daughter and the grass cutter's wife. The woman referenced directly, not indirectly through a male, is the cinnamon peeler's mother-in-law, though her identity is still only gained through a woman who is already defined in terms of a man.

The lack of distinct identities also quickly becomes apparent. The men in the poem are only identified through their occupations—the cinnamon peeler, the grass cutter, the lime burner. Again, there is only one occurrence, in the fourth stanza, of brothers being defined without occupational terms, and, as with the mother, they are only defined in terms that are relational, which lead back, through the wife, to the cinnamon peeler. With men only defined by what they do, women are even further removed from any sort of personal identity since they are only referenced through men.

These characteristics might well agitate readers within modern Western cultures. Yet, Western readers are the target audience of the poem, demonstrated by the fact that it has been published within a novel as well as two collections of poetry in England, Canada, and the United States. When the poem was first published in 1982, these three countries had already made great strides toward gender equality. Each had made strides toward increasing opportunities for women in the workforce, progressive equalization of pay, and even electing women rising to high political positions, as with Margaret Thatcher, who became Great Britain's first female prime minister in 1979. Great value was also placed on individuality. Pop psychologists Carl Rogers and Richard Farson had long since made their award-winning film, *Journey into Self* (1968). Self-help books already comprised a sizeable genre in the publishing market. The prevailing sentiments of the time seem quite contrary to those exhibited in "The Cinnamon Peeler." However, "The Cinnamon Peeler" is clearly not viewed so simplistically. Otherwise, it would not be nearly as well respected. Cultural context plays a large role in making the sexism and identity loss easier to tolerate. As it is examined, a subtext of community and tradition is discovered.

"The Cinnamon Peeler" appeared for the first time in *Running in the Family*, Ondaatje's semi-autobiographical novel about his experiences during two long-term visits to the country of his origin, Sri Lanka (formerly Ceylon). It can safely be assumed that this poem portrays a Sri Lankan cinnamon peeler. It is also likely that he is Sinhalese, which is the dominant ethnicity on the island. Sri Lankan society is infused with a hierarchical caste system. The caste hierarchies of South Asia are difficult to define and can vary significantly. Tamara Gunasekera offers one definition in *Hierarchy and Egalitarianism: Caste, Class and Power in Sinhalese Peasant Society*:

> Castes are defined as groups possessing differential degrees of social honour and prestige. These groups place restrictions on marriage with individuals in other such groups, and membership in them is hereditary, depending on one or both parents being members of a given caste. In societies where caste is present, therefore, social honour and prestige or status accrue to an individual by virtue of his birth in a particular caste. Thus, in such societies, the status hierarchy consists of the caste hierarchy.

"The Cinnamon Peeler" alludes to several specific Sinhalese castes, which are often associated with occupation: the cinnamon peeler caste, the honey gatherer caste, the grass cutter caste, and the lime burner caste. The men of the cinnamon peeler caste, known in Sinhalese as Salagama, were all cinnamon peelers traditionally, though it is no longer necessarily the case today, or when Ondaatje was writing the poem. The Salagama is a somewhat prestigious caste. They are also fairly numerous. Reinterpreting the poem in this light brings out rich and beautiful connotations that soften the patriarchal and labor-oriented identities.

The first stanza evokes passionate, almost violent lovemaking with the line "I would ride your

> *If the cinnamon peeler were to 'touch' or make love to the lime burner's daughter, she would not be brought into the fold of cinnamon peelers but would remain in the lime burner caste.*

bed." Using the verb "ride" connotes a way in which humans exert their will over an animal, like a horse. Replacing the woman with "your bed" continues to dehumanize and objectify the cinnamon peeler's wife. However, if the focus is shifted to the man emitting yellow bark dusk, though it still implies the marking of territory and ownership, it can also signify the bringing of his wife into the fold of the cinnamon peeler caste. The act of love allows her to gain an entire community, a community that will be able to recognize her, according to the concepts stated in Janice Jiggins's *Caste and Family in the Politics of the Sinhalese*: "[Sinhalese] society possesses an intimacy ... that enables members of the same nominal caste to recognize each other as part of the same community." The riding of the bed becomes necessary for the sufficient broadcast of the sign of the Salagama.

The phrase "profession of my fingers / floating over you" in the second stanza, presumably the smell of cinnamon, could be interpreted as a type of claim to ownership. Within the context of caste, however, it can also be a proclamation of community and family, which provides additional measures of safety and security because to deal with one caste member is to deal with them all. As Jiggins states, castes are known "at times to act together, and to display a common response as a group to the demands and attitudes of other castes." The following stanza continues this idea by laying out the cinnamon peeler's wife's body in terms of land and urbanization, implying that she has been incorporated into something much larger than herself. This phenomenon is described by Jiggins as follows: "families are known to members of the caste throughout the island, and to varying degrees, each major caste has representatives in public life who offer patronage and seek to wield influence on its members' behalf." The divvying up of her body is not merely another way to objectify. It parallels the regional spread a caste can have throughout the island while still maintaining connection.

The fourth stanza makes a stronger statement when seen in the context of the Sinhalese caste society. With only a little extrapolation, the reason for the cinnamon peeler disguising the scent of his hands is clear: his future mother-in-law has a keen sense of smell and would have been able to detect the slightest physical contact between the lovers, which was clearly off limits. These circumstances bring with them a certain amount of charm and humor to which people in many different cultures can relate. By looking at the Sinhalese caste society view on marriage, another idea materializes. Jiggins puts forth the following view:

> Kinship and property descend in both the male and female lines, and marriage is held to establish a kinship bond not only between the husband and wife but between the kinsmen by marriage. Marriage is thus traditionally very much viewed as an alliance; it is sometimes used to reinforce the circle of kinship by renewing bonds of descent which have grown weak and to bring back distant relatives into close relationship.

Marriages are more like contractual agreements. They are arranged based on finances and prestige as well as familial and social ties. A marriage based on love and attraction is rare. The fact that the cinnamon peeler literally could not keep his hands off his bride-to-be indicates that something special and out of the ordinary has occurred.

When the lovers touch in the water and "remained free" and "blind of smell," it symbolizes being without caste. Therefore, when the wife jests at the husband's infidelity, infidelity actually having severe consequences among the Sinhalese, she is alluding to the fact that extramarital sex does not come with the full benefits of marital bonds. If the cinnamon peeler were to "touch" or make love to the lime burner's daughter, she would not be brought into the fold of cinnamon peelers but would remain in the lime burner caste.

The cultural reading of the poem lends power to the final stanza. It becomes more than just a woman reveling in the claim made by her husband through the scent of his profession. The cinnamon peeler's wife accepts the gift of an entire caste offered through her husband's love. There are also implications for the couple's posterity, as suggested when the poem reads "You touched / your belly to my hands." Their children will receive all the honor, class distinction, and communal ties of the Salagama, a gift from the mother through her acceptance of it from the father. The cinnamon peeler's wife is also telling her husband that she accepts that her children will be cinnamon peelers. She then invites him to celebrate these gifts with the two words: "Smell me."

Sinhalese caste culture moves the patriarchal domination and identity loss occurring in "The Cinnamon Peeler" farther into the background, making them easier for Western readers to look past. The fact that the poem starts with "If I were a cinnamon peeler" emphasizes the idea that Ondaatje's readers are outsiders looking in. This is similar to how the protagonist of *Running in the Family* feels, as quoted by Douglas Barbour in *Michael Ondaatje*: "I am the foreigner." However, the sentence is immediately followed by, "I am the prodigal who hates the foreigner." This distaste is somewhat manifest in the first line of the poem, "If I were a cinnamon peeler." It removes the readers, i.e., foreigners, from the characters of the poem by making it the fantasy of a foreigner, rendering any judgments passed on the characters as judgments passed on an outsider. It is the narrator who wants to lose himself in an occupation and the narrator who wishes to dominate and own his lover.

Barbour, in his critical analysis of Ondaatje's works, says "Ondaatje's texts seek to create a sensual and emotional awareness of the other's living, in the midst of his or her experience. To slip into the other body and feel what it's like." In "The Cinnamon Peeler" Ondaatje allows readers to "feel what it's like," especially when viewed through the lens of caste culture. However, he cultivates an awareness of the fact that the reader is still only experiencing art by framing it with the word "if"; it is a piece of art (the fantasy of the narrator) within art (the poem itself). It is as though Ondaatje wants to make it clear that art can only go so far in representing actual experience. Therefore, even as readers come to know how intimacy can be experienced among the Sinhalese, one must remember that one cannot truly know what it is like until one has lived it himself.

Source: Daniel Toronto, Critical Essay on "The Cinnamon Peeler," in *Poetry for Students*, Gale, 2003.

Tamara Fernando

Fernando is a Seattle-based editor. In this essay, Fernando argues that Ondaatje's poem explores the complexities of identity and displacement through the use of a mythical identity.

> "The cinnamon peeler's narrow and inescapable identity offers a sharp contrast to the nebulous, anonymous narrator who daydreams of being him."

In reviewing Michael Ondaatje's 1991 collection of poetry, *The Cinnamon Peeler: Selected Poems*, poet Cyril Dabydeen, referring to the "seemingly distinctive personae" that each poem in the collection seems to have, writes in *World Literature Today* that "Ondaatje essentially creates a mythos about himself." This "mythos"—the creation of new identities—characterizes much of Ondaatje's writing. His best-known example is the nameless, faceless, and nation-less burn victim in his Booker-prize winning novel *The English Patient*. As an immigrant to Canada from the South Asian island nation of Sri Lanka, Ondaatje has been ascribed a variety of often-conflicting identities as an immigrant writer. W. M. Verhoeven, writing about Ondaatje's ethnicity in *Mosaic, a Journal for the Interdisciplinary Study of Literature*, cites Arun Muhkerjee's complaint against Ondaatje for pandering to the mainstream and not writing enough about "his otherness." On the other hand, critic Tom Marshall, writing in his text *Harsh and Lovely Land: The Major Canadian Poets and the Making of a Canadian Tradition*, casts Ondaatje as an exotic outsider by calling his work "a heady mixture . . . strange and intriguing to Canadians." In the Canadian magazine *MacLean's*, Brian Johnson simply ignores the question of his ethnic and national identity by proclaiming him "a writer without borders." It is precisely this sense of borderlessness, or displacement, that fuels Ondaatje's work. Like many postcolonial and/or immigrant writers whose identities are indeterminate, Ondaatje is obsessed with identity, and his characteristic myth-making is one method by which his art dissects notions of identity. In his poem "The Cinnamon Peeler," he creates a mythical identity, the cinnamon peeler, through which he explores the issues of identity and displacement.

This poem itself takes the form of a daydream; the narrator wonders aloud to his lover what it would be like if he were someone else. With this first line, tensions and anxieties of identity and displacement are revealed in the sharp contrast drawn between the actual identity of the narrator (which is never revealed) and the person he dreams of becoming—a cinnamon peeler, one who has a specific and defined place in society.

Cinnamon is a spice that is native to Sri Lanka, a country where, in traditional societies, a man's profession was determined by the caste into which he was born. In such a strict caste system, there was little or no social mobility or mingling between the castes, and professions were handed down father to son through the generations. The world dreamed of by the narrator echoes this narrow, class-conscious society. Here, men are not known by name but rather by their profession and, by extension, their caste. It can be surmised that this imagined cinnamon peeler was born, and will die, a cinnamon peeler.

The absolute unambiguousness of the cinnamon peeler's identity is represented throughout the poem by the pervading odor of cinnamon. The unmistakable pungency of the spice is with the peeler constantly; he cannot help but "leave the yellow bark dust / on your pillow."

Cinnamon is the source of his livelihood and, thus, of his social identity, the only identity by which he is known. The hyperbolic permanence of the odor of cinnamon then becomes a metaphor for the permanence of the cinnamon peeler's station in life. It represents not only his livelihood, but also his caste and all the societal restrictions his caste places upon him. The cinnamon peeler's narrow and inescapable identity offers a sharp contrast to the nebulous, anonymous narrator who daydreams of being him.

Not only does the odor of cinnamon cling to the man, but it also marks the body of the woman to whom the narrator is speaking. The scent of cinnamon is passed on to her body by the touch of her husband.

It is no accident that the scent of cinnamon, transferred to the woman through the touch of her husband, marks her body as indelibly as it does his, for her identity, too, is imparted by her husband's livelihood and caste. In the society re-imagined in this poem, women play a subordinate role to men and are defined in terms of their relationship to their husbands. Thus, in the poem, one reads not only of "the cinnamon peeler's wife" but also of "the grass cutter's wife" and "the lime burner's daughter." Just as the cinnamon peeler does not have a given name, neither does his wife, but the woman's lack of individual identity holds with it the additional, powerful connotation of the subordination of women as passive possessions.

The theme of woman as possession is evident in the language used by the man to describe how he touches her body. In the third stanza, he describes her body in terms of geography. The narrator literally maps this woman with the scent of cinnamon, much like a colonizer marking his new territory. The narrator imparts the indelible pungency of cinnamon on to her body to mark her as his; the scent of cinnamon thus becomes her identifying feature, as well.

The identities attributed to the characters are constricting, even demeaning by today's western standards. These characters lack even the most basic markers of individuality, and the woman is further demeaned by the lack of recognition of her existence as an individual separate from her husband.

This constricting, seemingly inescapable identity is precisely the mythic identity the narrator not only dreams for himself, but which he also describes in a language of erotic desire. Although cinnamon has been interpreted thus far strictly as a symbol of the characters' inescapable identities, its sensual attributes should not be ignored. Ondaatje turns its pungent odor and the yellow bark dust left on a pillow into the residue of lovemaking. In metaphorically ascribing sensuality and desirability to these identifying roles, it may seem that the narrator is naïvely romanticizing his mythical world and ignoring the oppression of the type of society it mirrors. However, even though the idea of a concrete, socially ascribed identity seems to be idealized by the narrator, it also becomes characterized as a source of oppression. For even as it is described sensually, the presence of cinnamon is almost too overpowering to bear. The woman's breasts and shoulders "reek" with its scent no matter what he does to rid himself of the smell. In the fifth stanza, the couple resorts to touching each other under water to escape from the scent.

Here, the poem shifts from one extreme to another, from the narrator's dream of bodies marked so strongly by the scent of cinnamon to these individualized bodies, underwater, liberated of the spice's identifying scent. In the water, the couple is free of the earth, and this freedom connotes a complete detachment from the land, their village, their caste.

But, this image is abruptly interrupted by the woman who suddenly "climb[s] the bank." She leaves the water to return to the land. At this instance, the course of the poem shifts. The woman becomes an active participant, asserting her own voice.

Until now, the woman has merely been the narrator's object, directly addressed in the poem but voiceless. She has also been the passive recipient of his touch and identified more as his possession than as an independent individual. When she finally speaks, however, she does not cast off the identity.

Although the woman recognizes the "wounding" effect of the social constrictions placed upon her, she chooses to embrace the resulting scars as her own. By the poem's end, she is able to assert her own individuality despite still being defined only in relation to her husband. Stepping out of passivity and subordination, she asserts herself by "touching [her] belly to [his] hands" and saying: "I am the cinnamon peeler's wife. Smell me."

This final line brings the poem to something of a balance between the desire for social definition and the repulsion against its constrictions. The woman, when she is finally allowed to assert her voice, asserts her individuality in the simplest but clearest of ways: by calling herself "I." She further asserts her individuality by the imperative, "Smell me." Again, she signifies her individuality by using the word "me," and she demands that it be *she* who is sensed, not the cinnamon that outwardly marks her. It is no longer the all-pervasive cinnamon that is being smelled; rather, it is the woman herself who is being recognized. It is her *self* that triumphs over the identifications that mark her, even if her identity is still recognized in relation to her position in society.

"The Cinnamon Peeler" opened with an idealization of a mythical identity. In a way, the woman's ultimate, but all-too-easy individual triumph, is also an idealization. It may be that for Ondaatje, only in the realm of a mythical world can such triumph not only be actualized but sustained, and thus the poem does not ever wake up from the daydream of its imagined world. In closing the poem this way, Ondaatje is able to strike a balance between the tensions of displacement by portraying an evolved, complex self-awareness that asserts individualism even as it recognizes the inextricable part social identity plays in the shaping of the self.

Source: Tamara Fernando, Critical Essay on "The Cinnamon Peeler," in *Poetry for Students*, Gale, 2003.

Diane Wakoski

In the following essay, Wakoski discusses the similarities and differences between the poetic styles of Ondaatje and Walt Whitman.

It is ironic that Michael Ondaatje is a writer who exemplifies every aspect of the Whitman tradition in American poetry, for he is a Canadian Writer, though once removed, since he was born and spent his boyhood in Ceylon (now Sri Lanka). His exotic story is told in a work of prose, *Running in the Family*, which most people read as if it were poetry. Indeed, Ondaatje is a melting pot of techniques, and his work, as Whitman said of his own, "contains multitudes."

Ondaatje's writing can take the form of intense lyric poems, as in "Kim at Half an Inch":

Brain is numbed
is body touch
and smell, warped light

hooked so close
her left eye
is only a golden blur
her ear a vast
musical instrument of flesh

The moon spills off my shoulder
slides into her face

It also can look like prose but work as poetic language and the retelling or making of myth, as does what is perhaps his best-known book, *The Collected Works of Billy the Kid*, which won the Governor-General's award in 1971. Moving in and out of imagined landscape, portrait and documentary, and anecdote and legend, Ondaatje writes for the eye and the ear simultaneously. A critic reviewing his work for *Books in Canada* in 1982 said that "each new book of Michael Ondaatje's seems wholly different from those that preceded it, and wholly the same . . . the characters keep outgrowing the confines of fact."

Like Whitman, Ondaatje is a writer of democratic vistas. He is fascinated by the lives of common people who do uncommon things, such as Billy the Kid, or figures from the world of jazz like Buddy Bolden, the subject of *Coming through Slaughter*. His own family seems impersonally related to him, as with Whitman's eye he sees equally both the large and the small, the close and the distant. Also like Whitman, he is fascinated by the taboos and peculiarities that combine to give him a voice that is unique but also universal.

Unlike Whitman, however, Ondaatje has a dark, witty side that makes his poetic voice irreverent, though rarely abrasive. His language alternates

> *Moving in and out of imagined landscape, portrait and documentary, and anecdote and legend, Ondaatje writes for the eye and the ear simultaneously.*

between the short lines of lyric and the long lines that actually become prose or prose poetry. His work lends itself to theater, and he has made several films as well. Yet his identity is as a poet, for it is the voice that is central in Ondaatje's work, a voice giving him control over both interiors and exteriors, as in these lines from *The Collected Works of Billy the Kid*:

> I am here with the range for everything
> corpuscle muscle hair
> hands that need the rub of metal
> those senses that
> that want to crash things with an axe
> that listen to deep buried veins in our palms
> those who move in dreams over your women night
> near you, every paw, the invisible hooves
> the mind's invisible blackout the intricate never
> the body's waiting rut.

What Ondaatje also possesses is a gift to draw on the myths of American culture in such a way that the reader can understand the depth of common experience. From a young outlaw of the American West to a strange, neurasthenic New Orleans jazz trumpet player to his eccentric relatives with their pet cobra warming itself on the radio in Sri Lanka, Ondaatje writes with lyric intensity about the differences we all share.

Source: Diane Wakoski, "Ondaatje, Michael," in *Contemporary Poets*, 7th ed., edited by Thomas Riggs, St. James Press, 2001, pp. 891–92.

Ann Mandel

In the following essay, Mandel examines Ondaatje's life and writings.

Winner of two Governor General's awards for poetry, Michael Ondaatje is one of the most brilliant and acclaimed of that impressive group of Canadian poets who first published in the 1960s, a group that includes Margaret Atwood, Gwen MacEwen, and B. P. Nichol. Ondaatje's widely praised books range from collections of tightly crafted lyrics to a narrative mixing poetry, prose, and fictional documentary, and a novel of lyric intensity. Using myth, legend, and anecdote drawn from the Wild West, the jazz world, film, and newspapers, his books have had wide popular appeal while at the same time occasioning considerable analysis by critics in Canada and elsewhere. The world of his poems has been called "surreal, absurd, inchoate, dynamic," "a dark, chaotic, but life-giving universe," and "the dangerous cognitive region which lies between reportage and myth."

Philip Michael Ondaatje was born in Colombo, Ceylon (now Sri Lanka), to Philip Mervyn and Enid Gratiaen Ondaatje. His paternal grandfather was a wealthy tea planter with a family estate in Kegalle. Ondaatje remembers "a great childhood" filled with aunts, uncles, many houses, and, judging from the stories he recounts in his autobiographical *Running in the Family* (1982), gossip and eccentricity. In his poem "Light" he tells of his grandmother "who went to a dance in a muslin dress / with fireflies captured and embedded in the cloth," and in "Letters & Other World" he speaks lovingly of his father's life as a "terrifying comedy" of alcohol and outrageous acts. In Colombo Ondaatje attended St. Thomas College. His parents separated in 1948, and in 1952 Ondaatje followed his mother, brother, and sister to London, England, where he attended Dulwich College. Dissatisfied eventually with the English school system which kept him trying "O" levels in maths when he wanted to study English, he immigrated to Canada at the age of nineteen, joining his brother Christopher already living in Montreal.

He entered Bishop's University, Lennoxville, majoring in English and history. It was there, finally able to concentrate on English literature and influenced by a teacher, Arthur Motyer, who "aroused an enthusiasm for literature," that Ondaatje began to write. It was there, too, that simultaneously with his reading of Browning, Eliot, Yeats, and younger modern poets, he came in contact with contemporary Canadian poets, notably D. G. Jones. It was his sense that Canada had "no big history," no weighty literary tradition, which freed Ondaatje to try to write.

A concluding year at the University of Toronto, at the end of which Ondaatje earned his B.A., brought him into contact with poet Raymond Souster, who included Ondaatje's work in his important anthology of young poets, *New Wave Canada* (1966). When Ondaatje won the university's Epstein Award for Poetry poet Wayne Clifford brought him to the attention of Coach House press. Coach House, a small but influential publisher of finely designed books, offered to publish one of Ondaatje's manuscripts, and though he refused then, it was with Coach House that his first collection, *The Dainty Monsters*, was published in 1967. From 1965 to 1967 he completed an M.A. at Queen's University, with a thesis on Edwin Muir ("because there was very little stuff written on him"), edited a university magazine, the *Mitre*, and wrote many of the poems included in his first book.

In 1964 Ondaatje married Kim Jones, an artist, and two children (Quentin and Griffin, for whom Dennis Lee wrote a children's poem) were born in the next two years. His wife had four children by a previous marriage, and the daily life of family and friends provided subject matter for many poems in his first book and in the 1973 volume *Rat Jelly*.

The Dainty Monsters, its title taken from a poem by Baudelaire, is divided into two sections: "Over the Garden Wall," thirty-six lyrics in which this domestic world collides with, or is transformed into, an exotic, violent, disorienting vision; and "Troy Town," nine poems centered on mythic and historical figures such as Lilith, Philoctetes, and Elizabeth I. The first section, with its plentiful animal imagery, concerns the "civilized magic" of family life. This magic can become extravagant: a dragon gets entangled in the badminton net, manticores clog Toronto sewers, a camel bites off a woman's left breast, pigs become poets, and strange, as yet unrecognized gods alter and reshape landscape, genetics, and the color and mood of a moment. Forces inside the body match forces outside it as all of the external world is involved in human visceral activity. Jungles and gorillas coexist with cocktails and cars, birds fly like watches, clocks swagger, zoo gibbons move like billiard balls, cars chomp on bushes with chrome teeth. Just as the natural world ranges from the domestic dog to the uncaged leopard, so each body or organism, animal or human, has the ability to hold within itself "rivers of collected suns, / jungles of force, coloured birds" as well as urges toward the suicidal refinement of overbreeding. As Sheila Watson has remarked in an article published in *Open Letter* (Winter 1974–1975), Ondaatje "is aware that all life maintains itself by functional specialization of some kind and as often as not loses itself for the same reason." Similarly, poetry is no absolute: it breaks the moment it seeks to record. It must, therefore, be sensitive above all to changes—to the altering moment, to the transforming imagination, and to the demands of an age when, as Ondaatje writes in *The Dainty Monsters*, "bombs are shaped like cedars." In some poems in the second section the poet imagines the characters of legendary figures: Prometheus in his martyred pain attracting mermaids at dusk, Lilith rioting with corrupted unicorns in Eden. Others are monologues in which historical characters—Helen, Elizabeth I—speak their lives and emotions. Formally these poems reflect Ondaatje's interest in longer discontinuous structures, but as far as subject matter is concerned, they represent a conclusion to one stage of his career. As Ondaatje recalls it, his friend the poet David McFadden told him "no more Greek stuff," and he took that advice.

The Dainty Monsters, published in an edition of 500 copies, received more attention than most first books of poetry. Reviewers were especially impressed by Ondaatje's startling imagery. The volume is still in print, as are all his major books.

In *The Dainty Monsters* Ondaatje began his exploration of the intersection of animal, human, and machine worlds and of the intricate meshing of primitive, violent forces and ordered, exact responses. The book also, in direct references and in its imagery, suggests an interest in the visual arts, especially in the paintings of Henri Rousseau. Ondaatje's second book, *The Man with Seven Toes* (1969), had its origins in a series of drawings the Australian artist Sidney Nolan had done, based on the life of Mrs. Eliza Fraser, a Scottish lady who was shipwrecked off the Queensland coast, lived among aborigines, and was helped to civilization by an escaped convict to whom she promised free-

> "The world of his poems has been called 'surreal, absurd, inchoate, dynamic,' 'a dark, chaotic, but life-giving universe,' and 'the dangerous cognitive region which lies between reportage and myth.'"

dom, then promptly threatened to betray. Ondaatje began with these drawings and Nolan's series of paintings of Ned Kelly, together with a sense of the Australian landscape as it is evoked in Alan Moorehead's books and a brief account of the Eliza Fraser story of Colin MacInnes. He began working on the poem in the fall of 1966, after spending a hot dusty summer working on a road gang—"the nearest thing to desert I could get"—and completed the poem about the time *The Dainty Monsters* was published. The book, a fine limited edition of 300 copies published by Coach House Press, appeared in 1969.

The Man with Seven Toes is Ondaatje's first major attempt at a long sequence, thirty-three short lyrics and a concluding ballad, prefaced by a striking reproduction of Canadian artist Jack Chambers's *Man and Dog*, which visually suggests something of the loneliness, agony, and violent rich beauty in the poems. The woman of the poems is nameless, left in the desert by a departing train which hums "like a low bird." She comes across fantastically decorated aborigines, is raped, and escapes with Potter, the convict. Their trek takes them through swamp where teeth like "ideal knives" take off some of Potter's toes and snakes with "bracelets of teeth" hang in the leaves; they proceed into the hot plain, where Potter kills a sleeping wolf by biting open its vein. When they are found, the woman says only "god has saved me."

The poems move from a narrator's voice in and out of the minds of the convict and woman, sometimes describing what happens, at others reflecting emotions. In the first poem she is merely a woman too tired to call after the receding train, but in the imagery of her responses to the rape, of the slaughter of animals, of the rape itself, the spilling of semen and blood are confused in ways that fuse terror, beauty, rich colors, sexuality, and death. And after her rescue, resting in the civilized Royal Hotel, she moves her hands over her body, "sensing herself like a map." While she sleeps, a bird is chopped up in a ceiling fan and scattered about the room. Her acceptance of violent death coincides with her acceptance of her sexual body, though she has rejected the moral dimension of her experience.

The poem conveys Ondaatje's acute awareness of song and the spoken voice. It has been performed as a dramatic reading for three speakers, first in Vancouver in 1968, then at Stratford in 1969. The second staging was directed by Paul Thompson in Toronto, with whom Ondaatje later worked on the 1971 adaptation and staging of *The Collected Works of Billy the Kid*, on the making of the 1972 film, *The Clinton Special*, and on the 1980 stage adaptation of *Coming through Slaughter*.

In 1967 Ondaatje became an instructor in English at the University of Western Ontario in London. During the summer of 1968, while staying in Ganonoque, Ontario, he wrote *Leonard Cohen* (1970), a short critical study of the poet and novelist who had recently become known as a songwriter and performer. Ondaatje has said that Cohen was the most important influence on him as a young writer and on his generation, especially through the novel *The Favourite Game* (1963), which seemed refreshingly unelitist. Ondaatje's was the first book-length study of Cohen and remains an important work on that writer, though the book also illuminates Ondaatje and his work. He is clearly close to Cohen, sharing Cohen's love of the sensuous startling image, his understanding of the detached mind of the artist, of the authentic fakery of art, and, as Ondaatje writes of Cohen, of the necessity of promoting "our own private cells of anarchy."

Shortly after completing *The Man with Seven Toes*, Ondaatje, feeling dissatisfied with the form of that work, began to browse through Edmund Wilson's *Patriotic Gore* (1962) with the vague intention of writing a Civil War story or poem. Somehow deflected west, he wrote a few poems using the voice of Billy the Kid and, as he described it in a 1975 interview with Sam Solecki for *Rune*, "moved from these to being dissatisfied with the limits of lyric; so I moved to prose and interviews and so on." The legend of Billy merged with Ondaatje's memories of childhood cowboys-and-Indians games in Ceylon, and he wrote over a period of about two years, taking another year to edit and rearrange his materials. *The Collected Works of Billy the Kid: Left Handed Poems* appeared in 1970, designed by Coach House and published by House of Anansi, another small but important Canadian press.

Winner of the Governor General's Award for 1970, *The Collected Works of Billy the Kid* has become Ondaatje's most celebrated work, praised by critics and readers and roundly condemned—to his delight—by federal MPs for dealing with an *American* hero and outlaw. The familiar Wild West characters are in this volume—Billy the Kid, sheriff Pat Garrett, and other historical characters taken from Walter Burns's *The Saga of Billy the Kid* (1926)—but the focus is not on the historical outlaw nor on the Wild West motif. The book has been interpreted by some as a parable of the artist/outlaw, but Ondaatje has commented that though Billy may be on some instinctual level an artist, he did not intend to create a "portrait of the artist." Rather, the book continues thematically his exploration of the ambiguous and often paradoxical area between biology and mechanization, movement and stasis, chaotic life and the framed artistic moment. The artist in the book is not Billy but Ondaatje himself as writer, shaping and faking material, bringing into the poems some of his own experiences while at the same time standing apart, watching his characters feel and act, and, in the end, leaving them as he wakes in his hotel room alone.

The book includes poems, prose, photographs and other illustrations, interviews, and a comic-book legend. It begins with Billy's list of the dead, including his own death in the future at the hands of Pat Garrett. The narrative sections, funny, witty, full of strange stories, tell of such events as Garrett's gunning down Tom O'Folliard, Billy's pastoral sojourns on the Chisum ranch in Texas, his arrest, ride to trial and escape, Garrett's peculiar self-education in French and alcoholism, and finally Billy's murder. In the lyrics and especially in the frame of the story, Ondaatje's concerns become clear. Before the text, there is a framed blank square and a quotation from the great frontier photographer L. A. Huffman about the development of a technique which allowed him to take photographs of moving things from a moving horse. The book concludes with a small framed picture of Ondaatje, aged about six, wearing a cowboy outfit. The volume's subtitle, *Left Handed Poems*, refers to Billy's hands, small, smooth, white, and trained by finger exercises twelve hours a day, the hands of a murderer who is a courteous dandy, a gentle lover, a man sensitive to every nerve in his body, every sense extending to the whole sensual world: a man with "the range for everything." Pat Garrett, the lawman whose hands are scarred and burned, is a "sane assassin," an "academic murderer" who decided what is right and "forgot all morals." Garrett's morals are mechanical, insane in their neutrality. Billy reflects that he himself can watch "the stomach of clocks / shift their wheels and pins into each other / and emerge living, for hours," but insane images blossom in his own brain, and he knows that in all ordered things, the course of the stars, "the clean speed of machines," "one altered move ... will make them maniac." Awareness and exactitude imply stress; the frame holds within it the breaking moment. It is better to be in motion.

Inside the small boy Michael Ondaatje are Garrett's and Billy's future legend; the three are held inside the book; the structure in its altering forms collects them all.

Canadian critics described *The Collected Works of Billy the Kid* as "one of the best books ... in a long time," "profound in its dimensions," and praised the originality of the form. The critic for the *New York Times*, reviewing the American edition, published in 1970, called it "carefully crafted and thoroughly literate," though a "miniature." It has sold at least 20,500 copies in Canada and is currently in print in both Canada and the United States. In one American anthology, *Modernism in Literature* (1977), the entire book is republished in facsimile as an example of contemporary impressionism, literature which, through ambiguity, calls attention to itself as a conscious construct and insists on the relativity of experience.

The Collected Works of Billy the Kid evolved into a play, beginning with radio and stage readings. Ondaatje reshaped, cut, and added songs, and the play, in its present form, was first performed by the Toronto Free Theatre in October 1974, directed by Martin Kinch. It was performed at the Brooklyn Academy, New York, in October 1975 and continues to be presented in many countries.

Given the visual quality and inspiration of Ondaatje's work, it was natural for him to turn to film. One effort, using family and friends as cast, involves the dognapping of the family bassett hound, Wallace, and bears the title *Carry on Crime and Punishment* (1972). A more serious effort is a thirty-five-minute film, *Sons of Captain Poetry* (1970), on Canadian sound and concrete poet B. P. Nichol, made when *The Collected Works of Billy the Kid* was going to press. It is an entertaining and thoughtful introduction to the impulses behind sound and concrete poetry and an appreciative homage to a man from whom Ondaatje says he has learned much.

After finishing *The Dainty Monsters* and during the writing of his two subsequent books, Ondaatje continued to write short lyrics, collected in 1973 in *Rat Jelly*. Published by Coach House, the book has a stunning cover taken from a nursery school stained-glass window, depicting a pieman who clearly has sinister designs on Simple Simon. The book is divided into three sections, "Families," "Live Bait," and "White Dwarfs," which contain domestic poems, animal poems, and poems about art respectively. The first two sections continue the themes of the previous books, though the structure and line are generally more relaxed, the tone more humorous and casual. Ondaatje's genius for vivid images is here: his wife's ear is "a vast / musical instrument of flesh"; bats "organize the air / with thick blinks of travel"; a window "tries to split with cold," a moth in his pajamas is the poet's heart "breaking loose." Violent events explode into everyday life: "At night the gold and black slashed bees come / pluck my head away"; a woman's naked back during lovemaking is a wrecked aircraft scattered across sand; the fridge contains a live rat pie. In the second section the deaths of animals are related to man's hate for his own animality and mortality: men kill to "fool themselves alive." It is the third section of *Rat Jelly* which is perhaps the most interesting in that it contains several poems explicitly on art and the relationship of art to experience. In "King Kong meets Wallace Stevens" these two figures are humorously juxtaposed: Stevens all insurance and thought, Kong whose "mind is nowhere." As the poem develops, it is the poet who "is thinking chaos is thinking fences," whose blood is bellowing in his head. Ondaatje's constructed beast loose in the city is the poem as anarchic animal, fashioned in the poet's subversive imagination. The poem entitled "The gate in his head" contains lines which have often been cited as Ondaatje's clearest aesthetic statement. Looking at a blurred photograph of a gull, the poet writes:

> And this is all this writing should be then,
> The beautiful formed things caught at the wrong moment
> so they are shapeless, awkward
> moving to the clear.

Certainly these lines reflect his wish to catch movement and to capture life without killing it, as clarity or the certainty of, say, Garrett's morals does. In "White Dwarfs," the concluding poem in the book, the poet speaks of his heroes as those who have "no social fuel," who die in "the ether peripheries," who are not easy to describe, existing in "the perfect white between the words." Silence is the perfect poetry, the silence of a star imploding after its brilliant parading in an unknown universe.

In 1971 Ondaatje left the University of Western Ontario ("they wanted me to do a Ph.D. and I didn't want to") and took an assistant professorship at Glendon College, Toronto. In a Toronto *Globe and Mail* interview in 1974, Ondaatje reported that he was working on a prose work about different characters in the 1930s. That work may yet see print, but the book which did appear in 1976 was *Coming through Slaughter*, a novel about New Orleans jazz musician Buddy Bolden, a cornetist who went mad in 1907. The book, as Ondaatje disclosed in a 1977 interview for *Books in Canada*, was begun in London, triggered by a newspaper clipping describing "Buddy Bolden, who became a legend when he went berserk in a parade." Ondaatje worked on it for several years, especially during summers on the family farm near Verona, Ontario. In 1973, well after he had started on the book, Ondaatje went to Louisiana to do research and absorb the geography of Bolden's life. Very little is, in fact, known about Bolden: in the novel, on one page, Ondaatje lists the available facts. He used tapes of jazzmen remembering Bolden, books about New Orleans's Storyville district and the period, and the records of the hospital where Bolden lived, mad, until his death in 1931. But as in his work on Billy the Kid, Ondaatje's interest is not historical. He has altered dates, brought people together who never met, and polished facts "to suit the truth of fiction," as he comments in the book's acknowledgements. For him, "the facts start suggesting things, almost breed," and the landscape of the book is "a totally mental landscape ... of names and rumours."

The book is in large part "a statement about the artist," Ondaatje noted in a 1980 interview published in *Eclipse*, though Bolden is an individual, not a generalized artist. It is, according to Ondaatje, "a very private book," in which an identification between author and character is made explicit in the text—"The photograph moves and becomes a mirror"—but it is also a controlled and impersonal creation, examining the tensions that exist among kinds of art, within certain artists, and within himself. By Ondaatje's account, one germ of *Coming through Slaughter* was the tension he observed among some of the London, Ontario, painters who were his friends, especially between Greg Curnoe and Jack Chambers, one a "local" and the other a "classical" artist.

The book follows Bolden from New Orleans, where he barbers during the day, plays cornet at night, his two-year disappearance from family and the world of music, to his discovery by his policeman friend, Webb, his return to friends and music, and his explosion into madness. The structure is unchronological. The first section is mainly narrative, much of the second takes place in Bolden's mind, the third alternates interior monologue with narrative, and the final pages mix Bolden's thoughts in various mental hospitals with historical documentation, narrative, and explicit comments of the novelist. The book ends, as *The Collected Works of*

What Do I Read Next?

- *Food of Sri Lanka: Authentic Recipes from the Island of Gems* (2001), by Douglas Bullis and Wendy Hutton, is a cookbook that offers recipes from the little-known Sri Lankan cuisine.

- In *The Emperor of Scent: A Story of Obsession, Perfume, and the Last Mystery of the Senses* (2003), journalist Chandler Burr chronicles the struggle that scientist Luca Turin faces when trying to get the scientific community to accept his new theory of smell. In addition to the main theme, the book examines the history of scent and olfactory chemistry and also gives anecdotes from the perfume industry.

- In Chitra Divakaruni's first novel, *The Mistress of Spices* (1997), Tilo is a young Indian woman who ends up on a remote island, where she is taught the magical, curative properties of spices. She is sent to Oakland, California, as a spice mistress, destined to live alone while she heals others with her gift. However, when she meets an American man who sees through her old-woman disguise and falls in love with her, she must choose between love and duty.

- In Joanne Harris's novel *Chocolat* (1999), Vianne Rocher, a choclatier, opens a chocolate shop in a repressed French town during the Lenten season. Over the course of the novel, Vianne and her daughter Anouk win over many of the townspeople through the magic and mystery of their chocolate confections.

- Most critics consider Ondaatje's *The Collected Works of Billy the Kid: Left-Handed Poems* (1970) to be the author's most important volume of poetry. The collection combines verse, prose, photographs, and drawings in a fictionalized biography of William Bonney, the famous American outlaw who went by the name of Billy the Kid.

- In *The Monkey King & Other Stories* (1998), editor Griffin Ondaatje collects an anthology of Sri Lankan folk tales, each retold by a contemporary. Michael Ondaatje contributes two stories, "The Vulture" and "Angulimala."

- *The English Patient* (1992), Ondaatje's most famous work, is a complex World War II novel that follows the story of a Canadian nurse, who stays in the remains of a bombed Italian convent to tend to a severely burned patient.

Billy the Kid does, with the writer alone in a room: "Thirty-one years old. There are no prizes."

Bolden's relationship with Webb parallels structurally that of Billy and Garrett. Bolden's other relationships—with Nora, his wife, and with Robin Brewitt, the woman he comes to love during his retreat, with various other musicians, and especially with Bellocq, a photographer of Storyville's prostitutes—all develop aspects of Bolden as man and as musician. He is an "unprofessional" player, the loudest, the roughest, his music "immediate, dated in half an hour . . . showing all the possibilities in the middle of the story." His playing appears formless, but only because "he tore apart the plot" trying to describe something in a multitude of ways, the music a direct extension of his life. His life is haunted by fears of certainty: "He did nothing but leap into the mass of changes and explore them." Bolden is the totally social, unthinking, chaotic man and artist until he meets Bellocq, who introduces him to privacy, calculated art, the silence beyond the social world. Bellocq eventually commits suicide. After Webb "rescues" Bolden from his self-imposed absence from music, Bolden retreats to a cottage alone, and in his mental addresses to Webb, he meditates on his muse and his life. He thinks about the temptation to silence and about the music of John Robichaux, whose formal complete structures "dominated . . . audiences," a tyranny Bolden loathes. Instead, he wants audiences to "come in where they pleased and leave when they pleased and somehow hear the germs of the start and all the possible endings." In his silence Bolden grows theoretical, and, returning to the "20th century game of fame," he brings self-consciousness into his uncertainties. He compares himself, needing and loathing an audience, with the sad transient mattress prostitutes, selling a wrecked talent. On his fifth morning home, playing in a parade, he sees a woman strut into the procession, and he begins to play for, at, her: she becomes all audiences, all the youth, energy, sexuality he once had, all women, all pure cold art: "this is what I wanted, always, loss of privacy in the playing." He "overblows" his cornet, hemorrhages, and collapses, his goal realized, for he has utterly become his music. Bolden is released into madness and a calm serenity. In the passage in which Ondaatje connects himself to Bolden, he suggests that the temptations of silence, madness, and death have also been his, and, by implication, that Bolden's art, aesthetics, and tensions are his, too.

During the writing of *Coming through Slaughter*, Ondaatje directed and edited a film about Theatre Passe Muraille's play *The Farm Show*, an actor-generated theater presentation based on the actors' experiences in a farming community. Ondaatje's interest in his film *The Clinton Special* is the play's merging of document, local gossip, and re-creation of these materials, a process which continues to hold his attention.

At the close of 1976 Ondaatje went to India for a Commonwealth Literature conference, the closest he had been to his birthplace in twenty-four years. On sabbatical in January 1978, he traveled to Sri Lanka for a five-month visit with his sister and relatives. The closing section of *There's a Trick with a Knife I'm Learning to Do* (his 1979 volume of selected poems covering the years 1963 to 1978 that won the Governor General's Award for poetry in 1980) contains new poems, some of which are based on this trip. Others further his concern with local history, and there are a few poems which develop his sense of the seductive, silent moon-world of night.

The final poem takes up his family history, a subject that Ondaatje continued to explore in his next book. He began a journal during his first trip to Sri Lanka and continued it while he was there, recording family stories he barely remembered. By the time he spent a second period in Sri Lanka in 1979 and 1980, he had become deeply involved in the lives and stories of his family history, a history he had ignored for years. *Running in the Family*, which he has refused to consign to any one genre—"the book," he claims, "is not a history but a portrait or 'gesture'"—furthers Ondaatje's experimentation in writing along the borders that separate history, story, and myth. At the same time it is an autobiographical quest, through memory and the tangled scandals and legends of family and a lost colonial world, for parents and the origins of his imagination.

Sri Lanka, fabled and invaded by Portuguese, Dutch, and English as Serendip, Taprobane, and Ceylon, peopled by a mix of Sinhalese, Tamil, and European, provides the tropical setting in which Ondaatje writes and records the memories and gossip of aunts, family friends, sisters and brothers, the history of his parents' courtship and divorce, the antic acts of his grandmother, Lalla, and the doings, "so whimsical, so busy," of earlier generations of Ceylonese society. History is shaped by conversation, anecdote, judgment, by its usefulness as family backdrop and to retelling the family's stories. Combining fiction, fact, poetry, and photographs, Ondaatje evokes the jungles, natural and social, in which his earliest memories grew. His father, an outrageous alcoholic whom he never knew as an adult, especially haunts his son's story. "I think all of our lives have been shaped by what went on before us," writes Ondaatje. Nevertheless, in imagination resides the power to bestow a countering magic on the past, which the writer uses to grant his flower-stealing grandmother the kind of death she always wanted. The book was praised by critics as much for its recreation of a particular society as for its stylistic exploration of the relationship between history and the poetic imagination.

Ondaatje spent the summer of 1979 teaching at the University of Hawaii. In 1980, as he continued his writing about his Sri Lankan family, his Canadian family situation changed radically when he separated from his wife and began to live with Linda Spalding. In *Secular Love* (1984), a collection of lyrics and lyric sequences, the pain of the marriage breakup and the sensual and emotional growth of new love make their way into the poems. One of the book's four sections, "Claude Glass," was published in 1979 as one of Coach House's manuscript editions. The book as a whole explores various landscapes: nighttime, moonlit, and rain-filled natural landscapes, the landscapes of love, a lover, a new life, and language. Like Billy the Kid with "the range for everything" and Bolden exploring chaos and change, the poet wants to know and see completely everything in his altering, altered life, from the "tiny leather toes" of geckos to the "scarred / skin boat" of another's body to the "syllables / in a loon sentence" signaling the lost and found moments which trace and locate a life. Again merging autobiography and poetics, the writer looks for a language which, like the love he seeks, names but does not dominate, which connects but does not control.

In June 1981 Ondaatje went to Australia as winner of the Canada-Australia Exchange award. He continues to be interested in theater and film and has written a screenplay for Robert Kroetsch's 1975 novel *Badlands*, which remains unproduced. Experimentation with the long poem has resulted in "Elimination Dance," a potentially endless comic poem taking off from a high-school dance ritual. One (unpublished) "elimination" is "All those bad poets who claim me as an early influence." He has worked for some years as an editor at Coach House, seeing through the press a number of important Canadian books; his own involvement in the design and production of his books is, by his own admission, obsessive.

He is now a professor at Glendon College, where he teaches Canadian and American literatures, contemporary literature in translation, and creative writing. In February and March of 1986 he spent four weeks teaching and lecturing at universities in Rome and Turin. In 1987 a novel that he had been working on for over three years was published in Canada, the United Kingdom, and the United States. Called *In the Skin of a Lion*, it draws its title from the *Epic of Gilgamesh*: "The joyful will stoop with sorrow, and when you have gone to the earth I will let my hair grow long for your sake, I will wander through the wilderness in the skin of a lion." According to Ondaatje in a 1987 *Quill and Quire* interview with Barbara Turner, it is his "first formal novel." Dealing with many of the social issues that most concern him—the "gulf between rich and poor, the conditions of the labour force, racism . . . in Canada"—the novel provides a historical glimpse of Toronto in the early years of the twentieth century. "I suddenly thought," says the author of the process of composing the book, "of a vista of Upper America where you had five or six people interweaving and treading . . . but somehow connected at certain times." The narrator of the novel not only tells his own story but also observes the lives of others: the immigrant workers who (without speaking the language of the community) build a bridge, the Bloor Street Viaduct, and the powerful Ambrose Small and his sometime lover Clara. What the narrator learns about life, he says, he learns in these years of tension: years of construction that placed the lives of the powerless in danger, years when the powerful were nonetheless susceptible to forces beyond their control. The historical millionaire Andrew Small disappeared at the height of his power in 1919 and was never found. The novel uses this event and the fictional lives of the years leading up to it to question the disparities between the character of life lived and the official versions of recorded history and culture.

Though Ondaatje is always insistent about the help he has received from other writers and friends, he is clearly an original writer, and his work has been received with enthusiasm by both scholars and general audiences. His importance lies, precisely, in his ability to combine a private, highly charged, sometimes dark vision with witty linguistic leaps and welcoming humor.

Source: Ann Mandel, "Michael Ondaatje," in *Dictionary of Literary Biography*, Vol. 60, *Canadian Writers Since 1960, Second Series*, edited by W. H. New, Gale Research, 1987, pp. 273–81.

Sources

Barbour, Douglas, "Secular Love," in *Michael Ondaatje*, Twayne's World Authors Series, No. 835, Twayne Publishers, 1993, pp. 137, 145.

Dabydeen, Cyril, Review of "The Cinnamon Peeler," in *World Literature Today*, Vol. 66, No. 2, Spring 1992, pp. 348–49.

Gunasekera, Tamara, *Hierarchy and Egalitarianism: Caste, Class and Power in Sinhalese Peasant Society*, Athlone Press, 1994, p. 7.

Hulse, Michael, "Worlds in Collision," in the *Times Literary Supplement*, No. 4405, September 4, 1987, p. 948.

Jiggins, Janice, *Caste and Family in the Politics of the Sinhalese, 1947–1976*, Cambridge University Press, 1979, p. 20.

Johnson, Brian D., "MacLean's Honour Roll 2000," in *MacLean's*, December 18, 2000, p. 67.

King-Edwards, Lucille, "On the Brink," in *Books in Canada*, Vol. 13, No. 10, December 1984, pp. 16–17.

Mandel, Ann, "Michael Ondaatje," in *Dictionary of Literary Biography*, Vol. 60, *Canadian Writers Since 1960, Second Series*, edited by W. H. New, Gale Research, 1987, pp. 273–81.

Marshall, Tom, *Harsh and Lovely Land: The Major Canadian Poets and the Making of a Canadian Tradition*, University of British Columbia Press, 1979, pp. 114–49.

Ondaatje, Michael, "The Cinnamon Peeler," in *The Cinnamon Peeler: Selected Poems*, Vintage International, 1997, pp. 154–55.

Solecki, Sam, "Coming Through," in the *Canadian Forum*, Vol. 64, No. 745, January 1985, pp. 32–34.

Verhoeven, W. M., "How Hyphenated Can You Get?: A Critique of Pure Ethnicity," in *Mosaic: A Journal for the In-*

terdisciplinary Study of Literature, Vol. 29, No. 3, September 1996, pp. 97–116.

Further Reading

Jewinski, Ed, *Michael Ondaatje: Express Yourself Beautifully*, Canadian Biography Series, ECW Press, 1994.

In this illustrated biography of Ondaatje, Jewinski discusses how Ondaatje's writing is usually inspired by a single intense image and relates this trend to the author's own intense life. The book explores Ondaatje's relationships with his family and links these relationships to his later works.

Le Guerer, Annick, *Scent: The Mysterious and Essential Powers of Smell*, Kodansha International, 1994.

Le Guerer explores the historical and cultural relationship among the sense of smell and mythology, religion, psychology, and other areas. This book also includes some sections on the relationship of scent to seduction and magic.

Rouby, Catherine, Benoist Schaal, Danièle Dubois, Rémi Gervais, and A. Holley, eds., *Olfaction, Taste, and Cognition*, Cambridge University Press, 2002.

In this first multidisciplinary research anthology, more than fifty specialists discuss smell, taste, and cognition as it relates to neuroscience, psychology, anthropology, philosophy, and linguistics.

Seneviratne, H. L., ed., *Identity, Consciousness, and the Past: Forging of Caste and Community in India and Sri Lanka*, Oxford University Press, 1997.

This collection of nine essays explores the historical and anthropological issues associated with Sri Lanka, Ondaatje's birthplace and the setting of the poem.

The City Limits

A. R. Ammons
1971

Like much of A. R. Ammons's poetry, "The City Limits" explores the uneasy relationship between modern civilization and the natural world. The images that Ammons uses in this poem, such as his consideration of the sound of "birds' bones" or of the "glow-blue" of the bodies of flies, make readers aware of the subtle things in the natural world that ordinarily would go unnoticed. He also draws readers' attention to dark, fearsome, and unpleasant aspects of the world around them, such as the "guts of natural slaughter" that flies feed on and the "dark work of the deepest cells," an allusion to cancer. It is typical of Ammons's poetry that he is able to show the duality of the way that humans view nature. After making his readers uncomfortable, Ammons ends by making a convincing case that understanding can make fear of nature "calmly turn to praise."

This poem was first published in 1971, when Ammons's reputation as a major American poet was already established. It is available in his *Collected Poems, 1951–1971*. For the following thirty years, before his death in 2001, Ammons continued to be an innovator, changing styles and producing a varied legacy of poems ranging from book-length to just a few lines long. Throughout the last half of the twentieth century, he was considered to be a central figure among the growing number of poets who embrace the spiritual aspects of science and nature.

A. R. Ammons

Author Biography

Archie Randolph Ammons was born on February 18, 1926, at his parents' farmhouse near Whiteville, North Carolina. His childhood was spent with his parents and two older sisters on the family's tobacco farm, which his grandfather had built. It was during these formative years that he developed the understanding of nature and appreciation of its complexity that is evident in almost all of his poems. After graduating from Whiteville High School in 1943, he went to work in the navy shipyard at Wilmington, North Carolina. He enrolled in the Navy in 1944 and did a tour of duty in the South Pacific during the end of World War II. While in the Navy, during the long night watches, Ammons began to write poetry.

When the war was over, Ammons took advantage of the G. I. Bill, a law that subsidized college tuition for veterans. He attended Wake Forest University, changing his major often between pre-medicine, biology, chemistry, and general science. In 1949, he graduated with a bachelor of science degree, and soon after he was married. After a few years of graduate school at the University of California at Berkley, he went to work for a small company in southern New Jersey that made glass products for laboratories. He was there for twelve years, during which time his first two poetry collections were published. At a poetry reading at Cornell University, he discussed the idea of teaching with another faculty member. The next year he was hired, the start of a long-term relationship between Ammons and Cornell that was to last for the rest of his life.

Ammons has won the National Book Award twice, first for *Collected Poems, 1951–1971* (1972) and second for the book-length poem *Garbage* (1993). In 1993, the Poetry Society awarded Ammons the Robert Frost Medal in recognition of his life's work. "The City Limits" can be found in *Briefings: Poems Small and Easy* (1971), in which it was first published, and in *Collected Poems, 1951–1971*. Ammons died in Ithaca, New York, on February 25, 2001, at the age of seventy-five.

Poem Text

When you consider the radiance, that it does not
  withhold
itself but pours its abundance without selection into
  every
nook and cranny not overhung or hidden; when
  you consider
that birds' bones make no awful noise against the
  light but
lie low in the light as in a high testimony; when   5
  you consider
the radiance, that it will look into the guiltiest

swervings of the weaving heart and bear itself upon
  them,
not flinching into disguise or darkening; when you
  consider
the abundance of such resource as illuminates the
  glow-blue
bodies and gold-skeined wings of flies swarming   10
  the dumped
guts of a natural slaughter or the coil of shit and in
  no
way winces from its storms of generosity; when
  you consider

that air or vacuum, snow or shale, squid or wolf,
  rose or lichen,
each is accepted into as much light as it will take,
  then
the heart moves roomier, the man stands and looks   15
  about, the

leaf does not increase itself above the grass, and
  the dark
work of the deepest cells is of a tune with May
  bushes
and fear lit by the breadth of such calmly turns to
  praise.

Poem Summary

Lines 1–3

The first stanza of "The City Limits" does not consist of just one unit of language: it starts with a conjunctive phrase, "When you consider," and finishes that idea in the middle of line 3, starting another phrase, again with the words "when you consider," before the stanza's end. By compiling one incomplete thought upon another before coming out with the main grammatical point, the poem goads readers to guess what they are supposed to find out in the end after they have considered all of the things being listed.

In this first stanza, readers are told that the poem's point will come out after they have considered a phenomenon that is defined as "the radiance." Radiance can be used to refer to light, and it can also sometimes refer to heat. It is first clearly identified as light in line 3, which says that the radiance is excluded from areas that are "overhung or hidden." Since the radiance is blocked out by overhangs, readers can assume that it comes from above, like sunlight.

Lines 4–6

The second phrase submitted for readers' consideration has been introduced in line 3, but it is fully realized in lines 4 through 5. Here, the poem brings up the image of "birds' bones." It mixes sensory images by bringing up the sound of the bones in line 4 and considers how that sound exists within the visual realm of light. The understatement "no awful noise" seems to imply that the beating of birds' wings does make a sound, and that it is in fact unpleasant, but that it just does not reach the level of "awful." This is just one way in which the poem shows an acceptance of the harshness of nature. In line 5, there is a contrast drawn between the heights that birds could reach in flight and the fact that they spend their time in the sun low near the earth.

The end of this stanza repeats the phrase that started the poem, "When you consider the radiance." It changes direction after that one introductory phrase, though. Instead of going on to identify the radiance, as it did in the first line, line 6 brings up a moral judgement, guilt. Ending with the phrase "the guiltiest" draws attention to the concept of guilt, and it calls on readers' curiosity to find out what guilty thing or things this radiance is examining.

Lines 7–9

In saying that the "radiance" that shines from above can look into the heart, this poem plays with

Media Adaptations

- The Modern Poetry Association of Chicago released a seven-cassette collection of poets discussing their craft with their peers. The collection is titled *Poets in Person* (1991). It includes a half-hour interview between Ammons and Alice Fulton.

- In 1984, Ammons read several of his poems for the radio series *New Letters on the Air*, produced by the literary journal *New Letters*. This program, hosted by Judy Ray, was released on cassette by *New Letters*.

- The American Academy of Poets maintains a web page about Ammons at http://www.poets.org/poets/poets.cfm?prmID=49 that includes links to poems and biographical information as well as an in-depth profile of the poet from their Summer 1998 issue.

the idea of mixed metaphors. Before this stanza, the radiance has been used to mean the sun; the heart, however, is not exposed to sunshine. Therefore, readers are forced to recognize a more abstract meaning to the idea of radiance, to know it as something that has access to human emotions, which are, symbolically at least, held within "the weaving heart." This understanding of human emotions is not the most important thing for the natural world's radiance; the poem goes on, past the complexity of the human heart to the complexity of a fly.

In line 9, the fly is described but not identified. Readers are introduced to positive elements, such as abundance, illumination, and the cool image of an object glowing blue. Coming after the human heart, these respectful descriptions seem to indicate something that has superior significance, a worldly object that deserves even more consideration than the labyrinth of human emotion.

Lines 10–12

The break between the third and fourth stanzas serves to make the glowing blue object that has yet to be defined seem even more mysterious to readers. The fourth stanza begins by building this object up even further, saying that it has "gold-skeined wings." The word "skein" is usually used to refer to a coil of thread, indicating the fineness and fragility of a fly's wings, while the emphasis on their gold color makes the fly sound extremely valuable. This impression is contradicted, of course, when the poem finally gets around to letting readers know that it is a fly being described. The reversal of expectation becomes even clearer in line 11, when the poem contrasts the positive aspects of the fly with its filthy actions, such as swarming onto the guts of dead animals or onto excrement. While the poem does introduce these gruesome aspects of the fly's life, it generally approves of the fly because, as it points out in line 12, the fly seems to appreciate the things that are made available to it. The poem does show, in stanza 3, that humans have a place in the greater scheme of nature, but it shows in stanza 4 that even the simple functions of a lowly fly are as important as the emotions that some humans find all-important.

Lines 13–15

In this stanza, the contrasts that have been alluded to before are presented in a quick list, which pairs opposites together to show that the natural world has room for much diversity. Air is paired with vacuum, which is defined as the absence of air; snow, which is a light, floating object, is paired with shale, which is a dark, heavy rock; soft oceanic squids are coupled with sharp, mountain-dwelling wolves; beautiful and delicate roses are contrasted with an unstoppable and unnoticed moss, lichen. Line 14 finally gets to the poem's overall point: that the light of the sun, its radiance, shines down upon all things evenly, with no favoritism from the sun. This main idea of universal equality marks the end of the list of phrases that each starts "when you consider," and the poem's language finally moves past that repetitive language and, in line 14, completes the phrases that begin with "when," moving on to what happens "then."

What happens after all of the considering, according to the poem, is the acceptance of the situations Ammons describes here makes a human a better person. As before, the poem uses the idea of the "heart" in line 15 to stand for all human emotion: saying that it "moves roomier" shows an acknowledgement that human potential is less limited once one accepts the varieties of nature.

Lines 16–18

In stanza 6, the poem offers three ways in which nature collects its contradictory elements in order to create something more grand than humans expect from it. The phrase "the / leaf does not increase itself above the grass," in line 16, has symbolic implications: leaves naturally grow toward the sun and, of course, blot out the sun for the grass below, but they do not "increase themselves," which may be read as the idea that they do not destroy the grass for the sake of their own ego. In line 17, Ammons hints at nature at its worst with the idea of "dark works" within "the deepest cells"; he pairs this frightening mystery, however, with the simple and obvious beauty of a bush growing in the springtime. In the last line, the poem shows the ultimate benefit of this new way of viewing things that it proposes: by seeing all things in their proper perspective in nature, fear of nature's immensity turns to praise of its complex system, where everything has its place.

Themes

Paradox

This poem centers much of its argument around the fact that nature has room to hold seemingly paradoxical situations at the same time. It starts out by pointing out things that do not seem to fit easily together, such as the solidity of birds' bones when contrasted with the insubstantial nature of sunlight, or the secrets of the human heart co-existing with the physical world at large. At about the middle of the poem, though, the poem becomes more clearly focused on the opposites found in nature. The fly is examined in two ways, first as a thing of beauty and then as a lowly scavenger that feeds thankfully on others' waste. Once that specific paradox has been introduced, the poem unleashes a list of paired items that illustrate the contrasts found in nature: air and vacuum, snow and shale, squids and wolves, roses and lichen. In acknowledging that the world is able to contain such seemingly contradictory situations, "The City Limits" seeks to break down the limits of human thought: the "breadth of such" referred to in line 18 opens the door for more possibility than humans generally recognize.

Acceptance and Belonging

This poem operates within a commonly-held notion that human emotions are categorically different than things found in nature. Here, the scope of nature is represented as "the radiance," an image that is primarily based on light but that also implies the sort of unseen glow, like radiation, that can permeate anything. The extremes of human emotion are represented in the poem as "the guiltiest swervings of the weaving heart." Many philosophical systems, particularly in Western civilization, separate humanity from nature, recognizing contact between them but not identifying them as part of the same overall system.

In the end, the poem suggests that seeing how humanity belongs to nature will allow people to transform their fear of the world into praise for it. This is not a case of the larger entity, nature, allowing the smaller, humanity, into its limited terrain but of humans admitting that they belong to the same system as everything else. Using the phrase "when you consider" five times in the first four stanzas emphasizes the fact that humanity's acceptance into the world at large is a matter of human thought being readjusted, allowing the poem's readers to see, or consider, how much people are involved in the same physical processes that rule all other things in the universe.

Fear

In "The City Limits," fear is said to stem from the "breadth" of the physical world. In a sense, human fear seems to stem from the knowledge that humanity is outnumbered in the world. It is humans who have made up the idea that there is a difference between nature and humanity; when a poem like this one points out that all of the things in nature, down to the "dark work of the deepest cells," are "of a tune" with each other, then the prospect of being left outside of that majority can indeed be very intimidating. The cure for such fear offered in the poem is to view the wholeness of nature as acceptance, not opposition. Light is offered to all things, including humans, and accepted by them. The element of competition is removed. The poem predicts that considering nature this way will change fear into praise, as humans see that they are not outside of the natural system but part of it.

Self-Discovery

A key moment in this poem comes in the fifth stanza, with the revelation of what all of the aforementioned considering will lead to. "The heart moves roomier," Ammons explains, and "the man stands and looks about." The implication is that the man has previously been narrow and unaware of his surroundings, but that examining nature beyond oneself leads one to discover what one really is. Disgust at the fly's habits or fear of the unknown "dark" parts of the world are all considered part of the process of self-discovery in this poem, with humans coming to know who they really are, not through self-centered concentration, but through examination of the world beyond them.

Style

Sprung Rhythm

"The City Limits" uses a poetic form called Sprung Rhythm. This form requires only that the same number of stressed syllables occurs on each line of the poem. The unstressed syllables are not counted, and can vary from line to line. The effect that this creates is one of simultaneous order, because of the consistency in accented syllables, and disorder, because of the variable number of overall syllables per line. In this case, the duality between order and disorder in the poem's form mirrors its message about the irrational and rational aspects of the universe coexisting as one.

Topics for Further Study

- Read a psychology report about how sunlight affects humans and report on the current theories.

- The fourth stanza of this poem focuses on flies and their habits. Research one species of fly common to your geographical area and prepare some sort of visual presentation to help your classmates get to know this fly better.

- This poem was first published when the environmental movement was new. Participate in an environmentally friendly activity or similar event and prepare an audio tape collage of the voices of local environmental leaders.

- Choose one line from this poem that you find crucial and expand it into your own poem, with three lines per stanza. Try to take your ideas in a different direction than the one Ammons explores.

Each line of "The City Limits" has eight stressed syllables. One-syllable words are sometimes accented, sometimes not; two-syllable words will usually have just one accented syllable; and words with more than two syllables will often have a second syllable that is stressed, though to a lesser degree than the primary accent. Therefore, the first line reads, "*When* you con-*si*-der the *ra*-di-*ance, that* it *does not* with-*hold*." Line fifteen could be scanned as such: "the *heart moves roo*-mier, the *man stands and looks* a-*bout*, the. . . ." This sort of consistency is understated and seldom noticed, but readers tend to feel its effect whether they know it or not.

Refrain

Ammons uses the phrase "when you consider" as a refrain. It appears often throughout this poem, reminding readers that they are being presented with a subject that they might not have thought about before, or at least have probably given too little consideration. Repeating a refrain often works in poetry in the same way that it does in music: regardless of the actual words being repeated, the very act of repetition gives readers a sense of the author's control, reminding them of the fact that somebody has arranged the thoughts being presented. In "The City Limits," this refrain establishes a voice for the poem's speaker. It is a gentle and thoughtful voice, one that is not about to rush readers to see things a particular way but is instead offering them suggestions.

Historical Context

Environmentalism

There is no specific moment marking an actual beginning to America's awareness of the delicate balance between nature and society, but there is also no doubt that the environmental movement came to national importance in the 1970s. That was when the general population became conscious of two intertwined ideas: human dependence on non-renewable resources, and the environment's inability to absorb the pollutants that were discarded into it.

Environmental awareness had appeared in intellectual works throughout the country's history, most notably in the writings of Henry David Thoreau, whose 1845 book *Walden* documented his attempt to live naturally in the woods, simplifying his life by freeing himself of the trappings of society. In the following century, small movements sprung up, mostly over local causes, protesting specific abuses of the environment. The world's first protected National Park, Yellowstone, was set aside by Congressional fiat in 1972; the Audubon Society, a collection of bird enthusiasts, was first formed in 1885 to oppose unregulated hunting; the Sierra Club was formed in 1892. Overall, however, as America expanded westward toward the Pacific coast in the nineteenth century and grew to economic and military dominance throughout the First and Second World Wars, there was not much sense of urgency about the natural limits on society.

One of the greatest influences on the environmental movement was the publication, in 1962, of *Silent Spring*, by zoologist Rachel Carson. Focusing on the effects of pesticides and insecticides on songbirds, Carson's book provided a clear overview of humanity's place in the ecosystem. It was widely successful, and to this day is considered one of the definitive texts about ecology. Decades later, *Time* magazine named Carson one of the 100 most influential women of the twentieth century.

The 1960s marked a turbulent and difficult time for America. Lingering resentments over racial segregation in the South drew attention to the fact that those who held economic and political power could not always be trusted to care for the well being of everybody. The military superiority that had impressed the world during the century's two Great Wars proved to be fallible when tangled up in the jungles of the tiny country of Vietnam. Questions about those in authority went hand in hand with a spiritual love for the splendors of the earth, which society was debasing. The country's young people, particularly college students, learned how to organize political opposition from their involvement in the Civil Rights movement and anti-war protest groups.

Throughout the 1960s, public awareness of environmental issues was raised. Air and water pollution were recognized as health threats. The United States government established the Environmental Protection Agency (EPA) in 1970, to coordinate efforts to contain pollution. Bills that favored clean air, clean water, and protection of endangered species were introduced into Congress by the end of the sixties. March 21, 1970, marked the first Earth Day, a holiday promoted by a coalition of concerned environmental groups in order to raise global awareness of the environment. An estimated

Compare & Contrast

- **1970s:** New government laws are being passed to restrict water and air pollution and to protect forests and endangered species.

  Today: Few new environmental laws are passed; instead, existing laws are repealed as being unfair to local businesses.

- **1970s:** The activities of cells are considered to be among nature's greatest mysteries.

  Today: Even with the recent completion of the Human Genome Project, all questions about cellular activity are not answered; however, scientists have a good sense of how information is transmitted throughout the body.

- **1970s:** Americans are eating more and more beef: per capita consumption of beef rises almost 50 percent between the early sixties and mid seventies, when it reaches its all-time high.

  Today: Knowledge about the effects of red meat on the body have caused a shift in the American diet to lighter meats; still, the nation's reliance on fast food has caused an increase in American obesity.

- **1970s:** One aspect of the "hippie" movement of the 1960s is the call to "return to nature," indicating a distrust of political and social values.

  Today: The word "natural" retains its positive connotation and is used to sell millions of dollars in food and health remedies. Independently-run health food stores are supplanted by publicly-traded chains.

---

20 million people across the world participated in demonstrations and events to mark the occasion. This event is celebrated every year, keeping environmental awareness at the forefront of public consciousness.

Critical Overview

"The City Limits" is one of A. R. Ammons's most famous poems. It came at the time in Ammons's life when he was first enjoying wide critical praise. The book that it first appeared in, *Briefings: Poems Small and Easy*, is considered one of his best, showing off his vast intellectual understanding of the natural world and his sharp poetic sensibilities. It was then included in *Collected Poems, 1951–1971*, which reached a wide audience after winning the National Book Award. Geoffrey Hartman announces at the beginning of his review of the book for the *New York Times Book Review* that "with these *Collected Poems* a lag in reputation is overcome. A. R. Ammons's 400 pages of poetry, written over the space of a generation, manifest an energy, wit and an amazing *compounding* of mind with nature that cannot be overlooked." "The City Limits" is one of Ammons's most frequently reprinted poems.

One of the poem's most strident admirers is the literary critic Harold Bloom. In his introduction to a book of essays about Ammons, Bloom refers to the poet as "the central poet of my generation." Foremost among the works that Bloom admires Ammons for is "The City Limits," which he considers an "extraordinary poem." For him, this one poem marks a mastery of style, with Ammons showing an ability to disappear as a speaker, to let the poem's imagery speak for itself. The poet Robert Pinsky, on the other hand, questions the philosophy that the poem espouses. His essay on Ammons, from his book *The Situation of Poetry*, points out that "[i]f fear ever turns 'calmly' to anything, being 'of a tune with May bushes' is a lamely rhetorical motive for such turning.... Moreover, it is the 'breadth of the natural world, and its radiance, which kindle such fear." In other words, Pinsky finds the poem self-contradictory, calling it "romantically affirmative" but "less convincing" than other of Ammons works.

Criticism

David Kelly

Kelly is a creative writing and literature instructor at two colleges in Illinois. In this essay, Kelly considers whether the "radiance" referred to in the poem is as comforting as Ammons wants it to be.

A. R. Ammons's reputation grew over the course of the nearly fifty years that he was publishing poetry, mostly because of two key elements. The first was his elasticity and curiosity as an artist: he went through phases but never settled on any one style as being the "right" one, choosing instead to constantly experiment. He was versatile enough to produce a four-line poem or a poem like *Tape for the Turn of the Year* (written on a roll of adding machine tape, three inches by one hundred feet), displaying equal craft in each. The second aspect that Ammons is remembered for is his drive to define with his poetry that meeting place between humanity and nature. He is generally considered to be a modern master of the nature poem, although opinions do vary: most critics recognize his work as the successor of the Emersonian tradition of Transcendentalism, the first and possibly strongest strain of philosophy produced in America, but a few see in Ammons's work little more insight into the natural world than one could glean from a subscription to a science magazine.

Ammons's poem "The City Limits" is a showcase for only the latter of these tendencies. It is structurally sound but has nothing remarkable about its style that would make a reader aware of his skill with different forms. The most interesting thing about it is the way that it approaches theology. It makes suppositions about the natural world and presents an inconsistency in traditional human understanding, which it ends up apparently settling. It is only after some examination that it becomes clear that the poem actually has less to say than one might first assume.

It would be hard to deny that what the poem refers to as "radiance" is something like what people in the Judeo-Christian tradition usually mean when they talk about God. Like God, this radiance is omniscient: it is described in the first stanza as being like sunlight, kept out of areas that are "overhung or hidden," but by the second and third stanzas it is credited with the ability to reach beyond the limits of the physical world, to "look into the guiltiest / swervings of the weaving heart and bear itself upon them." When Ammons presents this light as a unifying force, a constant that runs throughout the universe, it is difficult to not think that he means it to fill the function of God.

Like many images of God, the radiance is considered to have benevolent intentions: it brings warmth and light to all things of the Earth, uniting them as soon as they have been touched by it. This touch is not forced upon them, as "each is accepted into as much light as it will take." Still, even without working at it, the radiance is, by its very existence, able to calm strife. Because they have both been touched by this light, things that may seem completely unrelated to one another are, as the poem puts it in the last stanza, "of a tune" with each other. This is, at least, what the poem claims.

Contemporary readers certainly respond better to a passive, non-judgmental, accepting sort of radiance than they do to a God who can be pleased or displeased. God is generally thought to have a will, which the radiance apparently lacks. In this respect, "The City Limits" replaces old-fashioned moral judgements with amorality. It presents a world where all, in the judgement of the radiant sunshine, is equally good and acceptable. While God finds certain behaviors displeasing, the radiance does not, as the poem puts it, "withhold" itself. It is active only in the sense that it goes to all things and offers itself to them, but it does so with no particular agenda to promote, no desire to make things any different than they are currently. This radiance goes everywhere and deals with all things equally, with no distinction for "good" or "bad."

Within the poem, opposites are brought together by being touched by the same radiant light from above. That much is easy to understand and accept. The poem complicates the matter, though, with its reference to the "city" in its title, which pointedly raises a distinction between nature and humanity. There is no further mention of "city" after the title, leaving readers little to go on when they try to guess what Ammons meant the city to represent, or why he mentioned it in a place of such significance as the title if it was not his intention to focus on that idea.

It is fairly routine in poetry about nature to use the city to remind readers of nature's opposite, which is the man-made world, built from ideas that nature apparently never intended. This is the world that humans (including, of course, poets) are familiar with, one which some humans consider an accomplishment, to be looked upon with pride. Ammons gives the impression here that the city is simply not a good enough way for people to experience the world, which he defines here by its limits. He contrasts the city, with its limitations, to the limitless reach of radiant light.

It would be oversimplifying, almost to an insulting degree, to think that Ammons wrote this poem to show his readers how much smaller the creations of humanity are when compared to the vastness of the universe in general. Clearly, humanity is just one part of the whole of existence. Ammons may aim to remind his readers to keep their egos in check, but there is nothing new about the idea, nothing so complex that it would require an entire poem about it. When "nature" is taken to mean all things, seen and unseen, known and unknown, then it almost goes without saying that humans and their cities are limited.

In "The City Limits," there is a reference to the fear that comes to people when they see how wide the natural world is and how limited the protection they can hope for when they gather in cities with others. The poem offers examples of things that humans try to avoid, to block out of their lives, including the aforementioned guilt; the "dumped / guts of a natural slaughter"; the excrement that flies feed on; and, by the slightest hint, the vacuum, shale, wolf, and lichen that are either considered unpleasant or just overlooked in civilized life. When these are combined with less threatening elements, such as "gold-skeined wings" and air, snow, squid, roses, and finally May bushes, the natural world is recognized to have an honest completeness that people in cities are denied. The poem proposes that humans could, if they accepted all of this variety with the same impartiality that sunlight has, make fear go away.

Is this possible, or even desirable? In the less significant examples, accepting the unpleasant but necessary aspects of life does indeed make sense: turning away from the fly or the wolf's natural tendencies, or burying guilt deep within one's heart, actually does prove to be a senseless denial of reality. But this poem actually goes so far as to name cancer ("the dark work of the deepest cells") one of the things that should be praised, not feared, simply because it exists under the same sun as May bushes. Perhaps there are some things in the natural world that should be rejected. Perhaps human experience should be limited.

The problem with replacing God with radiance is that radiance, though it sounds pleasant enough, explains nothing. This might be one of the poem's points: traditional views of what God is always end up creating systems of values that eventually force

> "The poem's position that all is right just because the positive and negative coexist, or because they both accept the radiance, can be comforting, disturbing, or just ridiculous, depending on how the pieces of experience relate to each other."

people to reject some very real experiences. But taking an accepting attitude toward all things is not really the strong philosophical stance that it might at first seem to be. The poem's position that all is right just because the positive and negative coexist, or because they both accept the radiance, can be comforting, disturbing, or just ridiculous, depending on how the pieces of experience relate to each other. This is the one thing that Ammons does not address. Readers are not told about any grand scheme, such as a religious system might devise. They are only told that they should not fear because the more threatening things are "of a tune" with those that they find comforting.

There is no real answer to the question of what "of a tune" means. If, as the phrase implies, the varieties of experience are all in one large system, working together like notes in a musical chord, then there would actually be room in that tune for things, like cancer, that would not lead one to abandon fear for admiration. If the phrase means that everything should be considered harmonious exactly because it exists, then what does the sun's radiance do to explain this? "Of a tune" asserts a positive feeling in order to tell readers to feel positive, but it does not really give any reason for them to do so.

In some ways, it is more disappointing to see through the grand statements of an uplifting poem and find them hollow than it is to read a poem that never tries to give a positive message. The overall point of "The City Limits" is that humans should be open to the natural world, not fear it. That is a message that we would all like to believe, but the poem does not really prove its point: it only makes it with language that makes us want to believe it. We would all like to believe that having the sun shine on us protects us, but the only way to do that is to ignore the natural things that we need protection from.

Source: David Kelly, Critical Essay on "The City Limits," in *Poetry for Students*, Gale, 2003.

Mark White

White is a Seattle-based publisher, editor, and teacher. In this essay, White examines the Old Testament influences on Ammons's poem and argues its status as an ars poetica.

"The City Limits" is one of A. R. Ammons's most highly praised and discussed poems. First appearing in his 1971 collection, *Briefings*, and then again two years later in his National Book Award–winning *Collected Poems: 1951–1971*, the poem earned the immediate respect and awe of many, including critic Harold Bloom, who, in the introduction to his *Modern Critical Views of A. R. Ammons*, called it "extraordinary." Poet Richard Howard who, in his review of Ammons entitled "The Spent Seer Consigns Order to the Vehicle of Change," wrote that it was the "greatest poem" of *Briefings*.

While there is general agreement that the poem addresses significant religious and spiritual themes, there has been less agreement as to the particulars of the poem's meaning. Bloom points to Ralph Waldo Emerson's transcendentalist (one who believes that there is a unified soul in man and nature and that God is immanent in both) influence in the poem, while others interpret it more overtly on the basis of either its Eastern or Christian religious overtones. Because of the overlap of transcendentalism with both Eastern and Christian beliefs, none of these views are necessarily mutually exclusive. However, few critics have commented on the poem's Biblical Old Testament influence. Additionally, there has been surprisingly little discussion as to what extent the poem can be considered an *ars poetica*: in other words, how much of "The City Limits" is Ammons's own statement about the creation and art of poetry? Although these ideas may seem at first to be unrelated, they both find a connection in the notion of "creation," and an exploration of that shared thread may shed some unexpected light on what is one of Ammons's finest poems.

That "The City Limits" has religious or spiritual overtones becomes readily evident after a cursory reading of the poem. Words like "radiance," "abundance," "testimony," and "praise" collectively connote a transcendent tone often found in religious and spiritual works. That the phrase "fear ... calmly turns to praise" closes off the poem only enhances this reading. Reading the poem aloud for its rhythms gives one the feeling of a song of praise or of a sermon being read from a church or temple pulpit.

The structure of "The City Limits," with the rhythm that the poem's punctuation and line lengths demand, along with its repetition, is based on the form of a litany, a liturgical prayer with a series of repetitions.

One of Ammons's trademark characteristics was his extensive use of colons and semicolons in his work; it is a rare Ammons poem that employs more than a few periods. His 200-page *Tape for the Turn of the Year*, for instance, does not have a single period, and *Sphere: The Form of a Motion*, a work of 1,800 lines, concludes with a period but otherwise uses colons and semicolons exclusively. Whereas a period forces the reader to come to a full stop in both his or her reading and thought process, commas, colons, and semicolons force pauses of varying lengths and indicate to the reader that what precedes the punctuation mark is directly related to what follows. True to Ammons's form, the only period in "The City Limits" is at the end. This use of punctuation both speeds the poem's rhythm and ties its various ideas together.

A poem's rhythm and speed are not only dictated by punctuation. Other elements, such as the stanza and line lengths, also come into play. The single sentence that makes up "The City Limits" is broken into six unrhymed tercets (a three-line stanza), each made up of lines between thirteen and seventeen syllables. Although the stanza and line breaks each give the reading a slight pause, the long lines, like the punctuation, give the poem a more prose-like, less interrupted reading. Much like a preacher whose sermon flows from one thought to the next, Ammons wants the reader of this poem to move unabated, from the "radiance" of the first line to the "praise" of the last, pausing only slightly in between and never fully stopping.

The most telling formal conceit that recalls a litany is the poem's parallel structure. "The City Limits" comprises five "when you consider" clauses that culminate in a "then" conclusion. This use of parallelism—in this case, the repetitive use of the "when" clause—is a common rhetorical device in poetry. Walt Whitman used the technique extensively, and it is employed widely by Christian preachers, perhaps most famously by those inspired by the southern Baptist tradition. Parallelism is also a common technique found in traditional Hebrew poetry and is also found extensively throughout the Bible, especially in the Old Testament.

Ammons was, in fact, raised in the South by a Methodist mother and a Baptist father. The sermons that he recalls attending as a child, which he referred to in an interview with Cynthia Haythe as "religious saturation," profoundly impacted him. Although not widely considered a Christian poet, Ammons wrote several poems in his career that are explicit in their Christian themes, for example, "Hymn" and "Christmas Eve." The word "radiance," with its quality of light and a connotation of having a celestial origin, is closely tied both to the Christian tradition with Jesus (He says, "I am the light of the world" in The Gospel of John, 8:12) and with the process of enlightenment in many Eastern traditions, such as Buddhism and Hinduism. "The City Limits," with a "radiance ... [that] does not withhold / itself but pours its abundance without selection," describes a light that is offered without prejudice and is accepted by all who are willing to receive it—"into every / nook and cranny not overhung or hidden"—and as such can certainly be thought of in either a Christian or an Eastern context.

The poem is also deeply tied to the Old Testament tradition, a reading that is closely tied to the interpretation that it can also be read as an *ars poetica* for Ammons.

As previously mentioned, the poem's rhetorical structure can be found extensively throughout the Bible's Old Testament, but the poem is linked to the Old Testament in other ways as well. "The City Limits" recalls the first book of the Bible, Genesis, in the way that it lists the wide range of elements and creatures in the process of being created to populate the world. Ammons's list—"air or vacuum, snow or shale, squid or wolf, rose or lichen"—is no less representative of nature's, or God's, elements than the Bible's waters, earth, vegetation, fish, birds, and "living creatures of every kind: cattle and creeping things and wild animals of the earth." Like the creations of Genesis, which exist equally beneath the light God has created, Ammons's creations receive "the radiance" uniformly.

Another Old Testament element of this poem is some of its tonal characteristics. Despite much of

> *The inspiration that drives Ammons as poet, like the Old Testament God, turns its eyes upon the natural world indiscriminately, upon its creations as well as its destructions."*

its radiant feel, one cannot ignore the death-evoking "birds' bones" or "dumped guts of natural slaughter." These tones are those of the retributive God who turned disbelievers into pillars of salt and beset plagues upon the earth; these are not the New Testament tones of the all-forgiving father of Jesus.

Just as the God of the Old Testament worked with a forceful hand, so too is there a profound "weight" to the work that the "radiance" is performing here. In the first stanza, the light characteristically "pours its abundance" onto the world, but, in the second and third stanzas, that same light "look[s] into the guiltiest / swervings of the weaving heart" and "bear[s] itself upon them." By the fourth stanza, it is offering up "storms of generosity." This is not a "forgiving" light; this is a light that recognizes how humans contrive to manage their guilty affairs, and this is a light that "bear[s]" down and exerts pressure upon them. This is a light with profound weight and influence, a light that "storms" as well as "pours." With the connotations of death and violence, the poem is deep in the realm of the Old Testament. There is no hint of the New Testament themes of resurrection or immortality here: the bird has died and turned to bones, and flies feed off the remains of natural violence.

How does this Biblical reading fit into the idea that this poem can be read as an *ars poetica*? To begin with, Ammons was well known for addressing the art of poetry in his poems; many of his poems address his poetic theories. So much so, in fact, that critic Stephen Cushman calls *ars poetica* Ammons's "characteristic mode."

Taken on one literal level, "The City Limits" can be read as a "nature poem." As the title suggests, the setting is at the city limits, among the flora and fauna of the rural world. Ammons is simply listing what can be discovered in nature and how such a discovery can change a man, force his heart to move "roomier" and his "fear . . . [to turn] to praise."

If one reads the "limits" of the title as a verb, then the meaning is altered significantly. In this light, the title suggests that the city is "limiting," or that it "limits." What does the city limit? Spiritual growth and understanding, perhaps, or perhaps the poetic imagination.

There is no question that nature, and not civilization, fueled Ammons's writing; society as such seldom entered his poems. When they are not explicitly addressing his own poetic theories, Ammons's poems are almost exclusively populated by elements of the natural world. In Haythe's interview, Ammons was quoted as saying that the city represented for him "the artificial, the limited, the defined, the stalled."

With "limits" interpreted as a verb, it is possible to read the poem as Ammons's response as to where his poetic inspiration comes from, or, rather, where it does not come from. It does not come from civilization but from nature. Ammons's poetic inspiration is derived from the natural world and spreads its "radiance" back on the disparate elements of that world uniformly. The rank stench of excrement has as much chance of being woven into a poem as does the perfumed scent of a flower. Ammons does not rank nature's creations or its destructions; they all have equal chance of being realized into poems.

The God of the Old Testament reigned over all no matter how great or how small. His was the power to create and destroy, and the natural world is a testament to that power. The inspiration that drives Ammons as poet, like the Old Testament God, turns its eyes upon the natural world indiscriminately, upon its creations as well as its destructions. It is not an inspiration that tiptoes through rose gardens; rather, like the Old Testament God, it "pours," and "bears," and "storms" down upon the world relentlessly.

Just as the God of Genesis saw everything that he had made and praised it as being "very good," Ammons has turned the light of his inspiration on all of that creation and turned it into a song of praise.

Source: Mark White, Critical Essay on "The City Limits," in *Poetry for Students*, Gale, 2003.

Bonnie Costello

In the following essay excerpt, Costello describes "The City Limits" as an "eloquent example" of Ammons's mastery of poetic technique.

Ammons will return to the stance of the pilgrim throughout his career, but beginning with his second book, *Expressions of Sea Level,* a different stance begins to emerge, one relatively impersonal, comprehensive, and didactic. Where the medium of the pilgrim poet is ritual gesture, the medium of the sage is abstract proposition and example. The revelation of pattern dominates here over the articulation of self. Problems of identity fall away and the self becomes a node of consciousness through which the shape of the world reveals itself. Where nature in the pilgrim phase is variously the ally or antagonist to the poet's will, here it is the embodiment of dynamic design, often articulated in abstract titles. Critics have emphasized Ammons's interest in "ecological naturalism," and certainly the greater particularity, the assimilation of "facts" from the biological and earth sciences, and especially the emphasis on cycles, habitats, and cooperative behaviors in the natural world, resonate with developments in the environmental movement. Still, the natural environment is not the subject of these poems so much as a resource for exemplifying and troping their subject, which is "the form of a motion."

Ammons draws on natural imagery to give authority to his vision of pattern, and to remove it from the social and psychological attachments it inevitably has when embodied in human institutions. There remains an experiential element to these meditations in which knowledge is a process, incomplete and subject to the shifting conditions of observer and observed world. But an expansive, visionary posture and generalizing impulse prevail. The prophet-subject identifies with motion rather than being subject to it. Ammons's particular challenge is to reconcile this Thoreauvian idea of dwelling with his Emersonian emphasis on motion. "Can we make a home in motion?" he asks throughout his career, and explicitly and affirmatively in *Sphere: The Form of a Motion* (1974). In what I am calling the sage poems he begins to identify the text and the landscape as parts of a dynamic patterning where mind and world, thought and its object, become intertwined. Neither is firmly grounded in the other. Thus the power terms that motor the narrative of subject/object relations in the pilgrim poems fall away. While Ammons remains attached to a figure of "mirroring mind" it is clear that the model of cognition is not really the mirror but something more mobile and improvisatory (rather than ritualized, as before). Mapping may be the operative term for what the mind does, rather than mirroring, if we accept the map as an instrument of navigation rather than an objective diagram of reality.

Designed though it is to convey a Whitmanian plurality, the prophetic stance remains selective in the nature to which it attends. This phase is initiated with "expressions of sea level," not sermons on mountaintops. Ammons grew up in the mountains of North Carolina, but from early on he eschewed the iconology of the mountain, which in our culture has signified stability, endurance, remote imperial power, sublimity, and transcendence. The early poems of dispersal involve a repeated dismantling of hierarchical organizations. A poem still in the pilgrim mode, "Mountain Talk," makes this preference explicit, glancing at the "massive symmetry and rest" of the mountain and its "changeless prospect," but rejecting its "unalterable view," and he repeats it in "A Little Thing Like That" from *Brink Road* (1996): "I have always felt, / as one should, I think, shy / of mountains." In this middle phase Ammons need not dismantle hierarchical orders because he has set his gaze where nothing builds too high. In giving the seashore a central role, Ammons follows an American tradition of leveled, horizontal relations, of many as one, and of a permeable boundary between stability and flux. The seashore is precisely not a home, though it may be a habitat. It provides a simple, generally uniform, horizontal image with a maximum of local change and adjustment. It thus becomes an ideal figure for a decentered world. It is in this gnomic phase that the colon arises as a major signature of Ammons's work, a sign with multiple, ambiguous significations, marking permeable boundaries, tentative sponsorships, as well as analogical possibilities. Similarly, the preposition "of" emerges in this phase to create metaphors yoking concrete and abstract terms and to override the subject/object dichotomy.

Ammons's walk poems, central to this phase, are in a sense what the pilgrim poems grow into. The sage's poems are not emblematic (they do not convey idea by reducing and abstracting image), but analogical. The sage moves freely in and out of a representational scene, geography of mind and geography of landscape, text and referent, allowing for the play of contingent vision without restriction to a narrow perspective. In the pilgrim poems the one/many relation is experienced as a crisis or problem, whereas the walk poems present this relation as a primary dynamic of form. The pilgrim figure seeks a home, whether by mastery or by submission; he seeks to colonize or become accepted into the infinite. The prophet figure in the walk poems already identifies with the movement he conveys. Since the one/many is not a problem to be resolved but a reality to be apprehended and experienced, these poems are less sequential or narrative than they are serial and reiterative. Since the speaker identifies with the movement of reality, he does not need to discover it in a teleological process, but rather enacts it in an improvisatory process backed by a confident metonymic system. The tendency to evoke an infinite unity at the end, without claiming a "final vision" for the poet, is

What Do I Read Next?

- *Garbage* (1993), Ammons's book-length poem in eighteen chapters, is considered a modern masterpiece. It won the National Book Award in 1993.

- A contemporary poet whose writings have often been compared to Ammons's is Pattiann Rogers. The best works of her career have been collected in the *Song of the World Becoming: Poems, New and Collected, 1971–2001* (2001).

- Critics considering Ammons's poetry usually draw a connection to the work of American poet Walt Whitman. Their styles are seldom similar, but both men share a common sensibility about the natural world. Whitman's masterpiece, *Leaves of Grass*, was published in 1855 and has been in print continuously since then.

- Diane Ackerman writes long essays that combine ideas of nature and philosophy in much the same way that Ammons's poetry does. One of her most widely read and accessible books is *A Natural History of the Senses* (1990).

- Much of Ammons's best nonfiction writing is collected in *Set in Motion: Essays, Interviews, and Dialogs* (1997), published by University of Michigan Press. It includes a lengthy interview from the renowned *Paris Review* interviews.

> *The heavy enjambment works with the lexical diversity to maximize freedom in form and to create the sense of expansion the poem wishes to convey emotionally.*

even clearer in "Saliences" than in the more famous "Corson's Inlet":

> where not a single thing endures,
> the overall reassures;
> ...
> earth brings to grief
> much in an hour that sang, leaped, swirled,
> yet keeps a round
> quiet turning,
> beyond loss or gain,
> beyond concern for the separate reach.

One feels that the poem's own rounding off is confirmed here, despite the clamor against the "separate reach."

The precursor to Ammons's prophetic voice is clearly Whitman, and, like Whitman, Ammons tends to identify the one/many paradigm with America. This is particularly true in "One: Many" which, like most of the prophetic poems, announces its procedure:

> To maintain balance
> between one and many by
> keeping in operation both one and many.

The poem again locates vision initially in the experiential, and in a descriptive, narrative form. "I tried to summarize a moment's events," he tells us, and goes on to instantiate the one/many in terms of a description of natural objects and events at "creek shore." This section of the poem then embodies the one/many balance even as it stands, in terms of the poem as a whole, for the one, yielding in the next section to the transpersonal many of the American continent and its *e pluribus unum*. Careful not to make his path across the continent a "straight line," the prophetic mind zigzags from California to Maine and from Michigan to Kansas, integrating cultural and natural images and overriding all dualities. The device of the list becomes, again as in Whitman's poetry, a major formal embodiment of the one/many balance, and Ammons's use of it is careful. In this poem the list has a centrifugal force out from the I, so that the I is released even as it continually penetrates back into the plurality through anaphora ("I tried to think. . . ."; "I considered. . . ."). The list functions oppositely in the second section, where the I does not provide the hub from which details spin out, but rather intrudes with personal commentary upon the manifest plurality:

> Art Museum, Prudential Building, Knickerbocker Hotel
> (where Cummings stayed);
> of North Carolina's
> Pamlico and Albemarle Sounds, outer banks, shoals,
> telephone wire loads of swallows,
> of Columbus County
> where fresh-dug peanuts
> are boiled
> in iron pots, salt filtering
> in through boiled-clean shells (a delicacy
> true
> as artichokes or Jersey
> asparagus): and on and on through the villages.

The parenthesis, like the colon, becomes a device for interpenetration of the one and the many.

Because Ammons is constantly announcing his own practices, criticism has seemed very redundant. But in the behavior of the poem, rather than in its subject matter or discursive content, we find aesthetic and emotional satisfaction. "Poetry is action," and "poetry recommends," by its behavior, "certain kinds of behavior." Ammons's reflexivity is itself a particular kind of poetic behavior. "Terrain," for instance, after launching a description by way of metaphor ("the soul is a region without definite boundaries"), enters into the second term, forgetting its sponsorship. But, within that second term, the one/many dynamic, which is the real subject of the poem, is reiterated in landscape terms. The soul/body or self/landscape dichotomy is transposed into a network of landscape relations, and duality vanishes. The gnomic proposition that opens the poem yields to a perceptual/experiential model as the poet uses present tense to bring forward the landscape, reversing tenor and vehicle. The "like" in the line "It floats (self-adjusting) like a continental mass" recalls us to the initial metaphor, but the sponsorship of simile is weak and yields altogether to description, which enfolds simile rather than extending it: "river systems thrown like winter tree-shadows." Nature's internal resemblances displace a Cartesian model of mirroring mind. The correspondences of soul/region convert to correspondences within the geography itself—"where it towers most / extending its deepest mantling base." The second stanza of this poem adjusts the intersections that have become too symmetrical, so that "floods unbalancing / gut it, silt altering the / distribution of weight." "Weight" brings us back from illusion to the presence of the poem; we feel the weight not in the referential silt but in the "nature of content"—the weight of the "soul," which is the subject of the poem. This extraordinary interpenetration of consciousness and its object returns us, cyclically, to the poem's opening, but only momentarily.

The poem seeks other means of mapping the one/many/one paradigm. The images of imbalance are followed by images of dissolution:

> a growth into
> destruction of growth,
> change of character,
> invasion of peat by poplar and oak: semi-precious
> stones and precious metals drop from muddy water
> into mud.

The region is coming apart into multiplicity and separateness (after the earlier symmetry and correspondence). The landscape endures a kind of crisis of multiplicity and separateness—"whirlwinds move through it / or stand spinning like separate orders: the moon / comes: / there are barren spots: bogs, rising / by self-accretion from themselves." But if the orders that initiate the poem are entropic, the stanza recuperates with a structure of collision moving toward the "poise" of "countercurrents." The stanza divisions mark an overall pattern presiding in the shifts in focus and organization. The stanza I have quoted moves away from the large geographic model of continental plates and river systems to a more local model of "habitat." The "region" is now far more liquid—it does not just contain lakes and rivers and marshes but is itself "a crust afloat." In this model the sponsoring unity ("the soul" or "continental mass") gives way to "a precise ecology of forms / mutually to some extent / tolerable"—a strange phrase in which precision and approximation must somehow become compatible. But at the same time this "precision" moves to an increasingly imprecise language, a mysticism of "the soul" quite different from earlier geological references. Description turns back into heightened metaphor and visionary stance: "foam to the deep and other-natured: / but deeper than depth, too: a vacancy and swirl: // it may be spherical, light and knowledge merely / the iris and opening / to the dark methods of its sight." The phrase "whirls and stands still" cues the poem to rest in the interpenetration of imagination and earth: "the moon comes: terrain." This gesture marks the poem's unity, providing a double refrain—one internal to the poem, one echoing the title to complete a cycle.

As "Terrain" indicates, particularity in the prophetic phase derives from enumerative rather than descriptive rhetoric. The most eloquent example is "City Limits," which realizes vision in form. The relation of one and many inheres in the play of the unifying syntax and pluralizing diction: "when you // consider that air or vacuum, snow or shale, squid or wolf, rose or lichen, / each is accepted into as much light as it will take." The heavy enjambment works with the lexical diversity to maximize freedom in form and to create the sense of expansion the poem wishes to convey emotionally. What Randall Jarrell said of Whitman applies here: Ammons's lists are "little systems as beautifully and astonishingly organized as the rings and satellites of Saturn." Here the polarities indicate not only range, but also tension resolved, dualities overcome—good and evil, life and death, nature and culture, high and low. Collisions in the diction ("natural slaughter," "storms of generosity," "gold-skeined wings of flies") have a liberating effect within the constancy of "the radiance." Collisions become chords in the one / many harmony. The coordinating conjunction "or" creates an array of oppositions held in tension: "snow or shale" in textural or "rose or lichen" in visual parallel. Not too much is made of these arrangements. They remain local and metamorphic, yielding to other terms of connection. Similarly the anaphora that binds the list shifts its position in the line so that litany does not become harangue.

The pleasures of the prophetic phase are many and it is still the phase readers most associate with Ammons. It delights in the revival of form in inexhaustible substance, the rediscovery of pattern in particulars. "Scope is beyond me" not because the beholder's vision fails but because motion is the essential nature of this pattern. What this mode gives up, largely, is the self's direct, experiential engagement with the life it beholds. Motion remains theoretical, a matter of spectacle rather than impact. For all their apparent spontaneity and contingency, these are poems of thoughts more than thinking, life viewed more than felt. By making a home in motion, in its form, the sage evades its force....

Source: Bonnie Costello, "Ammons: Pilgrim, Sage, Ordinary Man," in *Raritan*, Vol. 21, No. 3, Winter 2002, pp. 130–58.

> "Aesthetic involvement in our physical world and the processes of assembly and disassembly are Ammons's perennial concerns."

Daniel Hoffmann
Martha Sutro

In the following essay, Hoffman and Sutro examine the canon of Ammons's work in the tradition of American Romantic poetry.

A. R. Ammons is an American Romantic in the tradition of Emerson and Whitman. He is committed to free and open forms and to the amassing of the exact details experience provides rather than to the extrusion from it of any a priori order. His favorite subject is the relation of a man to nature as perceived by a solitary wanderer along the beaches and rural fields of New Jersey, where Ammons grew up. Because of the cumulative nature of his technique, Ammons's work shows to best advantage in poems of some magnitude. Perhaps the best, and best known, of these is the title poem from *Corsons Inlet*, in which, describing a walk along a tidal stream, the speaker says,

> I was released from forms,
> from the perpendiculars,
> straight lines, blocks, boxes, binds
> of thought
> into the hues, shading, rises, flowing bends and blends of
> sight . . .

Here as elsewhere Ammons accepts only what is possible to a sensibility attuned to the immediacy of experience, for he admits that "scope eludes my grasp, that there is no finality of vision, / that I have perceived nothing completely, / that tomorrow a new walk is a new walk."

Another kind of poem characteristic of Ammons is the brief metaphysical fable, in which there are surprising colloquies between an interlocutor and mountains, winds, or trees, as in "Mansion":

> So it came time
> for me to cede myself
> and I chose
> the wind
> to be delivered to.
> The wind was glad
> and said it needed all
> the body
> it could get
> to show its motions with . . .

The philosophical implications in these poems are explicit in "What This Mode of Motion Said," a meditation upon permanence and change phrased as a cadenza on Emerson's poem "Brahma."

Ammons's *Collected Poems 1951–1971* was chosen for the National Book award in 1973. Not included in this compendious volume is his book-length *Tape for the Turn of the Year*, a free-flowing imaginative journal composed in very short lines and written on a roll of adding machine tape. The combination here of memory, introspection, and observation rendered in ever changing musical phrasing is impressive. Such expansiveness is Ammons's métier. *Sphere: The Form of a Motion* is a long poem in 155 twelve-line stanzas that comprise one unbroken sentence. Taking Whitman and Stevens as his models, Ammons combines the all-inclusive sensibility of the one with the meditative philosophical discourse of the other, as these excerpts may suggest:

> . . . the identifying oneness of populations, peoples: I
> know my own—the thrown peripheries, the stragglers, the cheated,
> maimed, afflicted (I know their eyes, pain's melting amazement)
>
> the weak, disoriented, the sick, hurt, the castaways, the
> needful needless: I know them: I love them, I am theirs . . .
>
> the purpose of the motion of a poem is to bring the focused,
> awakened mind to no-motion, to a still contemplation of the
> whole motion, all the motions, of the poem . . .
>
> . . . by intensifying the alertness
>
> of the conscious mind even while it permits itself to sink,
> to be lowered down the ladder of structured motions to the
> refreshing energies of the deeper self . . .
> the non-verbal
> energy at that moment released, transformed back through the
> verbal, the sayable poem . . .

Ammons continued to revel in both long wandering poems and shorter lyrics in his volume *Sumerian Vistas*. As he points out in "The Ridge

Farm," a meditative poem of fifty-one stanzas, "I like nature poetry / where the brooks are never damned up . . . " His work is consistent in its experimentation with open forms and in its celebration of living processes and of the identity of man with nature.

Perhaps Ammons's most profound study of culture, human behavior, and the physical world is his 1993 fin de siècle long poem titled *Garbage*, in which he attempts to link science, spirituality, and philosophy as modes through which to evaluate garbage. Ammons garbage has a force that brings communities together. Refuse expresses something essential about us; it is the originating point of communal consciousness and survival. His desire to know "simple people doing simple things, the normal, everyday routine of life and how these people thought about it" finds him recognizing "a monstrous surrounding of / gathering—the putrid, the castoff, the used, / / the mucked up—all arriving for final assessment." Historian, archeologist, culturalist, environmentalist, and—for this book's project—garbologist, Ammons uses the figure of "curvature," which shows that "it all wraps back around," to cast the net wide enough to consider the various angles of garbage, even though the central figure of the book is the garbage dump itself.

Aesthetic involvement in our physical world and the processes of assembly and disassembly are Ammons's perennial concerns. In *Brink Road* he approaches a world largely unpeopled but still in motion and perpetuity: " . . . a snowflake / streaks / out of the hanging gray, / winter's first whitening: white on white let it be, / then, flake / to petal— to hold for a / minute or so." Often compared with Robert Frost and e. e. cummings, Ammons has a voice that sometimes hits a note with a Zen ring to it. In "Saying Saying Away" he revealingly contends that poems "flow into a place where the distinction between meaning and being is erased into the meaning of / being."

Winner of the National Book award in both 1973 and 1993 and recipient of the Robert Frost medal for the Poetry Society of America for his life's work, Ammons has had a prolific career that has carried him to his long volume *Glare*, which has the tone of a kind of diary looping evenly, meditatively, seemingly inconsequentially back to itself. At its best moments it moves with a Wordsworthian grace typical of Ammons's early work:

> if you can
> send no word silently healing, I

mean if it is not proper or realistic
to send word, actual lips saying
these broken sounds, why, may we be
allowed to suppose that we can work
this stuff out the best we can and
having felt out our sins to their
deepest definitations, may we walk with
you as along a line of trees, every
now and then your clarity and warmth
shattering across our shadowed way.

Source: Daniel Hoffmann and Martha Sutro, "Ammons, A. R.," in *Contemporary Poets*, 7th ed., edited by Thomas Riggs, St. James Press, 2001, pp. 24–25.

Sources

Bloom, Harold, "Introduction," in *A. R. Ammons*, Modern Critical Views series, Chelsea House Publishers, 1986, pp. 1–31.

Cushman, Stephen, "A. R. Ammons, or the Rigid Lines of the Free and Easy," in *Critical Essays on A. R. Ammons*, edited by Robert Kirschten, G. K. Hall, 1997, pp. 271–308.

Hartman, Geoffrey, Review of *Collected Poems: 1951– 1971*, in the *New York Times Book Review*, November 19, 1972, pp. 39–40.

Haythe, Cynthia, "An Interview with A. R. Ammons," in *Critical Essays on A. R. Ammons*, edited by Robert Kirschten, G. K. Hall, 1997, pp. 83–96.

Howard, Richard, "The Spent Seer Consigns Order to the Vehicle of Change," in *A. R. Ammons*, edited by Harold Bloom, Modern Critical Views series, Chelsea House Publishers, 1986, pp. 33–56.

Pinsky, Robert, "Ammons," in *The Situation of Poetry*, Princeton University Press, 1976.

Further Reading

Cushman, Stephen, "A. R. Ammons, or the Rigid Lines of the Free and Easy," in *Critical Essays on A. R. Ammons*, edited by Robert Kirschten, G. K. Hall, 1997, pp. 271–308, originally published in *Fictions of Form in American Poetry*, Princeton University Press, 1993, pp. 149–86.
> Cushman examines one section of one of Ammons's longer works, showing the interplay between free verse and the poet's sense of structure, which sneaks into his work at discreet moments.

Holder, Alan, "Plundering Stranger," in *A. R. Ammons*, Twayne's United States Authors Series, No. 303, Twayne Publishers, 1978, pp. 74–89.
> In this relatively early survey of Ammons's works, Holder focuses on the various ways in which nature is used in the poet's works.

Kirschten, Robert, "Ammons's Sumerian Songs: Desert Laments and Eastern Quests," in his *Approaching Prayer:*

Ritual and the Shape of Myth in A. R. Ammons and James Dickey, Louisiana State University Press, 1998.

> In this article, Kirschten, who has written much about Ammons, writes about Ammons in terms of the similarities between his ideas and Eastern philosophy.

Schneider, Steven P., *A. R. Ammons and the Poetics of Widening Scope*, Fairleigh Dickinson University Press, 1994.

> Schneider examines the ways in which Ammons's overall poetic vision can be seen in the imagery, form, and subject matter of his poems.

His Speed and Strength

Alicia Ostriker
1980

"His Speed and Strength," published in Alicia Ostriker's 1980 collection *The Mother/Child Papers*, is a mother's meditation on both her son's maturation and the human race's survival. The poem's setting, its references to popular culture, and its conversational diction all belong to contemporary America. The speaker's allusions to mythical goddesses and poet Walt Whitman, however, signal the timeless relevance of the mother's thoughts. In her book of essays, *Writing Like a Woman*, Ostriker says of the period in which she wrote this poem: "It was impossible [in the 1970s] to avoid meditating on the meaning of having a boy child in time of war, or to avoid knowing that 'time of war' means all of human history." In the poem, the mother watches her son display "speed and strength" on his bicycle and at the town pool. She fancies herself a modern version of the ancient goddesses Niké and Juno as she competes with and protects her son. Through a series of ordinary images, the mother observes the masculine and feminine traits that compose her son's emerging adult identity. The poem implies that our culture opposes these traits at its own peril. On the one hand, the mother is proud of her son's developing speed, strength, and competitiveness—all traditionally masculine traits. But, since these traits also suit boys to become war fodder, the mother hopes to nurture in her son a (traditionally feminine) sense of connection to other people and things. If he maintains this connection, his strength may serve constructive, not destructive, ends. The son shows

Alicia Ostriker

concern for his mother and a sense of connection to other boys as he goes off to play. Seeing both masculine and feminine traits in her son and imagining herself as both a goddess of military victory and a goddess of motherhood, the speaker implies that her son will also successfully connect and integrate diverse traits.

Author Biography

Ostriker was born in Brooklyn, New York, on November 11, 1937, to David Suskin and Beatrice Linnick Suskin. Her father was employed by the New York City Department of Parks. Ostriker's mother wrote poetry and read Shakespeare and Browning to her daughter, who soon began writing her own poetry as well as showing an interest in drawing. Initially, Ostriker had hoped to be an artist, and she studied art as a teenager and young adult. Two of her books, *Songs* (1969) and *A Dream of Springtime* (1979), feature her own graphics on the covers.

Ostriker received her bachelor's degree in English from Brandeis University in 1959 and her master's and doctorate from the University of Wisconsin. Her dissertation became her first critical book, *Vision and Verse in William Blake* (1965); later, she edited and annotated Blake's complete poems for Penguin Press. In 1965, Ostriker began teaching at Rutgers University.

Poem Text

His speed and strength, which is the strength of ten
years, races me home from the pool.
First I am ahead, Niké, on my bicycle,
no hands, and the *Times* crossword tucked in my
    rack,
then he is ahead, the Green Hornet,   5
buzzing up Witherspoon,
flashing around the corner to Nassau Street.

At noon sharp he demonstrated his neat
one-and-a-half flips off the board:
Oh, brave. Did you see me, he wanted to know.   10
And I doing my backstroke laps was Juno
Oceanus, then for a while I watched some black
and white boys wrestling and joking, teammates,
    wet
plums and peaches touching each other as if

it is not necessary to make hate,   15
as if Whitman was right and there is no death.
A big wind at our backs, it is lovely, the maple
    boughs
ride up and down like ships. Do you mind
if I take off, he says. I'll catch you later,
see you, I shout and wave, as he peels   20
away, pedaling hard, rocket and pilot.

Poem Summary

Lines 1–2

In these lines, the speaker introduces a boy's physical speed and strength, repeating the word "strength" twice for emphasis. The poet reinforces the sense of speed by using alliteration, beginning nearby words with the same "s" sound. The traits of speed and strength signal other masculine traits about which the speaker is both proud and concerned. With the first line, Ostriker invokes the expression "the strength of ten men," but she uses enjambment, wrapping the sentence onto the next line, to create two meanings at once. First, the poet causes readers to complete the phrase "the strength of ten" in their heads with "men." She thereby introduces themes of manhood and great strength without stating them directly. Next, by beginning the second line with "years," the poet deflates the heroic phrase and reveals that "he" is only a boy of ten. Though the word "years" holds comic surprise here, the poet causes readers to keep both ideas in their heads: the boy is only ten, but he will grow into a strong man one day just around the corner. Poets often use enjambment to create two meanings from one sentence or phrase.

Lines 3–4

These lines set a tone of playfulness and companionship between the speaker and the boy. That the mother is first ahead of and then outdistanced by the boy shows that she fosters his sense of competition and that he will soon grow faster and stronger than she. For the moment, however, they are equal. In line 3, the speaker characterizes herself as the Greek goddess Niké, who represented winged victory, or speed, and whose image commemorated military victories in particular. This allusion, together with the themes of manhood, begins the poem's subtle meditation on masculinity and war. The speaker's mention of the "*Times* crossword" suggests both that this is a leisurely day and that the mother enjoys intellectual as well as physical challenges.

Lines 5–7

The rest of the first stanza shows the boy's competitive energy as he races out of sight. Comparing the boy to "the Green Hornet," a popular radio adventure series of the 1930s and 1940s, the speaker again highlights and gently deflates the boy's super-manly aspirations. Like Superman, the Green Hornet was a newspaperman by day and a masked crime-fighter by night. Playing on the name "Hornet," the speaker watches the boy "buzz" and "flash" away like an insect. This also identifies the speaker as a member of an earlier generation who heard, or has heard of, that radio show. The names "Witherspoon" and "Nassau Street" locate the poem in Princeton, New Jersey, where those main streets meet.

Lines 8–9

In stanza 2, the setting shifts to the town pool. The speaker's mention of "noon sharp" may have several implications. Noon is poised between morning and afternoon, as the boy is poised between childhood and adulthood. The sun at that hour approaches its peak strength, as the boy approaches his. This moment is recorded exactly in time with the precision of a mother, recalling events in her own and her child's shared lives. The boy's precise flip again reminds the reader of his maturing physical agility.

Line 10

This line identifies the speaker as a mother and the boy as her son. The slightly sarcastic cheer, "Oh, brave," indicates a mother's blend of pride and teasing toward her children. The boy's need for his mother to see, approve, and acclaim his feat is characteristic of child. Note that his "demand," "Did you see me," has no question mark, though, because it is not really a question. This mother does not seem to respond, and the boy does not seem to need her to. The words and punctuation in line 10, then, reinforce the theme of a boy poised on the verge of manhood: the boy is still a child who needs and wants his mother's approval, but he is almost beyond this stage.

Line 11

Here, the speaker imagines herself as the Roman goddess Juno. Juno was the wife of Jupiter, queen of the gods, and the goddess of married women and childbirth. (In Greek legend, Juno is named Hera and her husband is known as Zeus.) In myth, Juno is fiercely jealous of her unfaithful husband Jupiter and uses her powers primarily to punish the women with whom he cavorts. Thus, most references to Juno imply a jealous, wrathful, implacable woman. By referring to Juno luxuriously doing the backstroke, the speaker reinterprets and revises the traditional myth of this goddess. The mother in this poem shows none of those negative traits, so a relaxed, accepting, loving Juno emerges in these lines.

Line 12

The poet may separate the name "Juno Oceanus" on two lines because of rhythm and/or meaning. Line 11 has eleven syllables already; adding the four syllables of "Oceanus" would disturb this stanza's rhythm of mostly ten and eleven syllable lines. The poet also may have enjambed "Oceanus," writing the name on the next line, to create a dual meaning. Oceanus was a mythical male figure who fathered thousands of sea nymphs and river gods. He was a powerful but kindly old titan who ruled the oceans before Jupiter and his brothers took over the heavens and earth. By conceiving of "Juno Oceanus," the speaker envisions a new, dualistic, mythic figure who is both female and male, mother and father, and a ruler of the heavens and the seas. By splitting the name over two lines, the poet underscores this dual nature. This new mythic figure who encompasses male and female provides a model for the son to emulate as he combines masculine and feminine qualities in himself.

Lines 13–14

The rest of line 12 through the end of the stanza presents images of earthly oppositions synthesized into a harmonious whole. The speaker watches boys of two races, whom she compares to two types of fruit, play roughly and softly. Each difference the speaker identifies is balanced by similarities: the boys are all boys, "teammates," and all like fruit. The speaker may compare the boys to "plums and peaches" in part because these are summer fruits (and it is summer in the poem). Also, fruits are often associated with the freshness of youth, femininity and sexuality, since the story of Eve eating the apple in the Garden of Eden. By describing the boys this way, the speaker suggests that she sees how their youthful play contains opposite elements—femininity and sexuality—of which they are not yet aware. The last words of the second stanza, "as if," emphasize that the image of the boys as "teammates" is more the speaker's hopeful vision than a reality.

Line 15

The speaker ends stanza 2 with "as if" also in order to make the first line of stanza three a bold declaration of her vision of human relations. The third stanza's assurance balances the second stanza's tentative ending. Denying the need for strife between races of people, the speaker indirectly reminds the reader that this mother's contemplations take place during or shortly after the Vietnam War. The words "make hate" echo the Vietnam-era slogan: "make love, not war."

Line 16

In this line, the speaker refers to Walt Whitman, an American poet who wrote exuberant poetry in the 1800s about the connectedness of all life. Repeating "as if" to add on to her first wish, the speaker links the idea of racial and human harmony to Whitman's idea that "there is no death." Whitman's poems assert that every individual joins the earth in death and lives on in "leaves of grass," trees, and other life forms. Humans also live on, according to Whitman, by nurturing their own children and imagining future generations. When writers allude to previous writers, they often intend to invoke that writer's outlook on life rather than any specific poem or story. By alluding to a famous, visionary poet who believed that all life forms, differences, and contradictions were connected in a vibrant whole, Ostriker reminds the reader that there is a tradition of thought in this vein. Not only mothers, hoping their sons will not be killed in war, envision the world as so interconnected. Looking back from this line to line 14, the reader can see that the phrase "touching each other" means more than the boys' literal, physical contact as they wrestle. In light of the reference to Whitman, the boys "touch each other" spiritually as well, insofar as each life is linked to the universe.

Lines 17–18

This line creates an expansive feeling. It is the longest line in the poem. Whitman's poems had enormously long lines that strove to encompass everything, and Ostriker may be echoing his style here. These lines also provide a breath of fresh air by simply describing the wind in the trees; all the other lines describe the boy or the mother's thoughts. When the speaker uses a simile to compare maple boughs to "ships," she implies that the wind is like an ocean on which the boughs "ride." Without stating this likeness between the wind and the ocean, the speaker shows how different elements (water and air) are, like people of different races or genders, indivisibly connected. The word "ships" might invoke associations with the military.

Line 19

Here, the boy again asks his mother a question without a question mark or quotation marks. The punctuation in these lines reinforces the ideas that the boy is growing up and that he is nevertheless similar and connected to his mother. "He says" rather than "he asks" in line 19 shows the boy again asserting his decision rather than asking permission. The phrase "I'll catch you later" on the same line at first appears to be spoken by the boy, but the period after he speaks and the comma after "later" and "see you" indicate that the mother speaks this phrase. By omitting quotation marks, the poet forces the reader to look closely to distinguish who is speaking. The use of slang—"take off," "catch you"—by both the son and mother also makes it hard to tell them apart. The poet writes these lines without quotation marks and in the same slang diction purposely, to suggest that the son and mother are, like many other diverse elements in this poem, intimately connected.

Lines 20–21

The final two lines connect several of the poem's metaphors. The expression, he "peels away" reminds the reader of the fruit metaphor from stanza two. Because the other boys by the pool are associated with fruit in the mother's mind, the words "peel away" suggest that the son goes off to join the other boys in their play. The son's wish to play with boys rather than his mother is a final sign that he is leaving childhood and growing up. The last words of the poem, "rocket and pilot" again invoke images of war, since rockets were created for war. The mention of a rocket also makes literal the son's metaphor for leaving: "taking off." Though the mother waves happily as he speeds away, her vision of him as both "rocket," the instrument of war, and "pilot," an agent of war, is an ominous ending to the poem.

Themes

Masculine versus Feminine

As the title implies, this poem is concerned with issues of masculinity, at least in the traditionally accepted sense. In the poem, the narrator describes a day in which she spent time with her son at the local community swimming pool. In this scene, the narrator underscores the "speed and strength" of her son in several ways. At the beginning of the poem, the mother remembers how her son raced her home from the swimming pool. The race begins in the mother's favor: "First I am ahead, Niké, on my bicycle." The reference to Niké, the Greek goddess of victory, indicates that the narrator might win this race. Yet, the son soon prevails: "then he is ahead, the Green Hornet," a reference to a popular comic book male superhero. The differences between the two styles of competing are profound. While the mother rides her bicycle with "no hands, and the *Times* crossword tucked in my rack," indicating a lack of concern for winning, the boy is described as "buzzing" up a street and "flashing around the corner."

Traditionally, masculinity is associated with strength, competitiveness, and bravery, while femininity is associated with weakness and peace. Although the identification of these traits as specifically male has been hotly debated and has been labeled a stereotypical approach by some, Ostriker sticks to the traditional associations in this poem. This continues as Ostriker describes what the actual swim at the pool was like. While the mother is leisurely "doing my backstroke laps," the boy is performing impressive "one-and-a-half flips off the board." The boy is concerned with knowing whether or not his mother saw his acrobatics.

Racial Conflict

Ostriker also discusses, at least in a subtle sense, the fact that mother and son live in a world filled with racial hatred. Ostriker describes the mother's reaction when she sees a bunch of "black / and white boys wrestling and joking, teammates." The wrestling is once again an indication of the inherent aggressive male tendencies that Ostriker is underscoring. Yet, in the context of the poem, the wrestling between African American boys and white boys also serves to highlight the fact that these two groups, in the adult world at least, are locked in a racial struggle. The poet comments on this when she notes that the boys are "touching each other as if / it is not necessary to make hate." The poet knows that, although these boys are friends here in the sheltered environment of the pool, when they grow up and enter the adult world, they may become enemies, involved in the same racial conflict that adults are.

Childhood

It is their childhood that protects the boys from this adult hate that pervades society. As the poem

Topics for Further Study

- Research and discuss the differences between men and women, in terms of speed and strength. Organize your research into a short report, using charts, graphs, and other graphics wherever possible.

- Research the differences between male and female styles of communication. Imagine that you are a member of the opposite sex. Now, write a journal entry that describes the difficulties you have communicating with someone from the opposite sex (i.e., your actual sex).

- Choose one female athlete, from any point in history, who has competed successfully with men. Write a short biography about this woman.

- Read any of the classic texts from Carl Jung or other modern researchers who were among the first to discuss the psychological differences between men and women. Compare the ideas in this text to the latest research concerning the differences between the sexes.

progresses, one might think that perhaps there is hope for this generation of males, that maybe they can succeed peacefully where their parents' generation has not. Yet, at the end of the poem, Ostriker leaves her readers with an image that predicts the future, war-like tendencies of the boy: "he peels / away, pedaling hard, rocket and pilot." The use of these terms underscores the idea of physical war, which was a global fear when Ostriker wrote this poem, during the ideological conflict known as the Cold War. While the mother is content to focus on the "big wind at our backs" as they ride home and is not concerned with riding faster, the boy chooses to go faster, racing out of his childhood and into his adult life. One can determine, from the cues that Ostriker gives readers in the poem, that this future will likely be based on the boy's desire to achieve greater feats of speed and strength.

Style

"His Speed and Strength" is written from the first person point of view, which means that the speaker refers to herself as "I." The "I" who narrates a poem or story is often a fictional persona or character, rather than the author. In this poem, however, Ostriker seems to refer to her own son and their real hometown in New Jersey. This poem is written in free verse, which means that it does not have a regular pattern of rhymes or meter. The poem is divided into three stanzas that each have seven lines. The number of syllables and the rhythm in each line are irregular.

To determine whether a poem is written in free verse or a set form, readers can scan the meter, highlighting the syllables that are emphasized when spoken aloud. The first three lines of "His Speed and Strength" use four types of stresses: iambs, trochees, spondees, and anapests.

The first line can be read as using two iambs, one trochee, and two iambs. Or, if one stresses "is" instead of "which," then there are five iambs in a row; this is called iambic pentameter. The second line has three feet made up of a spondee and two anapests.

If you cannot find a regular pattern of stresses, rhyme, or feet in the first few lines, the poem is probably written in free verse. Though Ostriker's poem does not have a regular meter, many lines have the same number of syllables. Lines 4, 7, 10, 11, 12, 13, 14, 16, 19, and 21 all have eleven syllables. The first line of each stanza has 10 syllables. Since most of the poem's lines are approximately the same length, the poem has consistency despite varying stresses. This structure parallels the poem's themes of continuity amid variation.

Historical Context

The Cold War

Ostriker wrote "His Speed and Strength" during a time when the world was anything but peaceful. Following the dropping of atomic bombs on Japan by the United States at the end of World War II in 1945, several countries quickly rushed to create their own atomic and nuclear arsenals. For the next four decades, this struggle polarized itself in an escalating conflict between the communist Soviet Union and the democratic United States. The resulting tension between these two countries—and between communism and democracy in general—was labeled the Cold War, and for good reason. Although much of the period was technically spent in peacetime, the pervasive feeling of suspicion and paranoia that was generated by this clash of superpowers made many feel that they were fighting a war. This feeling was still strong in 1980 when Ostriker published "His Speed and Strength."

The 1980 Moscow Olympics

The Cold War hatred between communist and democratic societies affected athletes too. When the Soviet Union invaded Afghanistan in 1979, United States President Jimmy Carter instituted a boycott of the 1980 Summer Olympics, which were being held in Moscow that year. The resulting boycott—which ultimately affected 5,000 athletes representing more than 80 nations—was the biggest Olympic boycott in history. As a result of the reduced number of athletes, the 1980 Olympics were not very impressive. The Soviet Union dominated the highly politicized Games, taking home 195 total medals, including 80 gold medals, but the performances by many athletes left much to be desired and were often not up to previous Olympic quality. This was due in part to the fact that those athletes who did attend the Olympics also faced a rowdy crowd and cheating by the officials.

Reagan Is Elected

Hostilities between the Soviet Union and the United States increased after the 1980 election of United States President Ronald Reagan. Formerly

Compare & Contrast

- **Late 1970s/Early 1980s:** Following the Civil Rights movement of the 1950s and 1960s, African Americans and other minorities move into positions of political and economic power in America.

  Today: While African Americans and other minorities have made several gains on the path to equality, race relations remains a tense issue. Following attacks by Middle Eastern terrorists on American soil in 2001, hate crimes against Americans of Middle Eastern heritage increase.

- **Late 1970s/Early 1980s:** Following the second wave of feminism in the 1960s and 1970s, women in some parts of the world have more choices on how to live their lives, and many try to balance work and family roles. High-profile women are recognized in both traditionally feminine and masculine roles. Mother Theresa of Calcutta receives the 1979 Nobel Prize for Peace. The same year, Margaret Thatcher becomes Europe's first woman prime minister. She is noted for her combative political style.

  Today: The current state of the achievements of feminism is debated. Although women occupy many power roles traditionally held by men, such as CEO positions in major companies, others choose to become housewives. New studies indicate that women may experience infertility problems after their late twenties, prompting some people to speculate that women may once again have to choose between career and family. During the last half of the Clinton presidency, Madeleine Albright, a female politician noted for her aggressive political style, becomes the first American woman to hold the position of secretary of state.

- **Late 1970s/Early 1980s:** British Prime Minister Margaret Thatcher and American President Ronald Reagan join forces in the Cold War struggle against communism in general and the Soviet Union in particular.

  Today: British Prime Minister Tony Blair and American President George W. Bush join forces in the struggle against terrorism in general and Iraq in particular.

---

a Hollywood actor, Reagan's charisma and strong will had helped him win the California governor's race twice. Anybody who doubted his ability to compete with big-name politicians for the presidential bid was soon proved wrong, after a memorable debate during the Republican primaries, when the moderator attempted to shut off Reagan's microphone. Reagan's forceful reply and public display of strength helped him win over the public. He ultimately won the presidency against Democratic incumbent Carter, who tried to blast Reagan during his campaign by depicting Reagan as a warmonger. Reagan's focus on massive amounts of defense funding soon proved that he was, in fact, interested in arming the United States for potential war with the Soviet Union. With the help of tough international allies, like British Prime Minister Margaret Thatcher, Reagan faced off with the Soviet Union, placing America on what appeared to be the path to World War III. Besides talking tough, Reagan's image also made him seem to be powerful when it came to negotiating with hostile terrorists. After his inaugural ceremony in 1981, it was announced that Iran had agreed to release its American hostages.

Critical Overview

Although there is little criticism on "His Speed and Strength," several scholars have outlined characteristic themes and issues in Ostriker's poetry. Moreover, Ostriker has written critical books about poetry, which help illuminate her work. Critic Janet Ruth Heller in her essay, "Exploring the Depths of

Relationships in Alicia Ostriker's Poetry," analyzes Ostriker's treatment of the "ambivalence" and "tensions in intimate relationships," such as those between men and women or between parents and children. These tensions and divisions are revealed in poems about miscommunication, ambivalence, suppressed anger, invisibility, silence, uncertainty, and duality, particularly within women who are both mothers and writers. In her critical book *Stealing the Language: The Emergence of Women's Poetry in America*, Ostriker finds these and other recurring images of division in poetry by women from the 1600s to the present. In "His Speed and Strength," the mother recognizes dualistic traits in her son, but rather than causing tension within him or between mother and son, his duality gives the mother hope for his future wholeness.

Focusing perhaps on poems such as this, other reviewers argue that Ostriker's poems resolve tensions between and within people and between public and private life. In "His Speed and Strength," motherhood appears to be as, or more, powerful than the forces, such as war, that disturb the eternal process. Ostriker's poetry frequently focuses on women's lives and aspirations, myths of femininity, and relationships between men and women. When Ostriker began writing poetry in the 1960s, there were few poems about female experiences, such as pregnancy, birth, and motherhood, next to all the poems about male experiences of war, heroism, and love. The stories of female experiences that Ostriker did find in her years in college and graduate school were often rooted in ancient myths that portrayed women in negative and stereotypical ways. Like the women poets she studies, Ostriker seeks to create "revisionary myths," replacing negative myths about women with new and revised stories of women's authority and power. When the speaker in Ostriker's poem refers to herself as the goddesses Niké and Juno, she attempts to modernize and transform the negative connotations associated with these mythic female figures. Where Ostriker's criticism explores how female identity and consciousness has been represented in literature so far, her poetry envisions and creates new images of womanhood.

Criticism

Ryan D. Poquette

Poquette has a bachelor's degree in English and specializes in writing about literature. In the following essay, Poquette discusses Ostriker's poem in relation to its historical context and events in the poet's own life.

On the surface, it appears that Ostriker's poem, "His Speed and Strength," is primarily about the differences between men and women. Ostriker draws on the traditional stereotypes of men and women, emphasizing male aggression and female passivity. There is, however, a darker side to this poem, which starts with the title itself. Although the poem does contrast men and women, or rather, a mother and son, it is really a poem about the cultural factors that determine how male "speed and strength" are used in American society, namely for military purposes. One can understand this better by examining the historical and autobiographical contexts within which Ostriker wrote the poem.

The poem was first published in 1980 in Ostriker's poetry collection, *The Mother/Child Papers*. Yet, Ostriker began writing the book much earlier. As Amy Williams notes in her entry on Ostriker in the *Dictionary of Literary Biography*, the book "was a ten-year project" that Ostriker began in 1970. That year, the United States was embroiled in one of its most bitter Cold War conflicts—the Vietnam War. Officially, the American participation in the war took place from 1968 to 1973. Like many other Cold War hostilities, however, the Vietnam War was rooted in events that took place much earlier. The conflict in Vietnam actually began in 1946, shortly after World War II ended. World War II left many areas in Southeast Asia unstable, and over the next two decades the United States unofficially provided military support to South Vietnam and its allies who were fighting Communist forces in North Vietnam. United States policy during this time period emphasized this type of support, as an attempt to stop the spread of Communism in Southeast Asia.

Many of the poems in Ostriker's book underscore or comment on events that took place during this very unpopular conflict. Indeed, most critics, including Williams, highlight the book's connection to the war. Williams says, "she contrasts the events of her own life with the Vietnam War." "His Speed and Strength" is more subtle in its approach, and does not link directly to any one event in the Vietnam War. Instead, it discusses war in general.

The poem contains many allusions to war or aggression, starting with mythological associations. In the first stanza, the poet discusses a mother's bike race with her son, saying "First I am ahead, Niké, on my bicycle." In Greek mythology, Niké is the goddess of victory. Although victory can apply to many situations, such as winning a competition, much of Greek mythology deals with conflict and war, so one can assume that Ostriker's use of Niké is meant to be an allusion to war.

On a similar note, later in the poem, Ostriker alludes to a Roman goddess, when she is describing the mother's day at the pool: "And I doing my backstroke laps was Juno." In Roman mythology, Juno is the Roman goddess of light, birth, women, and marriage. She is also the wife of Jupiter, the chief Roman god, who rules over all of the other gods, enforcing his dominance when necessary. By referring to herself as Juno, the poet is underscoring, albeit in a subtle way, the mother's connection to her son and his male dominance and power. She is demonstrating her femininity by leisurely taking laps around the pool, while he is demonstrating his masculinity with his impressive "one-and-a-half flips off the board," an ultra-male symbol of competition and athletic prowess.

Still later in the poem, Ostriker references another general war theme—hate. When she is discussing the groups of boys "wrestling," another symbol of male aggression, she notes that they are also "joking," and that they are "touching each other as if / it is not necessary to make hate." On the surface, this statement seems to apply only to the racial conflicts that were evident in the United States at this point. It is not uncommon for the white boys and African American boys to be joking around, because they are, to some extent, less aware of the racial hatred that many adults experienced in America at this point. This statement, however, also underscores the war theme. War, by its very nature, generally involves hate. It is hard for a soldier to kill his enemies if he does not harbor some negative feelings toward them. For this reason, many governments, including the United States during the Vietnam War, created propaganda that was designed to breed hatred of the North Vietnamese. When Ostriker uses the phrase "make hate," she is referring to this deliberate attempt to create a negative view of another country or race during a war.

The poem also relies on some images of military equipment to underscore the war theme. In the last stanza, the poet is observing the scenery on their bike ride back from the swimming pool. She notes that they ride with "A big wind at our backs, it is lovely, the maple boughs / ride up and down like ships." In another poem, this observation could be attributed to the poet's creativity, comparing the bobbing tree branches to ships rocking gently on the waves in a large body of water. In the context

> *By associating the boy in the poem directly with military weaponry such as rockets, the poet is noting that this ten-year-old boy may someday be groomed for military service.*"

of this poem, however, her use of the ships is, once again, meant to underscore a darker meaning. During the Vietnam War, the use of naval warships formed a crucial part of the United States attack strategy. As coastal countries, North and South Vietnam could be accessed by the sea, and the American government used this geographic aspect to its advantage, off-loading soldiers and weapons to the two countries.

Ostriker uses a more direct military reference in the final part of the poem, when she talks about the boy taking off during their ride home, "pedaling hard, rocket and pilot." By comparing the boy's bicycle to a rocket and the boy himself to a pilot who is navigating the rocket, the poet is directly linking the boy to the war. This is Ostriker's way of commenting on the Selective Service system that drafted thousands of young men into military service, in an attempt to feed the war machine. Even before the Vietnam War began, the United States sent an increasing number of American soldiers to Southeast Asia, posing as nonaggressive military advisors. By the time that the United States officially entered the war, it had stationed hundreds of thousands of soldiers in the area. As J. M. Roberts notes in his *Twentieth Century: The History of the World, 1901 to 2000*, "In 1968 there were over half a million American servicemen in Vietnam." In order to meet these numbers, the United States government relied on the Selective Service system to conscript young American men into the military.

At this point, one can see that the poet is worried about the destiny of American males. Throughout the poem, Ostriker notes the male focus on strength, competition, and aggression, all factors that make a good soldier. By associating the boy in the poem directly with military weaponry such as rockets, the poet is noting that this ten-year-old boy may someday be groomed for military service.

To better understand the poet's fear for the boy, one must examine certain aspects of the poet's own life, namely, the birth of her son, Gabriel. As Judith Pierce Rosenberg notes in her 1993 profile of Ostriker in *Belles Lettres*, Ostriker started the book after the birth of her son, "a few days after the United States invaded Cambodia and four student protesters were shot by members of the National Guard at Kent State University." Ostriker is worried in general for all American males, but specifically for her son. If he grows up a stereotypical male, encouraged to be competitive and aggressive, he might be recruited to be a soldier, as the boy in the poem surely will. If, on the other hand, her son tries to protest this cultural stereotype and speak out against war itself, he could be shot, as the student protesters were. Ostriker seems to be saying that the male emphasis on speed and strength can ultimately work against them by leading to their early deaths.

During the course of writing her book, Ostriker and the rest of the American public witnessed some changes in the Selective Service system. The practice of active drafting during peacetime ended in 1973, after the Vietnam War, providing some hope for mothers like Ostriker that their sons might be safe. However, in 1980, the year that Ostriker published her poem, the United States reinstituted draft registration, giving the government the right to draft young men in the future, if necessary, for wartime purposes, validating once again the fears of mothers such as Ostriker.

Source: Ryan D. Poquette, Critical Essay on "His Speed and Strength," in *Poetry for Students*, Gale, 2003.

Joyce Hart

Hart is a published writer who focuses on literary themes. In this essay, Hart examines Ostriker's poem as a way of better understanding the effects of mid-twentieth-century social movements and the Vietnam War on the role of motherhood.

Ostriker, the author of "His Speed and Strength," has often stated that she views the writing of poetry more as a diagnostic tool than as a remedy. Although both concepts are closely connected, Ostriker makes it clear that she relies on her poetry to tell her what she is feeling rather than to cure a specific distress that she is aware of. Her poems, in other words, inform her. The words that bubble up to the surface in the form of a poem announce, or call to her attention, something that is troubling her deep within her psyche before she can fully put her finger on what it is.

Ostriker's poem "His Speed and Strength" could be such a poem. It was published in the collection *The Mother/Child Papers* in 1980, ten years after Ostriker's son was born, ten years after four students were shot at Kent State for protesting the Vietnam War, and just a little more than ten years after Martin Luther King was assassinated. In the same year that her son was born, the first Women's Equality Day was celebrated in commemoration of the fiftieth anniversary of women's right to vote. The decade between the birth of Ostriker's son and the publication of this poem, in other words, was saturated with events that could well have caused a sense of unease in anyone's psyche. The times were turbulent, and Ostriker, a feminist, was giving birth in the middle of it, trying to make sense of it all.

Ostriker had to come to grips with the horrendous atrocities of a highly criticized and protested international war, while on a national level, she had to face the rampant racism that had infected her society, a fact that many white people had hitherto tried to ignore. But even more particular to this poem is what women had to face on a more personal level. Women of Ostriker's generation were trying to redefine themselves and their roles, not only in society but also on a much smaller and more intimate scale, in the family.

The image of the 1950s mother still influenced many soon-to-be-married women of Ostriker's age, but that image was in the process of collapsing; and yet no other icon had successfully been adopted. Few young 1970s feminists had any clues as to how women were, on one hand, supposed to demand equal rights in a traditionally patriarchal society and, on the other, to raise a family. At times, these two concepts seemed diametrically opposed. The emerging feminist fought for her right for advanced degrees, for better wages in the workforce, as well as for the controversial right to abortion. The feminist sentiment in those early days was often interpreted to mean that women should not marry at an early age as their 1940s and 1950s mothers had but rather that they should gain access to the business world that had previously been dominated by their male counterparts. The consequence of this belief often meant that women delayed childbirth, if they had children at all. This left other women, those who had decided to marry and to have children early in their lives, with a sense of guilt, as if they had betrayed their own feminist beliefs. Hidden somewhere in their psyches was the idea that having children was somehow detrimental to women's progress. The role of motherhood tended to define the unliberated women of the previous generations.

So while many women of Ostriker's generation were beginning to celebrate the delay of childbearing, believing that having children was one of the reasons women were being held back, Ostriker gave birth to a son. In doing so, she appeared to be going against the tide of feminism, so through her poem, she tries to analyze how she feels about motherhood. Does motherhood entrap her? Does it deny her freedom? Has she turned her back on feminism by giving birth? It is possible that these were the questions that were surfacing in her mind as Ostriker wrote this poem.

From the very first line of the poem, rather than bemoaning motherhood, Ostriker celebrates it through the figure of her son. She begins by honoring him. She admires his ten-year-old speed and strength, which, by the way, she emphasizes by using this same phrase as the title of her poem, making it the focus of the entire piece. She honors his power not just because he is blessed with it but also because his strength challenges her in a lot of different ways. The challenge that his youthful energy offers is not a typical one in which either the son or the mother will be singularly victorious, but rather one in which they both will benefit. Ostriker makes this clear by having the narrator of the poem not only admire her son's strength but to be inspired by it.

To begin with, here is a woman, a mother, riding a bike. This is an act which in the 1970s was still considered a child's activity. The adult sport of biking had not yet been popularized. So for readers of this poem, when it was first published, the image of a mom on a bike racing her son paints a different picture than it might today. To the reader of the 1970s, this immediately portrays a woman who is filled with awe of a child's world. The woman in this poem is very comfortable with herself; to further this image, the narrator confides that not only is this mother racing her son on a bicycle, she is riding with "no hands." Some readers might interpret this by stating that she is showing off. However, someone else reading this poem might conclude that this woman must either be very confident in herself or that she does not really care about who will win the race between her son and herself. Another possibility might be that this mother is merely enjoying her sense of freedom in acting childlike. Whatever image comes to mind, the overall feeling

> *She not only embraces motherhood here, she takes motherhood to a higher realm. It is through motherhood, she states, that people create these new little souls and train them in new ways. Thus motherhood becomes a sacred duty."*

that is portrayed is one of comfort. This woman is comfortable in her role as mother.

She remains comfortable even when her son passes her. The narrator first states that the mother is "ahead" in the bicycle race for home, but then her son catches her and shortly afterward buzzes past her. With this portrayal of the so-called bicycle race, Ostriker reflects on the natural path of parenthood. The mother is ahead, in a sense, when the child is first born. Her newborn baby is totally dependent on her and must learn all the basics of survival: to eat, to walk, to run, to talk. Then as both the mother and the child age, the young boy gains strength and eventually passes her. But this is not something to regret. This is something to celebrate. Mother and child, although they share a path for a while, have different lives to lead. As she sits back on the seat of her bike, with the "*Times* crossword" puzzle "tucked" in her "rack," her son flashes past her, fast as the "Green Hornet." Her son has energy to burn. She is in more of a meditative mode. He pierces time in his rush toward the future. In contrast, she, in the middle years of her life, reflects equally on her experience of the past and the dreams, as embodied in her son, that lie "ahead" of her.

With these images, Ostriker shows that bearing children does not hold her back from becoming fully developed and confident as a woman any more than a mother might hold back her son from maturing. Mother and child are separate entities, each surviving off their own strength but at the same time encouraging one another through their separate journeys. Children do not erode a woman's role, Ostriker appears to be saying, they enhance it. They give as much as they take.

Furthering this idea is the next image that Ostriker advances in the second stanza of her poem. Here the mother and the son are at the swimming pool, where the mother watches her son perform his "neat one-and-a-half flips" off the diving board. She congratulates him with the words "oh, brave." The narrator demonstrates the mother's feelings by having her refer to Juno, the goddess and wife of Jupiter, and Oceanus, the god of the sea. In other words, in experiencing the courage of her son, the mother feels godlike; for it was through her that her son entered this world. Motherhood, Ostriker's poem states, has elevated her; has, in some way, enhanced her mortality; has blessed her. It is off of her, as if she is the springboard (the diving board), that her son jumps, soars, and spins, exhibiting his bravery to the world.

As depicted in the actions of some children nearby, Ostriker touches on the confusion of war and racism that was infiltrating her world when she wrote this poem. However, through the children (and obliquely through motherhood) she brings the concept of hope into her poem. She watches "some black and white boys wrestling," a sight that could have potentially represented conflict; but Ostriker turns this conflict into fun by stating that the boys were "joking, teammates," who were using the act of wrestling as an excuse to touch each other, thus proving that "it is not necessary to make hate." If there is any hope in the world that people will come to accept one another and turn their hate into love and sharing, Ostriker sees it in the children. She not only embraces motherhood here, she takes motherhood to a higher realm. It is through motherhood, she states, that people create these new little souls and train them in new ways. Thus motherhood becomes a sacred duty.

In the third stanza, Ostriker elaborates this point by referring to the poet Walt Whitman's thoughts as espoused in his "A Song of Myself." In that poem, Whitman is talking to a child who asks him to explain what grass is. In trying to clarify it to the child, Whitman meanders through many different thoughts, but in the end he uses the youngest sprout of grass, the regeneration of grass, as a symbol that there really is no such thing as death. In the same way, Ostriker implies, children bring immortality to their parents. What possible calling could be higher or more purposeful than that?

She then ends her poem with her son asking if it is all right with her if he "takes off." She watches him as he "peels away," as if he has been attached to her but is learning to pull away on his own. He is her son. He came into this world through her, but he is becoming his own "rocket and pilot." He has developed his own means to propel himself and is steering that vehicle into the future.

Her poem, in the end, shows that the role of mother is not diametrically opposed to feminist beliefs. Rather, it might more clearly personify them. Feminism does not mean that women should "race" against men and try to beat them. It does not mean that women who enjoy motherhood relinquish their opportunity to make their voices heard in the world. Feminism, as found in this poem, might well mean that women and men can work together; that nurturing others is not a weakness but rather a strength; and that motherhood, although it comes without a salary and does not require a college degree, is an honorable and self-satisfying profession.

Source: Joyce Hart, Critical Essay on "His Speed and Strength," in *Poetry for Students*, Gale, 2003.

Amy Williams

In the following essay, Williams discusses Ostriker's life and writings.

Like several women poets in her generation, including Sandra Gilbert, Adrienne Rich, Audre Lorde, and Alice Walker, Alicia Ostriker also writes as a literary critic. Clear and lyrical, her poetry combines intelligence and passion. Speaking in the tradition of Walt Whitman, she recreates the American experience in each of her volumes. Her voice is personal, honest, and strong; her poetry incorporates family experiences, social and political views, and a driving spirit that speaks for growth and, at times, with rage.

Ostriker's urban background contributes to the forcefulness of her work. Born in Brooklyn on 11 November 1937, she was a "Depression baby" and grew up in Manhattan housing projects. Her parents, David and Beatrice Linnick Suskin, both earned degrees in English from Brooklyn College. Her father worked for the New York City Department of Parks; her mother, who wrote poetry and read William Shakespeare and Robert Browning to her daughter, tutored students in English and math and later became a folk-dance teacher. Alicia began writing poetry in childhood and enjoyed drawing as well. Her earliest hope was to be an artist: she studied art as a teenager and young adult and continues to carry a sketchbook on her travels. Two of her books—*Songs* (1969) and *A Dream of Springtime* (1979)—feature her graphics in the cover designs.

Ostriker received her B.A. in English from Brandeis University in 1959, and her M.A. and Ph.D. from the University of Wisconsin (1961, 1964). Her dissertation, on William Blake, became her first critical book, *Vision and Verse in William Blake* (1965); she later edited and annotated Blake's complete poems for Penguin (1977). Blake has continued to influence Ostriker as a person and poet. Ostriker began teaching at Rutgers University in 1965 and now holds the rank of full professor.

Much of the work in her first collection, *Songs*, was written during her student years. The voice is relatively formal, reflecting the influences of John Keats, Gerard Manley Hopkins, and W. H. Auden, as well as Whitman and Blake. Imagist and free-verse poems mingle somewhat tentatively with traditional, metrical poetry.

In Ostriker's second and third volumes of poetry—the chapbook *Once More out of Darkness* (1971) and *A Dream of Springtime*—a more personal voice emerges, which captures the mind of the reader more readily. For these books, Ostriker composed consistently in free verse. The title poem of *Once More Out of Darkness* is a meditation on pregnancy and childbirth. *A Dream of Springtime* begins with a sequence of autobiographical poems designed to enable her to exorcise her childhood and become "freed from it." The organization of the book moves concentrically from the self, to the family, to teaching experiences, to the larger world of politics and history. Reviewer Valerie Trueblood calls Ostriker "one of the most intelligent and lyrical of American poets," who has given herself the "difficult assignment" of creating "an intellectually bearable picture of domestic security" while at the same time assigning herself "the equally ticklish (for poetry) job of publicizing national folly and soft spots of the culture" (*Iowa Review*, Spring 1982).

By the end of the book Ostriker emerges from the confined walls of her past and finds herself in the spring of her life. The title poem "A Dream of Springtime" reflects her movement into spring and its cold, watery vigor that wakes her senses: "The creek, swollen and excited from the melting / Freshets that are trickling into it everywhere / Like a beautiful woman unafraid is dashing / Over the stones." Nonetheless, Ostriker calls her attempt to reconcile herself to her childhood only "partially successful" but an important step in her development as a poet.

Not until *The Mother/Child Papers* (1980) did Ostriker fully reach her medium. In this book she contrasts the events of her own life with the Viet-

> *Her voice is personal, honest, and strong; her poetry incorporates family experiences, social and political views, and a driving spirit that speaks for growth and, at times, with rage."*

nam War. The book begins after the birth of her son, Gabriel, in 1970, but also focuses on the other members of her family: her husband, Jeremiah P. Ostriker, an astrophysicist, to whom she was married in December 1958; and her daughters, Rebecca and Eve, born in 1963 and 1965. Mary Kinzie in the *American Poetry Review* commends Ostriker on how her "work details the achievement of a connection between personal history and public fact" (July/August 1981). James McGowan in the *Hiram Poetry Review* (Fall/Winter 1982) calls the book "a product of a whole person, which is not to say a perfect person, but one alive to present, past, future, to the body and its mystifying requirements and capacities." Confronting her roles as mother, wife, and professor, Ostriker explores her identity as a woman. As she points out in the essay "A Wild Surmise: Motherhood and Poetry" in her book *Writing Like a Woman* (1983), "the advantage of motherhood for a woman artist is that it puts her in immediate and inescapable contact with the sources of life, death, beauty, growth and corruption."

The Mother/Child Papers was a ten-year project. At its inception, Ostriker had only a vague idea of what she wanted to accomplish; she struggled intermittently with it while teaching and raising her family. The offer of the Los Angeles poet and editor of Momentum Press, Bill Mohr, to publish the manuscript if she could finish it, enabled her to define its ultimate shape. The book is experimental, divided into four sections, all of which build on the artist's experience as mother.

The first section, written in prose, juxtaposes the impact of the Cambodian invasion and the shooting of student protestors at Kent State University with the birth of Ostriker's son in the ster-

What Do I Read Next?

- Betty Friedan's controversial *The Feminine Mystique* (1963) helped to launch the modern women's movement. The book shatters the myth that post–World War II housewives were happy taking care of their husbands and children. Friedan labeled this misconception the feminine mystique and used her book to reveal the pain and frustration that many women faced when their needs were placed below the needs of their families.

- Charlotte Perkins Gilman's *Herland* (1915) describes a feminist utopia. In the idealistic world that Gilman creates, women rule their own country, where they do not need men to reproduce. Three male explorers from the United States find this isolated country and name it Herland. The men are surprised to find that the women are equal to them and are shocked when the women do not respond to the same types of charms that work on women in the United States.

- John Gray's *Men Are from Mars, Women Are from Venus: A Practical Guide for Improving Communication and Getting What You Want in Your Relationships* (1992) is a bestselling self-help book that discusses the differences between male and female styles of communication.

- Ostriker's poetry collection titled *The Imaginary Lover* (1986), like many of her works, explores feminist themes, including the relations between men and women.

- Ostriker's *Stealing the Language: The Emergence of Women Poets in America* (1986) is her best-known work of feminist literary criticism. This controversial book explores the idea that women's writing is distinct from men's writing because it focuses on issues that are central to the female gender.

- In her essay *A Room of One's Own* (1929), Virginia Woolf argues that for women writers to achieve the same greatness that male writers have, these women need an income and privacy. In addition, Woolf discusses the fact that the idealistic and powerful portrayals of women in fiction have historically differed from the slave-like situations that many women face in real life.

---

ile environment of an American hospital, where, during labor, she was given an unwanted spinal injection that deprived her of the ability to "give birth to my child, myself." Ostriker recreates the personal world of mother and infant in section 2, alternating their voices and molding them together in their own private sphere, separate from the rest of the world yet vulnerable to its incursions: "We open all the windows / the sunlight wraps us like gauze."

Part 3 of *The Mother/Child Papers* consists of a series of poems, written over a ten-year span, that captures the environment of the family and confronts the issue of "devouring Time, an enemy familiar to all mothers" (*Writing Like a Woman*). In "The Spaces" time is stressed, and the chaos of the outside world seems to threaten the secure nucleus of the family. The speaker overhears her husband discussing "the mass of the universe" and the possibility that it might "implode . . . back to the original fireball" it once was. As this discussion continues, her mind closes in on her own universe and her family's private world: "Gabriel runs upstairs. Rebecca is reading. Eve takes the hat back, . . . / Outside my window, the whole street dark and snowy."

Ostriker ties the work together in part 4 by stressing the connection between motherhood and art. In the final poem of the book, she recreates the experience of a woman in labor who enjoys her pain and is "comfortable" as she "rides with this work / for hours, for days / for the duration of this / dream." The mother is seen as the source of life's energy and of the universe beginning its never-ending process.

Ostriker continues to confront her role as a woman in her next collection of poems, *A Woman Under the Surface* (1982). X. J. Kennedy commended her "wit, verve and energy" (*Poetry*, March 1983). Lynda Koolish called the book "Cool, cerebral, studied. Passionate visceral, immediate ... cold and fiery at the same time ... the central metaphor of *A Woman Under the Surface* is a surfacing, emerging woman" (*San Francisco Chronicle*, 6 September 1983).

Written while Ostriker was working on her critical book *Writing Like a Woman*, this 1982 collection clearly reflects the world of women's poetry and Ostriker's indebtedness to it. The first poem, "The Waiting Room," suggests the bond of fear many women share: "We think of our breasts and cervixes. / We glance, shading our eyelids, at each other." Ostriker imagines a female ritual: "Perhaps we should sit on the floor. / They might have music for us. A woman dancer / Might perform, in the center of the circle." But the ritual is not pleasant: "What would she do? / Would she pretend to rip the breasts from her body?" Even this vision of unity is punctured as a woman's scream permeates the room from inside the office; the scream suggests the need these women have to express themselves and the satisfaction of a release that is sometimes denied them.

In "The Exchange" a mysteriously powerful woman emerges from underwater to murder the speaker's children and husband. In "The Diver," on the other hand, as in Adrienne Rich's poem "Diving into the Wreck," the female diver's body "is saying a kind of prayer." Ostriker's diver feels safe: "Nobody laughs, under the surface. / Nobody says the diver is a fool." Losing her name yet finding her space and her identity, "she extends her arms and kicks her feet," escaped from "the heat" and confinement of a surface world. Other poems in this volume touch on art—as in the poems to Henri Matisse, Vincent van Gogh, and Claude Monet—and myth, as in Ostriker's rewritten versions of the stories of Eros and Psyche, Orpheus and Euridice, and Odysseus and Penelope.

Ostriker continues to speak in her feminist voice in *The Imaginary Lover* (1986) and goes one step further. In an anonymous review in *Publisher's Weekly*, her poetry was described as "a poetry of commitment, not so much to womankind as to humankind.... When the voice of this rational, scholarly woman rises to crescendo, a tide of sweet human emotion lifts the poem into the realm of true experience with Keatsian intensity" (24 October 1984).

Written while Ostriker was researching her second feminist book of criticism, *Stealing the Language: the Emergence of Women Poets in America* (1986), the collection reflects the influences of Rich and H. D. In *The Imaginary Lover* Ostriker confronts the fantasies, both beautiful and horrible, that accompany womanhood. A long poem, "The War of Men and Women" explores the difficulty of male-female relations as "an archeology of pain." Several poems look at mother-daughter relationships from the perspective of the mother and that of the daughter; several are portraits of marriage. In the final poem of this book, Ostriker creates a woman's imaginary lover. Like the lovers in H. D.'s poetry, he is androgynous: "Oh imaginary lover, oh father-mother." He is not, however, the speaker's male counterpart, but rather the "form in the mind / On whom, as on a screen, I project designs." It is through this projected perception that the speaker becomes "the flock of puffy doves / ... in a magician's hat" capable of the liberty of flight.

Green Age (1989) is Ostriker's most visionary and most successful collection. As Gail Mazur wrote in *Poetry*, "The poems are expressions of the hungry search for her real and spiritual place in the world.... A tough empathy informs the poems—she is no softer on others than she is on herself" (July 1990).

The three sections of the book confront personal time, history and politics, and inner spirituality. The speaker's voice in many of these poems is full of an anger that requires healing transformation. The energy for survival is reflected through the female character of "A Young Woman, a Tree," who has withstood her harsh surroundings and has developed a "Mutant appetite for pollutants." She is that city tree that can "feel its thousand orgasms each spring" and "stretch its limbs during the windy days." This woman takes a hungry bite of the world and experiences its pleasures, despite the pain of encroaching time. Another theme is the need for feminist spirituality in the face of traditional religion. Ostriker suffers in her Jewish heritage, for as a woman she is both the "vessel" of religious lineage and deprived of spiritual participation in male-dominated Jewish ritual and intellectual life. "A Meditation in Seven Days" considers and challenges the roles of women and femaleness within Judaism, concluding with a vision of potential change: "Fearful, I see my hand is on the latch / I am the woman, and about to enter." The final poem of *Green Age*, "Move," captures the mood of Ostriker's continuing quest for identity as woman and poet:

> When we reach the place we'll know
> We are in the right spot, somehow, like a breath
> Entering a singer's chest, that shapes itself
> For the song that is to follow.

> *While her work is grounded in her identity as both woman and feminist, her poems are not restricted to the recording of female experiences or consciousness.*

The poetry of Alicia Ostriker consistently challenges limitations. For discovery to take place there must be movement, and Ostriker refuses to stand still; each volume tries to uncover anew what must be learned in order to gain wisdom, experience, and identity. She is a poet who breaks down walls.

Source: Amy Williams, "Alicia Ostriker," in *Dictionary of Literary Biography*, Vol. 120, *American Poets Since World War II, Third Series*, edited by R. S. Gwynn, Gale Research, 1992, pp. 239–42.

Anne F. Herzog

In the following essay, Herzog discusses Ostriker's role as both poet and critic.

Throughout her career, poet-critic Alicia Ostriker has resisted the pressures which privilege one creative identity over the other, poet before the critic or critic before the poet. Her life's writing—five scholarly books, eight books of poetry and a ninth book (*The Nakedness of the Fathers: Biblical Visions and Revisions*, 1994) which marvelously blends both prose and poetry—steadfastly refuses the prevalent cultural rift between poets and scholars. In a beautifully crafted autobiographical essay, "Five Uneasy Pieces" (1997), she writes: "I have tried to make my criticism and poetry feed each other. To write intelligent poems and passionate criticism." Reviewing her critical and poetic accomplishments, one cannot help but conclude that she has succeeded.

Her critical-scholarly career began with the publication of Vision and Verse in William Blake (1965), a meticulous analysis of Blake's prosody which still serves as an invaluable resource in the study of Blake's technique. Ostriker's choice of Blake as a poetic mentor reveals much about her early (and enduring) poetic tastes. In "The Road of Excess: My William Blake," Ostriker traces the history of her "romance with Blake":

> What did I like? First of all, Blake had the reputation of being "mad." I liked that. He wrote as an outsider; I liked that because I was one myself. His white-hot intellectual energy excited me, along with his flashing wit and irony, his capacity for joy and delight.

She continues to detail her recognition of Blake's own masculinist biases which propelled her towards a search for the women poets who could articulate what Blake could not. Reflecting on her successful search, she recounts, "I found a radical collective voice and vision equivalent to Blake's—equivalently outrageous, critical of our mind-forged manacles, determined to explore and rethink everything, and inventing poetic forms to embody new visions." Ostriker has gone on from this epiphany to write two significant books which detail her growing passion for the works of women poets: *Writing Like a Woman* (1983) and *Stealing the Language of Poetry: The Emergence of Women's Poetry in America* (1986). The latter is particularly noteworthy in its ambitious mapping of an identifiable tradition of women's poetry in America, beginning with Anne Bradstreet and continuing to the 1980s. According to James E. B. Breslin, "*Stealing the Language* is literary history as it should be written—based on an extraordinary range of reading, written with passionate involvement, grounded in acute readings of particular poems and filled with provocative general statement."

Critical responses to Ostriker's poetry are quick to remark on what feminist scholar Elaine Showalter calls her "unwavering intelligence" as well as her "compassionate and ironic" voice. In terms of focus and thematic concerns, her books of poetry vary widely. While her work is grounded in her identity as both woman and feminist, her poems are not restricted to the recording of female experiences or consciousness. As a *Publisher's Weekly* reviewer comments, "Hers is a poetry of commitment, not so much to womankind as to humankind." Diana Hume George notes that Ostriker's "prophetic" vision "makes her return endlessly to the ordinary, phenomenal world, inhabited by women and men like herself, where the real work must be done."

In "Five Uneasy Pieces," Ostriker describes the affirmative, life-embracing vision under girding poetry:

> ... there was always a part of me for which everything—everything, the brick building of public housing, cracked sidewalks, delivery trucks, subways,

luminous sky of clouds, wicked people—was spectacle. Glorious theater. The vitality of those hard streets, poverty and ignorance bawling through our lives, was a sight to behold. The swing and punch of the bad language I was told not to imitate was live music to my ears, far more interesting than proper English. Literature—any art—exists to embody such perception. Exists to praise what is. For nothing.

Thus, we find in one of her earliest books, "Sonnet. To Tell the Truth," an ironic poem about the brick Housing Authority buildings" of her childhood in Brooklyn, New York, "For whose loveliness no soul had planned"; or alternately, her meditation on "the kindliness of old men ... something incommunicably vast," as she remembers the lost grandfathers and older male friends who nurtured the young girl-child, "Petted me, taught me checkers patiently." She concludes, "It seems to me then God's a grandfather; / Infinite tenderness, infinite distance— / I don't a minute mean that I believe this! / It's but a way to talk about old men" ("Old Men").

Ostriker writes poems about marriage, struggles for intimacy, childbirth, the necessary, painful separations between parent and child, teaching, art, aging, losses, desire, and more. Throughout, her love of the world is unabated. In "Hating the World," she tells a former student, "Do you know, to hate the world / Makes you my enemy?," while in "The Death of Ghazals," we read: "Where there's life there's hope. We bequeath this hope / To our children, along with our warm tears." Ostriker's persistent poetic faith in the face of hard truths culminates in her 1996 collection, *The Crack in Everything*, where among other poems of beauty and survival she includes "The Mastectomy Poems," created from her own experience with breast cancer. "You never think it will happen to you, / What happens every day to other women," she begins. In them, Ostriker fulfills her own poetic mandate: "to press the spirit forth / Unrepentant, struggling to praise / Our hopeless bodies, our hopeless world" ("The Book of Life").

Most recently, Ostriker's poetry and criticism have focused on her identity as both woman and Jew. She states in *People of the Book: Thirty Scholars Reflect on Their Jewish Identity* that she feels "a preoccupation amounting to obsession with Judaism, the Bible, God." In "Five Uneasy Pieces," Ostriker places her current work "in the tradition of midrash," retelling the Biblical narratives in search of a spiritual home within Judaism. *The Nakedness of the Fathers* (1994) is a remarkable testament to the passion and intelligence of Ostriker's career, ample evidence of the poetic and critical distances she has traveled and a clue to where she may be heading. Refuting accusations of blasphemy, witchery, ignorance or insanity, Ostriker writes:

> I remember things, and sometimes I remember
> My time when I was powerful, bringing birth
> My time when I was just, composing law
> My time playing before the throne
> When my name was woman of valor
> When my name was wisdom
> And what if I say the Torah is
> My well of living waters
> Mine

Source: Anne F. Herzog, "Ostriker, Alicia," in *Contemporary Women Poets*, edited by Pamela L. Shelton, St. James Press, 1998, pp. 271–73.

Sources

Cook, Pamela, "Secrets and Manifestos: Alicia Ostriker's Poetry and Politics," in *Borderlands: Texas Poetry Review*, Vol. 2, Spring 1993, pp. 80–86.

Heller, Janet Ruth, "Exploring the Depths of Relationships in Alicia Ostriker's Poetry," in *Literature and Psychology*, Vol. 38, No. 1–2, 1992, pp. 71–83.

Ostriker, Alicia, "His Speed and Strength," in *The Little Space: Poems Selected and New, 1968–1998*, University of Pittsburgh Press, 1998, p. 44.

———, *Stealing the Language: The Emergence of Women's Poetry in America*, Beacon Press, 1986.

———, *Writing Like a Woman*, University of Michigan Press, 1983.

Roberts, J. M., *Twentieth Century: The History of the World, 1901 to 2000*, Penguin Books, 1999, p. 673.

Rosenberg, Judith Pierce, "Profile: Alicia Suskin Ostriker," in *Belles Lettres*, Vol. 8, No. 3, Spring 1993, pp. 26–29.

Williams, Amy, "Alicia Ostriker," in *Dictionary of Literary Biography*, Vol. 120, *American Poets Since World War II, Third Series*, Gale Research, 1992, pp. 239–42.

Further Reading

Helgesen, Sally, *The Female Advantage: Women's Ways of Leadership*, Currency/Doubleday, 1995.
> Helgesen explores how women's management styles differ from their male counterparts. The author says that women, who tend to lead via a relationship web, are better suited for the modern business environment than men, who tend to lead via old-fashioned hierarchies. The book also provides in-depth profiles of four women executives who became successful as a result of their female qualities of leadership.

Hill, Gareth S., *Masculine and Feminine: The Natural Flow of Opposites in the Psyche*, Shambhala Publications, 1992.

This book offers a comprehensive analysis of the masculine and the feminine, drawing on the original psychological theories of Carl Jung as well as on non-Jungian approaches.

Kallen, Stuart A., ed., *The 1980s*, Cultural History of the United States through the Decades series, Lucent Books, 1999.

Each book in this series examines a specific decade through theme-based chapters, which place events in a cultural context. Among other topics, the 1980s volume discusses the Reagan presidency, the fall of Communism, the rise of Wall Street and corporate power, and the computer revolution. The book also includes a bibliography and a detailed chronology of events.

Moir, Anne, and David Jessel, *Brain Sex: The Real Difference between Men and Women*, Lyle Stuart, 1991.

In this groundbreaking book, Moir, a geneticist, and Jessel, a BBC-TV writer-producer, discuss the differences between male and female brains, identifying the innate abilities of each.

Schneir, Miriam, ed., *Feminism in Our Time: The Essential Writings, World War II to the Present*, Vintage Books, 1994.

This anthology focuses on contemporary writings from the second half of the twentieth century and features fifty selections, including many excerpts from longer works. Schneir also provides commentary on the writings.

Ithaka

C. P. Cavafy
1911

The first version of "Ithaka" was probably written in 1894. Cavafy revised the poem in 1910, and it was first published in 1911. The first English translation was published in 1924, and there have been a number of different translations since then. The poem can be found in Cavafy's *Collected Poems*, translated by Edmund Keeley and Philip Sherrard, edited by George Savidis, Princeton University Press, 1980.

"Ithaka" is an unrhymed poem of five stanzas that employ conversational, everyday language. The narrator, probably a man who has traveled a lot, addresses either Odysseus, the hero of Homer's epic poem the *Odyssey*, or an imaginary modern traveler or reader. The narrator tells the traveler that what is really important is not Ithaka, the island home that was the goal of Odysseus's years of wandering, but the journey itself. It is the journey that must be fully enjoyed at every moment, using all the resources of senses and intellect, because the goal itself is likely to be disappointing.

Cavafy enjoys a reputation as one of the finest of modern Greek poets. "Ithaka" is one of his best-known poems and is considered to express his outlook on life.

Author Biography

Constantine Peter Cavafy was born on April 17, 1863, in Alexandria, Egypt. He was a Greek citizen, the ninth and last child of Peter (an importer and exporter) and Hariklia Cavafy. His parents had settled in Alexandria in the mid-1850s. After his father died in 1870, Cavafy's mother moved the family to Liverpool, England, where her two eldest sons managed the family business.

From the age of nine to sixteen, Cavafy lived in England, where he developed a love for the writing of William Shakespeare, Robert Browning, and Oscar Wilde. The family business did not prosper, and the family was compelled to move back to Alexandria in 1880. Two years later, Cavafy's mother and some of his eight siblings moved again, to Constantinople. It was in Constantinople that Cavafy wrote his first poems.

In 1885, having received little formal education, Cavafy eventually rejoined his older brothers in Alexandria and became a newspaper correspondent for *Telegraphos*. In 1888, he began working as his brother's assistant at the Egyptian Stock Exchange. Within four years, he became a clerk at the Ministry of Public Works. Cavafy remained at the ministry for the next thirty years, eventually becoming its assistant director. He retired in 1922.

Although he began publishing poems in 1896 and continued to do so until 1932, a year before his death, it was a long time before Cavafy received much literary recognition beyond Alexandria. In his lifetime, he did not offer a single volume of poetry for sale. He printed pamphlets of his work privately and distributed them to friends and relatives. Only in his later years did he become sufficiently well known for Western visitors to seek him out in Alexandria.

In 1926, Cavafy received the Order of the Phoenix from the Greek government. In 1930, he was appointed to the International Committee for the Rupert Brooke memorial statue that was placed on the island of Skyros.

On April 29, 1933, eleven years after leaving the ministry, Cavafy died of cancer of the larynx.

The first collected edition of his poems was published in 1935 and first translated into English in 1948. In subsequent years, Cavafy became recognized as one of the foremost Greek poets of the twentieth century.

Poem Text

As you set out for Ithaka
hope your road is a long one,
full of adventure, full of discovery.
Laistrygonians, Cyclops,
angry Poseidon—don't be afraid of them: 5
you'll never find things like that on your way
as long as you keep your thoughts raised high,
as long as a rare excitement
stirs your spirit and your body.
Laistrygonians, Cyclops,   10
wild Poseidon—you won't encounter them
unless you bring them along inside your soul,
unless your soul sets them up in front of you.

Hope your road is a long one.
May there be many summer mornings when,   15
with what pleasure, what joy,
you enter harbors you're seeing for the first time:
may you stop at Phoenician trading stations
to buy fine things,
mother of pearl and coral, amber and ebony,   20
sensual perfume of every kind—
as many sensual perfumes as you can;
and may you visit many Egyptian cities
to learn and go on learning from their scholars.

Keep Ithaka always in your mind.   25
Arriving there is what you're destined for.
But don't hurry the journey at all.
Better if it lasts for years,
so you're old by the time you reach the island,
wealthy with all you've gained on the way,   30
not expecting Ithaka to make you rich.
Ithaka gave you the marvelous journey.
Without her you wouldn't have set out.
She has nothing left to give you now.

And if you find her poor, Ithaka won't have fooled you.   35
Wise as you will have become, so full of experience,
you'll have understood by then what these Ithakas mean.

Poem Summary

Stanza 1

"Ithaka" begins with the poet addressing the reader directly in the second person, as "you," and offering a piece of advice. The character addressed is not identified. He could be Odysseus, the hero of Homer's epic poem the *Odyssey*, but the poet is also addressing any reader of the poem.

The poet states that as the traveler sets out on his journey, he must hope that it is a long one, full of adventure and discovery. The destination of the journey is Ithaka. Ithaka is the island off the western coast of Greece to which Odysseus returned after the Trojan war. Odysseus's journey was a long and difficult one. It was ten years before he was able to rejoin his wife Penelope in Ithaka. However, Ithaka in this poem can also be understood as the destination of any journey, and it can be further understood metaphorically as a journey through life.

In line 4, the poet mentions two of the obstacles that Odysseus encountered in the *Odyssey*. First are the Laistrygonians, who were half-men and half-giants, who devoured many of Odysseus's crew. Second are the Cyclops, who were giants with just one eye, placed in the middle of their foreheads. One of the Cyclops, Polyphemus, took Odysseus and his men prisoner and ate six of them before Odysseus escaped with the remaining six men.

In line 5, the poet mentions another of the forces that obstructed Odysseus's return. This is Poseidon, who was the Greek god of the sea. He is referred to as angry because in the *Odyssey* Poseidon was angry that Odysseus had blinded Polyphemus, who was Poseidon's son.

In the *Odyssey*, each of these three types of beings are powerful and seek to delay or destroy Odysseus. But, in line 5 of "Ithaka," the poet bids his reader not to be afraid of them. In lines 6 and 7, he explains why. If the traveler keeps his thoughts "raised high," he will never encounter any challenge resembling those monsters. The poet is implying that it is always necessary to be optimistic and hopeful.

Lines 8–11 repeat the same idea with one variation. This time, the poet explains that Laistrygonians, Cyclops, or Poseidon will not appear as long as the traveler's spirit and body are stirred by a "rare excitement." In another translation of the poem, this phrase is rendered as "fine emotion"; yet another translation uses the phrase "noble emotion." The idea is that in order to ensure that he is not waylaid by monsters, the traveler must always continue to experience the thrill of being alive.

Lines 12 and 13 add a caveat: such beings will only appear if the traveler summons them up from within his own soul, if he allows them to dwell inside him.

Stanza 2

The poet returns to the hope expressed in line 2 of the first stanza, that the traveler's journey (whether that of Odysseus or any reader of the poem) is a long one. He hopes, in line 2, that there will be many summers when the traveler feels joy on the journey, when he see places he has never seen before.

The poet then imagines various places where a person might stop, such as a Phoenician trading station. Phoenicia was the coastal district of ancient Syria and is now the coast of modern Lebanon. Its ports were centers of trade in the ancient world. The poet states that many beautiful things may be purchased there, including precious stones such as mother of pearl and coral, and every kind of perfume. The poet also hopes the reader may visit Egyptian cities and learn from the scholars who live there. In the ancient world, Egypt was a center of learning, especially its capital city, Alexandria, which was one of the largest cities in the world and contained the largest library.

Stanza 3

The first line of this stanza contains another piece of advice. Odysseus, or any traveler on a journey, must always keep Ithaka in mind, because it is his or her final destination. The traveler will certainly arrive there. But, says the poet, do not hurry the journey. It is better if the journey lasts for years, so that the traveler is old by the time he reaches home and also wealthy from all he has accumulated on his travels. Then, he will not expect Ithaka to make him rich.

The poet states that it is enough that Ithaka was the reason for making the journey in the first place. Without it, Odysseus or other voyagers would never have started. When Odysseus finally does arrive, the city has lost its charm for him; he finds less pleasure in being there then what he had hoped for and imagined.

Stanza 4

The poet reemphasizes the message of the previous stanza. If the traveler, having arrived home in Ithaka, finds it to be a poor place, it does not mean that Ithaka has been deceptive. The traveler has not been fooled because he will have become wise and full of experience. He will therefore know what is meant by Ithaka, and by all destinations—all Ithakas—that people strive to reach. The implication is that he will have learned that the prize is all in the experience of the journey, not the final destination.

Themes

Life as a Journey

The theme of the poem may be summed up in one phrase: it is better to journey than to arrive. Life should not be wasted in always contemplating the goal of one's endeavors or in building up hopes and schemes for the future but in enjoying the journey. An obsession with the final goal can blind a

Topics for Further Study

- Compare and contrast Cavafy's "Ithaka" with Lord Alfred Tennyson's "Ulysses." In what ways are the two poems similar and how do they differ?

- Read the sections of the *Odyssey* in which the Laistrygonians and the Cyclops appear. What do you think these creatures represented to Cavafy? Why did Cavafy choose to mention these, of all the obstacles that Odysseus encountered, in his poem? Write an essay explaining your choices.

- It is often said that "life is a journey, not a destination." What is meant by this phrase and what meaning might it have in your own life?

- Write your own poem to a modern Odysseus, or any traveler, giving him what you think is the most appropriate advice for his journey. Use the form of Cavafy's poem, including the use of the second person, as a guide.

- Describe a recent achievement of your own in any field of endeavor, splitting the account into two sections: the process (the journey) and the completed task (the destination). Decide which was more valuable to you, the journey or the destination. Can you think of an occasion where you did not achieve your intended goal but still found value in the process of trying to achieve it?

person to the real business of living, which is to enjoy every minute that is available.

There is also the hint that life can be disappointing. The goals people strive for, their Ithakas, may not yield what they hoped for. Therefore, it is better not to have expectations. The poet counsels that there is no pot of gold at the end of the rainbow: Ithaka may be poor, with nothing to give. Perhaps, he also implies that a person should not have lofty ideals or strive to realize perfection in life, whether for oneself or for society (as a political activist might, for example).

Yet, it is human to have ambitions and expectations, to strive to achieve. As the poet states in stanza 3, without having an "Ithaka," a goal, in mind, there would be no reason to act at all, no reason to embark on the journey of life.

The poet has a recipe for enjoying the journey that involves the cultivation of a certain habit of mind. The whole person—body, mind, spirit, even soul—must be fully engaged in the life it is living. A person must keep his or her "thoughts raised high," which means that the mind must not give in to melancholy or disappointment or the sordid aspects of life. The poet may also have in mind the contemplation of art, which leads the mind to the higher levels of the human spirit, rather than allowing it to sink to the depths of which it is capable.

Another prerequisite for happiness on the journey is what the poet calls "rare excitement." This might be explained as a certain attitude to the experiences that life produces. A person must cultivate the ability to respond to situations and experiences as if they were entirely new and fresh, never before seen, and therefore an object of wonder and delight. The opposite would be to respond in a tired, mundane way, influenced by habit and custom.

The last part of the recipe for a fulfilling journey is to enjoy the sensual aspects of life ("as many sensual perfumes as you can"), to value beautiful things (symbolized by the precious stones), and to cultivate the intellect. The latter is suggested by the advice to learn and "go on learning" from the scholars in Egypt. The way this is phrased is significant. A person can never say that he or she has learned enough. Learning is an ongoing process with no final end in sight.

The advice given here could be summed up as the need to use everything that a human being has been given to perceive, enjoy, and understand the world. The aim is to live in the actualities of the present moment, not in the imagined future.

The Odyssey

Cavafy puts all this advice in context by setting it against the background of the *Odyssey*, one of the world's great travel narratives. He reverses the meaning of the *Odyssey* while at the same time advancing a psychological interpretation of some of its episodes.

In Homer's epic poem, Odysseus always longs for home. He does not enjoy his long journey, which is full of perils. Even the sensual delights and the prospect of immortality offered him by the enchantress Kalypso mean nothing to him. He continues to look to his home in Ithaka for peace, security, and love.

In "Ithaka," however, the reverse is true: it is the journey that is valued; the destination is dismissed as of no importance. The first lines of the poem clearly show the ironic way Cavafy treats the *Odyssey*:

> As you set out for Ithaka,
> hope your road is a long one,
> full of adventure, full of discovery.

This is the opposite of what Odysseus was hoping for. He wanted a quick voyage home, not one full of adventure.

Cavafy also suggests that the monsters Odysseus encounters are all creations of the human mind. Scholars identify the land of the Laistrygonians with Sicily's West Coast and the land of the Cyclops with an area near Naples called the Phlegrean Fields. In "Ithaka," however, the dwelling places of these monsters are not physical places but states of mind. If a man follows the poet's prescription for happiness, such personal demons will not arise in his psyche. The human mind has the power to create them and to dissolve them.

Style

Metaphor

Although the island of Ithaka will always be associated with the homeland of Odysseus, in this poem, Cavafy uses the place name in an additional sense. Just as the journey to Ithaka is a metaphor for the human journey through life, so Ithaka is a metaphor for all destinations. It represents all the goals and ideals that humans strive for, all the expectations of a reward to be received in the future for actions performed in the present. This metaphorical meaning of Ithaka is clear not only from the context in which the word is used but also because the last line refers to Ithaka not in the singular but in plural, "Ithakas."

Repetition

Apart from this overarching use of the journey as a metaphor for human life, Cavafy uses little figurative language. The language has a conversational flavor, and the poem employs the rhythms of natural speech. Cavafy's main rhetorical device in the poem is repetition. In the first stanza, the poet repeats the names of the characters from the *Odyssey*—Laistrygonians, Cyclops, and Poseidon—in order to emphasize how they may be avoided. The repetition of "as long as" in lines 7 and 8 of stanza 1 is echoed by the repetition of "unless" at the beginning of lines 12 and 13. The effect suggests that the traveler needs repeated reinforcement before he is ready to hear and absorb the message the poet offers.

A similar effect is gained by the repetition in the second stanza of "sensual perfume" in lines 21 and 22. It helps to drive home a theme of the poem, that fulfillment lies in the sensual experiences of the moment, not an imagined goal in the future.

Historical Context

Modern Greek Literature

When Greece was under Turkish rule in the eighteenth century, Greek literature virtually disappeared. It was awakened following the Greek War of Independence (1821–1827). As Greek national pride grew, there was a strong movement amongst writers to use the demotic form of the Greek language. Demotic is the popular form of Greek used by the ordinary person. However, there were also many writers who passionately believed in the preservation of the classical literary language. The controversial debate continued throughout the nineteenth century and into the twentieth. Many Greek intellectuals argued that using the demotic language was the only way to preserve Greek literature and develop Greek culture. But, feelings ran high on both sides. In 1903, university students rioted in Athens when a translation of the *New Testament* in demotic Greek was serialized in a newspaper. More riots followed several years later when Aeschylus's ancient Greek trilogy the *Oresteia* was performed in demotic Greek. The Greek government did not recognize the demotic form of the language until 1917, and only then was it taught in schools.

Cavafy aligned himself for the most part with the movement for demotic Greek, which is the language used in "Ithaka." He was a contributor to the magazine of a youth group called *Nea Zoe* (*New Life*), which existed to promote demotic Greek literature. Cavafy's poetry appeared in *Nea Zoe* for a decade. However, Cavafy also valued the purist, or classical form of the language, which was part of his family and class heritage.

Alexandria

Alexandria is a cosmopolitan city with a long history. Not only is it the city where Cavafy wrote "Ithaka," it is probably one of the unnamed

Compare & Contrast

- **Ancient Times:** A thousand years before Alexandria is founded, a small Egyptian town called Rhakotis exists at the same site. Alexander the Great founds Alexandria in 331 B.C.

  Cavafy's Lifetime: In the nineteenth century, Alexandria grows in size, wealth, and importance as a port city. But, in 1882, the British fleet bombards it. This marks the beginning of British dominance in Egypt, which lasts well into the twentieth century.

  Today: Alexandria is the second largest city and the main port of Egypt. It has a population of four million and is the most ethnically and culturally diverse of the Egyptian cities.

- **Ancient Times:** Homer and the later poets and dramatists of ancient Greece become the foundation of the Western literary tradition.

  Cavafy's Lifetime: Contemporary Greek literature is little known outside the borders of Greece.

  Today: Cavafy enjoys a worldwide reputation as one of Greece's finest poets. The Greek novelist Nikos Kazantzakis also has an international reputation, and two Greek poets, George Seferis and Odysseus Elytis, are winners of the Nobel Prize in literature.

- **Ancient Times:** Civilization exists on Ithaca in 2700 B.C., as shown by pottery fragments. This is fifteen hundred years before Odysseus is said to have ruled the kingdom. The kingdom of Odysseus probably includes the neighboring island of Kefalonia as well as Ithaca.

  Cavafy's Lifetime: In 1864, Ithaca finally breaks free of British rule and unites with Greece. This initiates a period, lasting up to the 1930s, in which the island is systematically excavated. In 1930, a female mask of clay with Odysseus's name engraved on it is found in Louizos cave in Polis. In another excavation, at the Aetos area, archeologists find ruins of ancient temples, everyday articles and objects of worship from the ninth, eighth, and seventh centuries B.C. Many different types of coins from the fourth and third centuries B.C. are also found, some of which refer to Odysseus as well as to various gods.

  Today: Ithaca has a population of only two thousand people, but it offers the tourist familiar with the *Odyssey* many attractions, including the bay of Dexia (Homer's harbor of Phorkys, where the Phaecians left the sleeping Odysseus on the beach); a ruined site known locally as Odysseus's Castle, and the Plateau of Marathia, where Odysseus's loyal servant Eumaeus kept his swine. A statue of Odysseus stands in the village of Stavros.

Egyptian cities referred to in the poem as a seat of learning in ancient times.

Alexandria did not exist in the time of Odysseus or Homer (who wrote about events several centuries in the past). It was built in 331 B.C., on the orders of Alexander the Great. After Alexander died, the Ptolemies ruled Egypt for several generations, and this was a glorious period in the history of the city. It was known for its architecture and as a center for natural sciences, mathematics, and literary scholarship. In 250 B.C., the state-supported library contained four hundred thousand volumes, the largest collection in the ancient world. Cavafy wrote a poem, "The Glory of the Ptolemies," in praise of that period in the history of the city.

In Cavafy's lifetime, Alexandria had largely lost the glories of its past. After it was bombarded by the British in 1882, it fell primarily under British control. The Greek community there was in decline, although E. M. Forster, the English novelist who lived in Alexandria during World War I (he was also a friend of Cavafy), was still able to write in his *Alexandria: A History and a Guide* (1922) that whatever elements of modern culture could be found in Alexandria were due to its Greek community.

Critical Overview

"Ithaka" has long been recognized as one of Cavafy's finest poems, and one that expresses his outlook on life. It was first admired by T. S. Eliot, who published the first translation of "Ithaka" into English in his literary periodical *Criterion* in 1924. Since then, almost every writer on Cavafy has had something to say about the poem, which has appeared in at least four different English translations, each of which contains subtle differences.

Jane Lagoudis Pinchin, in *Alexandria Still*, evaluates the different translations of the poem, including the first published translation, by George Valassopoulo, and the translations by Rae Dalven and John Mavrogordato. Pinchin prefers Mavrogordato's version of the last line of the poem ("You will have understood the meaning of an Ithaka") to Dalven's version ("You must surely have understood by then what Ithacas mean"). Pinchin comments, "Dalven *does* sound a bit impatient with her dim voyager."

Edmund Keeley, in *Cavafy's Alexandria: Study of a Myth in Progress*, points out that Cavafy "turn[s] the myths of history around to show us what may lie behind the facade most familiar to us."

C. M. Bowra comments briefly that the poem is "a lesson on all long searches." He also notes that in this and certain other poems of Cavafy, the "instructive, moral note is never quite absent . . . and gives them a certain stiffness and formality."

Peter Bien argues that the theme of "Ithaka," that the process is more important than the goal, sounds affirmative but is in fact a tragic view of life. He states, "Though affirmative in spirit, it is at the same time rigorously pessimistic, for it denies as illusory all the comforts invented by man: eternity, order, decorum, absolute good, morality, justice."

For C. Capri-Karka, in *Love and the Symbolic Journey in the Poetry of Cavafy, Eliot, and Seferis*, the poem "presents sensual pleasure as the center of man's existence." Using passages from other poems by Cavafy, Capri-Karka suggests that the precious stones and other fine things that the poet urges the voyager to collect are symbolic of erotic pleasure.

"Ithaka" has resonated with readers and scholars for generations. It was read aloud at the funeral of Jacqueline Kennedy Onassis in 1994.

Odysseus encounters Sirens on his journey home to Ithaka

Criticism

Bryan Aubrey

Aubrey holds a Ph.D. in English and has published many articles on twentieth century literature. In this essay, Aubrey discusses the range of possible meanings implied by the term Ithaka and compares the poem to Tennyson's "Ulysses" and W. H. Auden's "Atlantis."

It is often said that human beings live mostly in the past or in the future, but never the present. As individuals, humans spend much of their available mental energy analyzing, dissecting, and often regretting the past, or planning, dreaming about, and often fearing the future. An observer from outer space, were such a being privy to the workings of the human mind, might be baffled as to why these denizens of planet Earth exert themselves and attempt to work their will upon events that do not in fact exist, since the past has vanished into nothing and the future is only an idea in a myriad of separate individual minds.

Well aware of this tendency, the narrator of "Ithaka" attempts to persuade Odysseus, or any modern voyager on the sea of life, to abandon the

> "The tone not only of 'Ithaka' but of many other Cavafy poems suggests not the ecstasy of such moments but an awareness that they must always pass and live on only in the memory."

mirage of living in the future. He seeks to persuade him of the richness of the present moment, the "now" of immediate sensual experience. Everything else is likely to disappoint and is in a sense unreal, a mere mental construct not grounded in true experience.

Yet, "Ithaka" does not strike the reader as a joyful poem. In spite of its approving nods to the marvels to be found in the Phoenician trading port and to the pleasure to be gained from the moment the voyager enters a harbor he has never seen before, it seems tinged with melancholy and world-weariness. In the narrator's tone, there is something of the wistfulness, the regretful wisdom of the old that looks back on pleasures lost or not taken and now forever beyond reach. One can almost hear the narrator saying he wished he had valued more highly that "rare excitement," those precious stones, those sensual perfumes, when he himself was young.

What are "these Ithakas" of which the narrator holds such a low opinion? The more the term is pondered, the more it expands into multiple levels of meaning. For the narrator, Ithakas would seem to be all the things that people invent to postpone real living, defined as being in the sensual moment, looking neither forward nor backward. All Utopias or paradises that people dream of attaining or building are types of Ithakas. Ithakas too are philosophies that build metaphysical systems about the origins and goals and higher purposes of human life. They are, one suspects the narrator would say, mere stories, clever inventions, that take men and women away from the real stuff of life, the immediate experience of being alive in the flesh, now, sensitive to beauty, with five senses receiving in every moment the fullness that life has to offer.

This is not a worldview that has much time for religion either. If there is nothing of value other than the immediate sensual experience, then it would seem that the kind of moral code that religions prescribe is not applicable. Equally unnecessary would be the variety of religious beliefs in an afterlife, since an afterlife would surely qualify as another Ithaka—something longed for at the end of a journey.

The idea for expressing such thoughts by means of the *Odyssey* might have been suggested to Cavafy by a passage in Dante's *Divine Comedy* or by the poem "Ulysses," by Victorian English poet Alfred, Lord Tennyson. In Canto XXVI of Dante's *Hell* (Book I of the *Divine Comedy*), Dante depicts Ulysses (Odysseus) as being restless and dissatisfied after his return to Ithaka. Domesticity does not satisfy him, so he rounds up his old comrades and sets sail for one more round of exploration and adventure. After seeing many more wonders, his ship finally goes down in a storm, and he is drowned. Dante places Ulysses in Hell because he advised others to practice trickery and fraud. He was, after all, known in the *Odyssey* as the crafty Odysseus, and it was he who devised the stratagem of the Trojan Horse and also advised the Greeks to steal the sacred statue of Palladium on which the safety of Troy depended.

Tennyson took up this theme of the eternal explorer in "Ulysses," which was one of two poems he wrote based on the *Odyssey*. (The other was "The Lotos–Eaters.") Tennyson's Ulysses, like Dante's, has discovered to his cost what the narrator of Cavafy's "Ithaka" urged: the journey is always much more rewarding than the destination:

> It little profits that an idle king,
> By this still hearth, among these barren crags,
> Matched with an aged wife, I mete and dole
> Unequal laws unto a savage race,
> That hoard, and sleep, and feed, and know not me.

The reality of Ulysses' life back home in Ithaka seems hardly worth the many years of voyaging that it took him to get there. "She [Ithaka] has nothing left to give you now," said the narrator of "Ithaka," and here is the proof. Ulysses is fed up. He is an adventurer by nature, and he cannot sit still in peace and contentment for long. The journeying is all.

The parallel with "Ithaka" is a close one, but there is a difference. In Tennyson's poem, Ulysses is motivated by a desire for knowledge rather than sensual experience. He desires "To follow knowledge like a sinking star, / Beyond the utmost bound of human thought." Although Cavafy's narrator does indeed value the store of learning to be found amongst the scholars in Egyptian cities, the emphasis in the poem is more on sensual enjoyment than intellectual endeavor. This is not so prominent in Tennyson's poem, although one can imagine the narrator of "Ithaka" applauding the declaration Tennyson gives to his ancient mariner: "I will drink / Life to the lees." This shows that, as the wise old narrator of "Ithaka" promised, he has understood the meaning of all Ithakas. The voyage is the thing. Destinations disappoint.

If Tennyson may have been an influence on Cavafy's poem, Cavafy's "Ithaka" has in its turn worked its influence on another twentieth century poet who admired his work, W. H. Auden. Auden's poem "Atlantis" follows the same idea as "Ithaka," although the destination is not Odysseus's island but the mythical lost civilization of Atlantis. Auden adopts the same form Cavafy used for "Ithaka," employing a narrator to directly address the traveler in the second person, offering advice and instruction. Edmund Keeley, in his book *Cavafy's Alexandria: Study of a Myth in Progress* defines this form, which Cavafy used several times in his poems of this period, as "didactic monologue."

Like Cavafy's advice about Egyptian scholars, Auden's narrator advises his ancient traveler to consult the "witty scholars" if storms drive him ashore in Ionia. (He offers no tips, however, on how to avoid stirring up the anger of Poseidon.) More relevant is the third stanza of Auden's poem, which advises the traveler what he should do if he is forced ashore at Thrace. This region east of Macedonia was home of the worshipers of Dionysus, the god of wine and ecstasy:

> If, later, you run aground
> Among the headlands of Thrace
> Where with torches all night long
> A naked barbaric race
> Leaps frenziedly to the sound
> Of conch and dissonant gong;
> On that stony savage shore
> Strip off your clothes and dance, for
> Unless you are capable
> Of forgetting completely
> About Atlantis, you will
> Never finish your journey.

Here is the "rare excitement," the sensual enjoyment, that Cavafy's narrator advises his Odysseus to seek, in which thoughts of the destination are swallowed up in the immediacy of the moment. One can almost see the narrator of "Ithaka" smiling his approval. And yet it would probably be a wry smile, tinged with regret. The tone not only of "Ithaka" but of many other Cavafy poems suggests not the ecstasy of such moments but an awareness that they must always pass and live on only in the memory. It is this that gives many of Cavafy's poems a touch of melancholy, of yearning for what once was or might have been: "My life's joy and incense: recollection of those hours / when I found and captured pleasure as I wanted it" ("To Sensual Pleasure").

This "incense" is the equivalent of the "sensual perfume" of "Ithaka." It does not stay. Ithaka beckons, although Ithaka has nothing to offer that can match it.

Source: Bryan Aubrey, Critical Essay on "Ithaka," in *Poetry for Students*, Gale, 2003.

Roderick Beaton

In the following essay, Beaton discusses the treatment and effect of time in Cavafy's poems.

Solemnly asked his opinion of his own work, C. P. Cavafy towards the end of his life is said to have replied, 'Cavafy in my opinion is an ultra-modern poet, a poet of future generations.' History has proved him right, but the tone of the reply also reveals an important ingredient of the unique poetic voice that is Cavafy's: a gentle mockery of all pretension, even that of the poet interviewed about his own work, and a light-hearted concealment of his true self at the very moment when he appears about to lay his cards on the table. 'Cavafy,' he says, not 'I,' as if 'Cavafy' were someone different.

Cavafy's poetry is distinguished by many subtle forms of irony, and also by an intriguing self-effacement in poems that purport to tell of personal experience and feeling. The subject matter of his poems is equally unusual. Approximately half of what that he published in his lifetime (consisting of 154 fairly short poems) and a similar proportion of those published posthumously, are devoted to subjects taken from Greek history, chiefly between 340 BC and AD 1453, while the remainder deal more or less explicitly with homosexual encounters against a backdrop of contemporary Alexandria.

Cavafy's uniqueness has posed a problem for critics, for whom he continues to exercise a profound fascination. To many his erotic poetry is a disreputable appendage to more 'sublime' poetry dedicated to the Greek past, but Cavafy's uncompromisingly 'historical' treatment of that past has also disconcerted many. And those critics who have not chosen to ignore the erotic poems have been hard put to identify the source of powerful emotion, felt by many readers, in response to poems from which all reference to love is lacking, and the sordidness and triviality of the sexual encounters evoked are freely confessed.

> "Time takes away and alienates all real experience, but through art the poet can sometimes regain it in the creation of a poem, though what is regained is both more and less than the original."

The common denominator between Cavafy's two principal preoccupations, the distant Greek past and contemporary homosexual experiences, is time, which plays a major role in both types of poem. Often it appears that the true subject of the erotic poems is not the experience described so much as its loss to the passage of time. Time takes away and alienates all real experience, but through art the poet can sometimes regain it in the creation of a poem, though what is regained is both more and less than the original. More, because, as the poet frankly says in several of these poems, he is free to touch up reality in the imaginative act of writing; less, because, no matter how 'perfect' an experience can become thus imaginatively recreated, it is only imaginary, the real thing remaining lost to the past. This sense of 'lost to the past' is central, too, to Cavafy's historical poems, in which he juxtaposes vivid pictures of flesh-and-blood, fallible human beings with a chillingly historical sense of how remote they are, and how futile are these people's preoccupations now.

In their treatment of time, *all* Cavafy's poems can be said to belong to this third type, into which he once said his work could be divided, namely 'philosophical' poetry.

Source: Roderick Beaton, "Cavafy, C. P.," in *Reference Guide to World Literature*, 2d ed., edited by Lesley Henderson, St. James Press, 1995, pp. 249–50.

C. Capri-Karka

In the following introduction to her dissertation, Capri-Karka discusses "Ithaca" as a turning point in Cavafy's work, one where the poet began to be more open about his personal life—specifically, his homosexuality.

"Ithaca" is considered not only central for the theme of the journey but also the "brain" of Cavafy's whole work—if one can extend here the symbolism used by Stuart Gilbert for the ninth episode, of James Joyce's *Ulysses*. It is for this reason that Cavafy is referred to by many critics as "the poet of 'Ithaca.'" The poem works on two levels: on the most immediate, Cavafy emphasizes sensual pleasure and celebrates the journey from harbor to harbor; on the more general level, one can see the poem as a condensed expression of Cavafy's view of the world. To use Rex Warner's words for it, "what is emphasized in 'Ithaca' is the immense value of individual experience rather than the strained pursuit of an ideal or the heights and depths of cataclysmic events."

"Ithaca," published in 1911, marks a turning point in Cavafy's poetic development, as pointed out by I. A. Sareyannis, G. Seferis and G. Savidis. The poet himself drew a line separating his work "before 1911" from the rest. The publication of "Ithaca" coincides with Cavafy's decision to start speaking more freely about himself. Actually, as we know from the poet's personal notes, published only recently, Cavafy had come to terms with his homosexuality, or had been "liberated," as he put it, as early as 1902, but recognizing the power of prejudice he did not dare to reveal the truth until much later; and when he did, it was a very gradual process. Poems unequivocally identifying his erotic preferences appeared only after 1918. Several of the poems written before 1910 were not published until many years later and some were not published at all during the poet's lifetime.

Of the poems that he did publish before 1910 very few can be considered erotic, and they are usually symbolic or deal with abstractions ("Longings," "Voices"). Another group of poems published during this period is related to the symbolic journey in the sense that they express an unfulfilled desire for escape and a journey. They are cryptic and symbolic; the predominant mood is one of fear, frustration and despair, but it is hidden under a restrained tone and a laconic style that translations cannot fully convey. They deal with various forms of imprisonment, frustrated hopes for escape and liberation, external and internal conflicts, etc. In the "Walls," the protagonist finds himself imprisoned with no chance of escape. In the "Trojans" and "The Windows" there is some hope of liberation, but it does not last long. In these poems, Cavafy presents man cut off from the world, alienated and isolated by walls, besieged like the Trojans, fearing invasion from outside as a constant threat, and with only one desperate thought: escape.

This desire for an escape, a journey to another place and a new beginning is expressed in the first stanza of "The City," but in the second the journey turns into a nightmare as the persona realizes that the city, like the Furies, would pursue him wherever he goes.

A comparison of these poems, published before 1910, to those also written during the same period but published much later or not published by the poet at all reveals the agonizing process of gradual liberation that Cavafy had to go through before he could set out on his journey to Ithaca.

The date for Cavafy's personal or private liberation is set, as already mentioned, at 1902, on the basis of a note written in 1902 by the poet saying "I have been liberated." However, an examination of his poems suggests that this is an arbitrary date and that his change in attitude, both private and public, was very gradual and extended over a period of several years.

One may actually wonder why Cavafy, who according to his biographers was a homosexual from a very early age, was "liberated" only at the age of forty. The answer must be found in his background, which was classical Greek and Christian. The poet once said that he never had any metaphysical tendencies, but, as his biographer R. Liddell remarks, Cavafy "was not enough of a materialist to be without fear of the unknown." Growing up and living in a family and a society that functions within certain laws and convictions results in a conditioning of the individual that cannot be easily dismissed. One can logically reach a decision, but erasing from the subconscious the accumulated fears, guilt and insecurity is a very slow and painful process, especially when it takes place under the constant persecution of a society not ready to accept the change. It is true that Cavafy grew up in Alexandria, where the mixture of races, nationalities and religions created a certain neutrality, but the moral principles of his immediate environment were more restrictive. Had he lived in Greece, he would probably never have been liberated. The anguish involved in this process cannot be conceived by modern generations which have grown up in a more permissive society where the old values have lost much of their meaning.

One can find many indications of the fact that Cavafy still carried his subconscious burden of guilt in poems written long after 1902 and published after 1911 or not published at all, such as "He Swears" (written in 1905 and published in 1915). These indications gradually disappear in his later poetry. This does not mean of course that these poems do not represent significant steps toward liberation, as Cavafy became more and more explicit about his erotic tendencies. A number of poems written mostly before 1902 and dealing with historical or esthetic subjects contain some carefully worded hints about the poet's sexual preferences. For instance, within the context of esthetic abstractions are included expressions of admiration for Greek gods or heroes considered as prototypes of male beauty. One can mention in this group "Before the State of Endymion," "One of their Gods," "Sculptor of Tyana," "The Glory of the Ptolemies," "Ionic," and "Orophernes," all published in the period between 1911 and 1918.

Much more explicit and very significant for the evaluation of the way in which Cavafy really felt at that time are some of the poems written during the same period but never released for publication by the poet during his lifetime. In "Strengthening the Spirit," for instance, we find the first expression of the idea on which "Ithaca" was built, that "pleasures will have much to teach" man and that "law and custom" must be violated. In "Hidden Things," on the other hand, he describes his predicament of this period, the fact that he cannot "act freely" and that his writings are "veiled." The unpublished poem "On the Stairs" (1904) is an example of his fears, his hesitations and frustrations. Although he did have affairs at that time, he could not get rid of his anxiety and his feeling of persecution. In a less

> "The poem works on two levels: on the most immediate, Cavafy emphasizes sensual pleasure and celebrates the journey from harbor to harbor; on the more general level, one can see the poem as a condensed expression of Cavafy's view of the world."

oppressive society the encounter would probably have led to an adventure; instead it led to a poem, and even that he did not dare publish. Later in his life he did write and publish poems about encounters between strangers that did result in affairs ("The Window of the Tobacco Shop," "He Asked about the Quality").

Written in 1905–1908 were also a few exquisite erotic poems which leave no doubt about "the form of [sensual pleasure]" but which were written in an elevated style without explicit details and were published in 1912–1917. Included in this group are the poems "I Went," "One Night," "Days of 1903" and "Come Back."

With the publication of "Ithaca" in 1911 Cavafy established the theoretical framework into which one can fit all of these previous poems as well as those that follow. He declared that the final destination of the journey is not important; what is important is sensual pleasure, that the journey should be full of joy, adventure and sensual delights. The poem's symbolism covers a much wider area than that of the journey. It implies that there is no goal in life, that personal experience is more important and that life is its own justification.

In the decade that followed "Ithaca," Cavafy wrote many of his most affirmative erotic poems. He had overcome his inhibitions and was at peace with himself; and although his difficulties with society were not entirely over, he expressed himself more freely. His life and his poetry during this period seem to be more or less an application of the principles spelled out in "Ithaca." He was traveling "from harbor to harbor" enjoying with "rare excitement" the sensual pleasures of the journey and transforming them into art. The predominant mood in these poems is one of fulfilment and glorification of the senses.

This decade starts with "I've Looked So Much. . . ." (1911), in which he tells us that his vision overflows with beauty, and continues with "Ithaca," expressing the euphoria of the adventure. Even the symbolic poem "The God Abandons Antony" (1910), which represents the end of the journey, is the summing up of a life rich with happy experiences. The symbolic departure from a harbor in "In the Street" (1913) is also represented as a strong intoxication with pleasure. Another departure is presented in "Returning [Home] from Greece" (1914), in which the literal departure is at the same time a symbolic one, as the protagonist abandons the principles that Greece represents (classical restraint) and sails toward Alexandria and its more uninhibited way of life. The adventurous wandering from harbor to harbor is emphasized or implied in poems like "Passing Through" (1914), "Body, Remember. . . ." (1916) and "Gray" (1917). In "Passing Through" the protagonist abandons himself to a life of pleasure, his body overcome by "forbidden erotic ecstasy." Also in "Body, Remember," the protagonist's, indulgence in past pleasure is nothing else but a happy recollection or his journey from harbor to harbor. And the poem "Gray" contains the justification of his preference for many harbors.

Some of the above poems, as well as a few others written during the same decade, are journeys to the past. In this period, Cavafy is not an old man who recollects his distant past and for whom memory is a therapy. The poet vividly recalls happy moments even of a recent past, as for instance in "To Sensual Pleasure" (1913), where he feels the need to celebrate the journey and the fulfilment as he departs from a harbor. After "Walls" and the claustrophobic feeling and imprisonment of his early period, it is natural for him to write poems like "Body, Remember" and "To Sensual Pleasure" in order to reaffirm an uninhibited eroticism. It is this kind of affirmation that he describes in the poem "Outside the House" (1917), in which the view of an old building brings back joy and sensuous memories—the spell of love transforms the house and its environment into a magic place.

Very characteristic of Cavafy is his preference for transient affairs. As W. H. Auden writes, "The erotic world he depicts is one of casual pickups and short-lived affairs," but the poet refuses to pretend that he feels unhappy or guilty about it. Rex Warner, stressing the poet's realism and acceptance of life, notes that "if we are to take the poet's own word for it, love affairs of a disreputable character were a source of immense inspiration." Other critics, like George Seferis and Edmund Keeley, express a different point of view. Seferis sees in Cavafy's poetry an "unresurrected Adonis," and Keeley writes that sterility, frustration and loss are the prevailing attributes of actual experience in Cavafy's contemporary city. They both see him "condemned" to such ephemeral affairs. In my view, however, sterility for Cavafy is irrelevant, and transience means renewal. He believed that prolongation of a love affair would result in deterioration. This becomes clear in poems such as "Before Time Altered Them," "Gray," etc. Peter Bien, discussing in the context of "Ithaca" Cavafy's belief in the value of individual experience, observes that the acceptance of life as its own justification on the one hand "constituted Cavafy's own freedom and enabled him to be strangely animated and 'yea-saying,'" and on the other it meant denying "as illusory all the comforts invented by man: eternity, order, decorum, absolute good, morality, justice." He concludes that this outlook, though "affirmative in spirit . . . is at the same time rigorously pessimistic." It is true that Cavafy belonged to a generation which grew up with these values, and in my view the process of his liberation was for this reason a gradual and painful struggle. He was tormented by remorse, dilemmas and conflicts. Once "liberated," however, he can no longer be considered a pessimist. He was not an idealist who was deprived of the comfort offered by the old values. Order, decorum, morality were not really comforts for him but rather the source of his oppression and isolation, and denying them must have been accompanied by a kind of relief. This view is based on the poet's previously unpublished work, which appeared only recently, and more particularly on the poem "Hidden Things," in which he envisions a "more perfect society."

> On the subject of pessimism I would say: Cavafy has before him a reality which he sees and expresses in the most [dry] manner. This reality (of memory, of old age, of lost pleasure, of deceit), whether raw, dry, or whatever, cannot be called pessimistic.

According to G. Lechonitis, Cavafy himself has denied that his poems were pessimistic.

A large number of poems of this period can be characterized as "journeys to the past" in which Cavafy travels back in time "mixing memory and desire," in Eliot's phrase. The attitude is again for the most part positive, as the poet recollects happy memories: as in "Body, Remember," "Long Ago," etc. Sometimes the poet travels back not to his own past but through history to recreate portraits of historical or pseudohistorical figures. His historical poems are for the most part objective and realistic and are set predominantly in the Hellenistic period because, as he explained himself, this period "is more immoral, more free, and permits me to move my characters as I want." His purpose often is to uncover human motives, which he does with irony and political cynicism.

Of the several historical poems that Cavafy has written, of special interest to this study are those in which the poet weaves "homosexual suggestions into the historical context." In poems such as "Orophernes" or "Caesarion," he selects as his subjects minor historical figures who appeal to him. What fascinates him with Orophernes is the youth's exceptional beauty, while he identifies with Caesarion, who was one of the persecuted of history. In the "Glory of the Ptolemies" the first thing the king asserts of himself is that he is "a complete master of the art of pleasure." In "Favor of Alexander Balas" the protagonist boasts about the fact that he is the favorite of the Syrian king and shows an excessive arrogance by declaring that he dominates all Antioch.

Sometimes, however, his voyage back to history is an ingenious device for speaking about homosexual love in a dignified manner by using an objective correlative from history. This is particularly tree about his several epitaphs ("Tomb of Ignatios," "Tomb of Lanis," "In the Month of Athyr," etc.). A young man's epitaph is a dignified portrait, far back in the distance of time. The austerity of the form and the archaic language that Cavafy uses add to this effect.

During this decade, Cavafy was not unaware of the possible dangers and complications of uninhibited hedonism. But these complications appear only in very few poems of this period and mostly after 1917 ("Tomb of Iasis," "The Twenty-fifth Year of his Life").

In the decade 1920–1930 the complications and unpleasant situations increased as Cavafy was growing older. Art was therapy for him, a redeemer of time; he continued his voyages to the past evoking intoxicating memories. Since the fleeting moment was the essence of his life, he wanted to make it immortal through his art.

In this last decade and until his death, Cavafy wrote an increasing number of sad poems describing sometimes in realistic detail unpleasant or painful situations. The journey from harbor to harbor in the poems "In Despair" (1923), "In the Tavernas" (1926) and "Days of 1896" (1925) takes a different, unpleasant turn. In the first two of these poems the journey is not a beautiful adventure but rather an effort at adjustment after a sentimental setback. In the third, "Days of 1896," after the social degradation of the protagonist and the loss of his job, his wandering from harbor to harbor is more of a drifting than a delightful voyage.

Some of the poems of this period are journeys to the past and have a more or less therapeutic purpose for the aging poet, like "To Call up the Shades" (1920), "I Brought to Art" (1921)—where art plays a complementary role in life—or "On the Ship" (1919), in which the poet travels back to the past to revive the memory of a young man as he looks at a pencil portrait.

What Do I Read Next?

- Homer's *Odyssey* is considered by many to be the first great adventure story in Western literature, and its influence on poets and writers throughout the centuries cannot be overestimated. Although there are many translations of the epic, the version by Robert Fitzgerald, first published in 1961, has been highly acclaimed.

- If Cavafy is modern Greece's best known poet in the English-speaking world, Nikos Kazantzakis is its best known novelist. His *Zorba the Greek* (1952) is the story of a Greek workman who accompanies the narrator, a young writer, to a mine on Crete and becomes his best friend and inspiration. Zorba is considered by many to be one of the great characters of twentieth century fiction.

- *Voices of Modern Greece* (1982), edited by Edmund Keeley and Philip Sherrard, is an anthology of major poets of modern Greece. The editors selected poems that translate most successfully into English and are also representative of the best work of poets such as Cavafy, Angelos Sikelianos, George Seferis, Odysseus Elytis, and Nikos Gatsos.

- *Modern Greek Poetry* (1973), edited and translated by Kimon Friar, is a larger anthology than that of Keeley and Sherrard and is indispensable for anyone wanting to understand the full range of modern Greek poetry.

Some other poems of this period are spiritual journeys of a different kind in which the purpose of the poet is to emphasize his erotic preferences. In "Picture of a 23-Year-Old Painted by his Friend of the Same Age, an Amateur" (1928), he assumes the role of a painter and after giving shape to a handsome young man ("He's managed to capture perfectly / the sensual [tone] he wanted") he lets his mind wander to the "exquisite erotic pleasure" this youth is made for. The same thing happens in "In an Old Book" (1922), where the poet, looking at a watercolor portrait, imagines that the youth in the picture is destined only for homosexual love.

In most of the sad poems of this period there is an acceptance and even some possible consolation. The memory of the lost lover "saves" the protagonist of "In the Tavernas," while in "In Despair" the abandoned lover seeks new experiences, trying to recapture the old sensation. Only in very few poems does despair reach what one might call "the 'Waste Land' feeling" because, in contrast to earlier poems, there is a serious emotional involvement. The situations that led to this feeling include prematurely terminated affairs ("Kleitos' Illness," 1926), one-sided love ("A Young Poet in his Twenty-fourth Year," 1928) and the death of a lover ("Myris: Alexandria, A.D. 340," 1929; "Lovely White Flowers," 1929).

Cavafy admits in his poetry the dangers of excess, but since he places sensual pleasure at the center of existence he defies the consequences. Although in some epitaphs and other poems he implies that excess kills, in his "Longings" he twists the subject the other way around, suggesting indirectly that suppression of desire is also equivalent to death.

Even in this period in which, the sad poems predominate, however, Cavafy wrote some poems of affirmation and fulfilment ("He Came to Read," 1924; "Two Young Men, 23 to 24 Years Old," 1927).

The gradual change in attitude in Cavafy's erotic poems—from imprisonment and attempts at escape in the early period, through the affirmation of the journey from harbor to harbor on the way to Ithaca, and to the complications of the journey in the last decade—is summarized also in the words and phrases that the poet uses in describing similar situations. One example is the reference to a brothel as the "ill-famed house" in the unpublished "On the Stairs" but as the "house of pleasure" in the 1915 poem "And I Lounged and Lay on their Beds." Also, the narrator in "The Photograph" (1913) abhors the idea that the young man who was photographed leads a "degrading, vulgar life," while in "Sophist Leaving Syria," written in 1926, he admires Mevis, "the best looking, the most adored young man/in all Antioch," because selling his body he gets the highest price of all the young men leading the same life.

In the poems before 1910 homosexual love is not mentioned explicitly. Between 1919 and 1920 it is referred to as "illicit pleasure" ("In the Street;"

"Their Beginning," 1915). But in the last decade, after 1920, its is described as an "exquisite erotic pleasure" ("Picture of a 23-Year-Old Painted by his Friend of the Same Age, An Amateur"; "Theatre of Sidon [A.D. 400]," 1923). In the latter poem he explains further what kind of pleasure he has in mind, using in an ironic tone the everyday vocabulary on the subject: the "[exquisite erotic] pleasure, / the kind that leads toward a condemned, a barren love." The same kind of ironic and almost provocative tone is used in "In an Old Book," where he says that the young man whose watercolor portrait he is describing "was not destined for those / who love in ways that are more or less healthy" but was made for "beds / that common morality calls shameless."

Finally, in "Days of 1896," written in 1925, which is a clear defense of homosexually, he almost creates a new terminology in order to justify the young protagonist after he has realistically presented him as being déclassé and an outcast. He takes the word "pure," which has Christian connotations, and gives it a different meaning: the flesh is pure not when it is intact, immaculate, but only when ones does not betray it by resisting his desires. Thus, he reverses the traditional moral code by placing sensuality above honor and reputation, instead of honor and reputation above sensuality.

In contrast to his contemporary Greek poets, who were predominantly romantic, Cavafy, following the opposite direction, developed a laconic, objective and almost antipoetic style. This is acknowledged by all of his critics. In his erotic poems, however, most critics trace an element of sentimentality. Timos Malanos finds his late erotic poems inferior in their explicitness and sentimentality. Edmund Keeley and Kimon Friar also discuss this sentimentality; Friar writes that "occasionally . . . a surprising sentimentality intrudes." Peter Bien, referring to this excess of emotion, comments that most of the erotic poems "show remarkable control; and it would be entirely misleading to dwell on Cavafy's occasional lapses." Cavafy was a very severe editor of himself, destroying hundreds of poems every year. In my view, his use of emotion was not accidental. Since in all of his other poetry he appears as an enemy of sentimentality, he apparently thought that an erotic poem should not be written in a dry style, and only in his love poems did he permit himself to be occasionally sentimental, when he wanted to express an extremely strong feeling. Some of these poems, especially of the last decade, when complications of love were his themes, are portraits of unique pathos and tenderness. For instance, "A Young Poet in his Twenty-fourth Year," although referring to an "abnormal form of pleasure," is a superb study of one-sided love. Also, "Lovely White Flowers," undeniably sentimental, is an exquisite poem praised as one of Cavafy's best by Seferis, I.A. Sareyannis and Robert Liddell.

The perfection of Cavafy's art was a long, complex and tortuous process. This "fastidious poet who handled words as if they were pearls" went through many stages of severe self-editing in order to find his unique tone. This straggle to perfect the form paralleled the agonizing process reflected in the content of his poetry, as Cavafy was subject in his personal life to endless fluctuations, dilemmas and crises until he reached his complete liberation and adjustment.

Cavafy's journey in Alexandria may have turned out to be more complicated than he had predicted in his "Ithaca," but he dared to say the truth about human erotic experience with an unprecedented intensity.

Of the 153 poems collected for publication by Cavafy himself and the seventy-five that appeared recently, those dealing directly with the journey on the literal level are not many but include some of his most significant statements ("Ithaca," "The God Abandons Antony," "Returning [Home] from Greece"). The great majority of the other poems of Cavafy are indirectly related to the journey, as defined in the first section, on the symbolic level only by the fact that they are erotic.

As Cavafy grew older, he moved from a cryptic or allegorical form of expression on this subject to a more open and frank one. On this basis it is convenient to divide his work into three periods: before 1910, 1910 to 1920, and 1920 to 1932. This chronological division will be followed in the discussion of the poems related to the journey because it permits a better insight into the poet's changing attitudes on the subject. The chronological order will be based on the date on which each poem was written rather than that on which it was published, because it is more interesting to follow the poet's own development rather than the change in the public image he chose to project, although the latter will also be discussed.

Source: C. Capri-Karka, "Introduction," in *Love and the Symbolic Journey in the Poetry of Cavafy, Eliot, and Seferis*, Pella Publishing Company, 1982, pp. 19–28.

Sources

Auden, W. H., *Selected Poetry of W. H. Auden*, Random House, 1958, pp. 71–73.

Bien, Peter, *Constantine Cavafy*, Columbia University Press, 1964.

Bowra, C. M., "Constantine Cavafy and the Greek Past," in *The Creative Experiment*, Macmillan, 1949, pp. 29–60.

Capri-Karka, C., *Love and the Symbolic Journey in the Poetry of Cavafy, Eliot, and Seferis*, Pella Publishing Company, 1982.

Cavafy, C. P., *Collected Poems*, translated by Edmund Keeley and Philip Sherrard, edited by George Savidis, Princeton University Press, 1980.

———, *The Complete Poems of Cavafy*, translated by Rae Dalven, Harcourt, Brace & World, 1961.

———, *Poems of C. P. Cavafy*, translated by John Mavrogordato, Chatto and Windus, 1951.

Forster, E. M., *Alexandria: A History and a Guide*, with an introduction by Lawrence Durrell, Michael Haag, 1982.

Keeley, Edmund, *Cavafy's Alexandria: Study of a Myth in Progress*, Harvard University Press, 1976.

Pinchin, Jane Lagoudis, *Alexandria Still: Forster, Durrell, and Cavafy*, Princeton University Press, 1977.

Tennyson, Alfred, Lord, "Ulysses," in *The Norton Anthology of English Literature*, 4th ed., Vol. 2, Norton, 1979, pp. 1110–11.

Further Reading

Auden, W. H., "Introduction," in *The Complete Poems of Cavafy*, translated by Rae Dalven, Harcourt, Brace & World, 1961.
   Auden acknowledges that Cavafy has been an influence on his own writing and discusses the distinctive tone of voice in Cavafy's poems that makes his work instantly recognizable.

Forster, E. M., *Two Cheers for Democracy*, Penguin, 1965.
   Forster was a personal friend of Cavafy and admired his work. This book contains a very readable essay on Cavafy's poetry and gives insight into the man as well. (The essay was omitted from American editions of this book.)

Liddell, Robert, *Cavafy: A Critical Biography*, Duckworth, 1974.
   This is the only biography of Cavafy in English. It gives a detailed and sympathetic account of his difficult life, discussing his relationships with his six brothers and demanding mother, his homosexuality, and the mundane office job in which he worked for most of his life.

Ruehlen, Petroula Kephala, "Constantine Cavafy: A European Poet," in *Nine Essays in Modern Literature*, edited by Donald E. Stanford, Louisiana State University Press, 1965, pp. 36–62.
   Ruehlen argues that Cavafy should be considered a European poet, in the sense that he is culturally and emotionally within the Western tradition. Ruehlen argues that the two criteria for calling a poet European are maturity and comprehensiveness.

Once Again I Prove the Theory of Relativity

Sandra Cisneros

1994

Sandra Cisneros's poem "Once Again I Prove the Theory of Relativity" is from her third book of poetry, *Loose Woman* (1994). The poem is a celebration of romantic love. The female speaker imagines how excited and delighted she would be if her lover were to return. She lets her mind and heart contemplate all the things she would do for him and how well she would treat him and relates how beautiful he is. She says she would dote on him and make sure she fully got to know him before he departed again, as she knows he would.

Cisneros is noted not only for her poems but also for her novels and short stories. She typically portrays strong, independent women of Mexican American heritage, who refuse to conform to traditional male expectations of how women should behave and what their place in society should be. "Once Again I Prove the Theory of Relativity" is not exactly a typical Cisneros piece, since it does not emphasize the Chicano or feminist aspect of her work. Instead, it is a heartfelt expression of the ideal of romantic love. It reveals the heightened perceptions and intensity of sensual and emotional responses that such love calls forth. It also expresses the realization that in such intense experiences of love, whether they last or not, lie the seeds of creativity and art.

Author Biography

Sandra Cisneros was born December 20, 1954, in Chicago, Illinois, the daughter of a Mexican

Sandra Cisneros

father and Mexican American mother. She was the only daughter in a family of seven. Because her father missed his homeland, the family frequently moved from Chicago to Mexico City and then back again, leaving Cisneros often feeling homeless. She developed a love of reading and, as early as the fifth grade, had plans to go to college. During childhood and adolescence, she also began writing poems and stories.

In 1976, Cisneros earned a bachelor of arts degree from Loyola University of Chicago and then attended the University of Iowa Writers' Workshop, graduating in 1978 with a master of fine arts degree. It was while studying in Iowa that Cisneros began writing about her experiences as a Latina woman living outside mainstream American culture.

Cisneros taught at the Latino Youth Alternative High School in Chicago, and was a college recruiter and counselor for minority students at Loyola University, but her passion was for writing. In 1980, her first book of poems, *Bad Boys*, was published. In 1982, she received a fellowship from the National Endowment for the Arts. This endowment enabled her to continue working on *The House on Mango Street* (1984), which took her five years to complete. A collection of vignettes about the coming-of-age of a Latina woman in Chicago, *The House on Mango Street* won the American Book Award from the Before Columbus Foundation. The novel was a popular success, selling more than two million copies over the next two decades.

Having made her mark on the national literary scene, Cisneros published a book of poetry, *My Wicked, Wicked Ways* (1987), and a volume of short stories, *Woman Hollering Creek and Other Stories* (1991). In 1988 she was awarded a second fellowship from the National Endowment for the Arts. Cisneros also taught as a visiting writer at various universities, including California State University, Chico (1987–1988); the University of California, Berkeley (1988); the University of California, Irvine (1990); and the University of New Mexico, Albuquerque (1991).

In 1994, Cisneros wrote a bilingual juvenile book, *Hairs: Pelitos*, illustrated by Terry Ybanez, and the same year published her third collection of poems, *Loose Woman*, which contains the poem "Once Again I Prove the Theory of Relativity." Cisneros did not publish again until 2002, when her second novel, *Caramelo*, appeared. *Caramelo*, which took Cisneros nine years to write, is a multigenerational saga and historical novel about Latino immigration to the United States.

Poem Summary

Stanza 1

"Once Again I Prove the Theory of Relativity" begins with the speaker imagining the return of someone she obviously loves deeply. Addressing the absent lover directly, she imagines how she would act toward him if he returned. First, she would treat him like a valuable work of art, such as a piece by Matisse that had been considered lost. Henri Matisse was a French painter and sculptor who lived from 1869 to 1954. The speaker would also honor her returning lover by seating him on a couch like a pasha. A pasha was a Turkish title of rank or honor, placed after a person's name. The speaker then says she would dance a Sevillana, which is a dance from Seville, Spain that can be performed by a single female dancer. She would also leap around like a Taiwanese diva. Diva literally means goddess, and the term is often applied to female vocal stars in pop and opera. Taiwan has a number of young, female pop stars who are often called divas. They are known for their energetic and athletic performances on stage.

Next, the speaker says she would bang cymbals like in a Chinese opera. Chinese opera makes frequent use of percussion instruments. The persona of the poem would also "roar like a Fellini soundtrack." Federico Fellini (1920–1993) was an Italian film director, famous for innovative films such as *La strada*, *La dolce vita*, and *Otto e mezzo (8-1/2)*. Nino Rota wrote the music for Fellini's films, which contribute greatly to their impact. The two men had a long collaboration, which ended only with Rota's death in 1979. The poem's speaker says she would also laugh like the little dog in the nursery rhyme that watched the cow jump over the moon.

Stanza 2

The speaker continues to address her absent lover. If he were to return, she would be a clown and tell funny stories. She would paint clouds on the walls of her home—an image that presumably expresses her desire to show artistic creativity. She would put the best linen on the bed for him and observe him while he sleeps. During this time, she would hold her breath, which is a way of saying that she would be very quiet so as not to awaken him.

Stanza 3

The speaker breaks off from addressing her loved one directly and, using a series of similes, muses on the beauty of her beloved. Her beloved is like the "color inside an ear" or "like a conch shell." A conch shell is a spiral, one-piece shell of certain sea mollusks or any large shell used as a horn for calling. The third simile used to convey the beauty of her beloved is a nude by Modigliani. Amedeo Modigliani (1884–1920) was a French painter known for his distinctive portraits and nudes.

Stanza 4

In this stanza, the speaker returns to addressing her beloved. She declares that this time she will cut off some of his hair, so that even if he leaves her again, some part of him will remain. This image sparks a memory for the speaker of how soft her lover's hair is, the softest that can be imagined.

Stanza 5

The speaker continues with another set of actions she would perform if the beloved returned. She would present him with flowers and fruit, including parrot tulips and papaya. Parrot tulips have petals that are feathered, curled, twisted, or waved. The flowers are large and brightly colored. The papaya is a tropical tree that produces large yellow-orange fruit, like a melon.

Media Adaptations

- Cisneros made an audio recording of *Loose Woman*, issued in 1994 by Random House Audio.

The speaker then says she would laugh at the stories her returning lover told, though she could equally well be silent in his presence. She knows her lover is aware such an act of silence in his presence is normally hard for her.

Stanza 6

The speaker seems to have no illusions about her lover. She knows when he grows tired of her or the place they live, he will leave. He could go anywhere, and she names places far away and near: Patagonia, a region in Argentina and Chile; Cairo, Egypt; Istanbul, Turkey; Katmandu, the capital city of Nepal; and finally Laredo, Texas, a town on the United States-Mexico border with a large Mexican American population.

Projecting into the future, the speaker imagines what she will gain by her lover's return, even if he later departs again. She will have savored him like a tasty food, memorized everything about him, and tasted his essence ("held you under my tongue"). She will have learned him by heart. Here the poet plays on the usual meaning of the expression "learn by heart," which means to learn by memorizing. Since the poet has already mentioned memorizing, this phrase placed here means that the speaker learned all about her lover through her heart, through love.

The speaker's conclusion is that when her loved one leaves, all her knowledge and love of him will yield their fruit in the poetry she will write. He will become her muse.

Themes

Romantic Love

The title of the poem, "Once Again I Prove the Theory of Relativity" is meant humorously. It

Topics for Further Study

- The poem is an expression of romantic love. What is the nature of romantic love? What are its characteristics? Is romantic love the supreme kind of love, or are there other kinds of love that are equally valuable?

- Research the lives of three Chicano authors or other authors of color (African American, Asian American, Native American, etc.). Based on your research and your own or your friends' experiences, detail some challenges faced by someone growing up with a dual cultural identity. Provide examples of ways someone can be an American and at the same time preserve one's original cultural heritage.

- The poem suggests that creativity springs from love remembered. What else inspires poets to write poems, or novelists to write novels? Read several interviews with your favorite authors. What state of mind does a person have to be in to be creative? Provide examples from the interviews, along with your own ideas.

- Compare "Once Again I Prove the Theory of Relativity" with another love poem of your choice. What are the similarities and differences between the two? Which poem is more effective at conveying its meaning? Why?

---

refers to Albert Einstein's special theory of relativity, published in 1905, and his general theory of relativity, developed in 1915 and 1916. Using calculations based on the postulate of the uniform speed of light and the relativity of motion (the motion of something can be determined only by its relation to something else), Einstein showed that time is measured differently for people moving relative to one another. At speeds of light, time would slow to near zero.

In the popular mind, Einstein's theory, which is too complex for most laymen to understand in detail, has given rise to the idea that under certain circumstances, time might flow backward rather than forward. The actual physics of this notion is not important for the poem. Cisneros merely uses the idea as a jumping-off point for her speaker to imagine that, since time might run backwards, her lost lover might return.

Using this premise, the poem explores the many ways in which love can be expressed, and the lover can appreciate the beloved. There is an emphasis on the freedom love brings, as well as the feelings of exultation and lightness, of exhilaration, and of the intensity of sensual experience. This kind of love animates a person and enlivens her physically. Love is exciting. It makes the persona of the poem dance and leap with enthusiasm and do things she would not normally do. Love energizes.

The love revealed by the poem is also a grand sentiment, an expansive emotion. It stimulates in the lover the flamboyant expression of her feelings, and it can also enlarge her beyond her normal self and beyond her usual cultural boundaries. She can be a Spanish dancer or a Taiwanese diva, or she can take part in a Chinese opera. Her voice can be like the roar of music on a film soundtrack. When she loves, she leaves her small, individual self behind. She becomes universal.

Certain kinds of love, such as intensely felt romantic love, tend to worship and idealize the beloved. Such is the case in this poem. The persona idealizes the beauty of her lover ("How beautiful you are"). She is so enchanted by him that she would be content simply to watch him sleep. She wants to cut off a lock of his hair so that part of her beloved will always remain with her. She would do whatever he wanted. Her own needs would somehow slip into the background as she spent all her energy attending to him, honoring him, being the woman that she thinks he wants her to be. She would not be angry when, tired of her attention, he left again. She honors his restless spirit and would accept his loss without rancor. At least she would have her memories.

At the same time, there is a suggestion of unreality about the way the persona speaks of her love. It may strike some readers as a flight of the imagination that is too exaggerated, too extreme, and too fragile to survive the test of real experience. Such a view might note that behind the unabashed expression of devotion and love, this poem has an untold story—that these two people had a romantic relationship before, which did not, for unknown reasons, endure and would not (as the speaker recounts) endure again, even if the lover were to return.

Love as the Origin of Art

The last two lines of the poem suggest that love is the fuel of art and creativity. The memory of a love so deeply felt, absorbed into the fibers of the lover's being, even if the desired relationship does not last, will inspire her to write poetry. Or perhaps it would be truer to say that it is the loss of love that will inspire her. It is, after all, the loss of her love and her hopes for his return that has inspired the entire poem. So, underlying the tribute to love is perhaps a sadder reality. Love may not endure in the flesh, but it can be transformed into art.

Style

Visual Design

The poem is written with an awareness of how it appears on the printed page, in particular in relation to the line breaks. For example, the first line contains only one word, "If." The rest of the phrase, "you came back," follows on line 2. There is no grammatical reason for splitting up the phrase in this manner. The same device is used to begin the fifth stanza. The effect is to place much greater emphasis on that one word "if" then would otherwise be the case and makes it clear that the desire of the speaker is to be taken more as fantasy than realistic hope. The arrangement of the line is also a cue for the reader, when reading the poem aloud, as to where to place emphasis and pauses.

The design of the printed page is also important in stanzas 4 and 6. In stanza 4, in which the persona imagines cutting a lock of her beloved's hair so that he will never leave her, the lines become progressively shorter.

The visual design suggests something other than what the lines actually say: they depict the reality that the lover seeks to avert. Her beloved is going to depart, whatever she does, so the line shortens with each statement, as if he is slipping from her grasp in spite of all her efforts.

A similar effect is apparent in stanza 6, which deals directly with the beloved's inevitable departure:

> off you'd go to Patagonia
> Cairo Istanbul
> Katmandu
> Laredo

Each line gets shorter, as if the speaker's hold on her lover is diminishing with each place she names. He is fading into the distance.

Punctuation

The poem is written with almost no punctuation. There are no periods to mark the ends of sentences, the ends of stanzas, or even the end of the poem. There are clues, however, about where periods might fall, had they been used: when a sentence "ends," the following line begins with a capital letter.

It is difficult to know the poet's intent for her lack of punctuation. Perhaps it makes the poem more spontaneous, as if it is an unrestrained outpouring of idealized love and emotion that cannot even pause for a comma or a period. In the few instances when punctuation is used, as in "Ah, the softest hair / Ah, the softest," the effect is to slow down the reader and provide a moment of quiet contemplation.

Simile

This relatively short poem contains no less than ten similes. A simile is a figure of speech in which two things that appear dissimilar are compared in such a way that some similarity between them is exposed. A single voice can hardly "roar like a Fellini soundtrack," for example, but the comparison gives a sense of how the persona's delight at her returning lover can transform her, make her bigger than her everyday self.

A series of three striking similes compares the beauty of the beloved to various physical phenomena and to the creations of art. Another interesting simile is the comparison of the persona to a sunflower as she watches her sleeping beloved. A sunflower turns its face to the light, following the movement of the sun across the sky. So too the speaker watches and follows with her eyes the movement of her lover as he sleeps. The syntax of the two lines "I'd hold my breath and watch / you move like a sunflower" suggests that the comparison of the sunflower is with the beloved, not the lover, but it makes little sense for the random movements of a sleeping man to be compared to a sunflower. The simile seems far more appropriate if it is taken to refer to the lover following her "sun," the beloved.

Historical Context

Latino/a and Chicano/a Literature in the United States

Chicano (Mexican American) literature began to establish itself in the United States in the 1960s.

This period, sometimes known as the Chicano Renaissance, was in part inspired by the Civil Rights movement. Chicano writers emphasized the need for political action to provide equal opportunities for Chicanos. One of the leading figures in this movement was Tomás Rivera (1935–1984), whose novel *y no se lo trago la tierra/And the Earth Did Not Part* (1971) told of the hardships endured by Mexican American migrant workers. In 1972, Rudolfo Anaya (1937–) published *Bless Me, Ultima*, which has become one of the most popular of all Mexican American novels.

In the 1980s, mainstream publishers became more willing to publish works by Chicano and other Latino writers (such as Cuban Americans or Puerto Ricans), in part because of the movement in colleges and universities known as multiculturalism, in which efforts were made to reshape the literary canon to better reflect cultural diversity in America. Minority authors were thus given a better chance of being published and acquiring a large readership. It was during the 1980s that Chicano poet Gary Soto (1952–) made his mark nationally, and a number of Mexican American women writers found their literary voices, including Lorna Dee Cervantes (1954–), Gloria Anzaldua (1942–), Denise Chavez (1948–), and Sandra Cisneros. These women writers successfully articulated the desires and experiences of Mexican American women. They challenged the values of the patriarchal societies in which they were raised, while at the same time affirming their distinctive Mexican American heritage.

It was in the 1990s that Latino literature made its biggest breakthroughs into mainstream literary publishing and readership. In 1990 Oscar Hijuelos (1951–) became the first Latino to win the Pulitzer Prize for fiction, for his novel *The Mambo Kings Play Songs of Love*, which follows two Cuban immigrants who come to New York. *How the Garcia Girls Lost Their Accents* (1992) by Julia Alvarez (1950–) traces the lives of four sisters who immigrated to Miami from the Dominican Republic. The novel found a wide readership and won critical acclaim.

In an interview published in 1993 in *Booklist*, however, Cisneros argues that there is still a long way to go before Latino writers can gain the recognition and readership they deserve. She says she feels a responsibility to promote the work of the large number of as-yet-unknown Latino writers. She looks forward to a time when Latinos will be in influential positions in publishing and journalism and will be able to make decisions about which books get published and reviewed. She states,

There should be working-class writers, people of color, making the decisions that affect us all, whether it's determining funding in the arts or deciding what should be published or what is considered quality literature.

Although during the 1990s there were many anthologies of Latino writing published, Cisneros was wary of allowing her work to be included in anthologies with the word "Hispanic" in the title. Her reasoning was because such titles tended to marginalize the works as "ethnic literature" rather than taking them into the mainstream.

Critical Overview

Cisneros has attracted more attention for her novel *The House on Mango Street* and her short-story collection *Woman Hollering Creek* (1991) than for her poetry, which has been largely ignored by academic critics. A *Publishers Weekly* reviewer notes similarities between the poems in *Loose Woman* and Cisneros's coming-of-age novel *The House on Mango Street*: "We meet again a powerful, fiercely independent woman of Mexican heritage." The reviewer concludes, however, the poems cannot match the "depth, the complexity and the lyrical magic" of Cisneros's novels and short stories.

Susan Smith Nash in *World Literature Today* comments on the "sometimes rather flat, unadorned diction and the earthy explorations into the nature of desire" that characterize the poems in *Loose Woman*. Nash describes the "heightened awareness of the textures, colors, and physical sensations of the world" revealed by the poems. Because all the poems in *Loose Woman* express different aspects of the female experience and challenge conventional notions of identity, Nash also notes, "the reader gains the opportunity to celebrate the diversity of human experience."

Criticism

Bryan Aubrey

Aubrey holds a Ph.D. in English and has published many articles on twentieth-century literature. In this essay, Aubrey discusses Cisneros's poem in the context of other poems in her collection Loose Woman.

In her poetry, Cisneros likes to speak directly from the heart, to the heart. Her poems are not complex; the diction is straightforward and the meanings of the poems usually reveal themselves on the first reading. There is rarely a need to tease out allusions or hidden themes; the punch is delivered quickly and with force. Anyone who has ever been in love, for example, will instantly recognize the symptoms described in "Once Again I Prove the Theory of Relativity": the self in a state of wild abandon; the beloved contemplated as if he or she were a god; the intense feelings that create a kind of sacred space between two people, upon which the mundane aspects of life cannot intrude. The poem conveys a spontaneity and charm, almost a youthful naïveté, that suggests real experience. It gives the impression of having been written quickly, in the flush of that one overpowering and exhilarating emotion, whether felt at the time or vividly recalled later. And yet, the poem may not be quite what it first appears.

Cisneros sheds light on her method of composition, as well as making some revealing remarks about her poems, in an interview with Martha Satz published in *Southwest Review*. Cisneros says she wrote many of the poems published in *Loose Woman* for her private satisfaction only, never intending them to be published. She believes that her public life as a writer centers around her novels. As a poet, she feels free to explore the most intimate aspects of her psyche without a thought of how the results will be received by others: "The reason I write it is not to publish it but to get the thorn out of the soul of my heart." Cisneros takes inspiration from Emily Dickinson, another poet who did not write for publication. Cisneros notes, "[Dickinson] knew that the true reason one writes poetry and works at the craft is simply to write that poem."

Cisneros also comments in the same interview that in her poetry she does not decide what to write beforehand; the words just spill out, and she does not even feel in conscious control of the process. She writes what the inner levels of her psyche prompt her to write. Most readers would probably agree that many of the sixty poems in *Loose Woman* do indeed give this impression. These are not poems that have been much revised and reworked or agonized over. They are like quick snapshots of certain moods, attitudes, emotions, and situations. Taken together, they present a many-sided portrait of the experience of being a woman involved in the affairs of the heart.

"Once Again I Prove the Theory of Relativity" presents one of the more innocent aspects of that many-sided portrait. The reader would hardly guess

> *This persona is pliant rather than self-assertive and romantic rather than overtly sexual although fully aware of the sacredness of the body and the gifts it can bestow."*

from that poem the persona Cisneros adopts in many of the other poems. "With *Loose Woman*," Cisneros tells Satz, "I entered a realm where I am writing from a dangerous fountainhead." By this, she means the sexual aspects of her poems, which she thought that men might find threatening: "I strike terror among the men. / I can't be bothered what they think," she writes in "Loose Woman."

The title of the collection is meant, at least in one sense, ironically. "Loose woman" is how the persona of the poems thinks she might be described from a male, conservative, traditional standpoint; it is how a certain type of man might view her. From her point of view, "loose woman," as the poem of that title makes clear, is a label she bears with pride because for her it means being free from repressive, restricted ideas about how a woman should think and behave.

It is as well to remember that Cisneros was raised in a Mexican American community, in which patriarchal attitudes were the norm. These attitudes included the belief that a woman's place was in the home, sex was mainly for the pleasure of the male, and it was right for men to have freedom, privileges, and power that were denied to women. Cisneros once quipped that not only was she the only daughter in her family—she has six brothers—she was also "only a daughter." (She also takes care to note that her mother raised her in a nontraditional way, always allowing her time to study and fighting for her right to have a college education.) Given this traditional patriarchal context, the persona that Cisneros adopts in *Loose Woman*—of an independent woman who can be defiant, passionate, angry, raunchy, and ribald and is ready to indulge in sexual pleasure herself—is a threat to the accepted way of things. As the persona states in "Night Madness

Poem," "I'm the crazy lady they warned you about."

In many of these poems, Cisneros clearly alludes to her Mexican heritage. "You Bring out the Mexican in Me" is typical, with its liberal spattering of Spanish words—a common device in these poems, though absent from "Once Again I Prove the Theory of Relativity"—and its allusions to Mexico's pre-Christian pagan history. By invoking some of the potent symbols of Mexico's indigenous religions, such as the "filth goddess" Tlazoltéotl, she conveys a kind of on-the-edge, primordial wildness, a sultry, essentially female life-force springing up from ancient streams and ready to disconcert any man who does not understand it or who tries to stand in its way. This is the authentic Cisneros, feminist-woman-of-color persona, and it is the dominant voice in the collection. Here, for example, is the persona's opinion of marriage and husbands, from the poem "Extreme Unction":

> Husband.
> Balm for the occasional
> itch. But I'm witch now.
> Wife makes me wince.

There is another voice in *Loose Woman*, one that does not insist so much on challenging cultural taboos. This is a more romantic, feminine voice, tinged often with longing and regret and a certain vulnerability. It occurs only occasionally, but it can be heard, for example, in "Waiting for a Lover," in which the persona nervously awaits the arrival of her new date, wondering what will happen: "You're new. / You can't hurt me yet." As she gets ready she continues:

> I can't think.
> Dress myself in slinky black,
> my 14-karat hoops and my velvet spikes.
> Smoke two cigars.
> I'm doing loopity loops.

There is nothing feminist or Chicana about these statements; they could be any woman ready to embark on a new courtship (although perhaps the smoking of two cigars marks this lady as a little out of the ordinary!).

A similar voice is heard in "Why I Didn't," in which the persona pulls back from a sexual involvement with her friend:

> Oh I'm scared all right
> Haven't you noticed. I'm
> only shy when I like a man.

When this feminine voice allows full reign to her feelings, the result is "Once Again I Prove the Theory of Relativity," in which all diffidence and fear is overcome in the exuberant celebration of love. This persona is pliant rather than self-assertive and romantic rather than overtly sexual although fully aware of the sacredness of the body and the gifts it can bestow. Intoxicated by this pure, idealistic love for a man, she is ready to indulge his every whim and accept without reproach his inevitable wandering. She elevates herself to the level of infinite love that sees no fault. Yet, it should also be noted that this is a poem addressed to an absent lover, and, as the saying goes, absence makes the heart grow fonder. The poem is not a celebration of a here-and-now love relationship but of some imagined reunion at some time in the future. Despite its future orientation, it is more of a hymn to something past, something that has gone, and can now be safely enshrined and worshipped.

This seems to be a recurring theme in the poems of *Loose Woman*. They are rarely celebrations of here-and-now love but of love recalled or anticipated. The same idealization of an absent lover can be found in the first section of "Los Denudos: A Triptych," in which the speaker imagines a painting by Goya in which the female nude is replaced by her former lover. The flesh-and-blood man is turned into a work of art for the doting persona to contemplate.

Similarly, the theme in "Once Again I Prove the Theory of Relativity," that the memory of love inspires the writing of poetry, also occurs elsewhere in *Loose Woman*, notably in "My Nemesis Arrives after a Long Hiatus." This poem, which in fact is more about departure than arrival, contains the lines, "In the clatter of your departures / I write poems." To which we can compare, "So that when you leave / I'll write poems," which are the final two lines of "Once Again I Prove the Theory of Relativity."

It seems that for the persona of Cisneros's poems love may be a many-splendored thing, but it is perhaps better contemplated in retrospect, and not the least of its many fruits is the production of art.

Source: Bryan Aubrey, Critical Essay on "Once Again I Prove the Theory of Relativity," in *Poetry for Students*, Gale, 2003.

Carol Thomas

In the following essay, Thomas examines the essential qualities of Cisneros's writing.

For Sandra Cisneros, "our familia is our culture." Her stories and poems explore ethnicity, gender, language, and place where intimate and communal women-centered space provides ways of knowing the world of meaning and identity. Women's relationships, magic, myth, religion, and politics figure prominently in Cisneros' work, providing a rich matrix for her attempt to balance love and artistic work. In contrast to traditional representations of women, Cisneros foregrounds women characters who are often engaged to escape from the confinements of patriarchal determined roles common to two cultures, to interpret their own experience and redefine their lives. Her characters and situations are diverse and complex, reflecting realities that transcend stereotypes and categories. Once she found her own voice, Cisneros says, "I could speak up and celebrate my otherness as a woman, as a working-class person, as an American of Mexican descent" (*Mango*).

Cisneros' narrative style rejects traditional short story forms in favor of collage, often a mosaic of interrelated pieces, blending the sounds of poetry with oral story telling techniques. Her ingenious use of language includes the rhythm, sound, and syntax of Spanish, its sensibilities, emotional relationships to the natural world and inanimate objects, and its use of tender diminutives. She also uses the poetry of urban street slang, children's rhymes, and song creating her own innovative literary style at once musical, spontaneous, primal, and direct.

In her introduction to the 1994 edition of *Mango Street* she notes:

> The language of *Mango Street* is based on speech. It's very much an anti-academic voice—a child's voice, a girl's voice, a spoken voice, the voice of an American-Mexican. It's in this rebellious realm of antipoetics that I tried to create a poetic text with the most unofficial language I could find. I did it neither ingenuously nor naturally. It was as clear to me as if I were tossing a Molotov.

In the series of 44 brief, poetically charged vignettes which compose *Mango Street*, the voice of Esperanza Codero observes and documents the lives around her, women who look out the window and "sit their sadness on an elbow" ("My Name"). In this coming of age story, Esperanza writes about women who are alienated, confined, restricted, trapped by poverty, and often deserted by lovers and husbands. There is Rose Vargas, with too many kids and a husband who "left without even leaving a dollar for bologna or a note explaining how come" ("There Was an Old Woman She Had So Many Children She Didn't Know What to Do"), and Esperanza's own mother, "a smart cookie" who says, "I couldn've been somebody, you know?" She speaks two languages and can sing an opera but can't get down on the subway ("A Smart Cookie"). Esperanza's environment is characterized by both poverty and racism as well as the warmth, intimacy, and humor of her culture. She is nurtured and empowered by women who share stories and poems with her, who encourage her to keep writing because it will keep her free, who remind her never to forget who she is, that she "will always be Mango Street." As Esperanza's voice gains strength, she provides a powerful, carnal, poetic, and "unofficial text" which critiques traditional western discourse. Unlike the women around her, Esperanza escapes confinement and isolation, refusing to accept socioeconomic and gender-determined limitations. Instead, she discovers her inner poetic self and moves away from feelings of shame, away from silence towards artistic freedom and a fullness of identity. In the last story she says, "One day I will pack my bags of books and paper." But she leaves to return "for the ones I left behind. For the ones who cannot get out" ("Mango Says Goodbye Sometimes").

In *My Wicked Wicked Ways*, published in 1987, the voice of the youthful Esperanza merges with that of the grown woman/poet. "Tell me," she asks, "how does a woman who / a woman like me. / Daughter of / a daddy with no birthright in the matter. / What does a woman inherit / that tells her how / to go?" Her first felony she tells us is to have taken up with poetry, chucking the "life of the rolling pin or factory" (Preface). She says, "I've learned two things. / To let go / clean as kite string. / And never to wash a man's clothes. / These are my rules." ("For a Southern Man"). Her feminist Mexican American voice is playful, street smart, vigorous, and original continuing to transgress the dominant discourse of canonical standards, linguistically and ideologically.

> "Cisneros' narrative style rejects traditional short story forms in favor of collage, often a mosaic of interrelated pieces, blending the sounds of poetry with oral story telling techniques."

In *Woman Hollering Creek*, published in 1991, in contrast to those living on Mango Street, women struggle to take control of their lives in a place where love sours, men leave, and becoming a female artist is an arduous struggle. Against a background of *telenovelas*, religion, magic, and art, women find ways to escape and transform their lives. Clemencia, an artist rejected by her white married lover, paints and repaints his portrait, engaging in an imaginary conversation: "You think I went hobbling along with my life, whining like some twangy country-and-western when you went back for her. But I've been waiting. Making the world look at you from my eyes. And if that's not power, what is?" ("Never Marry a Mexican"). In "The Eyes of Zapata," the general's long time lover patiently waits for him, turning herself "into the soul of a *tecolote*" (owl), keeping "vigil in the branches of a purple jacaranda outside your door to make sure no one would do my Miliano harm while he slept." Invoking magic, offering a prayer in "*mexicano* to the old gods," and a plea to La Virgen, Ines endures. In the final story, Cisneros contrasts a highly educated Chicana artist with a young man whose poetic sensibilities challenge her values and perspectives. Lupe asks Flavio to make love to her in "*That* language. That sweep of palm leaves and fringed shawls. That startled fluttering like the heart of a goldfinch or a fan," not in English "with its starched r's and g's. English with its crisp linen syllables. English crunchy as apples, resilient and stiff as sailcloth. But Spanish whirred like silk, rolled and puckered and hissed" ("*Bien Pretty*").

In *Loose Woman*, her most recent book of poetry, Cisneros' lyricism is characterized by sassy deftness and precision of language. She's a woman who talks back. Addressing her lover she says: "You bring out the Mexican in me. / The hunkered thick dark spiral. / The core of a hear howl. / The bitter bile. / The tequila *lagrimas* on Saturday all / through next weekend Sunday." In the title poem Cisneros warns she is a woman-on-the-loose, both b—— and beast: "I'm an aim-well / shoot-sharp / sharp-tongued /sharp-thinking, / fast-speaking, / foot-loose, / loose-tongued, / let-lose, / woman-on-the-loose, / loose woman. / Beware, honey." In these poems Cisneros is concerned with women's erotic power, the joy of the female "Sinew / and twist of flesh, / helix of desire and vanity" ("Well, If You Insist"). She deftly explores and celebrates the wonder, possibilities, and consequences of being Mexican American and a woman—tough, independent, free-spirited, revolutionary and loose.

"I have always believed that, when a man writes a record of a series of events, he should begin by giving certain information about himself: his age, where he was born, whether he be short or tall or fat or thin," Ann Petry wrote in her 1947 novel, *Country Place*. "This information offers a clue as to how much of what a man writes is to be accepted as truth, and how much should be discarded as being the result of personable bias. For fat men do not write the same kind of books that thin men write; the point of view of tall men is unlike that of short men." In each of her works Cisneros throws the literary equivalent of a Molotov cocktail into Western discourse aimed at revolutionizing its monocultural representational system. Within her Chicana feminist alternative discourse, she privileges the wondrous and particular lives of those often defined as other, the *different*, those perceived as marginalized, as less than. She then illuminates these untold lives. When asked if she is Esperanza, she replies, "Yes, and no. And then again, perhaps maybe. One thing I know for certain, you, the reader, are Esperanza." And she asks a reader, will you learn to be "the human being you are not ashamed of?" Sandra Cisneros' work is not only original, unrelenting, and eloquent, it is essential.

Source: Carol Thomas, "Cisneros, Sandra," in *Contemporary Women Poets*, edited by Pamela L. Shelton, St. James Press, 1998, pp. 63–64.

Cynthia Tompkins

In the following essay, Tompkins discusses Cisneros's life and writings.

Sandra Cisneros, poet and short-story writer, is best known for *The House on Mango Street* (1983), a Chicana novel of initiation, which won the Before Columbus American Book Award in 1985. In this lyrical novella Cisneros challenges the conventions of the bildungsroman by weaving the protagonist's quest for selfhood into the fabric of the community. Such a dual focus is usual in Cisneros's poetry and prose, in which a multiplicity of voices illustrate the ways the individual engages in the discourses and social practices of Chicano culture. Additionally, by focusing on the socialization processes of the female in Chicano culture, Cisneros explores racism in the dominant culture as well as patriarchal oppression in the Latino community.

Born to working-class parents (her father an upholsterer, her mother a factory worker), Cisneros grew up as the only girl among six brothers on Chicago's South Side. Out of necessity, she learned to make herself heard, recalling in an 11 January

1993 interview, "You had to be fast and you had to be funny—you had to be a *storyteller*." Since her Mexican father missed his homeland and would frequently sojourn there for periods of time, the family was often disrupted and moved from one ghetto neighborhood to another many times during her childhood. In 1969 her parents managed to buy a cramped two-story bungalow in a Puerto Rican neighborhood on the city's North Side, an ugly red house similar to the one Cisneros portrays in *The House on Mango Street*.

Responding to questions concerning the autobiographical nature of *The House on Mango Street*, Cisneros in the spring 1991 *Americas Review* observed, "All fiction is non-fiction. Every piece of fiction is based on something that really happened.... They're all stories I lived, or witnessed, or heard." Nevertheless, the central idea of her novel had a specific literary inspiration. In a seminar at the Iowa Writers Program, Cisneros participated in a discussion of Gaston Bachelard's *La Poétique de l'éspace* (1958; translated as *The Poetics of Space*, 1964) and realized that her unique experience of the intersection of race, ethnicity, class, and gender separated her from the other students.

The House on Mango Street tells the story of a child named Esperanza (Hope) and her gradual realization of her own separate being. The tale of maturation is supported by Cisneros's use of the house as a symbol of familial consciousness, and the novel also depicts the lives, struggles, and concerns of Esperanza's immediate family, neighbors, and friends. As Erlinda González-Berry and Tey Diana Rebolledo point out, "we see the world through this child's eyes and we also see the child as she comes to an understanding of herself, her world, and her culture."

In a manner somewhat comparable to that of Sherwood Anderson's *Winesburg, Ohio* (1919) and Jean Toomer's *Cane* (1923), Cisneros's work mixes genres, for while each section achieves, in Ellen McCracken's words, "the intensity of the short story," the forty-four interrelated stories allow for a development of character and plot typical of the novel. Julián Olivares quotes Cisneros on her intent: "I wanted to write stories that were a cross between poetry and fiction.... Except I wanted to write a collection which could be read at any random point without having any knowledge of what came before or after. Or that could be read in a series to tell one big story. I wanted stories like poems, compact and lyrical and ending with a reverberation."

> "Perhaps most important, Cisneros grounds her revisionist feminist perspective in everyday experience by highlighting the stamina of the women she has known in real life."

The image of the house, as McCracken points out, is symbolic in three distinctive ways, first as it suggests a positive objectification of the self for Esperanza. Before her family moved into the house on Mango Street, Esperanza's teachers had made denigrating remarks about their living conditions. "'You live *there*?' ... I had to look where she pointed—the third floor, the paint peeling, wooden bars Papa had nailed on the windows so we wouldn't fall out.... The way she said it made me feel like nothing." Sister Superior reveals her prejudices by suggesting that as a Mexican, Esperanza must live in "a row of ugly 3-flats, the ones even the raggedy men are ashamed to go into." Thus, though far from perfect, the family's new home, according to McCracken, "represents a positive objectification of the self, the chance to redress humiliation and establish a dignified sense of her own personhood."

Cisneros also successfully dramatizes both the individual and the communal significance of owning a house. Such a basic human desire and need is especially crucial for economically oppressed minorities. The house Esperanza dreams of beyond her family home will still have a communal function. She vows that "one day I'll own my own house, but I won't forget who I am or where I came from. Passing bums will ask, Can I come in? I'll offer them the attic, ask them to stay." In a third distinctive motif Cisneros establishes a link between the image of the house and creativity, not only in the bedtime stories Esperanza's mother tells, but also in the daughter's wish for "a house quiet as snow, a space for myself to go, clean as paper before the poem."

Despite the generally positive symbolism of the house, Cisneros does explore issues of patriarchal and sexual violence. During the course of the novel, a woman is locked in by her husband, a young girl is brutally beaten by her father, and Esperanza is raped. But even as she "mourns her loss of innocence" Esperanza understands, as critic María Herrera-Sobek points out, that by romanticizing sexual relations, grown-up women are complicit in the male oppression of their sex.

Several positive role models, McCracken observes, help guide Esperanza's development. Minerva, barely two years older than Esperanza, writes poetry when not dealing with her two children and an abusive husband. In fact, Esperanza realizes that Minerva's writing allows her to transcend her predicament. Also, Esperanza's bedridden aunt encourages her, "You must keep writing. It will keep you free." And "las comadres" (godmothers or women close to the family circle) tell Esperanza that her art must be linked to the community: "When you leave you must remember always to come back . . . for the others. A circle, you understand? You will always be Esperanza. You will always be Mango Street. . . . You can't forget who you are." Writing, then, empowers Esperanza and strengthens her commitment to the community of Chicanas.

The House on Mango Street, in Ramón Saldívar's view, "represents from the simplicity of childhood vision the enormously complex process of the construction of [a woman's ethnic identity]. Posing the question of sexual difference within the urban working-class Chicano community, Cisneros's novel emphasizes the crucial roles of racial and material as well as ideological conditions of oppression." The need to address such pervasive conditions became clear to Chicana writers of the 1980s. After *The House on Mango Street* many Chicanas developed, according to Yvonne Yarbo-Bejarano, "a clear-sighted recognition of the unavoidably mutual overdetermination of the categories of race and class with that of gender in any attempted positioning of the Chicana subject."

Cisneros's willingness to experiment in different genres leads to stylistic and thematic crossovers. However, Cisneros regards writing poetry and prose as distinctly different: "writing poetry . . . you're looking at yourself *desnuda*. . . . [Y]ou've got to go beyond censorship . . . to get at that core of truth. . . . When you think: 'Oh my goodness, I didn't know I felt that!' that's when you stop. . . . That's a poem. It's quite a different process from writing fiction, because you know what you are going to say when you write fiction. To me, the definition of a story is something that someone wants to listen to."

My Wicked Wicked Ways (1987), Cisneros's most widely known collection, contains the poems published originally in a chapbook titled *Bad Boys*. Discussing the title of her work in the *Americas Review*, Cisneros observed, "These are poems in which I write about myself, not a man writing about me. It is . . . my life story as told by me, not according to a male point of view. And that's where I see perhaps the 'Wicked Wicked' of the title." Citing her novel, Cisneros acknowledges, "A lot of the themes from *Mango Street* are repeated: I leave my father's house, I don't get married, I travel to other countries, I can sleep with men if I want to, I can abandon them or choose not to sleep with them, and yes, I can fall in love and even be hurt by men—all of these things but as told by me. I am not the muse."

Both Cisneros's fiction and her poetry emphasize some dominant themes. In discussing the quest for cultural identity, Cisneros asserts that "it's very strange to be straddling these two cultures and to try to define some middle ground so that you don't commit suicide or you don't become so depressed or you don't self explode. There has to be some way for you to say: 'Alright, the life I'm leading is alright. I'm not betraying my culture. I'm not becoming Anglicized.'"

In a 1993 interview Cisneros attributes her devotion to feminism, another recurrent theme, to her Mexican American mother: "My mom did things that were very non-traditional—for one, she didn't force me to learn how to cook. She didn't interrupt me to do chores when I was reading or studying. And she always told me, 'make sure you can take care of yourself.' And that was very different from other women, who felt they had to prepare their daughters to be a wife." Yet she remains aware of the price exacted by a revisionist approach to traditional mores, recalling in the *Americas Review*, "I felt, as a teenager, that I could not inherit my culture intact without revising some parts of it. That did not mean I wanted to reject the entire culture, although my brothers and my father thought I did. . . . I know that part of the trauma that I went through from my teen years through the twenties up until very recently, and that other Latinas are going through too, is coming to terms with what Norma [Alarcón] calls 'reinventing ourselves,' revising ourselves. We accept our culture, but not without adapting ourselves as women."

For a Hispanic the question of cultural identity often involves language. Growing up, Cisneros spoke Spanish with her father and English with her mother. Her practice of interspersing Spanish terms and phrases in her writing, especially notable in *Woman Hollering Creek and Other Stories* (1991), which was written since her move to San Antonio, stems naturally from her bicultural background. Cisneros asserted in the 4 August 1991 *Chicago Tribune* that "if you're bilingual, you're doubly rich. You have two ways of looking at the world."

Again dramatizing the interconnection between the individual and the community through her focus on gender in interpersonal relationships, Cisneros in the twenty-two stories of *Woman Hollering Creek* explores the San Antonio setting, contrasting the socialization processes of *Mexicanas de éste y el otro lado* (Mexican women on both sides of the border) with those of their Anglo counterparts. The book's three major sections suggest a developmental progression from childhood to adulthood, and the thematic motifs of time, love, and religion also function as organizing principles.

The experience of cyclical and parallel patterns of time especially seems to be the collection's major unifying concept, as repeated actions and rites of passage allow Cisneros to make thematic interconnections. Time, for instance, appears as a metaphysical dilemma in "Eleven." The experience of immanence leads the child narrator to explore the notion of chronology: "when you wake up on your eleventh birthday you expect to feel eleven, but you don't. You open your eyes and everything's just like yesterday, only it's today." Cisneros's narrator also views the passage of time in a context of behavioral expectations: "some days you might say something stupid, and that's the part of you that's still ten. Or maybe some days you might need to sit on your mama's lap because you're scared, and that's the part of you that's five. And maybe one day when you're all grown up maybe you will need to cry like if you're three." Finally, the child understands that the resolution of the paradox lies in conceiving time as a process of accretion: "when you're eleven, you're also ten, and nine, and eight, and seven, and six, and five, and four, and three, and two, and one."

In "One Holy Night" the paradox of time is reflected in the characterization of Boy Baby, who "seemed boy and baby and man all at once." Similarly, his refutation of time—"the past and the future are the same thing"—is set against his proclaimed attempt to reenact ancient Mayan ways. The young female protagonist is told that she will become "Ixchel, his Queen" after undergoing a rite of passage, which turns out to be a rape. The experience is described as a clear-cut separation from the past: "something inside bit me, and I gave out a cry as if the other, the one I wouldn't be anymore, leapt out." The irony is underscored when the narrator, now a pregnant teenager who feels suspended in the present, says, "I don't think they understand how it is to be a girl. I don't think they know how it is to have to wait your whole life. I count the months for the baby to be born." A contrasting view of time is evident in "Eyes of Zapata," in which time becomes destiny. Zapata's long-standing lover, Inés Alfaro, states, "I . . . see our lives, clear and still, far away and near. And I see our future and our past, Miliano, one single thread already lived and nothing to be done about it."

Parallel temporal paradigms are articulated in "*Bien* Pretty." According to the narrator, an educated Latina from San Francisco confused about her ethnic identity, "we have to let go of our present way of life and search for our past, remember our destinies." Conversely, her Mexican lover argues, "You Americans have a strange way of thinking about time. . . . You think old ages end, but that's not so. It's ridiculous to think one age has overcome another. American time is running alongside the calendar of the sun, even if your world doesn't know it."

Distraught at discovering that her lover must return to Mexico to tend to a wife, a mistress, and seven children, the narrator seeks solace in *telenovelas* (soap operas). However, she substitutes the "passionate *and* powerful, tender and volatile, brave" women she has known in real life for the passive models on the screen. As a result, self-confidence returns, and aesthetic pleasure leads her to focus on the present, her *being* in the world: "the sky is throbbing. Blue, violet, peach, not holding still for one second. The sun setting . . . because it's today, today; with no thought of the future or past."

In keeping with the stereotype of the passionate Latina, many of the stories in *Woman Hollering Creek* revolve around love, Cisneros's second major organizing motif. To the author's credit, however, her approach is, for the most part, unorthodox. In "One Holy Night" love is defined as "a bad joke," as "a big black piano being pushed off the top of a three story building [while] you're waiting on the bottom to catch it," as "a top . . . spinning so fast . . . all that's left is the hum," and as a crazy man who "walked around all day with his harmonica in his mouth. . . . wheezing, in and out, in and out." The male lead of "*Bien* Pretty" defines love by means of a paradox, "I believe love is always eternal. Even if eternity is only five minutes." On the other hand, under the spell of *telenovelas*, the protagonist of "Woman Hollering Creek" lives for a masochistic version of passion, firmly believing that to "suffer for love is good. The pain all sweet somehow." It takes female bonding to help her break away from her predicament as a battered woman.

The link between time and love is established through a pattern of cyclical repetition. "Never Marry a Mexican" focuses on unrequited love. Seeking revenge for having been seduced by her teacher and smarting from a protracted but essentially unfulfilling love affair, the female protagonist repeats the pattern by having an affair with her lover's son, who at that point happens to be her student. Seduction initiated by males, however, is more common in Cisneros's fiction. In *"Bien Pretty"* Flavio acknowledges the existence of a wife, a mistress, and seven children in Mexico. In "Eyes of Zapata" Inés Alfaro is aware of the numerous "pastimes" who, in addition to his wife, compete with her for the General's attention.

Moreover, patterns of cyclical repetition connect time to male violence. Inés Alfaro's mother was murdered after being gang-raped; Boy Baby appears to have murdered eleven women; and the battered wife of "Woman Hollering Creek" recalls grisly stories that point to a pattern of socially condoned practices—"this woman found on the side of the interstate. This one pushed from a moving car. This one's cadaver, this one unconscious, this one beaten blue." In a much less brutal and depressing way, female power also takes on a cyclical pattern. Inés Alfaro acknowledges, "My Tía Chucha, she was the one who taught me to use my sight, just as her mother had taught her. The women in my family, we've always had the power to see with more than with our eyes."

Religion, the collection's third major unifying theme, might more accurately be defined as a faith in the intercession of certain spiritual figures in human dynamics. Though this cultural marker is treated in "Mericans" and "Anguiano Religious Articles," it is most developed in "Little Miracles, Kept Promises," where Cisneros offers an array of ex-votos (petitions addressed to religious figures and accompanied by promises to do penance in return for the granting of requests). These offers of penance in their very nature contain the nuggets of stories. Local color emerges from the popularity of certain saints as well as through references to healers and African deities. The twenty-two pseudo ex-votos in the story come from a wide range of people, including three heads of households, four young women, three grandparents, and a gay man.

The narrator, a Chicana artist who has been reading the ex-votos, rejects the traditional representation of the Virgin of Guadalupe and the passive endurance of pain endorsed by her mother and grandmother. "I wanted you bare-breasted, snakes in your hands. . . . All that self-sacrifice, all that silent suffering. Hell no. Not here. Not me." Her struggle against traditional mores, class values, and sexism results in a redefinition of and a challenge to the Catholic icon: "When I could see you in all your facets, all at once the Buddha, the Tao, the true Messiah, Yahweh, Allah, the Heart of the Sky, the Heart of the Earth, the Lord of the Near and Far, the Spirit, the Light, the Universe, I could love you." Thus Cisneros proves faithful to her purpose, as she defined it in a 20 May 1991 interview: "in my stories and life I am trying to show that U.S. Latinas have to reinvent, to remythologize, ourselves. A myth believed by almost everyone, even Latina women, is that they are passive, submissive, long-suffering, either a spit-fire or a Madonna. Yet those of us who are their daughters, mothers, sisters know that some of the fiercest women on this planet are Latina women."

Woman Hollering Creek won the P.E.N. Center West Award for best fiction in 1992. Also the winner of two National Endowment for the Arts Fellowships, Cisneros remarked on 20 December 1992 that "there are many Latino writers as talented as I am, but because we are published through small presses our books don't count. We are still the illegal aliens of the literary world." Cisneros has been a writer in residence at the University of Michigan in Ann Arbor and at the University of California at Irvine since she graduated with her master's degree from the writing program at the University of Iowa. Describing herself as "[n]obody's wife" and "nobody's mother" in 1993, the author currently "lives in a rambling Victorian painted in Mexican colors right on the San Antonio River amid pecan and mesquite trees."

Among other projects, Cisneros plans to write a second novel, "Caramelo," set in Mexico and the United States. In her December 1992 interview she said that her novel will focus on "Mexican love and the models we have of love." In a 4 August 1991 interview Cisneros asserted that she is also "particularly interested in exploring father-daughter relationships and aspects of growing up in 'the middle,' between Mexican and Mexican-American culture."

She wants to examine the notions that one culture holds about the other, "what one said when the other wasn't around." But her dream, she admitted in December 1992, is to write a Chicana feminist *telenovela* because "It's a way to reach a lot of people." Today Cisneros is perhaps the most visible Chicana in mainstream literary circles. The vividness of her vignettes and the lyrical quality of her prose attest to her craft, about which Melita Marie Garza notes, "Cisneros is as exacting in her writing as she is brazen in her criticism. She rewrites even her shortest stories about twenty-five times."

By re-creating a Chicana child's perspective, Cisneros has already made a significant contribution to the development of the Chicano literary tradition. Moreover, by focusing on the socialization processes of the Chicana, she has criticized and challenged major stereotypes. Perhaps most important, Cisneros grounds her revisionist feminist perspective in everyday experience by highlighting the stamina of the women she has known in real life. Finally, the broad range of voices that appears in her texts—from historical figures such as Emiliano Zapata to fictional gay lovers—attests to her continued success in developing a flexible, yet personal, style.

As shown by the six reprintings of *The House on Mango Street* (1983, 1984, 1985, 1986, 1988, and 1992), Cisneros's reading public is steadily increasing. Her endorsement of bilingualism in *Woman Hollering Creek* as well as her focus on interfacing cultures and her willingness to adopt the popular soap-opera style suggest that, though Cisneros has already carved herself a niche in American literature, the best may be yet to come.

Source: Cynthia Tompkins, "Sandra Cisneros," in *Dictionary of Literary Biography*, Vol. 152, *American Novelists Since World War II, Fourth Series*, edited by James Giles and Wanda Giles, Gale Research, 1995, pp. 35–41.

Eduardo F. Elías

In the following essay, Elías discusses Cisneros's personal history and her body of writing.

Sandra Cisneros considers herself a poet and a short-story writer, although she has also authored articles, interviews, and book reviews concerning Chicano writers. She began writing at age ten, and she is one of the few Chicano authors trained in a formal creative-writing program. At the University of Iowa Writers' Workshop she earned a Master of Fine Arts degree in 1978. She has taught creative writing at all levels and has experience in educational and arts administration. Her creative work, though not copious, has already been the subject of scholarly papers in the areas of Chicano and women's studies. She has read her poetry at the Colegio de México in Mexico City; at a symposium on Chicano literature at the Amerikanistik Universität in Erlangen, Germany; and over Swedish Educational Radio. Some of her poetry is included in a collection of younger Chicano poets published in Calcutta, India. She has garnered several grants and awards in the United States and abroad, and her book *The House on Mango Street* (1983) was praised, winning the 1985 Before Columbus American Book Award.

Cisneros is a native of Chicago, where she grew up and attended Loyola University, graduating in 1976 with a B.A. in English. Her father was born in Mexico City to a family of means; his wanderlust and lack of interest in schooling led him to travel broadly and to venture into the United States. By chance he traveled through Chicago, met Sandra's mother, and decided to settle there for life. He and his family were influential in Sandra's maturation. Her mother came from a family whose men had worked on the railroad. Sandra grew up in a working-class family, as the only girl surrounded by six brothers. Money was always in short supply, and they moved from house to house, from one ghetto neighborhood to another. In 1966 her parents borrowed enough money for a down payment on a small, ugly, two-story bungalow in a Puerto Rican neighborhood on the north side of Chicago. This move placed her in a stable environment, providing her with plenty of friends and neighbors who served as inspirations for the eccentric characters in *The House on Mango Street*.

The constant moving during her childhood, the frequent forays to Mexico to see her father's family, the poor surroundings, and the frequent changing of schools made young Cisneros a shy, introverted child with few friends. Her love of books came from her mother, who saw to it that the young poet had her first library card before she even knew how to read. It took her years to realize that some people actually purchased their books instead of borrowing them from the library. As a child she escaped into her readings and even viewed her life as a story in which she was the main character manipulated by a romantic narrator.

"I don't remember reading poetry," Cisneros admits. "The bulk of my reading was fiction, and Lewis Carroll was one of my favorites." As she wrote her first poems, modeling them on the rhythmic texts in her primary readers, she had no notion

> "Cisneros looks back on those years and admits she did not know she was a Chicana writer at the time, and if someone had labeled her thus, she would have denied it."

of formal structure, but her ear guided her in matters of rhyme and rhythm. After the sixth grade, however, Cisneros stopped writing for a while. In her junior year in high school she was exposed to works by the finest of British and American writers and by Latin-American poets who impressed her deeply. Finally, in her junior year at Loyola University, she was introduced to writers such as Donald Justice, James Wright, and Mark Strand, poets who had influenced a whole generation of Spanish writers, thus bringing Cisneros into touch with her cultural roots. She was also introduced to the Chicago poetry scene, where there was great interest in her work. She was encouraged to study in a creative-writing program and was admitted to the Iowa Writers' Workshop; she had hoped to study with Justice but discovered that he and Marvin Bell were on sabbatical leaves that academic year.

Cisneros looks back on those years and admits she did not know she was a Chicana writer at the time, and if someone had labeled her thus, she would have denied it. She did not see herself as different from the rest of the dominant culture. Her identity was Mexican, or perhaps Puerto Rican, because of the neighborhood she grew up in, but she mostly felt American—because all her reading was of mainstream literature, and she always wrote in English. Spanish was the private language of home, and she spoke it only with her father. Cisneros knew no Chicano writers in Chicago, and although she was the only Hispanic majoring in English at Loyola, she was unaware of being different—in spite of her appearance, which was considered exotic by her female classmates.

The two years at Iowa were influential on Cisneros's life and writing. She admits that the experience was terribly cruel to her as well as to many of the other first-year students, but it was also liberating. She had her share and fill of intimidating teachers and colleagues as well as some marvelous ones who helped and encouraged her. This was a time for Cisneros to mature emotionally, something she had neglected to do for some years—always having considered herself as somebody's daughter, lover, or friend. The poet struggled in these years with finding a voice for her writings. She imitated her teachers, her classmates, and what she calls the "terrible East-coast pretentiousness" that permeated the workshop, without finding satisfaction. An important friend at this time was Joy Harjo, a Native American from Oklahoma, who was well centered in her southwestern heritage and identity and who also felt lonely and displaced in the Iowa workshop. This friendship offered Cisneros the assurance that she had something to write about that would distinguish her from her classmates.

The bulk of Cisneros's early writing emerged in 1977 and 1978. She began writing a series of autobiographical sketches influenced by Vladimir Nabokov's memoirs. She purposely delighted in being iconoclastic, in adopting themes, styles, and verbal patterns directly opposed to those used by her classmates. *The House on Mango Street* was born this way, with a child's narrative voice that was to be Cisneros's poetic persona for several years.

The poem "Roosevelt Road," written in the summer of 1977, is most important to Cisneros because it forced her to confront the poverty and embarrassment she had lived with all her previous years and to admit the distinctiveness of this background as a positive resource that could nourish her writing. In this poem the language is completely straightforward and descriptive of the tenement housing where the poet lived as a child. Lines run into one another, so that the reader is compelled to follow the inherent rhythm, while working on the sense of the message:

> We lived on the third floor always
> because noise travelled down
> The milkman climbed up tired everyday
> with milk and eggs
> and sometimes sour cream.
> ....
> Mama said don't play in alleys
> because that's where dogs get rabies and
> bad girls babies
> Drunks carried knives
> but if you asked
> they'd give you money.
> ....
> How one time we found that dollar
> and a dead mouse in the stone wall
> where the morning glories climbed....

Once the journals *Nuestro* and *Revista Chicano-Riqueña* accepted her first poems, Cisneros gained enough confidence to submit her work to other publications. These early texts were more concerned with sound and timing, more with the *how* than with the *what*, of what she was saying. A case in point is "South Sangamon," in *My Wicked Wicked Ways* (1987), a poem which, when read aloud, corroborates the fact:

> His drunk cussing,
> her name all over the hallway
> and my name mixed in.
> He yelling from the other side open
> and she yelling from this side no.
> A long time of this
> and we say nothing
> just hoping he'd get tired and go.

Cisneros's master's thesis, titled "My Wicked, Wicked Ways" (Iowa, 1978), is full of such poems on a diversity of topics—daily events, self-identity, amorous experiences, and encounters with friends. Her penchant for sound is obvious, as is her representation of a world that is neither bourgeois nor mainstream. Revised and enlarged, the thesis was published as a book in 1987.

While Cisneros taught at Latino Youth Alternative High School in Chicago (July 1978–December 1980), she spent time on writing but never finished projects fully as collections. Her involvement with many aspects of student life was too draining and consumed her creative energy. However, one poem she wrote was selected to be posted on the Chicago area public buses, thus giving her much-needed exposure and publicity. Cisneros was also seduced by the adulation and applause awarded to writers who read their material at public performances. After a period of "too much performing" (in her words) in coffee-houses and school auditoriums, she gave up the lecture circuit to spend more time on her writing.

Another Chicano poet, Gary Soto, was instrumental in helping publish Cisneros's chapbook *Bad Boys* in 1980. The seven poems depict childhood scenes and experiences in the Mexican ghetto of Chicago. One poem, "The Blue Dress," is Cisneros's effort to paint a scene full of visual imagery that depicts a pregnant woman seen through the eyes of the expectant father. The language of these poems has a musical ring, with short, run-on lines and compact statements.

By the time that *The House on Mango Street* was ready for publication, Cisneros had outgrown the voice of the child narrator who recounts the tales in the book, but this 1983 work gave Cisneros her broadest exposure. It is dedicated to "the women," and, in forty-four short narratives, it recounts the experiences of a maturing adolescent girl discovering life around her in a Hispanic urban ghetto. There are many touching scenes that Esperanza, the young narrator, recounts: her experiences with the death of relatives and neighbors, for example, and with girlfriends who tell her about life. In "Hips," young Esperanza explains: "The bones just one day open. One day you might decide to have kids, and then where are you going to put them?" Esperanza identifies herself to her readers: "In English my name means hope. In Spanish it means too many letters." As the stories of Esperanza in her Hispanic barrio evolve, the child breezes through more and more maturing experiences.

The reader sees many portraits of colorful neighbors—Puerto Rican youths, fat ladies who do not speak English, childhood playmates—until finally Esperanza sees herself and her surrounding experiences with greater maturity. Thus the reader sees her at her first dance in the tale "Chanclas," where attention is first focused on the bulky, awkward saddle oxfords of a school-girl, then the vision is directed upward as Esperanza blossoms into a graceful and poised dancer, who draws everyone's glances. Esperanza retells humorous experiences about her first job and her eighth-grade girlfriend who marries; then Esperanza reveals more of her intimate self in the last two tales. In "A House of My Own" and "Mango Says Goodbye Sometimes," it is revealed that the adolescent has been nurturing a desire to flee the sordid, tragicomic environment where she has grown up. The image of the house is also useful to reveal the need for the narrator to find a self-identity.

An important contribution by Cisneros to Chicano letters is that this book about growing up offers a feminine view of the process, in contrast to that exemplified by leading works by men. As critics Erlinda Gonzales-Berry and Tey Diana Rebolledo have aptly pointed out, young Esperanza is a courageous character who must combat the socialization process imposed on females; the character breaks from the tradition of the usual protagonist of the female bildungsroman by consistently rejecting the models presented to her and seeking another way to be Chicana: "I have begun my own kind of war. Simple. Sure. I am one who leaves the table like a man, without putting back the chair or picking up the plate." Esperanza's experiences parallel those depicted by other Chicana writers.

In conversations about her life, Cisneros admits that up through her college years she had always felt that she was not her own person. Thus Esperanza yearns for "a house all my own.... Only a house quiet as snow, a space for myself to go, clean as paper before the poem." Cisneros's speaker feels the need to tell the world the stories about the girl who did not want to belong to that ugly house on Mango Street. Esperanza admits, at the conclusion of her stories, she is already too strong to be tied down by the house; she will leave and go far, only to come back some day for those stories and people that could not get away. The conclusion is that, in essence, Cisneros takes within her the memories from the house as she also carries her mementos from Mango Street, her bag of books and possessions. These are her roots, her inspirations, and the kernels of what Cisneros sensed, years ago in Iowa, that distinguished her from other American writers.

My Wicked Wicked Ways contains several texts that have been published singly. They show a different aspect of Cisneros's work. The speakers of several poems are adult women involved in relationships with a roguish male, Rodrigo. These poems are physically descriptive and sensuous—bordering on the erotic—and behind them lies a strong hand.

Woman Hollering Creek and Other Stories (1991) is a rare example of a work by a Chicana being published by a mainstream press. Writer Ann Beattie has said of this collection: "My prediction is that Sandra Cisneros will stride right into the spotlight—though an aura already surrounds her. These stories about how and why we mythologize love are revelations about the constant, small sadnesses that erode our facades, as well as those unpredictably epiphanic moments that lift our hearts from despair. A truly wonderful book."

Cisneros has been fortunate to earn several grants that have permitted her to devote herself full-time to her writing. In the spring of 1983 she was artist in residence at the Fondation Michael Karolyi in Vence, France. Earlier, in 1982, she received a National Endowment for the Arts grant, which she used to travel through Europe. During that time she began work on a series of poems she included in her 1987 book. Several of them are evidently based on fleeting encounters with men she met in her European travels. They are whimsical mementos of fleeting instances either enjoyed or lost. Still present are the familiar rhythm and musicality; the major change is in the themes and voice. Most definitely, she has outgrown the adolescent form of expression of her earlier writing.

In the late 1980s Cisneros completed a Paisano Dobie Fellowship in Austin, Texas, and then spent additional time in Texas. She also won first and third prizes for her short stories in the Segundo Concurso Nacional del Cuento Chicano, sponsored by the University of Arizona. Cisneros as a writer is growing rapidly. She feels that writers like herself, Soto, Lorna Dee Cervantes, and Alberto Ríos belong to a new school of technicians, new voices in Chicano poetry. Cisneros wants to maintain her distinctiveness and her dual inheritance and legacy, and not fuse into the American mainstream. She cannot tell in which direction her poetry will lead her; most recently she has expanded her writing to include essays. She hopes that years from now she will still be worthy of the title "poet" and that her peers will recognize her as such.

Source: Eduardo F. Elías, "Sandra Cisneros," in *Dictionary of Literary Biography*, Vol.122, *Chicano Writers, Second Series*, edited by Francisco A. Lomeli and Carl R. Shirley, Gale Research, 1992, pp. 77–81.

Pilar E. Rodriquez Aranda

In the following interview, Cisneros discusses her works, the autobiographical elements in them, and her evolution as a woman.

[Rodríguez Aranda]: *Lets start with what I call the soil where Sandra Cisneros' "wicked" seed germinated. Your first book,* The House on Mango Street, *is it autobiographical?*

[Cisneros]: That's a question that students always ask me because I do a lot of lectures in Universities. They always ask: "Is this a true story?" or, "How many of these stories are true?" And I have to say, "Well they're all true." All fiction is non-fiction. Every piece of fiction is based on something that really happened. On the other hand, it's not autobiography because my family would be the first one to confess: "Well it didn't happen that way." They always contradict my stories. They don't understand I'm not writing autobiography.

What I'm doing is I'm writing true stories. They're all stories I lived, or witnessed, or heard; stories that were told to me. I collected those stories and I arranged them in an order so they would be clear and cohesive. Because in real life, there's no order.

All fiction is giving order to that....

... to that disorder, yes. So, a lot of the events were composites of stories. Some of those stories happened to my mother, and I combined them with something that happened to me. Some of those stories unfortunately happened to me just like that.

Some of the stories were my students' when I was a counselor; women would confide in me and I was so overwhelmed with my inability to correct their lives that I wrote about them.

How did the idea of Mango Street *turn into a book?*

The House on Mango Street started when I was in graduate school, when I realized I didn't have a house. I was in this class, we were talking about memory and the imagination, about Gustave Bachelard's *Poetics of Space.* I remember sitting in the classroom, my face getting hot and I realized: "My god, I'm different! I'm different from everybody in this classroom." You know, you always grow up thinking something's different or something's wrong, but you don't know what it is. If you're raised in a multi-ethnic neighborhood you think that the whole world is multi-ethnic like that. According to what you see in the media, you think that that's the norm; you don't ever question that you're different or you're strange. It wasn't until I was twenty-two that it first hit me how different I really was. It wasn't as if I didn't know who I was. I knew I was a Mexican woman. But, I didn't think that had anything to do with why I felt so much imbalance in my life, whereas it had everything to do with it! My race, my gender, and my class! And it didn't make sense until that moment, sitting in that seminar. That's when I decided I would write about something my classmates couldn't write about. I couldn't write about what was going on in my life at that time. There was a lot of destructiveness; it was a very stressful time for that reason, and I was too close to it, so I chose to write about something I was far removed from, which was my childhood.

So you are and you're not "Esperanza," the main character in The House on Mango Street. *Now, at some point she says to herself that she's bad. Is that something you felt when you were her age?*

Certainly that black-white issue, good-bad, it's very prevalent in my work and in other Latinas. It's something I wasn't aware of until very recently. We're raised with a Mexican culture that has two role models: La Malinche y la Virgen de Guadalupe. And you know that's a hard route to go, one or the other, there's no in-betweens.

The in-between is not ours. All the other role models are outside our culture, they're Anglo. So if you want to get out of these two roles, you feel you're betraying you're people.

Exactly, you're told you're a traitor to your culture. And it's a horrible life to live. We're always straddling two countries, and we're always living in that kind of schizophrenia that I call, being a Mexican woman living in an American society, but not belonging to either culture. In some sense we're not Mexican and in some sense we're not American. I couldn't live in Mexico because my ideas are too ...

... progressive?

Yeah, too Americanized. On the other hand, I can't live in America, or I do live here but, in some ways, almost like a foreigner.

An outsider.

Yes. And it's very strange to be straddling these two cultures and to try to define some middle ground so that you don't commit suicide or you don't become so depressed or you don't self explode. There has to be some way for you to say: "Alright, the life I'm leading is alright, I'm not betraying my culture. I'm not becoming anglicized." I was saying this last night to two Latinas in San Antonio. It's so hard for us to live through our twenties because there's always this balancing act, we've got to define what we think is fine for ourselves instead of what our culture says.

At the same time, none of us wants to abandon our culture. We're very Mexican, we're all very Chicanas. Part of being Mexicana is that love and that affinity we have for our *cultura.* We're very family centered, and that family extends to the whole Raza. We don't want to be exiled from our people.

Even in the eighties, Mexican women feel there are all these expectations they must fulfill, like getting married, having children. Breaking with them doesn't mean you are bad, but society makes you feel that way. . . .

Part of it is our religion, because there's so much guilt. It's so hard being Catholic, and even though you don't call yourself Catholic anymore, you have vestiges of that guilt inside you; it's in your blood. Mexican religion is half western and half pagan; European Catholicism and Precolumbian religion all mixed in. It's a very strange Catholicism like nowhere else on the planet and it does strange things to you. There's no one sitting on your shoulder but you have the worst censor of all, and that's yourself.

I found it very hard to deal with redefining myself or controlling my own destiny or my own sexuality. I still wrestle with that theme, it's still the theme of my last book, *My Wicked Wicked Ways,* and in the new one that I've started and the one that comes after, so it's a ghost I'm still wrestling with.

> "*I used to think that writing was a way to exorcise those ghosts that inhabit the house that is ourselves.*"

Talking about ghosts, would you say that writing is a way of getting rid of your guilt, of saying: "You might think I'm wicked, but it's not about being wicked, it's about being me." Some kind of exorcism....

I used to think that writing was a way to exorcise those ghosts that inhabit the house that is ourselves. But now I understand that only the little ghosts leave. The big ghosts still live inside you, and what happens with writing—I think a more accurate metaphor would be to say—that you make your peace with those ghosts. You recognize they live there....

That they're part of you....

They're part of you and you can talk about them, and I think that it's a big step to be able to say: "Well, yeah, I'm haunted, ha! There's a little ghost there and we coexist."

Maybe I'll always be writing about this schizophrenia of being a Mexican American woman, it's something that in every stage of my life has affected me differently. I don't think it's something I could put to rest. I'll probably still be writing about being good or bad probably when I'm ninety-years old.

It didn't seem to me that in My Wicked Wicked Ways *there was a conflict over being a Hispanic woman. What I saw was the telling of different experiences, memories from childhood, travels, love affairs ... of course you can't get away from the fact that you are Mexican and that you experience life in a certain way because of this.*

These are poems in which I write about myself, not a man writing about me. It is my autobiography, my version, my life story as told by me, not according to a male point of view. And that's where I see perhaps the "Wicked Wicked" of the title.

A lot of the themes from *Mango Street* are repeated: I leave my father's house, I don't get married, I travel to other countries, I can sleep with men if I want to, I can abandon them or choose not to sleep with them, and yes, I can fall in love and even be hurt by men—all of these things but as told by me. I am not the muse.

Some men were disappointed because they thought the cover led them on. They thought it was a very sexy cover and they wanted ... I don't know what they wanted! But they felt disappointed by the book. The cover is of a woman appropriating her own sexuality. In some ways, that's also why it's wicked; the scene is trespassing that boundary by saying: "I defy you. I'm going to tell my own story."

You see, I grew up with six brothers and a father. So, in essence I feel like I grew up with seven fathers. To this day when any man tells me to do something in certain way, the hair on the back of my neck just stands up and I'll start screaming! Then I have to calm down and realize: "Well, alright, okay, you know where this came from, you don't even need an analyst to figure this one out!"

In Mango Street *there's a story called "Beautiful and Cruel," where Esperanza obviously feels an admiration towards the woman in the movies who was "beautiful and cruel," the one "with red red lips" whose power "is her own." Is that why you colored your lips on the black and white photograph of the cover of* My Wicked Wicked Ways?

I never thought about that. I was looking at women who are models of power. I suppose that for someone like Esperanza the only powerful women she would see would be the same type that Manuel Puig idolizes, those black and white screen stars. People like Rita Hayworth, the red-lip women that were beautiful. They didn't have to cling to someone, rather they snuff people out like cigarettes. They were the ones in control, and that was the only kind of role model I had for power. You had to have beauty, and if you didn't have that, you were lost. The cover was trying to play on the Errol Flynn years of film, the lettering and everything.

I got a lot of objections to that photo. People said, "Why did you paint the lips? It's a good photo." The photographer himself didn't want his photograph adulterated. But then, if the lips weren't painted then you'd think I was serious.

When did you realize that you wanted to be a writer or that you were a writer?

Everytime I say I'm a writer, it still surprises me. It's one of those things, that everytime you say it ... me suena muy curioso. It's like saying "I'm a faith healer." Sounds a little bit like a quack when you say it; something a little immodest, a little crazy, admitting you're a writer.

I guess the first time I legitimately started saying that's what I was instead of that's what I wanted to be was when I was in graduate school, when we all had the audacity to claim our major as what we were. But you never get used to saying it because we've always had to make our living other ways. I had to be a teacher, a counselor, I've had to work as an Arts Administrator, you know, all kinds of things just to make my living. The writing is always what you try to save energy for, it's your child. You hope you're not too exhausted so that you can come home to that child and give it everything you can.

It's hard to claim in this society that that's what you are. I feel a little more legitimate saying it these days after I've been doing it professionally for more than ten years. When I'm riding on a plane and I'm off to do a lecture somewhere and the person to the right of me says: "Well, what do you do?" I don't say "I'm a professor," because I only started doing that recently and that doesn't have anything to do with writing. I say "I'm a writer." And the next question always is: "Oh, do you publish?" That really makes me mad like you have to have your vitae with you. But it's nice to say, "Yes, I do."

There's a story in The House on Mango Street *where Esperanza goes to the fortuneteller, who tells her she sees a home in the heart. Did it become true for you, this home in the heart?*

The story impressed me very much because it is exactly what I found out, years after I'd written the book, that the house in essence becomes you. You are the house. But I didn't know that when I wrote it. The story is based on something that happened to me when I went to see a witchwoman once. Going to see that woman was so funny because I didn't understand half the s— she told me, and later on I tried to write a poem about her. The poem didn't work, but a lot of the lines stayed, including the title, so I decided, well, I'll write a story to include in *House on Mango Street*. Her response is at the end when Esperanza says: "Do you see anything else in the glass for my future?" and she says: "A home in the heart, I was right." I don't know where that came from. I just wrote it, and thought: "That sounds good. Kind of sounds like 'anchor of arms' and the other ambiguous answers that the witchwoman is giving the girl."

Two years after I wrote that, when the book finally came out, I was frightened because I had no idea how these pieces were going to fit together. I was making all of these little *cuentitos*, like little squares of a patchwork quilt, hoping that they would match, that somehow there wouldn't be a big hole in the middle. I said, "I think it's done but, *quién sabe!*" So when I saw the book complete, when I opened it and read it from front to back for the first time as a cold thing, in the order that it was, I looked and said, "Oh my goodness, *qué curioso!*" It is as if I knew all of these symbols.

I suppose a Jungian critic would argue: "Yes, you always do know in some sense. This writing comes from the same deep level that dreams and poetry come from, so maybe you're not conscious of it when you're writing, but your subconscious is aware."

It surprised me, and it's also a strange coincidence that I would write the things that eventually I would live. That, yes, I did find a home in the heart, just like Elenita, the witchwoman predicted. I hope that other women find that as well.

What is your home of your heart made of?

I've come this year to realize who I am, to feel very very strong and powerful, I am at peace with myself and I don't feel terrified by anyone, or by any terrible word that anyone would launch at me from either side of the border. I guess I've created a house made of bricks that no big bad wolf can blow down now.

I didn't feel that by the end of My Wicked Wicked Ways *you had that house yet.*

No, because, see, those poems were all written during the time I was writing *The House on Mango Street,* some of them before. They're poems that span from when I was twenty-one years old all the way through the age of thirty. It's a chronological book. If anything, I think that the new book, the *Loose Woman* book is more a celebration of that house in the heart, and *My Wicked Wicked Ways* I would say is in essence my wanderings in the desert.

The last poem in the book is the only one in Spanish. When I read this poem, maybe because my first language is Spanish—but I don't think it is only that—it felt to me the most vulnerable. Your language was more simple, direct, straight to the heart. The poem is called "Tantas Cosas Asustan, Tantas."

"So Many Things Terrify, So Many."

Do you write more in Spanish?

I never write in Spanish, y no es que no quiero sino que I don't have that same palate in Spanish that I do in English. No tengo esa facilidad. I think the only way you get that palate is by living in a culture where you hear it, where the language is not something in a book or in your dreams. It's on the loaf of bread that you buy, it's on the radio jingle, it's on the graffiti you see, it's on your ticket stub. It must be all encompassing.

You have two books published now and you're working on four.

I really have three books. I have a chap book, *Bad Boys*, that preceded this book of poetry and it's out of print now.

So, you are always getting some kind of criticism, comments, etc. How does that affect you? When you write, are you aware of an audience?

Well, sometimes, but not really. Poetry is a very different process from fiction. I feel in some ways that I'm more conscious of my audience when I'm writing fiction, and I'm not conscious of them when I'm writing poetry, or hardly. Poetry is the art of telling the truth, and fiction is the art of lying. The scariest thing to me is writing poetry, because you're looking at yourself *desnuda*. You're always looking at the part of you that you don't show anybody. You're looking at the part of you that maaaaybe you'd show your husband. The part that your siblings or your parents have never even seen. And that center, that terrifying center, is a poem. That's why you can't think of your audience, because if you do, they're going to censor your poem, in the way that if you think about yourself thinking about the poem, you'll censor the poem, see? That's why it's so horrible, because you've got to go beyond censorship when you write, you've got to go deeper, to a real subterranean level, to get at that core of truth. You don't even know what the truth is! You just have to keep writing and hope that you'll come upon something that shocks you. When you think: "Oh my goodness, I didn't know I felt that!" that's where you stop. That's the little piece of gold that you've been looking for. That's a poem. It's quite a different process from writing fiction, because you know what you're going to say when you write fiction. To me, the definition of a story is something that someone wants to listen to. If someone doesn't want to listen to you, then it's not a story.

I was reading an article discussing how there could be more audience for poetry, that one mistake is thinking that poetry is not storytelling.

Poetry can be storytelling. As a critic said, my poetry is very narrative, and is very poetic. I always denied when I wrote *House on Mango Street* that I was a fiction writer. I'd say: "I'm a poet, I just write this naively." But now I see how much of a storyteller I've always been. Because even though I wasn't writing stories, I was talking stories. I think it is very important to develop storytelling abilities. The way I teach writing is based on the oral word. I test all my stories out with my class. When I have every student in that class looking up and listening to me, I know I've got a good story. There's something in it that makes them want to listen. I ask my students, "Do you take notes in my class when I tell you stories?" They go, "No." "How many stories that I've told you, since the beginning of this semester, can you remember?" Ooooah! They all came back with these stories, they could remember them! "You didn't have to take notes. You didn't have to study, right? Why? See how wonderful stories are? You remember!"

You remember the ones that are important to you or that affect you, and you filter out the ones que no te sirven. It's just a nice thing about fiction. To me that's a test of what a good story is: if someone listens to you and if it stays with you. That's why fairy tales and myths are so important to a culture; that's why they get handed down. People don't need to write them down! I think that, even if we didn't have them written down, they would be alive as long as they fulfilled a function of being necessary to our lives. When they no longer spoke to us, then we'd forget.

I've always been interested in trying to understand the function of the myth. It's still kind of a puzzle to me. The way I see it now is that we're sort of in a crisis partly because we don't seem to have that many contemporary myths.

I think that there are urban myths, modern myths, only we can't tell which ones are really going to last. I think that maybe the visual is taking the place of the oral myth. Sometimes I have to make allusions in my class. If I said, "Now, do you remember when Rumple...?" They'd say: "Who?" or they more or less would know the story. Or if I'd make an allusion to the "Little Mermaid" or the "Snow Queen," which are very important fairytales to me, and an integral part of my childhood and my storytelling ability today! ... ¡No hombre! They didn't know what I was talking about. But if I made an illusion to Fred Flintstone, everyone knew who Fred Flintstone was. Ha, ha! It's kind of horrible in a way that I have to resort to the television characters to make a point. That was our common mythology, that's what we all had in common, television.

You've said a lot of positive things about your teaching, what else is in it for you, and does it sometimes get in the way of your writing?

What Do I Read Next?

- Cisneros's *The House on Mango Street* (1984) is a story about the coming-of-age of Esperanza, a Chicana growing up in an impoverished inner-city neighborhood in Chicago.

- *Bless Me, Ultima* (1972), by Rudolfo Anaya, is a classic of Chicano literature. It tells the story of a young Mexican American boy growing up in New Mexico and coming to terms with his dual cultural identity.

- *From Indians to Chicanos: The Dynamics of Mexican-American Culture* (1998; 2d ed.), by James Diego Vigil, is a readable introduction to the Mexican American experience in the United States. Vigil covers each stage of Mexican American history, from pre-Columbian and Spanish colonial times to Mexican independence and nationalism to the modern Anglo American period. He analyzes the social and cultural dynamics that shaped contemporary Chicano life.

- *Growing Up Chicana/o* (1995), edited by Tiffany Ana Lopez, contains twenty autobiographical essays and stories that explore the Mexican American experience from many angles. One of the essays is by Cisneros, who discusses her memories of growing up in Chicago.

- *Mirrors beneath the Earth: Short Fiction by Chicano Writers* (1992), edited by Ray Gonzalez, is a collection of thirty-one short stories by contemporary Chicano writers. It includes established figures such as Cisneros, Rudolfo Anaya, Denise Chavez, and Ana Castillo, as well as new writers such as Daniel Romero, Patricia Blanco, Ana Baca, and others.

I complain about my students and say how they're always sucking my blood. Ha! But they would never kill me or suck my blood if I didn't let them. I will work very hard for students that work hard for me; it's a contract thing, you know, you have to work for each other. I tell my students all the time that teaching and writing don't have anything to do with one another. And I say that because when I'm writing on a weekend, then that following week I'm kind of half-ass as a teacher: I didn't read through their stories well enough, I didn't have time to read them ahead of time, I read them in class for the first time, and so I have to steal their time in order to be a writer. When I'm teaching and doing a really kick-ass job that week, my private time gets stolen because I can't write. My creativity is going towards them and to my teaching and to my one-on-one with them. I never find a balance. I can't have it both ways, they don't have anything to do with one another.

On the one hand, I get encouraged to be a writer. They like it that I'm a writer, they like that I publish, that I lecture. Everywhere I've worked writing's always been kind of an interruption to my other duties. On the other hand, as a writer, I can't understand the priorities that academia has towards titles and towards time and deadlines, I don't work like that.

It helps that I call myself a writer because they think: "Oh well, she's just a writer, that's why she can't get her grades in on time," or "That's why she wears those funny clothes and has her hair so funny . . . she's a writer." The way universities are set up is very countercreative. The environment, the classroom, the times; the way that people have to leave when you're in the middle of a sentence to go to another class is countercreative. The fact that I have to be there on time boggles me. My students would get all upset if I'd come fifteen minutes late, and I'd say, "What are you so upset about? If I was in a cafe, would you leave?" They'd say, "Nooo." "I would wait for you. Why are you all so upset about?" You'd have to be there a certain time or right away they'd want to leave. That inflexibility with time to me doesn't make sense. I know that some of them might have to go to another class but that's not the way that I would like to do it. I would like to start the class when I get there and finish when we finish. Usually we don't run out ready in two hours, I want to go on. And I want to go out and drink with all of them, and have some coffee or beer after class, because I think the real learning keeps going.

We talk about that, we talk about what would we like if we could have any type of environment we would choose, and any kind of schedule. Sometimes we spend a whole class talking about what's important in making ourselves more creative and we come up with a whole, exaggerated list of demands, which we give to the chair: "We want a house by the country. . . ." It's fun to talk about those things because you start articulating what's important to you. Maybe we can't have a house in the country, but we realize we need a quiet space to write; alright, maybe we can't all go out and spend a weekend in Europe but we could take a trip to the next town by ourselves. I always feel that when we get off the track like that on a subject in class, it's important. I say: "Forget about my lesson plan because we're going to get on the track by going off the track." Some of my students don't like that about me, that I'll throw the lesson plan, or I won't have a lesson plan or I'll throw the whole syllabus out the window and say, "Well, that's not going to work, I've changed my mind." But it is precisely because I come from an anti-academic experience that I'm very good at teaching writing.

In The House on Mango Street *you were "bad," then you went through the times of figuring out who you were and you came out "wicked," and now you say you're working on being a "loose woman," how does that fit in with your solid brick house?*

I love that title: *Poemas Sueltos*. I was thinking of Jaime Sabines' book: *Poemas sueltos, Loose Poems,* because they didn't belong to any other collection. I started writing these poems after being with other women this last spring, and getting so energized. I had a whole series that I continued on through the summer and I thought: "These loose poems don't belong anywhere." I was in the bathroom in Mexico City, sitting on the pot and thinking, "What can I do with these poems, what would I call them? They're loose poems. But they're loose 'women' poems." You see? I'm reinventing the word "loose." I really feel that I'm the loose and I've cut free from a lot of things that anchored me. So, playing on that, the collection is called *Loose Woman*.

It is because your home in the heart is now so strong that you can be loose.

Yes. Like there is a poem called "New Tango," it's about how I like to dance alone. But the tango that I'm dancing is not a man over a woman, but a "new" tango that I dance by myself. Chronologically it follows the books as a true documentation of where the house of my heart is right now.

Source: Pilar E. Rodriquez Aranda, Interview with Sandra Cisneros, in *Americas Review*, Vol. XVIII, No. 1, Spring 1990, pp. 64–80.

Sources

Cisneros, Sandra, *Loose Woman*, Alfred A. Knopf, 1994.

Nash, Susan Smith, Review of *Loose Woman*, in *World Literature Today*, Vol. 69, No. 1, Winter 1995, pp. 145–46.

Niño, Raúl, "An Interview with Sandra Cisneros," in *Booklist*, Vol. 90, No. 1, September 1, 1993, pp. 36–37.

Review of *Loose Woman*, in *Publishers Weekly*, April 25, 1994, p. 61.

Satz, Martha, "Returning to One's House: An Interview with Sandra Cisneros," in *Southwest Review*, Vol. 82, No. 2, Spring 1997, pp. 166–85.

Further Reading

Cisneros, Sandra, "From a Writer's Notebook," in *Americas Review*, Vol. 15, No. 1, Spring 1987, pp. 69–79.
 This article includes three essays in which Cisneros discusses her motivations and development as a writer, her literary influences, and the differences between Spanish and English syntax.

Ganz, Robin, "Sandra Cisneros: Border Crossings and Beyond," in *MELUS*, Vol. 19, No. 1, Spring 1994, pp. 19–29.
 Ganz gives a review of Cisneros's life and work that discusses the origins of her literary career and assesses the nature of her achievements.

Jussawalla, Feroza, and Reed Way Dasenbrock, eds., *Interviews with Writers of the Post-Colonial World*, University Press of Mississippi, 1992.
 This work includes interviews with fourteen writers from a diverse group of nations, including Kenya, Nigeria, Somalia, India, Pakistan, New Zealand, and the Caribbean islands, as well as three Chicano writers from the United States, including Cisneros. Cisneros discusses her life and career as a Chicana writer in a mostly Anglo culture.

Mirriam-Goldberg, Caryn, *Sandra Cisneros: Latina Writer and Activist*, Enslow Publishers, 1998.
 Mirriam-Goldberg provides an enthusiastic survey of Cisneros's life and work, which emphasizes her perseverance in overcoming poverty and cultural biases. This work also discusses her political activities on behalf of Latino workers. Included along with the text are black-and-white photographs.

On Location in the Loire Valley

Diane Ackerman
1998

Diane Ackerman's poem "On Location in the Loire Valley" was published in her fifth volume of poetry, *I Praise My Destroyer* (1998). The poem is written in the form of a ghazal, which is a poetic form that has flourished for hundreds of years in Arabic, Persian, and Urdu literature. Most poets who write ghazals in English produce much looser forms than the traditional one, but Ackerman's "On Location in the Loire Valley" follows the traditional pattern quite closely. The poem appears to tell a story about a company of actors who are making a film on location in the Loire Valley in France. The poem also reflects, in a highly allusive manner, on the nature of human life—its transience, the search for communication, and its unanswerable questions.

Author Biography

Diane Ackerman was born October 7, 1948, in Waukegan, Illinois, the daughter of Sam (a restaurant owner) and Marcia (Tischler) Fink. She attended Boston University from 1966 to 1967, and then enrolled at Pennsylvania State University, from which she graduated in 1970 with a bachelor of arts degree. She pursued graduate study at Cornell University, graduating in 1973 with a master of fine arts degree. She went on to earn a master of arts degree in 1976, and a Ph.D. in English in 1978. She then held teaching positions at the University of Pittsburgh (1980–1983) and Washington

Diane Ackerman

University (1984–1986), and was a staff writer for the *New Yorker* from 1988 to 1994.

In 1976, Ackerman published *The Planets: A Cosmic Pastoral*, her first solo volume of poetry. It was followed by *Wife of Light* in 1978, *Lady Faustus* (1983), and *Jaguar of Sweet Laughter: New and Selected Poems* (1991).

In the early 1990s, Ackerman published two nonfiction works about natural history, *A Natural History of the Senses* (1990) and *The Moon by Whale Light, and Other Adventures among Bats, Penguins, Crocodilians, and Whales* (1991). These books established Ackerman's national reputation as a nature and science writer. *The Moon by Whale Light*, a collection of four essays previously written for the *New Yorker*, was selected by the *New York Times Book Review* as a "New and Noteworthy Book of the Year."

During the mid-1990s, Ackerman wrote three more nonfiction books: *A Natural History of Love* (1994), which explored romantic love from almost every possible angle; *The Rarest of the Rare: Vanishing Animals, Timeless Worlds* (1995); and *A Slender Thread: Crisis, Healing, and Nature* (1997), which was Ackerman's account of working the night shift of a suicide prevention hotline. In 1998, Ackerman produced her first volume of poetry in seven years, *I Praise My Destroyer. Origami Bridges: Poems of Psychoanalysis and Fire* was published in 2002.

Ackerman's other nonfiction works include *Deep Play* (1999), which examines how humans transcend the mundane daily world through "play" activities, including art and religion, and *A Natural History of My Garden* (2001), in which Ackerman observes the passage of the four seasons in her own garden. Along with her works of poetry and nonfiction, Ackerman has also written books for children, several plays, and several television documentaries. *The Senses of Animals: Poems* (2002, reissued as *Animal Sense*, 2003) is a highly praised book of poetry for children that includes illustrations by Peter Sis.

Ackerman has won numerous awards and prizes during her career, including the Wordsmith Award in 1992; the Golden Nose Award from the Olfactory Research Fund in 1994; and the John Burroughs Nature Award in 1998. She was named a "Literary Lion" by the New York Public Library in 1994.

Poem Summary

Couplet 1

The title of the poem, "On Location in the Loire Valley," suggests that it was prompted by some actors' experiences during a film-shoot in the Loire valley in France. The first line of the first couplet presents an image of mistletoe hanging in poplar trees. Mistletoe is a parasitic evergreen that grows on certain trees. The mistletoe absorbs water and mineral nutrients from the tree, damaging the tree. Some trees may be killed by an infestation of mistletoe. This is why in the poem the poplars "can't survive." The poet may use the phrase "clouds of mistletoe" because the abundance of the plant's white berries suggests clouds.

The second line of the couplet provides a consolation. The stately poplar trees, although festooned with the mistletoe that will kill them still have a beneficial effect on human life. They create a feeling of enchantment when a person looks at them.

Couplet 2

The Loire Valley is known for its many castles built during the medieval and Renaissance eras. Line 1 makes it clear that the film is being shot inside one of these castles. It is winter, the castle is extremely cold, and the actors and film crew are uncomfortable because of it. It feels as if cold steel is passing up their spines.

In line 2, the people in the castle shiver from the cold as they make the film. "Decant" means to pour something from one vessel into another. The actors pour their lives from one vessel (their real, everyday life) into another vessel, that of the film they are making.

Couplet 3

In line 1, there is a moment on the movie set when everyone is silent and motionless. Line 2 explains why. The sound engineers have to record what is called in film sound jargon, "room tone." Room tone is the unique sound that every room has when there is no human activity in it. It may be the hum of a computer, the creaks of furniture, the sound of an air conditioner or furnace, the sounds of traffic from outside. In this case in the castle perhaps it might be sounds from outside, such as the wind. Sound engineers will record at least thirty seconds of "room tone," which can then be later used in the film-editing process. If, for example, cuts are made in the original soundtrack, room tone can be inserted at that point so that the background sound will remain continuous.

The last sentence of couplet 2, "Soundmen record the silent rant of our lives," contains an oxymoron. An oxymoron is a figure of speech which combines contradictory terms. Since a "rant" is loud, wildly extravagant speech, it cannot logically be "silent." Perhaps the poet means that although speech has ceased, the "rant" in which the actors have been engaging (presumably dialogue in a scene from the movie) can still be felt and somehow heard (or sensed) in the silent room.

Couplet 4

In this couplet, the speaker of the poem describes his or her experience making the film. The speaker uses the first-person plural "we" to include all the people involved in the film. No precise meaning can be conclusively demonstrated, but perhaps "consort with chance" refers to the ins and outs of the storyline, in which, as in life, chance always plays a part. "Cascade through time" may refer to the actors' experience of acting in a film that is set in a different time than their own.

In line 2, "each trip" may refer to the different places to which the actors and film crew travel in the course of their filmmaking. To gallivant means to go about in search of amusement or excitement, so the phrase "the gallivant of our lives" may refer to the enjoyment they all had on these trips. The phrase might also be taken as a more general observation, that life is a continual chase after excitement.

Couplet 5

This couplet describes the end of the filming process. In the film, the actors have presented the passage of an entire life in a short space of time, "a whole life in miniature" in all its different aspects and relationships. A "small death at the end" may refer to the death of one of the characters in the film or to the severing of a relationship from the past. The line only makes suggestions; the reader can supply the details. The phrase "we adjourn to the constant of our lives" refers to the actors stepping out of the roles they played in the film and returning from their fictional selves to their real selves, the "constant" of their lives.

Couplet 6

This couplet is about the ways the moviemakers and actors part company. Farewells are awkward. It seems as if no one really feels sincere about what they say to each other, as if the whole process lacks any shred of genuine feeling. There is little conversation at mealtimes, and goodbyes are quickly said. So it is that the people "dismantle" their lives, as if their lives are like the film sets, erected for a certain purpose and taken apart and moved away when that purpose has been fulfilled. It is a mechanical process, without human warmth.

Couplet 7

The actors have now returned from their trip on location in the Loire Valley. They tell their loved ones about it, but exaggerate their exploits for the sake of telling a good story. Line 2 may be one of the stories they tell, about night drives through fog. The use of the word "nonchalant" to describe these trips suggests the exaggeration with which the stories are told. Nonchalant in this context probably means "unconcerned." The reader gets a picture of a group of people driving through thick fog but pretending it does not bother them at all.

Couplet 8

This couplet continues to encapsulate the adventures that the group of actors went through during the filming. "Alone with legendary art" might mean many things, but it suggests the artwork in the castle where part of the film was made. The same applies to "herding sheep in St. Michel," an act done in connection with the film. Line 2, "the wizardries of smell," is harder to explicate with any specificity. It certainly alludes to the well-known capacity of the sense of smell to evoke distinct memories and impressions, which give it a kind of wizard's power. The last thought in the couplet echoes the phrase "gallivant of our lives" from the fourth couplet. It suggests that there was a lot of good-humored teasing or pleasantries on the film set.

Couplet 9

The first thought, "the heart has a curfew," suggests there are some things that cannot be communicated. At some point the heart must, so to speak, shut down. This resembles a curfew, which is a time after which people must remain indoors. The speaker, and the other actors for whom he or she speaks, explains that they are able to tell people the external details of where they went and what they did, but they cannot explain who they were. Presumably this refers to the essence of the role each played in the film, although why they cannot explain this role is not made clear. An alternative meaning is possible too. Instead of describing the experiences on location, the speaker may be making a general reflection on life, that people cannot convey the deeper truths of their lives, or who they really are. This leads to the final statement, that their lives are pantomimes. A pantomime is a dramatic entertainment often based on a fairytale, or it may be a dumb show, in which actors express their meaning through action and gestures rather than words.

Couplet 10

This couplet is difficult to interpret because the two lines make up a fragment, not a complete sentence. In the absence of a subject and a verb, the meaning becomes problematic. The most likely interpretation seems to be that the couplet refers back to "but we cannot tell them who" in the previous couplet, meaning perhaps that they cannot fully explain the characters they portrayed in the film (or perhaps they cannot fully explain themselves). The speaker states what they were not, rather than what they were. They were not the "shadow family" they became. Nor can they fully convey the "shiver beneath the smile," which may refer to the cold conditions in which the film was made (mentioned in the second couplet). The first part of the final line, "not the people we clung to" remains difficult to explicate, however, unless it is referring again to the roles each actor played, in the sense that an actor "clings" to his character. On the other hand, if the couplet refers to the alternative meaning that is possible in couplet nine, and the speaker is making a general reflection on life, the couplet suggests that in spite of the "mad canter" of life, real knowledge of who we are and who we are dealing with in life remains elusive.

Themes

Death in Life

In a ghazal, the couplets can be read as self-contained poems, so there may be a multiplicity of themes rather than one. Sometimes the first couplet sets the tone for the remainder, although that is by no means always the case. In this ghazal, the first couplet creates an image of life being gradually destroyed by a parasite (mistletoe), and yet beauty is present too. The mistletoe decorates the trees and lends enchantment to life. This description of a natural phenomenon may metaphorically suggest that even if life is always a journey to death and death is present in life, life is still worth living.

The remainder of the poem, however, does not seem to extend or amplify this suggestion. The couplets that follow are like a series of snapshots of different moods, activities, and places. Some express enjoyment and light-heartedness (couplet 4) or a sense of wonder about life (couplet 8); others express discouragement and even cynicism about human relationships (couplet 6).

The Inability to Know

In the final two couplets, the thought seems to take a more serious and reflective tone, as if the speaker is meditating on the experience he or she shared with the other actors and filmmakers on location in the Loire Valley. The conclusion does not seem to be an optimistic one. Couplet 9 seems to hint with regret that in some profound way, the people in the poem (and by implication, all humans) are not able to fully communicate with each other. One final ingredient is missing; perhaps it is complete truthfulness to one's own experience of oneself and others. The refrain of "What a pantomime, our lives" suggests a certain ridiculousness about the lives evoked.

Perhaps the implication is that humans are all like characters in a film, acting some kind of role that has been appointed. Just as in a film the viewer sees only the moving images projected on the screen, never the screen itself, so too a person does not really know him or herself—that is, who he or she is underneath, beyond all the roles he or she is compelled to play in life.

The final couplet, although the meaning is obscure, contains phrases that suggest a negative or darker view of life: "shadow family"; "shiver beneath the smile"; and especially "the people we clung to in the mad canter of our lives." The images conjured up by this phrase suggest people clinging to each other out of need—the desire for affection or protection perhaps, in a life that cannot always be controlled, that hurtles along at a fast pace but is not wholly rational and cannot be fully understood. The effect of the poem is itself like the filmmaking it describes: scene after scene flashes by, there is variety and entertainment, but the answers to deeper questions about meaning and authenticity are more problematic.

Style

The Ghazal

The poem is written in the form of a ghazal. This poetic form has strict requirements, although Ackerman chose not to observe all of them. A traditional ghazal is a poem of five to fifteen couplets. Each couplet should be a self-contained poem that does not depend on the others for its meaning, although it is permissible to have all the couplets carry the same or similar theme. Because each couplet is self-contained, there should be no run-on lines, or enjambment, between couplets. The length of the lines must be the same. The second lines of each couplet must all end with the same word or words. This is the refrain. There must also be a rhyming pattern to the words that immediately precede the refrain.

The ghazal formula can be clearly seen in this poem. The refrain is "our lives." This phrase concludes all the couplets. The words before the refrain rhymes, at least in part, in each couplet: "enchant" (couplet 1), "decant" (2), "rant" (3), "gallivant" (4), "constant" (5), "dismantle" (6), "nonchalant" (7), "banter" (8), "pantomime" (9), and "canter" (10).

In strictly formulated ghazals, the first couplet must have the words of the refrain in both its lines, a requirement Ackerman chose not to follow. She settles for a rhyme instead, so "survive" (line 1) rhymes with "lives." She also inserts an additional rhyme, "can't" (line 1) rhyming with "enchant."

Alliteration

The poem also makes frequent use of alliteration, which is the repetition of initial consonants (this is not a requirement of the ghazal). "In stone castles, cold's steel," for example, the repetition in reverse order of the "s" and "c" sounds makes the phrase almost a tongue-twister. The "s" sounds are repeated in the phrase that follows, "straight up the spine." The combination of "s" and "c" sounds continues in "shivering to the core," and the "c" is heard again in "decant." Thus the entire couplet is built around the interplay of alliteration.

A similar effect is found in couplet 3, only this time the two initial consonants are "r" and "s." "Restlessness stops" at the end of line 1 is alliteratively echoed in reverse in "Soundmen record" and in "silent rant" in line 2. In couplet 4, the alliteration is with the letters "c" and "t," as in "consort with chance, cascade through time. / Each trip."

Topics for Further Study

- Research the formation of the ghazal in the eighth century. Explain what life was like at that time in India and what importance, if any, was placed on poetry. Is poetry held in high esteem in India today?

- Write a ghazal of your own, consisting of at least two couplets, following the standard rhyming formula. Then, write a ghazal in free verse couplets, making each couplet a complete expression of an idea.

- What are the advantages and disadvantages of writing in a strict poetic form like a ghazal (or a sonnet or a villanelle)? Why do modern writers usually prefer free verse to traditional poetic forms? Cite some contemporary examples of poets who use traditional forms and poets who use free verse.

- Based on your research, what place does poetry occupy in American cultural life today? Can poets and poetry influence society? Why or why not? Can you cite some examples?

Historical Context

The Ghazal

The ghazal originated in Arabic, Persian, Turkish, Urdu, and Pashto literature during the eighth century. The ghazal first appeared in the West in nineteenth-century German poetry. Poets who used the form included Schlegel and Goethe. Since the 1960s, ghazals have also been written in English.

One of the most famous writers of ghazals was Ghalib (1797–1869), who lived in Delhi, India and wrote in Urdu. Admiration for Ghalib's work has been responsible for stimulating an interest in the ghazal in English poetry over the last few decades. In the late 1960s and early 1970s, Adrienne Rich, W. S. Merwin, William Stafford, Mark Strand, and William Hunt, among others, all rendered ghazals by Ghalib into English. These poets have varied greatly over how closely to follow the form of the original, and most have opted not to use rhyme. In *Ghazals of Ghalib*, edited by Aijaz Ahmad, Rich made the following comment about Ghalib's ghazals: "The marvelous thing about these ghazals is precisely (for me) their capacity for both concentration and a gathering, cumulative effect." This twofold effect of epigrammatic concentration and cumulative meaning may be part of the reason that the ghazal has attracted other poets writing in English, such as Robert Bly and Denise Levertov, who are among those who have written loosely structured ghazals.

Free Verse and Formal Verse

In twentieth-century poetry, the dominant type of versification was free verse. Free verse is poetry that does not use traditional poetic meter with its rhythmic regularity. It employs differing line lengths and does not usually rhyme. During the period from about 1960 to 1980, the vast majority of poetry written by mainstream poets was in free verse. Poet and cultural critic Dana Gioia, writing in 1992 in *Can Poetry Matter?*, declares that "Literary journalism has long declared it [rhyme and meter] defunct, and most current anthologies present no work in traditional forms by Americans written after 1960." Gioia also notes that since 1960, only two new poetic forms have entered American poetry, the double dactyl and the ghazal, although he also notes that ghazals are "usually in a dilute unrhymed version of the Persian original."

Gioia also notes, however, signs of a revival of formal verse by young poets in the 1980s. First collections like Brad Leithauser's *Hundreds of Fireflies* (1982) and Vikram Seth's *The Golden Gate* (1986) are written entirely in formal verse and were well received by reviewers. Gioia himself published two poetry collections, *Daily Horoscope* (1986) and *The Gods of Winter* (1991) that employed both formal and free verse.

It is this category of poets—who make use of free verse but do not scorn traditional forms—to which Ackerman belongs. Although most of the poems in *I Praise My Destroyer* are written in free verse of varying types, Ackerman also shows a penchant for more formally structured verse. "On Location in the Loire Valley" is not the only poem written in a poetic form of foreign origin that has strict formal requirements. "Elegy," for example, is a villanelle, a French verse form that must have five tercets (three-line stanzas) and a final four-line stanza, as well as a precise rhyme scheme. Ackerman also employs rhyme in the couplets that compose "A Herbal" and "Timed Talk."

Critical Overview

Few volumes of poetry today win more than a handful of short reviews in the mainstream journals and magazines, but Ackerman's poetry has been routinely praised in reviews that do appear. Although he does not single out "On Location in the Loire Valley" directly for comment in his review of *I Praise My Destroyer*, John Taylor makes the following observation in *Poetry*: "Ackerman weaves intricate, colorful, often stunning linguistic tapestries. . . . her exuberant yokings of nouns and unexpected adjectives can likewise divert from quieter, more meditative feelings."

Similarly, in *Booklist* Donna Seaman comments that Ackerman "wears poetic forms like silk dresses that sway and cling in perfect accord to the stride of her lines." Seaman praises Ackerman's metaphors and humor and finds her poems "wholly original." In *Library Journal* Ann van Buren observes that "all of the poems [in *I Praise My Destroyer*] reflect intelligence, awareness, and the skillful employment of rhyme, meter, alliteration, and other poetic techniques."

However, Carolyn Kizer in *Michigan Quarterly Review* faults Ackerman for a tendency to be too "grandiose," and offers the view that "As a poet she is careless—including her grammar—and inclined to hyperbole." This comment is interesting in light of the puzzling grammar of the final couplet of "On Location in the Loire Valley."

Chateau Chambord, built by Henry II, in France's Loire Valley

Criticism

Bryan Aubrey

Aubrey holds a Ph.D. in English and has published many articles on twentieth-century literature. In this essay, Aubrey discusses the form of the traditional ghazal in Urdu. He also shows that although Ackerman's poem adheres closely to the traditional form, the ghazal has proved to be a highly flexible form when adapted by poets in English.

"On Location in the Loire Valley" is not only a remarkable exercise of formal technique in a little-known verse form, it is one of those poems that is thematically impossible to pin down. It seems to dance airily within its formal boundaries. At the same time as it delights in the comings and goings of life, it seems also to pose unanswerable questions, and in so doing it takes on a darker hue.

Ackerman's achievement is all the more remarkable because most of the ghazals that have appeared in English, whether translations of poems written in Urdu or original ghazals, have lacked some of the fundamental qualities that are traditionally associated with the form. For example, almost all English translations of the ghazals of the renowned nineteenth-century Indian poet Ghalib, who wrote in Urdu, employ neither a repeated refrain nor a rhyming word immediately before it. They are traditional ghazals only in the sense that they consist of several independent, self-contained couplets. The loss of certain structural elements is nearly inevitable in translations of any strict verse form from one language to another. However, there is one translation of Ghalib that does emerge in English as a recognizably traditional ghazal. The translation is by William Stafford in *Ghazals of Ghalib*.

This ghazal fulfills the formal requirement that the first couplet ends with the repeated refrain. This is known as the Quafia ("longer"). The Quafia appears at the end of the second line of each couplet. However, the repeated rhyming word (known as the Radif) before that refrain is absent from the translation.

One of the few poets other than Ackerman to write a ghazal complete with Quafia and Radif is the American poet John Hollander. In *Rhyme's Reason*, Hollander explains all the forms of English verse with self-descriptive examples.

If ghazals continue to be written in English, as seems likely, a distinctively English type of ghazal may emerge. In order for this to happen, poets writing in this mode will probably have to make more

> "Whether acclaimed or not, Ackerman's poem, because of its technical mastery of the form as well as its elusive, suggestive themes, certainly qualifies as one of the finest ghazals in the English language."

than a cursory study of the form and themes of the original Asian ghazals. This may in turn lead to more experimentation, which will stimulate the creative transformations that happen when an art form crosses a cultural boundary and takes root in new soil.

Scholars of the ghazal as it was practiced in India, where the form has been practiced since the twelfth century, offer many and varying analyses of the nature of the ghazal. One common practice is for the poet to identify or allude to himself in the final couplet, either by his own name or his pen name. For example, this is a translation (in *Masterpieces of Urdu Ghazal*) of a typical final couplet of Mir Taqi Mir, a prominent Indian poet of the eighteenth century who wrote in Urdu: "Your face, O Mir, is growing pale, / Have you, too, perchance, fallen in love?"

It seems unlikely that many poets writing in English will favor this overt reference to themselves. Indeed, in "On Location in the Loire Valley," Ackerman seems to undercut this tradition, since the implication of her final couplet, far from offering self-revelation, is that such a thing is not possible.

Some authorities, including Agha Shahid Ali, argue that each couplet should have a turn in the thought between lines 1 and 2. Line 2 should surprise the reader with a twist. Ackerman follows this practice in her first couplet: "Clouds of mistletoe hang in the poplars, which can't survive. / Still, decorated with ruin, they enchant our lives." The image of the mistletoe gradually killing the host tree in line 2 gives way to the surprising consolation of line 2. In other couplets, however, Ackerman does not follow this practice. The thought in the first line often continues to the caesura (a pause, indicated by a punctuation mark) in the second line.

Traditionally, each couplet in a ghazal is an independent poem, a complete expression of an idea. The couplets are not required to be related to each other; they need no consistency of theme. K. C. Kanda points out in his introduction to *Masterpieces of Urdu Ghazal* that this is one of the most fundamental traits of the ghazal. However, he also notes that some Indian writers of ghazals have challenged this convention, claiming that it has a stifling effect on the form. They have written ghazals in the style of a *nazm*, in which a single theme is developed throughout the sequence of couplets. In India, where the ghazal remains a vibrant form, this type of ghazal remains the exception rather than the rule, however.

In "On Location in the Loire Valley," Ackerman tends toward the *nazm* style. Although there is little thematic unity in the poem as a whole, she does tell a recognizable narrative of a film crew on location in a specific place. These couplets clearly build on each other to tell a story of sorts, even though many of them also act as independent poetic units.

The same is true for many of the poems written in English that go under the name of ghazal, although the range is very broad. Some ghazals in English abandon the couplet form. An example would be the "Sheffield Ghazals" by well-known American poet Galway Kinnell in his collection *Imperfect Thirst* (1994). These five poems explore the possibilities of the ghazal form as well as anyone writing in English today. Kinnell does not use couplets or rhymes. Each unit of free verse, one or two lines usually but on occasion three or four, often makes a self-contained, epigrammatic statement. "Passing the Cemetery," for example, begins, "Desire and act were a combination known as sin." Each subsequent verse unit makes a seemingly unrelated statement, and yet as the poem progresses, a thematic unity emerges, clustering around issues of sex, sin, and death. Interestingly, these unconventional ghazals conclude with one of the signature features of the original Urdu form. In each of the five, Kinnell addresses himself directly, using his first name, as if he is admonishing or reminding himself of certain realities that the ghazal has revealed.

The "Sheffield Ghazals" show that a prominent poet writing in the English language feels free to takes what is useful from the original form and discard what he considers unnecessary. The fact that, when originally published in the literary magazine *Ploughshares*, these ghazals were entitled "Sheffield Pastorals" shows how loosely the term ghazal can be interpreted.

This freedom of interpretation applies also to the question of the themes addressed by the ghazal. Traditionally, the theme of the ghazal was love (the term ghazal, according to K. C. Kanda, means in Arabic "talking to women"). Love could refer to love for the divine, as well as love for a person. Ghazals were also about beauty and wine (sometimes mystically understood as intoxication with the divine) and philosophical contemplation about life and death. Sometimes ghazals expressed political ideals or social and political satire.

Writers of ghazals in English, however, feel no such constraints on the themes they select. Ackerman's "On Location in the Loire Valley," as well as Kinnell's "Sheffield Ghazals," would be considered unusual in their themes by any traditional yardstick. The English-writing poet is likely to consider any topic about which he or she feels inspired to write to be a suitable theme for a ghazal.

Bearing that in mind, there seems to be every possibility that the ghazal will have staying power as a minor poetic form in literature written in English, comparable to the villanelle and the sestina, two intricate verse forms originating in France. However, it is not likely that the ghazal will attain the popularity that it has maintained in India for many centuries. Even today, that popularity shows no signs of diminishing. As Kanda states:

> During recent years there has been a remarkable revival of interest in the *ghazal*, as is evidenced by the rise, on both sides of the Indo-Pak border, of numerous singers of *ghazals*, whose performances at cultural gatherings, on the television screen, and on cassette players, are eagerly sought after.

There is many an American poet, of ghazals or not, who would welcome this kind of popular acclaim. Whether acclaimed or not, Ackerman's poem, because of its technical mastery of the form as well as its elusive, suggestive themes, certainly qualifies as one of the finest ghazals in the English language.

Source: Bryan Aubrey, Critical Essay on "On Location in the Loire Valley," in *Poetry for Students*, Gale, 2003.

Ryan D. Poquette

Poquette has a bachelor's degree in English and specializes in writing about literature. In the following essay, Poquette discusses Ackerman's use of juxtaposition and repetition in her poem.

"On Location in the Loire Valley" was first published in Ackerman's poetry collection, *I Praise My Destroyer*. This compelling title refers to death, and the entire volume is devoted to Ackerman's agnostic exploration of what human death means. Death is a process that humans have examined in countless ways. For Ackerman, this examination is done in a dispassionate, scientific manner, drawing on her skills as a naturalist. In his review of *I Praise My Destroyer* for *Poetry*, John Taylor notes that in these poems, "Ackerman opts for exalting the organic processes whereby entities such as ourselves come into existence, exist, then perish." Likewise, in her review of the collection for *Booklist*, Donna Seaman says that "naturalist Ackerman expresses her signature love for the world in all its seething glory." In "On Location in the Loire Valley," Ackerman does this by examining a litany of life experiences within the context of a film shoot, using juxtaposition and repetition to underscore the necessity of human experience.

When one first reads "On Location in the Loire Valley," the poem reveals itself to have a formal structure. It is composed of ten stanzas, each of which is no more than two or three lines. In addition, each stanza ends with the two words, "our lives." Poets, more so than any other writers, often make sure that each of their words count. There is so little space in most poems as compared to longer works, that poets tend to be economical in their selection of words and phrases. The fact that Ackerman chooses to end each stanza with the same phrase is significant and shows that she planned this effect carefully. This careful planning is evident throughout the other poems in the collection. Ann van Buren in her review of the book for *Library Journal* writes "All of the poems reflect intelligence, awareness, and the skillful employment of rhyme, meter, alliteration, and other poetic techniques."

In the case of "On Location in the Loire Valley," this attention to detail is evident from the first two words in the title, "On Location." With these two words, one can ascertain that the speaker is on a film shoot. Since the film shoot, an event that requires using a lot of technology, is staged in the Loire Valley—a rural, relatively undeveloped countryside in France—Ackerman is using juxtaposition right from the start.

In the first stanza, the speaker jumps right in and describes her experiences on the film shoot. The first image is one of a Christmas scene. One can imagine a film scene in which the actors are

> *If Ackerman is indeed trying to praise death in this poem, as she does in other poems in the collection, why does she try to make this point by using several negative examples?*

gathering around Christmas trees that have mistletoe on them. As the speaker notes, although the poplars are decorated with ruin, they "enchant" the film crew with their natural beauty. Right away, Ackerman is juxtaposing life, represented by the natural tree and mistletoe, with death. This is the dominant juxtaposition in the poem, which runs as an undercurrent throughout the narrative that describes the speaker's experiences on the film shoot. For example, in the fifth stanza, the speaker summarizes the film's narrative. One assumes that the film is a biography, which encapsulates the life of somebody within a short space of film time, just as Ackerman is encapsulating human life within the short space of her poem.

The film, and the process required to make it, have sparked the speaker's reflection on life and death. In some stanzas, the juxtaposition of life experiences and the inevitability of death is subtler. For example, in the second stanza, the speaker describes what it is like to film a scene in the cold, French castles. This stanza sets up an image of a group of actors who are freezing as they deliver their lines in the castle shoots. The word "decant" has a double meaning. In general, to decant means to pour something out. Decant can also mean to pour from one medium into another. In this case, the actors are pouring their lives, or life energy, into the film. People often talk of actors breathing life into a film. Ackerman is playing off this idea. Since a piece of film is inherently dead until something is recorded on it, the actors are literally giving the film life.

In addition to the juxtaposition of life and death, Ackerman also uses repetition. As noted above, each stanza ends with the phrase "our lives." It is tempting to view this repetition in a negative fashion. In most stanzas, the example ends with a dispassionate, and sometimes derogatory, commentary on human lives. For example, in the third stanza, "Soundmen record the silent rant of our lives." If humanity is just silently ranting, the poet seems to imply that it has no ultimate purpose. In another example, in the fifth stanza, the speaker says that, after the film shoot, "we adjourn to the constant of our lives." If human lives are constant, that implies that they are boring and monotonous. In other areas of the poem, "our lives" are dismantled. They are also described as "nonchalant" and full of "banter." These are not exactly positive descriptions of human experience. Ackerman seems to say that the human experience is, to a certain extent, a lonely one. A person can open himself or herself up to another human, but can never fully explain his or her life experience. This is why Ackerman notes that "The heart has a curfew," indicating that this restriction applies even to those in love.

With all of these negative descriptions, Ackerman seems to be saying that human lives are pointless and that humans live their lives out in a bunch of meaningless experiences, then die. Yet, Ackerman is more complex than this. As Taylor notes of the collection's praise of death "Psychologically ambiguous in their hintings at regret, these poems add another, more complex, more tantalizing, dimension to the resolve boldly expressed by Ackerman's title." If Ackerman is indeed trying to praise death in this poem, as she does in other poems in the collection, why does she try to make this point by using several negative examples?

To answer this question, one must look to the stanzas that open and close the poem. In the first stanza, Ackerman notes that even though the mistletoe and poplars will not live long, their impending death does "enchant our lives." This is a positive effect. After taking the reader through the eight middle stanzas, in which all of the human experiences she describes seem to have a negative undertone associated with death, the poet relents: "Not the shadow family we became, not the shiver beneath the smile, / not the people we clung to in the mad canter of our lives." Although this line is definitely "ambiguous," when it is juxtaposed with the rest of the poem, it seems as if the speaker is trying to take comfort in the same human experiences that she has just disparaged. During the film shoot, she has "clung to" her colleagues, whom she refers to as her "shadow family." The fact that the speaker refers to her film crew as family, even a shadow one, is significant, and it underscores the main point that the poet is trying to make. The inevitability of death should cause people to cherish the life experiences that they do have. The speaker indicates that humans' lives pass by quickly and end in death. She is saying that people need to appreciate all of their experiences, even if they are bittersweet. In the end, human experiences are all that one may have.

Source: Ryan D. Poquette, Critical Essay on "On Location in the Loire Valley," in *Poetry for Students*, Gale, 2003.

R. H. W. Dillard

In the following essay, Dillard discusses the themes and the passion behind Ackerman's poetry.

The work of Diane Ackerman in poetry and prose is a history of her extraordinary enthusiasms. Her memoirs recount her experiences on a cattle ranch (*Twilight of the Tenderfoot*) and in learning to fly (*On Extended Wings*), and, like her later books (*A Natural History of the Senses* and *A Natural History of Love*), they explore in depth and with intensity the full extent of the subject—its history, its detailed ins and outs, its poetry, and ultimately its meaning. She is a prodigious explorer of the world, if by "world" we mean, as she puts it, "the full sum of Creation." Her poetry is distinctive in finding its source in that same enthusiastic energy; she explores the world, inner and outer, with a scientist's poetic eye, recognizing, as the chaos scientist Mitchell Feigenbaum put it, that "art is a theory about the way the world looks to human beings."

Ackerman's book-length poems *The Planets: A Cosmic Pastoral* and *Reverse Thunder: A Dramatic Poem* are the most impressive results of her effort to draw scientific and poetic curiosity (and understanding) together into a unified field of electric language. The first is a long meditation on the planets in our solar system, and the second is a verse play about Juana Inés de la Cruz, a late seventeenth-century Mexican woman who actually lived Ackerman's ideal life as poet, scientist, and genuinely independent and creative thinker.

The Planets: A Cosmic Pastoral is a set of poetic explorations and meditations on the planets, Cape Canaveral, the asteroids, and even the blurry disappointment of the comet Kohoutek. In form and content it ranges widely and well—its science up-to-date and accurate and its poetry a display of dazzling wit. It roused Carl Sagan to say that it demonstrates "how closely compatible planetary exploration and poetry, science and art really are." It bridges the "two cultures" with a vigor and success not witnessed in English and American poetry since the eighteenth century, when Newton's *Opticks* and its implications excited poets and roused their imaginative responses.

> "Her poetry is distinctive in finding its source in that same enthusiastic energy; she explores the world, inner and outer, with a scientist's poetic eye, recognizing, as the chaos scientist Mitchell Feigenbaum put it, that 'art is a theory about the way the world looks to human beings.'"

At the end of *The Planets*, Ackerman returns to Earth "like a woman who, / waking too early each day, / finds it dark yet / and all the world asleep." This situation also sums up her dilemma as a poet, having pressed poetry into a service far beyond that of most of the poems of her contemporaries and now being faced with the choice of whether to join that sleeping world or to return to planetary exploration. In the poem she concludes, "But how could my clamorous heart / lie abed, knowing all of Creation / has been up for hours?"

Sister Juana Inés de la Cruz, the heroine of *Reverse Thunder*, faces that same dilemma and answers it in much the same way. She is tragically out of step with her place and time, but she triumphs in the work that she passes down to our time, when she finally can be (or almost can be) fully understood in all her complexity. This fascinating woman, as Ackerman pictures her, draws together in her life as a nun in seventeenth-century Mexico almost all of the conflicting and contradictory strands of life at that time. She is a nun who loves a man passionately, a believing Christian who explores the scientific view of the world, a spiritual and spirited poet who draws her inspiration from both the life of the body and of the mind, and a

What Do I Read Next?

- Ackerman's *Jaguar of Sweet Laughter: New & Selected Poems* (1993) contains 118 poems that show her ability to dazzle the reader with her skill with words and ideas without sacrificing the need to be understood. The collection also reveals her celebrated ability to incorporate scientific concepts into her poems about the natural world and imbue them with a sense of curiosity and wonder.

- In *Cultivating Delight: A Natural History of My Garden* (2002), Ackerman describes her garden in Ithaca, New York, through all the four seasons. She has her accustomed eye for small detail and writes in poetic prose that holds the reader's attention. In addition to the natural phenomena she describes so intricately, Ackerman is also effective in describing how the garden provides fuel for the human soul and spirit.

- *Ravishing DisUnities: Real Ghazals in English* (2000), edited by the late Agha Shahid Ali, is the first anthology of English-language ghazals. It contains work by well-known poets, including W. S. Merwin, and some newcomers. All the ghazals use the traditional refrain.

- *Daily Horoscope* (1986) was poet Dana Gioia's first collection. He has a reputation as one of the finest of the new formalists, poets who use traditional forms of rhyme and meter.

- Muhammad Daud Rahbar's *The Cup of Jamshid: A Collection of Original Ghazal Poetry* (1974), translated from Urdu by the author, contains ninety ghazals as well as an informative introduction.

- *The Lightning Should Have Fallen on Ghalib: Selected Poems of Ghalib* (1999), edited by Robert Bly and translated by Sunil Dutta, is a loosely translated selection of thirty ghazals by one of India's finest poets.

---

materialist who comes to understand that matter is so much more than it appears to be:

> If ever there was a good person in this world,
> one just or pure or altruistic or visionary,
> no matter who, or how many, or if only one,
> then purity, or justice or mercy or vision,
> is something of which matter is capable.
> That paradox of the apparent indifference
> of matter to such things as Good and Evil,
> and, yet, at the same time, the reality
> of its complete involvement:
> that's why beauty stuns and touches us.

In her collection of short poems, *Wife of Light* and *Lady Faustus*, and in the fifty-two new poems in *Jaguar of Sweet Laughter: New and Selected Poems*, Ackerman apparently strives to write as Sister Juana would if she were writing today, recognizing no limits to the range of her interests or her voice. Whether she is being earthy, playing a bluesy "Menstrual Rag" or singing the true joy of sex with a metaphysical force, or diving under the sea, flying an airplane, brooding over rivers and bridges, confessing the depth of her love, or speculating about the very nature of thought, her wit runs a full range, exhibiting mind, memory, sense, the senses, sensuality, sanity, ingenuity, acumen, real thought, witty banter, and productive persiflage. Her enthusiasm carries her forward but never beyond the bounds of genuine feeling and serious understanding.

As she put it in the title poem of her collection *Lady Faustus*:

> I itch all over. I rage to know
> what beings like me, stymied by death
> and leached by wonder, hug those campfires
> night allows,
> aching to know the fate of us all,
> wallflowers in a waltz of stars.

Source: R. H. W. Dillard, "Ackerman, Diane," in *Contemporary Poets*, 7th ed., edited by Thomas Riggs, St. James Press, 2001, pp. 6–7.

John Taylor

In the following review, Taylor discusses Ackerman's treatment of death and life in her collection I Praise My Destroyer.

I Praise My Destroyer faces up to death. As the title implies, plunging into the multivarious sensations of the quotidian is ultimately self-deceiving if one goes only halfway. Death cannot be ignored indefinitely while one is harvesting experience, however joyfully. For Diane Ackerman, death resembles a "horror lesson" noticed out of the corner of one's eye yet disbelieved until a cherished friend, family member or mentor—she commemorates Carl Sagan—suddenly passes away. Whence the increasing need, with age, to assimilate death into one's philosophy. Religious dogma of course offers pat solutions, but what about the agnostic whose only certitude is eschatological uncertainty? Confronting this dilemma with all the precision and enthusiasm for which her writings in the natural sciences have made her well known, Ackerman opts for exalting the organic processes whereby entities such as ourselves come into existence, exist, then perish.

The poet thereby praises "small daily marvels" as well as what ultimately destroys them (and us). Exalting life-in-death and death-in-life, she beckons us to "ransom each day," a courage-bolstering, even somewhat defiant, reinterpretation of Horace's "carpe diem." Death no longer looms so ominously—at least for a while, for in its purest formulation this metaphysical outlook could perhaps be maintained only by the strongest (or most insensitive) among us, not by the fragile.

This is where several gently erotic love poems come in. A few involve ephemeral affairs, thus entailing another kind of destruction. Within the metaphysics posited by Ackerman, these love poems show that we must come to terms not only with our demise, but also sometimes—and no less intensely—with the lover who fled "the love-brightened room for the tight, local orders of [his or her] life." We also die, perhaps even several times in the midst of life through amorous leave-takings and unrequited attractions. Psychologically ambiguous in their hintings at regret, these poems add another, more complex, more tantalizing, dimension to the resolve boldly expressed by Ackerman's title.

Ackerman weaves intricate, colorful, often stunning linguistic tapestries. Occasionally, self-indulgent declarations blur the focus ("darkest purple, a color ... which I love because of its emotional ambiguity"); her exuberant yokings of nouns and unexpected adjectives can likewise divert from quieter, more meditative feelings; and for all the good intentions of her opening "School Prayer," one recalls Andre Gide's warning that "it is with noble sentiments that bad literature gets written."

> *Exalting life-in-death and death-in-life, she beckons us to 'ransom each day,' a courage-bolstering, even somewhat defiant, reinterpretation of Horace's 'carpe diem.'"*

Yet many poems illustrate admirably that "wonder" is truly her "job," and the ten concluding "Cantos Vaqueros" superbly balance Ackerman's irrepressible curiosity about the outside world—here, cowboy life—with her desire to participate jubilantly in such a world, as a poet. "For if I won't leap up / and ride, who will?" she asks. "Who will say / what marvel [this life] was swept by?"

Source: John Taylor, Review of *I Praise My Destroyer*, in *Poetry*, Vol. 173, No. 2, December 1998, p. 182.

Julie Gleason Alford

In the following essay, Alford discusses Ackerman's life and writings.

Diane Ackerman is one of the most highly acclaimed lyric poets writing in the United States. Her poetry displays a mastery of language, lexical precision, and a vast range of poetic forms and voices. A passionate, disciplined writer, Ackerman creates poetry full of wit, compassion, courage, and fact; it is a poetry of wonder and celebration for the natural world and the human condition. "Ackerman is not interested in a poetry of irony or theory or intellectual distance," notes reviewer Michael McFee. "Her poems are immediate ... and accessible to anyone who has ever felt anything intensely" (National Public Radio, 7 July 1991). The fusion of science and art is one feature of Ackerman's poetry that makes her distinct from her contemporaries. To those who question the appropriateness or purpose of blending poetry with science, Ackerman replies: "Not to write about Nature in its widest sense, because quasars or corpuscles are not 'the proper realm of poetry,' as a critic once said to me, is not only irresponsible and philistine, it bankrupts the experience of living, it ignores much of life's fascination and variety. I'm a great fan of the Universe, which

> "The fusion of science and art is one feature of Ackerman's poetry that makes her distinct from her contemporaries."

I take literally: as one. All of it interests me, and it interests me in detail" (*Contemporary Poets*, 1991). Ackerman stretches the boundaries of what poets traditionally write about, producing collections of verse that contain a rich variety of voices, moods, and subjects. Among her favorite sources of inspiration are nature, flying, astronomy, travel, and love.

Ackerman was born on October 7, 1948 in Waukegan, Illinois. Her father, Sam Fink, was a shoe salesman and later ran one of the first McDonald's restaurant franchises. Her mother, Marsha Tischler Fink, "was—and is—a seasoned world traveler." In *The Moon by Whale Light* (1991), a collection of nature essays, Ackerman reflects on her childhood years and gives a humorous account of an incident that made her realize at a young age that she had poetic tendencies. As she and three schoolmates were walking through a plum orchard, "The trees were thick with plums," and she remarked that the dark plums were "huddled like bats." Her friends instantly recoiled. "The possibility of bats didn't frighten them," Ackerman recalls. "I frightened them: the elaborate fantasies I wove . . . ; my perverse insistence on drawing trees in colors other than green; my doing *boy* things like raising turtles. . . . And now this: plums that look like bats. . . . I remember flushing with wonder at the sight of my first metaphor—the living plums: the bats."

Her fascination with the natural world continued. In college, she studied science as well as literature. She began her undergraduate work in 1966 at Boston University but transferred to Pennsylvania State University the following year. She received her B.A. in English in 1970; then she entered Cornell University as a teaching assistant in 1971. At Cornell, Ackerman pursued academic studies for the next seven years, earning an M.F.A. in creative writing and an M.A. and Ph.D. in literature. She has taught writing at Cornell, Columbia, New York University, Washington University (in St. Louis, Missouri), the College of William and Mary, Ohio University and the University of Pittsburgh. At Washington University she was director of the Writer's Program from 1984 to 1986. Currently she is a staff writer for the *New Yorker* and lives in upstate New York.

Many prestigious literary awards and honors have been presented to Ackerman throughout her career. At Cornell she was awarded the Academy of American Poets Prize, Corson French Prize, Heerman-McCalmons Playwriting Prize, and the Corson-Bishop Poetry Prize. Her other awards include the Abbie Copps Poetry Prize (1974), the *Black Warrior Review* Poetry Prize (1981), and the Pushcart Prize (1984). She has received grants from the Rockefeller Foundation and the National Endowment for the Arts. In 1985 the Academy of American Poets honored her with the Peter I. B. Lavan Award. She received the Lowell Thomas Award in 1990. Ackerman has served as poetry judge in many poetry festivals and contests, on the board of directors for the Associated Writing Programs, and on the Planetary Society Advisory Board. In 1987 Ackerman was a judge in the AWP Award Series for Creative Nonfiction. She has also participated in several poetry panels, including those of the New York Foundation for the Arts (1987) and National Endowment for the Arts (1991).

Besides being a highly acclaimed poet, Ackerman is also a prose stylist. Her four books of nonfiction have been successful and have earned lavish praise from critics. Her first nonfiction book, *Twilight of the Tenderfoot* (1980), recounts her adventures at an authentic cattle ranch in New Mexico. Not content to rely on imagination, Ackerman left the quiet self-absorption of academia to experience the life of a cowhand. Her next work of prose, *On Extended Wings* (1985), is a memoir of her experiences as a student pilot. In a review of the book, Karen Rile wrote: "Diane Ackerman is a woman of letters, not numbers. When she gets her hands on the throttle, flying exceeds metaphor; it's the whole world; and yet nothing is mundane. This isn't simply a chronicle about learning how to fly; it's a poet's notebook with wings" (*St. Louis Post-Dispatch*, 8 September 1985). *On Extended Wings* was adapted for the stage by Norma Jean Giffen in 1987. *A Natural History of the Senses* (1990) is Ackerman's third and most critically acclaimed work of prose to date. A surprise best-seller, it has since been published in sixteen countries. The paperback edition was released in 1991 by Vintage. This encyclopedia of the senses is an intriguing assortment of history, biology, anthropology, cultural fact, and folklore, woven together with poetic inspiration to celebrate the faculties of human perception. *The Senses*, a five-hour PBS series based on this book, is in development. Her latest prose work, *The Moon by Whale Light*, has been highly praised.

Ackerman's nonfiction is a creative blend of journalism, science, and poetry; indeed, it is her poetic vision that makes her nonfiction so successful. Adventurous and endlessly curious, she may assume different roles at different times—pilot, journalist, astronomer, horsewoman, scuba diver—but she is always a poet. Ackerman explains her writing as a form of "celebration or prayer," a way to "enquire about the world."

An obsession with astronomy led to her first full-length book of poetry, *The Planets: A Cosmic Pastoral* (1976). In this collection Ackerman travels the scenic route through the universe, as she tours the country of the Milky Way and the landscape of space. Earth's moon ("Imagine something that big being dead") and all the planets of the solar system are explored in verse. Other subjects, such as comets and Cape Canaveral, are included as well.

Poetic imagery and metaphors interweave with scientific data. The planet Venus is described as "a buxom floozy with a pink boa; / mummy, whose black / sediment dessicates within; wasp star / to Mayan Galileos; / an outpatient / wrapped in postoperative gauze; / Cleopatra in high August—/ her flesh curling / in a heat mirage / light years / from Alexandria." Then, subtly, scientific fact creeps in among the rich poetic images: "Venus quietly mutates / in her ivory tower. / Deep within that / libidinous albedo / temperatures are hot enough to boil lead / pressures / 90 times more unyielding than Earth's." Later in the poem, readers also learn that Venus's atmosphere is forty miles thick and consists of sulphuric, hydrochloric, and hydrofluoric acids.

Although *The Planets* is liberally sprinkled with astronomical terms, phrases, and facts, the science does not distract but heightens reader interest and enhances the emotional value of the poems. Ackerman has the ability to take cold scientific fact and transform it into something fresh and poetic, compelling the reader to look at a thing in an exciting new way; her poetry intrigues, teaches, and delights at the same time. The overall feeling of *The Planets* is one of wonder and fascination. In the poem "Mars" a romantic, dreamy mood is created as the speaker bids her lover to fly with her to Utopia and the highlands of Tharis (regions on Mars):

> Once in a blue sun, when volcanoes
> heave up grit regular as pearls,
> and light runs riot, we'll watch
> the sun go darker than the sky,
> violet dust-tufts wheel on the horizon,
> amber cloudbanks pile, and the whole
> of color-crazed Mars ignite.

Critics hailed *The Planets* as an impressive debut and important work. Astronomer Carl Sagan said, "The work is scientifically accurate and even a convenient introduction to modern ideas on the planets, but much more important, it is spectacularly good poetry, clear, lyrical and soaring. . . . One of the triumphs of Ackerman's pastoral is the demonstration of how closely compatible planetary exploration and poetry, science and art really are" (*New Republic*, November 1976).

Ackerman's next two books of poetry, *Wife of Light* (1978) and *Lady Faustus* (1983), are rich and varied collections of short poems. Ackerman's range of interests appears limitless. The title *Wife of Light* is taken from a line in her poem "Period Piece," in which she begs the moon for deliverance from the depths and rages of mood caused by her menstrual cycle. Wit mingles with misery:

> Cares that daily fade or lie low
> hogged front-row-center in the bleachers
> of my despair and there, solemn
> as Kewpie dolls, began to heckle and hoot.

The last line of the poem provides the title of the book: "Moon, be merciful to your wife of light."

Nature often produces a sensual quality in Ackerman's love poems. "Driving through Farm Country at Sunset," which is frequently anthologized, exudes this quality. At first the poem seems to be simply a tribute to nature, to "farm country," as the persona describes the sights, smells, and sounds of the rural area she is driving through: manure, cut grass, honeysuckle, washloads blowing on a line, dogwoods, a sunlit mountainside, and the samba of a dragonfly in the "puffy-lidded dusk." But images of nature are sensuously intertwined with tranquil images of domestic life to evoke a sense of longing. In the last stanza the reader becomes aware that it is a love poem:

> Clouds begin to curdle overhead. And I want
> to lie down with you in this boggy dirt,
> our legs rubbing like locusts.'
> I want you here with the scallions
> sweet in the night air, to lie down with you
> heavy in my arms, and take root.

Wife of Light displays Ackerman's tremendous range of interests and moods, and also her range of voices. Some of the voices are historical, as in the witty verse "Anne Donne to Her Husband" and the sonnet "Quixote" ("life's torpor is the blazing savanna of my loins"). Ackerman manages to turn even mathematics into poetry in "Song of π." She assumes the persona of π (pi), the mathematical symbol that represents the ratio of the circumference of a circle to its diameter. The ratio can be carried to an infinite number of decimal places—it never rounds off—and Ackerman focuses on this unusual feature: "I barrel / out past horizon's bluff, / every digit pacing like a Tennessee Walker, / unable to break even, / come round...."

Lady Faustus, like *Wife of Light*, is broad in scope. Her romance with flying is one of the major sources of inspiration for the book. As a pilot, Ackerman experiences flight as a sort of rapture: "I am flight-luscious / I am kneeling on air" (from "Climbing Out"). Another pastime, scuba diving, provides inspiration for "A Fine, a Private Place." A man and woman make love underwater, "mask to mask, floating / with oceans of air between them, / she his sea-geisha / in an orange kimono / of belts and vests...." The ocean is a "blue boudoir," and sunlight cuts through the water "twisting its knives into corridors of light." The same enthusiasm and sense of adventure that impel her to experience the sky and the sea also move her to explore and celebrate everyday marvels closer to home. Wild strawberries, a goddaughter, soccer, whale songs, rivers, dinosaurs, and language labs are a few of the marvels she captures in verse.

Concerning flying and scuba diving, Ackerman admits she is often drawn to pastimes that many people find frightening; however, she does not consider herself a daredevil, or even particularly daring. As she said to Jesse Green, "I'm not reckless.... I'd be a bad role model to younger women if I were. There are people who *like* to touch the fabric of immortality every chance they get. I'm not one. I don't take unnecessary chances. But I don't let a little bit of danger stand between me and knowledge either." She also does not pursue danger for "cheap excitation." "For me," Ackerman writes in *Extended Wings*, "it's just a case of my curiosity leading with its chin: things fascinate me whether they are dangerous or not ... [;] there are some things you can learn about the world only from 5,000 feet above it, just as there are some things you can learn about the ocean only when you become part of its intricate fathoms."

Ackerman's innate, intense curiosity propels her into experiences that provide subject matter for her poems. Sometimes curiosity itself is the topic. One example is "Lady Faustus." In the opening lines of the poem, curiosity is expressed as a live entity, a thing barely controlled: "Devils be ready! My curiosity / stalks the outpost of its caution...." The intensity of her desire to know is compared to the sun's heat: "raw heat / fitful as a cautery / I, too, am burning with a lidless flame." Later, in *On Extended Wings*, Ackerman writes that her curiosity howls "like a caged dog." This image is originally found in the closing lines of "Lady Faustus":

> A kennelled dog croons in my chest.
> I itch all over. I rage to know
> what beings like me, stymied by death
> and leached by wonder, hug those campfires
> night allows,
> aching to know the fate of us all,
> wallflowers in a waltz of stars.

Both *Wife of Light* and *Lady Faustus* were extolled by critics for their vision and poetic range: "Lyrical description is Ackerman's strong suit. Rich melodies, almost voluptuous with sound and image, her best poems and songs of celebration ... stir and liberate all our best and kindest emotions" (*Publishers Weekly*, 29 July 1983).

Ackerman's next poetic work, published in 1988, is a long, dramatic poem, a play titled *Reverse Thunder*. She combines fact and fiction to portray the life of seventeenth-century nun Juana Inés de la Cruz, a remarkable woman and one of the best-known Spanish poets of that century. In de la Cruz, Ackerman has found a kindred spirit—a passionate, creative woman, independent in thought and action, whose raging enthusiasm for life did not allow her to conform to a conventional role. As R. W. H. Dillard writes, "This fascinating woman, as Ackerman pictures her, draws together in her life as a nun in 17th-century Mexico almost all of the conflicting and contradictory strands of life in that time; she is a nun who loves a man passionately, a believing Christian who explores the scientific view of the world, a spiritual and spirited poet who draws her inspiration from both the life of the body and of the mind." Besides being a poet, Sister Juana was also a musician, painter, and scientist. She read in several languages and taught astronomy and philosophy, which were considered profane by the church. Her library was the largest in the New World.

In the preface to *Reverse Thunder*, Ackerman writes: "Sister Juana Inés de la Cruz was an extraordinary woman who had the bad fortune to live during an era which demanded its women to be ordinary. She was a child prodigy with a gift and passion for learning at a time when education was not available to women." Such was the tragedy of

Juana's life; the triumph is her poetry, which has survived the centuries to tell her story.

The philosophy in most of Ackerman's work is that the passions for life, learning, and love are intertwined and often one and the same. *Reverse Thunder* contains two themes that reflect this philosophy. The first theme involves passion for life itself. With a conviction reminiscent of Walt Whitman, she emphasizes the importance of the here and now: the joys and wonders of Earth are, at best, as sweet as heaven's. Juana says. "To know this world well, / there's Heaven in all its marvels," and "A worldly woman knows Heaven as the suburb of each day."

Another theme found in *Reverse Thunder* is the affirmation of the power of love. Juana discovers that love is greater than her passion for learning and, ultimately, her passion for life: "My world that seemed so rich before him, / once I knew him, / was not enough. / It changed from a most that lived / only on air to an orient of petals."

This passion for life and the affirmation of love's power resonate throughout Ackerman's poetry. Both themes are aptly expressed in a poem from *The Planets*, "When You Take Me from This Good Rich Soil," which reflects the same spirited convictions of Juana Inés de la Cruz, even though Ackerman wrote this poem many years before *Reverse Thunder*. The poem acknowledges the existence of heaven, but love is recognized as the greater power: "No heaven could please me as my love / does.... / When, deep in the cathedral of my ribs, / love rings like a chant, I need no heaven." Appreciation for the secular and a raging passion for life are expressed in the closing lines:

> When you take me from this good rich soil,
> and my heart rumbles like the chambers
> of a gun to leave life's royal sweat
> for your numb peace, I'll be dragging at Earth
> With each cell's tiny ache, so you must
> rattle my bone-house until the spirit breaks.

Ackerman's *Jaguar of Sweet Laughter: New and Selected Poems* was published in 1991. She has grown with each book, and this is her finest collection of poems to date, "a heady and generous bouquet of 15 years of Ackerman's poetry," according to McFee. In the new poems Ackerman's muse leads her from rain forest to iceberg, from her backyard to Mars, as she writes of hummingbirds, orchids, Halley's Comet, deer, contact lenses, penguins, pilots, and love. *Jaguar* is a lush collection that revels in the exotic: "Unleash me and I am an ocelot / all appetite and fur" (from "Dinner at the Waldorf").

Highlights of the book include lyric sequences about the Amazon and Antarctica. The book ripples with adventure and sensuality: "when you kiss me, / my mouth softens into scarlet feathers— / an ibis with curved bill and small dark smile; / when you kiss me, / jaguars lope through my knees" (from "Beija-Flor"). As in previous collections, Ackerman's exceptional skill with voices is demonstrated. In "St. Louis Botanical Gardens" a personified orchid, "the world's most pampered flower," describes the luxuriant existence of the orchid exhibit:

> We dine
> on the equivalent of larks' tongues
> and chocolate. We are free
> from that slum of hummingbird and drizzle.
> Why bother with a mosquito's
> languid toilet? Why bother
> with the pooled vulgarity of the rain?

In a review of *Jaguar* Donna Seaman remarked, "Ackerman frees the exotic from the familiar, finds the familiar in the exotic, the large in the small, the personal in the vast" (*Booklist*, April 1, 1991). The corporeal is blended with the spiritual, the modern with the primitive, as Ackerman combines the poet's love of nature with a scientist's understanding of nature. "We Are Listening" is an excellent example. The "we" refers to humankind, listening with satellites and radios to the deep reaches of the universe, searching in "cosmic loneliness" for a sound, any sound. Ackerman interjects the creatural to emphasize the human feeling of insignificance as one faces the awesome silence and vastness of the universe:

> Small as tree frogs
> staking out one end
> of the endless swamp,
> we are listening
> through the longest night
> we imagine, which dawns
> between the life and times of stars.

The modern spiritual struggle is reflected in this poem, as "radio telescopes / roll their heads, as if in anguish"; humankind is affectionately referred to as "the small bipeds / with the giant dreams."

In *Jaguar* Ackerman acknowledges in verse a few of the poets who influenced her writing: Wallace Stevens, Sylvia Plath, and Walt Whitman. Ackerman's lexical dexterity and precision frequently move critics to compare her to Stevens. In Wallace Stevens she says that, at nineteen, she desired Dylan Thomas's "voluptuousness of mind" and Stevens's "sensuous rigor." In another poem she expresses admiration for Plath's intellect, talent, and "naturalist's eye," but not for the pain that

Plath "wore like a shroud." Ackerman refers to Plath as "the doll of insight we knew / to whom nearly all lady poets write, / a morbid Santa Claus who could die on cue." Of Plath's self-destruction Ackerman writes these chilling lines: "You wanted to unlock the weather system / in your cells, and one day you did." "Walt Whitman's Birthplace" recounts a metaphysical moment in which Ackerman draws inspiration from Whitman: "in an opera athletic as the land, / I drink from your source and swell as large as life."

Ackerman's unusual vision—the harmonious union of science and art—has made her a representative poetic voice of the twentieth century, a century in which science and technology have often separated people from nature and, thus, from themselves. In her poems, readers experience a reconnection with nature and an affirmation of life's glorious possibilities. George Garrett remarks (on the dust jacket of *Jaguar*) that "while a lot of fashionable poets have settled for a kind of whispering and mumbling in the monotonous dark, she has been making poems that can soar and sing, or talk straight and sure about interesting things, things that matter."

"Daring" is a word critics frequently apply to Ackerman and to her poetry because of her willingness to explore life and her refusal to shackle her writing to convention. Also, and perhaps more important, she has the courage to express passion and joyful exuberance for life at a time when intellectual distance and self-indulgent introspection is the vogue. In *Contemporary Poets* she states: "I try to give myself passionately, totally, to whatever I'm observing, with as much affectionate curiosity as I can muster, as a means to understanding a little better what being human is, and what it was like to have once been alive on the planet, how it felt in one's senses, passions and contemplations. I appear to have a lot of science in my work, I suppose, but I think of myself as a Nature writer, if what we mean by Nature is, as I've said, the full sum of Creation."

Poet, journalist, and prose stylist, Ackerman is a pioneer, exploring and opening fresh realms of thought for a new generation of poets, showing them that the only boundaries are ones they set for themselves. At the end of *The Planets*, she writes:

> I return to Earth now
> as if to a previous thought,
> alien and out of place,
> like a woman who,
> waking too early each day,
> finds it dark yet

> and all the world asleep.
> But how could my clamorous heart
> lie abed, knowing all of Creation
> has been up for hours?

Source: Julie Gleason Alford, "Diane Ackerman," in *Dictionary of Literary Biography*, Vol. 120, *American Poets Since World War II, Third Series*, edited by R. S. Gwynn, Gale Research, 1992, pp. 3–9.

Sources

Ackerman, Diane, "On Location in the Loire Valley," in *I Praise My Destroyer*, Random House, 1998, pp. 88–89.

Ahmad, Aijaz, *Ghazals of Ghalib*, Columbia University Press, 1971.

Gioia, Dana, *Can Poetry Matter? Essays on Poetry and American Culture*, Graywolf Press, 1992, pp. 31–45.

Hollander, John, *Rhyme's Reason: A Guide to English Verse*, Yale University Press, 1989, pp. 66–67.

Kanda, K. C., *Masterpieces of Urdu Ghazal: From the 17th to the 20th Century*, Sterling Publishers Private, 1990.

Kinnell, Galway, *Imperfect Thirst*, Houghton Mifflin, 1994, pp. 35–39.

Kizer, Carolyn, "Four Smart Poets," in *Michigan Quarterly Review*, Vol. 39, No. 1, Winter 2000, pp. 167–72.

Seaman, Donna, Review of *I Praise My Destroyer*, in *Booklist*, Vol. 94, No. 14, March 15, 1998, p. 1197.

Taylor, John, Review of *I Praise My Destroyer*, in *Poetry*, Vol. 173, No. 2, December 1998, p. 182.

van Buren, Ann, Review of *I Praise My Destroyer*, in *Library Journal*, Vol. 123, No. 5, March 15, 1998, p. 67.

Further Reading

Ali, Agha Shahid, *The Country without a Post Office*, Norton, 1997.
   This collection of poems contains three ghazals, two of which are original in English. They show what a traditional ghazal in English can be.

Gates, Barbara T., and Ann B. Shteir, "Interview with Diane Ackerman, 18 July 1994," in *Natural Eloquence: Women Reinscribe Science*, edited by Barbara T. Gates and Ann B. Shteir, University of Wisconsin Press, 1997, pp. 255–64.
   In this interview, Ackerman talks mainly about her nonfiction work rather than her poetry, especially *A Natural History of the Senses*, as well as *A Natural History of Love*.

Randhir, L. C., *Ghazal: The Beauty Eternal*, Milind Publications Private, 1982.
   This is a thorough analysis of the ghazal form in Urdu (English translations are supplied). It explains the

technical requirements of the form, its predominant imagery and themes, and its relationship with Indian music.

Rich, Adrienne, *The Fact of a Doorframe: Poems 1950–2001*, W. W. Norton, 2002.
 This volume includes thirteen ghazals, collectively entitled "Ghazals: Homage to Ghalib," written in unrhymed, discontinuous couplets. The evocative images, pithiness of thought, and occasional modern American idioms found in these poems create memorable English ghazals.

Ordinary Words

Ruth Stone

1999

Ruth Stone's poem "Ordinary Words" is the title poem of her 1999 collection *Ordinary Words*. A mere seventeen lines, the poem is broken into two stanzas of eleven and six free-verse lines respectively. The first stanza consists of the speaker's reminiscence of a time when she hurt another person with her words and a description of the pain and regret she continues to feel for that act, even though the person is now dead. The second stanza is a simile, comparing the music of an ancient reed (i.e., a flute) with the ability of a blind bird to recall its grief.

Stone uses common language in the poem. It is not full of literary allusions or references to high art. She is known for depicting in a direct manner the everyday experiences of joy and sorrow that all human beings experience. Stone's style makes the poem accessible to a wide audience. The lament she expresses in the poem is for her husband, novelist and poet Walter B. Stone, who committed suicide by hanging himself in 1959. Ordinary words refers to both Stone's own poetic vocabulary and to the name she called her husband at the beginning of the poem. The phrase suggests that ordinary words have the power to do great harm to others.

Author Biography

Ruth Stone has often been called "a poet's poet," though this has more to do with her relative obscurity than with any quality of her poetry. It has only been in the last few years that her work has gained the national attention it deserves. Born June 8, 1915, in Roanoke, Virginia, to musician Roger McDowell and poet and painter Ruth Ferguson Perkins, Stone was raised in Virginia and Indiana, where she spent long hours reading in her grandfather's library. Her parents nurtured her love for poetry. Her mother read her nursery rhymes and the poetry of Lord Alfred Tennyson, and her father read to her from the Bible. Stone received her formal education from the University of Illinois and Harvard University, from which she graduated with a bachelor of arts degree.

Although Stone began writing poems when she was six years old, she did not publish her first collection until she was in her mid-forties. *In An Iridescent Time* (1959) came out the same year her husband, novelist and poet Walter Stone, committed suicide. His death drastically changed her life. Having to raise their three daughters alone, Stone took teaching jobs wherever she could find them, moving her family around the country. She continued writing through her hardship and despair, producing a number of critically acclaimed, if under-read, volumes. These included *Topography and Other Poems* (1971); *Unknown Messages* (1973); *Cheap: New Poems and Ballads* (1975); *American Milk* (1986); *Second-Hand Coat: Poems New and Selected* (1987); and *Simplicity* (1995).

In 2000, Stone received the National Book Critics Circle Award for *Ordinary Words* (1999), the title poem of which—like so many of Stone's poems—details the love Stone still has for her late husband and the anguish his death caused her. Her next collection, *In the Next Galaxy* (2002), received the National Book Award for poetry, one of the nation's top literary prizes. In addition to her book awards, Stone has received a number of other awards and fellowships, including the Bess Hoskin Prize from *Poetry* magazine (1954); a Radcliffe Institute fellowship from Harvard University (1963–1965); a Robert Frost fellowship to the Breadloaf Writers' Conference (1963); the Shelley Memorial Award from the Poetry Society of America (1964); a Kenyon Review fellowship (1965); a grant from the Academy of Arts and Letters (1970); Guggenheim fellowships (1971–1972 and 1975–1976); a PEN Award (1974); the Delmore Schwartz Award (1983–1984); a Whiting Award (1986); and the Paterson Prize (1988).

Stone has taught at numerous universities, spending a few years in one place before moving

Ruth Stone

on to another. She did not settle down until 1989, when she was seventy-three, at which time the English department at the State University of New York, Binghamton, awarded her tenure.

Poem Summary

Stanza 1

Ruth Stone's "Ordinary Words" begins with the speaker describing an incident in which she calls someone a name. The speaker is commonly thought to be a version of Stone herself and the person she calls a name is commonly thought to be her deceased husband, Walter Stone. She uses the term "whatever" here to suggest that the name she used is not significant, but the fact that she committed the act is. The speaker says that her name-calling is no longer important because her husband is dead. She states this figuratively by saying, "your clothes have become / a bundle of rags." The statement "I paid with my life for that" means that she continues to regret the act because it stayed with her husband for a long time.

The eighth line signals a separation from the first part of the stanza, with the speaker suggesting

Media Adaptations

- Paris Press, which published *Ordinary Words*, issued *Poetry Alive!* (1991), a compact disc of Stone reading poems from *Ordinary Words* and *Simplicity*. The disc can be ordered by contacting Paris Press, P.O. Box 487, Ashfield, MA 01330.

that marriage was not all she believed it would be. "Dull dregs" signifies something that is left over. The last two lines, in which Stone uses the adjective "lackluster" as a noun, refer to the couple's sexual life.

Stanza 2

In this stanza, Stone breaks from the narrative of the first stanza and offers two seemingly dissimilar images: music from an ancient reed, and a bird. She links them together with a simile. "Similes use "like" or "as" to draw comparisons between dissimilar things. Here, Stone compares the music from an ancient reed, a flute, to the way "the blind bird remembers its sorrow." The bird is "in the mountains," where the speaker has never been, yet she is imagining the bird, suggesting a link between her and it. This comparison suggests that the speaker is in some way blind as well. Her emotional vision is muddy.

Themes

Memory

Memory is one tool poets use for inspiration. In Greek mythology, Mnemosyne was the muse of memory and the mother of the nine Muses. Memory is also the muse for "Ordinary Words." Stone begins her poem by recalling a specific incident from the past. She paints the memory of the event in broad brushstrokes. For example, she uses the word "whatever" to refer to the name she called her husband, and she employs general terms such as "clothes" and "middle-class beauty" rather than providing specifics about those terms. By describing her memory of the act in this vague way, Stone emphasizes that it is not so much the act itself she is remembering, but the emotional fallout from the act. She traces that fallout back in the last lines of the first stanza, depicting her marriage as a testing ground for herself, one in which she learned much about who she is.

Loss

Some of the most enduring and powerful poetry addresses loss—loss of love, loss of life, loss of self. "Ordinary Words" explores the emotional complexion of loss by detailing the speaker's remorse for something she said that she feels she should not have said. Sometimes people say things or behave a particular way because doing so allows them to be someone other than who they are. The speaker expresses this sentiment when she says, "Then I wanted to see what it felt like." Unfortunately, she cannot shake the feeling even after the person to whom she said the words has passed on. Not only does she have to live with having lost the other person, but she also has to live with losing the person she was before she "tried on" the words she used.

The poem also addresses another kind of loss: the loss of enthusiasm and freshness that often accompanies a new marriage. Stone expresses this loss in the phrases, "the dull dregs of ordinary marriage," and "The thick lackluster spread between our legs." The final stanza evokes the continuing feeling of loss by using a simile that has as its central image a "blind bird." Even though the bird has lost its sight, it has retained the feelings of sorrow, just as the poem's speaker has.

Language

Words matter, and can mean the difference between life and death. Stone's poem illustrates how words, once spoken, cannot be retracted, and how the consequences of what one says can last a lifetime. She highlights the sheer power of the spoken word's staying power when she writes that what she said "went behind your skull." This image vividly depicts the power of words to lodge themselves in the body, and to emotionally devastate not only the recipient of the words, but the speaker as well, who "paid with . . . [her] life for that."

Class

During the 1940s and 1950s, many Americans had great expectations for marriage and for the comforts that middle-class life would bring. By linking social class and beauty with marriage, Stone's poem perpetuates stereotypes of women who use their physical appearance to "land a husband." Stone's "middle-class beauty," however, only gets her "the dull dregs of ordinary marriage," which suggests disappointment and the desire for the marriage to have been otherwise.

Style

Apostrophe

An apostrophe is a figure of speech in which the speaker addresses someone as if the person were physically present, but is not. Throughout the poem, the speaker addresses an unnamed person in a conversational tone, calling him "you." Readers familiar with Stone's poetry know that the unnamed person is believed to be her husband; those not familiar with her poetry would not know this, but could arrive at that conclusion through deduction. The details used to describe the relationship between the speaker and the person addressed suggest an intimacy, as does the penultimate line of the first stanza, which figuratively describes the sexual relationship between the speaker and her husband. By using this form of address, Stone treats her readers as voyeurs of sort, who have privy to the writer's intense and personal emotional life. Apostrophes are often used to address abstract ideas as well; for example, when Thomas Hardy addresses love in his poem "I Said to Love."

Metaphor and Simile

At its most basic level, metaphor is a way of describing one thing in terms of something else. Stone employs a variety of metaphors in her poem. When she writes, "because your clothes have become / a bundle of rags," she does not mean that her husband is sloppy, but that he is dead. His clothes are rags because they have deteriorated over time. When she writes that her insult "went behind your skull," she means that her words hurt her husband deeply. She uses "skull" figuratively to emphasize the degree to which her name-calling penetrated his emotions and thinking. Whereas metaphors make implicit comparisons, similes make explicit ones. In the last stanza, Stone explicitly compares the sound of an ancient flute to the way a creature remembers sorrow, thus emphasizing the universal and transhistorical phenomenon of loss.

Topics for Further Study

- Stone's poem addresses the common human experience of regret. Make a list of three things that you regret having said to someone in the last year. Next, write a letter to that person, apologizing for what you said and trying to make things right.

- What is the "whatever" in the poem's first line? Brainstorm a list of words that the speaker might have used to insult the person addressed and then discuss why some words are more harmful than others.

- In groups: Make a list of your ideas about the institution of marriage, its benefits and drawbacks. Next, write a short essay speculating about your own future and marriage. Will you marry someone? What type of person will you choose? How old will you be? Will you have children? How many?

- Keep a diary for three months, noting all of the times you are happy and sad and why. At the end of the three months, read over your entries and see if you can discern a pattern for your feelings. Write a diary entry interpreting your moods for the time.

- Bring to class a piece of music that makes you feel melancholy and play it for your classmates. Discuss the qualities of the music that elicit sadness and the differences in responses from classmates.

Historical Context

1990s

When Stone's *Ordinary Words* was awarded the National Book Critics Circle Award for poetry (a prize voted on by book critics throughout the country), it was significant for several reasons. Then eighty-three years old, Stone was finally receiving long overdue recognition, and the collection was published by Paris Press, a small, young press founded by Jan Freeman to present the work of neglected women writers.

Starting a press and publishing poetry are risky endeavors. Book production in the United States is the highest in the world, and the number of people who buy contemporary poetry is very small.

One way small presses are able to generate interest in poetry titles is by sponsoring community outreach programs. Story Line Press, for example, runs the Rural Readers Project, an educational outreach program that sends nationally recognized authors into rural Oregon schools to teach writing and talk about literature. Paris Press has marketed Stone's books by sponsoring intergenerational readings with Stone and Stone's teenaged granddaughter Bianca at senior centers, middle schools, and high schools, in an effort to demonstrate poetry's vitality and relevance to everyday life.

Americans are concerned with growing old gracefully, and the aging of baby boomers along with an increase in life expectancy has led to a renewed interest in works by older writers. Papier-Mache Press's poetry anthology *When I Am an Old Woman I Shall Wear Purple* (1987), for example, is now in its forty-fifth printing and has sold more than 1.6 million copies. The anthology centers on the themes of aging and women's power.

Nonetheless, stereotypes about elderly people remain, and being old and female in America is not easy. Although older Americans have social security and Medicare, the poverty rate for elderly Americans hovers at around 13 percent and could rocket to 50 percent if the social security system collapses. Medicare does not cover long-term care or outpatient prescription drugs, and many elderly have to buy costly supplemental health insurance. Elderly women are worse off than their male counterparts. Because they have earned on average 30 percent less than men during their working lives, their social security payments and pensions are less. Women also live longer than men, meaning those who outlive their husbands and were dependent on them for income often suffer unless the husband had survivor's benefits.

Critical Overview

Many reviewers praised *Ordinary Words* while commenting on Stone's age and quirky voice. A *Publishers Weekly* critic, for example, notes, "Stone often writes as an aging observer," but also asserts that Stone's characters exhibit "a contagious hope." The critic further observes the collection's title poem "Ordinary Words" is "studded with socio-political zingers," and that "The ordinary, for Stone, turns out to be more than enough."

Reviewing *Ordinary Words* for *Library Journal*, Barbara Hoffert zeroes in on the inherent irony of the collection's title, noting that Stone's poetry, while exhibiting some wit, also shows "the darker side of life." Hoffert continues, "Ordinary words, these aren't."

New York Times reporter Dinitia Smith, in her article "Poetry That Captures a Tough 87 Years," reminds readers that Stone "is not a sweet old lady." Smith characterizes Stone's poetry as a form of "brutal honesty" and applauds her directness. "She writes uncompromisingly about passion and unbearable loss; about living in poverty and on the margins of experience," Smith says.

Smaller publications also noticed Stone's poetry collection. Reviewing the volume for *Poetry Flash*, Richard Silberg observes Stone's penchant for the unusual and unexpected: "Ruth Stone has one of the oddest, most exhilarating minds in contemporary poetry. You never know where the poem will leap next."

Criticism

Chris Semansky

Semansky's essays and reviews appear regularly in journals and newspapers. In this essay, Semansky considers the representation of marriage in Stone's poem.

Stone's poem, published in the 1990s, references her own marriage from the 1950s. American attitudes towards marriage in these two decades differ dramatically. In the 1950s, many Americans believed marriage was an essential component of the American dream. By the 1990s, however, marriage was simply one more option in an increasingly growing menu of life choices for Americans.

Stone not only calls readers' attention to her "ordinary marriage" but she also asserts that it was a way that her "middle-class beauty, test[ed] itself." By linking class with marriage, Stone brings to mind the image of the 1950s as an era of cookie-cutter houses, nine to five jobs, and picture-perfect families: Ozzie and Harriet writ large. In the late 1940s and early 1950s, America was in the midst of a postwar economic expansion, and soldiers who had married after returning from the war were now having children. The baby boom was on. Fueled by a lack of housing for returning veterans, developers began building on the outskirts of large cities. War contractor William J. Levitt's developments epitomized what would come to define the suburban experience. Between 1947 and 1951, Levitt converted a potato field in Levittown, Long Island into a development of seventeen-thousand Cape Cod houses that housed seventy-five-thousand people. Using prefabricated materials and package deals that included even the kitchen sink, Levitt was able to produce a four-and-one-half-room house for approximately $8,000.

For many people, living in suburban subdivisions such as Levittown meant living the American dream. The American middle class grew exponentially during this time—and so did expectations for the good life that it represented.

Stone suggests that the life that she expected did not materialize. She describes her marital relations as "The thick lackluster spread between our legs." However, in the very next line she writes, "We used the poor lovers to death," a somewhat ambiguous sentence, suggesting that either she and her husband had exhausted their sexual passion for each other, or that they continued to have a high degree of passion for each other. In either case, "Ordinary Words" evokes a profound sense of loss. It is not merely regret for having said something that hurt her husband's feelings, but sorrow for losing her partner and their life together.

Stone tackles the difficult subject of marriage, and she does it honestly. This is what makes the poem so profound and moving. She does not depict her marriage as paradisiacal, all bliss and no pain. Rather, she describes it as unremittingly ordinary, one in which both quarreling and the waxing and waning of sexual passion are part of the territory. The complex nature of her grief at losing this ordinary life is embodied in the last stanza in the images of the reed, the bird, and the mountains. This stanza works associatively, emotionally punctuating the description of the speaker's marriage and the hurtful things she said and could not take back.

At its simplest level, an image is a mental picture created in readers' mind by the writer's words. Images, however, can also relate to senses other than vision. Stone uses aural imagery in describing the sound of the ancient reed, a flute of sorts, and visual imagery in describing the mountains and bird. This is a difficult stanza because readers are not told what the connection is between the images and the details of the first stanza. What does it mean, "the blind bird remembers its sorrow?"

On its surface, the elements of the last stanza evoke an Asian scene of peacefulness and tranquility. One can imagine the poet Basho wandering the northern provinces of Honshu, penning a haiku at the end of a long day's journey. Stone's lines also have much in common with Basho's concept of *sabi*. Sabi refers to the speaker's awareness of the transitory nature of all things. The images of the unseen mountains and the "three notes in the early morning" elicit feelings of melancholy and the sensation of time passing, but the "blind bird remember[ing] its sorrow" suggests someone who has been wounded and cannot forget his or her hurt.

The images above are similar to the "deep images" that poets such as Robert Bly helped to popularize during the 1960s. Such images work through intuition to call up emotion and meaning and evoke a reality beyond that which can be seen. Poet-critic Robert Kelley coined the term "deep image" in 1961 to name the type of image that could fuse the experience of the poet's inner self and her outer world. Its predecessor was the imagery of poets Ezra Pound and William Carlos Williams, which attempted to cleanly describe the empirical world of things.

Bridging the gap between the inner world of emotion and outer world of things is what Stone does best in her poetry. In an interview with family friend Gowan Campbell for the online journal *12gauge.com*, Stone says this about her composing process:

> *That Stone was still writing about her husband in the 1990s speaks to the depth of her love and the power of her memory for the man and what her union with him represented."*

We speak—our brains speak for us, in a way. It's all very rapid. But it's not consciously considered, I think. It's just spontaneous. And I think that you have to be able to look at what has been in order to say something about the present moment. Even though poems come spontaneously too. It's some sort of door into your unconscious, I guess.

Whether she consciously came to the idea of naming her collection after "Ordinary Words" or not, the poem does function to represent many of the themes and subjects of the collection as a whole, chief among them the continuing presence of her dead husband in the life of the poet and her family. "Then," for example, the poem that directly precedes "Ordinary Words," describes how Stone and her daughters experienced his presence in things such as summer storms and an ermine who "visited" their house for the winter. "My trouble was I could not keep you dead," she writes.

That Stone was still writing about her husband in the 1990s speaks to the depth of her love and the power of her memory for the man and what her union with him represented. Meanwhile, since Walter Stone's death in 1959 the institution of marriage in America has undergone a sea of change. In the 1990s less than a quarter of American households were composed of a married couple and children, and the number of single mothers grew five times faster than married couples with children during the decade. According to Rose M. Kreider and Jason M. Fields in their report "Number, Timing, and Duration of Marriages and Divorces," Americans are filing for about 1 million divorces per year. Using U.S. Census information, Kreider and Fields note, "About 50 percent of first marriages for men under age 45 may end in divorce, and between 44 and 52 percent of women's first marriages may end in divorce for this age group."

It is not only the skyrocketing rate of divorce that distinguishes the 1990s from the 1950s, but the image of marriage as well. Many Americans no longer consider it a necessary ingredient for a satisfying life and an increasing number of people are choosing to remain single and not have children. These changing attitudes are reflected in popular culture. Whereas television shows of the 1950s such as *Ozzie and Harriet* and *Leave it to Beaver* portray the nuclear family as the cornerstone of a fulfilling life, television shows of the 1990s such as the immensely successful *Seinfeld* and *Friends* portray single life as an attractive alternative to marriage and children.

The change in attitudes towards marriage, however, does not diminish the emotional force and artistry of "Ordinary Words," which will speak to readers, single or married, for some time to come.

Source: Chris Semansky, Critical Essay on "Ordinary Words," in *Poetry for Students*, Gale, 2003.

Norman Friedman

In the following essay, Friedman discusses Stone's style and themes as they appear throughout the body of her work.

Although at age forty-four she was no beginner when she published her first book, *In an Iridescent Time*, in 1959, Ruth Stone was working largely within the elegant, formal conventions of that era, showing her respect for the likes of Ransom and Stevens. Thus, along with many other women poets of the 1950s—Sylvia Plath and Adrienne Rich—she began her career by expressing a female vision through a male medium.

Nevertheless, within the largely regular forms of these early poems there is heard a complex woman's voice compounded of the artful naivete of fable and tale and the deceptive simplicity of a sophisticated artist. The voice is as responsive to marriage, family, and human solitude as it is to animals, landscapes, and seasons. Given to gorgeous diction, eloquent syntax, and powerful statement, along with occasional colloquialisms, the book contains nothing callow or unformed, although today it appears marked by a somewhat overdone artfulness. This impression is confirmed by Stone's own changes as she has developed and explored the various possibilities of her special voice.

There was a conspicuous silence of twelve years before Stone's next book, *Topography and Other Poems*, appeared, and the single most determinative cause of the hiatus—as well as of its fruit—must have been her poet-scholar husband's unexpected suicide in 1959 when they were in England, leaving Stone and her three daughters to fend for themselves. She returns repeatedly here and in subsequent volumes to this devastating experience, and without either over- or underplaying it she somehow manages to survive and grow strong, as Hemingway's Frederic Henry says, in the broken places. Thus, there is a deepening of her emotional range, accompanied as we would expect by a corresponding roughening of rhythm and diction.

The more general poetic and political rebellions of the 1960s were no doubt operative as well, but Stone never becomes programmatic. A Keatsian poet "of Sensations rather than of Thoughts"—although like Keats she is certainly not without thought—so busy is she with her responses to the pressures of the lived life that she cannot afford time for philosophizing or moralizing.

Stone's second volume deals with her first attempts to absorb her husband's death, her reactions to the people around her, her return with her daughters to the seasons of Vermont, her subsequent travels, and her continuing growth as a poet, mother, and person. She begins by using more direct speech and unrhymed free verse lines of variable length, not, however, without her characteristic touches of elegance. In "Changing (For Marcia)" she writes to her eldest child, noticing the changes in her, and reflects, "Love cannot be still; / Listen. It's folly and wisdom; / Come and share."

That Stone had regained her voice and creative will at this time was shown four years later by the publication of *Cheap: New Poems and Ballads*. Here we find her risking relationships with others while still trying to deal with her husband's death and the loss of their life together, and she mines an iron vein of mordant wit to make bearable the bitterness. Some of her lines strike a late Plathian note of barely contained hysteria: "I hid sometimes in the closet among my own clothes" ("Loss"). But near a barn young bulls are bellowing ("Communion"), and solace is found in the germinative force of nature. "Cocks and Mares" concludes with a marvelous evocation of female power in wild mares.

Second-Hand Coat: Poems New and Selected, which came out in 1987, contains forty-six new poems. Along with exploring her evolving feelings about her lost husband, Stone probes more deeply into her childhood years and early family memories. Once again she balances between "fertility / futility" ("Pine Cones"), and in addition she reaches a new level of outrageous fantasy and satire. In "Some Things You'll Need to Know...." a "poetry factory" is described in which "the antiwar and human rights poems / are processed in the white room. / Everyone there wears sterile gauze."

The Solution, a chapbook of eighteen poems that came out two years later, in 1989, adds yet another new note—the emergence of Stone's other self, her doppelgänger, as in "The Rotten Sample." "Bird in the Gilbert's Tree" is truly remarkable, beginning with the question "What is the bird saying?" and continuing on to give in verbal form what is strictly nonverbal, a tour de force worthy of Lewis Carroll: "And you, my consort, my basket, / my broody decibels, / my lover in the lesser scales; / this is our tree, our vista, / our bagworms."

Who is the Widow's Muse? makes of the doppelgänger a dramatic and structural device in a sequence of fifty-two relatively short lyrics (perhaps for a year's cycle), plus a prefatory poem as introduction. Here the muse, a realistic—not to say caustic—voice, serves to limit and control the operatic tendency of the widow's voice in her endless quest for ways to come to terms with her husband's death. As a result the tone is a miraculous blend of desolation and laughter, a unique achievement. At the end, when the widow wants to write "one more" poem about her loss, the muse "shakes her head" and, in an almost unbearably compassionate gesture, "took the widow in her arms." The poem concludes, "'Now say it with me,' the muse said. / 'Once and for all . . . he is forever dead;.'" Thus is Stone solving, in her own particular way, the problem of expressing a female vision through a female idiom.

Stone's 1995 volume *Simplicity* contains the poems of *The Solutions* as well as a hundred pages of later work. Some still deal with her husband, but the rest derive from an independent inspiration, although it is of a rather somber mood, for at the age of eighty Stone has grown into a deep knowledge of suffering and survival. Her range is broad as well, shifting in a moment from the common to the cosmic, from the ordinary to the surreal. Riding a train or bus, she notes the passage of weather and the seasons, the isolation of those beside her, and the small towns and shops sliding by. She is the poet of hope in the midst of doom, of love as it encounters death, and of the apocalypse forthcoming

> *"Riding a train or bus, she notes the passage of weather and the seasons, the isolation of those beside her, and the small towns and shops sliding by. She is the poet of hope in the midst of doom, of love as it encounters death, and of the apocalypse forthcoming in the mundane."*

What Do I Read Next?

- In part, Stone's poem is an exploration of the expectations and disappointments of marriage in the 1950s. In *The Way We Never Were: American Families and the Nostalgia Trap* (2000), Stephanie Coontz argues against representations of the 1950s American family as wholesome and virtuous, claiming that notions of traditional family values are rooted more in myth than fact.

- Stone's first collection, *In an Iridescent Time* (1959), focuses on Stone's childhood family life.

- Stone won the National Book Award for poetry in 2002 for *In the Next Galaxy*, published by Copper Canyon Press.

- John Updike's novel *Rabbit, Run* (1960) follows the life of Harry Angstrom, a former star basketball player in high school, who is now in his mid-twenties, struggling in an unfulfilling marriage. Updike's (male) representation of marriage in the 1950s is a useful counterpoint to Stone's representation of marriage during that era.

---

in the mundane. "The Artist" is revelatory, showing the painter in his own painting—an old oriental scroll—climbing a mountain to reach a temple. Although he has been walking all day, he will not get there before dark, "and yet there is no way to stop him. He is / still going up and he is still only half way."

Four years later Stone published *Ordinary Words*, a new, beautiful full-length collection. Although she continues with many of her customary themes—her husband's death, a woman's poetry, the transcendent in the midst of the mundane, a mordant view of country life—she also reaches more toward a strange, unsettling, and profound theme of hysteria, chaos, and madness. So we read in "This" of a "glaze of vision fragmented." In "The Dark," about her sister's death from cancer, "we come to know / violent chaos at the pure brutal heart," and in "How They Got Her to Quiet Down" we learn of the madness of Aunt Mabel. The theme is found in other poems, for example, in "So What" ("For me the great truths are laced with hysteria") and in "Aesthetics of the Cattle Farm" ("A small funereal woods / into which a farmer dragged / the diseased cattle and left / them to fall to their knees"). Nevertheless there remains the balancing impulse, as in her description of a hummingbird "entering the wild furnace of the flower's heart" ("Hummingbirds") or in her touching descriptions in "The Ways of Daughters" or in "At the Museum, 1938," which concludes, "Outside, the great elms along the streets in Urbana, / their green arched cathedral canopies; the continuous / singing of birds among their breathing branches." And we see her now hard-earned intensity working equally well in both modes.

Source: Norman Friedman, "Stone, Ruth," in *Contemporary Poets*, 7th ed., edited by Thomas Riggs, St. James Press, 2001, pp. 1159–60.

Wendy Barker

In the following essay, Barker discusses Stone's life and writings.

Tillie Olson, in the *Iowa Review* collection *Extended Outlooks* (1982), calls Ruth Stone "one of the major poets" of the latter twentieth century, describing her poetic voice as "clear, pure, fierce." Olson is not alone in her high praise for this poet. Patricia Blake in *Time* (22 December 1980) singles out Stone as one of the most powerful and sensuous of woman poets writing since Sappho. Sandra M. Gilbert (in *Extended Outlooks*) praises the "terrible clarity of her vision," and Julie Fay in the *Women's Review of Books* (July 1989) insists that a place be made for Stone "among the better-known poets of [her] generation." Frances Mayes, reviewing Stone's 1987 book, *Second-Hand Coat*, in the *San Jose Mercury News* (10 July 1988), observes that Stone is not only "wise and abundantly gifted," but that, in addition, her poetry is "stunning work" that spans a "superb range of evocative experience."

Perhaps it is this wide range, one of Stone's best characteristics, that, paradoxically, has caused the work of this poet only recently to be given the attention it deserves. For the work of Stone is as difficult to categorize as the poetry of Emily Dickinson. Lush, lyrical, even at times Tennysonian in its music and meter, Stone's poetry is also, as Donald Hall has said in *Hungry Mind Review* (Spring 1988), "relentless as a Russian's."

Born on 8 June 1915 in Roanoke, Virginia, in her grandparents' house, Ruth Perkins Stone was surrounded by relatives who wrote poetry, painted, practiced law, and taught school. Intrigued by the large collection of books in her grandparents' library, Stone began reading at three. She attended kindergarten and first grade in Roanoke, but then moved to Indianapolis where she lived with her father's parents. Living at that time in her paternal grandparents' home in Indianapolis was Stone's aunt, Harriet, who played writing and drawing games with her niece. Together they wrote poems and drew comical cartoons: Stone refers to Aunt Harriet as "the best playmate I ever had." The poet's mother, Ruth Ferguson Perkins, encouraged her daughter's "play." This was a mother to whom poetry was an essential part of life: while nursing Ruth as a baby, she read the works of Alfred, Lord Tennyson aloud. As her child grew, she openly delighted in Ruth's irrepressible creativity.

Writing, poetry, drawing, and music also surrounded Ruth Stone during her childhood in Indianapolis. Her father, Roger McDowell Perkins, was a musician, a drummer who often practiced at home. As Stone tells it, on the nights he was not gambling, he would bring home an elegant box of the best chocolates and some new classical records. There would be music and candy while he read out loud to them, sometimes from the Bible, sometimes from humorous pieces by Bill Nye. He was "crazy about funny stuff," says Stone. Humor was, in fact, a large part of the pattern of family life in Indianapolis. At dinner parties, the poet remembers, her uncles told one funny, fascinating story after another. Every member of her father's family had an extraordinary sense of the ridiculous, an ability to see through the superficial.

And yet this family of English descent also played its part in polite Indianapolis society. Stone's paternal grandfather was a senator, and in keeping with the familial social position, his wife gave frequent formal tea parties. Stone remembers pouring tea, learning to be a lady, something she says she later "had to learn to forget."

Perhaps part of the fascination of Stone's poetry has to do with the counterpoint between a lyrical, ladylike gentility and a sharp, blunt, often bawdy ability to see into the core of experience. Indeed, the poetry of Stone is as informed by a knowledge of the sciences as it is by a novelist's eye for character, an artist's eye for color, and a musician's ear for sound. At the age of eight Stone read about meteors. Out in the grassy yard at night, she would lie on her back and study the stars. Once she found in the library a photograph of a galaxy that, as she puts it, "changed me terribly." When she read, in the *Phi Beta Kappa* magazine, an article about the new theory of the expanding universe, she became inquisitive about physics. She was also passionate about botany: "I wanted to absorb everything about the real world." When not intensely observing "real" phenomena, she read everything she could find; frequently she took encyclopedias and dictionaries to bed with her. She was, as she puts it, "obsessive about language."

It is no wonder then, with such passionate and diverse interests, that this poet's complex work has defied categorization. Diane Wakoski, in a paper delivered at the 1988 Modern Language Association convention, recognized Stone's poetry as embodying the comedic tradition of Dante, with its enormous range of human experience. As Wakoski put it, Stone is "opening the door to an American comedic verse." Stone's work could also be compared to William Shakespeare's plays, in that, immersed in the world of her poems, readers may find themselves moving inexplicably from laughter to tears and back to laughter again.

In an Iridescent Time (1959), Stone's first collection, includes poems written primarily while her husband, novelist and poet Walter B. Stone, was teaching at Vassar College. By that time the Stones had three children: Marcia, born in 1942; Phoebe, born in 1949; and Abigail, born in 1953. By 1959 Stone's reputation was established: in 1955 she won the Kenyon Review Fellowship in Poetry, received the Bess Hokin prize from *Poetry*, and recorded her poems at the Library of Congress. Individual poems had been published in the best magazines, including *Kenyon Review*, *Poetry*, the *New Yorker*, and *Partisan Review*.

Stone's first collection is aptly named: the poems are "iridescent," shimmering with music and echoes of Tennyson and the Romantics. These poems focus on youthful, exuberant family life, as in the title poem, in which the speaker remembers her mother, washing and hanging out to dry the brilliantly

> "Perhaps part of the fascination of Stone's poetry has to do with the counterpoint between a lyrical, ladylike gentility and a sharp, blunt, often bawdy ability to see into the core of experience."

colored "fluttering intimacies of life." The laundry in this poem shines in memory and gleams with the energy of the daughters who hone "their knuckles" on the washboard. The title poem is also characteristic of this collection in its formal qualities: "tub" rhymes with "rub-a-dub," and the girls shake the clothes "from the baskets two by two," draping them "Between the lilac bushes and the yew: / Brown gingham, pink, and skirts of Alice blue." The vitality and whimsy characteristic of this collection also spring from the opening poem, "When Wishes Were Fishes," in which the rhythm and meter gallop: "All that clapping and smacking of gulls, / And that slapping of tide on rock"; "Our senses twanged on the sea's gut string, / . . . and the young ladies in a flock / . . . ran the soprano scale and jumped the waves in a ring." The air is "suncharged" over the "kelp-smelling sea," at "the edge of the world and free."

Yet this shimmering world is not entirely free, not simply youthful and buoyant. The "Sunday wish" of the girls in "When Wishes Were Fishes" is "to bottle a dredged-up jellyfish"; though innocents, they are also becoming aware of the "Seaweed and dead fish" strewed on the sand. The sense of youthful vitality is underscored by a sense that all this lushness and youth cannot last, that something ominous is lurking close at hand.

In Stone's second volume of poetry, *Topography* (1971), such ominousness occupies the center of the collection, for this volume maps the territory of grief at its most acute. Written after the death of her husband, Walter, which occurred while the family was in England, *Topography* was published twelve years after her first book. In this second volume, music is still present, but rhyme is less frequent. Forms are less closed in this collection, as if to emphasize that nothing, not even the striking images of these poems, can contain the grief.

The poems that comprise *Topography* were, for the most part, written from 1963 to 1965, when the poet was a fellow of the Radcliffe Institute. The book opens with a short poem reflecting on marriage, "Dream of Light in the Shade": "Now that I am married I spend / My hours thinking about my husband. / I wind myself about his shelter." As if an echo from *In an Iridescent Time*, this poem, with its light touch and its wry attitude toward a wife's life, causes the rest of the volume to be read even more tragically, since the central fact underlying the book is that there is no longer anything to wind around, no longer any center, or any firm ground.

The second poem of *Topography* is "Arrivals and Departures," in which "the terminal echoes in the ears of a single traveler, / Meaningless as the rumble of the universe." *Topography* maps the journey from that arrival at the place of death, that departure from "normal" life initiated by the death of the mate. The speaker has been dropped off in this meaningless, rumbling "terminal," and must now map out alone both her destination and her itinerary. Imagery is stark: the counter in the terminal is wiped with a "grey rag," and the coffee bar is dirty. Everything has been spoiled, dirtied, and decayed. In "The Excuse," Stone writes: "It is so difficult to look at the deprived, or smell their decay, / But now I am among them. I too, am a leper, a warning." Poems in this collection contain images of "suckeddown refuse" ("Memory of Knowledge and Death at the Mother of Scholars"), "dead still fog" ("Fog: Cambridge"), and "repelling flesh" ("Being Human").

Yet, under the decay, under the almost devastating shock, the poems also trace the way out of this "terminal." One way is through the brutal honesty of many of these poems. "Denouement," for instance, maps the territory of anger following the death of a husband who took his own life: "After many years I knew who it was who had died. / Murderer, I whispered, you tricked me." But it is not only anger that is so powerfully mapped in these poems. In "Stasis" the poet says, "I wait for the touch of a miracle," and gradually, through the pages of *Topography*, small miracles do occur. Slow healing is the subject of poems such as "Reaching Out": "We hear the sound of a hammer in the pony shed, / And the clean slap of linens drying in the sun; / Climbing the grass path, / Reaching out before we are there / To know, nothing is changed." Old memories begin to surface, to shine into the present time, as in *In an Iridescent Time*; in "Green Apples" Stone writes: "In August we carried the old horsehair mattress / To the back porch / And slept with our children in a row...."

But for all its moments of stasis, of acceptance, even at times of brief happiness beyond the grief, *Topography* maps no simple country. Section 4, for instance, shows Stone's skill as a naturalist. In poems such as the comic "Pig Game," in which pigs, like poets, "live within / And scan without," and the determined "Habitat," in which the wolverine "is built for endurance," Stone moves beyond the shock and anger of early grief to a wide perspective and rich connections. There is also much humor here, especially in the nursery-rhyme-like poems such as "I Have Three Daughters." The title poem, "Topography," concludes the volume. Wry, wise, funny, and redolent with a sense of the possibilities that exist beyond the lost and mourned husband, the poem ends, "Yes, I remember the turning and holding, / The heavy geography; but map me again, Columbus."

Stone's 1975 book, *Cheap*, is characterized by a movement beyond "the terminal," beyond the paralysis that underlies much of *Topography*. These poems were written while Stone was slowly migrating across the country, from university to university. She taught at the University of Illinois (1971–1973), at Indiana University (1973–1974), and at Center College in Kentucky (1975). The changes since *In an Iridescent Time* are clear from the titles of poems. In Stone's first book, poems are titled "Snow," "Ballet," "Collage," "Swans"; in *Cheap*, poems are titled "Cocks and Mares," "Who's Out," "The Nose," "Bazook," "Bored on a Greyhound," and the much-anthologized "The Song of Absinthe Granny."

In *Cheap* Stone's humor comes into its own. *Topography* was less mannered, less lyrical than *In an Iridescent Time*; *Cheap* is even less so. The poet has moved through the country of grief and has emerged, seeing everything, right down to its frightening, funny core. Connections between human and nonhuman life are made even clearer—in "Vegetables I" eggplants are compared to decapitated human heads, "utterly drained of blood." In the market, they seem "to be smiling / In a shy embarrassed manner, / jostling among themselves." In "Vegetables II" Stone writes:

> It is the cutting room, the kitchen,
> Where I go like an addict
> To eat of death.
> The eggplant is silent.
> We put our heads together.
> You are so smooth and cool and purple,
> I say. Which of us will it be?

Such wryness and pithiness characterize this collection, which is tighter, more ironic, and wiser than either of the first two collections.

Styles and themes begun in the earlier volumes do continue. In the title poem, "Cheap," young love is the subject of fond scorn: "He was young and cheap ... I was easy in my sleep"; the boy and girl are "braying, galloping / Like a pair of mules," running "blind as moles." Marriage and betrayal continue as themes. In "Codicil" Stone writes of a widowed landlady who keeps all the eggs her ornithologist husband collected, comparing all the "secret muted shapes" of "unborn wisened eggs" to the stillborn possibilities for her own marriage. Stone continues to examine her widowhood in poems such as "Loss" ("I hid sometimes in the closet among my own clothes"), "Habit" ("Every day I dig you up ... I show you my old shy breasts"), and "The Innocent" ("I remember you / in the sound of an oak stake / Hammered into the frozen heart of the ground"). Other poems are lighter: "Tic Tac Toe" makes fun of all good intentions, of people "pulling in their stomachs and promising / To exercise more, drink less, grow brilliant."

Some poems in *Cheap* use the nursery-rhyme style of earlier poems. "Bargain," "The Tree," and "The Song of Absinthe Granny" all incorporate sing-song rhythms. Diana O'Hehir (in a paper delivered at the Modern Language Association convention, December 1988) observed that Stone's use of rhythms and comical word patterns, often coupled with terrifying subject matter, accounts for much of the poems' power. As O'Hehir put it, Stone "lures the reader in with the familiar rhythms of childhood, promises a pattern which the reader can join in on and follow along with, then yanks the entire structure out from under the feet," so that the reader is "surprised, startled, and made to follow gasping."

Surprising, startling, *Cheap* was the most direct, the most piercing of Stone's collections, until her *Second-Hand Coat: Poems New and Selected* was published in 1987. Here one finds a poet writing in her fullest power, relying upon craft, music, wisdom, and humor. "Orange Poem Praising Brown" captures the anxieties of the writer with admirable wit: "The quick poem jumped over the lazy woman. / There it goes flapping like an orange with peeling wings." A dialogue continues between the woman and the brown poem: "Watch it, the poem cried. You aren't wearing any pants.... / Praise my loose hung dangle, he said. Tell me about myself in oral fragments...." "Some Things You'll Need to Know before You Join the Union" is another comic poem for poets:

> At the poetry factory
> body poems are writhing and bleeding.
> ....
> The antiwar and human rights poems
> are processed in the white room.
> Everyone in there wears sterile gauze.
> These poems go for a lot.
> No one wants to mess up.
> There's expensive equipment involved.
> The workers have to be heavy,
> very heavy.
> These poems are packaged in cement.
> You frequently hear them drop with a dull thud.

Part of Stone's humor is based on the characters who populate this volume, characters who may remind readers of Fred and Ida of "Bazook" in *Cheap*. Stone's characters are outrageously funny, and very real, similar to those of Charles Dickens and Mark Twain. As Kevin Clark observed (in a paper delivered at the 1988 Modern Language Association convention), they are often grotesques, in which readers may recognize themselves. As in the poem "Bazook," many of the characters in *Second-Hand Coat* have gone "beserk" [*sic*]; but the poems question what is meant by "sanity" and "insanity." Mrs. Dubosky in "What Can You Do?"; Aunt Virginia in "Curtains"; Uncle, Little Ivan, and Aunt Bess in "The Miracle"; the Masons in "Sunday"—all are a little daft, yet, as Clark noted, they show readers the truth of who *they* are.

The humor of *Second-Hand Coat* also extends to the poems that show Stone as an avid student of contemporary science. Just as the young Stone took encyclopedias to bed with her, the mature Stone reads everything she can about astronomy, the new physics, the natural world, the galaxy, neurons, and protons. Much of the effect of these poems has to do with Stone's immense knowledge of the way the world actually works, and in many of these poems, she fuses the wacky humor and drummer's rhythms of her father, the lyricism of her mother's reading of Tennyson, and her own relentless curiosity, wit, and wisdom. "The bunya-bunya is a great louse that sucks," Stone begins in "From the Arboretum," a poem that goes on to show the intricacy of relatedness: "Rings of ants, bark beetles, sponge molds, / even cockroaches communicate in its armpits. / But it protests only with the voices of starlings, / their colony at its top in the forward brush. / To them it is only an old armchair, a brothel, the front porch." Other poems are even more obviously based on Stone's scientific knowledge. "Moving Right Along" begins, "At the molecular level, / in another dimension, oy, are you different! / That's where it all shreds / like Watergate." Like the new physicists who have come to the conclusion that there is no such thing as objectivity, that all depends on point of view, Stone questions the possibilities for clear answers in "At the Center"; "The center is simple, they say. / They say at the Fermi accelerator, / 'Rejoice. A clear and clean/explanation of matter is possible....'" The poem continues with the speaker's questioning: "Where is this place, / the center they speak of? Currants, / red as faraway suns, burn on the currant bush." The eyes of the beloved, now long dead, are "far underground," where they "fall apart, / while their particles still shoot like meteors / through space making their own isolated trajectories."

In *Second-Hand Coat* the grief of the widow is softened, muted. In "Curtains," another tragicomic poem, the speaker asks at the end, "See what you miss by being dead?" In "Winter" she asks, "Am I going toward you or away from you on this train?" "Message from Your Toes" begins, "Even in the absence of light / there is light. Even in the least electron / there are photons. / So in a larger sense you must consider your own toes...." Stone connects electron, photon, and toes in a poem that elicits laughter in the beginning and a deep sense of poignancy at the conclusion: "And your toes, passengers of the extreme / clustered on your dough-white body, / say how they miss his feet, the thin elegance of his ankles."

Often poignant, as in "Liebeslied," some of these poems are as lyrical as any in *In an Iridescent Time*. In "Names" the internal rhymes offer the reader as rich an inheritance as all the "plants on the mountain," with their names like "pennyroyal, boneset, / bedstraw, toadflax—from whom I did descend in perpetuity." The music in *Second-Hand Coat* is far more intricate than that of previous collections; sound in Stone's poetry deserves more study.

Second-Hand Coat is a book that, like the speaker's mother in the poem "Pokeberries" (as Donald Hall has observed), splits language in two. The next-to-last poem in the section of new poems in *Second-Hand Coat*, "Translations," may well be Stone's best poem to date. In it one sees the most powerful characteristics of the collection: a tone of forgiveness and understanding, and, through anger and aversion, a deep forgiving love.

There is also laughter. "Women Laughing," for instance, incorporates all the lyricism of *In an Iri-*

descent Time, with a new complexity, a richer, maturer vision:

> Laughter from women gathers like reeds in the river.
> A silence of light below their rhythm glazes the water.
> They are on a rim of silence looking into the river.
> Their laughter traces the water as kingfishers dipping
> circles within circles set the reeds clicking;
> and an upward rush of herons lifts out of the nests of laughter,
> their long stick-legs dangling, herons, rising out of the river.

Ruth Stone's poems are indeed "nests of laughter," of wisdom and humor. With *Second-Hand Coat* Stone's poems have not only moved far beyond personal grief but have also risen to the stature of perhaps the finest poetry being written today.

Source: Wendy Barker, "Ruth Stone," in *Dictionary of Literary Biography*, Vol. 105, *American Poets Since World War II, Second Series*, edited by R. S. Gwynn, Gale Research, 1991, pp. 241–46.

Sources

Campbell, Gowan, "A Conversation with Ruth Stone," in *12gauge.com*, http://www.12gauge.com/ (last accessed January 19, 2003).

Hoffert, Barbara, Review of *Ordinary Words*, in *Library Journal*, Vol. 125, Issue 7, April 15, 2000, p. 95.

Kreider, Rose M., and Jason M. Fields, "Number, Timing, and Duration of Marriages and Divorces," in *U.S. Census Bureau Current Population Reports*, February 2002, p. 18.

Review of *Ordinary Words*, in *Publishers Weekly*, Vol. 246, Issue 30, July 26, 1999, p. 86.

Silberg, Richard, Review of *Ordinary Words*, in *Poetry Flash*, November–December 1999, p. 47.

Smith, Dinitia, "Poetry That Captures a Tough 87 Years," in the *New York Times*, December 10, 2002, p. B1.

Stone, Ruth, "Then," in *Ordinary Words*, Paris Press, 1999, p. 31.

Further Reading

Barker, Wendy, "Ruth Stone," in *Dictionary of Literary Biography*, Vol. 105, *American Poets since World War II, Second Series*, edited by R. S. Gwynn, Gale Research, 1991, pp. 241–46.

> Barker offers a thorough overview of Stone's career through 1990 and includes a useful bibliography of secondary sources.

Barker, Wendy, and Sandra M. Gilbert, eds., *The House Is Made of Poetry: The Art of Ruth Stone*, Ad feminam series, Southern Illinois University Press, 1996.

> Barker and Gilbert collect essays on Stone's poetry by critics and poets such as Willis Barnstone and Diane Wakoski.

Bishop, Elizabeth, *The Complete Poems, 1927–1979*, Farrar Straus Giroux, 1983.

> Critics have often compared Stone's poetry to that of Elizabeth Bishop for its attention to detail and the ordinary things of life.

Gilbert, Sandra M., and Susan Gubar, "The War of the Words," in *No Man's Land: The Place of the Woman Writer in the Twentieth Century*, Vol. 1, Yale University Press, 1989.

> Gilbert and Gubar discuss Stone's place in relation to other women writers of the late twentieth century.

Perfect Light

Ted Hughes
1998

What astounds many readers about Ted Hughes's *Birthday Letters* (1998) is the tender, honest, and confessional voice that rises from the poems. Hughes is known for his emotional detachment from the situations about which he wrote, an aloofness of voice that reveals little about his speaker's sentiment and even less about his own. His language is often harsh and explicit in describing violence, whether in the natural world of animals or in human society, and his subjects avoid personal experience, particularly any overt reference to his wife, fellow poet Sylvia Plath. But then he published an entire book written in memory of her.

Birthday Letters includes eighty-eight poems composed over a twenty-five- to thirty-year period, and traces the couple's brief but saturated life together, from the first date and marriage to separation and suicide. Some of the poems are thought to have been inspired by specific letters and photographs of Plath that Hughes rediscovered while preparing her papers for sale to Smith College. "Perfect Light" is one such poem.

Based on a 1962 photo of Plath in a field of daffodils holding their two children, "Perfect Light" describes the physical scene and ends with an ominous metaphor suggesting the mother's inescapable fate. With atypical softness and sentimentality, Hughes addresses Plath directly as the "you" in the poem, portraying her in angelic terms and comparing her innocence to that of the children, before concluding that such a blissful moment was doomed to fade into a "perfect light." *Birth-*

day Letters is the only collection in which this poem appears.

Author Biography

Ted Hughes was born August 17, 1930, in the village of Mytholmroyd in West Yorkshire, England, but grew up in Mexborough. In school Hughes was encouraged to write poetry by teachers who recognized his talent, and he was later awarded a scholarship to Pembroke College, Cambridge, where he studied English literature. His fascination with animals and their connections to humankind caused him to change his major to anthropology, and after earning his bachelor's degree in 1954, he moved to London to work as a zoo attendant and gardener.

Hughes returned to Cambridge for a master's degree in the late 1950s. He fell in with the literary crowd and published several poems in local journals. At a party he met a young American Fulbright scholar named Sylvia Plath, who was also a poet, and the two were immediately drawn to one another. Within months they were married, so beginning a tumultuous relationship that neither could have anticipated would end in such tragedy.

The couple moved to America in 1957 and both taught at universities in Massachusetts. The same year, Hughes had his first collection of poetry published. In 1959 they moved back to England. They had a daughter in 1960 and a son in 1962, and seemed to live simple, pastoral lives without much money, encouraging one another's poetic efforts and enjoying their children. But a darker side of their marriage came to light when Hughes had an affair with a German woman, Assia Wevill. Plath committed suicide in 1963, a few months after her husband left her.

For years to come, Plath followers blamed Hughes's infidelity for her death, some even attending his readings only to stand up and shout, "Murderer!" when he took the stage. Tragedy struck Hughes again in 1969 when Wevill also committed suicide, adding to the anguish by first killing their two-year-old daughter.

A year later Hughes married again, moving with his wife to a farm in Devon where they raised sheep and cattle. For the next three decades, Hughes wrote prolifically, publishing poetry, drama, literary criticism, and works for children, though he was never able to escape completely his fate as Plath's

Ted Hughes

husband, and worse, as one of the reasons for her death.

Scholars, however, have long recognized Hughes's place as one of England's greatest poets of the twentieth century. He was made poet laureate of Great Britain in 1984, and was a recipient of many literary awards in his long career, including the Guinness Poetry Award in 1958 for *The Hawk in the Rain*, and the Whitbread Book of the Year Award in 1998 for *Birthday Letters*. *Birthday Letters*, which contains the bittersweet poem "Perfect Light," is Hughes's tribute to Plath—to their marriage, their love, their children, and their grievous ending. Only months after publication of *Birthday Letters*, Hughes died of cancer, October 28, 1998, in Devon.

Poem Summary

Line 1

In the first line of "Perfect Light," the speaker establishes the second-person address of the poem, talking directly to a "you" and implying that he is looking at a photograph of the person. Though he does not mention a picture specifically in this line, the phrase "There you are" suggests the premise and the rest of the poem confirms it. This opening line also contains the first use of the word "innocence," which will be used a total of three times and here refers to the innocent appearance of the woman in the photograph.

Lines 2–3

These two lines further establish the setting, explaining that the woman in the picture is "Sitting among [her] daffodils," the latter word another one that will appear repeatedly in the poem—five times to be exact. In line 2, the speaker reveals the picture specifically, suggesting that its subject appears "Posed" for a photograph that should be called "'Innocence.'" This second use of the word "innocence," coming so quickly after the first one, serves to emphasize the speaker's opinion that the woman is a symbol of purity and childlike naiveté.

Lines 4–5

The phrase "perfect light" is not only the title of the poem, but also appears two times within the poem. In line 4, it refers to the sunlight or daylight that shines on the face of the woman sitting in the field of flowers. The light is "perfect" for picture taking, and the speaker compares the woman's facial features to a daffodil. Line 5 contains the second and third uses of the word "daffodil," which create an ironic twist in the way they are presented with the word "Like." The first phrase—"Like a daffodil"—simply makes the comparison of physical beauty between the woman and the flower. The second phrase—"Like any one of those daffodils"—initially seems to make the same point, to be a repetition of the simile just used. The line immediately following, however, shows that the speaker has something different in mind.

Lines 6–7

The comparison in these lines is between the brief length of time that the ephemeral daffodils will exist in the field and the same short amount of time that the woman will have to live among them. These lines foreshadow her sorrowful fate but still reflect the soft tenderness of the speaker's feelings. Line 7 ends with an introduction of someone or something else in the photograph, something the woman holds in her arms.

Lines 8–10

The second subject in the picture is the woman's "new son," whom she holds "Like a teddy bear" against her. The child is only "a few weeks" old, or a few weeks "into his innocence," and while the third use of the word "innocence" describes the boy, the woman is still portrayed in her own childlike purity, like a little girl holding a teddy bear. The speaker further glorifies the mother and child by comparing them to the Virgin Mary and the baby Jesus. Now the woman and her son are not just innocent, but "Holy" as well.

Lines 11–13

These lines introduce the third person in the photograph, the woman's "daughter, barely two," sitting beside her mother and "laughing up" at her. At the end of line 12, the phrase "Like a daffodil" appears to modify the description of the little girl that comes just before it, but not so. The first word in line 13 is "You," meaning the woman, and this is again the person who is compared to the flower. This time her face is like a daffodil's when it turns downward, as she leans over to say something to her daughter.

Line 14

This final line of the first stanza marks a shift in the tone and setting of the poem. Whatever the woman says to her little girl cannot be understood by the speaker, and the camera of course cannot capture it either. The word "lost" is especially significant here in that it describes not only the woman's fate, but also that of the speaker, their marriage, even their love.

Lines 15–17

The gentle tone and pastoral imagery of the first stanza is replaced with a despairing voice and war images in the second stanza. In these first three lines, the speaker describes the hill on which the woman is sitting as a "moated fort hill, bigger than [her] house." A moat is generally constructed to protect a castle from assault, and this image suggests that the woman is in need of protection from something or someone. The "knowledge / Inside the hill" on which she and the children sit refers back to the final lines of the first stanza, in which she bowed her head to speak to her daughter. Whatever her words were, they are now kept secret by the earth that took them in.

Lines 18–20

The phrase "Failed to reach the picture" refers to the "knowledge" in line 15 and reemphasizes the fact that neither the speaker nor the camera knows what the woman said to her daughter. The speaker personifies time with military imagery, saying it comes toward her "like an infantryman / Returning slowly out of no-man's-land." The location of no-man's land is significant because it means the land between two warring parties, suggesting that the woman is caught up in the middle of her own private war, though what its cause is or who the armies are is not revealed.

Lines 21–22

The phrases "Bowed under something" and "never reached you" refer back to the woman's "next moment" in line 18. The notion that her future "never reached" her parallels the previous idea that the knowledge of her words "Failed to reach" or to be captured in the photograph. The final line of the poem again foretells the woman's fate in saying that her next moment "Simply melted into the perfect light." The phrase "perfect light" suggests something darker, something far from perfect.

Themes

The Brevity of Life

The repetition of the word "daffodils" in "Perfect Light" is more than a technique of style to make the poem cohesive. It is also evidence of the dominant theme that runs through many of the poems in *Birthday Letters*: life is preciously short, and even shorter for those who take their own life. The word appears five times in this poem. Three times the word "daffodils" is used with the word "like" to make a direct comparison between the subject, Plath, and the daffodils. Hughes presents such a powerful, recurrent connection between them that the flowers *become* his ill-fated wife as she becomes them. The basis of this relationship and the glue that holds it together is the brevity of life, both that of the daffodils and Plath's. In a poem called "Daffodils" from this collection, Hughes writes that "We knew we'd live for ever. We had not learned / What a fleeting glance of the everlasting / Daffodils are. . . . the rarest ephemera— / Our own days!" What a fleeting glance and rare ephemera Plath's life turned out to be. As "Perfect Light" declares, she had but one spring to live among her daffodils, and though the flowers would return the following year, Plath would not.

A theme purporting the shortness of human life may seem too obvious to be of much value, but it is made more complex here because the brevity is helped along by suicide. A poem about the death of an elderly person or someone who is killed or succumbs to disease is certainly worthwhile and not

Topics for Further Study

- Read some of Plath's poetry and compare the style and voice to that of Hughes's poems in *Birthday Letters*. What are the main similarities and differences?

- If the Hughes-Plath scandal had occurred today instead of in the early 1960s, how would it have been handled differently in the media and by British society? Would there be any difference in the British and American responses?

- For years, Plath fans placed blame for her death directly on Hughes. What does current psychology research suggest about the cause of most suicides? Is it right or wrong to blame the admittedly unfaithful husband for his wife's taking her own life?

- What effect does the repetition of the words "innocence" and "daffodils" have on the first stanza of this poem? Instead of these words, what other words may have been repeated for a similar effect?

unexpected. But in "Perfect Light," the grim reality of a woman's death by gassing herself in the kitchen oven is remarkably contrasted by the personification of her in tender spring flowers. Hughes had the advantage of writing this poem some years after Plath died; had he written it the same day the photograph was taken, he may have concentrated on the beauty of the daffodils and the serenity of the countryside, comparing only those items to his wife and children. As it was, however, the flowers came to represent something more pressing, something darker in their lives, and Hughes makes that clear through the repetition of one word.

Innocence versus Knowledge

Another compelling theme in this poem is the tension between innocence and knowledge, between the perfect light of blameless simplicity and the perfect light into which knowledge fades, leaving one blind to it. Throughout the entire first stanza, which is nearly twice as long as the second, Hughes stresses over and over again the innocent physical appearance and emotional demeanor of his wife, their children, and the overall setting of the photograph that inspired the work. If the poem ended after line 14, the theme would be only innocence and would conclude with an intriguing yet still expected outcome. But the second stanza presents an about-face, taking place inside the speaker's mind instead of within the setting of the photograph and exploring the effect of knowledge on the naiveté of both the speaker and the woman in the picture.

Knowledge is ironic here; it is both horrible and unattainable. It is horrible for the speaker because he can never know what words of wisdom, or simple, loving platitudes his wife spoke to their daughter as the picture was snapped. Just as sadly, it is unattainable for the woman because she is completely unaware of what her next moment will bring. If there must be a victor in the struggle between innocence and knowledge, Hughes awards the title to the latter, as he expresses by the end of the poem.

The word "innocence" is nowhere to be found in the second stanza. Something quite the opposite now dominates the scene, along with the concept of failure and inability. Neither knowledge nor time can make its destination, and both would-be recipients suffer for it—Plath with her life and Hughes with a lifetime of haunting memories and unanswered questions. The sudden shift from daffodils and teddy bears to an infantryman and no-man's land gives testament to the tormented emotions with which the poet was left after his first wife's suicide. It was also the knowledge that remained, a knowledge that came to dominate so much of Hughes's work, though he managed to conceal its direct source until the publication of *Birthday Letters*.

Style

Contemporary Free Verse

The style of "Perfect Light" is contemporary free verse, but that does not mean it is totally without any structured format. While the voice is conversational and the language is unadorned, the poem is driven by the force of repetition. This work revolves around three central, repeated words and ideas: the word "daffodil" is mentioned five times, "innocence" is mentioned three times, and the notion of inevitable failure appears twice in the second stanza. The first stanza becomes almost rote with daffodils and innocence, but the technique is very effective in driving home the speaker's frame of mind. He relates both flowers and tender naiveté to every aspect of his subject, and manages to keep the repetition from becoming monotonous by using the repeated words in ironic places. Both "daffodils" and "innocence" are paired with expected and unexpected partners, the daffodils expressing both physical beauty and a short life and innocence, foretelling a haunting, lifelong struggle to understand and overcome past misery.

In the second stanza, the technique of repetition is more somber and concentrates on the frustration of failure. "Failed to reach" and "never reached you" are phrases that are already effective by themselves, but they are made more forceful by appearing only three lines apart. In a relatively short poem, this technique works especially well, and in an otherwise typical free-verse effort, it adds cohesiveness where there may not seem to be any. Beyond the technique of simple repetition, "Perfect Light" is in line with ordinary contemporary free verse, containing no direct rhyme and following no pattern of meter or poetic form.

Historical Context

The premise of "Perfect Light" makes it clear that Hughes based the poem on a photograph taken in 1962, judging from the ages of his children in the picture. When he actually wrote the poem is anyone's guess, as the so-called "Sylvia" poems were written over a twenty-five- to thirty-year period. This particular poem, however, never appeared in any other collections during those decades, as others from *Birthday Letters* did, and may well have been penned later in his career. Hughes's incessant privacy makes it difficult to put an exact date on much of his autobiographical work, and it is unlikely that any social, cultural, or political events of the time had any effect on the poems inspired solely by his relationship with and love for his first wife. Nonetheless, despite his reclusive behavior, Hughes was certainly a citizen of the world while preparing this collection for publication in the 1990s, and that decade brought significant changes to his native Great Britain as it did to many nations across the globe.

From the outset, the British government was undergoing a shake-up as Prime Minister Margaret

Thatcher resigned in 1990 after her economic policies resulted in decaying inner cities, and her opposition to greater British intervention in Europe caused a revolt within her own Conservative party. The Conservatives, however, managed to hold onto power in the 1992 elections, as John Major came to power, bringing with him more moderate, middle-of-the-road policies than those of his predecessor. A central focus of Major was the ongoing conflict between the government and the Irish Republican Army of Northern Ireland. A peace initiative led to a cease-fire in 1994, but by 1996 renewed violence had erupted again. Peace talks began again in 1997 and within two years both sides had reached an agreement to end direct rule by the British government in Northern Ireland.

The early 1990s also saw the collapse of the Soviet Union and the official end of the Cold War between the United States and the Soviet Union. These events also had a positive impact on Great Britain, America's staunchest ally, particularly with a greater unification of Europe. But being an ally also meant supporting the United States in a time of war and in 1991, when the Americans bombed Iraq in Operation Desert Storm, the British were there as well.

Another critical development in Great Britain during the 1990s was the nation's participation in the European Union, or EU. While some Britons called for a limited role, others said the country should be vigorously active in the organization, but previous disputes with other member nations did not always make that possible. In 1996 an outbreak of mad cow disease in England worsened relationships when other EU nations banned the import of British beef. By 1999 the ban was lifted when the EU approved Britain's plans for controlling the disease, but France continued its own ban, further straining British-French relations. The two nations experienced an on-again-off-again relationship throughout the decade, with one high point being the completion of the Channel Tunnel project in 1994, which began in France eight years earlier. This tunnel linked England not only to France, but to the entire European mainland.

Still another point of contention in Great Britain was the proliferation of the "Euro" monetary system in the late 1990s, which some European countries embraced immediately and others more reluctantly accepted. A supporter of the new European currency, Labour Party leader Tony Blair became prime minister of Great Britain in 1997. Blair's move to decentralize the government was greatly supported, and Scotland and Wales established their own legislative bodies, giving them a more independent voice in their domestic affairs. Both houses of Parliament also voted to strip most hereditary peers of their right to vote in the House of Lords, a tradition of British government deemed impractical under the Blair administration. The popularity of Blair's government was made evident again a few years later when the Labour Party handed the Conservatives a sound defeat in the 2001 elections.

It is doubtful that the affairs of government or the economy bear any significance on Hughes's "Sylvia" poems, and just as unlikely that any gossip about Royal divorces or marriages, the tragic death of Princess Diana, or the creation of Dolly the cloned sheep in Scotland were any source of inspiration for such personal poetry. And while one can never completely discount the effect of culture or society on any individual, those who maintain a highly private life and derive creativity from within seem less susceptible to either. As poet laureate, Hughes was compelled to meet his public duties, but when it came to Plath, he was definitely one of the private ones.

Critical Overview

Unfortunate for both Hughes and poetry readers in general, the critical reception to his work has often been based more on the man's personal life than on the poet's talent for writing. But Hughes-the-ogre did not hit the presses until 1963 after Plath's death, meaning that Hughes-the-poet enjoyed at least six years of keen interest, even high praise, for his early poetry. Following the publication of his first collection, revered fellow poet W. S. Merwin lauded the young Hughes's work in "Something of His Own to Say," a 1957 article for the *New York Times Book Review*: "Mr. Hughes has the kind of talent that makes you wonder more than commonly where he will go from here, not because you can't guess but because you venture to hope."

As it turns out, it really was not possible to guess, for after the highly publicized scandal regarding Hughes's unfaithfulness to Plath and her subsequent suicide, many critics and scholars began reading his work more to find hidden references to the tragic marriage and violent ending than for mere poetic creativity. Those critics who did concentrate on the poems themselves highlighted the overuse of violent animal imagery, dark settings, and bleak themes, usually considering the vehemence and gloominess a reflection of the poet's personality. Nonetheless, Hughes's raw gift for poetry did not go unrecognized by British literati, and he was made poet laureate of the nation and awarded several prestigious awards over the years, despite the personal controversy.

After the publication of *New Selected Poems, 1957–1994*, a shift in criticism began. Hughes was finally recognized for having a side—a tender, reflective, loving side—that the public had not seen before. Writing a review of this collection for *World Literature Today*, critic Peter Firchow observes about the sixteen "Sylvia" poems in the "Uncollected" section at the end of the book: "Hughes had never before permitted so intimate a poetic glimpse into this much-excavated-and-speculated-about patch of his life.... [These poems] are by themselves worth the price of the entire collection."

In an article called "Owning the Facts of His Life: Ted Hughes's *Birthday Letters*," from the *Literary Review*, critic Carol Bere writes, "While there is little question that much of the impact of poems turns on the immediacy of biography ... this should not override the realization that *Birthday Letters* is a major work of poetry by Hughes, containing some of the most visceral, accessible writing that he has produced to date." Hughes would enjoy this kind of criticism only a few short months before his death, but perhaps the praise was at least a small satisfaction for him, even if it came much too late.

Criticism

Pamela Steed Hill

Hill is the author of a poetry collection, has published widely in literary journals, and is an editor for a university publications department. In the following essay, Hill addresses the turnaround in scholarly opinion on Hughes's personality after the publication of his last collection of poetry.

Now that both Plath and Hughes are dead, more fair and equitable analyses of their tragic relationship is being written than was ever afforded them while alive. This is especially true for Hughes, of course, who spent the last thirty-five years of his life fending off scornful reports of his marital infidelity and evading accusations of near-murder in Plath's death. Truly, he did not help himself much by refusing to be interviewed about the entire affair or about his reaction to the suicide and by having the gall to edit Plath's poetry and fiction, burn one of her journals, and limit access to all of it. Some say those were grounds enough to brand him an arrogant rogue and coldhearted brute for life. Perhaps Hughes's stony silence on this terrible episode was not an attempt to conceal how little he cared but, rather, how much he grieved. Perhaps his inhospitable aloofness was really painful insecurity. Maybe he loved his wife more than the world had a right to know.

Emory University in Atlanta now houses the two-and-a-half ton Hughes collection of manuscripts, journals, and letters acquired about a year before the poet's death. Opened exclusively to scholars in 1999, the archive has proven to be an eye-opener for those privileged to have seen the material that comprises it. In an article for the *Atlanta Journal-Constitution* titled "In a New Light," journalist Bo Emerson writes about the scholars' reactions, saying, "Their early verdict: Hughes is a different man and a different poet than we knew." One visiting researcher, poet Carolyn Wright (quoted in Emerson), notes that the writings present "a consistent voice, the voice of a man who is deeply, deeply marked by this violent death of this woman he loved so much." Summing up the previously undisclosed material most poignantly, Emerson asserts that "*Birthday Letters* was, in a way, the interview that Hughes never gave." From that final collection, the poem "Perfect Light" is an apt representative of what the poet may have felt in his heart but refused to speak with his tongue.

The primary evidence that "Perfect Light" was written with honesty and openness is that the subject of the poem is addressed directly. Hughes did not attempt to evade forthright expression by using a more distant third-person "she" or hiding behind any ambiguity in who the person he is speaking to really is. "There *you* are" (italics mine) starts this poem off with unmistakable candor from the speaker to Plath, essentially leaving the reader on the sidelines to be a mere observer of or eavesdropper on an intensely personal utterance. And consider this: *nineteen times* in this brief poem Hughes uses the word "you" or "your." Nineteen times in twenty-two lines he directly addresses his dead wife, creating such a compact, feverish attempt to communicate his feelings about her, for her, and to her that it seems almost overkill. Almost, but not quite. Here, what may appear to be exaggeration and overuse of a technique is really something as simple and honest as desperation. Repeating "you" and "your" over and over is the method of a man compelled to get his message across, not to the world, but to the only one who matters to him, dead or alive.

The first stanza of "Perfect Light" in particular is loaded with repeating words, and both "innocence" and "daffodils" embrace a tender affection and sweet lovingness that seem so unlikely coming from Hughes. How odd for a husband accused of driving his wife to suicide to compare her beauty to a flower, her gentleness to that of a child holding a teddy bear. This suspected lout even goes so far as to liken Plath to the mother of Jesus and to portray the entire family setting as not only pastoral and comforting, but supernatural and holy. The first fourteen lines of this poem are so saturated with sweetness that they beg for a touch of bitterness, or at least a good reason for their candy coating. And Hughes does not disappoint. Ironically, as sappy and sentimental as the first stanza is, it in no way can overshadow the brutal reality of grief and sorrow that permeates the second. Yet the poet does not lose his tenderness in the last eight lines, only the premise in which it exists.

If a sunlit field of daffodils and Plath's innocent appearance early on represent the youthful, sincere love of a young married couple, then the "moated fort hill" and infantryman returning from no-man's land later must symbolize the vulnerability and grief of the one left behind. But even in the midst of such harsh military verbiage, the tone is still soft, the voice still placid. Hughes turns to images of violence because he *must* in order to keep the poem honest. Plath may have died peacefully in her sleep when her lungs filled with gas from the oven, but the circumstances of such a demise are truly horrible. When one considers the entire situation, all of it reeks of violence and misery and pain. Like war. These images in the second stanza suggest a sudden and complete turnaround in the emotions of both Plath and Hughes, a change that neither could foresee nor, more sadly, prevent.

The sentiment of "Perfect Light" is not that of a man who had no feelings for his wife while she was alive and certainly not that of one who was unaffected by her death. While Plath fans were busy shouting down Hughes at his own poetry readings and chiseling his name off their heroine's tombstone, no one really knew what was going on inside the very private, estranged husband whose feelings must have run the gamut from guilt to exoneration, anger to grief. Still other more sober, nonjudgmental readers and critics allowed Hughes

> "What Hughes will really never know is why she did it. In spite of his obvious infidelity, in spite of the trouble between them, in spite of any painful influence his leaving had on her, why did she take her own life?"

the benefit of the doubt, at least in order to give the poet a fair chance to live his own life and create his own work, which was admittedly some of the best poetry of the time. It was as though they were willing to accept the fact that only Hughes would ever be the one to know how he really felt about Plath's suicide and public opinion did not matter. In the same vein, the "knowledge / Inside the hill" on which Plath was sitting in the "Perfect Light" photograph would forever be lost to Hughes who could not hear what words his wife had spoken to their daughter when the picture was taken. Most likely they were only benign phrases of love from a mother to a daughter, but casting them off misses the point. What Hughes will really never know is why she did it. In spite of his obvious infidelity, in spite of the trouble between them, in spite of any painful influence his leaving had on her, why did she take her own life?

This is undoubtedly a difficult question to answer regarding anyone who chooses suicide as a way out. First, one must ask, "A way out of *what*?" In Plath's case, many of her friends, mourners, and fans were quick to answer, "A life made miserable by her lousy husband." But how can one individual truly force such a final, self-imposed sentence on someone else, especially when that someone is a young mother with two beautiful children who surely adore her? The fact is Plath had problems long before she met Hughes. Her journals and her poems reflect a less-than-perfect childhood and a volatile relationship with both parents. Her autobiographical novel *The Bell Jar* portrays the life of an emotionally unstable young woman bent on self-destruction. And most importantly, at least in Hughes's defense, she had already attempted suicide in the early 1950s—years before ever meeting the young British poet. This, of course, is not to detract from the sorrowful fact of Plath's death nor to sympathize with an unfaithful husband who surely could have handled his personal life with less selfishness and more consideration of how his behavior would affect others. But to place wholesale blame on Hughes for his wife's suicide seems, at best, a reactionary move on the part of shocked and misinformed groupies, and, at worst, a pathetic attempt to further the cause of feminism by glamorizing the suicide and acting as judge and jury to publicly convict the "guilty." After *Birthday Letters*, some members of the jury have rescinded their verdict.

In the *Atlanta Journal-Constitution* article, Emerson contends that "Through it all, Hughes refused to explain himself or to be interviewed about Plath." It was likely this profound obstinacy that fed much of the accusatory outcry from a public already hungry for the juicy details. But would the condemned poet have been able to appease angry Plath supporters by laying open his heart on the matter? Would they have had sympathy for a thoughtless scoundrel who walked out on his wife and children for another woman if he had gone before a microphone and confessed his true love for the one he abandoned? Not likely. Hughes had every right and every reason to keep his private thoughts private, his personal grief personal. In the end, though, he came forward to let the world know that he did indeed love Plath and that he did indeed mourn her loss.

Source: Pamela Steed Hill, Critical Essay on "Perfect Light," in *Poetry for Students*, Gale, 2003.

Daniel Moran

Moran is a teacher of English and American literature. In this essay, Moran examines the ways in which Hughes's poem evokes a sense of "double time" in the viewer.

The literary and the visual arts are very similar. Each strives to capture a moment, tell a story or pin down something that would otherwise be lost in the flow of time. When a writer composes a piece of written work about a piece of visual art, neither of the original pieces remain unchanged: the written work affects how one views the visual and the visual work informs the way a reader approaches the written. Understanding this relationship is key to understanding Hughes's "Perfect Light" and its issues.

An historical example of this relationship between the visual and literary arts will suggest, by analogy, what happens to any reader of "Perfect Light" who knows the basic story of Sylvia Plath. In 1555, Pieter Brueghel painted "The Fall of Icarus," a work depicting the mythological character who flew too close to the sun on his man-made wings. The painting shows Icarus plummeting into the sea—but doing so far in the background. The foreground features scenes from the daily grind of peasant life: plowing and shepherding are given much more space on the canvas than Icarus, who is a mere speck near the horizon. Almost four-hundred years later (in 1938), W. H. Auden published "Musee de Beaux Arts," a poetic appreciation of Brueghel's painting and an insight into the vanity of human literal (and figurative) attempts at flight. The lines in which Auden praises the old masters (like Brueghel) because they "never forgot" that "dreadful martyrdom must run its course" in a "corner" or "some untidy spot" offer a critical commentary on the painting; they also, however, affect the way that any viewer of the painting will re-examine it. Reading Auden's poem affects the way a viewer sees Breughel's painting and, of course, looking at Breughel's painting will affect the way a reader understands Auden's poem. "The Fall of Icarus" and "Musee de Beaux Arts" exist independently from each other, yet they are welded together in a kind of artistic Gestalt.

Ted Hughes's "Perfect Light" works in much the same way as Auden's poem: it is the speaker's reaction to a work of visual art (in this case, a photograph) that changes the way the reader looks at and understands the work being described.

But what exactly changes? How does this change occur? A simple experiment will illustrate the change in a less profound but more immediate way: show anyone the photograph of Plath and her children on which the poem is based but do not identify the people in it. What does the unassuming viewer see? A woman, thirty or so, sitting in a field with two children (presumably her own). She is smiling at one of them, a girl; with her left arm she cradles an infant. The setting is pastoral; the daffodils in the foreground and held in the little girl's hand are in tune with the mood of the photograph. It is a picture of motherhood, of a quiet day in the country—or of "innocence," as Hughes labels it.

Now, tell the person to whom you have shown the photograph that the woman is Sylvia Plath, the poet who would commit suicide less than a year after the photograph was taken. Everything changes.

Her smile becomes more complex. The children become objects of pathos rather than only "cute kids." All of the ideas a viewer had about the photograph are exploded. The daffodils, once finishing touches on a bucolic scene, become ironic commentators on the people they surround; the viewer searches for clues or some indication in the photograph that suggests Plath's later fate.

The photograph has not changed, but the viewer has. What brought about this change? Knowledge. The discovery that the smiling woman in the photograph is dead and died at her own hand. The meanings of words and images are ambiguous and complex enough, but they become even more complex and ambiguous in the flow of time. This is not to suggest that a modern viewer's ideas about the photograph are more profound or complex, instead, they have been informed and shaped by the knowledge brought with time. Shakespeare's rousing play about Henry V conquering France meant one thing in 1599 and quite another in 1944, when England was in the throes of World War II.

"Perfect Light" works by evoking this sense of "double time," the sense that there are, in a way, two "versions" of the photograph. First, there is a kind of prelapsarian one in which Plath and her children seem posed "as in a picture" titled "Innocence," and a kind of postlapsarian version in which the viewer's knowledge of good and evil (and suicide) make Plath's smile more enigmatic. Knowledge is power, but it also pulls one out of paradise, in this case, the paradise of innocence where there is no suicide or torrent of emotions that need to be sorted out in verse.

The poem begins by addressing Plath directly: "There you are, in all your innocence, / Sitting among your daffodils, as in a picture / Posed as for the title: 'Innocence.'" To an innocent observer who had never heard of Sylvia Plath, Hughes's description would seem an apt one, but those who know her fate cannot be so comfortable. Plath *seems* posed "as in a picture" titled "Innocence," but she is not. Instead, she is posed for a picture with a much different and unspoken title, a title that would (if one could) encapsulate all of the contrary emotions felt by Hughes while viewing this photograph. The only way in which the photograph could be titled "Innocence" would be if the person bestowing the title were wholly unaware of its subject's tragic end. Yet, Plath's own innocence of what would be her fate can still be perceived by Hughes and it is his perception of this innocence that he tries to convey to the reader.

> "Knowledge is power, but it also pulls one out of paradise, in this case, the paradise of innocence where there is no suicide or torrent of emotions that need to be sorted out in verse."

The daffodils and "perfect light" of the title are similarly viewed as both innocent and ironic. Plath is, in one sense, like the daffodils surrounding her: beautiful and positioned so as to catch the rays of the sun just so. The light illuminates Plath's face "like a daffodil" while Plath turns her face to her daughter in the posture of a daffodil. However, such comparisons also invite another, more sobering one: "Like any of those daffodils / It was to be your only April on earth / Among your daffodils." As Robert Frost remarked, "Nothing gold can stay," and the thoughts of the natural death of the daffodils in the photograph serve as a reminder of the unnatural death of Plath. On one level, the April referred to here is the April of Chaucer's *Canterbury Tales*, a time of life and growth ("that Aprill, with his shoures soote"), but in another sense it is the April of Eliot's *The Waste Land* ("April is the cruelest month"). Both Aprils are present, in the photograph and the poem, simultaneously.

As Hughes's eye scans the photograph, it finds other details that suggest a longed-for (yet impossible to attain) prelapsarian view. Her "new son" is "Like a teddy bear" and "only a few weeks into his innocence"; he and Plath seem the epitome of "Mother and infant, as in the Holy portrait." The infant Jesus is, of course, a symbol of innocence, yet one is also reminded of another time in which the Virgin Mary held her son: the Pieta. Any depiction of the infant Jesus brings with it the knowledge of his ultimate fate on the cross, just as any photograph of Sylvia Plath brings with it the knowledge of her suicide.

The stanza break signifies the moment in Hughes's apprehension of the photograph when he deals directly with the fact that he is looking at a soon-to-be suicide: the "knowledge" that she would kill herself is "Inside the hill" on which she is posed. The landscape itself seems pregnant with meaning. Hughes remarks that this knowledge "Failed to reach the picture," but this is only true in one sense. While Plath is innocent of the knowledge of what she will do to herself, Hughes (and, by extension, any informed viewer) is not. The hill is compared to a "moated fort hill" to make it seem like a bastion of innocence, a place protected from the knowledge that time will bring. This knowledge, however, is "Inside the hill"—in other words, the very thing against which this bastion of innocence is supposed to stand has already corrupted it. One cannot pretend that the knowledge of Plath's suicide is not there. Thus, Plath's "next moment," a moment that would both disrupt the "perfect light" and bring her closer to her suicide, was "coming towards" her "like an infantryman / Returning slowly out of no-man's-land"—but never "reached" her. In other words, the moment is static, frozen in time by the photograph, and in that frozen moment, the violence that the "infantryman" time would bring to her is no match for the power of her innocence. Therefore, it "Simply melted into the perfect light." The poet thus stands in awe of Plath's innocence while simultaneously struggling with the knowledge that longs to assault such innocence. One cannot avoid the knowledge brought about by time, nor can one pretend that such knowledge does not affect one's perceptions of the past. Before Plath's suicide, the "perfect light" is that of perfect innocence; today, the light seen in that photograph is painful and ironic.

Source: Daniel Moran, Critical Essay on "Perfect Light," in *Poetry for Students*, Gale, 2003.

Lynda K. Bundtzen

In the following essay, Bundtzen examines Hughes's Birthday Letters *within the context of the myth of Orpheus and Eurydice to reveal Hughes's feelings about his deceased wife, poet Sylvia Plath.*

The task is now carried through bit by bit . . . while all the time the existence of the lost object is continued in the mind. Each single one of the memories and hopes which bound the libido to the object is brought up . . . and the detachment of the libido from accomplished. Why this process of carrying out the behest of reality bit by bit . . . should be so extraordinarily painful is not at all easy to explain . . . The fact is, however, that when the work of mourning is completed the ego becomes free and uninhibited again.

I see you there, clearer, more real
Than in any of the years in its shadow—
As if I saw you that once, then never again.

Reviewers of Ted Hughes's *Birthday Letters* have understandably been absorbed with biographical issues. Addressed to his American poet-wife Sylvia Plath thirty-five years after her death, these verse-letters hold the promise of providing answers to the many questions that biographers and critics have asked about the circumstances of their marriage, his desertion of her and their children for another woman in October 1962, and her suicide on 11 February 1963. Why, after a prolonged and obdurate silence about these matters has Hughes suddenly decided to tell what is presumably his side of the story—what A. Alvarez calls "scenes from a marriage, Hughes's take on the life they shared?" Are the poems, as Jacqueline Rose suggests, "calling for a response. Of understanding? Of sympathy?" and assuredly not from Plath, but more likely, from her readers and admirers who have found his silence "another sign of callousness" and his handling of her estate—the writing which she left unpublished when she committed suicide in 1963—highly suspect. His editing of her journals, his reconstruction of her *Ariel* volume, and his infamous disclosures about losing or destroying her final journals and an unfinished novel have all been seen as self-serving in one way or another. For many critics, Hughes censored those parts of Plath's journals which implicate him as a domineering husband; he mutilated her artistic intentions in *Ariel* to obscure his role as a villain in its poetic narrative; he destroyed valuable information about her final months in the journal which he burned; and he carelessly lost another journal and an unfinished novel because these works accuse him, point to him as the unfaithful one, the philandering and unfeeling husband. Are Hughes's *Birthday Letters* a confession? an apology? a catharsis? Do they provide information about Plath's final months and days? These are the questions initially raised in critical responses to their publication.

Symptomatic of reviewers' preoccupation with biographical accuracy is Katha Pollitt's description of the dilemma for Hughes's readers: "Inevitably, given the claims that these poems set the record straight, the question of truth arises." And Pollitt, with several other reviewers, is not convinced that Hughes is capable of objectivity and impartiality, or even of a modest and limited personal truth, especially not over the stretch of eighty-eight poems and two hundred pages of verse:

that intimate voice ... is overwhelmed by others: ranting, self-justifying, rambling, flaccid, bombastic. Incident after incident makes the same point: she was the sick one, I was the "nurse and protector." I didn't kill her—poetry, Fate, her obsession with her dead father killed her. The more Hughes insists on his own good intentions and the inevitability of Plath's suicide, the less convincing he becomes.

In a blistering review for the *New Republic* titled "Muck Funnel," James Wood likewise denounces *Birthday Letters* as boringly repetitious minor tantrums: "His poems are little epidemics of blame" that endlessly rebuke the dead Plath and her poems, and its "like listening to one half of a telephone call." The other side of the conversation is missing.

Even when a reviewer offers a more positive view of *Birthday Letters* as poetry rather than biographical evidence, as in Jack Kroll's praise of Hughes's "masterly arsenal of forms, rhythms and images," the laurel is quickly withdrawn because Hughes has not been as "merciless to himself" as he should have, has not submitted himself to the "deep self-examination" which would have provided answers to biographers who want to know, "Why did he leave? And what happened to drive Assia [Wevill, the other woman in the love triangle with his wife] to exactly the same self-destruction as Plath?" Similarly, even as Jacqueline Rose forgives the portent-laden plot of *Birthday Letters* that other reviewers have derided as evasive and "borrowed from the most familiar dirty magics," she reminds her reader of her own and other feminists' famous battles with Hughes and his sister, Olwyn, over interpreting Plath's work. She ends her review by asking him to end this feud with Plath's partisan women readers and to retract his wrong-headed and self-righteous "caricature" of feminists in *Birthday Letters* as, for example, hyenas feeding on Plath's corpse in "The Dogs Are Eating Your Mother."

As all this suggests, *Birthday Letters* has received very little interpretation based primarily on its literary values. He is a husband addressing his tragically dead wife, and this is why we have come to eavesdrop—to discover whether he wants belatedly to share his guilt for her suicide or to offer intimate glimpses into what seemed to be a closed chapter in his life. As Pollitt notes, "The storm of publicity surrounding *Birthday Letters* has turned into a kind of marital spin contest, an episode in the larger war between the sexes"; A. Alvarez complains that the volume is on the best-seller list " 'for all the wrong reasons. It's the Oprah Winfrey element.' " Critics do not wish to interpret the poetry so much as inquiring minds want to know all the gruesome and scandalous details.

Hughes's letters, however, are not simply the utterances of a bereaved husband invoking the haunting presence of a beloved spouse, but also poems addressed by one poet to another. In "Sam," for example, Hughes speculates that when Plath survived a ride on a runaway horse, it was the genius of poetry that saved her:

> What saved you? Maybe your poems
> Saved themselves, slung under that plunging neck,
> Hammocked in your body over the switchback road.

The poems which she wrote in her final months, Hughes suggests here, needed her to live long enough for them to be written, and by saving her, "saved themselves" from oblivion. She "couldn't have done it. / Something in you not you did it for itself." "It" was poetic destiny at work. Similarly, in "Flounders," he claims, "we / Only did what poetry told us to do," as if their lives were predetermined and their agency governed entirely by the Muse of their poetic marriage. Such assertions have no claim to factual truth, and, indeed, have been castigated as strategies for "fate playing"—manipulations by Hughes throughout *Birthday Letters* to escape responsibility and culpability for what happened in his marriage to Plath.

An alternative critical strategy begins by simply acknowledging the fictive nature of such assertions and then looks for a consistent patterning of poetic statements that offers an invented truth about what happened in their marriage. Hughes's "birthday letters" are embedded with myth, superstition, and folklore, with references to other poems, many of them by Plath, and they display an inordinate degree of literary self-consciousness. Further, when Hughes is not borrowing titles directly from Plath's poems—for example, "The Rabbit Catcher," "Totem," "Apprehensions"—he is engaging his wife's preoccupations with honeybees and Otto Plath, with the figure of Ariel and the other dramatis personae from Shakespeare's *Tempest*, and with Plath's overarching themes of death and rebirth, mourning and melancholia. *Birthday Letters* are both companion poems and adversarial poems, in conversation and argument with Plath as a fellow poet of grief and as the irretrievable wife, Eurydice, to Hughes's Orpheus.

> ... the lire you begged / To be given again, you would never recover, ever.

Throughout *Birthday Letters,* there is an implicit analogy between Hughes and Orpheus as the poet

> "By opposing her, he also releases himself from the melancholic and doomed poetic identity of Orpheus to complete a normal mourning process, simultaneously bidding final farewell to his dead wife."

who mourns for his lost wife Plath-Eurydice, who repeatedly fails to retrieve her from "Inside that numbness of the earth / [for] Our future trying to happen," and who eventually challenges Plath's grieving verse with his own poetry of loss. By opposing her, he also releases himself from the melancholic and doomed poetic identity of Orpheus to complete a normal mourning process, simultaneously bidding final farewell to his dead wife. In "A Picture of Otto," one of the final "letters," Hughes gives Plath back to her father, thereby lifting the mask that Plath imposed on him in her verse, in which the "ghost" of Otto Plath is

> ... inseparable from my shadow
> As long as your daughter's words can stir a candle.
> She could hardly tell us apart in the end.

At least one of Hughes's motives for writing *Birthday Letters* is to "tell" himself "apart" from Otto Plath in his poetic version of their marriage. Instead of joining his dead wife in the underworld, as Orpheus joins Eurydice in Ovid's *Metamorphoses*, Hughes descends to make peace with Otto Plath, meeting him "face to face in the dark adit / Where I have come looking for your daughter." The ghost of Orpheus in Ovid

> ... found Eurydice
> And took her in his arms with leaping heart.
> There hand in hand they stroll, the two together;
> Sometimes he follows as she walks in front,
> Sometimes he goes ahead and gazes back—No
> danger now—at his Eurydice.

The figure of Otto Plath, however, stands between Hughes and Plath, making such a reunion impossible, except on Plath's poetic terms, which deny Hughes an identity separate from her father. What Hughes has come to understand and accept is that she will always be her father's daughter:

> ... you [Otto Plath] never could have released her.
> I was a whole myth too late to replace you.
> This underworld, my friend, is her heart's home.
> Inseparable, here we must remain.

Everything forgiven and in common—

To hold his wife "in common" with her father is the fate that Plath's verse imposes on Hughes. Hughes's final line in "A Picture of Otto" compares the dead Plath with Wilfrid Owen in Owen's poem, "Strange Meeting," like Owen "Sleeping with his German as if alone." Plath, too, sleeps with her German father—her only company the supposed enemy whom she kills in her verse. The cold comfort of her poetic immortality is an eternity "as if alone" with presences she herself created for imaginary battles. As Owen is forever identified as the poet who died too young, a casualty of the Germans in World War I, so Plath is remembered as another poet who died too young, a casualty of her own obsession with the German daddy, Otto Plath.

Two Classical texts interwoven within the narrative of *Birthday Letters* further suggest that Hughes has appropriated an Orpheus-like identity for himself: these are the *Metamorphoses* of Ovid and *Book 4* of Virgil's *Georgics*. Hughes does not translate Ovid's version of the Orpheus and Eurydice myth for his own 1997 *Tales from Ovid*, but the elaborate narrative in *Birthday Letters* often seems ruled by mythic powers of transformation, inspired by an Ovidian "ether" invoked by the poet Hughes to explain his wife's poetic immortality. Even Plath's face is described in "18 Rugby Street" as continually metamorphosing, a shapeshifting shell for the restless spirit inside:

> A device for elastic extremes,
> A spirit mask transfigured every moment
> In its own seance, its own ether.

Plath's face is elementally protean—"a stage / For weathers and currents, the sun's play and the moon's"—and does not assume its final mask, "the face of a child—its scar / Like a Maker's flaw," until her death, "that final morning."

In the glossary for Hughes's *Tales,* Orpheus is described as the "Thracian bard, whose music could rouse emotion in wild beasts, trees and mountains; son of the Muse Calliope by either Apollo or Oeagrus, a king of Thrace, husband of Eurydice; after her death he wandered through the mountains of Thrace, playing his lyre." The wildness associated with Thrace has a parallel in the rough countryside and moors of Yorkshire, just as Orpheus' musical affinity for animals and nature may recall Yorkshire's native son, Hughes, also a poet of nature. In "The Owl," a "letter" remembering an early episode in his marriage to Plath, Hughes fascinates her with his Orpheus-like gifts: he rouses a predatory owl to swoop down on him by sucking "the throaty thin woe of a rabbit / Out of my wetted knuckle." Perhaps like Orpheus wooing Eurydice, Hughes "made my world perform its utmost for you."

Finally, while Hughes does not appropriate Ovid's framing narrative (Book X of the *Metamorphoses* opens with the story of Orpheus and Eurydice and ends, as we move into Book XI, with the story of Orpheus' death), he does rework the Thracian bard's longer tales as they appear in Ovid: the stories of Pygmalion, Myrrha, Venus and Adonis, and Atlanta also form a group in Hughes's *Tales from Ovid*. The story of Myrrha's attempted suicide and incestuous affair with her father, Cinyras, is especially pertinent to Hughes's understanding of Plath's suicide and her incestuous love for her father, Otto Plath. Myrrha's metamorphosis into a tree, a weeping myrrh, converges with Hughes's response to Plath's poem, "Elm" in which she assumes the voice of the tree in order to give figurative expression to her experience with shock treatments:

> I have suffered the atrocity of sunsets.
> Scorched to the root
> My red filaments burn and stand, a hand of wires.

Her anxiety "petrifies the will": "I am terrified by this dark thing / That sleeps in me." Akin to Hughes's narration of the birth of Adonis from the bole of his tree-mother Myrrha—"It heaves to rive a way out of its mother"—is his description of Plath's giving birth to Ariel's voice out of the process of composing "Elm": "the voice of Ariel emerges, fully-fledged, as a bird, 'a cry'":

> Nightly it flaps out
> Looking, with its hooks, for something to love.

Like Hughes's Adonis in the *Tales,* conceived by Myrrha after spending several nights with her father, Cinyras, Plath's Ariel-persona is, in his interpretation, the fruit of an incestuous bonding with her father in a classical underworld, followed by a strange metamorphosis:

> ... between the second of April [1962], when she entered her father's coffin under the Yew Tree [in the poem "Little Fugue"], and the nineteenth when she emerged as a terrible bird of love up through the "taproot" of the Elm Tree, she has made a journey of self-transformation from the Tree in the West to the Tree in the East. From a tree atone of the gates of the underworld in the sunset to a tree at another of the gates of the underworld in the dawn. As if she had travelled underground, like the sun in the night, from one to the other.

Hughes further describes this transformative journey by Plath as "the bereft love returning to life," as if Plath had revivified her dead father, but only by disinterring an erotic attachment that leads inevitably to her own suffering and sacrifice. As Hughes understands Plath's plight in "Elm," "The unalterable truth to this reality is the voice's deeper negative story. It explains why the bird in the Elm 'terrified' her with its 'malignity.'" Perhaps this also explains why Hughes's own mourning poems for Plath will enact a counter-ritual for expressing grief, at times anti-Ovidian in their handling of metamorphosis.

Another influence on Hughes's *Birthday Letters* may be Book 4 of Virgil's *Georgics*, a text commonly read by English schoolboys of his generation and one that specifically intertwines the craft of beekeeping with the myth of Orpheus and Eurydice. Here Virgil implicates Aristaeus, the classical patron of bees and beekeeping, in Orpheus' loss of Eurydice. As Hughes, in "The Bee God" and several other poems, blames Plath's father, Otto, the entomologist and expert on bees, for taking his wife away from him, so in the Georgics Orpheus' wrath is directed at the shepherd Aristaeus, whose lusty pursuit of Eurydice inadvertently causes her death. Aristaeus is punished when he loses all of his bees through famine and disease. Baffled at his misfortune, Aristaeus seeks oracular advice from Proteus, who explains why he has suffered this loss:

> "The anger that pursues you is divine,
> Grievous the sin you pay for. Piteous Orpheus
> It is that seeks to invoke this penalty
> Against you—did the Fates not interpose—
> Far less than you deserve, for bitter anguish
> At the sundering of his wife. You were the cause:
> To escape from your embrace across a stream
> Headlong she fled, nor did the poor doomed girl
> Notice before her feet, deep in the grass,
> The watcher on the bank, a monstrous serpent."

Aristaeus is advised by Proteus to make a sacrifice to "'The nymphs with whom [Eurydice] used to dance her rounds,'" who sent "'this wretched blight'" on his bees. From the "putrid flesh" of a bull which Aristaeus batters with a mallet until dead, a swarm of bees emerges to refurbish the ravaged hives of Aristaeus. Sacrifice reverses his misfortune and renews the life of his hives. Hughes reiterates this configuration of symbols and characters in *Birthday Letters,* adding to it an incestuous bond between Plath/Eurydice and Otto

Plath/Aristaeus. Like Orpheus, the poet-husband must contend with another maestro of bees, who comes between him and his youthful wife, as well as with a "monstrous serpent" that appears as a "great snake" and "a mamba, fatal" at their marriage ceremony in "The Rag Rug." In other poems, Otto Plath is a roaring minotaur, recalling the bull sacrificed by Aristaeus to renew his beehives. Otto Plath is also a "German cuckoo," like the bird which usurps another's nest to lay the egg that will hatch into the voice of Ariel—"fully-fledged, as a bird," or, as Hughes goes on to describe the father who cuckolds him in "The Table," "While I slept he snuggled / Shivering between us," a cold dead figure who robs their marriage bed of warmth and Hughes of his wife's body. Finally, in "Fairy Tale," he is an "Ogre" and once again Plath is a fledgling who "died each night to be with him, / As if you flew off into death."

Throughout *Birthday Letters,* Hughes reiterates and refashions the Virgilian theme of sacrifice to placate and appease. The figure of Orpheus-Hughes, however, stands in stark contrast to Aristaeus, to Plath's poetry of sacrifice, to her father's portrayal as a bellowing minotaur demanding human victims, and, finally, to the women who advised Plath in her final days—like the nymphs who were Eurydice's friends and wanted Aristaeus to be punished. Whereas for all of these figures in Hughes's narrative, sacrifice is a form of reparation—even an exchange of death for new life—Orpheus-Hughes's loss is depicted as irreparable, his grief implacable, and his longing unappeased by sacrifice. Only through the historical process of remembering important moments in their marriage and then permitting them to fade does *Birthday Letters* complete the process of healing grief.

> Step for step / I walked in the sleep / You tried to wake from.

The early poems in *Birthday Letters,* even as they move forward temporally—love at first sight, a whirlwind courtship, marriage, and honeymoon—are also frequently embedded both with narrative strands belonging to the Orpheus-Eurydice myth and freeze-frames or snapshots arresting motion and reminding readers of Orpheus' final, impulsive gaze at Eurydice. Memory and loss are conceived of as moments of backward-looking, briefly and stunningly vivid, then fading. Hence, in "St. Botolph's," Hughes remembers their first meeting:

> . . . —suddenly you.
> First sight. First snapshot isolated
> Unalterable, stilled in the camera's glare.

Almost immediately, however, Hughes leaps forward to the "years in its shadow— / As if I saw you that once, then never again," in which "its shadow" must be her death, the darkness that enfolds his "clearer, more real" poetic imagining of his first sight of her. As with so many moments of Plath's evocation in *Birthday Letters,* Hughes works with paradox, with absence that is palpable, with a "once" that is so real that its "never again" seems impossible—as impossible to accept as Orpheus' loss of Eurydice.

Another early "letter," "Carytids (I)," plays with the frozen animation of Greek statuary—the young virgins who are simultaneously supporting columns. Hughes is also looking backward at the first poem by Plath which he read, in which these maidens make their appearance. Because he "disliked" the poem "through the eyes of a stranger," he "missed everything" that he now recognizes he was meant to see. He foolishly

> . . . made nothing
> Of that massive, starless, mid-fall, falling
> Heaven of granite
>
> stopped, as if in a snapshot,
> By their hair.

In these artificed maids, he might have discerned the ghostly aura of his future wife, "Fragile, like the mantle of a gas-lamp," where "mantle" alludes to the caryatids' streaming hair as an architectural framing support, and also to the mantle of a gas lamp, a mesh bag that holds the burning gas of a gas lamp, yet instantly crumbles to powdery ash at the slightest touch. With his friends, too "careles / Of grave life," he saw "No stirring / Of omen" in the "Heaven of granite" held up by such "friable" creatures: a forewarning of the terrible fate also awaiting Plath. The pun in "grave life" alludes simultaneously to Plath's extraordinary posthumous life, the poetic immortality which Hughes has taken care of, and also to the seriousness and preciousness of life and the carelesnes of youth about it. Neither Orpheus nor Hughes anticipated how brief their marriages would be.

"Fate Playing" deals with an incident in Hughes's courtship of Plath—a planned rendezvous in London that almost went awry—and may also be read as a warning. The poem ominously enacts a version of the Orpheus-Eurydice myth. Fate disguises its oracular content by playfully reversing the roles of Hughes and Plath. As he emerges from a train at King's Cross, it is as if he has been pulled out of a dark underworld by the force of his wife's desire, suggested by

Hughes's repeated use of "molten" to describe the intensity of Plath's inner fire. On their wedding day, he will see her "Wrestling to contain your flames," and here, in "the flow of released passengers," he sees her

> ... molten face, your molten eyes
> And your exclamations, your flinging arms
> Your scattering tears
> As if I had come back from the dead
> Against every possibility, against
> Every negative but your own prayer
> To your own gods.

Even the taxi she has hired is a "chariot" driven by a "small god," and her "frenzied chariot-ride" may recall Persephone's kidnapping by Hades in a wagon, her descent as a young maiden, like Eurydice, into premature death. The poem ends with a miraculous thunderstorm, and Plath's joy at being reunited with her 'lost' husband is

> Like the first thunder cloudburst engulfing
> The drought in August
> When the whole cracked earth seems to quake
> And every leaf trembles
> And everything holds up its arms weeping.

The epic simile here invites us to read—to exaggerate—this minor skirmish with "fate playing" as artifice, equal to mythic Demeter's restoration of fertility to the earth when she is joyfully reunited with her daughter, Persephone, or to the mingled tears of joy and sorrow in Shakespearean recognition scenes. Hughes as Orpheus may well feel comfortable using the expansive epic simile, since Orpheus' mother was Calliope, the muse of epic poetry. He deploys this technique similarly to describe Plath's emotional response to Spain, too much of an underworld like the one that envelops Eurydice, a nightmare world of insubstantial spirits:

> ... you tried to wake up from
> And could not. I see you, in moonlight,
> Walking the empty wharf at Alicante
> Like a soul waiting for the ferry,
> A new soul, still not understanding,
> Thinking it is still your honeymoon
> In the happy world, with your whole life waiting,
> Happy, and all your poems still to be found.

Plath's Spain mimics Eurydice's limbo, that region between the world of the living and the world of shades, to which she will be ferried after all memories fade. Indeed, in "Moonwalk," Plath sleepwalks on their honeymoon through a landscape resembling a charnel house and speaks language belonging only to the dead. In her sleep, she mouths hieroglyphs from "tomb-Egyptian" that are "Like bits of beetles and spiders / Retched out by owls. Fluorescent, / Blue-black, splintered. Bat-skulls."

Hughes, like Orpheus gazing at his wife from the dimension of life and vital color, watches Plath wander through "a day pushed inside out. / Everything in negative." He dares not wake her and "could no more join you / Than on the sacrificial slab / That you were looking for." Plath's search in sleep for an altar—the "sacrificial slab"—presages her later desperate search for a god to whom she can dedicate her writing and, finally, her life.

The mythic Orpheus, famed for his ability to animate what is dead, to imbue nature with his song, is also famed as the poet who fails, who looks back at the crucial moment and loses Eurydice, who then fades, loses corporeality, and becomes a shade. Indeed, Orpheus might be defined as the poet who fails, whose verse is dedicated to a compulsion to repeat this failure, fixated as he is on the lyric moment when desire comes into being as longing and regret for what may never be. As Eurydice dies twice, so Plath figuratively dies many times in *Birthday Letters,* as if retreating from the vividly realized life which Hughes as poet-Orpheus briefly restores to her, fading again into a dark underworld, dematerializing as Eurydice did into shadows. Hence, in "The Blue Flannel Suit," Hughes relives her appearance and still concentration on the first morning when Plath teaches at Smith College, only to lose the memory of her in the shade of her loss: "as I am stilled / Permanently now, permanently / Bending so briefly at your open coffin." The paradoxical rocking between "permanently" and "briefly," between a "now" and an implicit forever, is commensurate to the realization of loss as a brief moment, even while its trauma is lasting. Even more moving is the ending to "Daffodils," a poem that returns to the first and only spring they would enjoy in their English home:

> We had not learned
> What a fleeting glance of the everlasting
> Daffodils are. Never identified
> The nuptial flight of the rarest ephemera—Our
> own days!

As with "The Blue Flannel Suit," his memory of this lost moment is at once fleeting and everlasting, ephemeral and eternal.

In an Orpheus-like reversal of a trope that conventionally celebrates spring rebirth, the "everlasting daffodils" come to haunt Hughes with her death and his loss, as "On that same groundswell of memory, fluttering / They return to forget" her every year. Only the "wedding-present scissors," which they lost while cutting daffodils in the garden, remember, but what they remember is her death: "April by April / Sinking deeper / Through the sod—an anchor, a cross of rust." For Plath, as for Eurydice, there is no

Christ-like resurrection; the scissors are a rusting anchor pulling her down and a symbol for a life prematurely cut short. As a symbol of the Plath-Hughes marriage, too, the scissors both contrast and complement the meaning of the daffodils. The scissors manifest the burial of memory, its gradual submergence, and the healing of an old wound, while the daffodils are "Wind-wounds, spasms from the dark earth," keeping Plath's loss fresh in the poet's heart. Indeed, many of Hughes's *Birthday Letters* may be read as "wind-wounds," with the wind as a familiar trope for poetic inspiration and wounds reminding the reader of lyric poetry's conventional relief of anguish through its expression.

This final phrase to capture daffodils also echoes Hughes's description of the birth of the windflower from Adonis' bloody wounds in *Tales from Ovid*: "His blood began to seethe—as bubbles thickly / Bulge out of hot mud." In the *Metamorphoses,* the "minstrel's songs" of Ovid's Orpheus end with this tale of Venus and Adonis and her mourning tribute to her lover, another life prematurely cut short, but immortalized by her in the spring return of a flower blooming from his blood:

> "Memorials of my sorrow,
> Adonis, shall endure; each passing year
> Your death repeated in the hearts of men
> Shall re-enact my grief and my lament.
> But now your blood shall change into a flower."

As Hughes renders this episode in his *Tales,* Venus promises, "'The circling year itself shall be your mourner,'" along with the "bright-blooded" windflower and its brief bloom: "Its petals cling so weakly, so ready to fall / Under the first light wind that kisses it." In contrast, the Orpheus of *Birthday Letters* wants to memorialize nature's forgetfulness in the daffodils, as if Hughes were engaged in a type of mourning that seeks release rather than Venus' enduring attachment to her loss—or, perhaps, Sylvia Plath's enduring attachment to her dead father. The pathetic fallacy of Venus' windflowers is painfully acknowledged as a failure.

While Hughes may be adopting an Orpheus identity for many of his lyrics, then, he does not seek Orpheus' fate. Indeed, it is precisely here that Hughes and Orpheus may be said to part ways. In Ovid, the melancholic Orpheus retreats from human company, especially women's, and ultimately incurs their wrath for ignoring their attentions:

> ... a frenzied hand
> Of Thracian women, wearing skins of beasts,
> From some high ridge of ground caught sight of him.
> "Look!" shouted one of them, tossing her hair
> That floated in the breeze, "Look, there he is,
> The man who scorns us!" and she threw her lance
> Full in Apollo's minstrel's face ...

Orpheus is sacrificed to the frenzy of these Maenads, his limbs torn apart, his voice "that held the rocks entranced" having no persuasive power over the scorned women. While Hughes has not escaped the wrath of feminists over the years, he portrays himself in *Birthday Letters* as at last freeing himself from a scene of sacrifice conceived originally by Plath.

> Your Aztec, Black Forest / God of the euphemism Grief.

The Orpheus disguise, then, is sustained long enough for Hughes to mourn Plath with an extravagance derived from ancient literary sources, to remember all of the key moments in his marriage to Plath with mythic embellishment; but, finally, he moves toward catharsis and dissolution of grief. As Freud describes normal mourning, "Each single one of the memories and hopes which bound the libido to the object is brought up and hyper-cathected, and the detachment of the libido from it accomplished." The term cathexis denotes an investment of emotional significance, while a hyper-cathexis is an exertion of counter-energy, an effort to dis-invest and take back the energy given to the lost love object. In *Birthday Letters*, counter-energy is exerted most strongly in poems in which Hughes engages Plath's own mourning verse. In "The God," he describes her muse as evolving out of her "panic of emptiness" as a writer, her anxiety over having no tale to tell, no story "that has to be told." To this "dead God / With a terrible voice," she first offers' "Little phials of the emptiness" and "Oblations to an absence. / Little sacrifices." Gradually, however, this terrible God wants more substantial and larger offerings, and, as Hughes describes this process in several poems, nothing will satiate Plath's fiery God but "blood gobbets of me" until,

> You fed the flames with the myrrh of your mother
> The frankincense of your father
> And your own amber and the tongues
> Of tire told their tale.

Only by giving up her father, mother, husband, and finally herself to this roaring beast of a god does Plath find her poetic narrative. Hughes can only watch

> ... everything go up
> In the flames of your sacrifice
> That finally caught you too till you
> Vanished, exploding
> Into the flames

Of the story of your God
Who embraced you
And your Mummy and your Daddy—Your
Aztec, Black Forest
God of the euphemism Grief.

Here Hughes indicts Plath for her inability to discriminate between grief and self-flagellation, between a normal mourning that gradually accepts loss and suicidal depression with its inevitable component of murderous aggression.

As Hughes portrays Plath's so-called "Grief," it is born out of her fear that she has no story to tell but the one given to her by her psychiatrist Ruth Beuscher about an Electracomplex:

Beutscher [sic]
Twanging the puppet strings
That waltzed you in air out of your mythical grave
To jig with your Daddy's bones on a kind of
tightrope . . .

Hughes accuses Plath of making "Grief" her excuse for relinquishing her agency and voice as a writer in order to perform and to please—even to pander to—others. In "Blood and Innocence," she willingly endures shock treatments because "They demanded it. Oh, no problem"; then "they" want her to come back from her suicide attempt so long as she does not mind a poetic reconstructive surgery that is monstrous: "Yourself by Frankenstein, stiff-kneed, / Matricidal, mask in swollen plaster." Still, "they" want more—the corpse of her father—and she is eager to oblige: "Why on earth didn't you say. / Daddy unearthed" in order for her to "howl" her childhood loss and then to avenge it by killing him again and dancing on his grave. "They" are never identified but at times resemble the doctors who, in Hughes's view, mismanaged her electroshock therapy and then patched her back together with Freudian theory, who encouraged her to "kill her mother and father so that she might be born again." At others, "they" are Plath's audience, the "peanut-crunching crowd" of "Lady Lazarus" who await the show which she is willing to put on for the sake of "some acknowledgement"; and they are Maenads, the feminists who are content only with finding someone to blame, who revel in dismemberment and sacrifice. They are "Grinning squabbling overjoyed" at the carnage that she performs, the rage against husband and father that she enacts in her poems.

The Maenad-feminists who have hounded him over the years find their inspiration in a Plath described by Hughes as "Catastrophic, arterial, doomed." His final poem, "Red" describes the bedroom that he shared with Plath in Court Green as

What Do I Read Next?

- *The Hawk in the Rain* (1957) is Hughes's first collection of poetry. It was met with some of the highest acclaim of any young poet of the time. It is worth reading today just to note the remarkable contrast to the poems from *Birthday Letters*, his last collection.

- Though published nearly three decades ago, Keith Sagar's *The Art of Ted Hughes* (1975) is still an intriguing, compact look at the poet's work in the first decade after Plath's death. It also includes a biography of Hughes's childhood and the author's take on Hughes's influence on Plath's poetry.

- Plath's autobiographical novel *The Bell Jar* (1963) was published under the pseudonym of Victoria Lucas a month before her death. The novel takes place in New York at the height of the Cold War, and the story of the heroine's breakdown and near death are modeled after Plath's own similar experience during the early 1950s, when she suffered from depression and made her first suicide attempt.

- Plath wrote a collection of poems, *Ariel* (1965), just prior to her death. It was edited by Hughes and published posthumously. Written feverishly in the months after Hughes left her, this book contains the infamous poems "Daddy" and "Lady Lazarus," among others. It has become one of the bestselling volumes of poetry published in England and America in the twentieth century.

"A judgement chamber" and "A throbbing cell. Aztec altar-temple." It is another scene of sacrifice from which he seeks release not only for himself, but also, in some ways, for Plath as she is remembered in literary history. His revulsion against Plath's poetic identity as a priestess of blood is evident in his description of the impact of her ghoulish appearance:

Your velvet long full skirt, a swathe of blood
A lavish burgundy.

> Your lips a dipped, deep crimson.
> You revelled in red.
> I felt it raw—like the crisp gauze edges
> Of a stiffening wound. I could touch
> The open rein in it, the crusted gleam.

Hughes ends *Birthday Letters* in flight from this portrait, mourning her adoption of a muse that needs to be fed with bloody sacrifice, when "Blue was your kindly spirit—not a ghoul / But electrified, a guardian, thoughtful." He prefers to remember Plath's genial spirit as fertile and forgiving, a guardian who is a healer, not an "open vein" and "stiffening wound," and a muse for a poet who chooses forgiveness over vengeance. Instead of the Aztec goddess bathed in red, Plath is pictured as a nurturing Madonna, whose "Kingfisher blue silks from San Francisco / Folded your pregnancy / In crucible caresses." Plath's true muse was a winged creature ("Blue was wings") like Shakespeare's "dainty" Ariel, an agent for executing Prospero's revenge who also inspires the magician-artist to pity the enemies in his power. Prospero might easily punish them, but, in response to Ariel's empathy, he muses:

> Hast thou, which art but air, a touch, a feeling
> Of their afflictions, and shall not myself,
> One of their kind, that relish all as sharply
> Passion as they, be kindlier mov'd than thou art?

Like Prospero, who knows that "The rarer action is / In virtue than in vengeance," Hughes bids farewell to his wife with tenderness and regret, because "the jewel you lost was blue." Instead of rage and accusation, then—often regarded as the predominant emotions of Plath's grieving verse—Hughes doubles the loss, gazing backward at his wife and fellow poet, knowing that she herself was a jewel which he failed to keep safe. Instead of a "bereft love returning to life," described by Hughes as Plath's inspiration for the *Ariel* poems, *Birthday Letters* ends with a "bereft love" being laid to final rest.

Source: Lynda K. Bundtzen, "Mourning Eurydice: Ted Hughes as Orpheus in *Birthday Letters*," in *Journal of Modern Literature*, Vol. 23, No. 3–4, Summer 2000, pp. 455–70.

Sources

Auden, W. H., "Musée de Beaux Arts" in *Collected Poems*, Random House, 1991.

Bere, Carol, "Owning the Facts of His Life: Ted Hughes's *Birthday Letters*," in *Literary Review*, Vol. 41, No. 4, Summer 1998, pp. 556–61.

Emerson, Bo, "In a New Light," in the *Atlanta Journal-Constitution*, March 19, 1999.

Firchow, Peter, Review of *New Selected Poems, 1957–1994*, in *World Literature Today*, Vol. 70, No. 2, Spring 1996, pp. 407–08.

Merwin, W. S., "Something of His Own to Say," in *New York Times Book Review*, October 6, 1957, p. 43.

Further Reading

Hughes, Ted, *New Selected Poems, 1957–1994*, Faber and Faber, 1995.

> When Hughes came out with this collection, many readers were surprised to find a selection at the end of this book of previously unpublished poems that were unmistakably written to and about his late wife Sylvia Plath. This comprehensive book provides an excellent overview of Hughes's entire career and a first glimpse of the much-sought "Sylvia" poems.

Plath, Sylvia, *The Unabridged Journals of Sylvia Plath*, edited by Karen V. Kukil, Anchor Books, 2000.

> Kukil, the supervisor of the Plath collection at Smith College, has carefully transcribed the journals Plath kept between 1950 and a few months prior to her suicide. There is perhaps no better way to try to understand her thoughts, emotions, and feelings about Hughes than to read them in her own words.

Scigaj, Leonard M., ed., *Critical Essays on Ted Hughes*, G. K. Hall, 1992.

> This book contains close to twenty essays by various critics, scholars, and poets and provides a good variety of Hughes analyses. Discussions include Hughes's performance as poet laureate, his poetic style, and several articles on his major volumes of poems.

Wagner, Erica, *Ariel's Gift: Ted Hughes, Sylvia Plath, and the Story of "Birthday Letters,"* Faber and Faber, 2000.

> Wagner's exploration of the intense, destructive relationship between Hughes and Plath is considered one of the fairest, most comprehensive looks at the lives of these two poets. She includes commentary to the poems in *Birthday Letters*, pointing out the actual events that inspired them and explaining how they relate to Plath's own work. This book is both a guide and a literary companion to Hughes's final collection.

Proem

Alfred, Lord Tennyson
1850

"Proem" was originally published as the introductory passage to Alfred, Lord Tennyson's book-length poem *In Memoriam A. H. H.* The complete poem consists of 131 sections and was written over the course of seventeen years, capturing the development of the poet's grief over the death of his friend Arthur Henry Hallam. The influence of Hallam's death can be seen in several of Tennyson's poems, including "Ulysses," "Tithonus," "The Two Voices," and "Break, break, break."

Tennyson met Hallam in the 1820s at Trinity College, Cambridge. Hallam was considered by his classmates to be one of the most promising scholars of the day, until his sudden death from a stroke in 1833, at age twenty-two. Hallam and Tennyson were close companions. They traveled through Europe together, and at the time of his death, Hallam was engaged to Tennyson's sister Emily.

In Memoriam A. H. H. is considered one of the single most influential poems of the Victorian age. It was a favorite of Queen Victoria's and her husband Prince Albert and was so admired by the royal couple that Tennyson was appointed poet laureate the year the poem was published. Throughout the last half of the century, *In Memoriam A. H. H.* was frequently quoted in church sermons, due to Tennyson's masterful control of the language and the poem's mournful contemplation of humanity's relationship to the eternal. In modern times, the poem is seldom read in its 2,868-line entirety, but individual sections like "Proem" are considered examples of Tennyson's poetry at its best.

Alfred, Lord Tennyson

Author Biography

Alfred, Lord Tennyson was born August 6, 1809, in Somersby, Lincolnshire, England. His father was a clergyman, the rector of Somersby, a profession for which he was not well suited and of which he was not fond. Tennyson was the fourth of twelve children. At an early age he showed a talent for writing, and began writing poetry by age eight. By the time he was eighteen, in 1827, he had published his first volume of poetry, *Poems by Two Brothers*. Though his older brothers Frederick and Charles wrote some of the poems in the book, most were by Alfred. The same year, Tennyson left home to attend Trinity College, Cambridge. There he gained recognition for his work, winning a major poetry prize.

While he was at Trinity, Tennyson became close friends with Arthur Henry Hallam, who was considered one of the school's outstanding literary talents. Hallam introduced Tennyson to Emily Sellwood, with whom the poet fell in love. In turn, Tennyson introduced Hallam to his sister, also named Emily, with whom Hallam fell in love.

Tennyson experienced a series of setbacks after his book *Poems, Chiefly Lyrical* was published in 1830. In 1831, Tennyson's father died. Tennyson's older brother Edward committed himself to a mental asylum, where he lived until his death in 1890. In 1832, Tennyson published *Poems*, which was harshly criticized in nearly every review. In 1833, Hallam died suddenly, at the age of twenty-two.

Tennyson was so shocked by Hallam's death that he vowed to publish no more poetry for ten years. During that time, he worked on *In Memoriam A. H. H.*, the work that "Proem" introduces. He started the first lines of it within days of hearing about Hallam's death.

Tennyson barely eked out a living, and was too poor to marry Emily Sellwood until the publication of *Poems* in 1843 made him financially independent. He married Emily in 1850, and Queen Victoria, influenced by the publication of *In Memoriam* that same year, appointed him to succeed William Wordsworth as poet laureate.

Tennyson lived the rest of his life in fame and prosperity. He wrote poetry, focusing on long romantic narratives, and a few plays, which were unsuccessful. He was one of the most famous and well-recognized men in England when he died October 6, 1892.

Poem Summary

Lines 1–4

The "Proem" for Tennyson's long poem *In Memoriam A. H. H.* literally opens with a strong beginning: the word "strong" emphasizes the speaker's awe and gives the poem a powerful tone. The phrase "Strong Son of God" can be read in two ways. The most obvious of these is that it is a reference to Jesus, who is referred to frequently in Christian doctrine as the Son of God. This emphasis on God's human element also serves to imply a human subject to the poem, perhaps Arthur Henry Hallam, who is not mentioned in "Proem," but whose initials appear in the title of the longer poem. Throughout the longer poem, readers find more evidence that Tennyson has drawn a connection between Christ and Hallam, whom he represents as a figure for the higher race of humanity that is expected to develop from Christ's prophesied second-coming.

The last three lines of this first stanza refer to the unknown aspects of God. Tennyson points out that human faith is based on a lack of direct experience, noting that people believe in God even though they cannot see Him.

Lines 5–8

Ancient and medieval astronomers believed that the Earth was surrounded by a series of transparent orbs, or spheres, that rotated around it, accounting for the change from night to day, which the poem refers to in line 5. Saying that they are God's is Tennyson's way of noting that God holds power over all the universe. Even more impressive is the power, noted in line 6, to make life, and the corresponding power to make death. Line 8 uses the image of a foot crushing a skull to show how God maintains control over the life that He has made.

Lines 9–12

Tennyson follows the brutal image of God's foot on man's skull with the declaration that God is in fact good and concerned and will not abandon humanity to the mechanical world. There is a slight shift in the voice of the poem's speaker from line 9, which refers to humanity as "us," to line 10, in which "man" is referred to as "him." This shift becomes clear in the rest of the stanza, in which the speaker shows that a normal person feels entitled to more than just death: the poem's speaker, on the other hand, is willing to accept anything that God decides to do for or to humanity. He has complete faith that, regardless what happens or how it seems at the time, God is just.

Lines 13–16

This stanza addresses one of the most basic tenets of Christian faith, that of free will. Line 13 refers back to the issue, raised in the first stanza, of Jesus being not just God but God's human son. This makes him, according to Tennyson, the ideal human. Having stressed God's dominance over all things in the universe in the previous stanzas, here the poem says twice, in lines 15 and 16, that humans control their own will.

Lines 17–20

"Little systems" in line 17 refers to all things that humans have created, from games to governments, arts, and sciences. Saying that they "have their day" emphasizes how temporary they are, how quickly they will be gone, in what must seem no more than a day in God's larger perspective. Calling these systems "broken lights of thee" in line 19 affirms that all things human are part of God, while line 20 asserts that even if these parts were all added together, the mystery of God would be still greater than their sum.

Lines 21–24

At the center of the poem, Tennyson explicitly states its main point: the fact that faith in God ex-

Media Adaptations

- The British actor Sir John Gielgud recorded "Proem" and other sections from *In Memoriam* on an audiocassette titled *Stanzas from "In Memoriam"* (1972). It was produced by the Tennyson Society and published by the Tennyson Research Centre.

ists independently of knowledge, because knowledge only applies to things that humans can experience. In line 22, all knowledge is referred to generally as things that can be seen. The lack of knowledge is presented as darkness, with faith a beam of light that cuts through it, giving the faithful person less reason to fear the world.

Lines 25–28

Having identified the differences between faith and knowledge, Tennyson asserts that the two must coexist. A purely religious poem might dismiss knowledge of the physical world as unimportant; here, though, Tennyson calls for increasing understanding of the physical world "more to more." He takes a stand against a purely worldly position, however, saying that reverence should grow at the same time that knowledge grows. Line 28 makes the assertion that a proper balance between "mind" and "soul" is the natural, original state of human understanding, implying that such a balance existed "before" the two aspects started growing.

Lines 29–32

This stanza returns to directly addressing God and asking for His assistance. The poem claims that humans are intellectually and physically insignificant, and then, in line 30, admits that humans often will either mock or fear God. Still, the poem asks God to accept human weakness and to ignore the insults humans direct at Him.

In line 32, what is usually referred to as the "world" is mentioned in the plural, "worlds." By calling mankind "thy vain worlds," Tennyson acknowledges all of the variations of social understanding, as in the expression that describes someone being "in his own world." While the God that Tennyson addresses in the poem is clearly a Christian God, this plurality indicates an understanding of the many different human perspectives, which understand existence so differently that they might as well be living on different planets.

Lines 33–36

The speaker of the poem asks God's forgiveness, pointing out the fact that his humble behavior cannot be an affront against God, who is too great to be affected by human affairs. Line 33 refers to "what seem'd my sin," while line 34 mentions "what seem'd my worth": both phrases point to the same element, that of human pride, which would make the poem's speaker think he is as important, if not more important, than God himself. In identifying sin and worth as mere illusion, the poem stresses the fact that God is far above such mundane things, which mean so much to humans. "Merit," the measure of human worth, is said to be only of value to humans, not to God.

Lines 37–40

As the poem nears its end, Tennyson finally mentions his grief for his dead friend, the "one removed," who is identified in the larger poem but not in this "Proem." Tennyson asks God's forgiveness for concentrating so much on another human being, excusing the lack of attention to God by showing how much his absent friend is connected to God. "Thy creature," he calls his friend, noting that his belief that his friend has gone to live with God in death makes him, in Tennyson's opinion, "worthier to be loved."

Lines 41–44

The last stanza apologizes for the poem's weakness in explaining the poet's ideas, characterizing his words as "wild and wandering cries." Addressing God, the poet begs forgiveness for being unable to discuss matters intelligently, identifying his problem as being caused by wasting his youth away when, presumably, he should have spent more time studying, so that his discussion of religious topics would be more solid. Ironically, it was with the dead friend whom he eulogizes in this poem that Tennyson spent much time in his youth, making him the cause of the time that he says was wasted. After apologizing for his intellectual shortcomings, he ends the poem by asking God to make him wise.

Themes

Free Will

In line 16, the speaker of Tennyson's "Proem" tells God, "Our wills are ours, to make them Thine." One of the central beliefs of the Judeo-Christian tradition, within which Tennyson wrote, is the understanding that human beings are able to make their own decisions and are not just the sum of their genetic predisposition and experiences. Without free will, humans would not be responsible for their sins or their good deeds but, like machines, would only behave according to external influences.

The poem asserts that humans have free will, and points out how this freedom, which could lead to bad behavior, is ultimately to God's benefit. Humans have the ability to choose to do God's bidding, which makes their worship of Him more significant than it would be if they had no choice. Being omnipotent, God does not need this explained to Him by Tennyson; the poem's description of free will may be phrased as an explanation, but it serves more as an acknowledgement of the responsibility humans have to actively, consciously obey the will of God.

The emphasis on free will fits in with the poem's overall analysis of the symbiotic relationship between knowledge and free will. If humans could have concrete knowledge of the nature of God and what God wants, then the obvious thing to do would be to follow God's bidding. Without any certainty, though, humans are able to, as the poem observes, mock God or fear Him. Worship becomes a greater achievement, one that is accomplished only through disciplined faith.

Reverence

The poem begins with strong praise of God, mentioning strength, love, and immortality in the very first line. Though it continues its praise, there is emphasis on the fact that reverence is based on uncertainty. In effect, the poem puts forth the idea that to revere God, one by definition does not *know* what one is talking about. Awkward as this position seems, it is one with which the poem is comfortable. Tennyson explains faith and how it contrasts with knowledge, and how there is much to existence that extends beyond humanity's limited knowledge. These explanations add together like a mathematical equation to support the idea that God is greater than humans can ever know.

In the poem's last stanza, the speaker of the poem subjugates himself completely to God, dismissing his own poetry as "wild and wandering cries" and "confusions of a wasted youth." Although the poem shows a disciplined attempt to make sense out of matters that go beyond human capacity, the poet still asks God's forgiveness, for fear that any of the things said in the poem might be wrong or might offend Him.

Mourning

Although death is mentioned frequently in "Proem," Tennyson does not mention the loss of any specific person until the tenth stanza, in which he asks God to "forgive my grief for one removed." Up to that point, death is discussed in terms of the human condition, as a way to show the contrast between the fleeting nature of human life and God's eternal existence, in order to give a context to humankind's limited knowledge. Death is referred to in the second stanza as a tool which God made and controls; in the fifth stanza it is mentioned to show how insignificant human life is; and in the eighth stanza there is a hint it is the fear of death that causes humans to turn from God.

When the idea of mourning is added to the poem, the discussion about God becomes more personalized. For most of the poem, Tennyson analyzes the fact that God cannot be known, but can only be experienced through blind faith. By noting his departed friend, "I trust he lives with Thee," Tennyson creates a connection between God's omnipotence and the limited capacity of humans. The fear and mocking of death explored earlier in the poem becomes irrelevant once Tennyson acknowledges death leads somewhere, and the meaningless void that follows death has meaning in this context. Although it is only mentioned late in the poem, the belief that Tennyson's friend's death is not meaningless, that death has led his friend to God, gives this poem a reason to tilt toward faith in God even when evidence and knowledge of God is lacking.

Style

Iambic Tetrameter

"Proem" is written in quatrains, which are four-line stanzas. It follows the rhyme scheme *abba*: the word at the end of the first line of each stanza rhymes with the word ending the last line, making the "a" rhyme, and the two middle lines end with the "b" rhyme. The lines follow an iambic tetrameter pattern. Iambic is a pattern of one unstressed syllable followed by a stressed syllable, as in "for*give*" and "em*brace*." This pattern is obviously subject to variation, especially at the beginnings of stanzas: outside of the context of the poem, the natural tendency for reading such phrases as "strong son" and "thine are" would be to put the stress on the first syllable, not the second. Tetrameter contains the Greek prefix "tetra," meaning "four": there are four iambs in each line. This metrical form is so strongly associated with Tennyson's poem *In Memoriam A. H. H.*, for which "Proem" is a preface, that it has been referred to as the *In Memoriam* stanza.

Monologue

In this poem, the speaker talks directly to God, asking for God's understanding and forgiveness and taking every possible opportunity to praise God. It

Topics for Further Study

- In 1850, the year that "Proem" was published, Tennyson became the poet laureate of England, replacing William Wordsworth. Research and report on how the differences in the two men's styles affected British literature.

- Research the seven stages of grief that have been outlined by Dr. Elisabeth Kübler-Ross and other psychiatrists. See which parts of the poem can be traced to each stage.

- The poem refers to the night and day as "orbs of light and shade." Look up the ancient theory that held that the sun and planets were held in spheres that surrounded the Earth and create a three-dimensional model to present this idea to your class.

- Near the end of the poem, Tennyson, one of Britain's most famous poets, asks God to forgive his "wild and wandering cries." Many of today's most popular musicians, by contrast, tend to brag about their achievements. Write a poem or essay that outlines your position on the importance of humility.

Compare & Contrast

- **1850s:** Great Britain is the world's political and economic leader.

  Today: Since the fall of the Soviet Union in 1991, America is the single remaining superpower in the world.

- **1850:** Most of the world is agricultural. The following year, Britain becomes the first nation in the world to have the majority of its population living in cities.

  Today: Most of the world's population is clustered into cities and their surrounding suburbs.

- **1850s:** Life expectancy in Great Britain is between 43 and 47 years. Tennyson lived almost twice this, though his friend Arthur Hallam, memorialized in this poem, lived less than half the average.

  Today: The average life expectancy for men in Great Britain is 75 years old; for women, it is 80.

- **1850s:** Tea outsells coffee for the first time in Great Britain, due in large part to the introduction of a new custom, afternoon tea, ten years earlier.

  Today: Though an afternoon break is often considered impractical in the international business climate, many British citizens still manage to find time for the traditional tea break.

- **1850s:** In a world with no mass media, the person holding the post of poet laureate is famous across Great Britain.

  Today: Poets are not as important to most citizens as musicians and movie stars; students interested in finding out about the current poet laureate can, however, learn background information within minutes from the Internet.

- **1850s:** If Tennyson wants to visit America, he can travel from London to New York on the fastest clipper ship of the time, arriving in ten days.

  Today: Travelling from London to New York on the Concorde can be done in less than three and a half hours.

---

follows a logical rhetorical structure, establishing God's greatness in the first three stanzas, then explaining the problem of free will, then explaining how faith can be used to help humans deal with things they cannot know, and finally referring to the speaker's personal grief over the death of his friend, which has been the unexamined reason behind all of these ruminations about existence. This monologue addresses God often, indicating it means to invoke God, to ask Him for help; but the poem can also be read as a display of the mental process through which grief takes a human mind in its quest for consolation.

Historical Context

Victoria and Albert

Tennyson is the poet most closely associated with the reign of Queen Victoria, and this poem in particular is considered representative of the Victorian age. Victoria was born in 1819, and in 1837, not yet twenty years old, she ascended to the throne of England, beginning a reign that would last nearly sixty-five years. She was politically active and involved in the business of running the country, even from the start.

In 1840 Victoria was married to Albert, her first cousin. It was an arranged marriage, but Victoria and Albert fell deeply in love and consulted with each other on all matters. It was Albert who first read Tennyson's *In Memoriam A. H. H.* and brought it to Victoria's attention, directly influencing Tennyson's 1850 appointment as poet laureate. Under Albert's influence, while still in her early twenties, Victoria changed from a liberal to a conservative political attitude, which affected the way England was governed in both domestic and international affairs. Victoria and Albert were married for twenty years, until Albert's death in 1861 from typhoid fever. After his death, Victoria remained devoted to Albert's memory, and she never remarried. Her popularity as a monarch grew as she aged, as England exerted its dominance over world affairs, becoming the world's most powerful country because of its strong navy and its colonization of Africa, India, and other territories that raised its financial power to ever-increasing heights.

Literary tastes changed during the time of Victoria's reign, reflecting the queen's tastes. The nineteenth century began with the romantic movement, which was initiated by Wordsworth and Coleridge and most frequently associated with Shelley, Keats, and Byron. Romantic poetry can be generalized as focusing on nature and on the importance of individual judgement and emotional reaction over the pressures of social institutions. Victorian literature, on the other hand, is generally concerned with how individuals fit into the social scheme, with formality and decorum. This poem, an introduction for a work written between 1833 and 1850, shows the influence of both eras. Tennyson has the romantic's sense of self-importance in his telling of his individual experience of grief, but he also expresses concern about the proper relationship with God and his fellow humans that came to characterize most literature during Victoria's reign.

The Industrial Age

At the same time Tennyson was writing this poem, England was undergoing a major change in basic economic structure, from agriculture to industrial production. Coal-powered machines made large-scale manufacturing possible, and this in turn created a surge in urban populations, which created a need for more jobs. London, for example, which had kept a stable population for centuries, grew fourfold between 1801 and 1841, from 598,000 to 2,420,000. New technologies made centralized industry possible: rail lines allowed manufacturers to produce items by the ton and transport them to distant points for sale; electric lighting (first invented in 1808) made it possible for workers to continue to labor beyond normal daylight hours; telegraphs allowed businesses to place orders and make arrangements in a fraction of the time it took to send representatives from one town to another.

The drawback of the industrial age was that rapid expansion caused cities to quickly became overpopulated with people, creating unsanitary conditions. Diseases such as typhus spread rapidly in crowded tenements, and the situation was made more perilous by the fact that workers, including children, worked long hours with little pay. Pollution was blinding, darkening the skies of industrial cities at midday. All of these conditions caused a crisis of faith: the benefits of industrialization turned out to be the cause of misery for millions of British citizens. Tennyson plays off this tension by contrasting knowledge with faith in this poem.

Critical Overview

Tennyson's poem *In Memoriam A. H. H.*, which "Proem" introduces, has always been considered one of Tennyson's most important works. George O. Marshall Jr., explained in 1963 in *A Tennyson Handbook*, "One of the most remarkable things about *In Memoriam* was its popularity with Tennyson's contemporaries. It seemed to be such a satisfactory answer to the problems of existence, especially those raised by the struggle between religion and science, that the Victorians clasped it to their bosoms to supplement the consolation offered by the Bible. This wholehearted acceptance of its teachings went from the highest to the lowest."

Marshall's account of the poem's reception is at odds, however, with that of G. M. Young, in his essay "The Age of Tennyson." Young's essay argues that Tennyson was less a Victorian poet than a modern one, explaining:

> *In Memoriam* was influential in extending his renown, but within limited range: many of its earliest readers disliked it, many did not understand it, and those who admired it most were not always the best judges of its poetry.

T. S. Eliot, writing in his *Selected Essays*, has declared that *In Memoriam*'s "technical merit alone is enough to ensure its perpetuity." Eliot also noted, "While Tennyson's technical competence is everywhere masterly and satisfying, *In Memoriam* is the least unapproachable of all his poems." Eliot's influence is evident in contemporary views of Tennyson's poem: while Tennyson's other works are critically respected, modern readers tend to take particular interest in the perspective taken by *In Memoriam*, which examines one person's grief (though Tennyson himself wanted readers to understand the views held by the speaker of the poem were not necessarily his own). This directness makes this poem, of all Tennyson's works, the most similar to the poetry with which twenty-first-century readers are familiar.

Criticism

David Kelly

Kelly is a creative writing and literature instructor at two colleges in Illinois. In this essay, Kelly explains why it is better to analyze Tennyson's poem without considering the larger work that it introduces.

The difficulty one finds in approaching a work like Alfred Lord Tennyson's "Proem" is one that troubles anyone practicing literary criticism and, in fact, anyone trying to understand life: how much should be examined at any one time? Even with an average poem, possibilities abound, since there exists any extent of background information that could be useful for helping readers comprehend the lines on the page in front of them. Biographical information is often referred to, and so are similar poems from the poet's canon, or poems written around the same time, or poems that clearly influence the subject matter.

"Proem" has all of these elements. It is the introduction to a longer piece, *In Memoriam A. H. H.*. The most obvious direction that a line of inquiry might be inclined to take is toward the larger poem, to see how this segment compares to the whole. Furthermore, this entire work deals with the most moving, significant event in Tennyson's otherwise stuffy literary life, the death of his dear friend Arthur Henry Hallam. The magnitude of this one event was so compelling to Tennyson that the bulk of his work in his important formative years, from twenty-four to forty, was spent trying to capture the experience in this one work. Most of Tennyson's poetry deals with subjects drawn from classical literature. The temptation to explore him through *In Memoriam* is strong, and could easily be justified as a rare opportunity that must not be ignored.

Finally, there is the fact that "Proem" is a part of the larger work, and should only be separated from it when absolutely necessary. One of the most influential poets in modern literature, T. S. Eliot, explicitly warned readers that it would be a mistake to break down *In Memoriam*, to examine any individual part, realizing the damage that such an act could do to the entire piece. In his discussion of *In Memoriam*, Eliot asserted that "the poem has to be comprehended as a whole. We may not memorize a few passages, we cannot find a 'fair sample'; we have to comprehend the whole of a poem which is essentially the length that it is." Given Eliot's stature, it might be a good idea to do just as he commands, assuming he knows best on poetic matters.

Those are the reasons for examining "Proem" in a larger context. There are also very good reasons, though, for letting this piece stand as an individual unit and examining it as such. For one thing, it was written separately, after the rest of the poem was already done. This introductory section ends with the date 1849, which shows it to have been one of the last pieces written. As much as Tennyson wanted it to be a part of *In Memoriam*, he also gave it some degree of autonomy by drawing attention to the fact that it was written out of sequence with the other sections that have been pieced together for this poem.

And, regardless of the poet's intentions, the fact remains that "Proem" actually stands independently. It has a definite beginning and end, assigned to it by the author: looking at this one segment without the context of the rest of the poem would not be anything like, as Eliot implies, taking a random section from the middle and pretending that it is supposed to have meaning. In a case like that, the reader defines what the piece is saying by defining its length, separating it from other information that it is tied to; in this case, though, it already has its own independent identity. As much as the case exists for looking around any one artistic piece in order to draw intellectual connections to the facts of the author's life or to other things that he wrote, still there is at least a reasonable case to be made for considering a poem like this as its own freestanding entity, in order to see what it, alone, says.

And that, ultimately, is the deciding factor. The piece does have a context, as every work of art will, but focusing too much on the context can actually drive readers away from its unique significance, putting them on the trail of research before they have given the work itself their fullest attention.

Examined on its own, "Proem" turns out to be less a memorial to Hallam than a general statement on the author's insecurity that surrounds his grief. There are two defining characteristics of this piece. One is the hazy way in which it approaches its own subject; if it were not in the context of a piece called *In Memoriam*, readers would not know until the end that it is written about the death of a friend. The other is the way that this poem begs for forgiveness at the end, just as the aspect of grief is being introduced, a show of humility that reflects the relationships that the poet has with both God and his departed friend.

Starting from the beginning, this does not seem at first to be a poem about grief, but about God. The first nine stanzas, spanning thirty-six lines, deal solely with the relationship between humans and God, focusing on the mysteries that lie beyond this life, and the proper attitude that one should take when contemplating the subject of the Almighty. This extended section, while seeming to be about praise, actually raises some questions about the speaker's devotion. The first is, of course, in the first line, which implies that the poet's verse might be aimed at someone other than who it identifies. On its own, the phrase "Son of God" traditionally refers to Jesus, who is described in these words in the New Testament. It is unusual though that the poet should address the Son of God here while the rest of the poem speaks of the reverence that is usually accorded to God proper, but it is not unusual enough to affect any reading of the poem. It is, however, coupled with "immortal Love" on the same line. This again could be explained as a description of Jesus, whose philosophy is described as being based on love, but it is a noticeably odd reference, and, coupled with the first phrase (and the fact that Tennyson has begun the poem with "strong," as if God's power is in any way comparable to anything) leaves the impression that the poem has another agenda than just calling on God for the sake of praise.

When the tenth stanza mentions "my grief for one removed," the poem's uncertainties come into sharper focus. Much of the talk of God up to that point has centered on death, and that, like the strange references in the first line, could be considered appropriate, but still seems strangely narrow. A reader who knows this poem to be part of a memorial already knows that the death of a friend is the reason for its existence, but without this foreknowledge, the first nine stanzas build a mystery about the speaker's obsession that the tenth and eleventh explain. The introduction of personal emotion at this late point shades what came before it. Suddenly, the poem is less a song of praise for God than it is a hopeless rant, as if the speaker has been trying in vain to ignore the looming subject of his friend's death and, in the end, can no longer suppress it.

This is why the most crucial aspect to "Proem" may well be its entreaties for forgiveness. These pop up suddenly and increase frequently: "forgive" starts the last three quatrains, and one additional occurrence starts the third line of stanza eleven, leaving readers with a final stanza in which half of the lines ask God for forgiveness. Despite the praise

> "For a person to fall prostrate before God like this is not at all unusual in poetry; what is unusual is that the pleas for mercy come only as the poet's love for his departed friend comes out."

of God mixed with acute consciousness of death in the first three quarters of the poem, and despite the grief that comes up quickly in the last section, when the death of the speaker's friend has finally been brought out into the open, the one overriding emotion that readers are left with is the author's humility. For a person to fall prostrate before God like this is not at all unusual in poetry; what is unusual is that the pleas for mercy come only as the poet's love for his departed friend comes out. The implication is that God would be displeased with the uncontrollable affection that the poem's speaker has for another person. Coming after so much discussion about the proper way to revere God, there is certainly more than a hint that the speaker's worldly love for his friend would detract from his reverence. Directly praising or lamenting his friend could never draw readers to understand the depth of emotions as are conveyed here; readers have to put the pieces together in order to see that the speaker of this poem is so powerfully grief-stricken that he fears that God will feel slighted or jealous, and he needs to beg forgiveness for the emotions that he cannot control.

These facts come from "Proem" itself; the rest of *In Memoriam* describes Arthur Hallam in a different way, and develops themes that are not yet begun in this opening section. To understand the poem in the larger context might be useful. Then again, it could be distracting: much of what makes the eleven stanzas of "Proem" effective is found in the delicate balance and pacing that these ideas have among each other. One need not know who Tennyson lost, how long he grieved, or how long he worked on the poem that follows this introduction in order to feel the poet's apprehension about a sorrow so great that all he can think to do about it is apologize.

Source: David Kelly, Critical Essay on "Proem," in *Poetry for Students*, Gale, 2003.

William E. Fredeman

In the following essay, Fredeman discusses the life and work of Tennyson.

More than any other Victorian writer, Tennyson has seemed the embodiment of his age, both to his contemporaries and to modern readers. In his own day he was said to be—with Queen Victoria and Gladstone—one of the three most famous living persons, a reputation no other poet writing in English has ever had. As official poetic spokesman for the reign of Victoria, he felt called upon to celebrate a quickly changing industrial and mercantile world with which he felt little in common, for his deepest sympathies were called forth by an unaltered rural England; the conflict between what he thought of as his duty to society and his allegiance to the eternal beauty of nature seems peculiarly Victorian. Even his most severe critics have always recognized his lyric gift for sound and cadence, a gift probably unequaled in the history of English poetry, but one so absolute that it has sometimes been mistaken for mere facility.

The lurid history of Tennyson's family is interesting in itself, but some knowledge of it is also essential for understanding the recurrence in his poetry of themes of madness, murder, avarice, miserliness, social climbing, marriages arranged for profit instead of love, and estrangements between families and friends.

Alfred Tennyson was born in the depths of Lincolnshire, the fourth son of the twelve children of the rector of Somersby, George Clayton Tennyson, a cultivated but embittered clergyman who took out his disappointment on his wife Elizabeth and his brood of children—on at least one occasion threatening to kill Alfred's elder brother Frederick. The rector had been pushed into the church by his own father, also named George, a rich and ambitious country solicitor intent on founding a great family dynasty that would rise above their modest origins into a place among the English aristocracy. Old Mr. Tennyson, aware that his eldest son, the rector, was unpromising material for the family struggle upward, made his second son, his favorite child, his chief heir. Tennyson's father, who had a strong streak of mental instability, reacted to his virtual disinheritance by taking to drink and drugs, making the home atmosphere so sour that the family spoke of the "black blood" of the Tennysons.

Part of the family heritage was a strain of epilepsy, a disease then thought to be brought on by sexual excess and therefore shameful. One of Tennyson's brothers was confined to an insane asylum most of his life, another had recurrent bouts of addiction to drugs, a third had to be put into a mental home because of his alcoholism, another was intermittently confined and died relatively young. Of the rest of the eleven children who reached maturity, all had at least one severe mental breakdown. During the first half of his life Alfred thought that he had inherited epilepsy from his father and that it was responsible for the trances into which he occasionally fell until he was well over forty years old.

It was in part to escape from the unhappy environment of Somersby rectory that Alfred began writing poetry long before he was sent to school, as did most of his talented brothers and sisters. All his life he used writing as a way of taking his mind from his troubles. One peculiar aspect of his method of composition was set, too, while he was still a boy: he would make up phrases or discrete lines as he walked, and store them in his memory until he had a proper setting for them. As this practice suggests, his primary consideration was more often rhythm and language than discursive meaning.

When he was not quite eighteen his first volume of poetry, *Poems by Two Brothers* (1827), was published. Alfred Tennyson wrote the major part of the volume, although it also contained poems by his two elder brothers, Frederick and Charles. It is a remarkable book for so young a poet, displaying great virtuosity of versification and the prodigality of imagery that was to mark his later works; but it is also derivative in its ideas, many of which came from his reading in his father's library. Few copies were sold, and there were only two brief reviews, but its publication confirmed Tennyson's determination to devote his life to poetry.

Most of Tennyson's early education was under the direction of his father, although he spent nearly four unhappy years at a nearby grammar school. His departure in 1827 to join his elder brothers at Trinity College, Cambridge, was due more to a desire to escape from Somersby than to a desire to undertake serious academic work. At Trinity he was living for the first time among young men of his own age who knew little of the problems that had beset him for so long; he was delighted to make new friends; he was extraordinarily handsome, intelligent, humorous, and gifted at impersonation; and soon he was at the center of an admiring group of young men interested in poetry and conversation. It was probably the happiest period of his life.

In part it was the urging of his friends, in part the insistence of his father that led the normally indolent Tennyson to retailor an old poem on the subject of Armageddon and submit it in the competition for the chancellor's gold medal for poetry; the announced subject was Timbuctoo. Tennyson's *Timbuctoo* is a strange poem, as the process of its creation would suggest. He uses the legendary city for a consideration of the relative validity of imagination and objective reality; Timbuctoo takes its magic from the mind of man, but it can turn to dust at the touch of the mundane. It is far from a successful poem, but it shows how deeply engaged its author was with the Romantic conception of poetry. Whatever its shortcomings, it won the chancellor's prize in the summer of 1829.

Probably more important than its success in the competition was the fact that the submission of the poem brought Tennyson into contact with the Trinity undergraduate usually regarded as the most brilliant man of his Cambridge generation, Arthur Henry Hallam. This was the beginning of four years of warm friendship between the two men, in some ways the most intense emotional experience of Tennyson's life. Despite the too knowing skepticism of the twentieth century about such matters, it is almost certain that there was nothing homosexual about the friendship: definitely not on a conscious level and probably not on any other. Indeed, it was surely the very absence of such overtones that made the warmth of their feelings acceptable to both men, and allowed them to express those feelings so freely.

Also in 1829 both Hallam and Tennyson became members of the secret society known as the Apostles, a group of roughly a dozen undergraduates who were usually regarded as the elite of the entire university. Tennyson's name has ever since been linked with the society, but the truth is that he dropped out of it after only a few meetings, although he retained his closeness with the other members and might even be said to have remained the poetic center of the group. The affection and acceptance he felt from his friends brought both a new warmth to Tennyson's personality and an increasing sensuousness to the poetry he was constantly writing when he was supposed to be devoting his time to his studies.

Hallam, too, wrote poetry, and the two friends planned on having their work published together;

> *More than any other Victorian writer, Tennyson has seemed the embodiment of his age, both to his contemporaries and to modern readers.*

but at the last moment Hallam's father, perhaps worried by some lyrics Arthur had written to a young lady with whom he had been in love, forbade him to include his poems. *Poems, Chiefly Lyrical* appeared in June 1830. The standard of the poems in the volume is uneven, and it has the self-centered, introspective quality that one might expect of the work of a twenty-year-old; but scattered among the other poems that would be forgotten if they had been written by someone else are several fine ones such as "The Kraken," "Ode to Memory," and—above all—"Mariana," which is the first of Tennyson's works to demonstrate fully his brilliant use of objects and landscapes to convey a state of strong emotion. That poem alone would be enough to justify the entire volume.

The reviews appeared slowly, but they were generally favorable. Both Tennyson and Hallam thought they should have come out more quickly, however, and Hallam reviewed the volume himself in the *Englishman's Magazine*, making up in his critical enthusiasm for having dropped out of being published with his friend.

The friendship between the young men was knotted even more tightly when Hallam fell in love with Tennyson's younger sister, Emily, while on a visit to Somersby. Since they were both so young, there was no chance of their marrying for some time, and meanwhile Hallam had to finish his undergraduate years at Trinity. All the Tennyson brothers and sisters, as well as their mother, seem to have taken instantly to Hallam, but he and Emily prudently said nothing of their love to either of their fathers. Dr. Tennyson was absent on the Continent most of the time, sent there by his father and his brother in the hope that he might get over his drinking and manage Somersby parish sensibly. Arthur's father, the distinguished historian Henry Hallam, had plans for his son that did not include marriage to the daughter of an obscure and alcoholic country clergyman.

In the summer of 1830 Tennyson and Hallam were involved in a harebrained scheme to take money and secret messages to revolutionaries plotting the overthrow of the Spanish king. Tennyson's political enthusiasm was considerably cooler than Hallam's, but he was glad to make his first trip abroad. They went through France to the Pyrenees, meeting the revolutionaries at the Spanish border. Even Hallam's idealistic fervor scarcely survived the disillusionment of realizing that the men they met were animated by motives as selfish as those of the royalist party against whom they were rebelling. Nonetheless, in the Pyrenees Tennyson marked out a new dimension of the metaphorical landscape that had already shown itself in *"Mariana,"* and for the rest of his life the mountains remained as a model for the classical scenery that so often formed the backdrop of his poetry. The Pyrenees generated such marvelous poems as *"Oenone,"* which he began writing there; *"The Lotos-Eaters,"* which was inspired by a waterfall in the mountains; and "The Eagle," which was born from the sight of the great birds circling above them as they climbed in the rocks. Above all, the little village of Cauteretz and the valley in which it lay remained more emotionally charged for Tennyson than any other place on earth. He came again and again to walk in the valley, and it provided him with imagery until his death more than sixty years later.

Early the following year Tennyson had to leave Cambridge because of the death of his father. Dr. Tennyson had totally deteriorated mentally and physically, and he left little but debts to his family, although he had enjoyed a good income and a large allowance from his father. Tennyson's grandfather naturally felt that it was hardly worth his while to keep Alfred and his two elder brothers at Cambridge when it was only too apparent that they were profiting little from their studies and showed no promise of ever being able to support themselves. The allowance he gave the family was generous enough, but it was not intended to support three idle grandsons at the university. Worse still, neither he nor Dr. Tennyson's brother Charles, who was now clearly marked out as the heir to his fortune, attended the rector's funeral, making the division in the family even more apparent. The widow and her eleven children were so improvident that they seemed incapable of living on the allowance, and they were certainly not able to support themselves otherwise.

This began a very bitter period of Tennyson's life. An annual gift of £100 from an aunt allowed him to live in a modest manner, but he refused his grandfather's offer to help him find a place in the church if he would be ordained. Tennyson said then, as he said all his life, that poetry was to be his career, however bleak the prospect of his ever earning a living. His third volume of poetry was published at the end of 1832, although the title page was dated 1833.

The 1832 *Poems* was a great step forward poetically and included the first versions of some of Tennyson's greatest works, such as *"The Lady of Shalott," "The Palace of Art," "A Dream of Fair Women," "The Hesperides,"* and three wonderful poems conceived in the Pyrenees, *"Oenone," "The Lotos-Eaters,"* and *"Mariana in the South."* The volume is notable for its consideration of the opposed attractions of isolated poetic creativity and social involvement; the former usually turns out to be the more attractive course, since it reflected Tennyson's own concerns, but the poems demonstrate as well his feeling of estrangement in being cut off from his contemporaries by the demands of his art.

The reviews of the volume were almost universally damning. One of the worst was written by Edward Bulwer (later Bulwer-Lytton), who was a friend of Tennyson's uncle Charles. The most vicious review, however, was written for the *Quarterly Review* by John Wilson Croker, who was proud that his brutal notice of *Endymion* years before was said to have been one of the chief causes of the death of Keats. Croker numbered Tennyson among the Cockney poets who imitated Keats, and he made veiled insinuations about the lack of masculinity of both Tennyson and his poems. Tennyson, who was abnormally thin-skinned about criticism, found some comfort in the steady affection and support of Hallam and the other Apostles.

Hallam and Emily Tennyson had by then made their engagement public knowledge, but they saw no way of marrying for a long time: the senior Hallam refused to increase his son's allowance sufficiently to support both of them; and when Arthur wrote to Emily's grandfather, he was answered in the third person with the indication that old Mr. Tennyson had no intention of giving them any more money. By the summer of 1833, Hallam's father had somewhat grudgingly accepted the engagement, but still without offering further financial help. The protracted unhappiness of both Arthur and Emily rubbed off on the whole Tennyson family.

That autumn, in what was meant as a gesture of gratitude and reconciliation to his father, Arthur Hallam accompanied him to the Continent. In Vienna Arthur died suddenly of apoplexy resulting from a congenital malformation of the brain. Emily Tennyson fell ill for nearly a year; the effects of Hallam's death were less apparent externally in Alfred but were perhaps even more catastrophic than for his sister.

The combination of the deaths of his father and his best friend, the brutal reviews of his poems, his conviction that both he and his family were in desperate poverty, his feelings of isolation in the depths of the country, and his ill-concealed fears that he might become a victim of epilepsy, madness, alcohol, and drugs, as others in his family had, or even that he might die like Hallam, was more than enough to upset the always fragile balance of Tennyson's emotions. "I suffered what seemed to me to shatter all my life so that I desired to die rather than to live," he said of that period. For a time he determined to leave England, and for ten years he refused to have any of his poetry published, since he was convinced that the world had no place for it.

Although he was adamant about not having it published, Tennyson continued to write poetry; and he did so even more single-mindedly than before. Hallam's death nearly crushed him, but it also provided the stimulus for a great outburst of some of the finest poems he ever wrote, many of them connected overtly or implicitly with the loss of his friend. *"Ulysses," "Morte d'Arthur," "Tithonus," "Tiresias," "Break, break, break," and "Oh! that 'twere possible"* all owe their inception to the passion of grief he felt but carefully hid from his intimates. Most important was the group of random individual poems he began writing about Hallam's death and his own feeling of loneliness in the universe as a result of it; the first of these "elegies," written in four-line stanzas of iambic tetrameter, was begun within two or three days of his hearing the news of Hallam's death. He continued to write them for seventeen years before collecting them to form what is perhaps the greatest of Victorian poems, *In Memoriam* (1850).

The death of his grandfather in 1835 confirmed Tennyson's fear of poverty, for the larger part of Mr. Tennyson's fortune went to Alfred's uncle Charles, who promptly changed his name to Tennyson d'Eyncourt and set about rebuilding his father's house into a grand Romantic castle, with the expectation of receiving a peerage to cap the family's climb to eminence. His hopes were never realized, but his great house, Bayons Manor, became a model for the home of the vulgar, nouveauriche characters in many of Tennyson's narrative poems, such as *Maud* (1855). Charles Tennyson d'Eyncourt's inheritance was the final wedge driving the two branches of the family apart; he and his nephew were never reconciled, but Alfred's dislike of him was probably even more influential than admiration would have been in keeping Charles as an immediate influence in so much of Alfred's poetry.

The details of Tennyson's romantic attachments in the years after Hallam's death are unclear, but he apparently had at least a flirtation with Rosa Baring, the pretty young daughter of a great banking family, some of whose members had rented Harrington Hall, a large house near Somersby. Tennyson wrote a dozen or so poems to her, but it is improbable that his affections were deeply involved. The poems suggest that her position made it impossible for him to be a serious suitor to her, but she may have been more important to him as a symbol of wealth and unavailability than as a flesh-and-blood young woman. Certainly, he seems not to have been crushed when she married another man.

In 1836, however, at the age of twenty-seven, Tennyson became seriously involved with Emily Sellwood, who was four years younger than he. By the following year they considered themselves engaged. Emily had been a friend of Tennyson's sisters, and one of her own sisters married his next older (and favorite) brother, Charles. Most of the correspondence between Tennyson and Emily has been destroyed, but from what remains it is clear that she was very much in love with him, although he apparently withheld himself somewhat in spite of his affection for her. He was worried about not having enough money to marry, but he seems also to have been much concerned with the trances into which he was still falling, which he thought were connected with the epilepsy from which other members of the family suffered. To marry, he thought, would mean passing on the disease to any children he might father.

In the summer of 1840 Tennyson broke off all relations with Emily. She continued to think of herself as engaged to him, but he abandoned any hope of marriage, either then or in the future. To spare her further embarrassment, the story was put out that her father had forbidden their marriage because of Tennyson's poverty; this legend has been perpetuated in the present century.

Through the second half of the 1830s and most of the 1840s Tennyson lived an unsettled, nomadic life. Nominally he made his home with his mother and his unmarried brothers and sisters, who continued to rent Somersby rectory until 1837, then moved successively to Essex and to Kent; but he was as often to be found in London, staying in cheap hotels or cadging a bed from friends who lived there. He was lonely and despondent, and he drank and smoked far too much. Many of those who had known him for years believed that his poetic inspiration had failed him and that his great early promise would remain unfulfilled; but this was to neglect the fact that when all else went wrong, he clung to the composition of poetry. He was steadily accumulating a backlog of unpublished poems, and he continued adding to his "elegies" to Hallam's memory.

One of the friends who worried away at Tennyson to have his work published was Edward FitzGerald, who loved both the poems and their author, although he was too stubborn to hide his feelings when a particular poem failed to win his approval. "Old Fitz" nagged at Tennyson, who in the spring of 1842 agreed to break his ten long years of silence.

The two volumes of *Poems* (1842) were destined to be the best-loved books Tennyson ever wrote. The first volume was made up of radically revised versions of the best poems from the 1832 volume, most of them in the form in which they are now known. The second volume contained new poems, among them some of those inspired by Hallam's death, as well as poems of widely varying styles, including the dramatic monologue *"St. Simeon Stylites"*; a group of Authurian poems; his first attempt to deal with rampant sexuality, *"The Vision of Sin"*; and the implicitly autobiographical narrative *"Locksley Hall,"* dealing with the evils of worldly marriages, which was to become one of his most popular poems during his lifetime.

After the reception of the 1832 *Poems* and after being unpublished for so long, Tennyson was naturally apprehensive about the reviews of the new poems; but nearly all were enthusiastic, making it clear that he was now the foremost poet of his generation. Edgar Allan Poe wrote guardedly, "I am not sure that Tennyson is not the greatest of poets."

But the bad luck that Tennyson seemed to invite struck again just as the favorable reviews were appearing. Two years earlier, expecting to make a fortune, he had invested his patrimony in a scheme to manufacture cheap wood carvings by steam-driven machines. In 1842 the scheme crashed, taking with it nearly everything that Tennyson owned, some £4,000. The shock set back any progress he had made in his emotional state over the past ten years, and in 1843 he had to go into a "hydropathic" establishment for seven months of treatment in the hope of curing his deep melancholia.

This was the first of several stays in "hydros" during the next five years. Copious applications of water inside and out, constant wrappings in cold, wet sheets, and enforced abstinence from tobacco and alcohol seemed to help him during each stay; but he would soon ruin any beneficial effects by his careless life once he had left the establishment, resuming his drinking and smoking to the despair of his friends. A rather more effective form of treatment was the £2,000 he received from an insurance policy at the death of the organizer of the wood-carving scheme. In 1845 he was granted a government civil list pension of £200 a year in recognition of both his poetic achievements and his apparent financial need. Tennyson was in reality released from having to worry about money, but the habit of years was too much for him; for the rest of his life he complained constantly of his poverty, although his poetry had made him a rich man by the time of his death. In 1845 the betterment of his fortunes brought with it no effort to resume his engagement to Emily Sellwood, showing that it was not financial want that kept them apart.

The Princess, which was published on Christmas 1847, was Tennyson's first attempt at a long narrative poem, a form that tempted him most of his life although it was less congenial to him temperamentally than the lyric. The ostensible theme is the education of women and the establishment of female colleges, but it is clear that Tennyson's interest in the subject runs out before the poem does, so that it gradually shifts to the consideration of what he thought of as the unnatural attempt of men and women to fulfill identical roles in society; only as the hero becomes more overtly masculine and the heroine takes on the traditional attributes of women is there a chance for their happiness. Considerably more successful than the main narrative are the thematic lyrics that Tennyson inserted into the action to show the growth of passion and between the cantos to indicate that the natural end of the sexes is to be parents of another generation in a thoroughly traditional manner. The subtitle, *A Medley*, was his way of anticipating charges of inconsistency in the structure of the poem. As always, the blank verse in which the main part of the poem is written is superb, and the interpolated lyrics include some of his most splendid short poems, such as *"Come down, O maid," "Now sleeps the crimson petal," "Sweet and low," "The splendour falls on castle walls,"* and *"Tears, idle tears."* The emotion of these lyrics does more than the straight narrative to convey the forward movement of the entire poem, and their brief perfection indicates well enough that his genius lay there rather than in the descriptions of persons and their actions; this was not, however, a lesson that Tennyson himself was capable of learning. The seriousness with which the reviewers wrote of the poem was adequate recognition of his importance, but many of them found the central question of feminine education to be insufficiently considered. The first edition was quickly sold out, and subsequent editions appeared almost every year for several decades.

Tennyson's last stay in a hydropathic hospital was in the summer of 1848, and though he was not completely cured of his illness, he was reassured about its nature. The doctor in charge apparently made a new diagnosis of his troubles, telling him that what he suffered from was not epilepsy but merely a form of gout that prefaced its attacks by a stimulation of the imagination that is very like the "aura" that often warns epileptics of the onset of a seizure. The trances that he had thought were mild epileptic fits were in fact only flashes of illumination over which he had no reason to worry. Had it been in Tennyson's nature to rejoice, he could have done so at this time, for there was no longer any reason for him to fear marriage, paternity, or the transmission of disease to his offspring. The habits of a lifetime, however, were too ingrained for him to shake them off at once. The real measure of his relief at being rid of his old fear of epilepsy is that he soon set about writing further sections to be inserted into new editions of *The Princess*, in which the hero is said to be the victim of "weird seizures" inherited from his family; at first he is terrified when he falls into trances, but he is at last released from the malady when he falls in love with Princess Ida. Not only this poem, but his three other major long works, *In Memoriam, Maud*, and *Idylls of the King* (1859), all deal in part with the meaning of trances, which are at first frightening but then are revealed to be pathways to the extrasensory, to be rejoiced over rather than feared. After his death Tennyson's wife and son burned many of his most personal letters, and in what remains there is little reference to his trances or his recovery from them; but the poems bear quiet testimony to the immense weight he must have felt lifted from his shoulders when he needed no longer worry about epilepsy.

Tennyson's luck at last seemed to be on the upturn. At the beginning of 1849 he received a large advance from his publisher with the idea that he would assemble and polish his "elegies" on Hallam, to be published as a whole poem. Before the year was over he had resumed communication with Emily Sellwood, and by the beginning of 1850 he was speaking confidently of marrying. On 1 June *In Memoriam* was published, and less than two weeks later he and Emily were married quietly at Shiplake Church. Improbable as it might seem for a man to whom little but bad fortune had come, both events were total successes.

The new Mrs. Tennyson was thirty-seven years old and in delicate health, but she was a woman of iron determination; she took over the running of the externals of her husband's life, freeing him from the practical details at which he was so inept. Her taste was conventional, and she may have curbed his religious questioning, his mild bohemianism, and the exuberance and experimentation of his poetry, but she also brought a kind of peace to his life without which he would not have been able to write at all. There is some evidence that Tennyson occasionally chafed at the responsibilities of marriage and paternity and at the loss of the vagrant freedom he had known, but there is nothing to indicate that he ever regretted his choice. It was probably not a particularly passionate marriage, but it was full of tenderness and affection. Three sons were born, of whom two, Hallam and Lionel, survived.

After a protracted honeymoon of some four months in the Lake Country, Tennyson returned to the south of England to find that the publication of *In Memoriam* had made him, without question, the major living poet. It had appeared anonymously, but his authorship was an open secret.

This vast poem (nearly 3,000 lines) is divided into 131 sections, with prologue and epilogue; the size is appropriate for what it undertakes, since in coming to terms with loss, grief, and the growth of consolation, it touches on most of the intellectual issues at the center of the Victorian consciousness: religion, immortality, geology, evolution, the relation of the intellect to the unconscious, the place of art in a workaday world, the individual versus society, the relation of man to nature, and as many others. The poem grew out of Tennyson's personal grief, but it attempts to speak for all men rather than for one. The structure often seems wayward, for in T. S. Eliot's famous phrase, it has "only the unity and continuity of a diary" instead of the clear direction of a philosophical statement. It was bound to be somewhat irregular since it was composed with no regard for either chronology or continuity and was for years not intended to be published. The vacillation in mood of the finished poem, however, is neither haphazard nor capricious, for it is put together to show the wild swoops between depression and elation that grief brings, the hesitant gropings toward philosophical justification of bereavement, the tentative little darts of conviction that may precede a settled belief in a beneficent world. It is intensely personal, but one must also believe Tennyson in his reiterated assertions that it was a poem, not the record of his own grief about Hallam; in short, that his own feelings had prompted the poem but were not necessarily accurately recorded in it.

To the most perceptive of the Victorians (and to modern readers) the poem was moving for its dramatic recreation of a mind indisposed to deal with the problems of contemporary life, and for the sheer beauty of so many of its sections. To a more naive, and far larger, group of readers it was a work of real utility, to be read like the Bible as a manual of consolation, and it is surely to that group that the poem owed its almost unbelievable popularity. Edition followed edition, and each brought Tennyson more fame and greater fortune.

Wordsworth, who had been poet laureate for seven years, had died in the spring of 1850. By the time Tennyson returned from his honeymoon, it must have seemed to many a foregone conclusion that he would be nominated as Wordsworth's successor. Tennyson knew that the prince consort, who advised the queen on such matters, was an admirer of his, and the night before receiving the letter offering the post, he dreamed that the prince kissed him on the cheek, and that he responded, "Very kind but very German." Early the following year he was presented to the queen as her poet laureate and kissed her hand, wearing the borrowed and too-tight court clothes that Wordsworth had worn for the same purpose on the occasion of his own presentation. The straining court suit was emblematic of the passing of the office from the greatest of Romantic poets to the greatest of the Victorians.

At the end of November 1853 Alfred and Emily Tennyson moved into the secluded big house on the Isle of Wight known as Farringford, which has ever since been associated with his name. Emily loved the remoteness and the fact that their clocks were not even synchronized with those elsewhere, but her husband sometimes had a recurrence of his old longing to be rattling around London. Most of the time, however, he was content to walk on the great chalk cliffs overlooking the sea, composing his poems as he tramped, their rhythm often deriving from his heavy tread.

It was perhaps his very isolation that made him so interested in the Crimean War, for he read the newspapers voraciously in order to keep current with world affairs. *"The Charge of the Light Brigade"* was one result in 1854 of his fascination with the heroism of that unpopular war. *Maud*, in which the hero redeems his misspent life by volunteering for service in the Crimea, was published the following year. In spite of that somewhat conventional-sounding conclusion, the poem is Tennyson's most experimental, for it tells a thoroughly dramatic narrative in self-contained lyrics; the reader must fill in the interstices of the story by inference. The lyrics are not even like one another in scansion, length, or style. The narrator of the poem is an unnamed young man whose father has committed suicide after being swindled by his partner. The son then falls in love with Maud, the daughter of the peccant partner; but since he is poor and she is rich, there is no possibility of their marrying. When he is bullied by her brother, he kills him in a duel. After Maud also dies the narrator goes temporarily insane; he finally realizes that he has been as selfish and evil as the society on which he has blamed his bad fortune. In an attempt to make up for his wasted life, he goes to the Crimea, with his subsequent death hinted at in the last section of the poem.

As always, Tennyson is not at his best in narrative, but the melodramatic content of the plot finally matters little in comparison with the startling originality of his attempt to extend the limits of lyricism in order to make it do the work of narrative and drama, to capitalize on his own apparently circumscribed gift in order to include social criticism, contemporary history, and moral comment in the lyric. In part it must have been a deliberate answer to those who complained that his art was too self-absorbed and negligent of the world around him.

The experimental quality of *Maud* has made it one of the most interesting of his poems to modern critics, but to Tennyson's contemporaries it seemed so unlike what they expected from the author of *In Memoriam* that they could neither understand nor love it. An age that was not accustomed to distinguishing between narrator and poet found it almost impossible not to believe that Tennyson was directly portraying his own thoughts and personal history in those of the central figure. The result was the worst critical abuse that Tennyson received after that directed at the 1832 *Poems*. One reviewer went so far as to say that *Maud* had one extra vowel in the title, and that it made no difference which was to be deleted. Tennyson's predictable response was to become defensive about the poem and to read it aloud at every opportunity in order to show how badly misunderstood both poem and poet were. Since it was a performance that took between two and three hours, the capitulation to its beauty that he often won thereby was probably due as much to weariness on the part of the hearer as to intellectual or aesthetic persuasion.

Ever since the publication of the 1842 *Poems* Tennyson had been something of a lion in literary circles, but after he became poet laureate he was equally in demand with society hostesses, who were more interested in his fame than in his poetic genius. For the rest of his life Tennyson was to be caught awkwardly between being unable to resist the flattery implied by their attentions and the knowledge that their admiration of him usually sprang from the wrong reasons. It was difficult for him to refuse invitations, but he felt subconsciously impelled when he accepted them to behave gruffly, even rudely, in order to demonstrate his independence. His wife's bad health usually made it impossible for her to accompany him, which probably increased his awkwardness. It all brought out the least attractive side of a fundamentally shy man, whose paroxysms of inability to deal with social situations made him seem selfish, bad-mannered, and assertive. In order to smooth his ruffled feathers, his hostesses and his friends would resort to heavy flattery, which only made him appear more arrogant. One of the saddest aspects of Tennyson's life is that his growing fame was almost in inverse ratio to his ability to maintain intimacy with others, so that by the end of his life he was a basically lonely man. All the innate charm, humor, intelligence, and liveliness were still there, but it took great understanding and patience on the part of his friends to bring them into the open.

Idylls of the King was published in 1859; it contained only four ("Enid," *"Vivien," "Elaine,"* and *"Guinevere"*) of the eventual twelve idylls. The matter of Arthur and Camelot had obsessed Tennyson since boyhood, and over the years it became a receptacle into which he poured his deepening feelings of the desecration of decency and of ancient English ideals by the gradual corruption of accepted morality. The decay of the Round Table came increasingly to seem to him an apt symbol of the decay of nineteenth-century England. It was no accident that the first full-length idyll had been "Morte d'Arthur," which ultimately became—with small additions—the final idyll in the completed cycle. It had been written at the time of the death of Arthur Hallam, who seemed to Tennyson "Ideal manhood closed in real man," as he wrote of King Arthur; no doubt both Hallam's character and Tennyson's grief at his death lent color to the entire poem.

Like *The Princess,*, *In Memoriam,* and *Maud,* the idylls were an assembly of poetry composed over a long time—in this case nearly half a century in all, for they were not finished until 1874 and were not all published until 1885. Taken collectively, they certainly constitute Tennyson's most ambitious poem, but not all critics would agree that the poem's success is equal to its intentions.

For a modern reader, long accustomed to the Arthurian legend by plays, musicals, films, and popular books, it is hard to realize that the story was relatively unfamiliar when Tennyson wrote. He worked hard at his preparation, reading most of the available sources, going to Wales and the west country of England to see the actual places connected with Arthur, and even learning sufficient Welsh to read some of the original documents. "There is no grander subject in the world," he wrote, and he meant his state of readiness to be equal to the loftiness of his themes, which explains in part why it took him so long to write the entire poem.

Although Tennyson always thought of the idylls as allegorical (his word was "parabolic"), he refused to make literal identifications between incidents, characters, or situations in the poems and what they stood for, except to indicate generally that by King Arthur he meant the soul and that the disintegration of the court and the Round Table showed the disruptive effect of the passions.

In all the time that he worked on the idylls Tennyson constantly refined their structure—by framing the main action between the coming of Arthur and his death, by repetition of verbal motifs, by making the incidents of the plot follow the course of the year from spring to winter, by making different idylls act as parallels or contrasts to each other, by trying to integrate the whole poem as closely as an extended musical composition. Considering how long he worked on the poem, the result is amazingly successful, although perhaps more so when the poem is represented schematically than in the actual experience of reading it.

As always, the imagery of the poem is superb. It is less successful in characterization and speech, which are often stilted and finally seem more Victorian than Arthurian. Even Arthur, who is meant to be the firm, heroic center of the poem, occasionally seems merely weak at the loss of his wife and the decay of the court rather than nobly forgiving. Individual idylls such as *"The Last Tournament"* and

"Gareth and Lynette" have considerable narrative force, but there is an almost fatal lack of forward movement in the poem as a whole.

The reviewers were divided between those who thought it a worthy companion of Malory and those who found it more playacting than drama, with the costumes failing to disguise Tennyson's contemporaries and their concerns. The division between critics still maintains that split of opinion, although it is probably taken more seriously in the 1980s than it was earlier in the twentieth century. Whether that attitude will last is impossible to predict.

In spite of the adverse reviews and the reservations of many of Tennyson's fellow poets, the sales of *Idylls of the King* in 1859 were enough to gladden the heart of any poet: 40,000 copies were printed initially and within a week or two more than a quarter of these were already sold; it was a pattern that was repeated with each succeeding volume as they appeared during the following decades.

The death of his admirer Prince Albert in 1861 prompted Tennyson to write a dedication to the *Idylls of the King* in his memory. The prince had taken an interest in Tennyson's poetry ever since 1847, when it is believed that he called on Tennyson when the poet was ill. He had written to ask for Tennyson's autograph in his own copy of *Idylls of the King*, and he had come over unannounced from Osborne, the royal residence on the Isle of Wight, to call on Tennyson at Farringford. In spite of the brevity of their acquaintance and its formality, Tennyson had been much moved by the prince's kindness and friendliness, and he had greatly admired the way Albert behaved in the difficult role of consort.

Four months after Albert's death the queen invited Tennyson to Osborne for an informal visit. Tennyson went with considerable trepidation, fearful that he might in some way transgress court etiquette, but his obvious shyness helped to make the visit a great success. It became the first of many occasions on which he visited the queen, and a genuine affection grew up on both sides. The queen treated Tennyson with what was great informality by her reserved standards, so that the relationship between monarch and laureate was probably more intimate that it has ever been before or since. She had an untutored and naive love of poetry, and he felt deep veneration for the throne; above all, each was a simple and unassuming person beneath a carapace of apparent arrogance, and each recognized the true simplicity of the other. It was almost certainly the queen's feeling for Tennyson that lay behind the unprecedented offer of a baronetcy four times beginning in 1865; Tennyson each time turned it down for himself while asking that if possible it be given to Hallam, his elder son, after his own death.

His extraordinary popularity was obvious in other ways as well. He was given honorary doctorates by Oxford and Edinburgh universities; Cambridge three times invited him to accept an honorary degree, but he modestly declined. The greatest men in the country competed for the honor of meeting and entertaining him. Thomas Carlyle and his wife had been good friends of Tennyson's since the 1840s, and Tennyson felt free to drop in on them unannounced, at last even having his own pipe kept for him in a convenient niche in the garden wall. He had met Robert Browning at about the same time as he had met Carlyle, and though the two greatest of Victorian poets always felt a certain reserve about each other's works, their mutual generosity in acknowledging genius was exemplary; Browning, like most of the friends Tennyson made in his maturity, was never an intimate, but their respect for each other never faltered. Tennyson was somewhat lukewarm in his response to the overtures of friendship made by Charles Dickens, even after he had stood as godfather for one of Dickens's sons. It is tempting to think that some of his reserve stemmed from an uneasy recognition of the similarity of their features that occasionally led to their being confused, particularly in photographs or portraits, which can hardly have been welcome to Tennyson's self-esteem.

Tennyson maintained a reluctant closeness with William Gladstone for nearly sixty years. It was generally accepted in London society that if a dinner was given for one of them, the other ought to be invited. Yet the truth was that they were never on an easy footing, and though they worked hard at being polite to each other, their edginess occasionally flared into unpleasantness before others. It is probable that some of their difficulties came from their friendship with Arthur Hallam when they were young men; Gladstone had been Hallam's best friend at Eton and felt left out after Hallam met Tennyson. To the end of their days the prime minister and the poet laureate were mildly jealous of their respective places in Hallam's affections so many years before. The feeling certainly colored Gladstone's reactions to Tennyson's poetry (which he occasionally reviewed), and nothing he could do ever made Tennyson trust Gladstone as a politician. The relationship hardly reflects well on either man.

Almost as if he felt that his position as laureate and the most popular serious poet in the English-speaking world were not enough, Tennyson deliberately tried to widen his appeal by speaking more directly to the common people of the country about the primary emotions and affections that he felt he shared with them. The most immediate result of his wish to be "the people's poet" was the 1864 volume whose title poem was *"Enoch Arden"* and which also contained another long narrative poem, *"Aylmer's Field."* These are full of the kinds of magnificent language and imagery that no other Victorian poet could have hoped to produce, but the sentiments occasionally seem easy and secondhand. The volume also contained a number of much more experimental translations and metrical innovations, as well as such wonderful lyrics as *"In the Valley of Cauteretz,"* which was written thirty-one years after he and Hallam had wandered through that beautiful countryside, and *"Tithonus."* There was no question that Tennyson was still a very great poet, but his ambition to be more than a lyricist often blinded him to his own limitations. His hope of becoming "the people's poet" was triumphantly realized; the volume had the largest sales of any during his lifetime. More than 40,000 copies were sold immediately after publication, and in the first year he made more than £8,000 from it, a sum equal to the income of many of the richest men in England.

Popularity of the kind he had earned had its innate disadvantages, and Tennyson was beginning to discover them as he was followed in the streets of London by admirers; at Farringford he complained of the total lack of privacy when the park walls were lined with craning tourists who sometimes even came up to the house and peered into the windows to watch the family at their meals. In 1867 he built a second house, Aldworth, on the southern slopes of Blackdown, a high hill near Haslemere, where the house was not visible except from miles away. Curiously, the house resembles a smaller version of Bayons Manor, the much-hated sham castle his uncle Charles Tennyson d'Eyncourt had built in the Lincolnshire woods. To his contemporaries it appeared unnecessarily grand for a second house, even slightly pretentious; today it seems emblematic of the seriousness with which Tennyson had come to regard his own public position in Victorian England, which was not his most attractive aspect. For the rest of his life he was to divide his time between Farringford and Aldworth, just as he divided his work between the essentially private, intimate lyricism at which he had always excelled and the poetry in which he felt obliged to speak to his countrymen on more public matters.

In the years between 1874 and 1882 Tennyson made yet another attempt to widen his poetic horizons. As the premier poet of England, he had been compared—probably inevitably—to Shakespeare, and he determined to write for the stage as his great predecessor had done. At the age of sixty-five he wrote his first play as a kind of continuation of Shakespeare's historical dramas. *Queen Mary* (1875) was produced in 1876 by Henry Irving, the foremost actor on the English stage; Irving himself played the main male role. It had been necessary to hack the play to a fraction of its original inordinate length in order to play it in one evening, and the result was hardly more dramatic than the original long version had been. In spite of the initial curiosity about Tennyson's first play, the audiences soon dwindled, and it was withdrawn after twenty-three performances; that was, however, a more respectable run than it would be today.

His next play, *Harold* (1876), about the early English king of that name, failed to find a producer during Tennyson's lifetime, although he had conscientiously worked at making it less sprawling than its predecessor. *Becket* (1884), finished in 1879, was a study of the martyred archbishop of Canterbury; Tennyson found the subject so fascinating that he once more wrote at length, in this case making a play considerably longer than an uncut *Hamlet*. Becket was, not surprisingly, not produced until 1893, the year after Tennyson's death. Following *Becket* in quick succession came *The Falcon* and *The Cup* (published together in 1884), *The Foresters* (1892), and *The Promise of May* (published in *Locksley Hall Sixty Years after, Etc.* in 1886), all of which abandoned the attempt to follow Shakespeare. On the stage only *The Cup* had any success, and that was in part due to the lavish settings and the acting of Irving and Ellen Terry. After the failure of *The Promise of May* (a rustic melodrama and the only prose work in his long career), Tennyson at last accepted the fact that nearly a decade of his life had been wasted in an experiment that had totally gone amiss. Today no one would read even the best of the plays, *Queen Mary* and *Becket*, if they were not the work of Tennyson. They betray the fact that he was not profound at understanding the characters of other persons or in writing speech that had the sound of conversation. Even the flashes of metaphor fail to redeem this reckless, admirable, but totally failed attempt to fit Tennyson's genius to another medium.

The climax of public recognition of Tennyson's achievement came in 1883 when Gladstone offered him a peerage. After a few days of consideration Tennyson accepted. Surprisingly, his first thought was to change his name to Baron Tennyson d'Eyncourt in an echo of his uncle's ambition, but he was discouraged by the College of Arms and finally settled on Baron Tennyson of Aldworth and Freshwater. Since he was nearly seventy-five when he assumed the title, he took little part in the activities of the House of Lords, but the appropriateness of his being ennobled was generally acknowledged. It was the first time in history that a man had been given a title for his services to poetry. Tennyson claimed that he took the peerage on behalf of all literature, not as personal recognition.

The rest of his life was spent in the glow of love that the public occasionally gives to a distinguished man who has reached a great age. He continued to write poetry nearly as assiduously as he had when young, and though some of it lacked the freshness of youth, there were occasional masterpieces that mocked the passing years. He had always felt what he once described as the "passion of the past," a longing for the days that had gone, either the great ages of earlier history or the more immediate past of his own life, and his poetic genius always had something nostalgic, even elegiac, at its heart. Many of the finest poems of his old age were written in memory of his friends as they died off, leaving him increasingly alone.

Of all the blows of mortality, the cruelest was the death from "jungle fever" of his younger son, Lionel, who had fallen ill in India and was returning by ship to England. Lionel died in the Red Sea, and his body was put into the waves "Beneath a hard Arabian moon / And alien stars." It took Tennyson two years to recover his equanimity sufficiently to write the poem from which those lines are taken: the magnificent elegy dedicated *"To the Marquis of Dufferin and Ava,"* who had been Lionel's host in India. Hauntingly, the poem is written in the same meter as *In Memoriam*, that masterpiece of his youth celebrating the death of another beloved young man, Arthur Hallam. There were also fine elegies to his brother Charles, to FitzGerald, and to several others, indicating the love he had felt for old friends even when he was frequently unable to express it adequately in person.

Lionel's death was the climax of Tennyson's sense of loss, and from that time until his own death he became increasingly troubled in his search for the proofs of immortality, even experimenting with spiritualism. His poetry of this period is saturated with the desperation of the search, sometimes in questioning, sometimes in dogmatic assertion that scarcely hides the fear underlying it. Yet there were moments of serenity, reflected in such beautiful poems as *"Demeter and Persephone,"* in which he uses the classical legend as a herald of the truth of Christianity. And there was, of course, *"Crossing the Bar,"* written in a few minutes as he sailed across the narrow band of water separating the Isle of Wight from the mainland. At his request, this grave little prayer of simple faith has ever since been placed at the end of editions of his poetry.

Tennyson continued to compose poetry during the last two years of his life; when he was too weak to write it down, his son or his wife would copy it for him. When he had a good day, he was still able to take long walks or even to venture to London. The year before his death he wrote a simple and delicate little poem, *"June Heather and Bracken,"* as an offering of love to his faithful wife; to her he dedicated his last volume of poetry, which was not published until a fortnight after his death. His friends noticed that he was gentler than he had been for years, and he made quiet reparation to some of those whom he had offended by thoughtless brusquerie.

On 6 October 1892, an hour or so after midnight, he died at Aldworth with the moon streaming in at the window overlooking the Sussex Weald, his finger holding open a volume of Shakespeare, his family surrounding the bed. A week later he was buried in the Poets' Corner of Westminster Abbey, near the graves of Browning and Chaucer. To most of England it seemed as if an era in poetry had passed, a divide as great as that a decade later when Queen Victoria died.

One of the most levelheaded summations of what he had meant to his contemporaries was made by Edmund Gosse on the occasion of Tennyson's eightieth birthday:

> He is wise and full of intelligence; but in mere intellectual capacity or attainment it is probable that there are many who excel him. This, then, is not the direction in which his greatness asserts itself. He has not headed a single moral reform nor inaugurated a single revolution of opinion; he has never pointed the way to undiscovered regions of thought; he has never stood on tip-toe to describe new worlds that his fellows were not tall enough to discover ahead. In all these directions he has been prompt to follow, quick to apprehend, but never himself a pioneer. Where then has his greatness lain? It has lain in the various perfections of his writing. He has written, on the whole, with more constant, unwearied, and unwearying ex-

cellence than any of his contemporaries.... He has expended the treasures of his native talent on broadening and deepening his own hold upon the English language, until that has become an instrument upon which he is able to play a greater variety of melodies to perfection than any other man.

But this is a kind of perfection that is hard to accept for anyone who is uneasy with poetry and feels that it ought to be the servant of something more utilitarian. Like most things Victorian, Tennyson's reputation suffered an eclipse in the early years of this century. In his case the decline was more severe than that of other Victorians because he had seemed so much the symbol of his age, so that for a time his name was nearly a joke. After two world wars had called into question most of the social values to which he had given only the most reluctant of support, readers were once more able to appreciate that he stood apart from his contemporaries. Now one can again admire without reservation one of the greatest lyric gifts in English literature, although it is unlikely that he will ever again seem quite the equal of Shakespeare.

When the best of his poetry is separated out from the second-rate work of the kind that any writer produces, Tennyson can be seen plainly as one of the half-dozen great poets in the English language, at least the equal of Wordsworth or Keats and probably far above any other Victorian. And that is precisely what his contemporaries thought.

Source: William E. Fredeman, "Alfred Tennyson," in *Dictionary of Literary Biography*, Vol. 32, *Victorian Poets before 1850*, edited by Ira B. Nadel, Gale Research, 1984, pp. 262–82.

Joanne P. Zuckermann

In the following essay, Zuckermann depicts In Memoriam *as a series of love poems influenced by Shakespeare's sonnets.*

Most of the few modern explanations of *In Memoriam* have, like E. B. Mattes' *In Memoriam: The Way of a Soul* and Graham Hough's "Natural Theology in *In Memoriam*", concerned themselves principally with the source and precise meaning of the poem's intellectual speculations. While inevitably admitting Tennyson's ultimate subjectivism, critics have concerned themselves little with the nature of the subjective experiences underlying the poem or the literary conventions governing their presentation.

In Memoriam is indeed in one sense a philosophical poem: it must have been amongst the works which prompted Jowett to say to Tennyson, just before the latter's death: "Your poetry has an element of philosophy more to be considered than any regular philosophy in England." But its philosophy is based not on the premise *Cogito, ergo sum,* but on the premise *Amo, ergo sumus,* and its relationship to a tradition of speculative or philosophical love poetry is clear. It is, in fact, one of the greatest series of love poems in the English language, and it seems to me that it can be most fruitfully approached by considering it as such, and by examining the literary conventions, the diction and the imagery through which the experiences of love and loss are presented and directed in the poem. This article is intended as the beginning of such an approach.

In Memoriam is both a traditional love poem and an evidently Victorian love poem. Interwoven with the depiction of the love of Tennyson and Hallam, which is sometimes presented in terms of an older and more obviously timeless tradition, are dozens of references to and vignettes of domestic love—of marriage, of parents and children, of brothers and sisters, of the widowed, and of the simple, rural love-tragedies which play such an important part in Victorian literature and popular writing. My aim in this article is to explore the way in which these conventions are blended, and to show how Tennyson builds up his philosophy not on the external intellectual supports which provide its flourishes and decorations and sometimes its tools, but on the simple, self-validating experience of human love. I wish, that is, to examine the poem on the kind of basis which Tennyson himself suggests in lyric XLIX, in which he indicates that it utilizes 'random influences,' 'From art, from nature and the schools,' but makes it clear that these are only the masks and tools of a personal emotional experience.

The poem in its final form is, of course, both personal and universal in its interest, and Tennyson said firmly that it was to be viewed as "a poem, *not* an actual biography," and that the "I" of the poem was sometimes to be regarded not as the poet, but as "the voice of the human race speaking through him." He conceived of it as a "kind of *Divina Comedia,* leading from despair to happiness." This latter description clearly refers not only to the structural outline of the poem and the fact that it is a carefully shaped whole rather than a mere diary of experience, but also to the role of a dead human beloved in leading the poet to a perception of universal truth and love; as Beatrice is to Dante, so Hallam is to Tennyson.

A sense of what one might almost call the poem's archaism, of its contact with older traditions of love poetry, was early noted by Sara Coleridge.

In contrasting the essential modernism of *The Prelude* (which she recognised even in the 1850 version, published in the same year as *In Memoriam*) with the less fundamentally original quality of *In Memoriam,* she commented on the "Petrarchanism" of the latter work. This is indeed one of many examples of a Victorian poet's reaching back to older traditions of love poetry. The Rossettis, of course, were under a special family influence: but one thinks too of the influence of Donne upon Browning, the greatest of the Victorian love-poets, and the allusions to Dante in "One Word More"; or one recalls Coventry Patmore, writing the best lyrics of *The Angel in the House* under the influence of the Metaphysicals. But the love poem which most pervasively influenced *In Memoriam,* which we knew that Tennyson read with special attention during the period of its composition, and which may even have helped to suggest its form, are undoubtedly Shakespeare's *Sonnets.*

Both the *Sonnets* and *In Memoriam* are series of lyric poems in a continuously used metrical form, in which a story is discerned through the lyric utterances rather than related in narrative form. In creating such a series, Tennyson has, as it were, accidentally stumbled upon an ideal solution to the problem of devising an appropriate form for a long poem, in an age which, if anything, rather overvalued the spontaneity of the brief lyric outburst. It has been frequently recognized that this was one of the problems confronting Victorian poets, and that the characteristic solution was to build up a longer poem out of shorter units. One sees this type of poetic form in such poems as *Maud, The Idylls of the King* and *The Ring and the Book,* and it is in some sense perpetuated in Yeats's rather Wordsworthian insistence that his total poetic output should be placed in a certain order and regarded as a single major work. Tennyson, however, has achieved perhaps the most perfect compromise between lyric spontaneity and major constructive art in *In Memoriam,* by taking a large group of highly personal poems, commenced without any view to publication, and arranging them in a series which must be read as a carefully structured whole. One of the few models which could really have helped to suggest such a solution is that of the sonnet sequence.

The resemblances between *In Memoriam* and Shakespeare's *Sonnets* are evident—the many meditative poems, the occasional poems referring to or commemorating an external event or an anniversary, the groups of lyrics on related themes which form smaller units within the larger work—but of course Tennyson has gone much further towards ordering his series than Shakespeare. His obvious model for the poem's larger structure is the major elegy, as represented by *Lycidas* (to which there are many resemblances and allusions) and *Adonais* (which Hallam has been the first to bring back to England in printed form). The models afforded by the sonnet sequence and the elegy fuse easily, since Shakespeare's sequence is so pervaded by the sense of time, transience and loss as to be almost anticipatorily elegiac. Sonnets like "Not marble nor the gilded monuments," "Since brass nor stone, nor earth, nor boundless sea," and "To me fair friend you never can be old" seem almost predestined models for elegiac poetry. One wonders too, in an idle and tentative way, if Shakespeare's reference to a three years' friendship in the last-mentioned sonnet might have suggested Tennyson's time-scheme of a three years' mourning, which does not, of course, correspond to the actual span of time covered by the poem. At all events, the completed *In Memoriam* combines much of the generalising bent of the classical, public elegy, which was usually written for a person not well known to the poet, with a much greater degree of the poignantly personal quality of the *Sonnets.*

Not that Shakespeare's *Sonnets* lack generalisation and universal validity: few works seem to speak so personally for every reader, or so convincingly of general truth. But their universality springs, paradoxically, from their very intimacy. By addressing them directly to the Friend and the Dark Lady, like letters, Shakespeare has reduced to a minimum the need for description and narrative, aimed at the unknowing and potentially unsympathetic world, which would particularise and restrict them: of the beauty which he promises so often to immortalise, he actually describes not so much as the colour of eyes and hair. What we hear is the voice of the basic emotion itself, expressing itself through universally recognised patterns of imagery. In the same way Tennyson, whilst giving poignancy by the occasional reference to hand or eye, offers no description of Hallam, and withholds even the most generalised account of his character and activities until late in the sequence. His lyrics are addressed to various friends, to God, to himself, to a number of personifications, and in some of the most crucial instances, to Hallam himself. Both sequences, Shakespeare's and Tennyson's are "overheard" poetry, and derive many of their most distinctive features from this fact.

The resemblance of *In Memoriam* to the *Sonnets* is particularly apparent in lyrics LX–LXV, and an examination of this group throws much light on the way in which the techniques of love poetry are made to serve Tennyson's special ends. In LX Tennyson compares himself, deserted by the dead Hallam, to:

> ... some poor girl whose heart is set
> On one whose rank exceeds her own.

The beloved moves on to his proper sphere, and she is left to find "the baseness of her lot," and "envying all who meet him there." In LXII Hallam is again likened to one who has outgrown a childhood sweetheart, although this time a girl below him in moral stature rather than mere social position. In LXIII Hallam's possible pitying memories of Tennyson are compared to the poet's love for his dog or horse, whilst in LXIV Hallam is seen as a great public figure, whose boyhood friend, left behind in their simple home, still wistfully broods on him and wonders if he remembers their relationship. The spirit throughout the group is one of the utmost humility and self-abnegation. The highborn lover, the public man, and the poet bestowing a little spare affection on his dog or horse, are all images of a higher being, moving in his "proper sphere" and wholly right in his attitude to those so far below him. The deserted girl in LX cries "How should he love a thing so low?" and Tennyson begins LXII by a direct renunciatory address to Hallam:

> Though if an eye that's downward cast
> Could make thee somewhat blench or fail,
> Then be my love an idle tale
> And fading legend of the past.

Yet throughout the section one feels, as one always does feel with this type of love poetry, that a tendency to blame the beloved or to demand more assertively some return of affection, has been overcome by strength of love, exercise of will, and magnanimity.

None of this is literally appropriate to Tennyson's situation. Hallam has not "deserted" him, however justifiably and properly: he has been snatched away by death. Unlike the highborn lover and the public man, he had no opportunity to make the false but romantically generous choice and count the world well lost for love. But an exclamation at the end of lyric LXI makes us recognise, early in the group, the provenance and nature of these emotions, and recall the situation in which they were literally appropriate:

> I loved thee, Spirit, and love, nor can
> The soul of Shakespeare love thee more.

It is almost as though Tennyson wishes at this point to render absolutely overt a resemblance which is present throughout the section in tone,

> "What we hear is the voice of the basic emotion itself, expressing itself through universally recognised patterns of imagery."

emotional quality and increased archaism of diction, but is not elsewhere thrust upon our attention by close verbal parallels or direct allusions. Thus alerted, we remark the similarity of the deserted girl of LX, all humility, yet still "Half jealous of she knows not what / And envying all who meet him there," to the Shakespeare of Sonnets 57 and 58, who dare not chide the beloved for his voluntary absences, but must "Like a sad slave stay, and think of naught / Save where you are how happy you make those." Similarly Tennyson in LXII, exonerating the beloved from even thinking about him if it would be a source of pain or trouble, echoes, although with an exact reversal of roles, the Shakespeare of 72:

> No longer think of me when I am dead
>
> for I love you so,
> That I in your sweet thoughts would be forgot,
> If thinking on me then should make you woe.

Lyric LXV deserves quoting in full, both as the climax of this section, and for the key it provides to Tennyson's method and achievement throughout *In Memoriam*. Here again the archaism of diction is unusually marked, and one notes the characteristically Shakespearean initial epithet, 'sweet,' and the Shakespearean sound-patterns of a line like the second in the last stanza:

> Sweet soul, do with me as thou wilt;
> I lull a fancy trouble-tost
> With 'Love's too precious to be lost,
> A little grain shall not be spilt.'
>
> And in that solace can I sing,
> Till out of painful phrases wrought
> There flutters up a happy thought,
> Self-balance on a lightsome wing;
>
> Since we deserved the name of friends,
> And thine effect so lives in me,
> A part of mine may live in thee
> And move thee on to nobler ends.

By treating love cut off by death in terms and images appropriate to love slighted or rejected, Tennyson has eventually come, in this lyric, to a sense of a continuing and mutual relationship, in which both he and Hallam can still give and receive. What reassures him, here and throughout the poem, is his sense that Hallam has survived in such a way that he can still make human claims upon him and humanly generous concessions to him. And this sense is expressed through, makes its impression upon the reader by means of, and is to some extent actually generated in Tennyson by, the diction and techniques of love poetry. Hallam is constantly addressed throughout the poem as though he were the living recipient of conventional love poetry, and this perhaps does more than anything else to establish the conviction of his survival. He is both addressed and spoken of in the third person in the language of such love poetry: "My Arthur," "Dearest," "My Love," "The man I held as half divine," "A little while from his embrace," "Mine, mine, for ever, ever mine,"—such epithets and phrases ring throughout the poem. Even the more neutral "friend" in such lines as "Since we deserved the name of friends," and "Unto me no second friend," takes on the power of love-language once the Shakespearean context is established. In the lyric just quoted in full, the nature of Tennyson's conviction is made particularly clear. It is self-validating and self-sustaining—"Self-balanced on a lightsome wing"; and it is not merely recorded in poetry, it is generated in part by the act of writing poetry; the poet creates it by singing, and it is wrought out of "phrases."

The group of lyrics we have been examining follows closely upon one of the poem's most serious and best-known outbreaks of doubt and questioning. In lyric LV the prodigal bounty of Nature has led Tennyson to reflect that "So careful of the type she seems, so careless of the single life," whilst in LVI geological evidence has pressed upon him the thought that not only is the individual doomed to die fruitlessly, but the race itself is heading for extinction. No speculative reply is attempted, no external counter-evidences are adduced: after a brief interlude, Tennyson produces, by way of answer to his doubts, the group of Shakespearean love-lyrics. Not that he wishes to suggest too great a certainty: he deliberately belittles his own achievement by the use of such words as "sing," "flutters," "fancy," "lightsome," in the concluding lyric of the section. But ultimately, of course, he did believe that the testimony of the imagination and the emotions was more valid than that of the reason, and in those lyrics in which he distinguishes between knowledge and wisdom, or shows us the heart leaping up "like a man in wrath" to answer the claims of the "freezing reason," he makes explicit his views. If *In Memoriam* were to be given a Shakespearean epigraph, it would come after all not from the *Sonnets* but from "The Phoenix and the Turtle": "Love hath reason, reason none." In later life his only anxiety about *In Memoriam* was that it suggested too much *speculative* certainty: he would almost have liked to add another section, which, by reopening the poem's intellectual doubt, would "throw man back to the more primitive impulses and feelings."

T. S. Eliot felt that Tennyson had gone further than he thus acknowledged, not merely suggesting too much purely speculative certainty, but essentially falsifying the record of his feelings. He called it a poem of religious despair, and commented that "Its faith is a poor thing." But the real key to Eliot's dislike of Tennyson's faith comes, I believe, earlier in his essay, and involves less a judgment of the strength or reality of that faith, or the effectiveness of its artistic expression, than a criticism of its nature and foundations. He writes: "Yet the renewal craved for seems at best but a continuance, or a substitute for the joys of friendship upon earth. His desire for immortality is never quite the desire for Eternal Life: his concern is for the loss of man rather than for the gain of God." This is a fair and perceptive comment on the poem, but not necessarily, as Eliot clearly intends it to be, a serious indictment of it. We are being offered not a literary assessment of the poem's value, but the statement of a conflict of opinion between an ascetic poet of renunciation, and a very different poet, who approaches a variety of religious experience not by renouncing, but by clinging to human love. It is, indeed, difficult to see what is, in Eliot's terms, "religious" about the poem's despair: in its despair and faith alike, it is a poem of human love before it is anything else.

Certainly the tendency which Eliot disapproves of is not peculiar to Tennyson: it is characteristic of the Victorian era. Writers as diverse as Elizabeth Barrett Browning, Robert Browning, Coventry Patmore, Christina Rossetti, Dante Gabriel Rossetti, Charles Kingsley and Charles Reade image the resumption in Heaven of human relationships severed by death, or treat romantic love as a guarantee of personal immortality. Even George Gissing bears negative testimony to the strength of the tradition, when he makes one of the characters in *New Grub Street* remark: "The days of romantic love are gone by. The scientific spirit has put an end to that kind of self-deception. Romantic love was inextricably blended with all sorts of superstitions—belief in personal immortality, in superior beings, in—in all the rest of it."

Walter Houghton, in *The Victorian Frame of Mind,* deals very briefly, at the end of his section on "Love," with the profound significance of idealized romantic love in Victorian literature. He points out that it could serve as a kind of substitute religion for some of the agnostics of the period, whilst men clinging to faith but troubled by doubts could use human love as a prop to their religion, treating it as a foretaste and guarantee of Heaven. But in such a general and wide-ranging survey of the period, Houghton is not able to investigate and develop the topic as fully as its importance merits. One might almost say that what the solitary, in his various guises of wanderer, seeker, outcast and hermit, was to the Romantic imagination, the pair, involved in a profound human relationship, was to the Victorian mind.

"Romantic love" implies an extreme idealization of human love, and an extreme insistence on fidelity and permanence, which is essentially "monogamous" even where the love is, as often in the medieval tradition, extra-marital. Thus defined it is not a prominent theme in Romantic poetry. It seems a gross over simplification, but not a total distortion, to suggest that the Romantic quest for permanence was carried on mainly in relation to nature, and that as science cut the ground from under the nature worshipper's feet, attention was transferred to romantic fidelity in love. It may be too facile to compare Wordsworth in "A slumber did my spirit steal" consigning the beloved to the custody of "rocks and stones and trees," with Tennyson in *In Memoriam* perceiving that "The hills are shadows and they flow / From form to form and nothing stands," and clinging to the individual human personality: but it indicates something of what was taking place.

Houghton, in discussing the interaction of religious impulses and romantic love, does not mention *In Memoriam.* In a sense this is scarcely surprising, since love-poetry is generally thought of as dealing with a romantic and physical attachment between a man and a woman. One perhaps invites misapprehension by linking *In Memoriam* with Shakespeare's *Sonnets* and discussing it as love poetry. After all, Tennyson does use a sexual relationship as a metaphor for his own relationship with Hallam on many occasions. Occasionally he takes on the male identity, but he casts himself as the female, the wife or the deserted girl, often enough to explain the delicious absurdity of one of the earliest reviews which commented: "These touching lines evidently come from the full heart of the widow of a military man." To suggest that there was anything consciously or overtly homosexual about the relationship is obviously absurd, and to speculate about its latent or suppressed tendencies is largely irrelevant to a consideration of *In Memoriam* as poetry: but nevertheless the fact that it celebrates a supreme love between men is of some importance in considering its scope and techniques.

Here, as in the matter of the poem's form, Tennyson seems to have had ready made for him a situation which other Victorian writers went out of their way to construct. He is celebrating a love relationship which both is and is not an ordinary romantic one. One might compare Browning's use of the relationship between Pompilia and Caponsacchi in *The Ring and the Book,* which borrows and transforms many motifs and conventions of romantic and chivalric poetry to present a special type of non-physical relationship. Or one might cite the minor example of *The Cloister and The Hearth,* in which a married man, believing his wife to be dead, takes the vows of a celibate priesthood, and must establish a special type of relationship with her when he rediscovers her. Both Browning and Reade show their lovers passing beyond death, looking to other than an earthly fruition of their love.

Most of the best love literature deals with unhappy or frustrated love, of course, because in such situations love becomes its own reward, and the writer is impelled to deal with the nature of the emotion and its profounder implications, rather than the mundane details of the relationship's consummation and continuation. But in relationships in which consummation and the daily trivia of shared existence are not merely denied but in some way out of the question, this effect is heightened. Browning and Reade deal with situations in which the straightforward living out of the relationship in commonplace domesticity is tabooed in a special way, and by taking priests as their heroes force us to place the romantic relationships in an explicitly religious context. But Tennyson had experienced a relationship with a similar value for poetry, and such a one as no Victorian writer would ever have created as a fiction: and he had the Shakespearean precedent for presenting this relationship through the conventions of romantic love poetry. *In Memoriam* is what it is, an exploration of human love in a religious context and against a background of loss and deprivation, not only because Hallam died, but because of the intrinsic nature of the relationship between the two, and the literary conventions available for its presentation.

Yet Tennyson does use, in abundance, the realistic and mundane domestic imagery which his theme removes from the central position in the poem. Perhaps its most prevalent images are the domestic ones of various kinds. The poem thus looks in two directions: towards the romantic, the ideal and unknowable through its theme of sublime love and premature death, and towards the practical business of living, the duties and domesticities of daily life, through its dominant imagery and many of its incidents. This is the familiar Tennysonian dichotomy—Ulysses and Telemachus raising their critic-branded heads—but the two strains are unusually well fused in this poem, since the domestic imagery accommodates both an exceedingly romantic view of marital love and fidelity, and an exceedingly practical view of marital and domestic duty.

A really full exploration of the domestic imagery of *In Memoriam* is certainly needed, but I wish to conclude this article with a brief examination of two examples of this aspect of the poem, the section in which personal immortality is first mentioned, and a few of the lyrics which deal directly with marriage.

It is very noticeable that the first intimations of faith and hope in *In Memoriam* arise in a domestic context. In lyric XVIII, when Hallam's body is finally brought home and buried, the stress is entirely on a purely pagan sense of homecoming:

> 'Tis well; 'tis something; we may stand
> Where he in English earth is laid,
> And from his ashes may be made
> The violet of his native land.

Tennyson was admittedly not present at Hallam's funeral, and so is unlikely to write about it in any detail, but the total absence of all religious reference, at a point where the lost beloved is being buried in a churchyard with Christian rites, is still striking. It is indeed necessary to the poem, which derives faith from love and loss, that the purely human experience of total grief should be established first.

The earliest explicitly religious references occur in the section dealing with the poem's first Christmas, beginning with lyric XXVIII. But the bells of this lyric, although they ring out the traditional message of "Peace and goodwill, goodwill and peace," call the poet's attention less to these words than to the fact that they are the bells of "four hamlets round." Their associations are local and biographical, and they bring Tennyson a measure of stability not because of their religious message, but because "they controlled me when a boy." In the last line he refers to them as "The merry, merry bells of Yule," giving the festival its pagan name.

In the next lyric the only mention of the church is a passing reference to "the cold baptismal font," from which the poet shrinks away to make a wreath for the home. The next lyric begins with a domestic celebration of Christmas, its centre not the altar but the hearth. The family try in vain to pretend merriment, and eventually, sitting hand in hand in a circle, they are moved to tears by a song which they sang the year before with Hallam. Then "a gentler feeling" comes upon them, and they are able to see death as peace and rest. Finally, after silence and tears:

> Our voices took a higher range;
> Once more we sang, 'They do not die
> Nor lose their mortal sympathy.
> Nor change to us, although they change.
>
> Rapt from the fickle and the frail
> With gather'd power, yet the same,
> Pierces the keen seraphic flame
> From orb to orb, from veil to veil.'

And then, and then only is Tennyson ready to conclude the lyric with a prayerful and explicitly Christian welcome to Christmas morning. Two things are noticeable here. Firstly, the family, like Tennyson in lyric XVI, *sing* their way to faith and solace, and at the climax of their experience, Tennyson invents the words of their song. Through the fusion of the family's song with the poet's lyric utterance, the singing of a domestic Christmas becomes a metaphor for what the poet himself is experiencing—the attainment of faith not through speculative reasoning but through surrender to artistic and emotional impulse. Secondly, the poet has selected an occasion ideally suited to his purpose, a major religious festival which was becoming, in Victorian England, very much the festival of the secular home and family, and has worked toward its religious meaning through its domestic celebration, in explicit isolation from the Church.

In the next two lyrics, XXXI and XXXII, the particularly rationally incredible miracle of the raising of Lazarus is simply accepted without comment and used as a basis for reflection, the domestic context being maintained by a focussing of attention on the relationship between Lazarus and his sister. After the interestingly ambiguous XXXIII, Tennyson attains a note of personal affirmation in lyric XXXIV:

> My own dim life should teach me this,
> That life shall live for evermore,
> Or earth is darkness at the core,
> And dust and ashes all that is.

This confident note will not be consistently maintained: even here the affirmation has the passion of despair, and soon the new-found faith will be probed and tested. But from this point onwards the notion of Hallam's personal survival is never long absent from the poem, and soon belief in it will begin to be strengthened by poems directly addressed to him.

Throughout the poem religious experience arises from, or is carefully related to a domestic context: one of the most striking examples is lyric XCV, in which the poet's visionary experience is carefully prepared for by an account of the preceding family scene on the lawn, with such concrete realistic details as "the fluttering urn." Domestic imagery is also frequently used metaphorically, most interestingly in those lyrics in which Hallam and Tennyson are compared to a married couple, in which it would, I think, be possible to show a steady and consistent development in the use of the image. In lyric XCVII the "marriage" of Hallam and Tennyson persists, unbroken by death, at once binding the poet to the remote but ever near ideal, and enabling him to carry on contentedly in his own lower sphere:

> Two partners of a married life—
> I look'd on these and thought of thee
> In vastness and in mystery,
> And of my spirit as of a wife.

The husband of this marriage is no longer the young man of their early days: he is rapt in deep thought, and despite their continuing union seems to have moved away from his wife—"He seems so near and yet so far," whilst "the faithless people" even say that he no longer loves her. But she treasures the withered violet he gave her years ago, and maintains a blind but unshakeable faith in his love. This is, of course, a purely human faith in the emotional constancy of a human being, but it is described in terms which inevitably suggest religious faith. Indeed, when the wife is contrasted with "the faithless people," one almost sees her as the Church as the Bride of Christ. In the strength of her faith, she is able to carry on a life of simple grace and usefulness, which is still somehow linked to and animated by her husband's larger sphere:

> For him she plays, to him she sings,
> Of early faith and plighted vows;
> She knows but matters of the house,
> And he, he knows a thousand things.

Again a domestic song becomes a metaphor for Tennyson's activity as poet, and reminds us of the crucial role this plays in sustaining his faith.

This lyric is full of the same humility and restrained self-abnegation as the Shakespearean group which we examined earlier. Tennyson is not, after all, in ordinary human terms, as confined, meek and ignorant as the wife of the poem, whatever he may be in relation to a beautiful spirit, and his placing himself on her level shows the willed humility of romantic love. And the wife in the lyric partially wills her belief: she sings "of plighted vows" rather than of purely spontaneous emotions, and she resolutely refuses to listen to "faithless people."

Indeed, *In Memoriam* as a whole does not simply depict spontaneous and irresistible emotion triumphing over the "freezing reason"; it is also, to some extent, a triumph of the will. The spontaneous instinct, the love which can sometimes leap intuitively across the barrier of death, is there; but it is confirmed and strengthened into a creed by the exercise of the will—at once the religious will to believe, the romantic will to remain faithful in love, and the artistic will to create. Certainly one can hardly help sensing, in reading the poem, that Tennyson believed in part because he wanted to believe, and it is this aspect of the poem which has disturbed most modern readers and critics, leading them to feel it valueless for them as a religious and philosophical document, and falsified as an emotional record.

But the view that faith is not merely a supernatural gift but a virtue, and loss of faith not merely a deprivation but a wilful sin, that faith depends in part on the will, is perfectly orthodox and traditional. This view became particularly important in the nineteenth century: we might recall the Pope's reflections in *The Ring and the Book,* or Bishop Blougram's willed choice between "a life of doubt diversified by faith" and "a life of faith diversified / by doubt." Or we may remember Coleridge arguing, in the *Biographia Literaria,* that religion, as the source of morality, must have a moral origin, and that "the evidence of its doctrines could not, like the truths of abstract science, be wholly independent of the will."

The same considerations apply to human "faith" or fidelity in love: one "falls in love," but the maintenance of the bond depends in part upon the will, and the "faithless one" has been traditionally regarded as reprehensible, as much under the code which governed "false Cressida" and "true

Troilus" as under religiously and socially sanctioned attitudes toward marriage like those prevailing in Victorian England. The exercise of the will in *In Memoriam* seems to me fundamentally of this kind: not the self-blinding of a stupid, cowardly or philosophically anti-rational man trampling on his own legitimate doubts, but the will of a romantic or chivalric lover, often imaged as a married lover, spurning temptations to infidelity. For this reason it seems not a means of falsification, but an essential part of the poem, of the emotions involved, and of the tradition to which the poem belongs.

The elegy ends with an epithalamium for Cecilia Tennyson and Edmund Lushington. Earlier in the poem Tennyson has avoided mention of orthodox religion in his treatment of Hallam's funeral, has not entered the church for the celebration of a festival so mysterious as Christmas, and has found the baptismal font, the source of a purely supernatural life, "cold." But now, when human love and domesticity move into the church in triumphal procession, for the celebration of a natural sacrament, ratified but not conferred by the Church, Tennyson can join the crowd and take part in the ceremonies. Cecilia, "Her feet, my darling, on the dead" and her ear to "the most living word of life," forms an almost physical link between past and future, death and life, human sorrow and divine consolation. But the words of the marriage ceremony actually quoted are lacking in all reference to the supernatural:

> The 'Wilt thou?' answer'd, and again
> The 'Wilt thou?' asked, till out of twain
> Her sweet 'I will' has made you one.

What has created the mysterious and indissoluble union, which the whole poem is now seen as leading up to, is not the supernatural activity of the Church, but the assent and resolve of the human will, ratifying and rendering permanent the romantic passion which was an essential accompaniment to this act of the will, but which could not have stood alone. Insofar as Cecilia and Edmund are symbolic equivalents of Hallam and Tennyson, Cecilia evidently stands for Tennyson, since she is his blood relative, and since he has most often depicted himself as the wife: and it should be noticed that it is Cecilia's "I will," in one sense dependent and responsive, but in another final and conclusive, which actually rivets the unbreakable link. And by then the poem has become Tennyson's "I will."

The writing of it had been an exercise both of art and of autotherapy, and in hitting upon its form, an elegy composed of a series of love-lyrics, Tennyson took a major step towards the solution of both his artistic and his personal problems. The faith and solace which he found, he found in part through singing of them: he learned to feel Hallam's presence by addressing him; and by addressing him in both the language of traditional love-poetry and the imagery of Victorian domestic fiction, he was able to give the fullest possible expression to his feelings, and to take in the widest possible range of interest. One of the major principles of the poem's unity is its inter-weaving of different modes and images of human love.

A fuller examination of *In Memoriam* as love poetry is obviously necessary. More attention needs to be given to the development of particular strands of imagery, to the distribution of archaic diction, to the shifts between "I" as the poet and "I" as "the voice of the human race speaking through him," and to the shifts between poems nominally addressed to different listeners, in particular the distribution and immediate context of the poems addressed directly to Hallam. But I hope that I have succeeded in indicating some of the lines of enquiry for such an approach to the poem.

Source: Joanne P. Zuckermann, "Tennyson's *In Memoriam* as Love Poetry," in *Dalhousie Review*, Vol. 51, No. 2, Summer 1971, pp. 202–17.

A. C. Bradley

In the following essay excerpt originally published in 1910, Bradley provides an explication of Tennyson's work, and explains its appeal to readers as the expression of a shared and common experience.

THE 'WAY OF THE SOUL.'

It is a fashion at present to ascribe the great popularity of *In Memoriam* entirely to the 'teaching' contained in it, and to declare that its peculiar position among English elegies has nothing to do with its poetic qualities. This is equivalent to an assertion that, if the so-called substance of the poem had been presented in common prose, the work would have gained the same hold upon the mass of educated readers that is now possessed by the poem itself. Such an assertion no one would make or consciously imply. The ordinary reader does not indeed attempt to separate the poetic qualities of a work from some other quality that appeals to him; much less does he read the work in terror of being affected by the latter; but imagination and diction and even versification can influence him much as they influence the people who talk about them, and

What Do I Read Next?

- The Norton Critical Edition of Tennyson's poem *In Memoriam* contains background and sources, along with critical essays. It was edited by Robert H. Ross and published in 1974 by W. W. Norton.

- Readers interested in this poem might want to compare Tennyson's style to the works of the man who inspired him. *Poems of Arthur Henry Hallam*, published in 1988 by AMS Press, reproduces Hallam's work.

- William Wordsworth, who preceded Tennyson as poet laureate of England and was one of the founders of the romantic movement, wrote a long poem titled *The Prelude*, which is similar in theme to *In Memoriam*. The first edition of Wordsworth's poem was published posthumously in 1850, the same year as Tennyson's poem.

- The poet's grandson, Charles Tennyson, wrote *Alfred Tennyson*, a biography that reflects its author's access to family-owned sources. It was published in 1968 by Archon Books.

- *Tennyson: The Growth of a Poet*, by Jerome Hamilton Buckley, combines biographical and critical analysis of Tennyson's life. It was published in 1960 and remains a standard source in Tennyson studies.

- At the same time Tennyson was laboring over *In Memoriam* in England, Emily Dickinson was writing poetry in the United States that was not published until years after her death. Many of Dickinson's poems deal with mortality. Fans of Tennyson's poem may be particularly interested in how the poem compares to Dickinson's "I Reason, Earth is Short," number XXIII in *The Complete Poems of Emily Dickinson*, first published in 1924 by Little, Brown.

---

he would never have taken *In Memoriam* to his heart if its consoling or uplifting thoughts had not also touched his fancy and sung in his ears. It is true, however, that he dwells upon these thoughts, and that the poem is often valued by him for its bearing upon his own life; and true again that this is one reason why he cares for it far more than for elegies certainly not inferior to it as poems. And perhaps here also many devotees of poetry may resemble him more than they suppose.

This peculiar position of *In Memoriam* seems to be connected with two facts. In the first place, it alone among the most famous English elegies is a poem inspired by deep personal feelings. Arthur Hallam was a youth of extraordinary promise, but he was also 'dear as the mother to the son.' The elegy on his death, therefore, unlike those on Edward King or Keats or Clough, bears the marks of a passionate grief and affection; and the poet's victory over sorrow, like his faith in immortality, is felt to be won in a struggle which has shaken the centre of his being. And then, as has been observed already, the grief and the struggle are portrayed in all their stages and phases throughout months and years; and each is depicted, not as it may have appeared when the victory was won, but as it was experienced then and there. In other elegies for example, scarcely anything is to be found resembling the earlier sections, which describe with such vividness and truth the varied feelings of a new grief; scarcely anything, again, like the night-poems, or the poem of the second anniversary, or those of the third springtime. Stanzas like these come home to readers who never cared for a poem before, and were never conscious of feeling poetically till sorrow opened their souls. Thus much of *In Memoriam* is nearer to ordinary life than most elegies can be, and many such readers have found in it an expression of their own feelings, or have looked to the experience which it embodies as a guide to a possible conquest over their own loss. 'This,' they say to themselves as they read, 'is what I dumbly feel. This man, so much greater than I, has suffered like me and has told me how he won his way to peace. Like me, he has been forced by his own disaster to meditate on "the riddle of the painful earth," and to ask whether the world can really be governed by a law of love, and is not rather the work of blind forces, indifferent to the value of all that they produce and destroy.'

A brief review, first of the experience recorded in *In Memoriam,* and then of the leading ideas employed in it, may be of interest to such readers, and even to others, as it may further the understanding of the poem from one point of view, although it has to break up for the time that unity of substance and form which is the essence of poetry.

The early sections portray a soul in the first anguish of loss. Its whole interest is fixed on one thing in the world; and, as this thing is taken away, the whole world is darkened. In the main, the description is one of a common experience, and the poem shows the issue of this experience in a particular case.

Such sorrow is often healed by forgetfulness. The soul, flinching from the pain of loss, or apprehensive of its danger, turns away, at first with difficulty, and afterwards with increasing ease, from the thought of the beloved dead. 'Time,' or the incessant stream of new impressions, helps it to forget. Its sorrow gradually perishes, and with its sorrow its love; and at last 'all it was is overworn,' and it stands whole and sound. It is not cynical to say that this is a frequent history, and that the ideas repelled in section XC are not seldom true.

Sometimes, again, the wound remains unhealed, although its pain is dulled. Here love neither dies nor changes its form; it remains a painful longing for something gone, nor would anything really satisfy it but the entire restoration of that which is gone. All the deeper life of the soul is absorbed in this love, which from its exclusively personal character is unable to coalesce with other interests and prevents their growth.

In neither of these extreme cases is there that victory of which the poet thinks even in the first shock of loss, when he remembers how it has been said

> That men may rise on stepping-stones
> Of their dead selves to higher things.

In the first case there is victory of a kind, but it is a victory which in the poet's eyes is defeat; the soul may be said to conquer its sorrow, but it does so by losing its love; it is a slave in the triumph of Time. In the second case, the 'self' refuses to die and conquers time, but for that very reason it is bound to the past and unable to rise to higher things. The experience portrayed in *In Memoriam* corresponds with neither case, but it resembles each in one particular. Sorrow is healed, but it is not healed by the loss of love: for the beloved dead is the object of continual thought, and when regret has passed away love is found to be not less but greater than before. On the other hand regret does pass away, and love does not merely look forward to reunion with its object but unites freely with other interests. It is evident that the possibility of this victory depends upon the fact that, while love does not die, there is something in the soul which does die. The self 'rises' only on the basis of a 'dead self.' In other words, love changes though it does not perish or fade; and with the change in it there is a corresponding change in the idea of its object. The poem exhibits this process of two-fold change.

At the beginning love desires simply that which was, the presence and companionship of the lost friend; and this it desires unchanged and in its entirety. It longs for the sight of the face, the sound of the voice, the pressure of the hand. These doubtless are desired as tokens of the soul; but as yet they are tokens essential to love, and that for which it pines is the soul as known and loved through them. If the mourner attempts to think of the dead apart from them, his heart remains cold, or he recoils: he finds that he is thinking of a phantom; 'an awful thought' instead of 'the human-hearted man he loved'; 'a spirit, not a breathing voice.' This he does not and cannot love. It is an object of awe, not of affection; the mere dead body is a thousand-fold dearer than this,—naturally, for this is not really a spirit, a thinking and loving soul, but a ghost. As then he is unable to think of the object of his love except as 'the hand, the lips, the eyes,' and 'the meeting of the morrow,' he feels that what he loves is simply gone and lost, and he finds his one relief in allowing fancy to play about the thought of the tokens that remain (see the poems to the ship).

The process of change consists largely in the conquest of the soul over its bondage to sense. So long as this bondage remains, its desire is fixed on that which really is dead, and it cannot advance. But gradually it resigns this longing, and turns more and more to that which is not dead. The first step in its advance is the perception that love itself is of infinite value and may survive the removal of the sensible presence of its object. But no sooner has this conviction been reached and embraced than suddenly the mourner is found to have transferred his interest from the sensible presence to the soul itself, while, on the other hand, the soul is no longer thought of as a mere awful phantom, but has become what the living friend had been, something both beloved and loving. This conquest is, indeed, achieved first in a moment of exaltation which cannot be maintained; but its result is never lost, and gradually strengthens. The feeling that the soul of the dead is something shadowy and awful departs for ever, and step by step the haunting desire for the bodily presence retires. Thought is concentrated on that which lives, the beauty of the beloved soul, seen in its remembered life on earth, and doubtless shown more fully elsewhere in a life that can be dimly imagined. At last the pining for what is gone dies completely away, but love is found to be but stronger for its death, and to be no longer a source of pain. It has grown to the dimensions of its object, and this object is not only distant and desired, but also present and possessed. And more—the past (which is not wholly past, since it lives and acts in the soul of the mourner) has lost its pang and retained its loveliness and power: 'the days that are no more' become a life in death instead of a 'death in life'; and even the light of the face, the sound of the voice, and the pressure of the hand, now that the absorbing desire for them is still, return in the quiet inward world.

Another aspect of this change is to be noticed. So long as the mourner's sorrow and desire are fixed on that which dies they withdraw his interest from all other things. His world seems to depend for its light on that which has passed away, and he cries, 'All is dark where thou art not.' But as his love and its object change and grow, this exclusiveness lessens and its shadow shrinks. His heart opens itself to other friendships; the sweetness of the spring returns; and the 'mighty hopes' for man's future which the friend had shared, live again as the dead friend ceases to be a silent voice and becomes a living soul. Nor do the reviving activities simply flourish side by side with love for this soul, and still less do they compete with it. Rather they are one with it. The dead man lives in the living, and 'moves him on to nobler ends.' It is at the bidding of the dead that he seeks a friendship for the years to come. His vision of the ideal man that is to be is a memory of the man that trod this planet with him in his youth. He had cried, 'All is dark where thou art not,' and now he cries,

> Thy voice is on the rolling air;
> I hear thee where the waters run;
> Thou standest in the rising sun,
> And in the setting thou art fair.

For the sake of clearness little has been so far said of the thoughts of the mourner regarding the life beyond death. These thoughts touch two main subjects, the hope of reunion, and the desire that the dead friend should think of the living and

> *It appears then that the victory over sorrow portrayed in the poem is dependent upon a change in the love felt by the living for the dead, and upon a corresponding change in the idea of the dead."*

should even communicate with him. The recurrent speculations on the state of the dead spring from this hope and this desire. They recur less frequently as the soul advances in its victory. This does not mean that the hope of reunion diminishes or ceases to be essential to the mourner's peace and faith; but speculation on the nature both of this reunion and of the present life of the dead is renounced, and at last even abruptly dismissed. The singer is content to be ignorant and to wait in faith.

It is not quite so with the desire that the dead friend should now remember the living, and should even communicate with him. True, this desire is at one moment put aside without unhappiness, and it ceases to be an urgent and disturbing force. But long after the pining for the bodily presence has been overcome, it remains and brings with it pain and even resentment. It seems to change from a hope of 'speech' or 'converse' to a wish that the dead should in some way be 'near' to or 'touch' the living; and thus it suggests the important group of sections XC.–XCV. Here the poet even wishes at first for a vision; and although he at once reflects that neither this nor any other appeal to sense could convince him that the dead was really with him, he does not surrender either here or later the idea of some more immediate contact of souls. On the other hand, he is not sure that the idea is realised, nor does his uncertainty disturb his peace. What he desires while he remains on earth is contact with 'that which is,' the reality which is half revealed and half concealed by nature and man's earthly life, and which, by its contact, convinces him of the reason and love that rule the world; and, as now he thinks of his friend as 'living in God,' he neither knows nor seeks to know whether that which touches him is to be called the soul of his friend or by some higher name.

It appears then that the victory over sorrow portrayed in the poem is dependent upon a change in the love felt by the living for the dead, and upon a corresponding change in the idea of the dead. And some readers may even be inclined to think that the change is so great that at last the dead friend has really ceased to be to the living an individual person. He is, they will say, in some dim fashion 'mixed with God and Nature,' and as completely lost in 'the general soul' as is Adonais in Shelley's pantheistic poem: and so the poet's love for him has not merely changed, it has perished, and its place has been taken by a feeling as vaguely general and as little personal as the object to which it is directed. As my purpose is neither to criticise nor to defend the poet's ideas, but simply to represent them, I will confine myself to pointing out that the poem itself flatly denies the charge thus brought against it, and by implication denies the validity of the antitheses on which the charge rests. It is quite true that, as the poet advances, he abandons all attempts to define the life beyond death, and to form an image of his friend, 'whate'er he be.' It is quite true also that he is conscious that his friend, at once human and divine, known and unknown, far and near, has become something 'strange,' and is 'darklier understood' than in the old days of earthly life. But it is equally clear that to the poet his friend is not a whit less himself because he is 'mixed with God and Nature,' and that he is only 'deeplier loved' as he becomes 'darklier understood.' And if the hope of reunion is less frequently expressed as the sense of present possession gains in strength, there is nothing in the poem to imply that it becomes less firm as the image of reunion becomes less definite. The reader may declare that it ought to do so; he may apply to the experience here portrayed his customary notions of human and divine, personal and impersonal, individual and general; and he may argue that whatever falls under one of these heads cannot fall under the other. But whether his ideas and his argument are true or false, the fact is certain that for the experience portrayed in *In Memoriam* (and, it may be added, in *Adonais* also) they do not hold. For the poets the soul of the dead, in being mingled with nature, does not lose its personality; in living in God it remains human and itself; it is still the object of a love as 'personal' as that which was given to

> the touch of a vanished hand,
> And the sound of a voice that is still.

Source: A. C. Bradley, "The 'Way of the Soul,'" in *A Commentary on Tennyson's "In Memoriam,"* Archon Books, 1966, pp. 36–48.

Sources

Eliot, T. S., "*In Memoriam*," in *Tennyson: A Collection of Critical Essays*, edited by Elizabeth Francis, Prentice-Hall, 1980, p. 133, originally published in *Selected Essays*, Faber and Faber, 1932.

Marshall, George O., Jr., "Tennyson the Teacher," in *A Tennyson Handbook*, Twayne Publishers, 1963, p. 122.

Young, G. M., "The Age of Tennyson," in *Critical Essays on the Poetry of Tennyson*, edited by John Killham, Barnes & Noble, 1960, p. 25.

Further Reading

Campbell, Matthew, *Rhythm and Will in Victorian Poetry*, Cambridge University Press, 1999.
    Campbell devotes an entire chapter to *In Memoriam*, putting its structure into context with the works of Tennyson's contemporaries.

Kingsley, C., "On *In Memoriam* (1850) and Earlier Works," in *Tennyson: The Critical Heritage*, edited by John D. Jump, Barnes & Noble, 1967, pp. 172–85.
    Reading a review of Tennyson's long poem from the time period when it was published gives a sense of what a departure the poem was from Tennyson's usual style and how uncertain Tennyson's reputation was before *In Memoriam* sealed his fame.

Tennyson, Charles, and Christine Falls, *Alfred Tennyson: An Annotated Bibliography*, University of Georgia Press, 1967.
    This book-length bibliography is several decades old, but it is useful as a reference to many studies of the poet published in the nineteenth and early twentieth centuries.

Turner, Paul, *Tennyson*, Routledge and Kegan Paul, 1976.
    What distinguishes this work from many other book-length analyses of Tennyson is the way that Turner presents his thoroughly researched background information in a style that is easy to follow.

Seven Seeds

Jill Bialosky
2001

"Seven Seeds" is a key poem at a turning point of Jill Bialosky's second book of poetry, *Subterranean*, published in 2001. It represents a high point of carefully woven verse and powerful meditation on themes such as motherhood, grief, and desire, for a poet who is rapidly emerging as a new talent. Although Bialosky's poetry does not clearly fit into a particular movement, this poem and many others in *Subterranean* establish a thoughtful female voice concerned with themes that range from secretive and personal to provocative and innovative.

"Seven Seeds" is one of the most important poems in the poet's writing about death and desire because it so fully combines the major mythological reference of *Subterranean* with the personal exploration of the speaker. In fact, in order to fully understand the poem, the reader must identify its references to the ancient Greek myth of Persephone's abduction by Hades, god of the underworld. Particularly important is the section of the myth from which the title comes, when Persephone eats seven pomegranate seeds while captive in the underworld; because of this act, she can go to her mother Demeter, the earth-goddess, but must return to her place in the underworld as the wife of Hades for part of each year.

Combining this myth with personal experience and universal themes of death, birth, and desire, Bialosky provides a poem of great interest to a modern reader or student of poetry. "Seven Seeds" is an excellent example of the use of a "conceit," or an elaborate, extended metaphor, and an allusion to an important theme from ancient mythology. This conceit, employed to develop new and complex thoughts that are highlighted in this entry, is characteristic of a sophisticated and engaging poetic style.

Author Biography

Jill Bialosky was born in 1957 in Cleveland, Ohio. She put herself through Ohio University in Athens, Ohio, where she majored in English and took her first poetry workshop. Then she studied for her master of fine arts degree at Johns Hopkins University and moved back to Cleveland. While working as a waitress, Bialosky tried to write poetry in her spare time, but soon decided instead to enter the University of Iowa's Writers' Workshop, earning her masters of fine arts degree there.

Bialosky began her career as an editor, eventually becoming a poet and then a novelist. Her first book, a collection of poetry on themes such as childhood and motherhood called *The End of Desire*, was published in 1997. In 1998, she coedited a collection of stories and essays called *Wanting a Child*, which was partly inspired by the fact that two of her children died from premature birth. Returning to poetry, Bialosky authored a collection entitled *Subterranean* (2001), which includes "Seven Seeds" and other meditations on desire, grief, and motherhood.

Bialosky's poems have been published in journals such as *Paris Review*, *American Poetry Review*, *Agni Review*, and *New Republic*. In 2002, she published her first novel, *House Under Snow*, which tells the story of three daughters and a mother coping with the father's death. The novel has been very favorably reviewed.

Bialosky has received many awards, including the Elliot Coleman Award in poetry, and was a finalist for the James Laughlin Prize from the Academy of American Poets.

Poem Summary

Lines 1–2

The first two lines of "Seven Seeds" establish a straightforward "simile," or a comparison using "like" or "as." Placed in a "walk-up" (which simply refers to an apartment which requires ascending one or more flights of stairs to reach), the speaker of the poem likens herself to a bird and her apartment to a nest. This comparison suggests that the speaker might be pregnant because female birds are confined to their nests in order to guard their eggs. Since birth and motherhood are among the most central themes in this collection of poetry as well as this particular poem, Bialosky is careful to introduce them in the opening lines.

Lines 3–10

Lines 3 to 7 employ the poetic technique called personification, by attributing human qualities to a non-human, in this case a cherry tree. Leaves have veins, but they do not have arteries. So, the image in these lines, that of the speaker describing sunlight pressing against a window and filtering through a cherry tree, invokes a theme of reversal. It may appear to the reader that the sun is coming inside the window, into the veins and arteries of the speaker, until the context is reversed and the light is suddenly placed outside. The reader may then wonder why the light cannot enter the room, why the traditionally strong honeysuckle flower is fading, and why the vines are "perishing," which is a strong and dark word with which to end the first stanza. One important resonance of this image is that, unlike the timeless and confined apartment, the natural garden experiences time and death.

The first four lines of the second stanza then make a rapid shift to flashes of imagery of a fetus. Fine downy hair, or fetal "lanugo," is present only in the ninth month of pregnancy, so this baby is about to be born. It is important that Bialosky's diction, or choice of words, surrounding this fetal hair includes "sprouted" immediately after she has given plants qualities of people. The poet is introducing the concept of mingling between birth and death, plants and people, and mothers and daughters.

Lines 11–15

Lines 11 to 15 describe another rapid shift as the speaker describes the passing of seasons. Bialosky reinforces that the speaker constantly sits in her apartment watching the sky; the poet describes a gradual increase of warmth until the last word of the second stanza, "bright." This is in stark contrast to the decay of the first stanza. It is therefore interesting that the style of the second stanza is much more abrupt, with many periods and stoppages, than the flowing first stanza. The enjambment, which is the term for a thought running over into the next line, in the first stanza is much smoother as well. All of this suggests that there is something unique in Bialosky's idea of birth and entering the bright world, and that she is establishing a reversal of expectation that will become clearer later in the poem.

Lines 16–17

Lines 16 to 17 seem to be saying that the speaker sacrifices her safe, confined space for a peek at the bright world. It is unclear where she will peek and why Bialosky chooses the word "bargain." This is the first moment in the poem when it is necessary to understand the mythological context in order to make sense of what is happening in the narrative. The myth of Persephone is extremely important to the entire poem, and these lines allude to the point when Demeter bargains with Zeus and Hades for the release of her daughter. A summary of the myth is included below, in the historical and cultural context section. For the story in full, see Book Five of Ovid's *Metamorphoses*. At this point in "Seven Seeds," it seems that the speaker sees herself as Demeter and imagines her unborn daughter as Persephone. But, these lines are confusing because the speaker simultaneously must be envisioning herself as Persephone peeking out of her confinement; otherwise Bialosky would use "her confinement" instead of "my confinement."

Lines 18–21

The next lines, 18 to 21, envision the speaker descending from her apartment. They extend the confusion over which mythological figure the speaker considers most like herself. In the myth, only Persephone actually descends into Hades and is offered the pomegranate seeds, and the fruit tempts only Persephone. The walk downstairs presumably leads outside, into the bright world, but since it is a descent and involves the pomegranate Persephone eats in the underworld, it is still unclear where the speaker and the baby are moving and which part each of them plays in the myth.

Lines 22–25

Lines 22 to 25 increase the confusion as they imagine a "she" figure brought to her mother's "meadow" and away from the underworld. At line 22, by combining the daughter "she" from line 9 with the Persephone "she" that tastes the fruit, Bialosky has reached the turning point of her poem. The mythological has merged with the personal. The "she" refers most explicitly to Persephone, but there are strong hints that it refers also to both the unborn daughter leaving her "underworld" of her mother's womb, as well as the speaker herself in this role as the female tempted by the pomegranate, since she empathizes so completely with this feeling that she acts it out by descending from the walk-up to the bright outdoors.

Also important at this turning point in line 22 is the contradictory imagery. The literal image seems to place the "mother's warm-bedded meadow" as the garden from stanza 1, outside of the confined womb of the "underworld." But there is a subtle suggestion that this may be reversed because "warm-bedded" seems to refer to the nest and the womb itself, while the descent downstairs implies that the underworld is, paradoxically, the bright outdoors. This is a difficult place in the poem; it is hard to distinguish what is happening and which female is being born and tempted and endangered—but Bialosky seems to be deliberately engaging confusion while thinking about such themes as birth and desire. The poet is exploring an idea that is prevalent in many poems in *Subterranean*: the desirability of a place like the underworld for a figure like Persephone or an unborn child, and the desire of the mother to bring her daughter into a different kind of "warm-bedded" confined space.

Lines 26–27

In lines 26 and 27, the speaker continues to imagine what it would have been like for the Persephone figure to have been tempted by the pomegranate seeds. It is important to note, however, that the speaker is producing a unique version of the myth itself. Bialosky warns the reader to be suspicious at this point by placing "Without foreknowledge" as a forethought to "of her doom"; the visual organization of the poem is the opposite of its literal meaning, which is a form of irony because the poet means the opposite of what she says. Different versions of the myth imply that Persephone may have known that she could not eat food from the underworld if she wanted to leave it; and the speaker certainly seems to have foreknowledge of her own doom as she leaves her confinement.

Lines 28–32

Lines 28 to 32, still imagining the temptation of leaving the underworld, provide a visual and rhythmic echo to the meaning of the passage. As Persephone eats more and more seeds, the lines become longer and have more syllables until she has eaten all the seeds and her lips are stained. The fact that the seeds stain her lips "crimson" is a particularly evocative image. First of all, it connects in color to the cherry tree in stanza 1; red symbolizes a loss of innocence in line with the concept of falling into darkness. Additionally, it represents the blood (through "veins and arteries") of life, and by now the reader should realize that Bialosky is not necessarily interested in condemning this sort of desire; she has been overturning assumptions about what is considered desirable since the first stanzas.

Line 33

In line 33, a declaration of the bright light outside, Bialosky brings the question of desire into focus and begins to resolve the reader's confusion over what she is trying to communicate. The italicization of "was" sets the line apart with surprise and revelation. It also places the speaker's extended imagination of the Persephone figure's temptation in the past and prepares her for a current enlightenment. The speaker's own experience of temptation by the bright light of the garden, despite the decaying honeysuckle and vines, allows her to relate to her daughter. The speaker seems to be coming to understand her daughter's desire to leave the womb in relation to Persephone's temptation by the crimson pomegranate of the underworld and in relation to the speaker's own desire to leave her confined apartment. This is a complex view of desire, one that is related to death and the underworld, connected to the womb, and tied to a blood-red loss of innocence as well as a bright light connected to a hazy idea of the outside garden or "warm-bedded meadow."

Lines 34–36

Lines 34 to 36 establish the final simile of the poem, comparing the bright light of the speaker's desire to apple seeds when an apple is sliced open. The image of light in line 34 "shut now in my brain" provides a natural progression from line meditation on complex and inverted forms of desire in line 33; it calls into question whether light, meaning, birth, and desire are internal or external—a thought that sheds further insight on the question Bialosky has been raising about the meaning of pregnancy. Then, in line 36, the bright light of desire is represented by seeds, which connote (or make the reader think of) birth and regeneration. And the fact that the apple has "flesh" in the same line links, again through the technique of personification, Bialosky's thoughts to the first stanza's cherry tree.

Lines 37–38

In lines 37 and 38, the reader ponders the significance of exposing this apple star of meaning and desire "to the elements." It seems paradoxical that the same light "shut now in my brain" is being compared to something "cut open and exposed to the elements," but it begins to make sense when the reader considers the progression of the poem towards the garden. Bialosky has already established that this garden is a place of decay and a location not frozen or confined by timelessness, unlike the womb or the underworld. The bright light that the speaker has attempted to enclose and shut in her brain is moving out, in the simile itself, to the elements, just as the child is ready to be born into the natural world.

Lines 39–40

Lines 39 and 40 presumably refer to the unborn child, although of course she could not literally have planted any seeds. But perhaps more confusingly, they allude to a "mother's grief" that has not been established in the poem itself. Bialosky meditates throughout *Subterranean* on child suicide, child death, and death from premature birth, but it is unnecessary to stick firmly with one of these sources from the evidence in this poem. In fact, from what has taken place so far in "Seven Seeds," this grief seems more likely to come from the mother's hesitancy to release her unborn daughter into the decaying garden of life (and death). It remains unexplained, however, and this mother's grief could also refer to the poet's themes of unconfined versus confined desire.

Lines 41–42

In the final two lines of the poem, the simile of the star of apple seeds and bright desire receives a final twist: the seeds have been planted in the garden to grow. This is interesting because it makes the poet's thematic thinking about desire even more complex, as it turns the external meaning gone from closed in the speaker's brain to "exposed to the elements" and back again into something internal and growing. Bialosky merges her thoughts about birth and desire just as she merged Persephone and her daughter into a single, tempted being, and she manages to communicate a variety of complex insights about how these two ideas are secretly related in various internal and external spaces.

Themes

Birth and Motherhood

"Seven Seeds" is a poem about a pregnant woman and the thoughts of both Persephone and the speaker's unborn daughter reside in the imagination of the mother herself. So one of the main themes of the poem is the consciousness of this mother—particularly how she reflects on the process of birth. In part she does so by imagining herself in the role of the child, desiring to come out of the womb but also finding a temptation to stay in this dark, confined, timeless place. Persephone's story provides a way for the mother to access her daughter's thoughts, as well as suggesting a variety of thoughts about how birth is connected with desire and temptation.

The bond between mother and daughter is something on which Bialosky is meditating very carefully, but she is also exploring themes suggested by the mythological reference to Persephone's temptation in the underworld. The poet is interested in the process of birth in the psyche of the mother, for example. When the speaker of "Seven Seeds" imagines Persephone's temptation in the lines "soon she would be brought / back to her mother's warm-bedded / meadow and released / from the underworld," Bialosky is making observations both about how a mother understands the birth process and how creation in general relates to death, temptation, and desire. The result is not a rigid argument, but a series of evocative observations, images, and unlikely associations, which displays Bialosky's unique perceptions about birth and what it is like to be a mother.

Desire

One of the themes Bialosky examines most thoroughly throughout *Subterranean* is the question of what constitutes desire—desire in love, as a mother, as an artist, and as a general or unspecified temptation. The speaker of the poem seems to desire the bright light outdoors, but she is also tempted by the interior, confined, indoor space. Similarly, Persephone (in the imagination of the speaker) desires to break from her confined underworld at the same time she desires the pomegranate seeds. Bialosky is exploring the duality of desire before she goes on to tie it to the "veins and arteries" of the cherry tree and the "crimson" lips of the mythical figure having succumbed to temptation. Desire is established as a complex idea, both dangerous and divine, related to grief and death but also to growth and creation.

Style

Mythological Allusion

Mythological allusion is a vital element of "Seven Seeds." Bialosky uses it so pervasively because it serves as a helpful metaphor for current

Topics for Further Study

- "Seven Seeds" uses a mythological allusion to reflect on modern emotions and themes. Research some poems by other authors engaging the same technique, such as W. H. Auden's "The Shield of Achilles" (1952) or Sylvia Plath's "The Disquieting Muses" (1957). Do these poets, or others you have chosen, use a similar approach to Bialosky when alluding to mythology? How do they differ?

- Read *Subterranean*. How does "Seven Seeds" fit into the collection and upon what themes does it touch that are explored more fully in the work as a whole? What is its importance compared to other poems in the work? Choose some other poems and compare their style and content with "Seven Seeds."

- Write a paper in which you discuss contemporary poetry. Find a volume that surveys a variety of modern poets, then do some reading and defend the ones you find most important, meaningful, or enjoyable. Does Bialosky fit into a particular movement?

- Write a poem of your own that uses a mythological reference and then write a short piece defending your poetic decisions. What themes and emotions does your poem convey? Why did you choose that particular myth to convey them?

ideas; it also allows her to add her thoughts to an ancient debate on universal themes. The Demeter-Persephone myth provides the poet with a common basis that readers can understand and allows her to allude to a series of images and thoughts outside the restricted and relatively small world of her current work. She is thereby able to develop something more than a simple impression, something that comments on the fundamental assumptions and values of Western society. Alluding to mythology also adds a sense of timelessness and erudition to the work, although some readers may not be familiar with the myth or its contemporary associations.

Personification

As noted in the poem summary above, Bialosky sometimes imbues non-human objects with human characteristics. The two main examples of this occur in lines 4–5, when leaves are given "arteries," and in lines 36–37, when an apple is given "flesh." This poetic technique, called personification, is very important to the successful development of poet's themes, particularly the idea of blending, combining, and weaving characters and events. Personification enhances Bialosky's ability to underscore the melding of the worlds of the speaker, her daughter, and Persephone, because it melds character to place and makes identity more fluid. For example, the first instance of personification allows the reader to imagine that the arteries of the speaker are extending into the garden, and the second instance binds the child in a physical way to her mother's brain, as well as the garden. Personification also serves as a connecting point for these key ideas, since a similar stylistic technique makes the reader think of its other instance, particularly in a case such as this where both examples are tied to the garden.

The other reason this device is particularly suitable for "Seven Seeds" is that a key character in the poem, Demeter, is an inherent example of personification. The earth goddess is, in a sense, the "garden" imbued with human characteristics. Bialosky uses this fact to bring the worlds of the poem much closer; because the reader sees the speaker's arteries move into the garden, he/she immediately fuses the speaker with ideas related to Demeter. The poet then goes on to combine natural and human imagery by placing them so close together and by using such phrases as "warm-bedded / meadow" that combine earth and garden with motherhood and home.

Visual Construction

The key stylistic devices in "Seven Seeds" are the extended comparisons that overlap and form layers in order to provide a complex and carefully structured visual poem. The speaker begins by comparing herself to a bird "confined to her nest." Immediately after this transformation of a person to an animal is the personification, imbuing a cherry tree with arteries. Then the second stanza begins by giving plant qualities (with the word "sprouted") to an unborn child. These layers of comparison continue until the simile in the lines thirty-five to thirty-eight of a star of apple seeds being compared to a light in the speaker's brain.

All of these comparisons are carefully employed in order to highlight thematic considerations, and to create a visual sense of the ideas in the poem. There is so much overlap and layering because the speaker overlaps her identity with those of her unborn daughter and the mythical figure of Persephone. For example, when Persephone's lips are stained crimson, the poet is visually connecting them to the cherry tree and the apple and therefore, by simile, to the objects of desire connected to the garden. This is a complex relationship the poet purposefully creates in order to express her ideas about what is connected in theme; this technique allows Bialosky to make her most important observations. She melds characters and ideas to suit her meditations, which are themselves complex themes that blend together. Following the comparison and visual connection of words and ideas allows for a much fuller understanding of both the style and the meaning of the poem.

Historical Context

Although many of her poems refer to the Midwest American homeland of her youth, Bialosky is part of the contemporary writing scene in New York City. She teaches a poetry workshop at Columbia University and has an influential role as a high-profile editor in the large publishing company W. W. Norton. But "Seven Seeds" is not easily associated with any particular aesthetic or poetic movement. It has loose connections to postmodernism, an influential theoretical movement involving (among other elements) the abandonment of a traditional linear narrative. But this can be largely attributed to this theory's general influence on contemporary works; although the poem questions identity and jumps between time periods, it has no characteristics that strictly identify it as "postmodern."

The reader knows "Seven Seeds" takes place in a walk-up apartment with a garden outside, but he/she is given no other clear context. A variety of cultural speculations are available from the other poems in *Subterranean*, such as a resonance of Midwestern American life for an adolescent; nevertheless, the literal location of "Seven Seeds" is not specified. Perhaps this is partly because it allows more freedom for the speaker to enter an ancient mythological role-play. In fact, the most important historical and cultural background for the poem is the sustained classical reference in stanzas 3 and 4.

The Myth of Persephone and Demeter

Sources provide varying reasons why the god of the underworld, Hades, seized Persephone from the meadow where she was playing, and raped her. Some say it was because he was struck in love at the order of the goddess Aphrodite, and some say he asked his brother Zeus beforehand if he could do so. In any case, the girl's mother Demeter, goddess of agriculture, became frantic and rendered the earth cold and barren of crops while searching for her lost daughter. Demeter came to the pool through which Hades had entered the underworld, but the naiad Cyane, who used to live there, had been melted into a pool after trying to stop Hades from carrying down his victim, and could not tell Demeter what had happened. On the tenth day, however, Demeter discovered that Hades had captured Persephone and brought her to the underworld in his chariot. The original Homeric hymn states that she heard this from Helios, the sun god, but Ovid's text mentions that she found out from Arethusa, a lover of the river god Alpheus.

When Demeter learned of Persephone's abduction, she immediately appealed to Zeus that Hades bring her daughter back to her, saying (in *Metamorphoses*) that her daughter did not deserve to have a robber for a husband. Zeus agrees that she can be released, but on one condition: the fates have forbidden anyone from eating food in the underworld before they are returned above, so Persephone must not have had anything to eat while with Hades. Demeter soon learns, however, that her daughter has already eaten seven pomegranate seeds—either because Hades forced them into her mouth or because she was tempted of her own will. Persephone must therefore become the wife of Hades. But Demeter is too upset and the earth is too barren; so, not wishing to see the balance between mother and daughter destroyed, Zeus decides to make a compromise. He decrees that Persephone may return to her mother for part of the year (either one-half or one-third, depending on the source); and this is why Demeter only allows crops to grow for part of the year.

Fountain of Persephone in Pozan, Poland

Bialosky's "varied and original" aesthetic, and presents a list of the poet's ambitious thematic goals, including "Desire, virginity, fertility and motherhood, . . . the passions of her life before children, the seductions of suicide, and the comforts of art."

Not all commentary has been solely positive. A *Publishers Weekly* critic points out that Bialosky's tendency to focus on the ground of conventional wisdom is not very compelling: "The poems work this ground with manic insistence, and, despite the fervid effort, harvest insights that are curiously banal." It goes on to claim that the collection is of "topical interest," and predicts that it will gather a good deal of attention in part because of Bialosky's high regard as an editor at W. W. Norton. A more long-term critical response remains to be seen.

Critical Overview

Bialosky's *Subterranean* has been generally quite favorably reviewed. Critics such as the well-known Harold Bloom are quoted on the back of the collection itself with superlatives about her voice and style. In *Library Journal*, Louis McKee praises

Criticism

Scott Trudell

Trudell is a freelance writer with a bachelor's degree in English literature. In the following essay, Trudell discusses Bialosky's unique use of the Demeter-Persephone myth in her poem.

The myth of Demeter and Persephone has been significant to American women's writing since the late nineteenth century. It provided a common groundwork for certain types of female artistic thinking during the industrial revolution, including the search for a feminine voice and identity within a male-dominated world. Josephine Donovan writes in her book *After the Fall: The Demeter-Persephone Myth in Wharton, Cather, and Glasgow* that the myth "allegorizes the transformation from a matricentric preindustrial culture—Demeter's realm—to a male-dominated capitalist-industrialist ethos, characterized by growing professionalism and bureaucracy: the realm of patriarchal captivity;" to the authors in the title, the ancient story was an appropriate metaphor for the female experience at this time of social upheaval. Donovan's book goes on to describe how authors such as these formed a tradition of interpreting the myth.

Bialosky, writing over a hundred years later, inevitably works out of this tradition as well. Her emphasis throughout *Subterranean* on the story of Demeter and her daughter is connected to this precedent for American female authors, and there are a variety of reasons why the myth is appropriate for Bialosky's poetic goals. One is the very personal element of her self-expression, in which the death of a child is a persistent theme; Bialosky lost two children to premature birth and has written about it in the collection of stories and essays she coedited, *Wanting a Child*. There is a sense in many of the poems in *Subterranean*, including "Seven Seeds," that she is thinking about the loss of a child, although in many cases she seems to be putting this death theme in the context of adolescent suicide as opposed to premature birth. In any case, in order to combine her personal interests with universalities related to birth, death, and desire, Bialosky consistently employs a unique and complexly layered version of the Persephone myth.

"Seven Seeds" comes at a particularly fragile moment in *Subterranean*, immediately after a prolonged exploration into the intimate connection between desire and death and a meditation on the creation and birth process. By the time the reader comes to "Seven Seeds," these themes have been assigned a complex and often ambiguous, yet carefully established, place within the Persephone "conceit" (or extended comparison). The first poems in the section rapidly shift from the mythological to the modern portrayal of a teenage girl figure, and Bialosky begins to establish a connection among chaos, pain, and creation; in "The Wrath of the Gods," the gods "decree that out of abundance / was pain, and from suffering / perhaps one day a child." "The Fate of Persephone" extends this idea and establishes the meaning of this myth in other contexts by stressing in the first section that "fruits / of the orchard, / flourished" only when Demeter "was full of her," which implies that Persephone is still within the womb and therefore that creation and fruition must be confined in order to be meaningful.

Bialosky is carefully setting up her ideas about birth and creation in passages such as these. A similar meditation continues in "The Circles, the Rings," as the speaker gets closer and closer to the beauty of artistic creation only by making increasingly perilous circles and rings in the ice. As before, this image of birth and creation is both very dangerous and very sexual: "so lost in the thrust and *glide, glide, glide*, the noxious, delirious, / blinding rhythm." This thinking becomes increasingly urgent until "Temptation," the poem immediately preceding "Seven Seeds," connects sexual imagery like "take possession" and "stab / so severe it sliced into the center / of my being" with creation, birth, and art.

These images and extended associations are extremely important to the meditation on captivity and confinement on the part of the speaker, her daughter, and Persephone, in "Seven Seeds." The poem dramatizes a journey out of confinement for both mother and daughter that is simultaneously a journey of artistic creation. This new and exciting birth, the bright light compared to a star of apple seeds and possibly the object of the mysterious "For one small peek" line beginning the third stanza, is such an important resonance of Bialosky's carefully chosen mythological metaphor because it perfectly suits her idea of the pomegranate seeds. Planted in the garden, these seven seeds comprise not just the simplistic submission to temptation in a more traditional version of the myth; they represent a complex and ambiguous host of ideas related simultaneously to birth, desire, death, and artistic creation.

Again, Bialosky has been developing the significance of her mythological allusion, with a unique emphasis, throughout the collection and particularly in section three. For example, Persephone herself (although this is not at all implicit in the traditional myth) is established in the second section of "The Fate of Persephone" to be "a girl too eager / for love"; this implies that she is either complicit in Hades's abduction or aroused by it in some way. The mythical daughter of Demeter, like the teenage girls in "The Fall" and "Adolescent Suicide," has some preconceived ideas about what she desires and what she will allow to stain "her lips crimson," as it is described in "Seven Seeds."

Indeed, Bialosky is establishing the womb and its double, the underworld, as the locations of desire and excitement. In "The Fall," it is "the eerie cavern of the backseat of a boy's car" where "Desire was indistinguishable from suffering"; this "eerie cavern" represents the underworld and will come back with further significance as the desire in "Seven Seeds" becomes indistinguishably connected to the suffering of the mother, the daughter, and the mythical figure of Persephone. "The Fall" goes on: "It was all this we ever wanted / offered up like a shiny pomegranate"; this more explicitly ties Bialosky's thoughts about the temptation of a young girl, or Persephone, to these pomegranate seeds. As with the previous examples illustrating Bialosky's process of assigning meaning to her idiosyncratic version of the myth, the poet continues to treat the seeds as "all this we ever wanted"—an excess of desire signifying both creation and death—in "Seven Seeds." They retain this ambiguity and serve as Persephone's ticket to straddling the world of desire (the underworld of her violent husband) and the "warm-bedded / meadow" of her mother.

Having illustrated such connections by the end of section three, the poet is free to experiment with further layers and twists on her associations in "Seven Seeds." Bialosky has already brought up the tendency for overbearing power on the part of the mother-figure, or Demeter, in "The Fate of Persephone," where the word "rape" inverts the savior mother with the evil abductor Hades: "(not even her mother / who raped the earth / in grief)." In "Seven Seeds," this inversion and experimentation with role-playing in the mythological allusion goes even further; the mother enacts her daughter's journey out of the womb and places herself in the role of Persephone, and eventually the daughter takes the role of her mother and the Demeter figure by planting the pomegranate seeds in the garden. This experimentation deeply complicates the mythological metaphor and throws into question which figure is creating, which is being tempted, which is dying, and which is being born.

In this complex meditation, Bialosky is building on and even overturning some of the common elements of this mythological tradition that goes back to authors like Edith Wharton. Josephine

> "Planted in the garden, these seven seeds comprise not just the simplistic submission to temptation in a more traditional version of the myth; they represent a complex and ambiguous host of ideas related simultaneously to birth, desire, death, and artistic creation."

Donovan goes on in her description of the use of this myth in nineteenth-century female writing: "Persephone represents the daughters who leave the sphere of the mothers and enter a period of patriarchal captivity, sealed by the eating of the pomegranate seed—which emblematizes the betrayal of the mothers." Bialosky makes some vital alterations to the traditional formula of the myth; daughters may enter a period of "patriarchal captivity," but by the end of "Seven Seeds" the daughter figure is planting the seeds of artistic creation herself. As the mother leaves the confined space of the protector and Demeter figure, envisioning herself as Persephone, the daughter is able (after some close calls with death, suicide, and temptation) to become "ignorant / of a mother's grief" and empowered in a way that the mother is not. Indeed, this final twist, during which the daughter takes seeds traditionally representing a fall into "patriarchal captivity" to be the seeds of her own creative powers, is such an interesting and meaningful way out of the world of the poem because it places the child into an active and creative position. Persephone has made her way out of the confined space of her mother's womb, (implicitly) out of her mother's confined poetic meditation, and out of the underworld of patriarchal captivity, into an entirely new creative space.

Source: Scott Trudell, Critical Essay on "Seven Seeds," in *Poetry for Students*, Gale, 2003.

Ryan D. Poquette

Poquette has a bachelor's degree in English and specializes in writing about literature. In the following essay, Poquette discusses Bialosky's use of imagery, symbolism, and allusion to underscore the impact of a woman's miscarriage.

Bialosky's "Seven Seeds" is a poem that encourages readers to dig deeper. When the poem begins, it is very cryptic. Even as it progresses and Bialosky gives sporadic clues about the poem's main theme, readers may not understand what the poet is telling them. It is only at the end, when the speaker reveals that she is reflecting on the death of her child the previous day that readers realize the speaker is talking about her recent miscarriage. Even if readers do not understand completely what Bialosky is describing as they read the poem, the vivid imagery keeps them hooked. It is this imagery, coupled with associated symbols and an effective allusion to a classical myth, which ultimately underscores the miscarriage theme and gives it maximum impact.

"Seven Seeds" is a poem about motherhood, a fact that is not readily apparent at the beginning of the poem. With her use of vivid imagery, Bialosky gives her readers steady clues throughout the poem. These images fall into one of four categories: fertility, motherhood and birth, life, and death. All these categories complement each other. Bialosky does not use these image systems in the order described above, which is the normal order of the life cycle. If Bialosky were to do this, the poem would be relatively straightforward, and readers who recognized the cycle might be able to guess that the poem is going to end with a death. Instead, Bialosky is very clever, weaving images from each category into the poem in various places and slowly building up to the revelation of her miscarriage.

The idea of fertility is highlighted from the very beginning with the poem's title: "Seven Seeds." Although the reader does not know what the seeds refer to at this point, seeds are a universal symbol for fertility and the beginning of growth. A symbol is a physical object, action, or gesture that also represents an abstract concept, without losing its original identity. Symbols appear in literature in one of two ways. They can be local symbols, meaning that their symbolism is derived only from within the context of a specific literary work. Symbols can also be universal, as the seeds are in this poem. The idea of seeds representing the beginning of growth is a traditional association that is widely recognized, regardless of context.

After the seed symbol in the title, Bialosky includes several other fertility images in the poem, most of which share the organic associations of the title. For example, in the first stanza, the speaker talks about "the cherry tree / in the little garden." A garden is typically thought of as a symbol of fertility because it is the site of creation and growth. This classical association dates back to the very beginning of humanity, even to the biblical account of the Garden of Eden and the creation of all life. Although the speaker seems to be casually observing the cherry tree, Bialosky is aware of these strong associations and is using them to underscore the depth of the woman's despair over her miscarriage. The speaker has been "confined to her nest" for several months during her pregnancy. After her miscarriage, she looks out her window and prepares to go outside. What does she see outside the window? A vibrant cherry tree in a garden. Seeing this symbol of fertility adds insult to the woman's injury over not being able to witness the birth of her own offspring.

If the reader has any doubt that this poem is about the intended birth of the speaker's child, the second stanza clears that up. The imagery in this stanza is direct and gives the reader a picture of a fetus growing inside its mother's womb. Again, the words that Bialosky uses, such as "sprouted," tie into the very natural, organic associations that she set up with her seeds and garden symbolism.

Although this child has not been born yet and never will be, the speaker does include some images that underscore the idea of life. For example, in the first stanza, the speaker watches the sun through the windows and notes that it is filtered through the "veins and arteries / on the leaves of the cherry tree." The speaker is describing the leaf in a human-like fashion, which again underscores the fact that the leaves on the tree are living, while her child is not.

The references to the tree lead to the most potent imagery in the poem, the imagery of death. Throughout the poem, the speaker includes subtle references to death, starting with the first description of the garden. While the cherry tree is alive, the honeysuckle is "fading" and the vines are "slowly perishing." These images indicate the impending death of these plants and specifically their death as the result of the encroaching winter season. It is shortly after this discussion of dying plants that the speaker chooses to start talking about her fetus, which she describes in the present tense, as if the fetus is still alive. This is significant, as it indicates that, while the fetus is dead, the miscarriage is too fresh in the speaker's mind and she is having a hard time letting go.

Dark thoughts start to creep into the speaker's mind. In addition to the death imagery in the garden, the speaker also invokes other images of death, most of them associated with a very potent allusion to the mythological figure of Persephone, who is also sometimes referred to as Proserpina or Proserpine. Although the specific details of the myth vary depending upon the source, the basic story of Persephone concerns her abduction by Hades (also known as Pluto), the god of the underworld. Persephone is the daughter of Demeter, the goddess of agriculture. When Demeter learns of her daughter's abduction, she is so distraught that she does not attend to her agricultural duties, and crops die. Although Demeter appeals to Zeus, who tells Hades that he must release Persephone, Hades tricks Persephone into eating a pomegranate in the underworld. Like Eve's eating of the apple in the biblical account of the Garden of Eden, Persephone's act has dire consequences. In her case, she now must live with Hades in the underworld for part of the year and can then live with her mother for the rest of the year. Most attribute this myth to the classical need to describe the seasonal renewal of life in the agricultural cycle, where crops are planted and grown in one part of the year, while the fields lie barren during the remainder of the year.

In the poem, Bialosky uses this classical allusion to great effect. The speaker starts talking about Persephone in the third stanza. "I know what it must have been like, to see the fruit held out," she says. Just as she is subtle in placing her image systems, Bialosky is also subtle in her allusions to Persephone. She never mentions the goddess by name. Instead, Bialosky uses oblique references to the Persephone myth to build on the poem's already established organic imagery. As a result, when the speaker talks about Persephone being returned to "her mother's warm-bedded / meadow and released / from the underworld," the reference has two meanings. Literally, the poet is describing Persephone's return from the underworld to the world that her mother controls. Yet, a "warm-bedded meadow," especially when it is referred to in a motherhood sense, is also a reference to a woman's womb, in this case, the womb of the speaker.

When the passage is viewed in this way, "the underworld" also takes on different connotations. In Greek and Roman mythology, the underworld is the land of the dead, where people go after they die. Bialosky flips this idea around. If a "warm-bedded / meadow" is an expectant mother's womb, then the "underworld" becomes the place that precedes the development of a human fetus in that womb. In other words, the speaker is referring to her unborn baby's development and saying that her unborn baby probably expects that it will soon take on human form and travel to the land of the living. One can find support for this idea by examining the second stanza. The speaker goes to great lengths to describe the development of her unborn fetus, listing specific details such as "downy hair" and "fetal lungs." Her focus on these human features, which the unborn fetus will now never develop, underscores the fact that her baby was at some threshold between life (the womb) and pre-life (the underworld) when the speaker had her miscarriage.

In the fourth stanza, the speaker continues her allusion to Persephone, talking about the fact that Persephone did not have "foreknowledge / of her doom" when she ate the seeds of the pomegranate.

What Do I Read Next?

- *Subterranean* (2001), the collection of poems from which "Seven Seeds" is drawn, should perhaps be read as a whole in order to fully appreciate any of its individual poems. The collection is a fluid and lyrical meditation on many of the themes discussed above.

- Book 5 of Ovid's *Metamorphoses* (1955), translated from the first-century Latin by Rolfe Humphries, provides one of the most compelling and readable versions of the Demeter-Persephone myth.

- Bialosky's first book of poems, *The End of Desire* (1997), is a sophisticated and thoughtful work, like her second collection, and is perhaps more intensely biographical.

- Edith Wharton's famous novel *The House of Mirth* (1905) employs the Demeter-Persephone myth to describe Lily Bart's downfall from high society.

> "Although the speaker says the seeds of the unborn child are being planted, they are really being buried."

Again, Bialosky is subtle and does not indicate that she is talking about a fruit, or that the fruit is a pomegranate. She expects that her readers will pick up on the allusion to Persephone eating the pomegranate. Because she does not name the fruit, Bialosky is able to create an even greater impact with her imagery. In the literal sense, she is describing Persephone eating the pomegranate, "the juice staining her lips crimson." Since a pomegranate is red inside, one could easily assume that Bialosky is referring only to the fruit's natural juice. Yet, just as the other references to Persephone have double meanings, so does this passage, a fact that can be determined from Bialosky's use of the word, "crimson." While crimson is another word for red, it is more commonly associated with blood. Since this poem is about a woman's miscarriage, the crimson juice of the fruit becomes a graphic reference to the speaker's own miscarriage.

The speaker continues this pattern later in the same stanza, when she discusses the "seeds inside the flesh / of an apple when it is cut / open and exposed to the elements." Again, she could just be talking about somebody slicing open an apple. But, within the context of this poem about miscarriage, the seeds indicate the speaker's unborn child. With the loss of her child, the speaker is in so much pain that she feels as if she has been cut open and her insides have been exposed. Although this is not literally true, one can see why the speaker chooses to use such words. Her unborn child was up until recently inside her, and therefore a part of her. Now, this child is dead and outside the speaker's body, where it is exposed to the elements.

As she does in the beginning, Bialosky uses a gardening image at the end of her poem. She notes that her child "took those seeds / and planted them in the garden." Again, Bialosky is reversing the symbolism that people have come to expect. As noted above, gardens are generally associated with fertility and life. Bialosky's clever use of death imagery and symbolism throughout the poem, as well as the Persephone allusion, indicate to the reader that there is going to be no birth here. Although the speaker says the seeds of the unborn child are being planted, they are really being buried. The speaker blames this on the unborn child itself, who is "ignorant / of a mother's grief," just as Persephone was ignorant of Demeter's profound grief. The speaker's unborn child will remain forever in seed form, never growing, as a result of the speaker's miscarriage, which halted the fetus's growth and development. Just as the garden in the beginning of the poem is starting to die, so is the garden at the end of the poem a garden that is focused on death, not life. Like Persephone, the speaker's child must return to the pre-life underworld. Unlike Persephone, however, the speaker's child will never return to the land of the living.

Source: Ryan D. Poquette, Critical Essay on "Seven Seeds," in *Poetry for Students*, Gale, 2003.

Sources

Bialosky, Jill, *Subterranean*, Knopf, 2001.

Donovan, Josephine, *After the Fall: The Demeter-Persephone Myth in Wharton, Cather, and Glasgow*, Pennsylvania State University Press, 1989, pp. 1–7.

McKee, Louis, Review of *Subterranean*, in *Library Journal*, December 2001, p. 130.

Review of *Subterranean*, in *Publishers Weekly*, December 17, 2001, p. 85.

Further Reading

Downing, Christine, ed., *Long Journey Home: Revisioning the Myth of Demeter and Persephone for Our Time*, Shambhala Publications, 2001.

> A collection of impressions about the Demeter-Persephone story, this work offers an interesting blend of fact and fiction about the ways in which the myth is important today.

Friebert, Stuart, David Walker, and David Young, eds., *A Field Guide to Contemporary Poetry and Poetics*, Oberlin College Press, 2001.

> The impressive range of poets contributing to this book provides it with a broad and thorough insight into the many elements of modern poetry.

Hardie, Phillip, ed., *The Cambridge Companion to Ovid*, Cambridge University Press, 2002.

> This critical text provides important historical information and commentary about the Roman author,

including his version of the Demeter-Persephone myth.

Homer, *The Homeric Hymn to Demeter: Translation, Commentary, and Interpretive Essays*, edited by Helene Foley, Princeton University Press, 1994.

    This edition of the most ancient source of the Demeter-Persephone myth provides helpful background and analytical material for the main mythological reference in "Seven Seeds."

Social Life

Tony Hoagland

1999

Tony Hoagland's poetry focuses primarily on contemporary issues in middle and upper class America, especially in middle class suburbia. His personal experience in this environment sometimes shows up in poems as straightforward autobiography and other times manifests itself in a generic "you" or "they" address, suggesting a shared experience within an entire generation. From politics and adultery to religion and sex, Hoagland's themes often resound of daytime talk shows and evening news, but the poems are also lined with an undercurrent of self-reflection and disillusionment, anger and hope. "Social Life," which first appeared in the spring 1999 issue of *Ploughshares*, aptly expresses the poet's take on contemporary society and behavior—here, in the form of party goers—but also offers an unusual shift in setting for his work. Typically content to deal with the material, plastic world of things and the people who use them, Hoagland searches for something different in "Social Life," something found only in the serenity, beauty, and wonder of the natural world.

Author Biography

Tony Hoagland was born Anthony Dey Hoagland on November 19, 1953, in Fort Bragg, North Carolina. Very little biographical information as of 2003 was available on Hoagland, yet scholars of his work point to various known autobiographical po-

ems that help draw a slim profile of him. Growing up in white, middle-class American suburbia—a theme in much of his poetic work—Hoagland seems to have been at odds with the wholesale materialism of his environment, viewing it with both cynicism and a desire to understand it. While his parents were able to provide him a comfortable childhood in the physical and monetary sense, Hoagland's poems tell the story of emotional upheavals within the family that mere money could not make up for. Apparently, his father intentionally ruined his own marriage (thus the title of Hoagland's first full-length collection, *Sweet Ruin*) and then died of a heart attack a short time later. At seventeen, the young poet lost his mother to cancer. Events at home, however, did not deter him from pursuing a college education, and he attended Williams College and the University of Iowa, eventually earning his master of fine arts degree at the University of Arizona in 1983. Not long after, Hoagland began a career in teaching English and poetry and has taught at several colleges and universities over the past two decades, including Arizona Western College, St. Mary's College in California, the University of Maine, and Warren Wilson College in North Carolina. Hoagland has also served on the English faculty at the University of Pittsburgh.

Though the quantity of Hoagland's publications has been relatively small, the quality of his work has not gone unnoticed. Between 1985 and 1990, he published three chapbooks of poems and turned some of the material in those books into *Sweet Ruin*, which was selected by poet Donald Justice as the winner of the Brittingham Prize in 1992. Hoagland's second collection, *Donkey Gospel: Poems*, was awarded the James Laughlin Award in 1997 and was published by Graywolf Press the following year. "Social Life" was published in 1999 in *Ploughshares*, the literary magazine of Emerson College in Boston. This poem was expected to be included in revised form in Hoagland's collection scheduled for publication in the fall of 2003.

Tony Hoagland

Poem Text

After the party ends another party begins
and the survivors of the first party climb
into the second one as if it were a lifeboat
to carry them away from their slowly sinking ship.

Behind me now my friend Richard   5
is getting a fresh drink, putting on more music
moving from group to group—smiles and
jokes, laughter, kissy-kiss—

It is not given to me to understand
the social pleasures of my species, but I think   10
what he gets from these affairs
is what bees get from flowers—a nudging of the stamen,

a sprinkle of pollen
about the head and shoulders—

whereas I prefer the feeling of going away, going   15
   away,
stretching out my distance from the voices and the lights
until the tether breaks and I

am in the wild sweet dark
where the sea breeze sizzles in the hedgetop
and the big weed heads whose names I never   20
   learned
lift and nod upon their stalks.

What I like about the trees is how
they do not talk about the failure of their parents
and what I like about the grasses is that
they are not grasses in recovery   25

and what I like about the flowers is
that they are not flowers in need of
empowerment or validation. They sway

upon their thorny stems
as if whatever was about to happen next tonight   30
was sure to be completely interesting—

the moon rising like an ivory tusk,
a few funky molecules of skunk

strolling through the air
to mingle with the aura of a honeysuckle bush,   35

and when they bump together in my nose,
I want to raise my head and sing,
*I'm a child in paradise again
when you touch me like that, baby,*

but instead, I stand still and listen   40
to the breeze departing from the upper story of a
    tree
and the hum of insects in the field,
letting everything else have a word, and then
    another word,

because silence is always good manners
and often a clever thing to say   45
when you are at a party.

Poem Summary

Lines 1–4

The first line of "Social Life" creates a tempo for the early part of the poem, almost begging to be read in a slow, monotonous tone in order to mimic the boringly repetitive behavior of typical party goers. One can hear the dreariness of routine in the voice of the speaker whose description of the party seems to say that after one thing ends, more of the same begins. The speaker adds to the already dismal scene by comparing the socialites to "survivors" of a boat wreck and the party they have been attending to the "slowly sinking ship" they managed to escape. The new party that starts is a "lifeboat" for the survivors of the first gathering, though one can easily imagine that it, too, will become a sinking ship before long.

Lines 5–8

These lines portray the activities at the party in more detail, and, again, there is an acute sense of treadmill behavior, of people doing expected things in expected manners while speaking expected words. The speaker's "friend Richard" is a model of the typical suburban socialite who circulates among party guests with "a fresh drink" in his hand, sharing small talk and gossip while everyone pretends to enjoy the chitchat. The phrase "moving from group to group" reminds one that party crowds often splinter into little cliques of guests, and the "smiles," "jokes," and "laughter" they emit are doubtfully genuine, particularly when an act as artificial and spurious as "kissy-kiss" is included. The notion of such idle chatter reappears at the end of the poem and lays the foundation for one of its most important themes.

Lines 9–10

These lines introduce the speaker for the first time as an "I," and the personal sentiment they reveal separates him from the rest of the usual party goers. He claims that it is "not given" to him to "understand / the social pleasures" of his entire "species," putting quite a distance between himself and those who share a common background with him. But, in citing his "species," the speaker does not really mean the entire human race, for the significant word here is "my." Rather, he refers to typical American suburbanites who have experienced a very similar environment and lifestyle as his own. Perhaps the last two words of line 10 also suggest a significant difference between the speaker and his more shallow peers—he is actually in a position to say, "I think."

Lines 11–14

These lines bring nature into the picture for the first time. In trying to understand how such seemingly pointless social behavior can be pleasurable for some people, the speaker compares this behavior to that of bees who extract pollen from flowers just to "sprinkle" a bit of it "about the head and shoulders." Obviously, the relationship between bees and flowers is not so frivolous—they depend on one another for procreation—but the implication here is that party goers who move from one group to another are actually seeking some sense of purpose, some excitement or broadening of their lives, even if it is only short-lived.

Lines 15–16

The distance between the speaker and the other party guests increases in these lines as he claims to "prefer the feeling of going away, going away" over listening to the petty banter, sincere or not, droning on all around him. The repetition of the phrase "going away" helps to emphasize distance, as does the notion of "stretching out." What the speaker wants to get away from are "the voices and the lights" that overwhelm most loud parties. The reference to "voices" and mindless chatter reiterate the sentiment in lines 7 and 8 about hollow conversations.

Lines 17–18

In line 17, the speaker implies that being at the party is like being trapped or tied down and that he must struggle with his bonds "until the tether breaks" and he is free—metaphorically speaking, of course. In reality, his body remains among the hubbub of music and chitchat and drinking, but his imagination has escaped to the "wild sweet dark" where the sounds in his ears are much different from those that inundate the party.

Lines 19–21

These three lines present a striking change of scenery, describing facets of nature that are simple and beautiful in their own right. In his mind, the speaker exchanges the din of party noises for the soothing sound of a "sea breeze" that "sizzles in the hedgetop," and he imagines tall weeds swaying in the gentle wind. In admitting that he "never learned" the names of the plants, he exposes his suburban roots again and implies that this ignorance is another malady of his "species."

Lines 22–28

These seven lines contain three parallel metaphors that contrast the nature of trees and grasses and flowers to the nature of human beings. With both cynicism and wit, the speaker manages to make his point—innocent plants are surely superior to phony people—without ever mentioning party goers or suburbanites or even humans specifically. Instead, he ridicules whiny party guests for how they are by praising the plants for how they are not. Trees are likable because "they do not talk about the failure of their parents." Obviously, the speaker has attended more than one gathering at which other guests complained about worthless mothers and fathers. He takes a sarcastic stab at self-professed alcoholics or addicts of one kind or another by lauding the grasses because "they are not grasses in recovery." Again, this is a response to too many unsolicited confessions from strangers at parties—strangers often seeking attention or sympathy by playing the oh-pitiful-me role. Finally, what the speaker likes about the flowers is that "they are not flowers in need of / empowerment or validation." That is, nature does not need praise or approval from humans to feel worthy about itself. Nature requires nothing of the speaker, demands nothing of him, unlike the party guests. The speaker is free to be silent in nature, appreciating the simplicity and grace of the flowers and trees. Furthermore, the speaker is free to be among the trees and grasses without feeling that he is being judged or needs to demand "validation" from them.

Lines 29–31

In these lines, the speaker furthers his idea of nature's superiority over certain human behaviors by implying that, within nature, things truly are

Media Adaptations

- A recording titled *Lunch Poems, Tony Hoagland, 10/7/99* (1999) was produced by the University of California, Berkeley, as a part of its monthly noon-time poetry reading series.

- The *Ploughshares* online literary journal at http://www.pshares.org/ as of 2003 links to twenty-four of its articles by or about Hoagland. These pages contain Hoagland's poems, reviews he has written, and articles in which he is mentioned by other poets and critics.

"completely interesting." Even the swaying flowers can anticipate and trust that "whatever was about to happen next" would be a genuine marvel of the natural world—just the opposite of the artificial compliments and feigned interest that permeate the human world of social interaction.

Lines 32–35

These lines provide exquisite examples of what is so remarkably and totally "interesting" about nature. For the first time, animals—other than man—are drawn into the picture with the crescent moon rising "like an ivory tusk" of an elephant and the "funky" odor of skunk "molecules" wafting through the air. The musty smell creates a wonderful contrast "with the aura of a honeysuckle bush" as the two scents "mingle" unimpeded in their natural environment.

Lines 36–39

These lines likely reflect back on the actual events of the party, particularly the music and typical sing-along by some guests. What makes the speaker so joyful he could "raise [his] head and sing" is the mixture of nature's raw odors "bump[ing] together" in his nose. The italicized lines appear as though they are lyrics to a song and their contemporary slang provides an apt irony to the setting, considering that they describe a man's gleeful union with nature, not a romantic encounter with another human being.

Lines 40–43

In these lines, the speaker draws closer to the central theme of the poem, opting to "stand still and listen" instead of singing his own tune out loud. What he hears is very comforting to him—the breeze blowing through the "upper story of a tree," the "hum of insects in the field"—but there is something else remarkable about these natural sounds: they take turns. The breeze blows, the bugs hum, and then something else chimes in and still something else after that, each one "letting everything else have a word, and then another word." This, then, is the ultimate illustration of the difference between the natural word and the human.

Lines 44–46

The last three lines of the poem provide a witty final blow to the common social life of men and women in contemporary suburban America. While maintaining one's "silence" in order to listen to someone else is "always good manners," it is a rare occasion at a loud party often filled with people who would rather hear themselves talk than anyone else. With this in mind, the speaker playfully suggests that coming right out and saying, "Silence is always good manners," at a party would add a clever twist to the event, even if its wry irony is lost on many of the revelers.

Themes

Self-Absorption

"Social Life" is not an enigmatic poem that attempts to hide its intended themes or disguise the message with irrelevant twists and esoteric metaphors. Instead, it very plainly makes two major points, the most dominant being human self-absorption and its pathetic results. The speaker's target is his own world, so he does not vainly exonerate himself from criticism but rather acknowledges his role within this world and admits that he is sometimes as guilty as the rest. But guilty of what? Largely, too much ego. While it is not fair to stereotype every individual who attends parties and other social gatherings, there is enough evidence of some typical behavior among certain factions to warrant the scrutiny. Most people have witnessed guests—and been guilty themselves—making the obligatory rounds at a party, with or without a drink in hand, oozing small talk, and pretending to be interested in what other people are saying when there is no genuine interest at all. Most people, too, have turned the tables at the first opportunity to begin talking about themselves, as though their own opinions, complaints, and platitudes are of more value than anything they have just heard. These are the people in Hoagland's poem. They mingle and drink, listen to music and chat, and tell jokes that may or may not be funny but everyone pretends that they are. The speaker's "friend Richard" is like the everyman of the contemporary suburban party scene—he moves "from group to group," smiling, laughing, joking, and planting insincere kisses on the cheeks (or just in the air) of people who act as if it is delightful. And though the speaker is present at the party, and therefore plays his own role in the charade, he cannot help but question the "social pleasures of [his] species."

Probably the greatest irony about being self-centered is that those who are guilty of it often point it out in everyone else but cannot see it in themselves. The party goers in "Social Life" complain about their parents, wear their "in recovery" status like it is a badge, and whine about not having any "empowerment or validation" in their lives. Amidst all the talk, no one is listening. The "good manners" of silence are lost in the din of self-absorbed chatter, and the result is a pathetic portrayal of life in middle class, suburban America: much materialism and ego, but even greater emptiness.

Nature in Suburban America

The other prominent theme in this poem is the role—or lack thereof—of nature in the suburbs. Surely, it exists, but many suburbanites do not seem to be aware of it. This point is seen most clearly in the marked contrast between the descriptions of the party indoors and those of the natural world outside. The speaker emphasizes the vast distance between them in his "going away, going away" to reach nature, which may consist only of flowers, trees, and weeds in somebody's yard, but it still provides a refreshing change of scenery. Whether the sea breeze, rising moon, or insects humming in a field are actually real or just a part of his imagination does not matter. What does matter is that the party guests do not appear to recognize nature, real or imagined. Even the speaker, who is also a product of the suburban environment, admits that he "never learned" the names of "big weed heads" that dot the surrounding landscape. This may seem an insignificant confession, but his simple ignorance is a symbol of a much larger failure. Contemporary society is out of touch with nature. While bees and flowers, the moon, even a skunk or two make appearances in cities and suburbs across America every day and night, many human inhabitants of these areas are blind to their presence. People cannot name the plants and animals that share their lawns and gardens, much less any of the more exotic species that may occasionally show up in a field or along the countryside. The guests at the party in "Social Life" are too caught up in their own little worlds to learn about the big one outside. The speaker represents hope, even for the plastic generation of which he is a part. After all, he may not be able to name the weeds that "lift and nod upon their stalks," but he does see them. He does appreciate them and recognize how unlike people they are—without complaint, without whining, without ego. But weeds, like all of nature, do not need recognition in order to achieve "validation"; they simply *are*, and that is enough.

Style

Contemporary Free Verse

"Social Life" is written in contemporary free verse with no rhyme or distinguishable meter. The stanzas are made up of two, three, or four lines, based on the subject and setting of each as opposed to any desire for structural consistency. In other words, Hoagland lets the events of the poem drive its format and is unconcerned with any established patterns of verse. One technique very evident in this poem, however, is the use of enjambment, or the continuation of a syntactic unit from one line or stanza to the next with no pause. For example, line 3 begins with the words "into the second one," but this phrase actually completes the thought begun in line 2 with "the survivors of the first party climb." Line 6 begins with the verb "is" but its subject is the last word in line 5, "Richard." One can find line-to-line enjambment throughout this entire work, but the technique also appears in stanza-to-stanza form. For instance, the fifth stanza ends with "and I" (line 17), and the sixth stanza completes the thought with "am in the wild sweet dark" (line 18). The eighth stanza ends with "They sway" (line 28), and the ninth tells how they sway: "upon their thorny stems" (line 29). The poem also contains a bit of alliteration (the repetition of consonant sounds) although it is not always clear whether the effect is intentional or accidental. For example, the *s* sound in the words "survivors" and "second" (lines 2 and 3) is most likely unplanned, but the repetition of the same sound in "slowly sinking ship" is a definite poetic technique. The tenth stanza provides a fairly strong example of assonance (the repetition of same or similar vowel sounds) with the recurrence of the *uh* sound. "Tusk," "skunk," "honey" and "suckle" all share the sound, and even "bush" is a close companion. Beyond these poetic efforts, though, "Social Life" is a solid example of verse that is both contemporary and free of formality.

Historical Context

Because this poem did not appear in a journal until 1999, it is more closely associated with present American culture and social ethics than with any historical perspective. That said, however, the brief span of years between those publications has

Topics for Further Study

- Write a poem about the kind of "social life" you have encountered or that your family leans toward. Is it much like Hoagland's or does it differ dramatically?

- Levittown is known as the first suburb in America, named after its founder and creator, William Levitt. Write an essay on this neighborhood, examining both its positive and negative reception, as well as how it sparked controversy over issues of race, gender, and economic status.

- In this poem, the speaker's friend, Richard, appears to represent the typical partygoer that Hoagland targets. If you had to create a psychological profile of Richard, based only on the information in the poem, how would you describe him? How fair do you believe your assessment can be and why?

- How important is the natural world of trees, flowers, and wild animals where you live? Should more emphasis be placed on them or do other matters take precedence?

brought significant and unimagined political, economic, and emotional change, not only for citizens of the United States, but throughout the world.

By some accounts, the decade of the 1990s is remembered as the "Narcissistic 90s," based on Americans' increasing material indulgence and a seemingly unlimited consumption of everything from trendy foods and gasoline to big houses and new computers. Middle class families moved in droves into "Monopoly board" communities, with houses pre-designed by contractors, offering little variety in appearance but touting such amenities as built-in microwave ovens, home offices, security alarms, Jacuzzi baths, and three-car garages. These new suburban neighborhoods sprang up quickly across the country, attracting many people with children who felt a greater sense of safety and a shared value for home ownership, as well as comfort and convenience. Many of the communities are located close to schools, shopping and entertainment centers, and various corporations, providing these families with all the suburbanite essentials and making it unnecessary to leave the general area. City planners and politicians have made an effort to attract more people and businesses to downtown areas to prevent the further decay of inner cities, but, for the most part, they have not been able to compete with the lure of the perceived security and personal convenience of the suburbs.

In the late 1990s, the American economy appeared to be undergoing limitless expansion. The stock market increased its value by an incredible margin, due largely to low inflation, stable interest rates, and a boom in high-technology industries. Never before had so many Americans been able to make money for a considerable length of time simply by owning stocks. Because of the boost in investment, many industries were able not only to recover from previous financial setbacks but also to achieve a growth status that would have seemed unthinkable only a few years earlier. From automobiles to high-tech computer hardware and software, manufacturers boasted record gains and a renewed sense of financial stability. Then came September 11, 2001.

Since the terrorist attacks on the World Trade Center in New York City and the Pentagon in Washington, D.C., many people have experienced only a sense of dread, vulnerability, and fear. Aside from the obvious shock and emotional anguish brought on by this catastrophic event, some Americans have also admitted a desire for spirituality over materialism, peace of mind over personal gain, honesty and integrity over self-indulgence and deceit. This is not to imply, of course, that the narcissism of the twentieth century's final decade has given way to some Pollyanna brotherhood and sisterhood throughout the country, but that perhaps more people have taken time to question what is truly valuable in their lives. Families still flock to the suburbs, yet there is a reborn sense of pride and determination in bringing back the spirit of city living and of refusing to let international extremists make Americans afraid of their own big towns. Despite the wave of emotions, however—from disbelief and fear to anger and determination—the state of the American mind cannot deny the state of the American economy.

After September 11, the stock market plunged and was slow to yet to recover. The United States and Britain led war with oil-rich Iraq resulted in the same market jitters that occurred in 1990 when Iraq attacked Kuwait, sparking the first Persian Gulf War. Unemployment rose in the United States, not only in blue-collar fields but in white-collar corporate positions as well. Despite the gloomy economic conditions, many factions of society persevered with business as usual. Entertainment and sports industries seemed undaunted, religious leaders rallied more and more supporters to their cause, and even the federal government made progress on strengthening bipartisanship and across-the-board policies. While it is safe to say that materialism and self-absorption were as much a part of the American fabric as baseball and apple pie, one may also assume that somewhere in the midst of mingling, music, and "kissy-kiss," everyone knew the world was a different place.

Critical Overview

With only two full-length collections to his credit at this point, Hoagland has not yet been afforded volumes of criticism, good or bad, within the annals of literary scholarship. But the fact that both books he has produced were selected for prestigious awards by prominent colleagues in American poetry speaks strongly of a positive reception. Writing a book review of *Sweet Ruin* in a 1992 issue of *Ploughshares*, poet and critic Steven Cramer says that "Hoagland's poems grapple with selfhood and manhood, but they also consider the mysteries of national identity—how the social and the personal mutually impinge." At the end of the critique, Cramer sums up his evaluation by declaring, "Hoagland's is some of the most sheerly enjoyable writing I've encountered in a long time." Six years later, in a *Library Journal* book review of *Donkey Gospel*, critic Frank Allen says that "Hoagland's second book ... is nothing if not imaginative. Invigorated by 'fine distress,' these graceful, perceptive poems gaze without blinking at what we hide from each other and ourselves when 'head and heart / are in different time zones.'" Allen's analysis of Hoagland's most recent book is that, "This award-winning collection illuminates conflicts between individual desire for self-actualization and the 'dark and soaring fact' of experience." From all accounts, his third collection, due out in 2003, is a much-anticipated work, and if "Social Life" is a fair representation of its contents, the book will likely garner as much praise and enthusiasm as the first two.

Criticism

Pamela Steed Hill

Hill is the author of a poetry collection, has published widely in literary journals, and is an editor for a university publications department. In the following essay, Hill examines Hoagland's portrayal of American middle-class emptiness and the spirituality of nature—viewed as polar opposites in this poem.

While there may not be a written manual on how to act at a typical contemporary party in suburban America, most party guests seem to have an innate sense of expectations and taboos. Just like the given laws and mores of a society, the common social gathering has its own set of do's and don'ts, such as *do* glide smoothly from group to group; *don't* sit in a corner contemplating the artwork on the walls. Breaking the rules can brand one a social outcast or, even worse, unsophisticated. In Hoagland's "Social Life," the speaker decides to take a chance with the rules, but he does so only in his mind, leaving him caught between the public expectations of materialism and a private longing for something more spiritual.

Even the title of this poem belies its content. Normally, the term "social life" evokes favorable images of togetherness, good times, and positive energy. Here, it translates into little more than trite conversation and pathetic behavior, and all of it with an aura of sadness hanging about. From the outset, the party goers are portrayed as weary "survivors" of a harrowing ordeal, which turns out to be simply the first party that has ended. The metaphoric scene is one of nearly drowned people clamoring onto a lifeboat while in the background their sinking ship slowly goes down—hardly a festive sight. Richard, the speaker's friend, appears to be enjoying himself, but the rote listing of his activities suggests that he is just going through the motions like everyone else: pouring a drink, putting on music, moving around the room, smiling, joking, laughing, kissing, etc. It all reeks of prescribed behavior and total insincerity. So, if these "social pleasures" are not pleasurable in the least, what is their purpose? The speaker is not sure he understands, but he has an idea.

The setting of the party is really the setting of contemporary, suburban America. In this world, *things* are important, not only concrete or tangible things, but also attitudes, desires, and topics of conversation—sort of an *emotional* materialism. The interesting difference between the objects that the guests are expected to possess and the sentiments or thoughts they possess is that the latter are hardly desirable. Big houses with all the latest gadgets, new cars leased yearly, big-screen TVs, fashionable clothing, and tasteful furniture may all be part of the suburban status quo, but apparently so are nagging dissatisfaction, self-absorption, and a need to complain. Social gatherings, then, become a refuge, a place for people to air their woes and at least pretend to commiserate with one another. This is when the pleasure comes in. As the reader learns inadvertently through descriptions of nature, the people in Hoagland's poem grumble about how their parents have failed them, solicit sympathy regarding their "recovery" period from some kind of substance abuse, and blame a lack of "empowerment or validation" for their feelings of emptiness and insignificance. Having a safe harbor where they can share these complaints is comforting and, therefore, pleasurable. After all, such moaning may not be so well received at work or at home with the family, but it is perfectly acceptable at a party where everyone is doing it.

If the analysis seems too harsh or overly generalized, it may be tempered by the degree of sympathy, if not sorrow, that Hoagland implies with the flowers and bees metaphor he uses to describe the social pleasures of his "species." All the party goers really get from "these affairs" is a little "nudging of the stamen, / a sprinkle of pollen / about the head and shoulders." Aside from the obvious sexual innuendo, there is a pathetic sense of *this is all we are asking for* among the guests. They do not demand any life-changing inspiration from one another—no rewards, promises, or answers. Instead,

> "There are no pretenses between the plants and animals, no kissy-kiss between geography and the weather. Instead, something quite remarkable is going on out there: nature is living in harmony with itself."

they seek only a short moment of time to feel important, to be rejuvenated and worthy of "pollination." No one seems to be fooled into thinking any of it is permanent.

The speaker is especially perceptive in recognizing the party behavior for what it reflects—the dull, empty lives of middle-class suburbia—and he is determined not to succumb to it himself. Since he is obviously an invited guest at the event, one can assume he is a part of the crowd, that he shares a similar environment and similar values. Yet he also knows that something is missing, and he steps outside to find it. There, among the sea breeze and weeds, the trees and grasses and flowers, the moon and the scent of skunk, he finds an aura of something higher, something magnificent and spiritual. He finds things that are natural in the utmost sense. There are no pretenses between the plants and animals, no kissy-kiss between geography and the weather. Instead, something quite remarkable is going on out there: nature is living in harmony with itself. Perhaps most extraordinary, it is respecting all parts of itself, actually taking turns within its ranks, from the breeze whistling through the treetops to insects humming in the field. The fact that these movements and sounds let each other "have a word, and then another word" is fascinating to a human being who struggles for genuine respect and fairness among his own kind. How could humans, supposedly the most intelligent of all inhabitants of the earth, fall so short in the process of simply being themselves and getting along with others? Are those two goals at odds with each other in the human world?

The cynical answer is that when human beings are allowed to be themselves then, naturally, they will consider their own situations and agendas of paramount importance and find fault with the same in others. The more congenial answer is that humankind needs to learn only one great lesson from nature, and then harmony may be achievable: be quiet. Be silent while other people have their say and maybe something unexpected will be heard. Maybe the voices will be worth taking turns to hear. The climax of "Social Life" comes in the final three lines of the poem when the big punch is delivered: "silence is always good manners," and especially at a party. This is the exact place in suburban America where it rarely happens. As the speaker so aptly points out, this is a loud place, not only because of the music on the stereo but also from the din of idle chitchat that permeates the room. Undoubtedly, people are talking over top of one another, not hearing what someone else is saying but trying to make themselves heard as they go on and on about their families or jobs or aches and pains and politics, or anything else. The current common phrase *It's all about me* is personified many times over in this setting. Outside, nature may be saying *It's all about everything* and proving it by letting everything be.

If public complaining and confessing fills some material need, perhaps only silence can fill the spiritual need. Hoagland's "Social Life" points in that direction. The irony of the title, the lush descriptions of nature, and the witty little biting comment at the end all add up to a very unflattering appraisal of middle-class suburbia. Feelings of emptiness, however, are not exclusive to this particular part of American society, for people from all backgrounds and all locations can attest to the same. The difference lies more in how individuals or groups deal with emptiness rather than who feels it and who does not. The people at the party try to talk it away. They seem to believe that the more they talk, the less they will have to think about the real problem. What the speaker has figured out, though, is that this method is only digging the hole deeper, making it tougher to fill up with anything but emptiness. He has learned to take a lesson from nature, to reach a level of spiritual fulfillment by being quiet long enough to absorb real serenity and peace of mind. This is the lesson he wishes for his fellow suburbanites, but his assessment of their endless gabbing leaves little room for hope.

Source: Pamela Steed Hill, Critical Essay on "Social Life," in *Poetry for Students*, Gale, 2003.

Adrian Blevins

Blevins has published essays and poems in many magazines, journals, and anthologies and teaches writing at Roanoke College. In this essay, Blevins warns that reading Hoagland's poem as a mere celebration of the natural world would undermine its more serious intentions.

Although some critics will be tempted to place "Social Life" in the pastoral tradition by reading it as an idealization of the natural world, an understanding of Hoagland's main concerns and techniques will uncover the poem's more complicated intention, which is to expose the conflict between mind and body. Camille Paglia, writing in *Sexual Personae: Art and Decadence from Nefertiti to Emily Dickinson*, calls this conflict humankind's "supreme... problem." Hoagland engages the prehistoric attempt to subdue the dark powers of nature with the civilizing forces of culture to insist that it is incorrect and dangerous to make distinctions between these two powers. In other words, "Social Life" does not compare the weeds to people to celebrate the weeds; a celebration of weeds would seem to Hoagland ridiculous. Instead, Hoagland borrows gestures from the Wordsworthian pastoral tradition to expose man's consciousness of his being both body and mind because it is this consciousness that makes him man.

"Social Life" does seem at first to want to argue that the activities of flowers and trees are preferable to the activities of humans at parties. The speaker praises the trees and grasses because they are without afflictions. The natural world also differs from the world of human experience in "Social Life" in that it is indifferent enough to be content. Yet, the speaker's feigned guess that what his friend Richard "gets from these affairs" emphasizes the poem's recognition that man seeks in his social activities the same natural pleasure that bees and flowers seek in theirs. Only when the poem shifts from its initial comparative base to its speaker's attempt to separate himself from "the voices and the lights" does it rise to the level of its most acute meaning, which concerns the conflict between the process of mind and the process of body that only man must suffer.

To see how the natural images in "Social Life" work, it is important to understand that Hoagland often reverses the process of personification that describes animals and other natural objects by comparing them to humans. When James Wright says in a famous poem like "A Blessing" that ponies in a field "love each other," he is giving animals human characteristics in order to reveal that they are like humans. Hoagland, however, uses images from the natural world to comment on the ways in which humans are not only like animals, but how they are animals. For example, when Hoagland closes his poem "Game" by saying that "the unmown field is foaming at the mouth with flowers," his goal is not to suggest that the field is excited or animated. Instead, by turning regular alfalfa into "Jennifer alfalfa"

What Do I Read Next?

- The Academy of American Poets at http://www.poets.org/ maintains a page called "Citation: 1997 James Laughlin Award." Written by late poet William Matthews, this article offers insight into why he and other members of the award committee selected Hoagland's *Donkey Gospel* to receive the 1997 prize. Matthews quotes sections of a few poems from the book and offers critiques on each.

- *Some Ether* (2000) is the title of poet Nick Flynn's first collection. His work has received considerable attention by critics and fellow poets, including Hoagland.

- Noted journalist, demographer, and political analyst G. Scott Thomas examines the massive power shift from the cities to suburbia in *The United States of Suburbia: How the Suburbs Took Control of America and What They Plan to Do with It* (2000). He argues that the dividing line between the two Americas, which used to be racial, has become more economic and geographic and that voters in the suburbs control the nation's elections.

- In *The High Price of Materialism* (2002), psychology professor Tim Kasser argues that a materialistic orientation toward the world contributes to low self-esteem, depression, antisocial behavior, and even a greater tendency to get physically ill. Though statistically and scientifically based, Kasser's prose is very accessible and his theories are intriguing.

> *A broad understanding of both Hoagland's approach and his major concerns shows that 'Social Life' seeks to place its speaker in the space between longing (body) and thought (mind) to reveal man's most profound psychological challenge.*

and a regular cloud into a "Jennifer-shaped cloud," his goal is to comment on his own interests in and obsessions with describing the way all humans frame the world in the context of their own interests and obsessions and therefore seem to be "foaming at the mouth" over "the energy / which gushes through all things."

In the fifth stanza of "Social Life," the speaker states that he "prefer[s] the feeling of going away" to being at a party. Yet, in stanzas 11 and 12, he states that while he is away he "want[s] to raise [his] head and sing." That is, he says he to wants come as close to the natural world as humans can get and praise human union in song. Instead, the speaker "stand[s] still and listens" and "let[s] everything else have a word." The peacefulness of these two stanzas, especially in comparison to the false expressions of the humans seems to imply that "going away" is a suitable way to contend with the din and clatter of human social ritual. But, because the speaker says he is listening and smelling instead of singing, "Social Life" is not really interested in offering solutions to the problem of "the social pleasures of [the human] species." Rather, the poem wants to express the conflict that man must ride between his desire to sing about the beauty of the "the wild sweet dark" and "letting everything else have a word." Paglia talks about the conflict between mind and body by recalling what the Greek gods Apollo and Dionysus commonly represent in the Western aesthetic tradition:

The quarrel between Apollo and Dionysus is the quarrel between the higher cortex and the older limbic and reptilian brains. Art reflects on and resolves the external human dilemma of order verses energy. In the west, Apollo and Dionysus strive for victory. Apollo marks the boundary lines that are civilization but that lead to convention, constraint, oppression. Dionysus is energy unbound, mad, callous, destructive, wasteful. Apollo is law, history, tradition, the dignity and safety of custom and form. Dionysus is the new, exhilarating but rude, sweeping all away to begin again. Apollo is a tyrant, Dionysus is a vandal.

In "Social Life," Hoagland straddles the space between his need to sing of the Dionysian space that parties represent and his Apollonian contempt for disorder. This theme is addressed again and again in Hoagland's poems, as for example "Lawrence" from *Donkey Gospel*, which celebrates D. H. Lawrence's talent for making humans "seem magnificent" in their "inability to subdue the body." Thus, when in "Social Life" the speaker says that he "listen[s] / to the breeze departing from the upper story of a tree / and the hum of insects in the field, / letting everything else have a word, and then another word," Hoagland is being extremely ironic, since the poem that records the experience is, in the end, the last word.

Hoagland's ability to mix modes of discourse, a technique the critic Steven Cramer described in a *Ploughshares* review as "muscular, conversational lines spring[ing] from narrative passages to metaphorical clusters to speculative meditations," also reveals the tensions and counterbalances that represent the mind/body split that is one of Hoagland's major concerns. In other words, in most of his poems, Hoagland uses the logic and order of Apollo to construct a coherent metaphorical and rhetorical whole to describe an overwhelmingly Dionysian sensibility. In "Social Life," discursive lines such as "It is not given to me to understand / the social pleasures of my species" are married to narrative, time-framing passages like "behind me now my friend Richard / is getting a fresh drink." These knots of discourse are linked by the metaphorical cluster of the lifeboat that becomes the ship that becomes the vessel on which the speaker can join "the wild sweet dark." These clusters can be said to construct the poem's lyrical center, or the place where time in the poem seems to stop. The mix here produces pleasure at the sensual level of music and rhythm but also serves the purposes of meaning by reenacting mankind's most profound dilemma, which concerns the mind/body split that separates man from other animals.

In his Academy of American Poets citation for awarding *Donkey Gospel* the James Laughlin Award in 1997, William Matthews noted "a gaudy crash between dictions" in Hoagland's work. Although Hoagland does not merge idiomatic and conversational diction with more elevated word choices in "Social Life," the attraction to multiple tones can be seen in the clash between an idiomatic or conversational phrase like "kissy-kiss" and far more lyrical lines like "the wild sweet dark / where the sea breeze sizzles in the hedgetop." Thus, it can be seen that Hoagland's technique reveals his content in his diction as well as in his merging of the various modes of discourse.

Although it would not be fair to say that Hoagland opposes the natural world, it is clear that his work is so solidly bound to the human experience that a pastoral reading of "Social Life" would seriously underestimate the poem's intentions. A broad understanding of both Hoagland's approach and his major concerns shows that "Social Life" seeks to place its speaker in the space between longing (body) and thought (mind) to reveal man's most profound psychological challenge. The poem's most gorgeous irony is that its speaker has the last word by "writing" this poem. Thus, one can see Paglia's claim that "poetry is the connecting link between mind and body" illustrated in "Social Life."

Source: Adrian Blevins, Critical Essay on "Social Life," in *Poetry for Students*, Gale, 2003.

Burton Hatlen

In the following essay, Hatlen discusses the "geography" of Hoagland's poetry and his writing style as it appears throughout his works.

The total quantity of Tony Hoagland's poetry is relatively small. Three slim chapbooks were incorporated in large part into the full-length book *Sweet Ruin*, selected by Donald Justice as the 1992 winner of the Brittingham prize. In addition, Hoagland has published other poems in various magazines. But the body of Hoagland's work is fine-honed, and it has won considerable admiration not only from Justice but also from critics like Carl Dennis and Carolyn Kizer. Hoagland's poems characteristically open with dramatic flair: "When I think of what I know about America, / I think of kissing my best friend's wife / in the parking lot of the zoo one afternoon...." or "That was the summer my best friend / called me a faggot on the telephone, / hung up, and vanished from the earth...." These openings suggest the narrative mode in which Hoagland likes to work, and the need to find out

> *The geography of Hoagland's poetry is white, middle-class suburban, post-1960s. Hoagland explores this region with a pervasive irony, a bravura wit, and sometimes a probing self-awareness."*

what happens draws the reader into the poem. Hoagland develops his narratives in longish poems, almost always more than a page and sometimes as long as three pages, that normally resolve themselves in a wry, epigrammatic twist that implicitly acknowledges the insolubility of the initial premise; after you kiss your best friend's wife or after your best friend calls you a faggot, there is no going back.

The geography of Hoagland's poetry is white, middle-class suburban, post-1960s. Hoagland explores this region with a pervasive irony, a bravura wit, and sometimes a probing self-awareness. Many of the poems seem to be autobiographical, edging toward the confessional. Hoagland, or his invented persona, tells us not only about his best friends but also about how his father deliberately ruined (thus the title of this book) his own marriage and was then struck down by a heart attack; about how, at age seventeen, the young poet watched his mother shrivel away with cancer; about his grandmother Bernice, who believed that "people with good manners / naturally had yachts, knew how to waltz / and dribbled French into their sentences / like salad dressing"; about "that architect, my brother," who "lost his voice, and then his wife / because he was too proud to say, "'Please, don't go'"; about the rock concerts that filled his ears and those of his friends with scar tissue; and about many, many girlfriends. Sometimes the "I" becomes a "you" to imply that these experiences are typical of a generation and a particular social group. Thus, in one poem we read of "the night your girlfriend / first disappeared beneath the sheets / to take you in her red, wet mouth / with an amethystine sweetness / and a surprising expertise, / then came up for a kiss / as her reward...."

In the most resonant of Hoagland's poems the thin and somewhat brittle social surface opens up to reveal unexpected depths. Sometimes the depths are religious, for God, it seems, is keeping an eye on us. In one marvelously delicate poem the poet shares a late-night cigarette with God, and in this moment "things"—the cluttered American middle-class life, not only the cars and the microwaves but all the responsibilities and human entanglements too—fall away, and we find ourselves in the presence of a great and blessed emptiness:

> One does so much
> building up, so much feverish acquiring,
> but really, it is all aimed
> at a condition of exhausted
> simplicity, isn't it?
> We don't love things.

The poet realizes that, at least in our sleep, we can escape the tyranny of things. All about him (and God) are "bodies / falling from the precipice of sleep," who for a few hours do not

> remember how to suffer
> or how to run from it.
> They are like the stars,
> or potted plants, or salty oceanic waves.

It seems that even in American suburbia getting and having can sometimes fade away to allow a few moments of simple being, although the reference to potted plants seems to twist the poem back toward irony.

In a few of his later poems Hoagland chooses to probe beneath the surface of American middle-class life in quest not of spiritual depths but of the social and economic underpinnings of this way of life. In "From This Height," for example, we are invited to observe a seduction scene that takes place beside a hot tub in an eighth-floor condominium. The speaker, caught up in the elegance of his surroundings, suddenly finds himself looking through this veneer as he recognizes that

> we are on top of a pyramid
> of all the facts
> that make this possible:
> the furnace heats the water,
> the truck that hauled the fuel,
> the artery of highway
> blasted through the mountains....

At the bottom, the speaker realizes, down there "inside history's body / the slaves are still singing in the dark." The speaker cannot think of anything to do with this knowledge except to kiss the girl and eat another mouthful of the "high calorie paté ... / which, considering the price, / would be a sin / not to enjoy." But while the speaker of the poem seeks to deflect his new awareness with cynical wit, the poem seems to ask another kind of response from us—to move beyond cynicism and to act on this new and bitter knowledge.

Source: Burton Hatlen, "Hoagland, Tony," in *Contemporary Poets*, 7th ed., edited by Thomas Riggs, St. James Press, 2001, pp. 538–39.

Sources

Allen, Frank, Review of *Donkey Gospel*, in *Library Journal*, Vol. 123, No. 9, May 15, 1998, p. 88.

Cramer, Steven, Review of *Sweet Ruin*, in *Ploughshares*, Vol. 18, No. 4, Winter 1992, p. 236.

Hoagland, Tony, *Donkey Gospel*, Graywolf Press, 1998, pp. 14, 15, 32.

———, "Social Life," in *Ploughshares*, Vol. 25, No. 1, Spring 1999, pp. 173–74.

Matthews, William, *Citation for the 1997 James Laughlin Award*, Academy of American Poets, www.poets.org (last accessed March 21, 2003).

Paglia, Camille, *Sexual Personae: Art and Decadence from Nefertiti to Emily Dickinson*, Vintage Books, 1991, pp. 1, 18, 96–97.

Wright, James, *Above the River: The Complete Poems*, Noonday Press, 1990, p. 143.

Further Reading

Hoagland, Tony, *Donkey Gospel*, Graywolf Press, 1998.
  The poems in Hoagland's second full-length collection deal primarily with the male desire for sexual prowess and machismo, while at the same time trying to deal with issues such as homosexuality, feminism, and other contemporary concerns. The poet's sexually explicit language in this collection is not for the easily offended.

———, "On Disproportion," in *Poets Teaching Poets: Self and the World*, edited by Gregory Orr and Ellen Bryant Voigt, University of Michigan Press, 1996.
  In this collection of sixteen essays by contemporary poets, subjects range from a defense of the lyric form to Sylvia Plath's bees. Hoagland's contribution is helpful in understanding poetry created from seemingly disparate angles, thus, disproportionate, but not negatively so.

———, *Sweet Ruin*, University of Wisconsin Press, 1992.
  Hoagland's first collection is highly autobiographical and centers around his father's quest to ruin his own marriage by committing adultery. But, the poems also expand into Hoagland's own romantic exploits and attempt to connect the deeply personal with

the openly social and political, particularly in contemporary America.

Lyons, Paul, *Class of '66: Living in Suburban Middle America*, Temple University Press, 1994.

Though the high school class of 1966 was a few years prior to Hoagland's own graduation, the lives of the subjects in this book parallel those examined in much of the poet's work. Here, Lyons looks at what happened to a select group of white, middle-class suburban kids who grew up in the era of Vietnam and the Civil Rights movement. His findings should be surprising to most readers.

somewhere i have never travelled,gladly beyond

e. e. cummings

1931

Edward Estlin Cummings, known to most of his readers as e. e. cummings, first published "somewhere i have never travelled,gladly beyond" in 1931 in his poetry collection, *ViVa*. As with all of his other poems, the author did not give this poem an actual title. For purposes of identification, editors simply refer to each of cummings's poems by its first line. The poem is very clearly a love poem, and cummings is renowned for his love poetry. Critics, however, have singled this poem out as one of cummings's best love poems.

The poem details the profound feelings of love that the speaker has for his beloved, and his wonder over this mysterious power that the woman has over him. Over the course of the short poem, the speaker examines and praises this power, and notes how his beloved has transformed him. The speaker in the poem may or may not be cummings himself, although the intensity of emotion expressed in the poem leads one to believe that the poet is describing his own experiences. When cummings published "somewhere i have never travelled,gladly beyond," he had been married to Anne Barton for two years. While Barton might have been the source of the poem's inspiration, this inspiration would have been short-lived, for cummings and Barton divorced a year later, in 1932. A current copy of the poem can be found in *E. E. Cummings: Complete Poems 1904–1962*, which was published in hardcover by Liveright in 1994.

Author Biography

Born in Cambridge, Massachusetts, in 1894, cummings spent his childhood in that city, where his father Edward Cummings was a sociology professor at Harvard and a Unitarian clergyman. From an early age, cummings showed a strong interest in poetry and art, which was encouraged by his mother Rebecca. Cummings attended Harvard University from 1911 to 1915 and joined the editorial board of the *Harvard Monthly*, a college literary magazine. While in college, he became fascinated by avant-garde art, modernism, and cubism, and he began incorporating elements of these styles into his own poetry and paintings. He received a bachelor's degree in 1915 and a master's the following year. His first published poems appeared in the anthology *Eight Harvard Poets* in 1917. These eight pieces feature the experimental verse forms and the lower-case personal pronoun "i" that were to become his trademark. The copyeditor of the book, however, mistook cummings's intentions as typographical errors and made "corrections." During World War I, cummings volunteered for the French-based Norton-Harjes Ambulance Service. As a result of his disregard of regulations and his attempts to outwit the wartime censors in his letters home, cummings spent four months in an internment camp in Normandy on suspicion of treason. Although he found his detention amusing and even enjoyable, his father made use of his contacts in government to secure his son's release. Cummings returned to New York and pursued painting but was drafted in 1918. He spent about a year at Camp Danvers, Massachusetts, during which time he wrote prolifically. Beginning around this time, cummings, with the knowledge and approval of his friend Schofield Thayer, had an affair with Schofield's wife Elaine. Cummings's daughter Nancy was born in 1919, but she was given Thayer's name. Cummings and Elaine Thayer married in 1924, at which time cummings legally adopted Nancy. During the 1920s and 1930s, he traveled widely in Europe, alternately living in Paris and New York and developing parallel careers as a poet and a painter. He published his first poetry collection, *Tulips and Chimneys*, in 1923. Politically liberal with leftist leanings, cummings visited the Soviet Union in 1931 to learn about that government's system of art subsidies. He was very disillusioned, however, by the regimentation and lack of personal and artistic freedom he encountered there. As a result, he abandoned his liberal views and became deeply conservative on social and political issues. Cummings continued to write steadily throughout the 1940s and 1950s, reaching his greatest popularity during this period and winning a number of honors, including the Shelley Memorial Award for poetry in 1944, the Charles Eliot Norton Professorship at Harvard for the academic year 1952–1953, and the Bollingen Prize for Poetry in 1958. Despite such successes, however, he never achieved a steady income. Cummings continued to give poetry readings to college audiences across the United States until his death in 1962.

e. e. cummings

Poem Text

somewhere i have never travelled,gladly beyond
any experience,your eyes have their silence:
in your most frail gesture are things which enclose
    me,
or which I cannot touch because they are too near

your slightest look easily will unclose me   5
though i have closed myself as fingers,
you open always petal by petal myself as Spring
    opens
(touching skilfully,mysteriously) her first rose

or if your wish be to close me,i and
my life will shut very beautifully,suddenly,   10

as when the heart of this flower imagines
the snow carefully everywhere descending;

nothing which we are to perceive in this world
    equals
the power of your intense fragility:whose texture
compels me with colour of its countries,   15
rendering death and forever with each breathing

(i do not know what it is about you that closes
and opens;only something in me understands
the voice of your eyes is deeper than all roses)
nobody,not even the rain,has such small hands   20

Poem Summary

Stanza 1

"somewhere i have never travelled,gladly beyond" begins with the title words. The words, "somewhere" and "travelled," imply that the speaker is about to tell the reader about a journey that he has taken or will take. This journey is a happy one, as the word "gladly" indicates, although the reader does not know at this point the destination of this journey. In the end of the first line and beginning of the second line, the poet clarifies that this journey is "beyond / any experience" that he has ever had. He also, curiously, notes that "your eyes have their silence." The "your" indicates that the speaker is talking to another person, who for some reason has silent eyes. The reader can determine that the poet is discussing metaphysical concepts, abstract ideas that cannot be experienced by one's physical senses. In the real world, eyes do not have the capability of producing noise, so they are, by default, silent. The discussion of the person's eyes, along with the use of the word "gladly," gives readers their first indication that this might be a love poem. Eyes are thought by many to be a window into a person's soul, and poets often describe their lovers' eyes in positive terms.

In the third line, the use of the words "frail gesture" indicates that the person to whom the speaker is dedicating this poem is most likely a woman. At the time this poem was written, frailty was often used to describe womanhood. While this idea has since become a negative stereotype to many, readers in cummings's time would have recognized this frailty as a compliment to the woman in the poem. The speaker notes that this woman's frail gestures contain "things which enclose me," or which he "cannot touch because they are too near." The speaker is not saying that these things are literally enclosing him. Instead, these things—the feelings that are produced in the speaker by this woman's enchanting glance—are so powerful that he feels enclosed by them. At the same time, although these feelings surround him, he cannot touch them, because they are so all-consuming that they have become a deeply ingrained part of him. At this point, the reader can see that when the speaker discusses the "somewhere" to which he is travelling, he is not talking about a literal, physical journey. Rather, his journey is metaphysical, and the woman's eyes are the means by which the speaker makes this journey.

Stanza 2

The speaker underscores the power of the woman's glance with the first two lines of the second stanza. The speaker notes that the woman can easily "unclose," or open him, even though he has up until that point "closed myself as fingers." Here, the speaker is talking about the power of love to change a person's perspective. The speaker could be talking about his feelings about love. Perhaps he has been hurt in the past and so has closed himself off from the idea of love. Or, he could be closed in the sense of being pessimistic about the current state of society. When cummings wrote the poem, the United States was in the grip of the Great Depression, a financial disaster that changed the lives and moods of many. In any case, the speaker's love for this woman has opened him up, and he is basking in these new emotions. In the third line of the stanza, the speaker elaborates on how the woman opens him up, using the analogy of a rose opening up in spring. In this poem, however, the speaker personifies the season of spring. Poets use personification when they give human-like qualities to nonhuman items. When the poet notes that "Spring opens / (touching skilfully,mysteriously) her first rose," he is referring to spring as a person, who is physically opening up the rose.

Stanza 3

The speaker continues his discussion of the woman's power, noting that just as she can easily open him up, "if your wish be to close me, i and / my life will shut very beautifully,suddenly." The speaker is in the woman's complete control, to the point that she has power over his life and his death. While death is generally considered a negative concept, in the context of this poem, the speaker describes it as beautiful, equating his hypothetical death with the impending death of a flower, which "imagines / the snow carefully everywhere descending." Again, the poet uses personification. While a flower is alive in the organic sense, it does not have the human quality of imagination. By describing the rose in this way, the poet paints a unique picture. The rose, coming to the end of its seasonal life in the fall, is imagining the snow that will soon be falling, a sign of the flower's impending and unavoidable death in winter. Since the lifecycle of the rose is eternal (the flower will experience a rebirth again in spring) its death is not tragic. By equating his own hypothetical death at his lover's hands with the rose's death, the speaker's death is not tragic, either. It is important that the speaker does this. A discussion of death could very easily give this love poem a negative mood. By referring to death "beautifully," the poem retains the positive mood that it established with the word "gladly" in the first stanza.

Stanza 4

In the first line of the fourth stanza, the speaker alludes to the metaphysical quality of the woman's power, by noting that "nothing which we are to perceive in this world equals / the power of your intense fragility." Again, this woman's fragility, or femininity, is so powerful that it transcends the physical world. The speaker examines the "texture" of this femininity, which he says "compels" him with the "colour of its countries." A reader may at first be confused by the use of the word, "countries." The speaker does not literally mean that the woman's intense femininity is composed of countries, in a geographic sense. Rather, by referring to the woman in this way, the speaker makes the woman seem larger than life, as if her feminine powers occupy a metaphysical world of their own. The speaker has already referred to the physical "world" in the first line of this stanza. Now, in this feminine, metaphysical world, he examines the countries, or specific details that make up this woman's femininity, and they fascinate him. In the last line of the stanza, he notes that these feminine qualities can render "death and forever with each breathing." Here, the speaker builds on the idea of the previous stanza, underscoring the power that the woman has over his life and death.

Stanza 5

As the speaker notes in the final stanza, as much as he examines the specific aspects of the woman's femininity, he does not know "what it is about you that closes / and opens." The speaker is unsure how the woman has such a power over him, how she can open him or close him, how she can control his life and death so easily. This is not a bad thing. The speaker does not want to know. He

Media Adaptations

- *E. E. Cummings: A Poetry Collection* is an audiocassette that gathers selections from the poet's work. Published in 2001, the collection features poems read by cummings. It is available from HarperAudio.

- The *Great Voices Audio Collection* (1994) is an audiocassette that gathers selections from four writers: Ernest Hemingway, Anais Nin, James Joyce, and cummings. Each writer reads his or her own work. In the case of cummings, the poet reads from his *XAIPE* collection. The audiobook is available from HarperAudio.

is caught up in the mystery of the woman's power and knows only that "something in me understands / the voice of your eyes is deeper than all roses)." Previously in the poem, the speaker has equated his lover's power to the power that spring has to open a rose. Now, he is saying that his lover's power is even stronger than this natural, seasonal power. In one final, potent image, the speaker underscores the idea that this woman's power is unmatched by anything in nature: "nobody,not even the rain,has such small hands." The speaker is personifying the rain, and imagining it as the "hands" that spring uses to open roses. While this is an impressive natural power, the speaker says that his lover is even more impressive. Her "hands" are smaller, which in this context means that the woman has the ability to open up the speaker to an even deeper extent than that of a rose opened by the spring rains.

Themes

Love

It is very clear from the beginning that this poem is a love poem about the poet's beloved. Although the language is cryptic at first, as it is in many of cummings's poems, in the second line of the poem he identifies the subject of the poem by

Topics for Further Study

- Some commentators have called cummings a unique poet. Read through several other avant-garde or experimental poetry by different poets and try to find a poem that is similar to the entry poem. Compare the two poems in terms of punctuation, grammar, and style.

- Read more about cummings's life and write a short biography about the woman who you think is the subject of the poem.

- Cummings wrote this poem during the era known as the Great Depression in the United States. Compare cummings's poetry during this time period with other depression-era poetry. Discuss any trends that you find in this poetry.

- In the poem, the poet is amazed at how his lover has been able to change his perspective about life. Research the physiology and psychology of love and discuss why you think love has this effect. Use your research to support your claims.

---

saying, "your eyes have their silence." A poet's reference to the eyes of his beloved is an age-old tradition. The eyes are commonly thought to be the windows into a person's soul, and much love poetry has been written about eyes. Cummings continues his profession of love and underscores the power of his beloved's eyes by noting that "your slightest look will easily unclose me / though i have closed myself as fingers." The poet is noting the power of love to change a person, in this case, change the poet from a closed person to an open one. As is common in love poetry, the poet expresses his adoration for his beloved by making her seem larger than life. In addition to having the power to change him from a closed man to an open one, this unnamed woman also has the power to do the reverse: "if your wish be to close me, i and / my life will shut very beautifully, suddenly." At the same time, the poet notes that this powerful woman is also very feminine, in the frail sense that his contemporary readers would have understood. Cummings says "nothing which we are to perceive in this world equals / the power of your intense fragility." The poem is also very sensual, using the image of a blooming rose, which is often given sexual connotations by writers.

Nature

Cummings's discussion of his adoration for his beloved goes hand-in-hand with his love of nature. When he is describing how easy it is for his lover's glance to open him up, if she wishes, cummings compares this process to a natural one, the blooming of a rose: "you open always petal by petal myself as Spring opens / (touching skilfully, mysteriously) her first rose." Cummings continues the natural allusions when he talks about his lover closing him. He notes that if this were to happen, it would be the same "as when the heart of this flower imagines / the snow carefully everywhere descending." In other words, cummings is linking the opening of himself to a flower's blooming in Spring, while the closing of himself is associated with a flower's death, as winter arrives and snow falls.

While the poet is infatuated with nature, he also notes that his beloved is more beautiful and her glance is more powerful than nature. He first talks about this idea in the context of the roses that he discussed earlier in the poem. He notes, "the voice of your eyes is deeper than all roses." His lover's eyes literally speak to this poet, as roses often speak to others, though in a symbolic sense. The poet expands on this idea when he incorporates another emblem of nature—rain. Cummings says "nobody, not even the rain, has such small hands." The rain is one of the natural catalysts that help a rose to bloom. The rain drops, which cummings is referring to as "hands," help to open the roses during their blooming, as if they are literally hands that pull open the petals. Yet, the poet is saying that his beloved's skilful power to open him up rivals even that of nature to open up the flower.

Faith

Throughout all of his professions of love, the poet does not express a desire to understand why his lover has such power over him and why he has such faith in her. In fact, he appreciates the fact that the origins of his faith in his lover's power remain shrouded in mystery. The poet is traveling "gladly beyond / any experience" that he has ever had. In other words, he is in the metaphysical world, the only place where intangible concepts such as love and faith can be examined. Physically, nobody can identify how people fall in love or generate their faith in that love. The poet, however, is not trying to understand the origin of his faith, even though he examines it throughout the poem. Love's mystery, which he equates with nature's mystery—as when "Spring opens (touching skilfully, mysteriously) her first rose"—is more beautiful because it remains mysterious. As he notes at the end of the poem, "(i do not know what it is about you that closes / and opens." For the poet, this is the way he prefers it. If the poet knew exactly where and why these intense feelings of his originated, it would steal some of the passion that he feels by blindly following his faith in his beloved.

Style

Imagery

For a reader who is new to cummings, or who is new to poetry, this poem may seem confusing at first. While the poem contains concrete images of objects such as eyes and roses, the ways that the poet chooses to describe them are often unusual or contradictory. For example, in the first stanza, the speaker talks about things that he "cannot touch because they are too near." This seems paradoxical at first, and hard to imagine, because if something is very close to somebody, that person should be able to touch it. When the reader realizes that cummings is speaking in metaphysical terms, the poem starts to make more sense, as do its image systems, which collectively evoke a sense of intense love and passion. Cummings uses two main image systems in his poem—human anatomy and nature. The poem's focus on anatomical imagery is apparent from the second line, when the speaker discusses his beloved's eyes. These eyes have such a power over the speaker that one look can easily "unclose" him. Likewise, a "frail gesture" made by the woman evokes powerful feelings from the speaker. The poem ends with anatomical imagery, as the speaker discusses "the voice of your eyes" and "small hands" that rival the manipulative powers of nature.

While even nature is ultimately shown to be inferior to the speaker's beloved in this final stanza, it plays an important part in the poem's imagery in the second and third stanzas. Here, the speaker uses the natural image of nature controlling a flower's lifecycle—opening in spring; dying in winter—to express the power that his beloved has over his own life. By using natural images to first establish the power of nature, these final images indicate even more effectively that the woman's powers are superior to those of nature.

Symbolism

A symbol is a physical object, action, or gesture that also represents an abstract concept, without losing its original identity. Symbols appear in literature in one of two ways. They can be local symbols, meaning that their significance is only relevant within a specific literary work. They can also be universal symbols, meaning that their significance is based on traditional associations that are widely recognized, regardless of context. In this poem, cummings relies mainly on universal symbols, which add a subtext, or second meaning, to the poem. As with the imagery, these symbols are taken from nature. The rose is a flower commonly associated with love and romance, so the blooming roses help to symbolize the speaker's blooming love. The flower symbolism runs deeper than that, however. Budding flowers are also a common symbol used to signify sexual love. Since many of cummings's poems, especially his early works, were erotic in nature, his use of a known sexual symbol was probably intentional.

Yet, cummings flips the common sexual symbolism around. Generally, when a writer uses a budding flower to symbolize sexual love, it is associated with women, who physically open themselves to men during sexual intercourse. Cummings seems to hint at this symbolism, when he organizes one of the lines in the second stanza as follows: "you open always petal by petal myself." The first two words, "you open," at first seem to be talking about the woman opening up. As the line progresses, however, the reader can see that it is the woman doing the opening. Cummings could have been grammatically correct and written the line as follows: "you always open me petal by petal." By structuring the line as he did, however, cummings gives the line, and the poem, a unique symbolism that, once again, underscores the power that the woman has over the speaker.

Historical Context

The Great Depression

When cummings wrote his poem in the early 1930s, America was in the grips of the Great Depression, a massive economic disaster that affected the entire country. As a result, many people did not have the luxury of being in awe over love, as cummings is in the poem. Most were focused on basic survival. Although the exact causes of the Great Depression are still debated, most historians agree

Compare & Contrast

- **Late 1920s–Early 1930s:** The world escalates toward a world war, in large part due to the rise to power of Adolf Hitler and the Nazi Party.

    Today: The world is engaged in a war on terrorism, in large part focusing on Middle Eastern figureheads such as Saddam Hussein of Iraq.

- **Late 1920s–Early 1930s:** During the Great Depression, most Americans focus on the struggle to survive and feed their families, so there is little time for quiet reflection about love and other feelings.

    Today: Despite a massive recession that leaves many Americans jobless, people take time out to appreciate love and other feelings. In fact, although some men still fit the stereotype of being a tough-guy male who bottles up his feelings, the self-help revolution of the late twentieth century has encouraged everybody, men included, to get in touch with their feelings.

- **Late 1920s–Early 1930s:** Americans are encouraged to be conservative with their sexuality.

    Today: Despite the very real threat of lethal venereal diseases like AIDS, it is a very sexually free time. Sensual images and words can be found in most major media, including television, radio, and print ads.

---

that the Stock Market Crash of 1929 helped to usher in this huge economic downturn. As the country began to have increasing financial troubles, however, President Herbert Hoover, along with many others, refused to provide federal aid to struggling individuals. The Hoover administration felt that the crisis was only temporary, and that in any case, it would not help Americans to give them handouts. Unfortunately, the situation only got worse. As the jobless rate rose, starvation and suicide became an issue for many families. Millions of families migrated to try to find a better life and available work in other regions of the country, but in many cases, they found neither, and instead set up shelters on vacant lots in other cities and towns, which came to be known as Hoovervilles—after President Hoover, who many blamed for the depression.

The Rise of Hitler and the Nazi Party

At the same time, the world was recovering from the financial and emotional impact of World War I, while trying to prevent another world war. Although war was technically outlawed by the Kellogg-Briand Pact, some countries refused to disarm, while others had disarmed and wished to arm again for their own protection. In addition, Germany, one of the primary aggressors in the First World War, was made to pay large reparations for its role in the war. Unfortunately, when the Great Depression hit America, it also affected other countries, including Germany, which was having its own financial problems. The Germans, inspired by Adolf Hitler and frustrated over their own rising unemployment, became increasingly hostile on the issue of war reparations payments. This issue helped Hitler and his Nazi Party gain in popularity, especially when the worldwide depression in the early 1930s affected Germany's ability to make its reparations payments. In addition to rebelling against making reparations, Hitler also spoke out against Jews, blaming the rising rate of German unemployment on Jewish businessmen. This was the beginning of an ethnic-cleansing policy that would eventually take the lives of millions of Jews. Following such horrific acts, many felt that the innocence of humanity was gone. After the war's end in 1945, however, many Americans tried to avoid these unpleasant thoughts and focus on the simple things in life, including love.

Critical Overview

When discussing the critical reception of "somewhere i have never travelled,gladly beyond," one should first examine cummings's overall reputation, since his poetry has often been described in absolute positive or negative terms, especially in the first half of his career when he wrote "somewhere i have never travelled,gladly beyond." Cummings's unique structural style and unconventional use of punctuation was disturbing to many of his contemporary critics, and people tended to either love his poetry or hate it. As R. P. Blackmur notes in his influential 1931 article for the *Hound & Horn*, "Critics have commonly said, when they understood Mr. Cummings' vocabulary at all, that he has enriched the language with a new idiom." At the same time, Blackmur also indicates that the "typographical peculiarities" of Cummings's poetry "have caught and irritated public attention." The negativity aimed toward cummings's poetry can also be seen, indirectly, in the relative lack of formal criticism of the poet, especially during these early decades.

In subsequent decades, as more poets began to employ unconventional forms and techniques, cummings's reputation also improved. As Robert E. Maurer notes in his 1955 article for the *Bucknell Review*, "It is unfortunate that most of the critical appraisals of Cummings' poetry were made early, shortly after his first books were published." Maurer disputes the idea that cummings did not know poetic rules, and so chose to use gimmicks in his writing. Maurer says, "He is instead a prime example of the old adage that an artist must know all the rules before he can break them." Likewise, in *E. E. Cummings: An Introduction to the Poetry* (1979), Rushworth M. Kidder notes that "It is important to recognize . . . that the spatial arrangements of [cummings'] poems are the work neither of a whimsical fancy nor a lust for novelty."

Today, cummings is widely regarded as one of the great twentieth-century poets. In addition, while his poem, "somewhere i have never travelled,gladly beyond," has not been examined in great detail by many critics, the poem has become one of cummings's most well-known poems and has become a favorite with readers.

Criticism

Ryan D. Poquette

Poquette has a bachelor's degree in English and specializes in writing about literature. In the following essay, Poquette discusses cummings's use of punctuation in his poem.

Many people first think of cummings's uses of language, especially his odd methods of punctuation, when they think of the poet. In fact, his unconventional approach to poetry inspired the wrath of many conservative critics during his lifetime. As S. V. Baum notes in his 1954 *South Atlantic Quarterly* article, "E. E. Cummings has served as the indispensable whipping boy for those who are outraged by the nature of modern poetry." Yet, cummings has also been acknowledged, especially recently, as one of the great modern love poets. In turn, the poem, "somewhere i have never travelled,gladly beyond," is often thought of as one of cummings's best love poems. As Robert K. Johnson notes in his 1994 entry on the poem in the *Reference Guide to American Literature*, it "exemplifies Cummings's many poems in praise of love." It is cummings's unique use of language that makes "somewhere i have never travelled,gladly beyond" such a potent statement on the powerful qualities of love.

It is apparent from a first glance at the poem that cummings follows his own rules when it comes to the use of language. This is most noticeable in his lack of spaces. The first line reads "somewhere i have never travelled,gladly beyond," a sentence construct that lacks proper grammar. Normally, when a writer uses a comma, he or she includes a space after it, to set the preceding phrase apart from the words that come after it. In this first line, however, cummings runs all of the words and the comma together. In fact, he continues this throughout the poem anywhere there is a comma in the middle of a line. One may wonder at first, as some critics have, whether cummings is doing this just to be individualistic. Yet, if one examines this odd use of punctuation in relation to cummings's theme of love, it makes sense why he is running all of the words together. Cummings is so enamored of his beloved that he does not want to even take the customary pauses that punctuation marks, such as commas, introduce into a line of poetry.

One can also find support for this idea by examining the poem's periods—or lack thereof. Poets use periods in different ways within their poetry. Some use them mid-line, to force readers to slow down in their reading. Others use them at the ends of lines to finish thoughts. At the very least, however, poets often use a period or some other end mark such as a question mark to close out the poem and signal to the reader that they have finished the examination of their subject. In "somewhere i have never travelled,gladly beyond," cummings does not do this. In fact, he does not include any periods at

> "It is as if cummings is trying to let readers inside his mind, so that they can follow his unorganized thoughts as he is having them. In novels, this is a technique known as stream of consciousness, and it involves literally going inside a character's head and following his or her jumbled thoughts."

any point in the poem. It is as if he wants to indicate grammatically the timeless quality of his love, which will never end.

Cummings's lack of capitalization also underscores this idea. Just as there are no periods in the poem, there are also no capitalized words. While poets vary in their use of capitals, they will often at the very least capitalize the first word of the first line, to indicate that it is the beginning of the poem. In fact, in cummings's time, poets were expected to do much more. Baum says "Academic procedure obligates the poet to capitalize the initial letter in every line and the pronoun *I* wherever it may occur." Cummings, however, ignored this rule, as he ignored most other poetic rules. He did this for various reasons. Within the context of "somewhere i have never travelled,gladly beyond," he does not capitalize any words, including the first word of the first line. The overall effect makes it seem as if the poem has no beginning. When this effect is combined with the effect created by the lack of a period at the end of the poem, it makes it seem as the poem has no beginning or end. The poem is eternal, just as the poet's love is eternal.

The lack of capitalization, specifically in the pronoun "I," also supports the poet's extreme devotion to his lover. As Baum notes of cummings's poetry in general, "By rejecting the pronoun *I* Cummings assumes a casual humility." This idea is well suited to "somewhere i have never travelled,gladly beyond," because the poet is completely humble. He is totally signing away any power he has over himself, even his life and death, to his beloved. Therefore, it is appropriate for him not to capitalize the pronoun that indicates himself. Likewise, the total lack of capitalization in the poem underscores the poet's feelings of humility. He is so meek that he does not capitalize any of the words in the poem. It is as if he does not want to call attention to any one part of the poem. He wants to emphasize, and wants his readers to understand, the all-consuming power of his lover's beauty and influence, which affects him so deeply that he cannot even give special emphasis to one element through the use of capitalization. This idea underscores the eternal, timeless quality of his love.

That said, however, the poet does use another form of punctuation, the parentheses, to emphasize certain moments within this eternal time scale. This is a common technique in cummings's poetry. Baum says "One of the most important elements in Cummings's technique of immediacy is the set of parenthetical marks." To Baum, this is cummings's attempt to describe the effect of "all-at-oneness" that happens when people perceive a specific moment in time. Baum sees cummings's attempts to do this as a function of "his extreme honesty as a poet," which compels cummings "to describe the complex unit of experience without the presence of falsifying temporal order." In other words, when people describe a moment of their experience, it can be described several different ways, so people generally just choose one and talk about the experience from this angle. Or, they talk about the experience in different ways, but not all at once. They say one observation, then another observation that addresses a different aspect.

For cummings, however, this is not good enough. He wants to describe everything that he is feeling all at once. So he uses parentheses to indicate that the parenthetical information is all part of the same momentary experience. For example, in "somewhere i have never travelled,gladly beyond," cummings describes how the power of his lover's glance can open him up "as Spring opens / (touching skilfully,mysteriously) her first rose." In reality, the information contained in the parenthetical and nonparenthetical portions of cummings's description explains two different aspects of a flower's blooming. One describes the physical action of Spring actually opening the rose. The other underscores the expertise and mystery of this same act, even as it happens. In a normal conversation, somebody would probably describe the fact that the rose opened, *then* discuss the mysterious aspects of this natural process. As Baum notes, however, this type of description imposes a false temporal order that does not exist naturally, and cummings refuses to do this.

Likewise, in the other use of parenthetical text in the poem, cummings offers an acknowledgement of the mystery of the power his lover holds over him, even as he is discussing that power. Cummings says "(i do not know what it is about you that closes / and opens;only something in me understands / the voice of your eyes is deeper than all roses)." It is as if cummings is trying to let readers inside his mind, so that they can follow his unorganized thoughts as he is having them. In novels, this is a technique known as stream of consciousness, and it involves literally going inside a character's head and following his or her jumbled thoughts. Cummings mimics this effect in his use of parenthetical descriptions, as if he does not want the reader to miss out on any part of the experience that he is having as he thinks about the power and mystery of his beloved.

In the end, this is the key to understanding cummings's love poem. He uses the various forms of punctuation that are at his disposal—including spaces, periods, capitalization, and parentheses—in unconventional ways, in an attempt to let readers inside his mind. The poet's goal is have readers experience the depth and potency of his love in the same way that he is experiencing it.

Source: Ryan D. Poquette, Critical Essay on "somewhere i have never travelled,gladly beyond," in *Poetry for Students*, Gale, 2003.

Bryan Aubrey

Aubrey holds a Ph.D. in English and has published many articles on twentieth century literature. In this essay, Aubrey discusses cummings's poem as an exploration of transcendental love and spiritual knowledge.

Cummings's love poems are celebrations of a many-leveled intimacy between a man and a woman. Many of them also reveal a mystical longing for transcendence that grows out of the experience of love. Transcendence is the experience of a dimension of life that is beyond all everyday categories, something that feels utterly complete, is timeless and silent, and conveys the feeling of being at the very root and essence of existence, beyond all distinctions of subject and object, of "I" and "you."

"somewhere i have never travelled,gladly beyond" is one such poem. At its most immediate level, it is a poem that honors an inexplicable mystery:

> *No amount of seminars, books, or workshops on how to find love can teach this experience to anyone.*

how, through the experience of love, one human being can awaken something in the beloved that nothing or no one else has ever managed to touch. Lovers will recognize this experience, the sense that one's whole being has opened up to the call from another, and that nothing can now be hidden or held back. No amount of seminars, books, or workshops on how to find love can teach this experience to anyone. It just happens when it happens, and it often leaves the person, as the speaker in the poem testifies, lost in wonder at the mystery of it and searching for words to express what is inexpressible.

It is at this point that the experience of being in love, of knowing and being known at the deepest levels not of personality but of soul, comes close to some types of mystical experience and parallels the language—cosmic, boundless, paradoxical—in which such experiences are expressed. It is at this meeting point of the sensual and the mystical, attained through love, that many of cummings's poems seem to hover, at the place where words give way to the wordless, talk gives way to silence, and there is a paradoxical experience of an empty fullness in which all meaning is contained and is also at rest.

What is this experience, referred to in the first stanza, of which the poet speaks? Perhaps the key phrase is "your eyes have their silence." It is not difficult to imagine the situation: two lovers sit gazing into each other's eyes. It is often said that eyes are the windows of the soul, and humans have always known the power of eye-to-eye contact. Anyone who has ever gazed steadily into the eyes of another will testify that it can produce a feeling of deep communion and primal sympathy between the two people, the sense that "I and this person are one," existing in a timeless, silent ocean of consciousness. If this kind of eye contact is conducted as a spiritual exercise with a friend or even a complete stranger, the effect can be very similar. In fact, the practice of "gazing" was used by the thirteenth century Sufi poet and mystic Rumi in his relationship with his spiritual master Shams-i-Tabriz. As Rumi gazed into the eyes of the master, there was a spiritual transmission; the prolonged eye contact dissolved the smallness of the individual self and allowed Rumi an experience of the totality of infinite love. Rumi wrote of an experience like this (quoted in Harvey):

> One look from you, and I look
> At you in all things
> Looking back at me: those eyes
> in which all things live and burn

This puts in mind line 5 of "somewhere i have never travelled,gladly beyond," in which the lover says to the beloved, "your slightest look easily will unclose me." The respected Indian spiritual teacher Ramana Maharshi, quoted in Will Johnson's *Rumi: Gazing on the Beloved*, once put it this way: "When the eyes of the student meet the gaze of the teacher, words of instruction are no longer necessary."

This, or something similar to it, seems to be the core experience out of which the poem arises. Seen in this light, the statement in line 1, that the speaker has never traveled to this "somewhere," suggests that such an experience is beyond the everyday, ego-bound self, cummings's "i," which consists of an unruly collection of thoughts, desires, feelings and memories. This "i" can indeed never travel to this "place," which exists as a completely different mode of timeless consciousness and which supplies anyone who becomes aware of it with a new sense of who he or she really is. Cummings said this fairly explicitly in another of his later poems, "stand with your lover on the ending earth," in which the "i" this time represents the higher awareness:

> —how fortunate are you and i, whose home
> is timelessness: we who have wandered down
> from fragrant mountains of eternal now

This is the real self that exists in timelessness, and which is simply overlooked or forgotten when the individual "wanders down" and focuses his or her attention on the things that exist in the endlessly repetitive tick-tock of "time time time time time" as cummings puts it in the poem quoted above.

Given all this, the metaphor of a journey in line 1 of "somewhere i have never travelled,gladly beyond" gets turned on its head, for it is not possible to go on a journey to discover something that is already present here and now. This is why the spiritual journey is often described in Eastern mystical literature (the *Upanishads*, for example) as a pathless path; the only way it can be expressed is through paradox. Cummings suggested as much in another of his posthumously published poems, "seeker of truth":

> seeker of truth
>
> follow no path
> all paths lead where
>
> truth is here

The second phrase of "somewhere i have never travelled,gladly beyond" implies another paradox in the same vein. What does it mean if something is "beyond any experience" and yet can be described as the silence discernible in the eyes of (it is to be assumed) the beloved? This is an experience that is paradoxically an un-experience, or a nonexperience, which conveys the inadequacy of the usual categories in which perceptual experiences are described.

Another paradox occurs in line 4, following the mysterious "things" conveyed by the beloved's "frail gestures" which "enclose" the speaker but which he "cannot touch because they are too near." What does it mean to say that one cannot touch something because it is too near? It may suggest that an emotion or feeling opened up in the speaker by the transforming presence of the beloved is so intimate, so delicate and subtle, that he cannot lay hold of it; to touch it, to try to articulate it in words, would be to destroy it. The phrase also suggests something even deeper. To touch something implies a separation between the toucher and the object touched. If something is so near that it cannot be touched, there is no separation between the subject and the object. The phrase thus becomes an image of oneness, of absolute union between the speaker and some previously unknown, and precious, aspect of life.

Cummings enjoyed lacing his poems with paradoxes such as these, and there has been some complaint from critics that he overused the device. In the view of Carl Bode, writing in *Critical Essays on E. E. Cummings*, cummings's paradoxes, rather than enriching his poems, "created a barrier between cummings and his reader because of the way [they] defeated even the most assiduous attempts to make out the poem's meaning."

There may be some truth in this assertion, but the paradoxes in this poem seem clearly aimed at establishing a transcendental frame of reference with which to grasp the main thrust of meaning.

"[T]he power of your intense fragility" is almost exactly the same as the paradox "strong fragile" which cummings used in his early poem "my love is building a building," and which was one of the examples that aroused Bode's displeasure. It expresses at once strength and weakness, and yet it is not devoid of meaning. The transcendental context is clear: this "intense fragility" of the beloved is like nothing that can be encountered in the everyday world of experience. It is fragile because it is likely to break up at any moment, in the sense that it is constantly leading the lover on to something beyond his customary self. This is the experience of completely open awareness that is at the heart of the poem, and which is clearly evoked, again through paradox, in the fourth line of this stanza.

In that paradox, "death and forever," the speaker dies to all smallness, all limitations, all petty concerns of life and is reborn into "forever," a state of consciousness that is complete and eternal. As L. S. Dembo, in his essay, "E. E. Cummings: The Now Man," put it: "To die in time and be reborn in timelessness is the poetic aim of life." This paradox of dying into life is a common one in religious and mystical thought. It is found in this poem by Rumi for example (quoted in Harvey's *The Way of Passion*):

> To die in life is to become life.
> The wind stops skirting you
> And enters; all the roses, suddenly,
> Are blooming in your skull.

This is a particularly interesting example since the metaphor of the opening, rebirthing self as a flowering rose is also used by cummings in the poem under consideration: "you open always petal by petal myself as Spring opens / (touching skilfully,mysteriously)her first rose." Cummings returns to this metaphor in the final stanza, but in a clever twist he transcends it as he comes back for the third time in the poem to the image of the beloved's eyes: "the voice of your eyes is deeper than all roses." In other words, the deepest truth leaves all images and metaphors behind. It is truly inexpressible, beyond the resources of language to capture. But it can be intuitively known, and its presence is always healing, even if the speaker has "closed [him]self as fingers." He would have agreed with Rumi's fellow Sufi poet Hafiz, quoted in *The Gift: Poems by Hafiz, the Great Sufi Master*, who in one poem to the divine wrote:

> I have
> Seen you heal
> A hundred deep wounds with one glance
> From your spectacular eyes.

This elucidation of the paradoxes of "somewhere i have never travelled,gladly beyond" does not absolve the poem of some of its weaknesses.

Bode and others have accused cummings of indulging in "casually semi-private writing" which would be hard to explicate unless the poet himself decided to explain it. It is difficult, for example, to ascribe much meaning to "colour of its countries" in stanza 5, or to avoid the conclusion that the words were chosen largely because of their alliteration. And the final line, "nobody,not even the rain,has such small hands" also seems a very private one. One is reminded of a lecture given by the poet Robert Graves in 1955, in which he offered 1 pound in cash to any member of the audience who could make sense of one of Dylan Thomas's more obscure lines. (Thomas is a poet who resembles cummings at many points.) Of cummings's line, it might properly be asked, In what sense does rain have hands, whether small or not? Be that as it may, it would be churlish to end with harsh criticism of a poem that moves so tenderly, so mysteriously, and with such humility, into the realm of transcendental love and spiritual knowledge.

Source: Bryan Aubrey, Critical Essay on "somewhere i have never travelled,gladly beyond," in *Poetry for Students*, Gale, 2003.

William Heyen

In the following essay excerpt, Heyen reacts to critical evaluations of Cummings by other critics and calls "somewhere i have never travelled . . . " "among the finest and most profound poems on the theme of love ever written."

E. E. Cummings' *100 Selected Poems* was published in 1959. This selection, which includes work from *Tulips and Chimneys* (1923) through *Xaipe* (1950), was made by Cummings himself. These were the poems, no doubt, that he considered his best and perhaps most representative. I'd like to talk about a few of the lyrics in this volume, and to move from them to critical considerations that they inevitably raise.

I am now three sentences deep into my talk and already almost forced to stop. For there is a sense in which, from Cummings' point of view, from the assumptions and visions of his life and life's work, poems *do not* inevitably raise critical considerations. Poems are poems, and they are to be taken for what they are or are to be left alone. And when mind starts tampering with them, Cummings would say, we'll have the same situation as occurs in one of his poems when the "doting / fingers of / prurient philosophers" poke and prod the earth to no avail. In the first of his *i: six nonlectures* (1953) Cummings quotes Rainer Maria Rilke:

"Works of art are of an infinite loneliness and with nothing to be so little reached as with criticism. Only love can grasp and hold and fairly judge them." This is said so well and it sounds so good that it may be true, but I don't know just what "love" is; or, at least, I think that part of the love I bring to any poem is the result of something more than pure feeling. But this is to quarrel, of course, more with Cummings than with Rilke.

John Logan, an American poet who has written what is to my mind the single finest essay on Cummings, will allow me to get at least my hands unstuck from this tarbaby of a dilemma. In "The Organ-Grinder and the Cockatoo: An Introduction to E. E. Cummings" (*Modern American Poetry: Essays in Criticism,* ed. Jerome Mazzaro, 1970), Logan says that when Yvor Winters charged that Cummings "understands little about poetry," Winters missed the whole point. "It is not Cummings' job," says Logan, "to understand poetry; it's his job to write it; and it is up to the critics to understand and to derive whatever new machinery they need to talk about the poems...." So, Logan will at least allow me to talk about the poet he believes to be "the most provocative, the most humane, the most inventive, the funniest, and the least understood" of his generation. I don't know whether I'm ready or ever will be to erect "new machinery," but at least I am not slapped in the face as I am by so many of Cummings' poems which accuse me of being a "most-people" with a 2 + 2 = 4 mentality should I ever attempt anything sensible or logical. For Cummings, of course, this irascibility in the face of criticism may be more of a mask than a true self. Certainly, one of his ploys is hyperbole. Richard Wilbur, in fact, tells a very winning story about visiting Cummings in Greenwich Village, about Cummings nonchalantly mentioning some sort of article on him by a fellow named Blackmur which he hadn't seen, and about seeing a whole stack of *Hound and Horn,* the magazine with Blackmur's essay, in a corner. Cummings probably was more aware of criticism than he cared to admit. Although he was a loner, and although he persisted in his stylistic and thematic leaps and glides like a single salmon making its way upstream, many of his poems, like the one beginning "mr youse needn't be so spry / concernin questions arty," may be masks and defenses. In any case, I trust that Cummings' ghost wouldn't be offended by something a professor of mine used to say: "The major purpose of criticism is that sooner or later someone should say something."

When I think of Cummings, the first poem I think about is No. 28 from the selected volume. First collected in *is 5* (1926), it argues the mathematics of that title:

> since feeling is first
> who pays any attention
> to the syntax of things
> will never wholly kiss you;
>
> wholly to be a fool
> while Spring is in the world
>
> my blood approves,
> and kisses are a better fate
> than wisdom
> lady i swear by all flowers. Don't cry
> —the best gesture of my brain is less than
> your eyelids' flutter which says
>
> we are for each other: then
> laugh, leaning back in my arms
> for life's not a paragraph
>
> And death i think is no parenthesis

I am more than fond of this poem. I think it is imaginative and compelling, convincing and even deep. But what I have realized, and this is to strike to the center of the matter on my mind, is that it sometimes seems as though I could not possibly appreciate this poem or much of Cummings if I did not read it as though Cummings were masking himself in hyperbole, as though he deliberately or not established a persona and an emotional and mental world for his persona to inhabit. I want to read this poem as though it speaks better than its speaker knows. I want to say that its essential thrust is its duplicity. I want to say that Cummings does not go as far as many of his critics have said he has gone in denying rationality, intelligence, logic; that these abstractions are indeed his whipping boys, but in a more complex way than Cummings has been given credit for.

Certainly, any poem is a fiction; it is a poem's burden to convince us of the truth of what I. A. Richards called its "pseudo-statements." When Robert Frost says "Something there is that doesn't love a wall," his poem, to be successful, has to convince me, through its images and sounds and languages, that there is indeed something in nature that wants walls down. Whether or not (and I suspect not) there *is* some natural force that detests walls is beside the point. The fiction has to be convincing, at least temporarily. Frost himself defined poetry as "a momentary stay against confusion." In "Directive" he tells us to follow him and to "Drink and be whole again beyond confusion." Poetry, to my mind, is a refuge from chaos; even when poems seek to embody chaos, they give shape to it. But while every poem is a fictional construct, the problem is that so many of Cummings' poems as-

What Do I Read Next?

- In the decade before cummings wrote "somewhere i have never travelled,gladly beyond," another avant-garde artistic movement, surrealism, gained force. *Surrealist Painters and Poets* (2001), edited by Mary Ann Caws, offers a good introduction to the works of surrealist painters and poets from this era, including some rare letters and essays that are hard to find elsewhere.

- Although cummings is best known for his poetry, he also wrote other works, including *Eimi* (1933), a travel diary of his trip to the Soviet Union in 1931. Up until that point, cummings had been a supporter of communism but changed his views after witnessing the Soviet dictatorship that masqueraded as a communist government. The book is a scathing review of the Soviet Union and its policies.

- Cummings's eccentric, experimental style was evident in his first poetry collection, *Tulips and Chimneys* (1923). While the initial reviews of the collection were mixed, many recognized cummings's poetic talent even at this early stage in his career.

- *The Outlaw Bible of American Poetry* (1999), edited by Alan Kaufman and S. A. Griffin, is a wide-ranging anthology of avant-garde and experimental American poetry from the 1950s to today. Selections include works from more than two hundred poets.

---

sume the same insistent hatred for rationality that they seem in the end to be speaking the poet's own narrow belief.

> since feeling is first / who pays any attention / to the syntax of things / will never wholly kiss you. . . .

It is not true that feeling is always first. It seems to me that emotions often arise after thought. But Cummings' first line is the given of his poem, his speaker's assumption. It is very important, of course, that he convince his listener that he is right. For this is a seduction poem. He is telling his lady to make good use of time, to act from feeling, to abandon her "syntax" in the matters of, perhaps, time and the steps of proper courtship. Our Romeo has only words—I think of Ogden Nash's famous seduction poem: "Candy is dandy, / but liquor is quicker"—and one of the delights for us in visualizing the dramatic situation of this poem is in anticipating whether or not our swain will be successful in petting or bedding his lady. This is a digression of sorts, but the poem can be read as a defense of spontaneous poetry, as a confrontation between poet and muse. What it should not be read as is a blanket condemnation of rationality. Mind was a villain for Cummings when it became dissociated from feeling, when it made bombs or political systems without regard to humane consequences.

Cummings' speaker in this poem finds perfect words and a wonderful sort of reasoning to convince his lady. He tells her that she will never really be kissed until she is kissed without forethought, that kisses are better than wisdom, that his brain's best gesture is nothing next to the flutter of her eyelids. Then he tells her that he knows, probably better than she does, just how she feels, that her eyes give her away. Then come the clinchers, the old visions of worms trying the chastity of virgins in their graves: "life's not a paragraph"—i.e., it is not something formal and organized and part of a larger composition; it is all we have. "And death I think is no parenthesis"—he argues, at the same time, that death is not parenthetical, is not a bit of extra information. Death is the final arbiter of everything. As Cummings writes in another poem, doom "will smooth entirely our minds." What lady could resist the Gatsby-like plaintiveness of that last parenthetical statement uttered so offhandedly and matter-of-factly? What lady, in fact, could resist the inexorable logic of this poem?

What we have here, then, is a carefully contrived and logical lyric that argues feeling and the abandonment of inhibition to larger forces. What we have, also, is a conventional lyric, one reminiscent of seventeenth-century love songs or even of the songs of the medieval troubadors. I hear this conventional quality often in Cummings, in a poem like "All in green went my love riding" (No. 2), for example, or in "if i have made, my lady, intricate" (No. 29).

But to return to what I see to be the central problem of any consideration of Cummings: "since feeling is first" is one of any number of Cummings' poems that seem to argue against any display of rationality, mentality, intelligence, thought; that is, against the processes of the upper mind. Cummings is often considered charming and primitive and shallow as a thinker. And worse: an antiintellectual. Norman Friedman, Cummings' first book-length critic, has said that many important critics—Edmund Wilson, Randall Jarrell, Louis Untermeyer, John Crowe Ransom, F. O. Matthiessen—have just not known what to make of Cummings. Roy Harvey Pearce in *The Continuity of American Poetry* (1961) calls Cummings "hyperconsciously lyrical" and is among those who have not been able to justify Cummings' typography. (James Dickey says he is not interested in this aspect of Cummings; Richard Wilbur sees Cummings' experiments as basically reductive, a sacrifice of the ear to the eye; Max Eastman forty years ago saw Cummings as a leading member of the "cult of unintelligibility," a poet who turned punctuation marks loose on a page like bacteria to eat the insides out of otherwise healthy words.) But the central problem in regard to Cummings is what seems to be his permanent adolescence in so stridently defending life against any intrusion by mind. Is it possible that Cummings really believes all of those escapist things he seems to be saying? Poem after poem tells us that we "shall above all things be glad and young" (No. 54), that "all ignorance toboggans into know / and trudges up to ignorance again" (No. 84), that "anything's righter / than books / could plan" (No. 88), that the supreme facts of existence are that scientists and thinkers are bad guys and that "girls with boys / to bed will go" (No. 47). Does he really believe, as he said in his introduction to new poems included in *Collected Poems* (1938), "Never the murdered finalities of wherewhen and yesno, impotent nongames of wrongright and rightwrong"? Is there as much pure and obstinate resolution in Cummings' universe as there seems to be? I don't think so. I think that just as Whitman declared himself to be a poet of body and soul but had to spend a greater amount of time on armpits and breasts because they had been neglected in poetry, Cummings has to emphasize feeling as opposed to thought. We had had enough thought in our poetry (indeed, in our whole society of passionless Cambridge ladies and politicians and scientists). And hyperbole on behalf of unimpeded emotion would help to balance the scales. Cummings relies on the shock value of unconventional statement presented no-holds-barred. Cummings' speakers speak what they believe now, and in hard words, as Emerson said any real man must. If Cummings' persona in "since feeling is first" seems to argue that any sort of mentality is useless and stupid, the poet I hear behind the poem's pose means what Emerson meant when he said that "Thinking is a partial act" and that a "man thinking" instead of a "thinking man" knew and felt that he had to live each moment of life to its utmost or he would lose his soul. The Cummings I hear is a reformer nagging and pleading for and bragging about a radical resolution of sensibility so that, as Thoreau says in *Walden,* life would be "like a fairy tale and the Arabian Nights' Entertainments. If we respected only what is inevitable and has a right to be, music and poetry would resound along the streets." In his 1946 essay "Lower Case Cummings" William Carlos Williams said that Cummings is addressing his language "to the private conscience of each of us in turn." Should any great number of us understand Cummings, said Williams, "the effect would be in effect a veritable revolution, shall we say, of morals? Of, do we dare to say, love?"

I would like at this point to quote from R. P. Blackmur, whose criticism of Cummings is archetypal:

> [In Cummings] there is no pretense at hardness of surface. We are admitted at once to the bare emotion. What is most striking, in every instance, about this emotion is the fact that, in so far as it exists at all, it is Mr. Cummings' emotion, so that our best knowledge of it must be, finally, our best guess. It is not an emotion resulting from the poem; it existed before the poem began and is a result of the poet's private life. Besides its inspiration, every element in the poem, and its final meaning as well, must be taken at face value or not at all. This is the extreme form, in poetry, of romantic egoism: whatever I experience is real and final, and whatever I say represents what I experience. Such a dogma is the natural counterpart of the denial of the intelligence.

Blackmur's chief complaint against Cummings is the deadness and personalism, though we may feel just the opposite, of Cummings' language, and even John Logan, chief among Cummings' admirers, admits that the older poet's vocabulary is "the least imaginative aspect of his work (coinages and composites aside.)" At the same time, Logan senses a great depth in many poems and tells us, in fact, that

"Freud's analysis of the punnings, splittings, and composings in the language of dreams and jokes provides an insight into some of Cummings' effects, which to my knowledge no student has yet followed out."

What strikes me as off the track of Cummings in Blackmur is his insistence that a Cummings poem "must be taken at face value or not at all," that the emotion of a poem "is Mr. Cummings' emotion." I think that this is far from true, that seldom, if ever, is Cummings' language so flat or private that I am left with only an emotion of resolution, so to speak, one that existed before the poem. The question is, with so many of Cummings' poems: What is the relation between the sensibility of the poet and his speaker's sensibility? I don't think there are any simple answers to this. Each poem may be a case in itself. I think that "since feeling is first" ought to be read as a sort of inquiry, though this is too philosophical a word, into the tenability of the poem's fictions, and not as a statement of Cummings' belief in the good sense that spontaneous sex makes in the face of death, or as just another Cummings poem celebrating the poet's own epicureanism. Cummings was a craftsman—he left behind, I read somewhere, 150 pages of drafts for a 50-line poem alone—and his poems are artifacts that often unfold several levels of irony. Given Cummings' aesthetic, his sense of the poem as an object, his labor to promote nuance and suggestion, we owe it to him to read the poems very carefully, masks and all, and not to throw them into one small basket labeled The Poet's Belief. Cummings was not, in general, a poet of the anticipated, stock emotion. Consider the depth of "if there are any heavens my mother will (all by herself) have / one" (No. 31), a poem that sounds the losses of the heaven of love. And consider "somewhere i have never travelled,gladly beyond / any experience" (No. 35). It seems to me that these two are among the finest and most profound poems on the theme of love ever written. At his best, Cummings is far from immature, and his mind is far from flimsy, whatever "since feeling is first" or similar poems initially suggest. Cleanth Brooks, in *Modern Poetry and the Tradition* (1939), can say that Robert Frost's voice issues from a character who may be described as "the sensitive New Englander, possessed of a natural wisdom; dry and laconic when serious; genial and whimsical when not; a character who is uneasy with hyperbole and prefers to use understatement to risking possible overstatement." Brooks can go on to say, and I think with justification, that "The range of Frost's poetry is pretty thoroughly delimited by the potentialities for experience possessed by such a character." I do not think, though attempts have been made, that Cummings will be caught in this way. The Cummings voice behind even what might be called the childhood poems, "in Just- / spring" (No. 4) and "who knows if the moon's" (No. 13), for example, is elusive.

I have mentioned the duplicity of many of Cummings' poems, the depth, or the level of irony inherent in them. I have also urged a close reading. To talk about one of the two love poems mentioned earlier, poems of obvious complexity, would load the argument and involve a long discussion. Blackmur also objects to Cummings' "tough guy" poems (poems of Jazz effects, tough dialects, barkers, prostitutes, etc.) as being purely surface poems which leave us with "the certainty that there was nothing to penetrate." There is no question but that Blackmur is sometimes correct. Two of Cummings' tough guy elegies come to mind, "i sing of olaf glad and big" (No. 30), and "rain or hail" (No. 78). Neither poem gives us much more than a surface. Neither poem is likely to demand particularly close attention. Also, sometimes when Cummings is just a fraction away from reaching an important theme, from coming to grips with an important issue, he seems to shy away, content with humor when much more is within reach. "spoke joe to jack" (No. 56) is such a poem. What Cummings gives us is a graphic description of a barroom fight over a girl. The last two lines, "jesus what blood / darling i said" edge toward the very complicated relationships between violence and sex, but the poem's potential seems abandoned. Also, many of Cummings' satirical poems, such as "'next to of course god america i'" (No. 24), are watery and thin, eliciting only stock responses. But often Cummings' poems are deceptively simple and we discover that what at first seemed an objective and bare statement involves much more. This is the case, I believe, with "raise the shade" (No. 10).

raise the shade
will youse dearie?
rain
wouldn't that

get yer goat but
we don't care do
we dearie we should
worry about the rain

huh
dearie?
yknow
I'm

> "To Cummings any poem and the life force that the poem manifested was an ecstasy and an intuition, not an induction. We cannot in any logical way argue with the transcendental assumptions that make Cummings' world what it is and his poems what they are."

sorry for awl the
poor girls that
get up god
knows when every
day of their
lives
aint you,
oo-oo. dearie

not so
hard dear

you're killing me

If we leave this poem in its own comic world where it seems to stand—and it is, plain and downright, a funny poem—we'll miss its larger importance, its high seriousness, its subtle art that raises it to the first rank of Cummings' poems. Cummings' persona here, probably a mistress or a prostitute on an all-nighter or sleeping with her pimp, speaks much better than she knows, and the poem becomes a wide psychological portrait in a few words and a brilliant example of dramatic irony. Immediately her diction, "youse" and "dearie," gives her away as uneducated, so ignorant that any sort of conscious irony on her part is impossible. But if someone says to us "I'm not a liar, I'm not a liar, I'm not a liar," we know that that person is protesting too much, that he is revealing more than he knows about himself, that he probably is a liar. Listen to our heroine here: "we don't care do / we dearie we should / worry about the rain / huh / dearie?" Her rhetorical questions are dead giveaways themselves, and Cummings stands behind her questions. Notice the ends of the lines: "we don't care do / we dearie we should . . . " And notice the end of the stanza: "worry about the rain . . . " She is lost, and knows it, even if this knowledge has not reached a conscious level. She also knows, or feels, that "god / knows when" other girls get up to work. She thinks of their routine as hard and dreary, but speaking in Cummings' chosen rhythms she reveals the monotony of her own affairs: "oo-oo. dearie / not so / hard dear . . . " In these terms, "you're killing me" becomes a deep statement, the poem's first line becomes a kind of prayer for any light on this waste land. But it is raining, of course, and her partner is not sufficiently interested in her slow death even to say one word.

G. S. Fraser, in a review of Cummings' *Poems: 1923–1954*, argued that what Cummings leaves out of his world is "the complex personal relationships of men and women. What Mr. Cummings seems to me to substitute for this fine traditional theme is, firstly, a celebration of the sexual appetites and achievements of the hearty male animal: and, secondly, the celebration of a kind of mystical attitude toward life in general. . . ." Fraser goes on to say that Cummings' "love poetry is, in a bad sense, impersonal. . . ." In general, I don't think this is true. To Cummings love is a serious and complex matter, difficult to fathom, fraught with darkness as we are reminded in "my father moved through dooms of love" (No. 62). In a poem like "raise the shade," it is the realm of possible love beyond this almost tragic scene that serves as the poem's foil. There are love poems in the Cummings canon as deep as we are likely to find anywhere. Impersonal? Only in the sense that Whitman's poems are impersonal, bulwarked by the faith that if he can truly speak for himself he will be speaking for us all.

I'd like to turn now to something suggested by Fraser's statement that Cummings' poetry celebrates "a kind of mystical attitude toward life." Fraser, by the way, also charges Cummings with "a youthful, not very well-balanced religiousness, a 'reverence for life' combined with a youthful refusal to accept death as a fact." I must admit that this last statement especially puzzles me, since I could argue that all of Cummings begins with the blunt fact of death and attempts to build from there. In any case, this question of Cummings' religiousness, his "mystical attitude toward life," is one that should be examined.

The truth is that Cummings often seems awfully unfashionable. He celebrates and affirms. He cherishes "mystery," one of his very favorite words, and spring and flowers. He prays that his heart be always open to little things, and he gives thanks to God for the grace of each amazing day. He tells us in his *i: six nonlectures* that he loved his parents and that they loved him—how out of step with the times is this?—and tells us that he considers himself no worthy specimen of the so-called lost generation. He insists on individuality. Rather than puzzle over good and evil, he seems to assume that we all know, if we allow our feelings full play, what is right and what is wrong. While Wallace Stevens could say that we need our minds to defend us, Cummings often seems to trust the beneficence of pure emotional Being. "Life, for eternal us, is now; and now," as he says in the introduction to his collected *Poems: 1923–1954,* "is much too busy being a little more than everything to seem anything, catastrophic included. . . ." It is difficult to know what to make of Cummings. Or is it? You know that old adage: if it has feathers like a duck and waddles like a duck and sounds like a duck and eats what a duck eats, it may very well be a duck. Cummings is a Transcendentalist. In *American Poets from the Puritans to the Present* (1968) Hyatt H. Waggoner argues, and to my mind absolutely convincingly, that Cummings' "poetry and prose give us the purest example of undiluted Emersonianism our century has yet provided." We have been slow to recognize this, and I'm not sure why. Perhaps we did not want to equate a writer as seemingly modern as Cummings, with all of his dazzle and virtuosity, with those nineteenth-century sages from Concord. But Cummings is a Transcendentalist, and to call him this, of course, is still not to button-hole him comfortably. He will elude all but general definition, as Whitman claimed to. He will never, as J. Alfred Prufrock, that most non-transcendental of all men, was, be pinned to a lepidopterist's wall.

I will not attempt to summarize the parallels Professor Waggoner draws between Cummings and Emersonian tradition. The point is that given his transcendental assumptions Thoreau, for example, and everything he says in *Walden* and elsewhere is absolutely unassailable. Criticism is beside the point. To complain that Cummings' pacifism, for example, is "not argued out," as Fraser complains, is beside the point. To talk about a "philosophy" or system of thought in regard to a poet who refuses all but illimitable Being is beside the point. Cummings has been speaking a different language from the one so many of his critics have been wanting to yoke him with. We cannot charge a Transcendentalist with unearned joy or sudden irrationality any more than we can charge a mystic. Cummings' transcendentalism explains his poems' tendencies to see society as being in conspiracy against its members, their celebrations of youth and the noble savage like Olaf who only knows that there are some things he will not eat. Cummings' transcendentalism explains his unconcern for consistency, his glorification of intuition, his optimism, even the undercurrent of satirical instruction as in "When serpents bargain for the right to squirm" (No. 89) and "Humanity i love you" (No. 16), poems whose life is rooted in the same love-hate for man and the same desire to lead the townspeople to freedom and happiness that generated *Walden.* Cummings' transcendentalism explains his "not very well-balanced religiousness." If we make the faithful leap and read Cummings in the spirit with which we read an essay by Emerson or Whitman's "Song of Myself," we will find that most of the critical objections seem to melt away. If we do not for any reason see fit to do this, his achievement often seems very thin indeed.

I see that I have made a sort of transcendentalist's circle, one that comes back to where it started but one that may not be entirely round. "Works of art"—this is Cummings quoting Rilke, as you'll recall—"are of an infinite loneliness and with nothing to be so little reached as with criticism. Only love can grasp and hold and fairly judge them." Cummings tilled the soil, as Emerson said every man must, that was given to him to till. To Cummings any poem and the life force that the poem manifested was an ecstasy and an intuition, not an induction. We cannot in any logical way argue with the transcendental assumptions that make Cummings' world what it is and his poems what they are. All we can do is to make a Cummings poem our own, to appreciate its crafts and mysteries as best we can and to come to love it, or we can reject it. His poem No. 96 begins "the great advantage of being alive / (instead of undying) is not so much / that mind no more can disprove than prove / what heart may feel and soul may touch," and ends:

> a billion brains may coax undeath
> from fancied fact and spaceful time—
> no heart can leap, no soul can breathe
> but by the sizeless truth of a dream
> whose sleep is the sky and the earth and the sea.
> For love are in you am in i are in we

Source: William Heyen, "In Consideration of Cummings," in *Southern Humanities Review*, Vol. 7, No. 2, Spring 1973, pp. 131–42.

Sources

Baum, S. V., "E. E. Cummings: The Technique of Immediacy," in *South Atlantic Quarterly*, Vol. 53, No. 1, January 1954, pp. 70–88.

Blackmur, R. P., "Notes on E. E. Cummings' Language," in the *Hound & Horn*, Vol. 4, No. 2, January–March 1931, pp. 163–92.

Bode, Carl, "E. E. Cummings: The World of 'Un,'" in *Critical Essays on E. E. Cummings*, edited by Guy Rotella, G. K. Hall, 1984, p. 83.

cummings, e. e., *Complete Poems, 1913–1962*, Harcourt Brace Jovanovich, 1972.

———, "somewhere i have travelled,gladly beyond," in *100 Selected Poems*, by e. e. cummings, Grove Weidenfeld, 1959, p. 44.

Dembo, L. S., "E. E. Cummings: The Now Man," in *Critical Essays on E. E. Cummings*, edited by Guy Rotella, G. K. Hall, 1984, p. 177.

Hafiz, *The Gift: Poems by the Great Sufi Master*, translated by Daniel Ladinsky, Penguin/Arkana, 1999, p. 88.

Harvey, Andrew, *Love's Fire: Re-Creations of Rumi*, Meeramma, 1988, p. 22.

———, *The Way of Passion: A Celebration of Rumi*, Frog, 1994, p. 105.

Johnson, Robert K., "Somewhere I Have Never Traveled, Gladly Beyond: Poem by E. E. Cummings, 1931," in *Reference Guide to American Literature*, 3d ed., edited by Jim Kamp, St. James Press, 1994.

Johnson, Will, *Rumi: Gazing at the Beloved*, Inner Traditions, 2003, pp. 2–3.

Kidder, Rushworth M., *E. E. Cummings: An Introduction to the Poetry*, Columbia University Press, 1979.

Maurer, Robert E., "Latter-Day Notes on E. E. Cummings' Language," in the *Bucknell Review*, May 1955.

Further Reading

Friedman, Norman, ed., *E. E. Cummings: A Collection of Critical Essays*, Prentice-Hall, 1972.
> Friedman, a noted cummings scholar, offers a selection of critical essays that examines several aspects of cummings's work.

Kennedy, David M., *Freedom from Fear: The American People in Depression and War, 1929–1945*, Oxford History of the United States series, No. 9, Oxford University Press, 2001.
> Kennedy, a Stanford history professor, chronicles the years during the Great Depression and Second World War, at times posing theses that directly contradict established views. This accessible, comprehensive study relies on an extensive number of both published accounts and primary sources to recreate this formative period in America's history.

Kennedy, Richard S., *Dreams in the Mirror: A Biography of E. E. Cummings*, Liveright, 1980.
> Kennedy's critical biography is noted for its insights into cummings's life. The comprehensive biography also includes drawings by cummings, comments from his daughter, and some previously unpublished poems.

Marks, Barry, *E. E. Cummings*, Twayne's United States Authors Series, No. 46, Twayne, 1963.
> Published shortly after cummings's death, this book gives a biographical and critical overview of the author's life and work.

True Night

Gary Snyder
1983

"True Night" by Gary Snyder was first published in 1983 in Snyder's collection of poems, *Axe Handles*. The poem tells a story of how the sleeping poet is awakened by the sound of raccoons in his kitchen. He gets out of bed and angrily chases the raccoons away. Then, in the stillness of the night outside the house, he becomes more reflective, to the point where he seems to become one with nature. After a while, he reminds himself that he should not get carried away by such introspective meditations. He needs his sleep and has responsibilities to his family. So, he returns to bed to sleep and await the dawning of a new day.

"True Night" is often considered the finest poem in *Axe Handles*, which was the first volume of poetry Snyder published for nine years following his Pulitzer Prize–winning collection *Turtle Island* in 1974. The poem illustrates some of Snyder's typical concerns: his appreciation of the natural world and his interest in Zen Buddhism and altered states of mind. The poem can be read metaphorically as a journey in consciousness from the dualities of the outer world to a state of oneness, followed by a return to the world of duality with an increased appreciation of its possibilities.

Author Biography

Gary Snyder was born on May 8, 1930, in San Francisco, California, the first of two children born to

Gary Snyder

Harold and Lois Snyder. His family moved to Washington and then to Oregon, and Snyder attended high school in Portland, Oregon. After graduation, he enrolled at Reed College, Portland, graduating in 1951 with a bachelor of arts degree in anthropology and literature. Snyder then entered a graduate program at Indiana University but left the following year and returned to San Francisco. In 1953, he entered the University of California, Berkeley, pursuing graduate study in Oriental languages. During this period, he also worked as a lumberjack, trail maker, and forest firewatcher. He also became part of a community of West Coast writers which included Allen Ginsberg and Jack Kerouac, who became the leaders of the Beat Generation in the 1950s.

In 1956, Snyder traveled to Japan to study Zen Buddhism and Japanese language. He remained abroad for most of the next twelve years, studying Zen and traveling to places such as India and Indonesia. It was during these years that his first two poetry collections, *Riprap* (1959) and *Myths & Texts* (1960), were published.

During the second part of the 1960s, when Snyder divided his time between the United States and Japan, he produced a steady stream of publications. These included *Riprap & Cold Mountain Poems* in 1965 (the Cold Mountain poems are Snyder's translations of poems by Han-Shan); *Six Sections from Mountains and Rivers without End* (1965); *A Range of Poems*, which included translations of the modern Japanese poet, Miyazawa Kenji (1966); *The Back Country* (1968); and *Regarding Wave* (1970). He also published a collection of essays titled *Earth House Hold: Technical Notes and Queries to Fellow Dharma Revolutionaries* (1969).

In 1971, Snyder built his own house along the Yuba River in the northern Sierra Nevada mountains. Three years later, he published *Turtle Island*, which was awarded the Pulitzer Prize for Poetry and established his national reputation. *Axe Handles*, which won the American Book Award from the Before Columbus Foundation, followed in 1983, as did *Passage through India*, a journal of the trip Snyder made to India in the 1960s.

In 1985, Snyder became a professor at the University of California, Davis, and three more poetry collections followed over the next decade: *Left out in the Rain: New Poems 1947–1986* (1986); *No Nature: New and Selected Poems* (1992); and *Mountains and Rivers without End* (1996), which Snyder had been working on for several decades. Snyder also published *The Real Work: Interviews & Talks, 1964–1979* (1980) and *The Practice of the Wild* (1990), a collection of essays which develop Snyder's ecological ideas. A representative selection of his work was published in 1999 as *The Gary Snyder Reader: Prose, Poetry, and Translations, 1952–1998*.

Poem Summary

Stanza 1

In the first line of "True Night," the poet is fast asleep in bed. Then, there is a clattering sound. Gradually, the poet is pulled awake by the persistent noise. As his mind focuses, he realizes that the sounds are caused by a raccoon that has entered the kitchen. Metal bowls are falling, jars are being pushed against each other, and many plates are also tumbling to the floor. Immediately, he springs up to take action. The word "ritual" suggests that this is not an isolated occurrence but has happened many times before.

The poet rises unsteadily from his bed, grabs a stick and dashes off in the darkness. He shouts angrily and describes himself as a "huge pounding demon," which must be the way the raccoon sees him. But, the raccoons—it now transpires that there are more than one—are too quick for him. They race around the corner, go out of the kitchen, and climb up a tree. The poet knows where they have gone because he hears a scratching sound.

Stanza 2

The poet stands at the foot of the tree. Two young raccoons perch on two dead limbs of the tree and peer down at him from both sides of the trunk. The poet rages and shouts at them for waking him up at night and for making a mess of the kitchen.

Stanza 3

The poet remains standing under the tree but now he is silent. He feels the chill of the night air on his bare flesh. The sensation on his skin seems to wake him up and make him aware of the sensations of the moment that are brought to him by the night. He is aware of his bare foot and the shape it is forming in the gravel as he stands. He is aware of himself with the stick in his hand. It is a moment of awareness that seems to freeze time.

Stanza 4

The poet observes the night. He notices long streaks of cloud that give way to "milky thin" moonlight. He notices the silhouette of the back of the branch of a black pine tree. The moon is full. Up in the hillside, the pine trees are all whispering (presumably as the breeze blows), and the crickets are still singing. But, their song is heard only faintly, from their "cold coves" somewhere in the dark.

Stanza 5

The poet turns and walks slowly back down the path, heading back for bed. He feels chilly and gets goosebumps and his hair blows in the breeze. Then, he repeats his observation of the previous strophe, about the moonlight glow that emanates from around the streaky clouds, and the rustling sound from the pine trees. At that moment, he feels almost ready to dissolve into the night. In a simile, he compares himself to a dandelion head that is about to spread its seeds on the wind. Another simile follows, as he compares himself to a sea anemone that is open and waving in cool water.

Stanza 6

The poet thinks of his own life. He is fifty years old. The next lines are ambiguous. If the lines are read literally, they reveal the poet to be an artisan who works with his hands. The adverb "still" may suggest a tone of regret, that even though he is middle-aged, this is still his occupation. On the other hand, the lines might be interpreted metaphorically. They would then suggest that the poet is a man who works in practical ways in the day-to-day material world, doing what is necessary, rather than being someone who can get carried away by the mystical sense of the presence of the night.

Stanza 7

Here, the poet remembers his sleeping family, including his children at the "shadow pool." This phrase may suggest a place where the shadows of the night comes together (pool), or it might even be a reference to a swimming pool, although that seems unlikely. The poet also remembers his lover, with whom he has lived for many years. The poet follows this with the phrase "True night," which is part of the previous sentence. The fact that it is given a line all to itself shows its significance. Although the syntax is a little puzzling, it is likely that the poet is emphasizing that sleeping during the night, rather than staying awake and immersing oneself in the night's mysterious presence, is the better way for humans to live. This is confirmed by the last two lines of the strophe, which state that it is not advisable to stay awake too long in the night.

Stanzas 8–9

This stanza explains more of what was obliquely suggested in the previous stanza. The night now seems less attractive. The poet's feet are "dusty" and his hair is tangled (in contrast to the "loose waving hair" of stanza five). He goes back to bed, knowing that he still needs more sleep. He needs to be fresh for when the new day dawns. By placing the last line in its own stanza (stanza 9), he invests it with a special significance.

Themes

Shifts of Consciousness

The poem depicts a mental process that involves profound shifts in the poet's consciousness. Although the poet tells a story about an outer event—how his sleep was disturbed by raccoons in the kitchen—he also simultaneously describes the inner workings of his own mind. When the poem begins, he is asleep and possibly dreaming (he refers to sleep and the bed itself as a "dream womb"), which means that he either has no conscious awareness (sleep), or an illusory one (dreams).

When he is first awakened by the sounds of the disturbance in the kitchen, he becomes angry.

Topics for Further Study

- Research Zen Buddhism and describe its origins and main tenets. How would you describe the Zen Buddhist method and purpose of meditating? What is a koan?

- Research shamanism in the Native American tradition. What is a shaman? What functions does a shaman perform? What is the shaman's place in traditional Native American culture, or in other cultures?

- Rewrite the first part of "True Night" from the point of view of the raccoons. Try to convey how they would experience the situation. What might they see, hear, touch, smell, taste, and sense?

- As humans build communities on ever-expanding areas of land, the natural habitats of wildlife are being displaced or altered. What is the impact of the presence of wildlife on property and residents? In what areas of the United States is the problem most acute? What can be done to alleviate the problem? Can humans and wildlife co-exist?

After he rises, he shouts and is ready to chase the raccoons away with a stick. He still shouts at them when they have escaped up a tree. This shows that the narrator is in the typical waking state of consciousness, in which consciousness is centered on the individual sense of "I," and everything else is seen as separate from it. The poet and the raccoon are different; they occupy different worlds, the human and the nonhuman; they are in opposition to each other. The gain of one—the raccoons' raid of the kitchen—is against the interests of the other—the human being who wants to sleep and to keep his home secure from intrusion.

But, this changes in the more reflective section of the poem that begins in stanza 3. Up to this point, the poet has been locked into an adversarial, ego-bound mode of consciousness. He is concerned only with the ego's need to control and shape the outer world to ensure its own comfort. Now, the stillness of the night begins to work on him. It is as if the raccoons, and his conflict with them, disappear from his awareness. They are not mentioned again. His consciousness shifts from a sense of separation from the world to a sense of oneness. Not only is he alive to all the sights and sounds of the night, no longer obsessed with the irritable workings of his own individual mind, he also seems able, so to speak, to dissolve into the night. He is in touch, a part of the natural world, no longer himself at all (in the limited, individual sense of the word), but connected to and a part of something much larger. The poet has become transparent, translucent, "open" to the natural world. All that held him fixed, rigid and apart from other things has vanished.

The last part of the poem is a journey back from this tranquil oneness with all things into a more practical awareness of the poet's responsibilities in the world. The poet does not mean merely that he must not waste his time idling outside in the beauty of the night because he needs his sleep. Although there is nothing wrong with this literal level of interpretation, the poet may have something deeper in mind. He seems to be suggesting that, although the experience he records of oneness with the natural world is a positive experience, life cannot be lived permanently in this state. The mind must return from oneness to duality, the day-to-day world. Each state has its own validity; neither is repudiated, and there must be a balance between the two in a person's life.

During the course of the poem, the poet has therefore journeyed from sleep to an agitated waking state of consciousness, to a serene contemplative mode of experience, and then back to sleep, enriched by the insights he has gained.

Style

Alliteration and Assonance

The poet uses a variety of poetic devices to create the effect he wants. In the first line, when the poet is fast asleep in bed, the assonance and alliteration, as well as the use of words of one syllable, create an effect that suggests a state of consciousness different from the normal waking state. The assonance is in the repetition of the "e" sounds in "sheath" and "sleep." These two words also show the use of alliteration, the repetition of initial consonants. The alliteration also occurs in the second part of the line, in "black" and "bed."

Onomatopoeia

In lines 3 and 4, "Comes a clatter / Comes a clatter," the alliteration and repetition create an onomatopoeic effect. (Onomatopoeia is the use of words that suggest their meaning by the sounds they make when spoken aloud.)

Simile

The poet also makes telling use of simile. A simile is a figure of speech in which one thing is compared to something else. The two items of comparison are mostly unalike, but the simile identifies one aspect in which they resemble each other. For example, in stanza 5 the poet compares himself to a "dandelion head" that is about to be blown away by the wind, and to a "sea anemone" that waves in the water. On the surface, there appears to be almost nothing that a human being has in common with either dandelion head or sea anemone. But, in the context of the poem, the simile does bring out one similarity. Neither dandelion nor sea anemone resists in any way the forces that play upon it—wind and water, respectively. They have no individual will or ego. Neither, in this situation, does the poet, who has surrendered entirely to the sensations of the night that play upon him.

Historical Context

The Environmental Movement

Snyder's collection *Turtle Island* (Turtle Island is the ancient Native American name for the North American continent), published in 1974, established him as a national voice in the environmental movement, which gathered considerable strength in the 1970s. Snyder lent his support to issues such as the need to combat industrial pollution caused by the burning of fossil fuels, the use of harmful chemicals in agriculture that taint the food supply, and the problem of nuclear waste.

By the time of the publication of *Axe Handles* in 1983, the environmental movement, which had been so successful in bringing environmental concerns to the awareness of the public, was going through a difficult period. In the view of environmentalists, the conservative administration of President Ronald Reagan championed the cause of industry and paid little attention to environmental concerns.

One environmental issue of the 1980s was acid rain, which is the increased acidity in rainfall, caused by sulfur dioxide emitted from coal-fired power plants. Environmental groups called for a 50 percent reduction of sulfur dioxide emissions, a call that was echoed by a report issued by the National Academy of Sciences. The Reagan administration opposed new regulations, however, arguing that more research on the causes of acid rain was needed.

The cleaning up of toxic waste sites was another issue in the 1980s. The Superfund was established in 1980 to help pay the costs of cleaning up polluted sites. In the early 1980s, however, the federal Environmental Protection Agency (EPA) came under fire from Democratic members of Congress for its administration of the Superfund. The EPA was accused of misusing funds and favoring the industries that cause the pollution. In 1983, there were 546 hazardous waste sites on the EPA's priority list.

In October 1983, the EPA issued a report stating that the "greenhouse effect," a warming trend in the earth due to the build up of carbon dioxide in the atmosphere, would begin to be felt in the 1990s. The greenhouse effect is now known as global warming, and despite dire warnings from scientists, the international community has still not taken any effective measures to combat it. It is predicted today, as it was in the 1980s, that global warming will have potentially catastrophic effects on coastlines, climate and agricultural production.

The Endangered Species Act (ESA) of 1973, which protected listed species (plants and animals) as well as the habitats they rely on, became a source of controversy during the 1980s. Many people argued that in many regions, the ESA restricted economic development to the point that an economic crisis was imminent. The conflict became fixed in the public mind as the "owl versus logging" issue. The owl in question was the Northern spotted owl, which in the 1980s was on the endangered species list. The timber industry vigorously argued that the protection of the spotted owl was costing thousands of jobs because of restrictions on logging. Although research published in the 1990s by a Massachusetts Institute of Technology research group established that this was not the case, for many years the issue polarized opinion on both sides.

There can be little doubt about which side of the issue Snyder was on. No reader of his poetry could fail to see that he has a deep respect for the integrity of each species of animal and plant life and values the ecological diversity that was threatened, not only in the 1980s but also today. "For

Compare & Contrast

- **1980s:** Zen Buddhism has a hundred-year history in the United States. There are many Zen centers in cities throughout the nation. Many people are attracted to Zen through the work of Snyder, who first became interested in Zen in the 1950s.

  Today: Zen Buddhism and other branches of Buddhism continue to grow steadily in the United States. The branch that has recently attracted most attention is Tibetan Buddhism. Much of this has been due to the popularity of the Dalai Lama and the publicity given to the cause of Tibet in its conflict with China by Hollywood personalities like Richard Gere, Martin Scorsese, and Steven Seagal.

- **1980s:** In *Axe Handles*, Snyder continues to advocate responsibility to a sense of community and shared culture. He admires cultures that consist of small, self-governing communities.

  Today: As *Bowling Alone: The Collapse and Revival of American Community* (2000), by Robert Putnam, demonstrates, Americans are becoming more and more isolated and disengaged from civic life. This is indicated by measures including how many times the average American votes, volunteers, goes to church, attends a club or union meeting, signs a community petition, or chats with a stranger.

- **1980s:** After a series of legislative successes in the 1970s that established regulations governing clean air and water, the environmentalist movement is on the defensive. The Reagan administration tends to favor business interests over environmental concerns.

  Today: The environmentalist movement is in a crisis. The Bush administration pursues a pro-business agenda and makes substantial efforts to ease environmental regulations. In 2001, the Bush energy plan emphasizes oil exploration and construction of coal and nuclear power plants. Energy conservation and the development of renewable energy receive little attention.

All," the last poem in *Axe Handles*, makes this abundantly clear. The poem restates the Pledge of Allegiance in a way that redefines the meaning of patriotism, and lays out an environmentalist view of what unity means in its fullest sense:

> I pledge allegiance to the soil
> of Turtle Island,
> and to the beings who thereon dwell
> one ecosystem
> in diversity
> under the sun
> With joyful interpenetration for all.

Critical Overview

Snyder's national reputation as a poet was established after his collection *Turtle Island* (1974) won the Pulitzer Prize in 1975. *Axe Handles*, which was Snyder's first collection of poems since *Turtle Island*, sold thirty thousand copies within six months of publication in 1983. For modern poetry, which does not in general create much public interest, this represented huge sales. It showed that Snyder was one of the few modern poets who was read by ordinary poetry lovers and non-specialists as well as academic critics.

"True Night" was regarded by many as the finest poem in the collection. This was the view, for example, of Robert Schultz and David Wyatt, in "Gary Snyder and the Curve of Return" (reprinted in *Critical Essays on Gary Snyder*). For these critics, "True Night" "beautifully captures the tension between the urge to be out and away and the need to settle and stay."

In *Understanding Gary Snyder*, Patrick D. Murphy interpreted the meaning of the poem as follows: "To remain in the dark too long, to be carried away permanently into the wilderness of the land and his own mind, would be to renege on the various promises he had made in his life and his poetry." Murphy also suggested that the final lines of the poem, about the waking that comes with each dawn, might be interpreted in terms of the poet's increasing awareness of his responsibilities to his community and his obligation to the future.

Criticism

Bryan Aubrey

Aubrey holds a Ph.D. in English and has published many articles on twentieth century literature. In this essay, Aubrey discusses Snyder's poem in terms of Robert Bly's concept of "double consciousness," as well as shamanism and Zen Buddhism.

In the volume of poems he selected and introduced entitled *News of the Universe: Poems of Twofold Consciousness* (1980), poet Robert Bly sketches a history of poetry in terms of the kind of human awareness it expresses. What he calls the "old position," which includes most poetry written in the seventeenth and eighteenth centuries, assumes that consciousness existed only in humans and was best expressed through reason, or the intellect. Nature was separate from humans, who believed themselves to be superior to it. Bly calls this period "the peak of human arrogance." During the romantic era in the early nineteenth century, there was a concerted attack on this position, in the work of Goethe, Hölderlin and Novalis in Germany, and Blake, Wordsworth and others in England. The romantics were conscious of a unity in the universe beyond the subject-object relationship with which humans were conditioned to perceive the world. For the romantics, nature was alive with consciousness; it was not a dead thing separate from man. As Wordsworth put it in "Lines Written a Few Miles above Tintern Abbey," he felt:

> A presence that disturbs me with the joy
> Of elevated thoughts; a sense sublime
> Of something far more deeply interfused.
> Whose dwelling is the light of setting suns,
> And the round ocean and the living air,
> And the blue sky, and in the mind of man;
> A motion and a spirit, that impels
> All thinking things, all objects of all thought,
> And rolls through all things.

Bly finds the kind of unity of consciousness expressed in romanticism continuing as an underground stream even in the heyday of modernism in the early part of the twentieth century. He cites as examples the work of Robert Frost, William Carlos Williams, and D. H. Lawrence, among others. After World War II, fresh poetic voices took up the same vision, even though it was not (and still is not) the dominant poetic tradition in American literature. Bly calls this vision "double consciousness," meaning that the poet is aware not only of consciousness residing inside himself but also outside himself in the animal, plant and even mineral world. Quoting the poet Juan Ramón Jimenez, Bly also uses the term "full consciousness" to describe this way of perceiving self and world.

One of the poets named by Bly in this context is Snyder. It is this "full consciousness" that much of Snyder's poetry seems to capture, and this is very apparent in "True Night." The first part of the poem seems at first glance to be an example of what Bly means by the "old position": man trying to control nature, preparing to take a stick to it if any part of it should disturb his comfort, such as the attempted attack by the poet on the raccoons. But, a careful reading of these lines suggests that something else is at work also.

When the poet declares in lines 14 and 15 of stanza 1, "I'm a huge pounding demon / That roars at raccoons" he is surely describing himself not the way he sees himself, but how the raccoons must see him. It is the equivalent of a sudden switch in point of view, a bursting beyond the confines of the individual consciousness to see with the eyes of the "other." The persona of the poem actually seems unaware that this is happening and slips back into normal everyday consciousness immediately, but it is surely a significant moment. It recalls D. H. Lawrence's poem "Fish," a prolonged effort by the poet to penetrate the being of a fish, to project himself into "fish consciousness." The poem includes the following lines, after the poet imagines the horror experienced by the fish when caught: "And I, a many-fingered horror of daylight to him, / Have made him die." "The many-fingered horror" is the equivalent of the "pounding demon" in "True Night."

Snyder has had a long interest in the shamanism often associated with the Native American tradition. It is this that gives him the gift, poetically speaking, of seeing into, or fully participating in, the consciousness of beings other than himself. In *The Real Work*, Snyder described shamanism as "a teaching from the nonhuman"; it involves "a sense of communication with all of life's network." It is this that is so prominent a feature of "True Night."

It is Snyder's equally long-held interest in Zen Buddhism that is responsible for the fact that "True Night" expresses in its middle section the kind of

> "Of course, the meaning of 'True Night,' as the concluding stanzas show, lies not so much in the experience of oneness with nature but in the need to return to the world of human relationships and responsibilities."

mental transformation, an emptying of the individual mind, that is the goal of meditation in the Buddhist and other Eastern religious traditions. This can be seen in the way that the poet gradually sinks into the essence of the night. This process can be understood metaphorically as the mind sinking into deeper levels of itself, where the restless ego is stilled and there is a sense of peace and oneness. In *The Real Work*, Snyder compares meditation, an act that takes the mind from surface levels to deeper levels, to the act of "still hunting":

> Still hunting is when you take a stand in the brush or some place and then become motionless, and then things begin to become alive, and pretty soon you begin to see the squirrels and sparrows and raccoons and rabbits that were there all the time but just, you know, duck out of the way when you look at them too closely.

This "still hunting" of the mind that leads to the loss of the individual self in the boundless expansiveness of (in the language of this poem) the night, is conveyed in subtle ways. It is accomplished not only through the words themselves, but in the punctuation and the arrangement of the words of the page. For example, at the end of stanza 4, in the lines "crickets still cricketting / Faint in cold coves in the dark," there is no punctuation mark after "dark" at the end of the line. Grammatically, a period is called for and would certainly have been used had this been prose writing. The lack of any punctuation at all creates for the reader an effect of open-endedness, the feeling that this particular "dark" may well go on and on without end.

The effect is repeated with even greater force at the end of stanza seven. There is no period, or any other punctuation mark, after "In this dark." A period is surely to be expected here, since the next stanza clearly begins a new sentence. The effect is to once more reinforce the meaning. The dark is endless; it represents, metaphorically speaking, an experience of eternity within the quiet of the poet's consciousness. The absence of punctuation, coupled with the expanse of white space on the page that immediately follows the phrase, helps to give the reader the experience of a "dark" that opens out (like the sea anemone in stanza five) into the endlessness of the blank white space on the page—the equivalent of the blank fullness/emptiness of the poet's own mind at this point.

A similar effect is noticeable in stanza 5, which has no punctuation at all until the period at the end, even though one might expect a period after either "hair" at the end of line 3, or after "pines," at the end of line 5, or even after "beds" at the end of line 2. The effect of the absence of punctuation is to make it impossible to sort out which subject (either "I turn" or "I feel") the dependent clauses belong to. The lack of punctuation conveys the seamlessness of the state of mind the poet describes. Just as the experience of oneness with nature is different from that of normal waking consciousness, since it breaks up the distinctions habitually made between self and world, so too the absence of punctuation thwarts the reader's expectations, leaving him or her without the usual guideposts that help to create meaning.

It is not unusual for Snyder to use methods such as this. As Jody Norton, in "The Importance of Nothing: Absence and Its Origins in the Poetry of Gary Snyder" (reprinted in *Critical Essays on Gary Snyder*), states:

> When conventionally required elements are omitted from linguistic structures ... their meanings are consequently problematized. But Snyder's procedures are aimed at more than merely confounding the understanding. His purpose is to use the grammatical, syntactical, and semantic spaces that permeate even language ... to make possible a kind of immediate knowing that language is not theoretically designed to produce.

Of course, the meaning of "True Night," as the concluding stanzas show, lies not so much in the experience of oneness with nature but in the need to return to the world of human relationships and responsibilities. No one can remain in that meditative state forever, because humans have to function in the world. People's bonds and relationships with each other are just as important as the mind-expanding practices of meditation.

Snyder addressed this issue in "The East West Interview," in *The Real Work*. He pointed out that the purpose of Zen meditation (zazen) is to experience the simplicity of being aware of oneself, of coming to know who one is without all the distracting thoughts and sense impressions that normally crowd into the mind. But, the aim is not to stay permanently in meditation, but to come back to everyday life, preferably maintaining spontaneously the experience of being gained during meditation. As Snyder says, "I still wouldn't sit [i.e. in meditation] ten hours a day unless somebody forced me, because there's too much other work in the world to be done. Somebody's got to grow the tomatoes."

It is this thought that is in the mind of the poet at the conclusion of "True Night." His enjoyment of his nocturnal excursion was profound, but there are others who depend on him, and they must have priority.

Source: Bryan Aubrey, Critical Essay on "True Night," in *Poetry for Students*, Gale, 2003.

John P. O'Grady

In the following essay, O'Grady discusses Snyder's life and works.

Gary Snyder is one of the most important American poets of the second half of the twentieth century. He has written with eloquence, intellectual power, and mythopoeic grandeur in celebration and defense of the natural world. In his *With Eye and Ear* (1970) the poet Kenneth Rexroth describes Snyder as "a master of challenge and confrontation, not because he seeks controversy but because his values are so conspicuous, so plainly stated in the context of simple, sensuous, impassioned fact that they cannot be dodged." Although Snyder has achieved renown for his role in introducing American readers to the literature and spirit of Asia, he is first and foremost a writer of the American West.

Gary Sherman Snyder was born in San Francisco on 8 May 1930, during the early months of the Great Depression. His mother, Lois Wilkey Snyder, was a Texan, some of whose ancestors had lived in Kansas; his father, Harold Snyder, was a native of Washington State. A year and a half after Snyder's birth the family moved to a farm north of Seattle, where they scratched out a meager income amid the stumps of a cutover forest. Snyder was deeply imbued with his parents' working-class, West-Coast, left-wing ideas, and in the rain forests and mountain landscapes of the Puget Sound region he came to the realization that the environment serves more complex human needs than that for natural resources. This recognition later emerged as his most profound theme, both as a writer and a political activist.

> "Although Snyder has achieved renown for his role in introducing American readers to the literature and spirit of Asia, he is first and foremost a writer of the American West."

From childhood Snyder was a voracious reader. His mother, a writer herself, encouraged her son's literary sensibility by taking him on weekly excursions to the public library in the University District of Seattle, where he would check out ten to twelve books a week. In his teenage years Snyder discovered the writings of John Muir and Robinson Jeffers, two authors widely regarded by critics as his literary precursors. While these writers served to focus his thinking along the lines of what he now refers to as "Bioregionalism," Snyder's aesthetic foundations had already been laid by his childhood reading of such Western writers as Stewart Edward White, H. L. Davis, Charles Erskin Scott Wood, and Oliver La Farge, as well as books, both ethnographic and literary, about Native American cultures.

At the beginning of World War II the Snyders moved to a low-income housing project in Portland, Oregon. When his parents' marriage dissolved near the end of the war, Snyder and his younger sister, Anthea, remained with their mother. Although he was living in the city, his feeling for the Western landscape was fortified by his view of the snowy "Guardian Peaks" of the Columbia—Mount Hood, Mount St. Helens, and Mount Adams—that hovered on the Portland horizon. In the summer of 1945 Snyder ascended Mount St. Helens as part of an old-style climbing party from the YMCA camp at Spirit Lake. The following year he joined the Mazamas, a mountaineering organization based in Portland; he went on to climb many of the highest peaks in the Northwest. His enthusiasm for the landscape of the Pacific Slope is echoed in the title of his magnum opus, *Mountains and Rivers without End* (1996).

Although he had a few bylines in the Lincoln High School student newspaper, Snyder's first formal publication appeared in 1946 in the mountaineering organization's annual, *Mazama*. "A Young Mazama's Idea of a Mount Hood Climb" is a tongue-in-cheek account of ascending the snow-capped 11,239-foot volcano and suggests that Snyder was something of a Young Turk among the postwar Northwest mountaineers. "You say you want to climb Mt. Hood?" he writes. "Don't do it! You had just better listen to me, because I'm an experienced mountaineer. I'm the one who can tell you which end of an ice axe you hold on to." After vigorously discouraging his readers from attempting the mountain, he concludes: "I'm climbing it again next week." The energy and sense of humor in this little-known essay are extraordinary for a sixteen-year-old author.

During the summer of 1947, near the base of Mount St. Helens, Snyder composed "Elk Trails," a poem that was not published until the 1986 collection *Left out in the Rain: New Poems 1947–1985*. Although a youthful effort, it anticipates the thrust of Snyder's lifework:

> Ancient, world-old Elk paths
> Narrow, dusty Elk paths
> Wide-trampled, muddy,
> Aimless ... wandering ...
> Everchanging Elk paths.

Some readers may detect a hint of the rhythms of Langston Hughes's "The Negro Speaks of Rivers" (1926) in these lines, but more important is Snyder's trademark fidelity to natural detail: this narrator will not describe anything he has not experienced himself:

> I have walked you, ancient trails,
> Along the narrow rocky ridges
> High above the mountains that
> Make up your world:
> Looking down on giant trees, silent
> In the purple shadows of ravines—
> Above the high, steep-slanting meadows
> Where sun-softened snowfields share the earth
> With flowers.

The speaker, a literary mountain man of sorts, becomes the reader's guide along the trail: he is levelheaded, skilled in woodcraft, and showing admirable restraint in his diction. At one point, however, he pushes the poem past the ordinary limits of natural history, suddenly identifying the elk as "A God coarse-haired, steel-muscled, / Thin-flanked and musky." Just as quickly, he brings his readers back to earth, where they find that this "God" is "Used to sleeping lonely / In the snow, or napping in the mountain grasses / On warm summer afternoons, high in the meadows"—exactly where one would expect to find an elk in the Western mountains. In this poem, as in many others in the Snyder canon, boundaries between realms of consciousness are not simply transgressed but are dissolved altogether, revealing the interconnectedness of all things. Some commentators have referred to this aspect of Snyder's work as his "ecological worldview," but such a label is too reductive for Snyder, whose independence of thought and spirit defy easy classification.

The conclusion of "Elk Trails" delivers an implicit Romantic critique of a human society that has fallen out of touch with nature and its ways, a theme that Snyder takes up repeatedly—perhaps most grandly in *Turtle Island* (1974), the volume for which he was awarded the 1975 Pulitzer Prize.

In the fall of 1947 Snyder entered Reed College in Portland on a scholarship. One of his professors, Lloyd Reynolds, had a passion for the art of calligraphy and the poetry of William Blake. Reynolds had a life-shaping influence not only on Snyder but also on several generations of writers who received their education at the small liberal-arts college. At Reed, Snyder made friends who shared his love for literature, including his fellow poets Lew Welch and Philip Whalen.

Important as formal education has been for him, Snyder's writings are at least as deeply rooted in the experience he acquired on the various jobs he has held, most of them outdoors. In 1949, during the summer between his sophomore and junior years, he shipped out as a merchant seaman; in 1950 he was employed excavating an archaeological site. "As I grew into young manhood in the Pacific Northwest," he reflects in *The Practice of the Wild* (1990), "advised by a cedar tree, learning the history of my region, practicing mountaineering, studying the native cultures, and inventing little rituals to keep my spirit sane, I was often supporting myself by the woodcutting skills I learned on the Depression stump-farm." Snyder cherishes a well-maintained tool as much as a well-placed word. He uses the phrase "the real work" to refer to his practice of poetry, a spiritual melding of literary and physical labor.

In 1950 Snyder married a Reed classmate, Alison Gass; they lived together for only two months.

Pursuing a dual major in literature and anthropology, he wrote a thesis in his senior year that analyzed a myth of the Haida, a coastal British Columbia native people. One of his former professors later remarked that it was the most photocopied Reed thesis of all time. It was published in 1979 as *He Who Hunted Birds in His Father's Village: The Dimensions of a Haida Myth*. The book is a scholarly work of some intrinsic interest, but it is most valuable for the light it sheds on the patterns of Snyder's development: by age twenty-one he had reached a level of intellectual sophistication rivaling that of most Ph.Ds. Clearly evident in this thesis is the poet's preoccupation with themes that recur in his work to the present day: Native American culture, the natural landscape, and the relationship between myth and literature. Yet, as Snyder himself cautions in the preface he wrote some twenty-seven years later, the essay "is about twentieth century occidental thinking as much as Dream Time, the Old Ways, or the Haida." Nevertheless, it conveys his respect for, and facility with, scholarly method.

After graduating from Reed in 1951 Snyder spent the summer working on a logging operation, setting choker cables and scaling timber on the Warm Springs Indian Reservation on the east side of the Oregon Cascades. Then he hitchhiked to Indiana University to begin graduate study in anthropology but remained there only a semester. In early 1952 he made his way to San Francisco and moved in with Whalen. That same year he and his wife were divorced.

In 1953 Snyder met Rexroth, who became a valued, albeit irascible, friend and mentor. Rexroth served as a sort of poetic elder for the young writers of Snyder's generation, presiding over the literary movement later known as the "San Francisco Renaissance," a loose affiliation of like-minded writers, artists, and intellectuals that also included Lawrence Ferlinghetti and Michael McClure. In a 1977 interview Snyder commented on those years: "San Francisco taught me what a city could be, and saved me from having to go to Europe." Also in 1953 Snyder took up residence in Berkeley and enrolled in the graduate school of the Department of East African Languages at the University of California; he remained there for the next three years but did not receive a degree.

Snyder was able to get away from the city each summer and find employment in the forests of the Pacific Slope. In the summer of 1952 he worked as a fire lookout on Crater Mountain in the Cascades of Washington, an experience that proved central to his aesthetic and spiritual development. Snyder chronicled the events of these summers in his diary and later published it as "Lookout's Journal," the opening section of his 1969 prose collection *Earth House Hold: Technical Notes & Queries for Fellow Dharma Revolutionaries*. He might have continued as a lookout for the Forest Service for several more summers, but he was denied subsequent employment because of his alleged communist sympathies.

In the summer of 1955 Snyder worked on a trail crew in Yosemite National Park. Although he had been writing poetry since high school, the poems that came to him in the Yosemite high country that summer were in a voice he recognized at once as uniquely his own. His first published volume, *Riprap* (1959), he explains in his "Statement on Poetics" in Donald M. Allen's 1960 anthology, *The New American Poetry*, "is really a class of poems I wrote under the influence of the geology of the Sierra Nevada and the daily trail-crew work of picking up and placing granite stones in tight cobble patterns on hard slab." The title poem, one of Snyder's best-known pieces, not only serves as a statement of his poetics but also provides a glimpse into the Western American backcountry cultural practice of trail-making:

> Lay down these words
> Before your mind like rocks.
> placed solid, by hands
> In choice of place, set
> Before the body of the mind
> in space and time:
> Solidity of bark, leaf, or wall
> riprap of things

In the opening of the volume the poet provides a sort of trail map to the poems that follow by defining *riprap* as "a cobble of stone laid on steep slick rock to make a trail for horses in the mountains." "Riprap" and the other Yosemite poems in the volume—"Piute Creek," "Milton by Firelight," "Above Pate Valley," "Water," and "Hay for the Horses"—remain favorites with his audience, which includes Park Service employees as well as academic literary critics. The book is dedicated to the men he worked with on the trail crew that summer and on the oil tanker *Sappa Creek* in 1957–1958. The backcountry poems in *Riprap* and subsequent volumes preserve something of the lore of the American West that otherwise might have been lost. In addition to their literary value, Snyder's writings are a trove of anthropological information on the American West in the latter half of the twentieth century.

In the fall of 1955 Snyder took up residence in Berkeley. There he met the poet Allen Ginsberg, who had recently moved from the East Coast. Soon Ginsberg's friend Jack Kerouac appeared on the scene. In October, Snyder participated in a poetry reading at the Six Gallery in San Francisco, where Ginsberg gave the inaugural performance of his poem *Howl*. In the early months of 1956 Snyder moved into a flimsy shack in a eucalyptus grove on a hillside in Marin County, north of San Francisco, converting the structure into a meditation hall where he and others could practice Zen Buddhism. Kerouac shared these quarters with Snyder during the month of April. In "Migration of Birds" in *Riprap* Snyder captures one of the more contemplative moments the two writers shared:

> I saw the redwood post
> Leaning in clod ground
> Tangled in a bush of yellow flowers
> Higher than my head, through which we push
> Every time we come inside—
> The shadow network of the sunshine
> through its vines. White-crowned sparrows
> Make tremendous singings in the trees
> The rooster down the valley crows and crows.
> Jack Kerouac outside, behind my back
> Reads the *Diamond Sutra* in the sun.

The straightforward description and understated emotion give the poem a quality that in Japanese literary aesthetics is called *yugen*, a term that translates as "quiet beauty" or "elegant simplicity." Snyder perfected this poetic technique early in his career, having encountered outstanding examples of it in his reading of classical Chinese and Japanese poetry. He also had native models in the poetry of Rexroth, especially in the latter's *The Phoenix and the Tortoise* (1944) and *The Signature of All Things* (1950). These two West Coast writers are, more than anyone else, responsible for bringing the influence of classical Buddhism into American poetry.

The events of this lively period in West Coast literary history were translated into fiction by Kerouac in his novel *The Dharma Bums* (1958), in which the character Japhy Ryder is based on Snyder. This fictional portrayal by his friend and literary compatriot proved both a boon and a curse to Snyder. The novel brought him a share of public attention, but the idealized characterization that emerges in these pages—of a youthful, upbeat, goatish, self-sufficient mountaineer-cum-Buddhist-saint—deflects attention from the real-life Snyder and his own concerns, concerns that are often far removed from those of Japhy Ryder. Years later, in *Jack's Book: An Oral Biography of Jack Kerouac* (1978), by Barry Gifford and Lawrence Lee, Snyder offered an astute summation of the importance of Kerouac's work—an analysis that applies equally to Snyder's prose and poetry: "Jack was, in a sense, a twentieth-century American mythographer. And that's why maybe those novels will stand up, because they will be one of the best statements of the myth of the twentieth century."

Snyder's association with Kerouac and with Ginsberg, who became a close lifelong friend, resulted in Snyder mistakenly being labeled a "Beat Poet," a designation he has robustly rejected. He maintained friendships with some of the leading figures of the Beat Generation, and he shared their skepticism about the political and social conservatism of the Eisenhower era; Snyder's work, however, in its political engagement and attention to nature, provides a sharp contrast to the apolitical and urban Beat aesthetic. Even so, Snyder's affiliation with Ginsberg and Kerouac constitutes an important chapter in the literary history of the West Coast. In profound and far-reaching ways, these writers who came together for a time in the mid 1950s in northern California achieved a critical mass of social and artistic awareness that soon exploded on a national level. What was called a renaissance in San Francisco in the 1950s became the "counterculture" of the 1960s, and it was all imagined first by these poets.

Snyder, however, was out of the country for much of the decade when his influence reached major proportions. In May 1956 he departed for Japan. In Kyoto he entered a Buddhist monastery and practiced Zen meditation. He soon left the monastery, but he took up residence nearby and continued his studies. His sojourn in Asia lasted until 1968 and was interrupted by a tour as a merchant seaman and occasional visits to the United States, including a teaching stint at the University of California. In Kyoto he found a lively community of Japanese and American artists and intellectuals, and he kept in close contact with his friends in the United States, who kept him informed of events during the tumultuous decade of the 1960s. He married the poet Joanne Kyger in 1960; they were divorced in 1965. In 1967 he married Masa Uehara in a ceremony on the rim of an active volcano off the coast of Japan. The couple had two sons, Kai in 1968 and Gen in 1969. The marriage ended in divorce in 1987.

While in Asia, Snyder published a steady stream of poetry and prose: *Myths & Texts* in 1960; *Six Sections from Mountains & Rivers without End* and a new edition of *Riprap*, which included his translations of the "Cold Mountain Poems" of the ancient Chinese poet Han Shan, in 1965; and *A Range of Poems* in 1966. In 1968 New Directions in New York published *The Back Country*, Snyder's first book to be brought out by a major U.S. publisher (it had been published in London in 1967). In 1969 the prose collection *Earth House Hold* was published, its title a play on the Greek root of the word *ecology*.

While all of these books to varying degrees provide insight into themes identifiably "Western" or "West Coast"—the natural environment, Native Americans, and strenuous labor in the woods—the most crucial volume in this regard is *Myths & Texts*, a long poetic sequence that Snyder composed between 1952 and 1956. The forty-eight poems are arranged in three sections, titled "Logging," "Hunting," and "Burning." In its nonlinear progression and abundance of allusion, most notably to Buddhist and Native American sources, *Myths & Texts* presents challenges to the reader akin to those found in modernist epics such as T. S. Eliot's *The Waste Land* (1922) and Ezra Pound's *Cantos* (1925–1968).

The last poem in *Myths & Texts* gives an insight into Snyder's poetics and his evolving vision for the American West. It is divided into two sections, "the text" and "the myth." The first section reads as a diary entry in verse:

> Sourdough mountain called a fire in:
> Up Thunder Creek, high on a ridge.
> Hiked eighteen hours, finally found
> A snag and a hundred feet around on fire

This part of the poem is descriptive and matter-of-fact, narrating the events of a particular day in the northern Cascades in the summer of 1952 when the speaker and others were called to fight a forest fire. By the end of this subsection, rain has come and extinguished the fire:

> We slept in mud and ashes,
> Woke at dawn, the fire was out,
> The sky was clear, we saw
> The last glimmer of the morning star.

In the way it hews closely to the facts, "the text" is historical and realistic in tone.

In contrast, "the myth"—which serves as the conclusion not only to the poem but also to the book—takes place on a nonspatial and ahistorical level of consciousness, as is immediately apparent in the opening lines: "Fire up Thunder Creek and the mountain— / troy's burning!" The physical realm, which is conditioned by space and time, is not abandoned altogether by the narrator—Thunder Creek, an actual stream in the Cascades of Washington, remains. With his mythic eye, however, the speaker sees far more going on in this watershed than any Forest Service management plan can account for; the poet directs attention to the numinous qualities that always attend ordinary events if consciousness is properly attuned. A signature quality of Snyder's poetics is that, while acknowledging the split between the historical and the mythical, he refuses to abandon one for the other. Instead, he shows how various realms of consciousness interpenetrate one another: "The mountains are your mind," he proclaims.

As the myth courses toward its conclusion, the speaker invokes Buddhist cosmology but arrives finally at an American myth by alluding to the last line of Henry David Thoreau's *Walden* (1854):

> Rain falls for centuries
> Soaking the loose rocks in space
> Sweet rain, the fire's out
> The black snag glistens in the rain
> & the last wisp of smoke floats up
> Into the absolute cold
> Into the spiral whorls of fire
> The storms of the Milky Way
> "Buddha incense in an empty world"
> Black pit cold and light-year
> Flame tongue of the dragon
> Licks the sun
> The sun is but a morning star

In *Myths & Texts*, as well as in his subsequent books, Snyder lends a new myth to the American West that supersedes the well-entrenched conquest narratives that glorify resource extraction and cultural extermination. In the preface to the 1978 edition of the book he writes: "The effort of this kind of poetry remains one of our most challenging enterprises: here on Occupied Turtle Island"—a term Snyder uses to refer to the North American continent, borrowed from a Seneca myth—"we are most of us a still rootless population of non-natives who don't even know the plants or where our water comes from."

On his return to California in 1968 Snyder homesteaded on land he had purchased with Ginsberg and others in the "Gold Country" of the Sierra Nevada foothills. In sharp contrast to the nineteenth-century gold-seekers, whose hydraulic mining operations gouged out vast swaths of terrain and silted up the region's clear-flowing rivers, Snyder, his family, and some like-minded neighbors sought a way of life that honored the nonhuman world. He called his house "Kitkitdizze," the local Indian word for an aromatic shrub usually referred to as "Mountain Misery"—a name suggestive of the cultural attitude the poet seeks to change. In his 1995 collection, *A Place in Space: Ethics, Aesthetics, and Watersheds. New and Selected Prose,* Snyder offers an optimistic reflection: "The need for ecological literacy, the sense of home watershed, and a better understanding of our stake in public lands are beginning to permeate the consciousness of the larger society."

Snyder's deepening commitment to a specific place in the American West is reflected in the books he published during the 1970s and 1980s. In *Regarding Wave* (1969), *Turtle Island, Axe Handles* (1983), and a substantial number of the poems in *Left out in the Rain: New Poems 1947–1985* he composed a body of poetry that puts him in the company of such landscape visionaries as John Muir, John Wesley Powell, and Mary Hunter Austin. In a 7 February 1978 letter to the San Francisco *Chronicle* Snyder explained, "I know it's hard for people still accustomed to thinking with an essentially European mindset to take 'place' seriously. But one of the exciting possibilities for the future will be the rise of an artistic consciousness that has begun to draw deeply on the spirit of the place."

A haunting manifestation of the spirit of place occurs in "For/From Lew," included in *Axe Handles.* The speaker encounters the ghost of Snyder's old friend and college classmate Welch, who disappeared into the thick forest and chaparral around Kitkitdizze in 1971, a presumed suicide:

> Lew Welch just turned up one day,
> live as you and me. "D——, Lew," I said,
> "you didn't shoot yourself after all."
> "Yes I did" he said,
> and even then I felt the tingling down my back.
> "Yes you did, too" I said—"I can feel it now."
> "Yeah" he said,
> "There's a basic fear between your world and
> mine. I don't know why.
> What I came to say was,
> teach the children about the cycles.
> The life cycles. All the other cycles.
> That's what it's about, and it's all forgot."

Dead but not gone, Snyder's friend becomes a genius loci, an intermediary between the human and nonhuman realms. Welch appears again in the penultimate poem in *No Nature: New and Selected Poems* (1992), "For Lew Welch in a Snowstorm." The speaker addresses Welch, observing how all people, things, and even words are subject to decay. The poem concludes:

> All those years and their moments—
> Crackling bacon, slamming car doors,
> Poems tried out on friends,
> Will be one more archive,
> One more shaky text.
>
> But life continues in the kitchen
> Where we still laugh and cook,
> Watching snow.

Individual lives pass, but life goes on. Although memory becomes an increasingly prominent subject in Snyder's later work, he does not indulge in sentimentality but ponders one of the fundamental tenets of Buddhism—that there is no inherent self-nature. This concept, in turn, becomes a major theme in the long poem *Mountains and Rivers without End.*

Forty years in the making and much anticipated by readers since early sections appeared in the 1960s, *Mountains and Rivers without End* is the great long poem of the West. Well received by reviewers, the book became, only one year after its publication, the subject of a year-long humanities seminar at Stanford University, a level of critical acknowledgment rare for a living writer. The book comprises thirty-nine poems woven into a complex tapestry, drawing on such sources as Buddhism, literature, anthropology, Native American myth, natural history, and the poet's experience. Although *Mountains and Rivers without End* opens with a poem devoted to a description of a Chinese landscape painting, the book's provenance is the American West. In an interview with John P. O'Grady that focused on his career as a West Coast writer, Snyder said of *Mountains and Rivers without End*: "In a sense, what I've done there is globalize the West.... it is a Western poem that starts and ends in the West, and never is far from it, but it uses the West, the Western landscape, almost as a metaphor for the whole planet—it becomes the whole planet."

Snyder's most recent volumes of prose, *The Practice of the Wild* and *A Place in Space*, reflect a lifetime of philosophical thought on the human relationship to place and are major contributions to environmental philosophy. While maintaining the highest scholarly standards, Snyder's philosophical writing is not filled with academic jargon; he conveys his ideas in a spare and direct style that retains all the rhetorical power of his poetry. His recurring theme of modern culture's need to "reinhabit" the North American continent is eloquently summarized in "The Rediscovery of Turtle Island" in *A Place in Space*:

> Ultimately we can all lay claim to the term native and the songs and dances, the beads and feathers, and the profound responsibilities that go with it. We are all indigenous to this planet, this mosaic of wild gar-

dens we are being called by nature and history to reinhabit in good spirit. Part of that responsibility is to choose a place. To restore the land one must live and work in a place. To work in a place is to work with others. People who work together in a place become a community, and a community, in time, grows a culture. To work on behalf of the wild is to restore culture.

In comparison to the abundance of critical analyses of Snyder's poetry, the response to his prose has lagged considerably. In the interview with O'Grady Snyder speculated that this neglect may be the result of the unfamiliar demands his books make upon readers: "There's an intellectual push there that is not part of mainstream intellectual life. There are a lot of ideas there that are new to a lot of people."

As he approached his seventieth birthday in 1999, Snyder's career showed no signs of slowing. He has long been acknowledged as a significant teacher as well as a poet, but it was not until 1986 that he formalized this aspect of his career by joining the faculty at the University of California, Davis, where, in addition to teaching literature and creative writing classes, he was instrumental in the founding of its Nature and Culture Program. With his wife, Carole Koda, whom he married in 1991, he continues to live at Kitkitdizze. The couple has been active in local environmental politics, working closely with their neighbors and the Bureau of Land Management in developing an innovative, cooperative management agreement for nearby public lands.

Snyder is editing his journals, which extend back to his teenage years. In early 1997 he was awarded the Bollingen Prize, the nation's most prestigious honor for a poet, and shortly thereafter he received the John Hay Award for Nature Writing. In conferring the Bollingen Prize, the judges observed:

> Gary Snyder, throughout a long and distinguished career, has been doing what he refers to in one poem as "the real work." "The real work" refers to writing poetry, an unprecedented kind of poetry, in which the most adventurous technique is put at the service of the great themes of nature and love. He has brought together the physical life and the inward life of the spirit to write poetry as solid and yet as constantly changing as the mountains and rivers of his American—and universal—landscape.

This otherwise excellent summary of Snyder's work neglects to mention how important the vast public lands of the American West have been to him. As a writer he has certainly put himself in the service of literature's "great themes," but more significantly he has put himself in the service of the nonhuman world, a constituency not ordinarily accorded a voice in mainstream American culture.

Gary Snyder's importance to the literature and the environmental philosophy of the American West has been great. In the words of another of his old friends, the writer and visionary thinker Alan Watts: "I can only say that a universe which has manifested Gary Snyder could never be called a failure."

Source: John P. O'Grady, "Gary Snyder," in *Dictionary of Literary Biography*, Vol. 212, *Twentieth-Century American Western Writers, Second Series*, edited by Richard H. Cracroft, Gale, 1999, pp. 269–77.

Kevin McGuirk

In the following essay, McGuirk discusses the life and poetry of Snyder.

As Wendell Berry writes in his contribution to *Gary Snyder: Dimensions of a Life* (1991), "One thing that distinguishes Gary Snyder among his literary contemporaries is his willingness to address himself, in his life and in his work, to hard practical questions." Snyder's work is informed by anarchist and union politics, Amerindian lore, Zen Buddhism, and a pragmatic commitment to and delight in the daily work that sustains community. It is important to emphasize the integrity but insufficiency of Snyder's poetry to his total cultural project. As is suggested by his title *The Practice of the Wild*, a 1990 essay collection, he wants to heal the division between practice, a cultural activity, and the wild by reading the wild itself as a culture. His aim in his work and in his life has been to envision and enact the reinhabitation of the American land on a sustainable basis. One of the most highly regarded postwar American poets, Snyder has produced a large body of poetry intelligible to the political and spiritual aspirations of many readers not normally concerned with poetry.

Snyder was born in San Francisco and raised in a poor family on a farm just north of Seattle during the Depression. His family tradition was radical on both sides—socialist and atheist. His mother studied writing at the University of Washington and introduced him to poetry. He attended Lincoln High School in Portland, where he spent his adolescent years with his younger sister, Anthea, and his mother, who worked as reporter. During these years he had his first experience of wilderness as a member of the Mazama Mountain Climbers. In 1957 he went to Reed College in Portland on a scholarship, where he met the poets Philip Whalen and Lew Welch, who became his lifelong friends, and majored in English and anthropology.

> "One of the most highly regarded postwar American poets, Snyder has produced a large body of poetry intelligible to the political and spiritual aspirations of many readers not normally concerned with poetry."

Although his literary education reflected the formalist criticism of the time, anthropology exposed him to other traditions and conceptions of the cultural role of literature. Already at this time he was recognized for his independence, unconventionality, industry, and learning. The 159 page honors thesis he wrote in 1951, *He Who Hunted Birds in His Father's Village: The Dimensions of a Haida Myth* (1979), examined the West Coast tribe's mythology from different methodological points of view and set him on the cross-cultural path he has followed in his work ever since. From 1950 to 1952 he was married to Alison Gass. In 1951 Snyder hitchhiked east to attend graduate school at Indiana University but dropped out after one semester, heading west again to enroll in Japanese and Chinese courses at the University of California at Berkeley in order to prepare himself for a trip to Japan to study Zen. He worked summers as a U.S. Forest Service lookout (1952–1953), a logging crewman in Oregon (1954), and a trail crewman in Yosemite National Park (1955), experiences that would inform his first published books.

In November 1955 Snyder participated in the famous Six Gallery reading in San Francisco, where his friend Allen Ginsberg read "Howl" publicly for the first time, a scene replayed in Jack Kerouac's Beat novel *The Dharma Bums* (1958). This novel, in which Snyder is fictionalized as Dharma hero Japhy Ryder, inaugurated Snyder's career as public figure well before he became famous as a poet and stamped him with a lingering, and ultimately limiting, Beat identity. The Beat writers' apparently freewheeling religiosity, their casual dress and manners, their adoption of jazz, and their experiments with sex and mind-altering drugs set them deliberately at odds with the establishment intelligentsia and cultural elite of the 1950s. One reviewer called them "the know-nothing Beats," but such a view belies the serious spiritual and political commitments of Snyder and many Beat figures.

The poems of *Riprap* (1959) present the young seeker-worker divesting himself of civilization—"All the junk that goes with being human / Drops away"—but an alternative vision is not clearly articulated as yet. In "Piute Greek" he encounters the sublime otherness of austere nature but is still unsure of his welcome there. What he is sure of is his deep respect for ordinary manual work and for his teachers among ordinary workers, to whom he dedicates the book. On the title page he defines the word *riprap* as "a cobble of stone laid on steep slick rock to make a trail for horses in the mountains." He makes it the central metaphor of the collection in the beginning of the title poem that is often taken as an *ars poetica*:

> Lay down these words
> Before your mind like rocks.
> placed solid, by hands
> In choice of place, set
> Before the body of the mind.

"Poetry," as Snyder writes in *Myths & Texts* (1960), is "a riprap on the slick rock of metaphysics." "Riprap" is significant first because it presents Snyder's solution to the Romantic problem of the relation between mind and nature, though his solution may be read as either advancing or diverging from that tradition: to give words in poems the qualities of things in nature. The poem is also important because it links the poetic solution to a life problem through a key Snyder concept: *work*. Snyder's "nature poetry" is not about aesthetic perception of a pristine nature but about work as an activity that mediates between humans and the material world. For Snyder the acts of the mind are grounded in physical activity. As he noted in his contribution to the classic anthology *The New American Poetry* (1960), "I've just recently come to realize that the rhythms of my poems follow the rhythms of the physical work I'm doing . . . at any given time."

Snyder writes in the American tradition articulated by William Carlos Williams in *Paterson* (1963), a poetry that discovers "no ideas but in things," or better, poetry as "a reply to Greek and Latin with the bare hands." Although as a West Coast poet he looks to Asia for supplements to his American experience rather than to Europe, he occasionally invokes the Western tradition to define his difference from it. In "Milton by Firelight," Satan is compared to the poet's trail-crew leader, Roy Marchbanks. The poem juxtaposes Satan's exclamation of despair upon seeing the unfallen Adam and Eve in the garden—"O hell, what do mine eyes / with grief behold?"—and a "Singlejack miner, who can sense / The vein and cleavage / In the very guts of rock." The juxtaposition provokes a question: "What use, Milton, a silly story / Of our lost general parents, eaters of fruit?" The crisis that captures Milton's imagination is rejected in favor of the grounded selves of the miner and an Indian boy who live in the context of the ancient sierras: "No paradise, no fall, / Only the weathering land." While Snyder finds among workers types of the poet-sage, he also looks to history. At Berkeley he translated the work of Han Shan (650–727), a hermit who lived during the T'ang dynasty, which he includes as "Cold Mountain Poems" in the collection *Riprap & Cold Mountain Poems* (1965). Han Shan "and his sidekick," Snyder writes, "became great favorites with Zen painters of later days—the scroll, the broom, the wild hair and laughter." Han Shan disdained ambition and the usual run of social life; instead, he chose a place in "a tangle of cliffs," where he reveled in "the pearl of the Buddha-nature." Cold Mountain becomes a metaphor for a life lived free and an expression of Buddhist metaphysics:

> Cold Mountain is a house
> Without beams or walls.
> The six doors left and right are open
> The hall is blue sky.
> The rooms all vacant and vague
> The east wall beats on the west wall
> At the center nothing.

Myths & Texts, which was begun in 1952 and finished in 1956, is a more systematic and ambitious volume. Except for the still unfinished "Mountains and Rivers without End," published in six sections in 1965, it is the only volume of his work conceived as a whole rather than as a collection. The book was written under the influence of Ezra Pound's *Cantos*, which Snyder read as an undergraduate. Snyder shares Pound's stress on concision, on the natural object as the adequate symbol, and on presentation rather than expression. Image-line units similar to Pound's—for example, a line such as "Thick frost on the pine bow"—are standard. The influence is structural as well as stylistic, most obviously in the organization of a variety of texts, modes, documents, and anecdotes according to the principle of juxtaposition, or collage, rather than narrative or exposition.

Myths & Texts has received less critical attention than either *Riprap* or subsequent books. It is more forbidding partly because of the absence of a consistent subjective center, or lyric "I"—the likable, straightforward speaker of the typical Snyder poem—and partly because of the inconclusiveness of its radically allusive poetics. It is less interesting as poetic autobiography than as technical experiment reflecting Snyder's early work experience and preoccupations. As Patrick Murphy observes in his essay on *Myths & Texts* in the collection *Critical Essays on Gary Snyder* (1991), which he edited, critics have observed two principals of structure underlying the poem: it is a quest, or, according to Lee Bartlett in "Gary Snyder's *Myths & Texts* and the Monomyth" (also published in *Critical Essays*), it is a three-part progression adding up to what Joseph Campbell calls a "monomyth." The book's three sections, "Logging," "Hunting," and "Burning," correspond, Bartlett argues, to "separation—initiation—return," a journey from an Apollonian vision of experience to a Dionysian one. Murphy argues that the volume is better understood as structured by the alternation and interpenetration of "texts," or phenomenal experience, and "myths," or cultural interpretations.

Part 1, "Logging," is based on Snyder's own logging experience in Oregon, but its thematic core is not personal. It comments on the exploitative and ultimately *culturally* destructive logging enterprise by juxtaposing different levels of experiences, texts, and myths. Thoreau declared that "The sun is but a morning star," but Snyder opens with a literalizing counter, stating that "the morning star is not a star"; he then cites a second position, that "The May Queen / Is the survival of / A pre-human rutting season" and tacitly relates this to images of contemporary San Francisco through juxtaposition: "Green comes out of the ground / Birds squabble / Young girls run mad with the pine bough." The second poem tells a different story in *its* selected myths and texts. Exodus 34:13—"But ye shall destroy their altars, break their images, and cut down their groves"—stands as a metonym for Western attitudes to the wild and to the investment of the wild with sacred meaning by premodern peoples. The "text" of this "myth" is that both in China and elsewhere ancient forests have long since been logged; "San Francisco 2 × 4s / were the woods around Seattle." In this poem the poet is waking "from bitter dreams" to the real world of logging: "250,000 board-feet a day / If both Cats keep working / & nobody gets hurt."

The second section, "Hunting," initiates a process of healing. Hunting describes a relationship with the natural world that may be either merely destructive or productive of integral relations. It is closely linked to shamanism, which is in turn linked to poetry. All three are cultural activities—forms of meditation or ritual—that aim to bring the hunter-shaman-poet into intimate contact with animals. "The shaman-poet," as Snyder writes in *Earth House Hold: Technical Notes & Queries for Fellow Dharma Revolutionaries* (1969), "is simply a man whose mind reaches easily out into all manners of shapes and other lives, and gives song to dreams." Shamanism is Snyder's metaphor for imagining an ideology of human-animal-wild relations to replace the mainline Western ideology.

The first poem of the Hunting section, "first shaman song," situates Snyder on an apparent vision-quest, fasting in isolation to achieve a dislocation of the self and open a chink to shamanistic wisdom. The section then enacts textually a shamanistic experience. In "this poem is for bear" Snyder retells a local native tale—shamanistic lore—about the union of a woman and a bear. Commenting on the story, the poet debunks his own potential, as if he is not yet ready for transformation. The critical piece in the section is "this poem is for deer." It depicts first the ugly practice of shooting deer from cars, in which Snyder has apparently been involved at least once, and moves toward an experience of expiation or *kenosis*: "Deer don't want to die for me. / I'll drink sea-water / Sleep on beach pebbles in the rain / Until the deer come down to die / in pity for my pain."

The third section opens with "second shaman song," in which the speaker initiates a second phase of his wilderness quest, "Quivering in nerve and muscle / Hung in the pelvic cradle / Bones propped against roots / A blind flicker of nerve. . . . / A mud-streaked thigh." The section then presents a series of purgative confrontations with evil, fear, and death that include "Maudgalyayana saw hell" and "Maitreya the future Buddha." One poem describes John Muir on Mount Ritter. Despairing of finding a foothold or handhold to lead him from the rock face, Muir discovers that "life blaze[es] / Forth again with a preternatural clearness. . . . every rift and flaw in / The rock was seen as through a microscope." Snyder achieves a vision of the Earth as feminine Buddhist Prajna: "The Mother whose body is the Universe / Whose breasts are Sun and Moon, / the statue of Prajna / From Java: the quiet smile, / The naked breasts."

The volume ends by juxtaposing the literal and mythical versions of an event. The final poem describes a fire on Sourdough Mountain that is fought all night. In the morning the firefighters "saw / the last glimmer of the morning star." Snyder gives the event mythical significance by alluding to the ancient city of Troy burning. He asserts that the "mountains are your mind" and sees "the last wisp of smoke float up / Into the absolute cold / Into the spiral whorls of fire / The storms of the Milky Way" as "'Buddha incense in an empty world.'" With this successful conclusion to the "alternation and interpenetration" of myth and text, he is able to say with Thoreau in the last line that "the sun is but a morning star" and look forward to regeneration.

Between 1956, when he won a First American Zen Centre scholarship, and 1968, when he returned to the United States permanently, Snyder spent most of his time in Kyoto, Japan, where he studied as a lay monk in the rigorous Rinzai sect of Zen under his beloved teacher Oda Sesso Roshi, who died in 1966. He was married to the poet Joanne Kyger between 1960 and 1964. *The Back Country* (1967) charts his experience of living in Japan, his visit to India with Kyger and Allen Ginsberg in 1962, and his first return to the United States in 1966. Along with *Regarding Wave* (1969) and *Earth House Hold*, a collection of notes, reviews, and essays, *The Back Country* established Snyder as a poet and extended his fame as a countercultural hero. The first critical article on his work was published in 1968.

Studying Zen as a lay monk in Kyoto, Snyder gradually came into contact with a Japanese Beat scene, a group of people calling themselves the Bum Academy, and developed an important friendship with the wandering poet and teacher Nanao Sakaki. He also met, in 1966, Masa Uehara, a graduate student in English at Ochanomizu Women's University. Following Sakaki with several others, Snyder and Masa settled on a sparsely populated volcanic island off the Japanese coast called Suwanose in 1967, where they established the Banyan Ashram, an experiment in communal living. With Sakaki acting as priest, Snyder and Masa were married on 6 August 1967 at 6:30 A.M. on the lip of the active volcano. The Suwanose experience is described in the last essay of *Earth House Hold*, concluding the movement from solitary seeker of *Riprap* to marriage and community. "It is possible at last," he writes, "for Masa and me to imagine a little what the ancient—archaic—mind and life of Japan were. And to see what could be restored to the life today." In December 1968 Snyder, Masa, and their new son, Kai, returned to the United States and set up residence in San Francisco. A second son, Gen, was born in 1969.

In some ways Snyder's least political volume, *The Back Country* covers about a decade of his life. The title can be read as referring to the wilderness, the unconscious, and the so-called backward countries of the East. The book is divided into four sections, "Far West," "Far East," "Kali," and "Back," which correspond roughly to Snyder's experiences in the American West, Japan, India, and to his return to the United States—or, in different terms, a journey from home, to otherness, to chaos and dread, and back to home on a different plane. As Charles Molesworth suggests in his book on Snyder, "If we realize the fourth section refers, among other things, to a return to America, and if we recognize in 'Kali' that much of the imagery and incidents are drawn from Snyder's visit to India in 1962, then obviously place becomes the central metaphor of the book." Place will increasingly form the basis for cultural vision in Snyder's work, and *The Back Country* as a whole traces his transformation from traveler to dweller, from alienated American to inhabitant of what he will call "Turtle Island."

"Far West" contains several of Snyder's best-known poems. "A Walk" seems like merely a casual anecdotal narrative of a hike in the woods, but it is significant in the way it concretizes values, encouraging engagement and satisfaction through its simple accumulation of particulars that, as Charles Altieri notes in *Enlarging the Temple* (1978), "require one another if they are to be appreciated fully":

> The tent flaps in the warm
> Early sun: I've eaten breakfast and I'll
> take a walk
> To Benson Lake. Packed a lunch,
> Goodbye. Hopping on creekbed boulders
> Up the rock throat three miles
> Piute Creek—
> In a steep gorge glacier-slick rattlesnake country
> Jump, land by a pool, trout skitter,
> The clear sky. Deer tracks.

Details accumulate, jostle, both in the walk and in the poem; they are completed in the arrival "At last," where he eats by the old cookstove of a trail crew. Not merely sensory, the process is in an ordinary and important sense customary: he repeats the basic but sacramental satisfactions of others before him.

The juxtaposition of such images is not merely reportorial; it should be emphasized that Snyder uses techniques he learned jointly from Pound and from Chinese poetics. As far back as his "Lookout's Journal," the opening piece in *Earth House Hold*, he noted a technical strategy based on a principal akin to Zen philosophy:

> form—leaving things out at the right spot
> ellipse, is emptiness[.]

Snyder uses gaps and spaces expressively to score the reading of the poem and give it a visual rhythm. Silences or gaps also admit the essential emptiness out of which, according to Zen, phenomena arise and into which they return.

"Burning the Small Dead" illustrates various potentials of the strategy:

> Burning the small dead
> branches
> ....
> a hundred summers
> snowmelt rock and air
> hiss in a twisted bough.
> sierra granite;
> mt. Ritter—
> black rock twice as old.
> Deneb, Altair
> windy fire[.]

Elisions, juxtapositions, spacing—these are as important as the words themselves. While the speaker is apparently burning branches, the poem seems to go on without him, more as a function of the activity itself. The relations configured in the poem, seemingly random, actually articulate an ethos, a view of relations in the world. The star Deneb and Altair and windy fire are set in apposition to one another, inviting the reader to discover identities and differences between them. Deneb and Altair are windy fire at the same time that they obviously have different references. As Altieri notes, "The process of the poem up to the last line is a continual pushing outward in time and space until the contemplative mind reaches the stars Deneb and Altair.... The last line then creates a fusion of two forces: it is a return to the limited space of the burning branches, but it is also a continuation beyond the stars to a kind of essence of fire." Phenomena are placed in relations that are local and cosmic, but the basis of their existence is emptiness.

The subsequent three sections of *The Back Country* chart Snyder's emotional and spiritual journey out and his return. In "Far East" Snyder appears as an observer in a strange culture, prompted by dislocation to a degree of self-reflection and retrospective meditation unusual in his poetry. In "Four Poems for Robin" he remembers an important relationship during his early years at Reed College. He concludes the last, "I feel ancient, as though I had / Lived many lives. // And may never now know / If I am a fool / Or have done what my / karma demands." The second section also includes "Six Years," a picture of one phase of his life in Japan reshuffled into a twelve-poem cycle representing a year, in which Snyder takes his predilection for the metonymic list to an extreme. The next section, "Kali," presents images of danger and evil that provoke an uncharacteristic yearning for "the safe place in a blanket burrow." "This Tokyo" represents Snyder at his bleakest. The meditation is opened and, more important, closed by the refrain "Peace war religion revolution / will not help." But "Back" elaborates a more positive vision, notably in "Through the Smoke Hole," a poem based on Hopi Indian cosmology. The kiva, a ceremonial structure, serves as an analogue for Snyder's own vision of a multiworld universe, while the kiva rituals for ensuring the continuity of community through life and death offer structures for Snyder's own movement beyond, if not exclusive of, the vision of "Kali" and toward the real work of building community in his native place.

Regarding Wave, written under the influence of his Japanese anarchist-visionary friends, sets Snyder firmly on a new communitarian course, celebrating a countercultural hero's version of family values. The collection begins with a poem titled "Wave," a meditation that associates the words *wave* and *wife*. The poem is a self-delighted unfolding of what it means to have a wife: the word, the woman, the "wyfman," the erotic, spiritual adventure that is "veiled; vibrating; vague":

> Ah, trembling spreading radiating wyf
> racing zebra
> catch me and fling me wide
> To the dancing grain of things
> of my mind!

The last phrase, "dancing grain of things / of my mind," nicely articulates the repetitions Snyder affirms as generated out of *wyf*, the repetition that occurs at once in things and in the things of the mind.

An exuberant formalism, or in Charles Olson's phrase, representation "by the *primitive-abstract*," dominates the book. Many poems elaborate a basic perception of formal and spiritual correspondences between different ontological planes. In "Song of the Tangle" lovers who "sit all folded" formally "repeat" the ancient temple and landscape at the center of which they sit: "Two thigh hills hold us at the fork / round mount center." Both the overgrown archaic temple and crotches of lovers are forms for discovery: "the tangle of the thigh // the brush / through which we push." "Song of the Slip," a poem arranged with every line centered on the page, proposes that the male's lovemaking completes a physical and spiritual harmony: "seedprow // moves in and makes home in the whole." When a son is born the poet stays home and discovers a new center: "From dawn til late at night / making a new world of ourselves / around this life."

Such formal design may seem to displace politics, as if the intuition of correspondence was also an intuition of a sufficient world. Thus, in "Everybody Lying on their Stomachs, Head toward the Candle, Reading, Sleeping, Drawing," as the poet's household forms a circle whose "plank shutter" is "set / Half-open on eternity," the social world is bypassed. But such intuitions of formal and spiritual shapelessness, as partly realized in erotic, family, and natural experience, provide the basis for a militant politics and poetics that envision such harmonies realized in society. *Regarding Wave* lays groundwork for the overtly political verse of later volumes. "Revolution in the Revolution in the Revolution" displays its formal repetition in a revisionary statement of political ideology:

> If the capitalists and imperialists
> are the exploiters, the masses are the workers.
> and the party
> is the communist.
> If civilization
> is the exploiter, the masses is nature.
> and the party
> is the poets.
> If the abstract rational intellect
> is the exploiter, the masses is the unconscious.
> and the party
> is the yogins.
> & POWER
> comes out of the seed-syllables of mantras.

This is a politics based on a kind of formalist logic—the substitution of new elements within the same formula. Mantras themselves are forms—more than contents—that produce a kind of elementary power through repetition. It is the kind of power that Snyder believes will drive political change.

In 1966 Snyder had bought with Allen Ginsberg one hundred acres of land on the San Juan Ridge near Nevada City in northern California. In 1970, with the help of a crew of ten, he built a home for his family there, naming it Kitkitdizze after some local vegetation. In "Buddhism and the Coming Revolution," an essay first written in 1961 and collected in *Earth House Hold*, Snyder states: "The mercy of the West has been social revolution; the mercy of the East has been individual insight into the basic self/void. We need both." Kitkitdizze and its region would be Snyder's place to develop a grounded Buddhism. Buddhism's essential perception of emptiness, its aim to look into the nature of things without prejudice, would be put to the service of a local, ecological politics informed by a planetary perspective.

What Do I Read Next?

- Buddhist teacher and community leader Thich Nhat Hanh, in *Peace Is Every Step: The Path of Mindfulness in Everyday Life* (1991), explains through stories, anecdotes, and meditations how spirituality can be lived in each moment of the day, in whatever circumstances a person finds oneself. He also provides some breathing exercises to facilitate spiritual awareness and peace of mind.

- *The Gary Snyder Reader* (1999), with an introduction by Jim Dodge, includes essays, interviews, and poetry culled from a creative life that has spanned over forty years. It serves as an excellent introduction to the range of Snyder's poetry as well as to his intellectual, social and political concerns.

- *Howl and Other Poems* (1956), by Allen Ginsberg, with an introduction by William Carlos Williams, contains the famous poem "Howl." This was first read by Ginsberg in a historic poetry reading in 1955 in San Francisco, in which Snyder also participated. Ginsberg went on to become a leading figure of the Beat Generation and a very influential personality in the radical social movements of the 1960s.

- Robert Bly's *Eating the Honey of Words: New and Selected Poems* (2000) is a collection of old and new poems by one of America's leading poets. Bly has written appreciatively about Snyder's poetry, and the range of his own work is extremely wide. Known also as the founder of the men's movement, Bly shares with Snyder an interest in spirituality, which he approaches from a mythic and psychological point of view.

- *The Complete Poems of Kenneth Rexroth* (2002), edited by Sam Hamill and Bradford Morrow, contains *The Signature of All Things*, which had a major influence on Snyder's early poetry and which Robert Bly has called one of the greatest of all American books. Rexroth, who died in 1982, is noted for his poems of nature, travel, political protest, and love. Like Snyder's poetry, *The Signature of All Things* shows a keen sense of how the material world is interpenetrated by consciousness and spirit.

Turtle Island (1974), Snyder's most successful and highly regarded book, won the Pulitzer Prize for 1975. The first complete book written after his permanent return to the United States, it has generated the most criticism of any of his books, partly because it marks a major turn in his career. The volume as a whole sets forth an explicit, sometimes militant ecopolitics, made urgent on one hand by the sense that a virtual war is being waged against the environment and on the other by the vision of sustainable life on Earth. Snyder's use of form changes as well, shifting away from his earlier emphasis on visual presentation to a more straightforward rhetorical mode. The fourth section of the book, called "Plain Talk," consists of four polemical or didactic essays. Instead of letting the images of nature "speak for themselves," Snyder now wishes "to bring a voice from the wilderness, my constituency. I wish to be a spokesman."

The book is prefaced by an opening prose salvo that explains the title and the poet's purpose in using it. Turtle Island is "the old/new name for the continent, based on many creation myths of the people who have been living here for millenia, and reapplied by some of them to 'North America' in recent years." The name must be changed, he argues, so "that we may see ourselves more accurately on this continent of watersheds and life-communities—plant zones, physiographic provinces, culture areas: following natural boundaries." Snyder calls for nothing less than the undoing of such confounding territorial markers as state lines and national borders, metonymies for civilization.

The poems, written in the service of what he calls "the real work," are revisionist histories, prophecies, spells, chants, prayers, jeremiads, and visions, as well as personal lyrics. "I Went into the Maverick Bar" describes his infiltration of a conservative establishment during a rest from the road: "My long hair was tucked up under a cap / I'd left the earring in the car." Cowboys, country music, a couple dancing, holding each other "like in High School dances / in the fifties"—Snyder acknowledges the innocent appeal of this world: "The short-haired joy and roughness— / America—your stupidity. / I could almost love you again." But out on the road "under the tough old stars" he "came back" to himself, "to the real work, to / 'What is to be done.'" The revolutionary aim of Snyder's work—not just in poetry—is indicated in the citation from Lenin. "Work" in being qualified by the adjective "real" becomes a master term for his cultural project.

American "stupidity" is not "real" because it is complicit in the destruction of the wild. In "The Call of the Wild" the wild is figured as the Native American trickster figure Coyote: amoral, unpredictable, always ungainsayable by human design. But Snyder's coyote is a real animal as well as a figure. The old man who doesn't like coyote "songs" puts out traps; the acidheads from the cities shut him out from their "oil-heated / Geodesic domes, that / Were stuck like warts / In the woods"; the government wages all-out war, "Across Asia first, / And next North America." The coyote is not a spirit that can survive the devastation of the wild. There is "A war against earth. / When it's done there'll be / no place // A Coyote could hide." The envoy reads: "I would like to say / Coyote is forever / Inside you. // But it's not true."

The question posed by this poem is who will inhabit the land: "my sons ask, who are we? / drying apples picked from homestead trees / drying berries, curing meat, / shooting arrows at a bale of straw." Up above "military jets head northeast, roaring every dawn. / my sons ask, who are they?" The poet challenges: "WE SHALL SEE / WHO KNOWS / HOW TO BE." Against the abstract innocence of a country bar and an invasive government, Snyder in "The Bath" celebrates the religious values of his new life of family in nature. Like "Burning the Small Dead," "The Bath" traces a movement from the commonplace phenomena to the apprehension of cosmic significance and back to an immediate reality invested with a larger meaning but in a more elaborate, personal, and ecstatic manner. The bath here is the family soak in the sauna, poet-father-husband-lover, two young sons, and wife-lover-cosmic-mother. The poem depends on juxtaposition, but its principal structural feature is a refrain, "is this our body?," that in its final rendering becomes the declarative "this is our body."

Consciously or not, Snyder echoes the Christian mass, which transforms ordinary bread and wine into the body of a dead savior by transforming the daily family bath into an event of religious significance.

Several of Snyder's most perceptive critics have seen the shift in *Turtle Island* as a problematic development. Either the political statements are not justified dramatically, as Altieri argues, or as Robert Kern suggests in *Critical Essays on Gary Snyder*, the statements seem like slogans because Snyder's style is made "for the quick, accurate, and reticent notation of metonymic detail that would provide no foothold for the subjective ego or analytic intellect." Michael Davidson cautions that in Snyder's turn toward a more explicit rhetorical intent "the attendant danger is that the poet will move from seer to prophet and begin to instruct where he might present." But this is only to beg the question of whether didacticism in general, and Snyder's didacticism in particular, must be considered intrinsically antipoetic.

Turtle Island, despite the limitations some critics find, can perhaps best be appreciated within its historical context. Snyder wrote the book after the bloom had gone off 1960s radicalism and in the midst of the first widely perceived ecological crisis, the oil shortage of the early 1970s. His trust in the body, in the goodness of natural impulses, in the ability of poetry to share in that goodness—a poetics of immediate experience—gives way in the 1970s to a more rhetorical style capable of dealing with the disappointments and complexities of new kinds of politics. At the same time, Snyder acknowledges both the temptation of rhetoric and its dangers, because, as he told Ekbert Faas, it may afford only a quick-fix of emotion and ideas "as against the work of doing it structurally. Convincing people with ideas is one system, the other is to change its structural basis."

Many critics have noted Snyder's tendency to elide the pronoun "I" in his poetry. For example, in "Six-Month Song in the Foothills" from *The Back Country* the preparation of tools for the spring is described. Instead of stating, "*I* am sharpening the saws," the "I" is elided, leaving only the participle: "In the cold shed sharpening saw." The speaker is a function of the work, a belief that can be related to Snyder's more general sense of how human subjectivity is derived. In *The Practice of the Wild* he writes:

> how could we *be* were it not for this planet that provided our very shape? Two conditions—gravity and a livable temperature range between freezing and boiling—have given us fluids and flesh. The trees we

climb and the ground we walk on have given us five fingers and toes. The 'place' ... gave us far-seeing eyes, the streams and breezes gave us versatile tongues and whorly ears. The land gave us a stride, and the lake a dive. The amazement gave us our kind of mind.

Snyder reverses the priority given to human subjectivity in Western philosophy; subjectivity is a derivative of natural processes. As Davidson suggests, the presentation of the natural ground of subjectivity would seem to be the appropriate mode for the poetry. Snyder observes in his contribution to the anthology *Naked Poetry* (1969) that "Each poem grows from an energy-mine-field-dance, and has its own inner grain. To let it grow, to let it speak for itself, is a large part of the work of the poet." A problem arises in *Turtle Island* because political activism in a modern nation-state is not given by nature. Nature lacks rhetorical skills, and this is why Snyder is compelled to assume a "legislative role" with the wild as his constituency. If the poets are the party of nature in a defensive war against civilization, they must marshal their rhetorical powers.

Underlying the rhetoric, however, is a perception both "primitive" and Buddhist that, as he says in "It Pleases," "The world does as it pleases." "Knowing that nothing need be done," he writes in "Plain Talk," "is where we begin to move from." As he suggests in "As for Poets," there is an earth poet, air poet, fire poet, water poet, and space poet, all with their peculiar gifts, but the ultimate place to be what Buddhists call "original mind," which encompasses matter and spirit, is the house without walls on Cold Mountain:

> A Mind Poet
> Stays in the house.
> The house is empty
> And it has no walls.
> The poem
> Is seen from all sides,
> Everywhere,
> At once.

Such freedom from anxiety—knowing that nothing *need* be done—permits one of Snyder's achievements, a lyric poetry outside the Romantic tradition. Snyder produces lyric speakers who, rather than exercise a lyric crisis of subjectivity in isolation, participate, with good humor and compassion, in collective and political endeavors.

In the nine years that passed between *Turtle Island* and his next major volume of poems, *Axe Handles* (1983), Snyder was building a life on the San Juan Ridge with his wife and sons, an activity honored in the new collection's dedication: "This book is for San Juan Ridge." The didacticism of the previous collection is tempered even as it becomes a central theme of *Axe Handles* "From/For Lew," a poem dedicated to his Reed College friend Lew Welch, exemplifies the content of instruction. Snyder, surprised Welch has not killed himself after all, sees his friend in a dream; but Welch actually is dead and has appeared only to ask Snyder to teach him the wisdom of cycles. Welch's appearance is itself one turn in the cycling of life, death, and knowledge.

In "Axe Handles" Snyder recalls teaching his son Kai how to shape a handle for his hatchet from a broken-off axe handle. The poem becomes a reflection on the transmission of both practical knowledge and the knowledge of knowledge, or culture. Snyder recalls Pound and quotes to his son: "When making an axe handle / the pattern is not far off": "And he sees." Now he recalls also Lu Ji of the fourth century A.D.:—"in making the handle / Of an axe / By cutting wood with an axe / The model is indeed near at hand"—and his Chinese teacher, Shihsiang, who translated it years ago:

> And I see: Pound was an axe,
> Chen was an axe, I am an axe
> And my son a handle, soon
> To be shaping again, model
> And tool, craft of culture,
> How we go on.

Two poems in the collection especially speak to the poles of Snyder's career, wandering and dwelling. "True Night," Robert Schultz and David Wyatt suggest in "Gary Snyder and the Curve of Return" from *Critical Essays on Gary Snyder*, articulates "the tension between the urge to be out and away and the need to settle and stay." Awakened from sleep to chase away raccoons from the kitchen, Snyder is arrested by the moment of stillness and emptiness: "I am all alive to the night. / Bare foot shaping on gravel / Stick in the hand forever." "Fifty years old," he reflects sardonically, "I still spend my time / Screwing nuts down on bolts." But he is pulled back, in Wyatt's words, by "a contrary motion," realizing that "One cannot stay too long awake / In this dark." Life is back with his family, "the waking that comes / Every day // With the dawn." The final poem, "For All," elaborates that insight as a statement of faith and purpose. Snyder is not primarily an ironic writer, but the light irony in this version of the pledge of allegiance to the American flag provides enough tension to make the poem more than a political program. It moves from exclamation, "ah to be alive"—the mind's amazement—to illustration through metonymic description of fording a stream.

This delighted kinetic experience of contiguity—not alienation, not fusion—opens to the single line, "I pledge allegiance":

> I pledge allegiance to the soil
> of Turtle Island,
> and to the beings who thereon dwell
> one ecosystem
> in diversity
> under the sun
> With joyful interpenetration for all.

A broadside of "for all" is posted on one wall of the North Columbia Cultural Center on San Juan Ridge.

In the spring of 1986 Snyder became a faculty member at the University of California at Davis, two hours' drive from his home. He has taught creative writing, literature, and wilderness thought and has been actively involved in bringing writers to the campus and in developing a program in nature and culture. This position freed him from the arduous poetry-reading circuit and gave him another area of activity, a broad scholarly community, and the encouragement to produce *Practice of the Wild*, a sustained work of prose distinct from his previous collections of occasional essays and talks. In 1991 Snyder's many friends and colleagues contributed to *Gary Snyder: Dimensions of a Life*, a book honoring the poet's sixtieth birthday. They testify to Snyder's worth as a teacher of Zen and as a model of pragmatism, courtesy, good sense, and leadership. He is praised for making his home a center for the recreative life of the San Juan community and for his generosity and honesty.

Although he has not produced a major volume of poetry since *Axe Handles*, Snyder in the fifteen-poem final section of *No Nature: New and Selected Poems* (1992), titled "No Nature," continues his "real work." Snyder seems to be looking back over his career in such poems as "On Climbing the Sierra Matterhorn Again after Thirty-One Years":

> Range after range of mountains
> Year after year after year.
> I am still in love.

"The cultural revolution is over," he says in "Building," a poem dedicated to his neighbors. But "this dance with Matter / Goes on: our buildings are solid, to live, to teach, to sit, / To sit, to know for sure the sound of a bell—/ This is history. This is outside history." Snyder again articulates a Buddhist perception: nothing need be done, yet it will be done:

> Buildings are built in the moment,
> they are constantly wet from the pool
> that renews all things
> naked and gleaming.

The last poem of the volume, "Ripples on the Surface," may reflect Snyder's exposure to poststructuralist thought at Davis, showing the latest inflection of Snyder's thinking on the relations between nature and culture:

> "Ripples on the surface of the water—
> were silver salmon passing under—different
> from the ripples caused by breezes"

Snyder asserts that nature has a signifying practice; because the ripples signify, Snyder concludes: "—Nature not a book, but a *performance*, a / high old culture." Culture is not a category of society only, not a structure set off from the wild: there is in a sense "No nature," only "Both together, one big empty house"—Cold Mountain.

Recent developments in cultural studies have made possible a less literary assessment of Snyder's work. Tim Dean's *Gary Snyder and the American Unconscious: Inhabiting the Ground* (1991) is the most ambitious work on Snyder to date, both in the critical, cultural, and theoretical materials it brings to a reading of a small selection of representative poems and in the claims it makes, not so much for Snyder's greatness as a poet but for his important role in the construction of American culture in the late twentieth century. For Dean, American culture is defined both by the central role of the land in its development and by the repression of its real relation to that land, which is one of exploitation. Snyder is significant because his principal address as poet and thinker is to that very relation, and his principal goal as cultural worker is the reinhabitation of the ground according to a different relation. His work reminds us over and over, as in *The Practice of the Wild*, that "It is not enough just to 'love nature' or to want to 'be in harmony with Gaia.'" In his 1990 interview with David Robertson, Snyder indicated that his next project would be the completion of his long poem begun in the late 1950s, "Mountains and Rivers without End."

Source: Kevin McGuirk, "Gary Snyder," in *Dictionary of Literary Biography*, Vol. 165, *American Poets Since World War II, Fourth Series*, edited by Joseph Conte, Gale Research, 1996, pp. 254–66.

Robert Schultz and David Wyatt

In the following essay excerpt, Schultz and Wyatt summarize Snyder's early work and provide in-depth coverage of Axe Handles, *the collection that contains "True Night."*

Published when he was 29, Snyder's first book ... empties the mind of the "damned memories" that clog it in an ascesis that marks the beginning of his quest. In *Riprap* (1959) he turns from America toward the East and begins the motion out and away that will preoccupy him for 15 years. *Myths & Texts* (1960) promotes Snyder's emerging vision of process in a dialectical structure which resolves that all form is a momentary stay, "stresses that come into being each instant." In a world where "It's all falling or burning" the experience of place is only a fiction, and there can be therefore nothing to return to. *Mountains and Rivers without End* (1965–) will contain 25 sections and is as yet unfinished. This may prove the major work of Snyder's career, though, as in Pound's *Cantos,* the poet can seem more committed to the theory than the poetry of this poem. The theory holds, in Snyder's words, that "every poem in *Mountains and Rivers* takes a different form and has a different strategy." A poem built upon the impulse of turning away from its own realized structures, *Mountain and Rivers* would seem a work about journeys, about "Passing / through." Its fascination however with what Snyder has called the "focal image" and with a realm above the Blue Sky also reaches toward permanence. These growing tensions as well as the poem's quality as a running rumination on all that Snyder holds dear place it at this point beyond any developmental model of Snyder's career.

The Back Country (1968) is in this argument the pivotal book, the one openly engaged with Snyder's own history of turning. What begins as a reprise of *Riprap*—in "Far West" Snyder amasses his reasons for moving and forgetting—proceeds by discovering an opposing impulse to return and remember. A poem like "Dodger Point Lookout" bears comparison to "Tintern Abbey" in its acceptance of meaning as a function of elapsed time. The return of the poet to a beloved spot five years later "brings it all back," and he admits that the conserving power of memory is what keeps him "sane."

Regarding Wave (1970) shores up the position gained in *The Back Country* by valorizing a new and conserving pattern—the wave—capable of storing and releasing the energy which Snyder had earlier discovered in the stream. A book about "What's Meant by Here." *Turtle Island* (1974) register Snyder's emerging commitment to a structure that stays in place. Homesteading replaces hitchhiking as the privileged human activity as Snyder's act of settlement in California expands into a sense of stewardship over the entire planet.

This rapid summary brings us back to *Axe Handles,* Snyder's first book of poems in nearly a decade and one in which he celebrates the whim and wisdom of middle age. In *Axe Handles* Snyder begins with work around the house and ends with journeys. Travel is now seen as the venturing out from a hearth, and thus the controlling metaphors ... are of structures that return or contain.

Axe Handles is divided into three parts, "Loops," "Little Songs for Gaia," and finally "Nets," which itself contains four sections. At first glance, the book may seem too intricate or arbitrary in its structure, but with further reading sections and subsections reveal important groupings of Snyder's current concerns. The book follows the poet's movement of mind as he attempts to discover a coherence among commitments that are personal, familial, and cultural in scope.

"True Night," the book's central poem and the concluding poem of the first section, most succinctly dramatizes the choice Snyder has made in favor of returning and settling. But the poems which surround it show the full content of the poet's choice. *Axe Handles* is a declaration of affiliations to an ideal of "home," an ideal that has grown in Snyder's imagination to include the full range of a life's attachments, from the most personal and local to the most public and distant. At the personal level, Snyder takes firm possession of his own biography, noting memories which reveal patterns of self-definition ("Look Back," "Soy Sauce," "Delicate Criss-crossing Beetle Trails Left in the Sand"). He writes of family and community with ideals of mutual support and teaching ("Changing Diapers," "Painting the North San Juan School"). He writes about the possibilities and limitations of government ("Talking Late with the Governor about the Budget"). He returns again and again to the mooring certainties of hard physical labor ("Working on the '58 Willys Pickup," "Getting in the Wood"). And, as ever, he writes with great attention to a natural order seen through the particularities of his home region (the book is dedicated "To San Juan Ridge").

Memory, family, community, teaching, government, and natural process: the subjects of *Axe Handles* necessarily involve Snyder in time and recurrence. The poet who began by relishing the obliterating sense of timelessness as he peered down alone through miles of air from Sourdough Lookout now gives special emphasis to the loops of cultural transmission, and *Axe Handles* begins with a coincidence which dramatizes for Snyder the "craft of culture." His son has asked for a hatchet handle, and while carving it with an axe Snyder remembers with a shock of recognition the Chinese phrase, "When making an axe handle the pattern is not far off." The lesson, first read in Ezra Pound and then studied again under Snyder's Japanese teacher, Chen, is now lived by the poet, and he writes:

> ... I see: Pound was an axe,
> Chen was an axe, I am an axe
> And my son a handle, soon
> To be shaping again, model
> And tool, craft of culture,
> How we go on.

The book's second poem reinforces the theme, as the spirit of Lew Welch returns from the dead to tell Snyder: " ... teach the children about the cycles. / The life cycles. All the other cycles. / That's what it's all about, and it's all forgot." And indeed, subsequent poems deal with integrities created by recurrence: the water cycle; the life cycle of a Douglas fir; loops of personal memory that illuminate present moments; and a pilgrimage of return to Japan to renew ties with Masa's family and, incidentally, to crisscross the path of Snyder's own earlier travels....

Imbued with a sense of nature's rigor, Snyder has chosen to live apart from what he takes to be the extravagance of his contemporaries. He frets comically about the $3.50 worth of kerosene required to soak his fence posts and wonders at the amount of fuel burned in displays of power by air defense jets. His alarm at our civilization's utter dependence upon a diminishing oil supply, in fact, arises in no fewer than five poems, making it one of the book's most insistent concerns. In "Alaska" he describes a trip to the oil pipeline, where he read the question, "Where will it all end?" spray-painted on the elevated tube. Later, dozing with his colleagues in a small plane, he suddenly noticed out the window "the mountains / Soaring higher yet, and quite awake."

The eerie presence of those mountains, immense and watchful, looms for Snyder as a premonition of inevitable retribution. According to the poet's sense of natural law, unnatural acts call forward inevitable consequences, and in several poems Snyder sounds a note of judgment. In "Money Goes Upstream," he is in a lecture hall, daydreaming about greed and corruption. Money, he thinks, is "an odd force ... in the world / *Not* a power / That seeks to own the source." It behaves unnaturally—"It dazzles and it slips us by. / It swims upstream." Therefore, those who place it too near the center of their lives become unmoored, possessed. Against this insidious influence Snyder poses his own ability to summon the corrective presence of nature:

> I can smell the grass, feel the stones with bare feet
> though I sit here shod and clothed
> with all the people. That's my power.

This power is two-fold: Snyder's firsthand knowledge of nature and its sufficiencies inoculates him from avarice, and his ability to summon what is not present keeps him ever close to the natural law from which he borrows his authority.

Snyder could hardly have traveled farther from his early absorption with moments of pure vision or sensation to the instinct for teaching—and judgment—so apparent in *Axe Handles*. The former experience is solitary and held out of time by its novelty and intensity, while "passing on" is communal and temporal, yet the poet still holds that our most fundamental knowledge is discovered in moments of experience which stand out of time. And, as if to reaffirm this fact, Snyder includes at the center of *Axe Handles* a sequence of lyrics which presents a gallery of such moments.

"Little Songs for Gaia," issued in an earlier version as a Copper Canyon Press chapbook (1979), is addressed to the earth goddess of Greek mythology. In it Snyder descends from the more general point of view which allows him to be discursive elsewhere in the book to write here with an unmixed particularity. The ecological point of view expressed in *Axe Handles* has grown out of a thousand individual experiences, and here Snyder reestablishes contact, zooming down to the thing, itself:

> Red soil—blue sky—white cloud—grainy granite,
> and
> Twenty thousand mountain miles of manzanita.
> Some beautiful tiny manzanita
> I saw a single, perfect, lovely,
> manzanita
> Ha.

Snyder, like Antaeus, renews his strength by touching ground, and that is what he does in this middle section, absorbed in description of his home region and his daily domestic life.

Elsewhere in the book readers may sometimes balk at Snyder's prose-like rhythms, which often conform only to the poet's clipped, trochaic manner of speech. But "Little Songs for Gaia" features some of the most accomplished lyric writing of Snyder's career whether he is presenting a dream of corn goddesses or a deer hit by a car:

> Dead doe lying in the rain
> on the shoulder
> in the gravel
> I see your stiff leg
> in the headlights
> by the roadside
> Dead doe lying in the rain

The circularity of this brief lyric fixes our attention, beginning and end, on the unfortunate deer, with the assonance of the spondee, "Dead doe," hammering home the image. In between, the four prepositional phrases are exactly parallel in rhythm, relentlessly locating the dead animal. And in between them, the kernel sentence, "I see your stiff leg," particularizes the doe efficiently and with poignance.

Elsewhere, Snyder even uses end rhyme to good effect:

> Log trucks go by at four in the morning
> as we roll in our sleeping bags
> dreaming of health.
> The log trucks remind us,
> as we think, dream and play
> Of the world that is carried away.

The surprise of the closural rhyme, which suddenly links the family's dreams and play with eventual loss, is largely responsible for the power of this brief lyric. Contributing to the effect, three consecutive anapests speed the final line, creating a sense of the poet's world quickly slipping away.

"Little Songs for Gaia" is made of glimpses— heightened moments of perception or feeling communicating an intimacy of contract with things which spices and sustains the life of the poet. Everywhere in this section Snyder is intent upon the particular and absorbed in the moment, attending to everything as to the flickers' call: "THIS! / THIS! / THIS! / in the cool pine breeze."

Snyder moves back from knowing to doing in the book's final section, "Nets," in which each of the four clusters of poems forms a rather loosely organized Poundian "ideogram." Taken together, these four clusters portray the "nets" of contemplation and activity in which Snyder is currently enmeshed.

The first, a bridge from the Gaia sequence, presents Snyder active and reverent in a natural world that flashes glimpses of deity. Walking a Yellowstone meadow, for instance, he observes its graceful creatures and ambiguously records the perception of a goddess-like presence:

> And I saw: the turn of the head, the glance of the
> eye, each gesture, each lift and stamp
> Of your high-arched feet.

Part II of "Nets" probes the possibilities and shortcomings of government. Snyder is skeptical (he seems to long for a more expansive governmental perspective when he notes that "The great pines on the Capitol grounds [in Sacramento] / Are less than a century old"), but he is willing to participate, and former California governor Jerry Brown, who appointed Snyder to the state Arts Council, is a sympathetic character in the book. Adding another piece of the cultural puzzle, part III juxtaposes "civilization" with more primitive ways of life, marking chiefly their differing relationships to the ecosystems which support them....

The allegiances pledged in *Axe Handles* are many—to family, community, culture, and planet. And to make such pledges Snyder has turned considerably from his earlier conception of the world as "all change, in thoughts, / As well as things" ("Riprap"). Within this earlier view, the poet's only recourse was to attempt to fix in words moments plucked out of the careering flux.

In *Axe Handles* there are many heightened moments seized out of time by language, but these are now seen to take their place within a broader continuity. Snyder still prizes moments when the self loses itself entirely in sensation, and a poem like "Getting in the Wood" shows how that early experience of transcendence survives into its new context. This passage in mid-poem contains no subject because the self is utterly absorbed in its work:

> The lean and heave on the peavey
> that breaks free the last of a bucked
> three-foot round,
> it lies flat on smashed oaklings—

Departing from the usual subject-predicate structure, Snyder's noun phrase presents only the effort itself and the object worked upon, with internal rhyme and skillfully managed rhythms communicating the strain of the job. The poet is happily lost in what he elsewhere calls the "relentless clarity at the heart of work," an experience which is for Snyder virtually a kind of meditation. At peace in his work, his attention is enthralled by "Wedge and sledge, peavey and maul, / little axe, canteen, piggy-back can / of saw-mix gas and oil for the chain, / knapsack of files and goggles and rags."

Snyder could be writing about his early logging days in a poem like this, which captures in words the grit and strain of sensation. But the distance he has traveled since those early days is revealed in the final stanza, in which the task at hand is shown to be a collective one, and in which Snyder emphasizes the continuities of family and community which the work helps to develop:

> the young men throw splits on the piles
> bodies hardening, learning the pace
> and the smell of tools from this delve
> in the winter
> death-topple of elderly oak.

This is a community task, with the young men learning and hardening to the jobs they will inherit when their elders pass, like the toppled oak. Here is the sense of continuity and cultural transmission which Snyder has acquired as a husband, father, and homesteader, a sense which has changed him over the course of his career from *dharma* hitchhiker to domestic visionary.

Source: Robert Schultz and David Wyatt, "Gary Snyder and the Curve of Return," in *Virginia Quarterly Review*, Vol. 62, No. 4, Autumn 1986, pp. 681–94.

Sources

Bly, Robert, ed., *News of the Universe: Poems of Twofold Consciousness*, Sierra Club Books, 1980.

Lawrence, D. H., *Selected Poems*, Penguin, 1971.

Murphy, Patrick D., ed., *Critical Essays on Gary Snyder*, G. K. Hall, 1991.

———, *A Place for Wayfaring: The Poetry and Prose of Gary Snyder*, Oregon State University Press, 2000.

———, *Understanding Gary Snyder*, University of South Carolina Press, 1992.

Schultz, Robert, and David Wyatt, "Gary Snyder and the Curve of Return," in *Critical Essays on Gary Snyder*, edited by Patrick D. Murphy, G. K. Hall, 1991.

Snyder, Gary, *The Real Work: Interviews & Talks, 1964–1979*, edited and with an introduction by William Scott McLean, New Directions, 1980.

———, *Regarding Wave*, Fulcrum Press, 1970.

Wordsworth, William, "Lines Written a Few Miles above Tintern Abbey," in *Lyrical Ballads*, edited by R. L. Brett and A. R. Jones, Methuen, 1971, pp. 113–18.

Further Reading

Halper, Jon, ed., *Gary Snyder: Dimensions of a Life*, Sierra Club Books, 1991.

> This book was published in honor of Snyder's sixtieth birthday; it is a collection of affectionate and appreciative essays written by Snyder's friends and colleagues. It covers varying aspects of Snyder's life and work.

Molesworth, Charles, *Gary Snyder's Vision: Poetry and the Real Work*, University of Missouri Press, 1983.

> This scholarly study, hampered by the lack of an index, emphasizes Snyder's political concerns, showing how he responds to and corrects the values of multinational capitalism. It was published before *Axe Handles* and so includes no discussion of that volume.

Snyder, Gary, *The Practice of the Wild*, North Point Press, 1990.

> This is a collection of nine essays that describe Snyder's many journeys into nature, both literal and metaphorical, and his thoughts on the interaction of nature and culture.

Steuding, Bob, *Gary Snyder*, Twayne's United States Authors Series, No. 274, Twayne Publishers, 1976.

> This is an excellent introduction to Snyder's poetry. It covers his major works up to and including *Turtle Island* and contains a useful annotated bibliography.

Glossary of Literary Terms

A

Abstract: Used as a noun, the term refers to a short summary or outline of a longer work. As an adjective applied to writing or literary works, abstract refers to words or phrases that name things not knowable through the five senses.

Accent: The emphasis or stress placed on a syllable in poetry. Traditional poetry commonly uses patterns of accented and unaccented syllables (known as feet) that create distinct rhythms. Much modern poetry uses less formal arrangements that create a sense of freedom and spontaneity.

Aestheticism: A literary and artistic movement of the nineteenth century. Followers of the movement believed that art should not be mixed with social, political, or moral teaching. The statement "art for art's sake" is a good summary of aestheticism. The movement had its roots in France, but it gained widespread importance in England in the last half of the nineteenth century, where it helped change the Victorian practice of including moral lessons in literature.

Affective Fallacy: An error in judging the merits or faults of a work of literature. The "error" results from stressing the importance of the work's effect upon the reader—that is, how it makes a reader "feel" emotionally, what it does as a literary work—instead of stressing its inner qualities as a created object, or what it "is."

Age of Johnson: The period in English literature between 1750 and 1798, named after the most prominent literary figure of the age, Samuel Johnson. Works written during this time are noted for their emphasis on "sensibility," or emotional quality. These works formed a transition between the rational works of the Age of Reason, or Neoclassical period, and the emphasis on individual feelings and responses of the Romantic period.

Age of Reason: See *Neoclassicism*

Age of Sensibility: See *Age of Johnson*

Agrarians: A group of Southern American writers of the 1930s and 1940s who fostered an economic and cultural program for the South based on agriculture, in opposition to the industrial society of the North. The term can refer to any group that promotes the value of farm life and agricultural society.

Alexandrine Meter: See *Meter*

Allegory: A narrative technique in which characters representing things or abstract ideas are used to convey a message or teach a lesson. Allegory is typically used to teach moral, ethical, or religious lessons but is sometimes used for satiric or political purposes.

Alliteration: A poetic device where the first consonant sounds or any vowel sounds in words or syllables are repeated.

Allusion: A reference to a familiar literary or historical person or event, used to make an idea more easily understood.

Amerind Literature: The writing and oral traditions of Native Americans. Native American literature was originally passed on by word of mouth, so it consisted largely of stories and events that were easily memorized. Amerind prose is often rhythmic like poetry because it was recited to the beat of a ceremonial drum.

Analogy: A comparison of two things made to explain something unfamiliar through its similarities to something familiar, or to prove one point based on the acceptedness of another. Similes and metaphors are types of analogies.

Anapest: See *Foot*

Angry Young Men: A group of British writers of the 1950s whose work expressed bitterness and disillusionment with society. Common to their work is an antihero who rebels against a corrupt social order and strives for personal integrity.

Anthropomorphism: The presentation of animals or objects in human shape or with human characteristics. The term is derived from the Greek word for "human form."

Antimasque: See *Masque*

Antithesis: The antithesis of something is its direct opposite. In literature, the use of antithesis as a figure of speech results in two statements that show a contrast through the balancing of two opposite ideas. Technically, it is the second portion of the statement that is defined as the "antithesis"; the first portion is the "thesis."

Apocrypha: Writings tentatively attributed to an author but not proven or universally accepted to be their works. The term was originally applied to certain books of the Bible that were not considered inspired and so were not included in the "sacred canon."

Apollonian and Dionysian: The two impulses believed to guide authors of dramatic tragedy. The Apollonian impulse is named after Apollo, the Greek god of light and beauty and the symbol of intellectual order. The Dionysian impulse is named after Dionysus, the Greek god of wine and the symbol of the unrestrained forces of nature. The Apollonian impulse is to create a rational, harmonious world, while the Dionysian is to express the irrational forces of personality.

Apostrophe: A statement, question, or request addressed to an inanimate object or concept or to a nonexistent or absent person.

Archetype: The word archetype is commonly used to describe an original pattern or model from which all other things of the same kind are made. This term was introduced to literary criticism from the psychology of Carl Jung. It expresses Jung's theory that behind every person's "unconscious," or repressed memories of the past, lies the "collective unconscious" of the human race: memories of the countless typical experiences of our ancestors. These memories are said to prompt illogical associations that trigger powerful emotions in the reader. Often, the emotional process is primitive, even primordial. Archetypes are the literary images that grow out of the "collective unconscious." They appear in literature as incidents and plots that repeat basic patterns of life. They may also appear as stereotyped characters.

Argument: The argument of a work is the author's subject matter or principal idea.

Art for Art's Sake: See *Aestheticism*

Assonance: The repetition of similar vowel sounds in poetry.

Audience: The people for whom a piece of literature is written. Authors usually write with a certain audience in mind, for example, children, members of a religious or ethnic group, or colleagues in a professional field. The term "audience" also applies to the people who gather to see or hear any performance, including plays, poetry readings, speeches, and concerts.

Automatic Writing: Writing carried out without a preconceived plan in an effort to capture every random thought. Authors who engage in automatic writing typically do not revise their work, preferring instead to preserve the revealed truth and beauty of spontaneous expression.

Avant-garde: A French term meaning "vanguard." It is used in literary criticism to describe new writing that rejects traditional approaches to literature in favor of innovations in style or content.

B

Ballad: A short poem that tells a simple story and has a repeated refrain. Ballads were originally intended to be sung. Early ballads, known as folk ballads, were passed down through generations, so their authors are often unknown. Later ballads composed by known authors are called literary ballads.

Baroque: A term used in literary criticism to describe literature that is complex or ornate in style or diction. Baroque works typically express tension, anxiety, and violent emotion. The term "Baroque Age" designates a period in Western European literature beginning in the late sixteenth century and ending about one hundred years later.

Works of this period often mirror the qualities of works more generally associated with the label "baroque" and sometimes feature elaborate conceits.

Baroque Age: See *Baroque*

Baroque Period: See *Baroque*

Beat Generation: See *Beat Movement*

Beat Movement: A period featuring a group of American poets and novelists of the 1950s and 1960s—including Jack Kerouac, Allen Ginsberg, Gregory Corso, William S. Burroughs, and Lawrence Ferlinghetti—who rejected established social and literary values. Using such techniques as stream-of-consciousness writing and jazz-influenced free verse and focusing on unusual or abnormal states of mind—generated by religious ecstasy or the use of drugs—the Beat writers aimed to create works that were unconventional in both form and subject matter.

Beat Poets: See *Beat Movement*

Beats, The: See *Beat Movement*

Belles-lettres: A French term meaning "fine letters" or "beautiful writing." It is often used as a synonym for literature, typically referring to imaginative and artistic rather than scientific or expository writing. Current usage sometimes restricts the meaning to light or humorous writing and appreciative essays about literature.

Black Aesthetic Movement: A period of artistic and literary development among African Americans in the 1960s and early 1970s. This was the first major African American artistic movement since the Harlem Renaissance and was closely paralleled by the civil rights and black power movements. The black aesthetic writers attempted to produce works of art that would be meaningful to the black masses. Key figures in black aesthetics included one of its founders, poet and playwright Amiri Baraka, formerly known as LeRoi Jones; poet and essayist Haki R. Madhubuti, formerly Don L. Lee; poet and playwright Sonia Sanchez; and dramatist Ed Bullins.

Black Arts Movement: See *Black Aesthetic Movement*

Black Comedy: See *Black Humor*

Black Humor: Writing that places grotesque elements side by side with humorous ones in an attempt to shock the reader, forcing him or her to laugh at the horrifying reality of a disordered world.

Black Mountain School: Black Mountain College and three of its instructors—Robert Creeley, Robert Duncan, and Charles Olson—were all influential in projective verse. Today poets working in projective verse are referred to as members of the Black Mountain school.

Blank Verse: Loosely, any unrhymed poetry, but more generally, unrhymed iambic pentameter verse (composed of lines of five two-syllable feet with the first syllable accented, the second unaccented). Blank verse has been used by poets since the Renaissance for its flexibility and its graceful, dignified tone.

Bloomsbury Group: A group of English writers, artists, and intellectuals who held informal artistic and philosophical discussions in Bloomsbury, a district of London, from around 1907 to the early 1930s. The Bloomsbury Group held no uniform philosophical beliefs but did commonly express an aversion to moral prudery and a desire for greater social tolerance.

Bon Mot: A French term meaning "good word." A *bon mot* is a witty remark or clever observation.

Breath Verse: See *Projective Verse*

Burlesque: Any literary work that uses exaggeration to make its subject appear ridiculous, either by treating a trivial subject with profound seriousness or by treating a dignified subject frivolously. The word "burlesque" may also be used as an adjective, as in "burlesque show," to mean "striptease act."

C

Cadence: The natural rhythm of language caused by the alternation of accented and unaccented syllables. Much modern poetry—notably free verse—deliberately manipulates cadence to create complex rhythmic effects.

Caesura: A pause in a line of poetry, usually occurring near the middle. It typically corresponds to a break in the natural rhythm or sense of the line but is sometimes shifted to create special meanings or rhythmic effects.

Canzone: A short Italian or Provencal lyric poem, commonly about love and often set to music. The *canzone* has no set form but typically contains five or six stanzas made up of seven to twenty lines of eleven syllables each. A shorter, five- to ten-line "envoy," or concluding stanza, completes the poem.

Carpe Diem: A Latin term meaning "seize the day." This is a traditional theme of poetry, especially lyrics. A *carpe diem* poem advises the reader or the person it addresses to live for today and enjoy the pleasures of the moment.

Catharsis: The release or purging of unwanted emotions—specifically fear and pity—brought about by exposure to art. The term was first used by the Greek philosopher Aristotle in his *Poetics* to refer to the desired effect of tragedy on spectators.

Celtic Renaissance: A period of Irish literary and cultural history at the end of the nineteenth century. Followers of the movement aimed to create a romantic vision of Celtic myth and legend. The most significant works of the Celtic Renaissance typically present a dreamy, unreal world, usually in reaction against the reality of contemporary problems.

Celtic Twilight: See *Celtic Renaissance*

Character: Broadly speaking, a person in a literary work. The actions of characters are what constitute the plot of a story, novel, or poem. There are numerous types of characters, ranging from simple, stereotypical figures to intricate, multifaceted ones. In the techniques of anthropomorphism and personification, animals—and even places or things—can assume aspects of character. "Characterization" is the process by which an author creates vivid, believable characters in a work of art. This may be done in a variety of ways, including (1) direct description of the character by the narrator; (2) the direct presentation of the speech, thoughts, or actions of the character; and (3) the responses of other characters to the character. The term "character" also refers to a form originated by the ancient Greek writer Theophrastus that later became popular in the seventeenth and eighteenth centuries. It is a short essay or sketch of a person who prominently displays a specific attribute or quality, such as miserliness or ambition.

Characterization: See *Character*

Classical: In its strictest definition in literary criticism, classicism refers to works of ancient Greek or Roman literature. The term may also be used to describe a literary work of recognized importance (a "classic") from any time period or literature that exhibits the traits of classicism.

Classicism: A term used in literary criticism to describe critical doctrines that have their roots in ancient Greek and Roman literature, philosophy, and art. Works associated with classicism typically exhibit restraint on the part of the author, unity of design and purpose, clarity, simplicity, logical organization, and respect for tradition.

Colloquialism: A word, phrase, or form of pronunciation that is acceptable in casual conversation but not in formal, written communication. It is considered more acceptable than slang.

Complaint: A lyric poem, popular in the Renaissance, in which the speaker expresses sorrow about his or her condition. Typically, the speaker's sadness is caused by an unresponsive lover, but some complaints cite other sources of unhappiness, such as poverty or fate.

Conceit: A clever and fanciful metaphor, usually expressed through elaborate and extended comparison, that presents a striking parallel between two seemingly dissimilar things—for example, elaborately comparing a beautiful woman to an object like a garden or the sun. The conceit was a popular device throughout the Elizabethan Age and Baroque Age and was the principal technique of the seventeenth-century English metaphysical poets. This usage of the word conceit is unrelated to the best-known definition of conceit as an arrogant attitude or behavior.

Concrete: Concrete is the opposite of abstract, and refers to a thing that actually exists or a description that allows the reader to experience an object or concept with the senses.

Concrete Poetry: Poetry in which visual elements play a large part in the poetic effect. Punctuation marks, letters, or words are arranged on a page to form a visual design: a cross, for example, or a bumblebee.

Confessional Poetry: A form of poetry in which the poet reveals very personal, intimate, sometimes shocking information about himself or herself.

Connotation: The impression that a word gives beyond its defined meaning. Connotations may be universally understood or may be significant only to a certain group.

Consonance: Consonance occurs in poetry when words appearing at the ends of two or more verses have similar final consonant sounds but have final vowel sounds that differ, as with "stuff" and "off."

Convention: Any widely accepted literary device, style, or form.

Corrido: A Mexican ballad.

Couplet: Two lines of poetry with the same rhyme and meter, often expressing a complete and self-contained thought.

Criticism: The systematic study and evaluation of literary works, usually based on a specific method or set of principles. An important part of literary studies since ancient times, the practice of criticism has given rise to numerous theories, methods, and "schools," sometimes producing conflicting, even contradictory, interpretations of literature in general as well as of individual works. Even such basic issues as what constitutes a poem or a novel have been the subject of much criticism over the centuries.

D

Dactyl: See *Foot*

Dadaism: A protest movement in art and literature founded by Tristan Tzara in 1916. Followers of the movement expressed their outrage at the destruction brought about by World War I by revolting against numerous forms of social convention. The Dadaists presented works marked by calculated madness and flamboyant nonsense. They stressed total freedom of expression, commonly through primitive displays of emotion and illogical, often senseless, poetry. The movement ended shortly after the war, when it was replaced by surrealism.

Decadent: See *Decadents*

Decadents: The followers of a nineteenth-century literary movement that had its beginnings in French aestheticism. Decadent literature displays a fascination with perverse and morbid states; a search for novelty and sensation—the "new thrill"; a preoccupation with mysticism; and a belief in the senselessness of human existence. The movement is closely associated with the doctrine Art for Art's Sake. The term "decadence" is sometimes used to denote a decline in the quality of art or literature following a period of greatness.

Deconstruction: A method of literary criticism developed by Jacques Derrida and characterized by multiple conflicting interpretations of a given work. Deconstructionists consider the impact of the language of a work and suggest that the true meaning of the work is not necessarily the meaning that the author intended.

Deduction: The process of reaching a conclusion through reasoning from general premises to a specific premise.

Denotation: The definition of a word, apart from the impressions or feelings it creates in the reader.

Diction: The selection and arrangement of words in a literary work. Either or both may vary depending on the desired effect. There are four general types of diction: "formal," used in scholarly or lofty writing; "informal," used in relaxed but educated conversation; "colloquial," used in everyday speech; and "slang," containing newly coined words and other terms not accepted in formal usage.

Didactic: A term used to describe works of literature that aim to teach some moral, religious, political, or practical lesson. Although didactic elements are often found in artistically pleasing works, the term "didactic" usually refers to literature in which the message is more important than the form. The term may also be used to criticize a work that the critic finds "overly didactic," that is, heavy-handed in its delivery of a lesson.

Dimeter: See *Meter*

Dionysian: See *Apollonian and Dionysian*

Discordia concours: A Latin phrase meaning "discord in harmony." The term was coined by the eighteenth-century English writer Samuel Johnson to describe "a combination of dissimilar images or discovery of occult resemblances in things apparently unlike." Johnson created the expression by reversing a phrase by the Latin poet Horace.

Dissonance: A combination of harsh or jarring sounds, especially in poetry. Although such combinations may be accidental, poets sometimes intentionally make them to achieve particular effects. Dissonance is also sometimes used to refer to close but not identical rhymes. When this is the case, the word functions as a synonym for consonance.

Double Entendre: A corruption of a French phrase meaning "double meaning." The term is used to indicate a word or phrase that is deliberately ambiguous, especially when one of the meanings is risque or improper.

Draft: Any preliminary version of a written work. An author may write dozens of drafts which are revised to form the final work, or he or she may write only one, with few or no revisions.

Dramatic Monologue: See *Monologue*

Dramatic Poetry: Any lyric work that employs elements of drama such as dialogue, conflict, or characterization, but excluding works that are intended for stage presentation.

Dream Allegory: See *Dream Vision*

Dream Vision: A literary convention, chiefly of the Middle Ages. In a dream vision a story is presented as a literal dream of the narrator. This device was commonly used to teach moral and religious lessons.

E

Eclogue: In classical literature, a poem featuring rural themes and structured as a dialogue among shepherds. Eclogues often took specific poetic forms, such as elegies or love poems. Some were written as the soliloquy of a shepherd. In later centuries, "eclogue" came to refer to any poem that was in the pastoral tradition or that had a dialogue or monologue structure.

Edwardian: Describes cultural conventions identified with the period of the reign of Edward VII of England (1901–1910). Writers of the Edwardian Age typically displayed a strong reaction against the propriety and conservatism of the Victorian Age. Their work often exhibits distrust of authority in religion, politics, and art and expresses strong doubts about the soundness of conventional values.

Edwardian Age: See *Edwardian*

Electra Complex: A daughter's amorous obsession with her father.

Elegy: A lyric poem that laments the death of a person or the eventual death of all people. In a conventional elegy, set in a classical world, the poet and subject are spoken of as shepherds. In modern criticism, the word elegy is often used to refer to a poem that is melancholy or mournfully contemplative.

Elizabethan Age: A period of great economic growth, religious controversy, and nationalism closely associated with the reign of Elizabeth I of England (1558–1603). The Elizabethan Age is considered a part of the general renaissance—that is, the flowering of arts and literature—that took place in Europe during the fourteenth through sixteenth centuries. The era is considered the golden age of English literature. The most important dramas in English and a great deal of lyric poetry were produced during this period, and modern English criticism began around this time.

Empathy: A sense of shared experience, including emotional and physical feelings, with someone or something other than oneself. Empathy is often used to describe the response of a reader to a literary character.

English Sonnet: See *Sonnet*

Enjambment: The running over of the sense and structure of a line of verse or a couplet into the following verse or couplet.

Enlightenment, The: An eighteenth-century philosophical movement. It began in France but had a wide impact throughout Europe and America. Thinkers of the Enlightenment valued reason and believed that both the individual and society could achieve a state of perfection. Corresponding to this essentially humanist vision was a resistance to religious authority.

Epic: A long narrative poem about the adventures of a hero of great historic or legendary importance. The setting is vast and the action is often given cosmic significance through the intervention of supernatural forces such as gods, angels, or demons. Epics are typically written in a classical style of grand simplicity with elaborate metaphors and allusions that enhance the symbolic importance of a hero's adventures.

Epic Simile: See *Homeric Simile*

Epigram: A saying that makes the speaker's point quickly and concisely.

Epilogue: A concluding statement or section of a literary work. In dramas, particularly those of the seventeenth and eighteenth centuries, the epilogue is a closing speech, often in verse, delivered by an actor at the end of a play and spoken directly to the audience.

Epiphany: A sudden revelation of truth inspired by a seemingly trivial incident.

Epitaph: An inscription on a tomb or tombstone, or a verse written on the occasion of a person's death. Epitaphs may be serious or humorous.

Epithalamion: A song or poem written to honor and commemorate a marriage ceremony.

Epithalamium: See *Epithalamion*

Epithet: A word or phrase, often disparaging or abusive, that expresses a character trait of someone or something.

Erziehungsroman: See *Bildungsroman*

Essay: A prose composition with a focused subject of discussion. The term was coined by Michel de Montaigne to describe his 1580 collection of brief, informal reflections on himself and on various topics relating to human nature. An essay can also be a long, systematic discourse.

Existentialism: A predominantly twentieth-century philosophy concerned with the nature and perception of human existence. There are two major strains of existentialist thought: atheistic and Christian. Followers of atheistic existentialism believe that the individual is alone in a godless universe and that the basic human condition is one of suffering and loneliness. Nevertheless, because there are no fixed values, individuals can create their own characters—indeed, they can shape themselves—through the exercise of free will. The atheistic strain culminates in and is popularly associated with the works of Jean-Paul Sartre. The Christian existentialists, on the other hand, believe that only in God may people find freedom from life's anguish. The two strains hold certain beliefs in common: that existence cannot be fully understood or described through empirical effort; that anguish is a universal element of life; that individuals must bear responsibility for their actions; and that there is no common standard of behavior or perception for religious and ethical matters.

Expatriates: See *Expatriatism*

Expatriatism: The practice of leaving one's country to live for an extended period in another country.

Exposition: Writing intended to explain the nature of an idea, thing, or theme. Expository writing is often combined with description, narration, or argument. In dramatic writing, the exposition is the introductory material which presents the characters, setting, and tone of the play.

Expressionism: An indistinct literary term, originally used to describe an early twentieth-century school of German painting. The term applies to almost any mode of unconventional, highly subjective writing that distorts reality in some way.

Extended Monologue: See *Monologue*

F

Feet: See *Foot*

Feminine Rhyme: See *Rhyme*

Fiction: Any story that is the product of imagination rather than a documentation of fact. Characters and events in such narratives may be based in real life but their ultimate form and configuration is a creation of the author.

Figurative Language: A technique in writing in which the author temporarily interrupts the order, construction, or meaning of the writing for a particular effect. This interruption takes the form of one or more figures of speech such as hyperbole, irony, or simile. Figurative language is the opposite of literal language, in which every word is truthful, accurate, and free of exaggeration or embellishment.

Figures of Speech: Writing that differs from customary conventions for construction, meaning, order, or significance for the purpose of a special meaning or effect. There are two major types of figures of speech: rhetorical figures, which do not make changes in the meaning of the words; and tropes, which do.

***Fin de siecle*:** A French term meaning "end of the century." The term is used to denote the last decade of the nineteenth century, a transition period when writers and other artists abandoned old conventions and looked for new techniques and objectives.

First Person: See *Point of View*

Folk Ballad: See *Ballad*

Folklore: Traditions and myths preserved in a culture or group of people. Typically, these are passed on by word of mouth in various forms—such as legends, songs, and proverbs—or preserved in customs and ceremonies. This term was first used by W. J. Thoms in 1846.

Folktale: A story originating in oral tradition. Folktales fall into a variety of categories, including legends, ghost stories, fairy tales, fables, and anecdotes based on historical figures and events.

Foot: The smallest unit of rhythm in a line of poetry. In English-language poetry, a foot is typically one accented syllable combined with one or two unaccented syllables.

Form: The pattern or construction of a work which identifies its genre and distinguishes it from other genres.

Formalism: In literary criticism, the belief that literature should follow prescribed rules of construction, such as those that govern the sonnet form.

Fourteener Meter: See *Meter*

Free Verse: Poetry that lacks regular metrical and rhyme patterns but that tries to capture the cadences of everyday speech. The form allows a poet to exploit a variety of rhythmical effects within a single poem.

Futurism: A flamboyant literary and artistic movement that developed in France, Italy, and Russia from 1908 through the 1920s. Futurist theater and poetry abandoned traditional literary forms. In their place, followers of the movement attempted to achieve total freedom of expression through bizarre imagery and deformed or newly invented words. The Futurists were self-consciously modern artists who attempted to incorporate the appearances and sounds of modern life into their work.

G

Genre: A category of literary work. In critical theory, genre may refer to both the content of a given work—tragedy, comedy, pastoral—and to its form, such as poetry, novel, or drama.

Genteel Tradition: A term coined by critic George Santayana to describe the literary practice of certain late nineteenth-century American writers, especially New Englanders. Followers of the Genteel

Tradition emphasized conventionality in social, religious, moral, and literary standards.

Georgian Age: See *Georgian Poets*

Georgian Period: See *Georgian Poets*

Georgian Poets: A loose grouping of English poets during the years 1912–1922. The Georgians reacted against certain literary schools and practices, especially Victorian wordiness, turn-of-the-century aestheticism, and contemporary urban realism. In their place, the Georgians embraced the nineteenth-century poetic practices of William Wordsworth and the other Lake Poets.

Georgic: A poem about farming and the farmer's way of life, named from Virgil's *Georgics*.

Gilded Age: A period in American history during the 1870s characterized by political corruption and materialism. A number of important novels of social and political criticism were written during this time.

Gothic: See *Gothicism*

Gothicism: In literary criticism, works characterized by a taste for the medieval or morbidly attractive. A gothic novel prominently features elements of horror, the supernatural, gloom, and violence: clanking chains, terror, charnel houses, ghosts, medieval castles, and mysteriously slamming doors. The term "gothic novel" is also applied to novels that lack elements of the traditional Gothic setting but that create a similar atmosphere of terror or dread.

Graveyard School: A group of eighteenth-century English poets who wrote long, picturesque meditations on death. Their works were designed to cause the reader to ponder immortality.

Great Chain of Being: The belief that all things and creatures in nature are organized in a hierarchy from inanimate objects at the bottom to God at the top. This system of belief was popular in the seventeenth and eighteenth centuries.

Grotesque: In literary criticism, the subject matter of a work or a style of expression characterized by exaggeration, deformity, freakishness, and disorder. The grotesque often includes an element of comic absurdity.

H

Haiku: The shortest form of Japanese poetry, constructed in three lines of five, seven, and five syllables respectively. The message of a *haiku* poem usually centers on some aspect of spirituality and provokes an emotional response in the reader.

Half Rhyme: See *Consonance*

Harlem Renaissance: The Harlem Renaissance of the 1920s is generally considered the first significant movement of black writers and artists in the United States. During this period, new and established black writers published more fiction and poetry than ever before, the first influential black literary journals were established, and black authors and artists received their first widespread recognition and serious critical appraisal. Among the major writers associated with this period are Claude McKay, Jean Toomer, Countee Cullen, Langston Hughes, Arna Bontemps, Nella Larsen, and Zora Neale Hurston.

Hellenism: Imitation of ancient Greek thought or styles. Also, an approach to life that focuses on the growth and development of the intellect. "Hellenism" is sometimes used to refer to the belief that reason can be applied to examine all human experience.

Heptameter: See *Meter*

Hero/Heroine: The principal sympathetic character (male or female) in a literary work. Heroes and heroines typically exhibit admirable traits: idealism, courage, and integrity, for example.

Heroic Couplet: A rhyming couplet written in iambic pentameter (a verse with five iambic feet).

Heroic Line: The meter and length of a line of verse in epic or heroic poetry. This varies by language and time period.

Heroine: See *Hero/Heroine*

Hexameter: See *Meter*

Historical Criticism: The study of a work based on its impact on the world of the time period in which it was written.

Hokku: See *Haiku*

Holocaust: See *Holocaust Literature*

Holocaust Literature: Literature influenced by or written about the Holocaust of World War II. Such literature includes true stories of survival in concentration camps, escape, and life after the war, as well as fictional works and poetry.

Homeric Simile: An elaborate, detailed comparison written as a simile many lines in length.

Horatian Satire: See *Satire*

Humanism: A philosophy that places faith in the dignity of humankind and rejects the medieval perception of the individual as a weak, fallen creature. "Humanists" typically believe in the perfectibility of human nature and view reason and education as the means to that end.

Humors: Mentions of the humors refer to the ancient Greek theory that a person's health and personality were determined by the balance of four basic fluids in the body: blood, phlegm, yellow bile, and black bile. A dominance of any fluid would cause extremes in behavior. An excess of blood created a sanguine person who was joyful, aggressive, and passionate; a phlegmatic person was shy, fearful, and sluggish; too much yellow bile led to a choleric temperament characterized by impatience, anger, bitterness, and stubbornness; and excessive black bile created melancholy, a state of laziness, gluttony, and lack of motivation.

Humours: See *Humors*

Hyperbole: In literary criticism, deliberate exaggeration used to achieve an effect.

I

Iamb: See *Foot*

Idiom: A word construction or verbal expression closely associated with a given language.

Image: A concrete representation of an object or sensory experience. Typically, such a representation helps evoke the feelings associated with the object or experience itself. Images are either "literal" or "figurative." Literal images are especially concrete and involve little or no extension of the obvious meaning of the words used to express them. Figurative images do not follow the literal meaning of the words exactly. Images in literature are usually visual, but the term "image" can also refer to the representation of any sensory experience.

Imagery: The array of images in a literary work. Also, figurative language.

Imagism: An English and American poetry movement that flourished between 1908 and 1917. The Imagists used precise, clearly presented images in their works. They also used common, everyday speech and aimed for conciseness, concrete imagery, and the creation of new rhythms.

In medias res: A Latin term meaning "in the middle of things." It refers to the technique of beginning a story at its midpoint and then using various flashback devices to reveal previous action.

Induction: The process of reaching a conclusion by reasoning from specific premises to form a general premise. Also, an introductory portion of a work of literature, especially a play.

Intentional Fallacy: The belief that judgments of a literary work based solely on an author's stated or implied intentions are false and misleading. Critics who believe in the concept of the intentional fallacy typically argue that the work itself is sufficient matter for interpretation, even though they may concede that an author's statement of purpose can be useful.

Interior Monologue: A narrative technique in which characters' thoughts are revealed in a way that appears to be uncontrolled by the author. The interior monologue typically aims to reveal the inner self of a character. It portrays emotional experiences as they occur at both a conscious and unconscious level. Images are often used to represent sensations or emotions.

Internal Rhyme: Rhyme that occurs within a single line of verse.

Irish Literary Renaissance: A late nineteenth- and early twentieth-century movement in Irish literature. Members of the movement aimed to reduce the influence of British culture in Ireland and create an Irish national literature.

Irony: In literary criticism, the effect of language in which the intended meaning is the opposite of what is stated.

Italian Sonnet: See *Sonnet*

J

Jacobean Age: The period of the reign of James I of England (1603–1625). The early literature of this period reflected the worldview of the Elizabethan Age, but a darker, more cynical attitude steadily grew in the art and literature of the Jacobean Age. This was an important time for English drama and poetry.

Jargon: Language that is used or understood only by a select group of people. Jargon may refer to terminology used in a certain profession, such as computer jargon, or it may refer to any nonsensical language that is not understood by most people.

Journalism: Writing intended for publication in a newspaper or magazine, or for broadcast on a radio or television program featuring news, sports, entertainment, or other timely material.

K

Knickerbocker Group: A somewhat indistinct group of New York writers of the first half of the nineteenth century. Members of the group were linked only by location and a common theme: New York life.

Kunstlerroman: See *Bildungsroman*

L

Lais: See *Lay*

Lake Poets: See *Lake School*

Lake School: These poets all lived in the Lake District of England at the turn of the nineteenth century. As a group, they followed no single "school" of thought or literary practice, although their works were uniformly disparaged by the *Edinburgh Review.*

Lay: A song or simple narrative poem. The form originated in medieval France. Early French *lais* were often based on the Celtic legends and other tales sung by Breton minstrels—thus the name of the "Breton lay." In fourteenth-century England, the term "lay" was used to describe short narratives written in imitation of the Breton lays.

Leitmotiv: See *Motif*

Literal Language: An author uses literal language when he or she writes without exaggerating or embellishing the subject matter and without any tools of figurative language.

Literary Ballad: See *Ballad*

Literature: Literature is broadly defined as any written or spoken material, but the term most often refers to creative works.

Lost Generation: A term first used by Gertrude Stein to describe the post-World War I generation of American writers: men and women haunted by a sense of betrayal and emptiness brought about by the destructiveness of the war.

Lyric Poetry: A poem expressing the subjective feelings and personal emotions of the poet. Such poetry is melodic, since it was originally accompanied by a lyre in recitals. Most Western poetry in the twentieth century may be classified as lyrical.

M

Mannerism: Exaggerated, artificial adherence to a literary manner or style. Also, a popular style of the visual arts of late sixteenth-century Europe that was marked by elongation of the human form and by intentional spatial distortion. Literary works that are self-consciously high-toned and artistic are often said to be "mannered."

Masculine Rhyme: See *Rhyme*

Measure: The foot, verse, or time sequence used in a literary work, especially a poem. Measure is often used somewhat incorrectly as a synonym for meter.

Metaphor: A figure of speech that expresses an idea through the image of another object. Metaphors suggest the essence of the first object by identifying it with certain qualities of the second object.

Metaphysical Conceit: See *Conceit*

Metaphysical Poetry: The body of poetry produced by a group of seventeenth-century English writers called the "Metaphysical Poets." The group includes John Donne and Andrew Marvell. The Metaphysical Poets made use of everyday speech, intellectual analysis, and unique imagery. They aimed to portray the ordinary conflicts and contradictions of life. Their poems often took the form of an argument, and many of them emphasize physical and religious love as well as the fleeting nature of life. Elaborate conceits are typical in metaphysical poetry.

Metaphysical Poets: See *Metaphysical Poetry*

Meter: In literary criticism, the repetition of sound patterns that creates a rhythm in poetry. The patterns are based on the number of syllables and the presence and absence of accents. The unit of rhythm in a line is called a foot. Types of meter are classified according to the number of feet in a line. These are the standard English lines: Monometer, one foot; Dimeter, two feet; Trimeter, three feet; Tetrameter, four feet; Pentameter, five feet; Hexameter, six feet (also called the Alexandrine); Heptameter, seven feet (also called the "Fourteener" when the feet are iambic).

Modernism: Modern literary practices. Also, the principles of a literary school that lasted from roughly the beginning of the twentieth century until the end of World War II. Modernism is defined by its rejection of the literary conventions of the nineteenth century and by its opposition to conventional morality, taste, traditions, and economic values.

Monologue: A composition, written or oral, by a single individual. More specifically, a speech given by a single individual in a drama or other public entertainment. It has no set length, although it is usually several or more lines long.

Monometer: See *Meter*

Mood: The prevailing emotions of a work or of the author in his or her creation of the work. The mood of a work is not always what might be expected based on its subject matter.

Motif: A theme, character type, image, metaphor, or other verbal element that recurs throughout a single work of literature or occurs in a number of different works over a period of time.

***Motiv*:** See *Motif*

Muckrakers: An early twentieth-century group of American writers. Typically, their works exposed the wrongdoings of big business and government in the United States.

Muses: Nine Greek mythological goddesses, the daughters of Zeus and Mnemosyne (Memory). Each muse patronized a specific area of the liberal arts and sciences. Calliope presided over epic poetry, Clio over history, Erato over love poetry, Euterpe over music or lyric poetry, Melpomene over tragedy, Polyhymnia over hymns to the gods, Terpsichore over dance, Thalia over comedy, and Urania over astronomy. Poets and writers traditionally made appeals to the Muses for inspiration in their work.

Myth: An anonymous tale emerging from the traditional beliefs of a culture or social unit. Myths use supernatural explanations for natural phenomena. They may also explain cosmic issues like creation and death. Collections of myths, known as mythologies, are common to all cultures and nations, but the best-known myths belong to the Norse, Roman, and Greek mythologies.

N

Narration: The telling of a series of events, real or invented. A narration may be either a simple narrative, in which the events are recounted chronologically, or a narrative with a plot, in which the account is given in a style reflecting the author's artistic concept of the story. Narration is sometimes used as a synonym for "storyline."

Narrative: A verse or prose accounting of an event or sequence of events, real or invented. The term is also used as an adjective in the sense "method of narration." For example, in literary criticism, the expression "narrative technique" usually refers to the way the author structures and presents his or her story.

Narrative Poetry: A nondramatic poem in which the author tells a story. Such poems may be of any length or level of complexity.

Narrator: The teller of a story. The narrator may be the author or a character in the story through whom the author speaks.

Naturalism: A literary movement of the late nineteenth and early twentieth centuries. The movement's major theorist, French novelist Emile Zola, envisioned a type of fiction that would examine human life with the objectivity of scientific inquiry. The Naturalists typically viewed human beings as either the products of "biological determinism," ruled by hereditary instincts and engaged in an endless struggle for survival, or as the products of "socioeconomic determinism," ruled by social and economic forces beyond their control. In their works, the Naturalists generally ignored the highest levels of society and focused on degradation: poverty, alcoholism, prostitution, insanity, and disease.

Negritude: A literary movement based on the concept of a shared cultural bond on the part of black Africans, wherever they may be in the world. It traces its origins to the former French colonies of Africa and the Caribbean. Negritude poets, novelists, and essayists generally stress four points in their writings: One, black alienation from traditional African culture can lead to feelings of inferiority. Two, European colonialism and Western education should be resisted. Three, black Africans should seek to affirm and define their own identity. Four, African culture can and should be reclaimed. Many Negritude writers also claim that blacks can make unique contributions to the world, based on a heightened appreciation of nature, rhythm, and human emotions—aspects of life they say are not so highly valued in the materialistic and rationalistic West.

Negro Renaissance: See *Harlem Renaissance*

Neoclassical Period: See *Neoclassicism*

Neoclassicism: In literary criticism, this term refers to the revival of the attitudes and styles of expression of classical literature. It is generally used to describe a period in European history beginning in the late seventeenth century and lasting until about 1800. In its purest form, Neoclassicism marked a return to order, proportion, restraint, logic, accuracy, and decorum. In England, where Neoclassicism perhaps was most popular, it reflected the influence of seventeenth-century French writers, especially dramatists. Neoclassical writers typically reacted against the intensity and enthusiasm of the Renaissance period. They wrote works that appealed to the intellect, using elevated language and classical literary forms such as satire and the ode. Neoclassical works were often governed by the classical goal of instruction.

Neoclassicists: See *Neoclassicism*

New Criticism: A movement in literary criticism, dating from the late 1920s, that stressed close textual analysis in the interpretation of works of literature. The New Critics saw little merit in historical and biographical analysis. Rather, they aimed to examine the text alone, free from the question of how external events—biographical or otherwise—may have helped shape it.

New Journalism: A type of writing in which the journalist presents factual information in a form usually used in fiction. New journalism emphasizes description, narration, and character development to bring readers closer to the human element of the story, and is often used in personality profiles and in-depth feature articles. It is not compatible with "straight" or "hard" newswriting, which is generally composed in a brief, fact-based style.

New Journalists: See *New Journalism*

New Negro Movement: See *Harlem Renaissance*

Noble Savage: The idea that primitive man is noble and good but becomes evil and corrupted as he becomes civilized. The concept of the noble savage originated in the Renaissance period but is more closely identified with such later writers as Jean-Jacques Rousseau and Aphra Behn.

O

Objective Correlative: An outward set of objects, a situation, or a chain of events corresponding to an inward experience and evoking this experience in the reader. The term frequently appears in modern criticism in discussions of authors' intended effects on the emotional responses of readers.

Objectivity: A quality in writing characterized by the absence of the author's opinion or feeling about the subject matter. Objectivity is an important factor in criticism.

Occasional Verse: Poetry written on the occasion of a significant historical or personal event. *Vers de societe* is sometimes called occasional verse although it is of a less serious nature.

Octave: A poem or stanza composed of eight lines. The term octave most often represents the first eight lines of a Petrarchan sonnet.

Ode: Name given to an extended lyric poem characterized by exalted emotion and dignified style. An ode usually concerns a single, serious theme. Most odes, but not all, are addressed to an object or individual. Odes are distinguished from other lyric poetic forms by their complex rhythmic and stanzaic patterns.

Oedipus Complex: A son's amorous obsession with his mother. The phrase is derived from the story of the ancient Theban hero Oedipus, who unknowingly killed his father and married his mother.

Omniscience: See *Point of View*

Onomatopoeia: The use of words whose sounds express or suggest their meaning. In its simplest sense, onomatopoeia may be represented by words that mimic the sounds they denote such as "hiss" or "meow." At a more subtle level, the pattern and rhythm of sounds and rhymes of a line or poem may be onomatopoeic.

Oral Tradition: See *Oral Transmission*

Oral Transmission: A process by which songs, ballads, folklore, and other material are transmitted by word of mouth. The tradition of oral transmission predates the written record systems of literate society. Oral transmission preserves material sometimes over generations, although often with variations. Memory plays a large part in the recitation and preservation of orally transmitted material.

Ottava Rima: An eight-line stanza of poetry composed in iambic pentameter (a five-foot line in which each foot consists of an unaccented syllable followed by an accented syllable), following the *abababcc* rhyme scheme.

Oxymoron: A phrase combining two contradictory terms. Oxymorons may be intentional or unintentional.

P

Pantheism: The idea that all things are both a manifestation or revelation of God and a part of God at the same time. Pantheism was a common attitude in the early societies of Egypt, India, and Greece—the term derives from the Greek *pan* meaning "all" and *theos* meaning "deity." It later became a significant part of the Christian faith.

Parable: A story intended to teach a moral lesson or answer an ethical question.

Paradox: A statement that appears illogical or contradictory at first, but may actually point to an underlying truth.

Parallelism: A method of comparison of two ideas in which each is developed in the same grammatical structure.

Parnassianism: A mid nineteenth-century movement in French literature. Followers of the movement stressed adherence to well-defined artistic forms as a reaction against the often chaotic expression of the artist's ego that dominated the work of the Romantics. The Parnassians also rejected the moral, ethical, and social themes exhibited in the works of French Romantics such as Victor Hugo. The aesthetic doctrines of the Parnassians strongly influenced the later symbolist and decadent movements.

Parody: In literary criticism, this term refers to an imitation of a serious literary work or the signature style of a particular author in a ridiculous manner. A typical parody adopts the style of the original and applies it to an inappropriate subject for humorous effect. Parody is a form of satire and could be considered the literary equivalent of a caricature or cartoon.

Pastoral: A term derived from the Latin word "pastor," meaning shepherd. A pastoral is a literary composition on a rural theme. The conventions of the pastoral were originated by the third-century Greek poet Theocritus, who wrote about the experiences, love affairs, and pastimes of Sicilian shepherds. In a pastoral, characters and language of a courtly nature are often placed in a simple setting. The term pastoral is also used to classify dramas, elegies, and lyrics that exhibit the use of country settings and shepherd characters.

Pathetic Fallacy: A term coined by English critic John Ruskin to identify writing that falsely endows nonhuman things with human intentions and feelings, such as "angry clouds" and "sad trees."

Pen Name: See *Pseudonym*

Pentameter: See *Meter*

Persona: A Latin term meaning "mask." *Personae* are the characters in a fictional work of literature. The *persona* generally functions as a mask through which the author tells a story in a voice other than his or her own. A *persona* is usually either a character in a story who acts as a narrator or an "implied author," a voice created by the author to act as the narrator for himself or herself.

Personae: See *Persona*

Personal Point of View: See *Point of View*

Personification: A figure of speech that gives human qualities to abstract ideas, animals, and inanimate objects.

Petrarchan Sonnet: See *Sonnet*

Phenomenology: A method of literary criticism based on the belief that things have no existence outside of human consciousness or awareness. Proponents of this theory believe that art is a process that takes place in the mind of the observer as he or she contemplates an object rather than a quality of the object itself.

Plagiarism: Claiming another person's written material as one's own. Plagiarism can take the form of direct, word-for-word copying or the theft of the substance or idea of the work.

Platonic Criticism: A form of criticism that stresses an artistic work's usefulness as an agent of social engineering rather than any quality or value of the work itself.

Platonism: The embracing of the doctrines of the philosopher Plato, popular among the poets of the Renaissance and the Romantic period. Platonism is more flexible than Aristotelian Criticism and places more emphasis on the supernatural and unknown aspects of life.

Plot: In literary criticism, this term refers to the pattern of events in a narrative or drama. In its simplest sense, the plot guides the author in composing the work and helps the reader follow the work. Typically, plots exhibit causality and unity and have a beginning, a middle, and an end. Sometimes, however, a plot may consist of a series of disconnected events, in which case it is known as an "episodic plot."

Poem: In its broadest sense, a composition utilizing rhyme, meter, concrete detail, and expressive language to create a literary experience with emotional and aesthetic appeal.

Poet: An author who writes poetry or verse. The term is also used to refer to an artist or writer who has an exceptional gift for expression, imagination, and energy in the making of art in any form.

Poete maudit: A term derived from Paul Verlaine's *Les poetes maudits* (*The Accursed Poets*), a collection of essays on the French symbolist writers Stephane Mallarme, Arthur Rimbaud, and Tristan Corbiere. In the sense intended by Verlaine, the poet is "accursed" for choosing to explore extremes of human experience outside of middle-class society.

Poetic Fallacy: See *Pathetic Fallacy*

Poetic Justice: An outcome in a literary work, not necessarily a poem, in which the good are rewarded and the evil are punished, especially in ways that particularly fit their virtues or crimes.

Poetic License: Distortions of fact and literary convention made by a writer—not always a poet—for the sake of the effect gained. Poetic license is closely related to the concept of "artistic freedom."

Poetics: This term has two closely related meanings. It denotes (1) an aesthetic theory in literary criticism about the essence of poetry or (2) rules prescribing the proper methods, content, style, or diction of poetry. The term poetics may also refer to theories about literature in general, not just poetry.

Poetry: In its broadest sense, writing that aims to present ideas and evoke an emotional experience in the reader through the use of meter, imagery, connotative and concrete words, and a carefully constructed structure based on rhythmic patterns. Poetry typically relies on words and expressions that have several layers of meaning. It also makes use of the effects of regular rhythm on the ear and may make a strong appeal to the senses through the use of imagery.

Point of View: The narrative perspective from which a literary work is presented to the reader. There are four traditional points of view. The "third person omniscient" gives the reader a "godlike" perspective, unrestricted by time or place, from which to see actions and look into the minds of characters. This allows the author to comment openly on characters and events in the work. The "third-person" point of view presents the events of the story from outside of any single character's perception, much like the omniscient point of view, but the reader must understand the action as it takes place and without any special insight into characters' minds or motivations. The "first person" or "personal" point of view relates events as they are perceived by a single character. The main character "tells" the story and may offer opinions about the action and characters which differ from those of the author. Much less common than omniscient, third person, and first person is the "second-person" point of view, wherein the author tells the story as if it is happening to the reader.

Polemic: A work in which the author takes a stand on a controversial subject, such as abortion or religion. Such works are often extremely argumentative or provocative.

Pornography: Writing intended to provoke feelings of lust in the reader. Such works are often condemned by critics and teachers, but those which can be shown to have literary value are viewed less harshly.

Post-Aesthetic Movement: An artistic response made by African Americans to the black aesthetic movement of the 1960s and early 1970s. Writers since that time have adopted a somewhat different tone in their work, with less emphasis placed on the disparity between black and white in the United States. In the words of post-aesthetic authors such as Toni Morrison, John Edgar Wideman, and Kristin Hunter, African Americans are portrayed as looking inward for answers to their own questions, rather than always looking to the outside world.

Postmodernism: Writing from the 1960s forward characterized by experimentation and continuing to apply some of the fundamentals of modernism, which included existentialism and alienation. Postmodernists have gone a step further in the rejection of tradition begun with the modernists by also rejecting traditional forms, preferring the antinovel over the novel and the antihero over the hero.

Pre-Raphaelites: A circle of writers and artists in mid nineteenth-century England. Valuing the pre-Renaissance artistic qualities of religious symbolism, lavish pictorialism, and natural sensuousness, the Pre-Raphaelites cultivated a sense of mystery and melancholy that influenced later writers associated with the Symbolist and Decadent movements.

Primitivism: The belief that primitive peoples were nobler and less flawed than civilized peoples because they had not been subjected to the corrupt influence of society.

Projective Verse: A form of free verse in which the poet's breathing pattern determines the lines of the poem. Poets who advocate projective verse are against all formal structures in writing, including meter and form.

Prologue: An introductory section of a literary work. It often contains information establishing the situation of the characters or presents information about the setting, time period, or action. In drama, the prologue is spoken by a chorus or by one of the principal characters.

Prose: A literary medium that attempts to mirror the language of everyday speech. It is distinguished from poetry by its use of unmetered, unrhymed language consisting of logically related sentences. Prose is usually grouped into paragraphs that form a cohesive whole such as an essay or a novel.

Prosopopoeia: See *Personification*

Protagonist: The central character of a story who serves as a focus for its themes and incidents and as the principal rationale for its development. The protagonist is sometimes referred to in discussions of modern literature as the hero or antihero.

Proverb: A brief, sage saying that expresses a truth about life in a striking manner.

Pseudonym: A name assumed by a writer, most often intended to prevent his or her identification as the author of a work. Two or more authors may work together under one pseudonym, or an author may use a different name for each genre he or she publishes in. Some publishing companies maintain "house pseudonyms," under which any number of authors may write installations in a series. Some authors also choose a pseudonym over their real names the way an actor may use a stage name.

Pun: A play on words that have similar sounds but different meanings.

Pure Poetry: poetry written without instructional intent or moral purpose that aims only to please a reader by its imagery or musical flow. The term pure poetry is used as the antonym of the term "didacticism."

Q

Quatrain: A four-line stanza of a poem or an entire poem consisting of four lines.

R

Realism: A nineteenth-century European literary movement that sought to portray familiar characters, situations, and settings in a realistic manner. This was done primarily by using an objective narrative point of view and through the buildup of accurate detail. The standard for success of any realistic work depends on how faithfully it transfers common experience into fictional forms. The realistic method may be altered or extended, as in stream of consciousness writing, to record highly subjective experience.

Refrain: A phrase repeated at intervals throughout a poem. A refrain may appear at the end of each stanza or at less regular intervals. It may be altered slightly at each appearance.

Renaissance: The period in European history that marked the end of the Middle Ages. It began in Italy in the late fourteenth century. In broad terms, it is usually seen as spanning the fourteenth, fifteenth, and sixteenth centuries, although it did not reach Great Britain, for example, until the 1480s or so. The Renaissance saw an awakening in almost every sphere of human activity, especially science, philosophy, and the arts. The period is best defined by the emergence of a general philosophy that emphasized the importance of the intellect, the individual, and world affairs. It contrasts strongly with the medieval worldview, characterized by the dominant concerns of faith, the social collective, and spiritual salvation.

Repartee: Conversation featuring snappy retorts and witticisms.

Restoration: See *Restoration Age*

Restoration Age: A period in English literature beginning with the crowning of Charles II in 1660 and running to about 1700. The era, which was characterized by a reaction against Puritanism, was the first great age of the comedy of manners. The finest literature of the era is typically witty and urbane, and often lewd.

Rhetoric: In literary criticism, this term denotes the art of ethical persuasion. In its strictest sense, rhetoric adheres to various principles developed since classical times for arranging facts and ideas in a clear, persuasive, appealing manner. The term is also used to refer to effective prose in general and theories of or methods for composing effective prose.

Rhetorical Question: A question intended to provoke thought, but not an expressed answer, in the reader. It is most commonly used in oratory and other persuasive genres.

Rhyme: When used as a noun in literary criticism, this term generally refers to a poem in which words sound identical or very similar and appear in parallel positions in two or more lines. Rhymes are classified into different types according to where they fall in a line or stanza or according to the degree of similarity they exhibit in their spellings and sounds. Some major types of rhyme are "masculine" rhyme, "feminine" rhyme, and "triple" rhyme. In a masculine rhyme, the rhyming sound falls in a single accented syllable, as with "heat" and "eat." Feminine rhyme is a rhyme of two syllables, one stressed and one unstressed, as with "merry" and "tarry." Triple rhyme matches the sound of the accented syllable and the two unaccented syllables that follow: "narrative" and "declarative."

Rhyme Royal: A stanza of seven lines composed in iambic pentameter and rhymed *ababbcc*. The name is said to be a tribute to King James I of Scotland, who made much use of the form in his poetry.

Rhyme Scheme: See *Rhyme*

Rhythm: A regular pattern of sound, time intervals, or events occurring in writing, most often and most discernably in poetry. Regular, reliable rhythm is known to be soothing to humans, while interrupted, unpredictable, or rapidly changing rhythm is disturbing. These effects are known to authors, who use them to produce a desired reaction in the reader.

Rococo: A style of European architecture that flourished in the eighteenth century, especially in

France. The most notable features of *rococo* are its extensive use of ornamentation and its themes of lightness, gaiety, and intimacy. In literary criticism, the term is often used disparagingly to refer to a decadent or overly ornamental style.

Romance:

Romantic Age: See *Romanticism*

Romanticism: This term has two widely accepted meanings. In historical criticism, it refers to a European intellectual and artistic movement of the late eighteenth and early nineteenth centuries that sought greater freedom of personal expression than that allowed by the strict rules of literary form and logic of the eighteenth-century Neoclassicists. The Romantics preferred emotional and imaginative expression to rational analysis. They considered the individual to be at the center of all experience and so placed him or her at the center of their art. The Romantics believed that the creative imagination reveals nobler truths—unique feelings and attitudes—than those that could be discovered by logic or by scientific examination. Both the natural world and the state of childhood were important sources for revelations of "eternal truths." "Romanticism" is also used as a general term to refer to a type of sensibility found in all periods of literary history and usually considered to be in opposition to the principles of classicism. In this sense, Romanticism signifies any work or philosophy in which the exotic or dreamlike figure strongly, or that is devoted to individualistic expression, self-analysis, or a pursuit of a higher realm of knowledge than can be discovered by human reason.

Romantics: See *Romanticism*

Russian Symbolism: A Russian poetic movement, derived from French symbolism, that flourished between 1894 and 1910. While some Russian Symbolists continued in the French tradition, stressing aestheticism and the importance of suggestion above didactic intent, others saw their craft as a form of mystical worship, and themselves as mediators between the supernatural and the mundane.

S

Satire: A work that uses ridicule, humor, and wit to criticize and provoke change in human nature and institutions. There are two major types of satire: "formal" or "direct" satire speaks directly to the reader or to a character in the work; "indirect" satire relies upon the ridiculous behavior of its characters to make its point. Formal satire is further divided into two manners: the "Horatian," which ridicules gently, and the "Juvenalian," which derides its subjects harshly and bitterly.

Scansion: The analysis or "scanning" of a poem to determine its meter and often its rhyme scheme. The most common system of scansion uses accents (slanted lines drawn above syllables) to show stressed syllables, breves (curved lines drawn above syllables) to show unstressed syllables, and vertical lines to separate each foot.

Second Person: See *Point of View*

Semiotics: The study of how literary forms and conventions affect the meaning of language.

Sestet: Any six-line poem or stanza.

Setting: The time, place, and culture in which the action of a narrative takes place. The elements of setting may include geographic location, characters' physical and mental environments, prevailing cultural attitudes, or the historical time in which the action takes place.

Shakespearean Sonnet: See *Sonnet*

Signifying Monkey: A popular trickster figure in black folklore, with hundreds of tales about this character documented since the nineteenth century.

Simile: A comparison, usually using "like" or "as," of two essentially dissimilar things, as in "coffee as cold as ice" or "He sounded like a broken record."

Slang: A type of informal verbal communication that is generally unacceptable for formal writing. Slang words and phrases are often colorful exaggerations used to emphasize the speaker's point; they may also be shortened versions of an often-used word or phrase.

Slant Rhyme: See *Consonance*

Slave Narrative: Autobiographical accounts of American slave life as told by escaped slaves. These works first appeared during the abolition movement of the 1830s through the 1850s.

Social Realism: See *Socialist Realism*

Socialist Realism: The Socialist Realism school of literary theory was proposed by Maxim Gorky and established as a dogma by the first Soviet Congress of Writers. It demanded adherence to a communist worldview in works of literature. Its doctrines required an objective viewpoint comprehensible to the working classes and themes of social struggle featuring strong proletarian heroes.

Soliloquy: A monologue in a drama used to give the audience information and to develop the speaker's character. It is typically a projection of the speaker's innermost thoughts. Usually delivered while the speaker is alone on stage, a soliloquy is intended to present an illusion of unspoken reflection.

Sonnet: A fourteen-line poem, usually composed in iambic pentameter, employing one of several rhyme schemes. There are three major types of sonnets, upon which all other variations of the form are based: the "Petrarchan" or "Italian" sonnet, the "Shakespearean" or "English" sonnet, and the "Spenserian" sonnet. A Petrarchan sonnet consists of an octave rhymed *abbaabba* and a "sestet" rhymed either *cdecde, cdccdc,* or *cdedce.* The octave poses a question or problem, relates a narrative, or puts forth a proposition; the sestet presents a solution to the problem, comments upon the narrative, or applies the proposition put forth in the octave. The Shakespearean sonnet is divided into three quatrains and a couplet rhymed *abab cdcd efef gg*. The couplet provides an epigrammatic comment on the narrative or problem put forth in the quatrains. The Spenserian sonnet uses three quatrains and a couplet like the Shakespearean, but links their three rhyme schemes in this way: *abab bcbc cdcd ee*. The Spenserian sonnet develops its theme in two parts like the Petrarchan, its final six lines resolving a problem, analyzing a narrative, or applying a proposition put forth in its first eight lines.

Spenserian Sonnet: See *Sonnet*

Spenserian Stanza: A nine-line stanza having eight verses in iambic pentameter, its ninth verse in iambic hexameter, and the rhyme scheme *ababbcbcc*.

Spondee: In poetry meter, a foot consisting of two long or stressed syllables occurring together. This form is quite rare in English verse, and is usually composed of two monosyllabic words.

Sprung Rhythm: Versification using a specific number of accented syllables per line but disregarding the number of unaccented syllables that fall in each line, producing an irregular rhythm in the poem.

Stanza: A subdivision of a poem consisting of lines grouped together, often in recurring patterns of rhyme, line length, and meter. Stanzas may also serve as units of thought in a poem much like paragraphs in prose.

Stereotype: A stereotype was originally the name for a duplication made during the printing process; this led to its modern definition as a person or thing that is (or is assumed to be) the same as all others of its type.

Stream of Consciousness: A narrative technique for rendering the inward experience of a character. This technique is designed to give the impression of an ever-changing series of thoughts, emotions, images, and memories in the spontaneous and seemingly illogical order that they occur in life.

Structuralism: A twentieth-century movement in literary criticism that examines how literary texts arrive at their meanings, rather than the meanings themselves. There are two major types of structuralist analysis: one examines the way patterns of linguistic structures unify a specific text and emphasize certain elements of that text, and the other interprets the way literary forms and conventions affect the meaning of language itself.

Structure: The form taken by a piece of literature. The structure may be made obvious for ease of understanding, as in nonfiction works, or may obscured for artistic purposes, as in some poetry or seemingly "unstructured" prose.

Sturm und Drang: A German term meaning "storm and stress." It refers to a German literary movement of the 1770s and 1780s that reacted against the order and rationalism of the enlightenment, focusing instead on the intense experience of extraordinary individuals.

Style: A writer's distinctive manner of arranging words to suit his or her ideas and purpose in writing. The unique imprint of the author's personality upon his or her writing, style is the product of an author's way of arranging ideas and his or her use of diction, different sentence structures, rhythm, figures of speech, rhetorical principles, and other elements of composition.

Subject: The person, event, or theme at the center of a work of literature. A work may have one or more subjects of each type, with shorter works tending to have fewer and longer works tending to have more.

Subjectivity: Writing that expresses the author's personal feelings about his subject, and which may or may not include factual information about the subject.

Surrealism: A term introduced to criticism by Guillaume Apollinaire and later adopted by Andre Breton. It refers to a French literary and artistic movement founded in the 1920s. The Surrealists sought to express unconscious thoughts and feelings in their works. The best-known technique used for achieving this aim was automatic writing—transcriptions of spontaneous outpourings from the unconscious. The Surrealists proposed to unify the contrary levels of conscious and unconscious, dream and reality, objectivity and subjectivity into a new level of "super-realism."

Suspense: A literary device in which the author maintains the audience's attention through the buildup of events, the outcome of which will soon be revealed.

Syllogism: A method of presenting a logical argument. In its most basic form, the syllogism consists of a major premise, a minor premise, and a conclusion.

Symbol: Something that suggests or stands for something else without losing its original identity. In literature, symbols combine their literal meaning with the suggestion of an abstract concept. Literary symbols are of two types: those that carry complex associations of meaning no matter what their contexts, and those that derive their suggestive meaning from their functions in specific literary works.

Symbolism: This term has two widely accepted meanings. In historical criticism, it denotes an early modernist literary movement initiated in France during the nineteenth century that reacted against the prevailing standards of realism. Writers in this movement aimed to evoke, indirectly and symbolically, an order of being beyond the material world of the five senses. Poetic expression of personal emotion figured strongly in the movement, typically by means of a private set of symbols uniquely identifiable with the individual poet. The principal aim of the Symbolists was to express in words the highly complex feelings that grew out of everyday contact with the world. In a broader sense, the term "symbolism" refers to the use of one object to represent another.

Symbolist: See *Symbolism*

Symbolist Movement: See *Symbolism*

Sympathetic Fallacy: See *Affective Fallacy*

T

Tanka: A form of Japanese poetry similar to *haiku*. A *tanka* is five lines long, with the lines containing five, seven, five, seven, and seven syllables respectively.

Terza Rima: A three-line stanza form in poetry in which the rhymes are made on the last word of each line in the following manner: the first and third lines of the first stanza, then the second line of the first stanza and the first and third lines of the second stanza, and so on with the middle line of any stanza rhyming with the first and third lines of the following stanza.

Tetrameter: See *Meter*

Textual Criticism: A branch of literary criticism that seeks to establish the authoritative text of a literary work. Textual critics typically compare all known manuscripts or printings of a single work in order to assess the meanings of differences and revisions. This procedure allows them to arrive at a definitive version that (supposedly) corresponds to the author's original intention.

Theme: The main point of a work of literature. The term is used interchangeably with thesis.

Thesis: A thesis is both an essay and the point argued in the essay. Thesis novels and thesis plays share the quality of containing a thesis which is supported through the action of the story.

Third Person: See *Point of View*

Tone: The author's attitude toward his or her audience may be deduced from the tone of the work. A formal tone may create distance or convey politeness, while an informal tone may encourage a friendly, intimate, or intrusive feeling in the reader. The author's attitude toward his or her subject matter may also be deduced from the tone of the words he or she uses in discussing it.

Tragedy: A drama in prose or poetry about a noble, courageous hero of excellent character who, because of some tragic character flaw or *hamartia*, brings ruin upon him- or herself. Tragedy treats its subjects in a dignified and serious manner, using poetic language to help evoke pity and fear and bring about catharsis, a purging of these emotions. The tragic form was practiced extensively by the ancient Greeks. In the Middle Ages, when classical works were virtually unknown, tragedy came to denote any works about the fall of persons from exalted to low conditions due to any reason: fate, vice, weakness, etc. According to the classical definition of tragedy, such works present the "pathetic"—that which evokes pity—rather than the tragic. The classical form of tragedy was revived in the sixteenth century; it flourished especially on the Elizabethan stage. In modern times, dramatists have attempted to adapt the form to the needs of modern society by drawing their heroes from the ranks of ordinary men and women and defining the nobility of these heroes in terms of spirit rather than exalted social standing.

Tragic Flaw: In a tragedy, the quality within the hero or heroine which leads to his or her downfall.

Transcendentalism: An American philosophical and religious movement, based in New England from around 1835 until the Civil War. Transcendentalism was a form of American romanticism that had its roots abroad in the works of Thomas Carlyle, Samuel Coleridge, and Johann Wolfgang von Goethe. The Transcendentalists stressed the importance of intuition and subjective experience in communication with God. They rejected religious dogma and texts in favor of mysticism and scientific naturalism. They pursued truths that lie beyond the "colorless" realms perceived by reason and the senses and were active social reformers in public education, women's rights, and the abolition of slavery.

Trickster: A character or figure common in Native American and African literature who uses his ingenuity to defeat enemies and escape difficult situations. Tricksters are most often animals, such as the spider, hare, or coyote, although they may take the form of humans as well.

Trimeter: See *Meter*

Triple Rhyme: See *Rhyme*

Trochee: See *Foot*

U

Understatement: See *Irony*

Unities: Strict rules of dramatic structure, formulated by Italian and French critics of the Renaissance and based loosely on the principles of drama discussed by Aristotle in his *Poetics*. Foremost among these rules were the three unities of action, time, and place that compelled a dramatist to: (1) construct a single plot with a beginning, middle, and end that details the causal relationships of action and character; (2) restrict the action to the events of a single day; and (3) limit the scene to a single place or city. The unities were observed faithfully by continental European writers until the Romantic Age, but they were never regularly observed in English drama. Modern dramatists are typically more concerned with a unity of impression or emotional effect than with any of the classical unities.

Urban Realism: A branch of realist writing that attempts to accurately reflect the often harsh facts of modern urban existence.

Utopia: A fictional perfect place, such as "paradise" or "heaven."

Utopian: See *Utopia*

Utopianism: See *Utopia*

V

Verisimilitude: Literally, the appearance of truth. In literary criticism, the term refers to aspects of a work of literature that seem true to the reader.

Vers de societe: See *Occasional Verse*

Vers libre: See *Free Verse*

Verse: A line of metered language, a line of a poem, or any work written in verse.

Versification: The writing of verse. Versification may also refer to the meter, rhyme, and other mechanical components of a poem.

Victorian: Refers broadly to the reign of Queen Victoria of England (1837–1901) and to anything with qualities typical of that era. For example, the qualities of smug narrowmindedness, bourgeois materialism, faith in social progress, and priggish morality are often considered Victorian. This stereotype is contradicted by such dramatic intellectual developments as the theories of Charles Darwin, Karl Marx, and Sigmund Freud (which stirred strong debates in England) and the critical attitudes of serious Victorian writers like Charles Dickens and George Eliot. In literature, the Victorian Period was the great age of the English novel, and the latter part of the era saw the rise of movements such as decadence and symbolism.

Victorian Age: See *Victorian*

Victorian Period: See *Victorian*

W

Weltanschauung: A German term referring to a person's worldview or philosophy.

Weltschmerz: A German term meaning "world pain." It describes a sense of anguish about the nature of existence, usually associated with a melancholy, pessimistic attitude.

Z

Zarzuela: A type of Spanish operetta.

Zeitgeist: A German term meaning "spirit of the time." It refers to the moral and intellectual trends of a given era.

Cumulative Author/Title Index

A

Ackerman, Diane
   On Location in the Loire Valley: V19
Acosta, Teresa Palomo
   My Mother Pieced Quilts: V12
Address to the Angels (Kumin): V18
The Afterlife (Collins): V18
An African Elegy (Duncan): V13
Ah, Are You Digging on My Grave? (Hardy): V4
Ai
   Reunions with a Ghost: V16
Akhmatova, Anna
   Midnight Verses: V18
Alabama Centennial (Madgett): V10
American Poetry (Simpson): V7
Ammons, A. R.
   The City Limits: V19
An Arundel Tomb (Larkin): V12
Anasazi (Snyder): V9
And What If I Spoke of Despair (Bass): V19
Angelou, Maya
   Harlem Hopscotch: V2
   On the Pulse of Morning: V3
Angle of Geese (Momaday): V2
Annabel Lee (Poe): V9
Anniversary (Harjo): V15
Anonymous
   Barbara Allan: V7
   Go Down, Moses: V11
   Lord Randal: V6
   The Seafarer: V8
   Sir Patrick Spens: V4
   Swing Low Sweet Chariot: V1
Anorexic (Boland): V12
Any Human to Another (Cullen): V3
A Pièd (McElroy): V3
Arnold, Matthew
   Dover Beach: V2
Ars Poetica (MacLeish): V5
The Arsenal at Springfield (Longfellow): V17
As I Walked Out One Evening (Auden): V4
Ashbery, John
   Paradoxes and Oxymorons: V11
Astonishment (Szymborska): V15
At the Bomb Testing Site (Stafford): V8
Atwood, Margaret
   Siren Song: V7
Auden, W. H.
   As I Walked Out One Evening: V4
   Funeral Blues: V10
   Musée des Beaux Arts: V1
   The Unknown Citizen: V3
Auto Wreck (Shapiro): V3
Autumn Begins in Martins Ferry, Ohio (Wright): V8

B

Ballad of Orange and Grape (Rukeyser): V10
Baraka, Amiri
   In Memory of Radio: V9
Barbara Allan (Anonymous): V7
Barbie Doll (Piercy): V9
Ballad of Birmingham (Randall): V5
Barrett, Elizabeth
   Sonnet 43: V2
The Base Stealer (Francis): V12
Bashō, Matsuo
   Falling Upon Earth: V2
   The Moon Glows the Same: V7
   Temple Bells Die Out: V18
Bass, Ellen
   And What If I Spoke of Despair: V19
The Bean Eaters (Brooks): V2
Because I Could Not Stop for Death (Dickinson): V2
Bedtime Story (MacBeth): V8
La Belle Dame sans Merci (Keats): V17
The Bells (Poe): V3
Beowulf (Wilbur): V11
Beware: Do Not Read This Poem (Reed): V6
Beware of Ruins (Hope): V8
Bialosky, Jill
   Seven Seeds: V19
Bidwell Ghost (Erdrich): V14
Birch Canoe (Revard): V5
Birches (Frost): V13
Birney, Earle
   Vancouver Lights: V8
A Birthday (Rossetti): V10
Bishop, Elizabeth
   Brazil, January 1, 1502: V6
   Filling Station: V12
Blackberrying (Plath): V15
Black Zodiac (Wright): V10
Blake, William
   The Lamb: V12
   The Tyger: V2
A Blessing (Wright): V7
Blood Oranges (Mueller): V13

The Blue Rim of Memory (Levertov): V17
Blumenthal, Michael
   Inventors: V7
Bly, Robert
   Come with Me: V6
   Driving to Town Late to Mail a Letter: V17
Boland, Eavan
   Anorexic: V12
The Boy (Hacker): V19
Bradstreet, Anne
   To My Dear and Loving Husband: V6
Brazil, January 1, 1502 (Bishop): V6
Bright Star! Would I Were Steadfast as Thou Art (Keats): V9
Brooke, Rupert
   The Soldier: V7
Brooks, Gwendolyn
   The Bean Eaters: V2
   The Sonnet-Ballad: V1
   Strong Men, Riding Horses: V4
   We Real Cool: V6
Brouwer, Joel
   Last Request: V14
Browning, Elizabeth Barrett
   Sonnet 43: V2
   Sonnet XXIX: V16
Browning, Robert
   My Last Duchess: V1
   Porphyria's Lover: V15
Burns, Robert
   A Red, Red Rose: V8
Business (Cruz): V16
The Bustle in a House (Dickinson): V10
Butcher Shop (Simic): V7
Byron, Lord
   The Destruction of Sennacherib: V1
   She Walks in Beauty: V14

C

The Canterbury Tales (Chaucer): V14
Cargoes (Masefield): V5
Carroll, Lewis
   Jabberwocky: V11
Carson, Anne
   New Rule: V18
Carver, Raymond
   The Cobweb: V17
Casey at the Bat (Thayer): V5
Cavafy, C. P.
   Ithaka: V19
Cavalry Crossing a Ford (Whitman): V13
The Charge of the Light Brigade (Tennyson): V1
Chaucer, Geoffrey
   The Canterbury Tales: V14
Chicago (Sandburg): V3

Childhood (Rilke): V19
Chocolates (Simpson): V11
The Cinnamon Peeler (Ondaatje): V19
Cisneros, Sandra
   Once Again I Prove the Theory of Relativity: V19
The City Limits (Ammons): V19
Clifton, Lucille
   Climbing: V14
   Miss Rosie: V1
Climbing (Clifton): V14
The Cobweb (Carver): V17
Coleridge, Samuel Taylor
   Kubla Khan: V5
   The Rime of the Ancient Mariner: V4
Colibrí (Espada): V16
Collins, Billy
   The Afterlife: V18
Come with Me (Bly): V6
The Constellation Orion (Kooser): V8
Concord Hymn (Emerson): V4
The Conquerors (McGinley): V13
The Continuous Life (Strand): V18
Cool Tombs (Sandburg): V6
The Country Without a Post Office (Shahid Ali): V18
Courage (Sexton): V14
The Courage That My Mother Had (Millay): V3
Crane, Stephen
   War Is Kind: V9
The Creation (Johnson): V1
The Cremation of Sam McGee (Service): V10
Cruz, Victor Hernandez
   Business: V16
Cullen, Countee
   Any Human to Another: V3
cummings, e. e.
   i was sitting in mcsorley's: V13
   l(a: V1
   maggie and milly and molly and may: V12
   old age sticks: V3
   somewhere i have never travelled,gladly beyond: V19
The Czar's Last Christmas Letter. A Barn in the Urals (Dubie): V12

D

The Darkling Thrush (Hardy): V18
Darwin in 1881 (Schnackenberg): V13
Dawe, Bruce
   Drifters: V10
Daylights (Warren): V13
Dear Reader (Tate): V10
The Death of the Ball Turret Gunner (Jarrell): V2

The Death of the Hired Man (Frost): V4
Deep Woods (Nemerov): V14
The Destruction of Sennacherib (Byron): V1
Dickey, James
   The Heaven of Animals: V6
   The Hospital Window: V11
Dickinson, Emily
   Because I Could Not Stop for Death: V2
   The Bustle in a House: V10
   "Hope" Is the Thing with Feathers: V3
   I felt a Funeral, in my Brain: V13
   I Heard a Fly Buzz—When I Died—: V5
   Much Madness Is Divinest Sense: V16
   My Life Closed Twice Before Its Close: V8
   A Narrow Fellow in the Grass: V11
   The Soul Selects Her Own Society: V1
   There's a Certain Slant of Light: V6
   This Is My Letter to the World: V4
Digging (Heaney): V5
Do Not Go Gentle into that Good Night (Thomas): V1
Donne, John
   Holy Sonnet 10: V2
   A Valediction: Forbidding Mourning: V11
Dove, Rita
   Geometry: V15
   This Life: V1
Dover Beach (Arnold): V2
Dream Variations (Hughes): V15
Drifters (Dawe): V10
A Drink of Water (Heaney): V8
Driving to Town Late to Mail a Letter (Bly): V17
Drought Year (Wright): V8
Dubie, Norman
   The Czar's Last Christmas Letter. A Barn in the Urals: V12
Du Bois, W. E. B.
   The Song of the Smoke: V13
Duncan, Robert
   An African Elegy: V13
Dugan, Alan
   How We Heard the Name: V10
Dulce et Decorum Est (Owen): V10
Duration (Paz): V18

E

The Eagle (Tennyson): V11
Early in the Morning (Lee): V17
Easter 1916 (Yeats): V5
Eating Poetry (Strand): V9

Elegy for My Father, Who is Not Dead (Hudgins): V14
Elegy Written in a Country Churchyard (Gray): V9
Eliot, T. S.
  Journey of the Magi: V7
  The Love Song of J. Alfred Prufrock: V1
Emerson, Ralph Waldo
  Concord Hymn: V4
  The Rhodora: V17
Erdrich, Louise
  Bidwell Ghost: V14
Espada, Martín
  Colibrí: V16
  We Live by What We See at Night: V13
Ethics (Pastan): V8
The Exhibit (Mueller): V9

F

Facing It (Komunyakaa): V5
Falling Upon Earth (Bashō): V2
A Far Cry from Africa (Walcott): V6
A Farewell to English (Hartnett): V10
Fenton, James
  The Milkfish Gatherers: V11
Fern Hill (Thomas): V3
Fifteen (Stafford): V2
Filling Station (Bishop): V12
Fire and Ice (Frost): V7
The Fish (Moore): V14
For a New Citizen of These United States (Lee): V15
For An Assyrian Frieze (Viereck): V9
For Jean Vincent D'abbadie, Baron St.-Castin (Nowlan): V12
For Jennifer, 6, on the Teton (Hugo): V17
For the Union Dead (Lowell): V7
For the White poets who would be Indian (Rose): V13
The Force That Through the Green Fuse Drives the Flower (Thomas): V8
Forché, Carolyn
  The Garden Shukkei-en: V18
Four Mountain Wolves (Silko): V9
Francis, Robert
  The Base Stealer: V12
Frost, Robert
  Birches: V13
  The Death of the Hired Man: V4
  Fire and Ice: V7
  Mending Wall: V5
  Nothing Gold Can Stay: V3
  Out, Out—: V10
  The Road Not Taken: V2
  Stopping by Woods on a Snowy Evening: V1
  The Wood-Pile: V6
Funeral Blues (Auden): V10

G

Gallagher, Tess
  I Stop Writing the Poem: V16
The Garden Shukkei-en (Forché): V18
Geometry (Dove): V15
Ginsberg, Allen
  A Supermarket in California: V5
Giovanni, Nikki
  Knoxville, Tennessee: V17
Glück, Louise
  The Gold Lily: V5
  The Mystery: V15
Go Down, Moses (Anonymous): V11
The Gold Lily (Glück): V5
A Grafted Tongue (Montague): V12
Graham, Jorie
  The Hiding Place: V10
  Mind: V17
Gray, Thomas
  Elegy Written in a Country Churchyard: V9
The Greatest Grandeur (Rogers): V18
Gunn, Thom
  The Missing: V9

H

H.D.
  Helen: V6
Hacker, Marilyn
  The Boy: V19
Hall, Donald
  Names of Horses: V8
Hardy, Thomas
  Ah, Are You Digging on My Grave?: V4
  The Darkling Thrush: V18
  The Man He Killed: V3
Harjo, Joy
  Anniversary: V15
Harlem (Hughes): V1
Harlem Hopscotch (Angelou): V2
Hartnett, Michael
  A Farewell to English: V10
Having a Coke with You (O'Hara): V12
Having it Out with Melancholy (Kenyon): V17
Hawk Roosting (Hughes): V4
Hayden, Robert
  Those Winter Sundays: V1
Heaney, Seamus
  Digging: V5
  A Drink of Water: V8
  Midnight: V2
  The Singer's House: V17
Hecht, Anthony
  "More Light! More Light!": V6
The Heaven of Animals (Dickey): V6
Helen (H.D.): V6

Herrick, Robert
  To the Virgins, to Make Much of Time: V13
The Hiding Place (Graham): V10
High Windows (Larkin): V3
The Highwayman (Noyes): V4
Hirshfield, Jane
  Three Times My Life Has Opened: V16
His Speed and Strength (Ostriker): V19
Hoagland, Tony
  Social Life: V19
Holmes, Oliver Wendell
  Old Ironsides: V9
Holy Sonnet 10 (Donne): V2
Hope, A. D.
  Beware of Ruins: V8
Hope Is a Tattered Flag (Sandburg): V12
"Hope" Is the Thing with Feathers (Dickinson): V3
The Horizons of Rooms (Merwin): V15
The Hospital Window (Dickey): V11
Housman, A. E.
  To an Athlete Dying Young: V7
  When I Was One-and-Twenty: V4
How We Heard the Name (Dugan): V10
Howe, Marie
  What Belongs to Us: V15
Hudgins, Andrew
  Elegy for My Father, Who is Not Dead: V14
Hugh Selwyn Mauberley (Pound): V16
Hughes, Langston
  Dream Variations: V15
  Harlem: V1
  Mother to Son: V3
  The Negro Speaks of Rivers: V10
  Theme for English B: V6
Hughes, Ted
  Hawk Roosting: V4
  Perfect Light: V19
Hugo, Richard
  For Jennifer, 6, on the Teton: V17
Hunger in New York City (Ortiz): V4
Huong, Ho Xuan
  Spring-Watching Pavilion: V18
Hurt Hawks (Jeffers): V3

I

I felt a Funeral, in my Brain (Dickinson): V13
I Go Back to May 1937 (Olds): V17
I Hear America Singing (Whitman): V3
I Heard a Fly Buzz—When I Died— (Dickinson): V5
I Stop Writing the Poem (Gallagher): V16

i was sitting in mcsorley's (cummings): V13
The Idea of Order at Key West (Stevens): V13
In a Station of the Metro (Pound): V2
Incident in a Rose Garden (Justice): V14
In Flanders Fields (McCrae): V5
In Memory of Radio (Baraka): V9
In the Land of Shinar (Levertov): V7
In the Suburbs (Simpson): V14
Inventors (Blumenthal): V7
An Irish Airman Foresees His Death (Yeats): V1
Island of the Three Marias (Ríos): V11
Ithaka (Cavafy): V19

J

Jabberwocky (Carroll): V11
Jarrell, Randall
   The Death of the Ball Turret Gunner: V2
Jeffers, Robinson
   Hurt Hawks: V3
   Shine Perishing Republic: V4
Johnson, James Weldon
   The Creation: V1
Journey of the Magi (Eliot): V7
Justice, Donald
   Incident in a Rose Garden: V14

K

Keats, John
   La Belle Dame sans Merci: V17
   Bright Star! Would I Were Steadfast as Thou Art: V9
   Ode on a Grecian Urn: V1
   Ode to a Nightingale: V3
   When I Have Fears that I May Cease to Be: V2
Kenyon, Jane
   Having it Out with Melancholy: V17
   "Trouble with Math in a One-Room Country School": V9
Kilroy (Viereck): V14
King James Bible
   Psalm 8: V9
   Psalm 23: V4
Kinnell, Galway
   Saint Francis and the Sow: V9
Kizer, Carolyn
   To an Unknown Poet: V18
Knoxville, Tennessee (Giovanni): V17
Kooser, Ted
   The Constellation Orion: V8
Komunyakaa, Yusef
   Facing It: V5
Kubla Khan (Coleridge): V5
Kumin, Maxine
   Address to the Angels: V18
Kunitz, Stanley
   The War Against the Trees: V11

L

l(a (cummings): V1
The Lady of Shalott (Tennyson): V15
The Lake Isle of Innisfree (Yeats): V15
The Lamb (Blake): V12
Lament for the Dorsets (Purdy): V5
Landscape with Tractor (Taylor): V10
Lanier, Sidney
   Song of the Chattahoochee: V14
Larkin, Philip
   An Arundel Tomb: V12
   High Windows: V3
   Toads: V4
The Last Question (Parker): V18
Last Request (Brouwer): V14
Lawrence, D. H.
   Piano: V6
Layton, Irving
   A Tall Man Executes a Jig: V12
Leda and the Swan (Yeats): V13
Lee, Li-Young
   Early in the Morning: V17
   For a New Citizen of These United States: V15
   The Weight of Sweetness: V11
Levertov, Denise
   The Blue Rim of Memory: V17
   In the Land of Shinar: V7
Leviathan (Merwin): V5
Levine, Philip
   Starlight: V8
Longfellow, Henry Wadsworth
   The Arsenal at Springfield: V17
   Paul Revere's Ride: V2
   A Psalm of Life: V7
Lord Randal (Anonymous): V6
Lorde, Audre
   What My Child Learns of the Sea: V16
Lost Sister (Song): V5
The Love Song of J. Alfred Prufrock (Eliot): V1
Lowell, Robert
   For the Union Dead: V7
   The Quaker Graveyard in Nantucket: V6

M

MacBeth, George
   Bedtime Story: V8
MacLeish, Archibald
   Ars Poetica: V5
Madgett, Naomi Long
   Alabama Centennial: V10
maggie and milly and molly and may (cummings): V12
The Man He Killed (Hardy): V3
A Martian Sends a Postcard Home (Raine): V7
Marvell, Andrew
   To His Coy Mistress: V5
Masefield, John
   Cargoes: V5
Matsuo Bashō
   Falling Upon Earth: V2
   The Moon Glows the Same: V7
   Temple Bells Die Out: V18
McCrae, John
   In Flanders Fields: V5
McElroy, Colleen
   A Pièd: V3
McGinley, Phyllis
   The Conquerors: V13
   Reactionary Essay on Applied Science: V9
McKay, Claude
   The Tropics in New York: V4
Meeting the British (Muldoon): V7
Mending Wall (Frost): V5
Merlin Enthralled (Wilbur): V16
Merriam, Eve
   Onomatopoeia: V6
Merwin, W. S.
   The Horizons of Rooms: V15
   Leviathan: V5
Midnight (Heaney): V2
Midnight Verses (Akhmatova): V18
The Milkfish Gatherers (Fenton): V11
Millay, Edna St. Vincent
   The Courage That My Mother Had: V3
   Wild Swans: V17
Milosz, Czeslaw
   Song of a Citizen: V16
Milton, John
   [On His Blindness] Sonnet 16: V3
   On His Having Arrived at the Age of Twenty-Three: V17
Mind (Graham): V17
Mirror (Plath): V1
Miss Rosie (Clifton): V1
The Missing (Gunn): V9
Momaday, N. Scott
   Angle of Geese: V2
   To a Child Running With Outstretched Arms in Canyon de Chelly: V11
Montague, John
   A Grafted Tongue: V12
The Moon Glows the Same (Bashō): V7
Moore, Marianne
   The Fish: V14
   Poetry: V17
"More Light! More Light!" (Hecht): V6
Mother to Son (Hughes): V3
Much Madness Is Divinest Sense (Dickinson): V16

Muldoon, Paul
  Meeting the British: V7
Mueller, Lisel
  Blood Oranges: V13
  The Exhibit: V9
Musée des Beaux Arts (Auden): V1
Music Lessons (Oliver): V8
My Father's Song (Ortiz): V16
My Last Duchess (Browning): V1
My Life Closed Twice Before Its Close (Dickinson): V8
My Mother Pieced Quilts (Acosta): V12
My Papa's Waltz (Roethke): V3
The Mystery (Glück): V15

N

Names of Horses (Hall): V8
A Narrow Fellow in the Grass (Dickinson): V11
The Negro Speaks of Rivers (Hughes): V10
Nemerov, Howard
  Deep Woods: V14
  The Phoenix: V10
Neruda, Pablo
  Tonight I Can Write: V11
New Rule (Carson): V18
Not Waving but Drowning (Smith): V3
Nothing Gold Can Stay (Frost): V3
Nowlan, Alden
  For Jean Vincent D'abbadie, Baron St.-Castin: V12
Noyes, Alfred
  The Highwayman: V4
The Nymph's Reply to the Shepherd (Raleigh): V14

O

O Captain! My Captain! (Whitman): V2
Ode on a Grecian Urn (Keats): V1
Ode to a Nightingale (Keats): V3
Ode to the West Wind (Shelley): V2
O'Hara, Frank
  Having a Coke with You: V12
  Why I Am Not a Painter: V8
old age sticks (cummings): V3
Old Ironsides (Holmes): V9
Olds, Sharon
  I Go Back to May 1937: V17
Oliver, Mary
  Music Lessons: V8
  Wild Geese: V15
On Freedom's Ground (Wilbur): V12
[On His Blindness] Sonnet 16 (Milton): V3
On His Having Arrived at the Age of Twenty-Three (Milton): V17
On Location in the Loire Valley (Ackerman): V19

On the Pulse of Morning (Angelou): V3
Once Again I Prove the Theory of Relativity (Cisneros): V19
Ondaatje, Michael
  The Cinnamon Peeler: V19
  To a Sad Daughter: V8
Onomatopoeia (Merriam): V6
Ordinary Words (Stone): V19
Ortiz, Simon
  Hunger in New York City: V4
  My Father's Song: V16
Ostriker, Alicia
  His Speed and Strength: V19
Out, Out— (Frost): V10
Overture to a Dance of Locomotives (Williams): V11
Owen, Wilfred
  Dulce et Decorum Est: V10
Oysters (Sexton): V4

P

Paradoxes and Oxymorons (Ashbery): V11
Parker, Dorothy
  The Last Question: V18
Pastan, Linda
  Ethics: V8
Paul Revere's Ride (Longfellow): V2
Paz, Octavio
  Duration: V18
Perfect Light (Hughes): V19
The Phoenix (Nemerov): V10
Piano (Lawrence): V6
Piercy, Marge
  Barbie Doll: V9
Pinsky, Robert
  Song of Reasons: V18
Plath, Sylvia
  Blackberrying: V15
  Mirror: V1
A Psalm of Life (Longfellow): V7
Poe, Edgar Allan
  Annabel Lee: V9
  The Bells: V3
  The Raven: V1
Poetry (Moore): V17
Pope, Alexander
  The Rape of the Lock: V12
Porphyria's Lover (Browning): V15
Pound, Ezra
  Hugh Selwyn Mauberley: V16
  In a Station of the Metro: V2
  The River-Merchant's Wife: A Letter: V8
Proem (Tennyson): V19
Psalm 8 (King James Bible): V9
Psalm 23 (King James Bible): V4
Purdy, Al
  Lament for the Dorsets: V5
  Wilderness Gothic: V12

Q

The Quaker Graveyard in Nantucket (Lowell): V6
Queen-Ann's-Lace (Williams): V6

R

Raine, Craig
  A Martian Sends a Postcard Home: V7
Raleigh, Walter, Sir
  The Nymph's Reply to the Shepherd: V14
Randall, Dudley
  Ballad of Birmingham: V5
The Rape of the Lock (Pope): V12
The Raven (Poe): V1
Reactionary Essay on Applied Science (McGinley): V9
A Red, Red Rose (Burns): V8
The Red Wheelbarrow (Williams): V1
Reed, Ishmael
  Beware: Do Not Read This Poem: V6
Remember (Rossetti): V14
Reunions with a Ghost (Ai): V16
Revard, Carter
  Birch Canoe: V5
The Rhodora (Emerson): V17
Rich, Adrienne
  Rusted Legacy: V15
Richard Cory (Robinson): V4
Rilke, Rainer Maria
  Childhood: V19
The Rime of the Ancient Mariner (Coleridge): V4
Ríos, Alberto
  Island of the Three Marias: V11
The River-Merchant's Wife: A Letter (Pound): V8
The Road Not Taken (Frost): V2
Robinson, E. A.
  Richard Cory: V4
Roethke, Theodore
  My Papa's Waltz: V3
Rogers, Pattiann
  The Greatest Grandeur: V18
Rose, Wendy
  For the White poets who would be Indian: V13
Rossetti, Christina
  A Birthday: V10
  Remember: V14
Rukeyser, Muriel
  Ballad of Orange and Grape: V10
Rusted Legacy (Rich): V15

S

Sailing to Byzantium (Yeats): V2
Saint Francis and the Sow (Kinnell): V9

Sandburg, Carl
   Chicago: V3
   Cool Tombs: V6
   Hope Is a Tattered Flag: V12
Schnackenberg, Gjertrud
   Darwin in 1881: V13
The Seafarer (Anonymous): V8
The Second Coming (Yeats): V7
Service, Robert W.
   The Cremation of Sam McGee: V10
Seven Seeds (Bialosky): V19
Sexton, Anne
   Courage: V14
   Oysters: V4
Shahid Ali, Agha
   The Country Without a Post Office: V18
Shakespeare, William
   Sonnet 18: V2
   Sonnet 19: V9
   Sonnet 29: V8
   Sonnet 30: V4
   Sonnet 55: V5
   Sonnet 116: V3
   Sonnet 130: V1
Shapiro, Karl
   Auto Wreck: V3
She Walks in Beauty (Byron): V14
Shelley, Percy Bysshe
   Ode to the West Wind: V2
Shine, Perishing Republic (Jeffers): V4
Silko, Leslie Marmon
   Four Mountain Wolves: V9
   Story from Bear Country: V16
Simic, Charles
   Butcher Shop: V7
Simpson, Louis
   American Poetry: V7
   Chocolates: V11
   In the Suburbs: V14
The Singer's House (Heaney): V17
Sir Patrick Spens (Anonymous): V4
Siren Song (Atwood): V7
60 (Tagore): V18
Small Town with One Road (Soto): V7
Smart and Final Iris (Tate): V15
Smith, Stevie
   Not Waving but Drowning: V3
Snyder, Gary
   Anasazi: V9
   True Night: V19
Social Life (Hoagland): V19
The Soldier (Brooke): V7
somewhere i have never travelled,gladly beyond (cummings): V19
Song, Cathy
   Lost Sister: V5
Song of a Citizen (Milosz): V16
Song of Reasons (Pinsky): V18
Song of the Chattahoochee (Lanier): V14

The Song of the Smoke (Du Bois): V13
Sonnet 16 [On His Blindness] (Milton): V3
Sonnet 18 (Shakespeare): V2
Sonnet 19 (Shakespeare): V9
Sonnet 30 (Shakespeare): V4
Sonnet 29 (Shakespeare): V8
Sonnet XXIX (Browning): V16
Sonnet 43 (Browning): V2
Sonnet 55 (Shakespeare): V5
Sonnet 116 (Shakespeare): V3
Sonnet 130 (Shakespeare): V1
The Sonnet-Ballad (Brooks): V1
Soto, Gary
   Small Town with One Road: V7
The Soul Selects Her Own Society (Dickinson): V1
Southbound on the Freeway (Swenson): V16
Spring-Watching Pavilion (Huong): V18
Stafford, William
   At the Bomb Testing Site: V8
   Fifteen: V2
   Ways to Live: V16
Starlight (Levine): V8
Stevens, Wallace
   The Idea of Order at Key West: V13
   Sunday Morning: V16
Stone, Ruth
   Ordinary Words: V19
Stopping by Woods on a Snowy Evening (Frost): V1
Story from Bear Country (Silko): V16
Strand, Mark
   The Continuous Life: V18
   Eating Poetry: V9
Strong Men, Riding Horses (Brooks): V4
Sunday Morning (Stevens): V16
A Supermarket in California (Ginsberg): V5
Swenson, May
   Southbound on the Freeway: V16
Swing Low Sweet Chariot (Anonymous): V1
Szymborska, Wislawa
   Astonishment: V15

T

Tagore, Rabindranath
   60: V18
A Tall Man Executes a Jig (Layton): V12
Tate, James
   Dear Reader: V10
   Smart and Final Iris: V15
Taylor, Henry
   Landscape with Tractor: V10
Tears, Idle Tears (Tennyson): V4

Teasdale, Sara
   There Will Come Soft Rains: V14
Temple Bells Die Out (Bashō): V18
Tennyson, Alfred, Lord
   The Charge of the Light Brigade: V1
   The Eagle: V11
   The Lady of Shalott: V15
   Proem: V19
   Tears, Idle Tears: V4
   Ulysses: V2
Thayer, Ernest Lawrence
   Casey at the Bat: V5
Theme for English B (Hughes): V6
There's a Certain Slant of Light (Dickinson): V6
There Will Come Soft Rains (Teasdale): V14
This Life (Dove): V1
Thomas, Dylan
   Do Not Go Gentle into that Good Night: V1
   Fern Hill: V3
   The Force That Through the Green Fuse Drives the Flower: V8
Those Winter Sundays (Hayden): V1
Three Times My Life Has Opened (Hirshfield): V16
Tintern Abbey (Wordsworth): V2
To a Child Running With Outstretched Arms in Canyon de Chelly (Momaday): V11
To a Sad Daughter (Ondaatje): V8
To an Athlete Dying Young (Housman): V7
To an Unknown Poet (Kizer): V18
To His Coy Mistress (Marvell): V5
To His Excellency General Washington (Wheatley): V13
To My Dear and Loving Husband (Bradstreet): V6
To the Virgins, to Make Much of Time (Herrick): V13
Toads (Larkin): V4
Tonight I Can Write (Neruda): V11
The Tropics in New York (McKay): V4
True Night (Snyder): V19
The Tyger (Blake): V2

U

Ulysses (Tennyson): V2
The Unknown Citizen (Auden): V3

V

A Valediction: Forbidding Mourning (Donne): V11
Vancouver Lights (Birney): V8
Viereck, Peter
   For An Assyrian Frieze: V9
   Kilroy: V14

W

Walcott, Derek
  A Far Cry from Africa: V6
The War Against the Trees (Kunitz): V11
War Is Kind (Crane): V9
Warren, Rosanna
  Daylights: V13
Ways to Live (Stafford): V16
We Live by What We See at Night (Espada): V13
We Real Cool (Brooks): V6
The Weight of Sweetness (Lee): V11
What Belongs to Us (Howe): V15
What My Child Learns of the Sea (Lorde): V16
Wheatley, Phillis
  To His Excellency General Washington: V13
When I Have Fears That I May Cease to Be (Keats): V2
When I Was One-and-Twenty (Housman): V4
Whitman, Walt
  Cavalry Crossing a Ford: V13
  I Hear America Singing: V3
  O Captain! My Captain!: V2
Why I Am Not a Painter (O'Hara): V8
Wilbur, Richard
  Beowulf: V11
  Merlin Enthralled: V16
  On Freedom's Ground: V12
Wild Geese (Oliver): V15
Wild Swans (Millay): V17
Wilderness Gothic (Purdy): V12
Williams, William Carlos
  Overture to a Dance of Locomotives: V11
  Queen-Ann's-Lace: V6
  The Red Wheelbarrow: V1
The Wood-Pile (Frost): V6

Wordsworth, William
  Lines Composed a Few Miles above Tintern Abbey: V2
Wright, Charles
  Black Zodiac: V10
Wright, James
  A Blessing: V7
  Autumn Begins in Martins Ferry, Ohio: V8
Wright, Judith
  Drought Year: V8

Y

Yeats, William Butler
  Easter 1916: V5
  An Irish Airman Foresees His Death: V1
  The Lake Isle of Innisfree: V15
  Leda and the Swan: V13
  Sailing to Byzantium: V2
  The Second Coming: V7

Cumulative Nationality/Ethnicity Index

Acoma Pueblo
Ortiz, Simon
   Hunger in New York City: V4
   My Father's Song: V16

African American
Ai
   Reunions with a Ghost: V16
Angelou, Maya
   Harlem Hopscotch: V2
   On the Pulse of Morning: V3
Baraka, Amiri
   In Memory of Radio: V9
Brooks, Gwendolyn
   The Bean Eaters: V2
   The Sonnet-Ballad: V1
   Strong Men, Riding Horses: V4
   We Real Cool: V6
Clifton, Lucille
   Climbing: V14
   Miss Rosie: V1
Cullen, Countee
   Any Human to Another: V3
Dove, Rita
   Geometry: V15
   This Life: V1
Giovanni, Nikki
   Knoxville, Tennessee: V17
Hayden, Robert
   Those Winter Sundays: V1
Hughes, Langston
   Dream Variations: V15
   Harlem: V1
   Mother to Son: V3
   The Negro Speaks of Rivers: V10
   Theme for English B: V6

Johnson, James Weldon
   The Creation: V1
Komunyakaa, Yusef
   Facing It: V5
Lorde, Audre
   What My Child Learns of the Sea: V16
Madgett, Naomi Long
   Alabama Centennial: V10
McElroy, Colleen
   A Pièd: V3
Randall, Dudley
   Ballad of Birmingham: V5
Reed, Ishmael
   Beware: Do Not Read This Poem: V6

American
Ackerman, Diane
   On Location in the Loire Valley: V19
Acosta, Teresa Palomo
   My Mother Pieced Quilts: V12
Ai
   Reunions with a Ghost: V16
Ammons, A. R.
   The City Limits: V19
Angelou, Maya
   Harlem Hopscotch: V2
   On the Pulse of Morning: V3
Ashbery, John
   Paradoxes and Oxymorons: V11
Auden, W. H.
   As I Walked Out One Evening: V4
   Musée des Beaux Arts: V1
   The Unknown Citizen: V3

Bass, Ellen
   And What If I Spoke of Despair: V19
Bialosky, Jill
   Seven Seeds: V19
Bishop, Elizabeth
   Brazil, January 1, 1502: V6
   Filling Station: V12
Blumenthal, Michael
   Inventors: V7
Bly, Robert
   Come with Me: V6
   Driving to Town Late to Mail a Letter: V17
Bradstreet, Anne
   To My Dear and Loving Husband: V6
Brooks, Gwendolyn
   The Bean Eaters: V2
   The Sonnet-Ballad: V1
   Strong Men, Riding Horses: V4
   We Real Cool: V6
Brouwer, Joel
   Last Request: V14
Carver, Raymond
   The Cobweb: V17
Cisneros, Sandra
   Once Again I Prove the Theory of Relativity: V19
Clifton, Lucille
   Climbing: V14
   Miss Rosie: V1
Collins, Billy
   The Afterlife: V18
Crane, Stephen
   War Is Kind: V9
Cruz, Victor Hernandez
   Business: V16

Cullen, Countee
    Any Human to Another: V3
cummings, e. e.
    i was sitting in mcsorley's: V13
    l(a: V1
    maggie and milly and molly and may: V12
    old age sticks: V3
    somewhere i have never travelled,gladly beyond: V19
Dickey, James
    The Heaven of Animals: V6
    The Hospital Window: V11
Dickinson, Emily
    Because I Could Not Stop for Death: V2
    The Bustle in a House: V10
    "Hope" Is the Thing with Feathers: V3
    I felt a Funeral, in my Brain: V13
    I Heard a Fly Buzz—When I Died—: V5
    Much Madness Is Divinest Sense: V16
    My Life Closed Twice Before Its Close: V8
    A Narrow Fellow in the Grass: V11
    The Soul Selects Her Own Society: V1
    There's a Certain Slant of Light: V6
    This Is My Letter to the World: V4
Dove, Rita
    Geometry: V15
    This Life: V1
Dubie, Norman
    The Czar's Last Christmas Letter. A Barn in the Urals: V12
Du Bois, W. E. B.
    The Song of the Smoke: V13
Dugan, Alan
    How We Heard the Name: V10
Duncan, Robert
    An African Elegy: V13
Eliot, T. S.
    Journey of the Magi: V7
    The Love Song of J. Alfred Prufrock: V1
Emerson, Ralph Waldo
    Concord Hymn: V4
    The Rhodora: V17
Erdrich, Louise
    Bidwell Ghost: V14
Espada, Martín
    Colibrí: V16
    We Live by What We See at Night: V13
Forché, Carolyn
    The Garden Shukkei-En: V18
Francis, Robert
    The Base Stealer: V12
Frost, Robert
    Birches: V13
    The Death of the Hired Man: V4
    Fire and Ice: V7
    Mending Wall: V5
    Nothing Gold Can Stay: V3
    Out, Out—: V10
    The Road Not Taken: V2
    Stopping by Woods on a Snowy Evening: V1
    The Wood-Pile: V6
Gallagher, Tess
    I Stop Writing the Poem: V16
Ginsberg, Allen
    A Supermarket in California: V5
Giovanni, Nikki
    Knoxville, Tennessee: V17
Glück, Louise
    The Gold Lily: V5
    The Mystery: V15
Graham, Jorie
    The Hiding Place: V10
    Mind: V17
Gunn, Thom
    The Missing: V9
H.D.
    Helen: V6
Hacker, Marilyn
    The Boy: V19
Hall, Donald
    Names of Horses: V8
Harjo, Joy
    Anniversary: V15
Hayden, Robert
    Those Winter Sundays: V1
Hecht, Anthony
    "More Light! More Light!": V6
Hirshfield, Jane
    Three Times My Life Has Opened: V16
Hoagland, Tony
    Social Life: V19
Holmes, Oliver Wendell
    Old Ironsides: V9
Howe, Marie
    What Belongs to Us: V15
Hudgins, Andrew
    Elegy for My Father, Who is Not Dead: V14
Hughes, Langston
    Dream Variations: V15
    Harlem: V1
    Mother to Son: V3
    The Negro Speaks of Rivers: V10
    Theme for English B: V6
Hugo, Richard
    For Jennifer, 6, on the Teton: V17
Jarrell, Randall
    The Death of the Ball Turret Gunner: V2
Jeffers, Robinson
    Hurt Hawks: V3
    Shine, Perishing Republic: V4
Johnson, James Weldon
    The Creation: V1
Justice, Donald
    Incident in a Rose Garden: V14
Kenyon, Jane
    Having it Out with Melancholy: V17
    "Trouble with Math in a One-Room Country School": V9
Kinnell, Galway
    Saint Francis and the Sow: V9
Kizer, Carolyn
    To An Unknown Poet: V18
Komunyakaa, Yusef
    Facing It: V5
Kooser, Ted
    The Constellation Orion: V8
Kumin, Maxine
    Address to the Angels: V18
Kunitz, Stanley
    The War Against the Trees: V11
Lanier, Sidney
    Song of the Chattahoochee: V14
Lee, Li-Young
    Early in the Morning: V17
    For a New Citizen of These United States: V15
    The Weight of Sweetness: V11
Levertov, Denise
    The Blue Rim of Memory: V17
    In the Land of Shinar: V7
Levine, Philip
    Starlight: V8
Longfellow, Henry Wadsworth
    The Arsenal at Springfield: V17
    Paul Revere's Ride: V2
    A Psalm of Life: V7
Lorde, Audre
    What My Child Learns of the Sea: V16
Lowell, Robert
    For the Union Dead: V7
    The Quaker Graveyard in Nantucket: V6
MacLeish, Archibald
    Ars Poetica: V5
Madgett, Naomi Long
    Alabama Centennial: V10
McElroy, Colleen
    A Pièd: V3
McGinley, Phyllis
    The Conquerors: V13
    Reactionary Essay on Applied Science: V9
McKay, Claude
    The Tropics in New York: V4
Merriam, Eve
    Onomatopoeia: V6
Merwin, W. S.
    The Horizons of Rooms: V15
    Leviathan: V5
Millay, Edna St. Vincent
    The Courage that My Mother Had: V3
    Wild Swans: V17

Momaday, N. Scott
  Angle of Geese: V2
  To a Child Running With Outstretched Arms in Canyon de Chelly: V11
Montague, John
  A Grafted Tongue: V12
Moore, Marianne
  The Fish: V14
  Poetry: V17
Mueller, Lisel
  The Exhibit: V9
Nemerov, Howard
  Deep Woods: V14
  The Phoenix: V10
O'Hara, Frank
  Having a Coke with You: V12
  Why I Am Not a Painter: V8
Olds, Sharon
  I Go Back to May 1937: V17
Oliver, Mary
  Music Lessons: V8
  Wild Geese: V15
Ortiz, Simon
  Hunger in New York City: V4
  My Father's Song: V16
Ostriker, Alicia
  His Speed and Strength: V19
Parker, Dorothy
  The Last Question: V18
Pastan, Linda
  Ethics: V8
Piercy, Marge
  Barbie Doll: V9
Pinsky, Robert
  Song of Reasons: V18
Plath, Sylvia
  Blackberrying: V15
  Mirror: V1
Poe, Edgar Allan
  Annabel Lee: V9
  The Bells: V3
  The Raven: V1
Pound, Ezra
  Hugh Selwyn Mauberley: V16
  In a Station of the Metro: V2
  The River-Merchant's Wife: A Letter: V8
Randall, Dudley
  Ballad of Birmingham: V5
Reed, Ishmael
  Beware: Do Not Read This Poem: V6
Revard, Carter
  Birch Canoe: V5
Rich, Adrienne
  Rusted Legacy: V15
Ríos, Alberto
  Island of the Three Marias: V11
Robinson, E. A.
  Richard Cory: V4
Roethke, Theodore
  My Papa's Waltz: V3
Rogers, Pattiann
  The Greatest Grandeur: V18
Rose, Wendy
  For the White poets who would be Indian: V13
Rukeyser, Muriel
  Ballad of Orange and Grape: V10
Sandburg, Carl
  Chicago: V3
  Cool Tombs: V6
  Hope Is a Tattered Flag: V12
Schnackenberg, Gjertrud
  Darwin in 1881: V13
Sexton, Anne
  Courage: V14
  Oysters: V4
Shapiro, Karl
  Auto Wreck: V3
Silko, Leslie Marmon
  Four Mountain Wolves: V9
  Story from Bear Country: V16
Simic, Charles
  Butcher Shop: V7
Simpson, Louis
  American Poetry: V7
  Chocolates: V11
  In the Suburbs: V14
Snyder, Gary
  Anasazi: V9
  True Night: V19
Song, Cathy
  Lost Sister: V5
Soto, Gary
  Small Town with One Road: V7
Stafford, William
  At the Bomb Testing Site: V8
  Fifteen: V2
  Ways to Live: V16
Stevens, Wallace
  The Idea of Order at Key West: V13
  Sunday Morning: V16
Stone, Ruth
  Ordinary Words: V19
Strand, Mark
  The Continuous Life: V18
Swenson, May
  Southbound on the Freeway: V16
Tate, James
  Dear Reader: V10
  Smart and Final Iris: V15
Taylor, Henry
  Landscape with Tractor: V10
Teasdale, Sara
  There Will Come Soft Rains: V14
Thayer, Ernest Lawrence
  Casey at the Bat: V5
Viereck, Peter
  For An Assyrian Frieze: V9
  Kilroy: V14
Warren, Rosanna
  Daylights: V13
Wheatley, Phillis
  To His Excellency General Washington: V13
Whitman, Walt
  Cavalry Crossing a Ford: V13
  I Hear America Singing: V3
  O Captain! My Captain!: V2
Wilbur, Richard
  Beowulf: V11
  Merlin Enthralled: V16
  On Freedom's Ground: V12
Williams, William Carlos
  Overture to a Dance of Locomotives: V11
  Queen-Ann's-Lace: V6
  The Red Wheelbarrow: V1
Wright, Charles
  Black Zodiac: V10
Wright, James
  A Blessing: V7
  Autumn Begins in Martins Ferry, Ohio: V8

Australian
Dawe, Bruce
  Drifters: V10
Hope, A. D.
  Beware of Ruins: V8
Wright, Judith
  Drought Year: V8

Canadian
Atwood, Margaret
  Siren Song: V7
Birney, Earle
  Vancouver Lights: V8
Carson, Anne
  New Rule: V18
Layton, Irving
  A Tall Man Executes a Jig: V12
McCrae, John
  In Flanders Fields: V5
Nowlan, Alden
  For Jean Vincent D'abbadie, Baron St.-Castin: V12
Purdy, Al
  Lament for the Dorsets: V5
  Wilderness Gothic: V12
Strand, Mark
  Eating Poetry: V9

Canadian, Sri Lankan
Ondaatje, Michael
  The Cinnamon Peeler: V19
  To a Sad Daughter: V8

Chilean
Neruda, Pablo
  Tonight I Can Write: V11

Egyptian, Greek

Cavafy, C. P.
   Ithaka: V19

English

Alleyn, Ellen
   A Birthday: V10
Arnold, Matthew
   Dover Beach: V2
Auden, W. H.
   As I Walked Out One Evening: V4
   Funeral Blues: V10
   Musée des Beaux Arts: V1
   The Unknown Citizen: V3
Blake, William
   The Lamb: V12
   The Tyger: V2
Bradstreet, Anne
   To My Dear and Loving Husband: V6
Brooke, Rupert
   The Soldier: V7
Browning, Elizabeth Barrett
   Sonnet XXIX: V16
   Sonnet 43: V2
Browning, Robert
   My Last Duchess: V1
   Porphyria's Lover: V15
Byron, Lord
   The Destruction of Sennacherib: V1
   She Walks in Beauty: V14
Carroll, Lewis
   Jabberwocky: V11
Chaucer, Geoffrey
   The Canterbury Tales: V14
Coleridge, Samuel Taylor
   Kubla Khan: V5
   The Rime of the Ancient Mariner: V4
Donne, John
   Holy Sonnet 10: V2
   A Valediction: Forbidding Mourning: V11
Eliot, T. S.
   Journey of the Magi: V7
   The Love Song of J. Alfred Prufrock: V1
Fenton, James
   The Milkfish Gatherers: V11
Gray, Thomas
   Elegy Written in a Country Churchyard: V9
Gunn, Thom
   The Missing: V9
Hardy, Thomas
   Ah, Are You Digging on My Grave?: V4
   The Darkling Thrush: V18
   The Man He Killed: V3
Herrick, Robert
   To the Virgins, to Make Much of Time: V13
Housman, A. E.
   To an Athlete Dying Young: V7
   When I Was One-and-Twenty: V4
Hughes, Ted
   Hawk Roosting: V4
   Perfect Light: V19
Keats, John
   La Belle Dame sans Merci: V17
   Bright Star! Would I Were Steadfast as Thou Art: V9
   Ode on a Grecian Urn: V1
   Ode to a Nightingale: V3
   When I Have Fears that I May Cease to Be: V2
Larkin, Philip
   An Arundel Tomb: V12
   High Windows: V3
   Toads: V4
Lawrence, D. H.
   Piano: V6
Levertov, Denise
   The Blue Rim of Memory: V17
Marvell, Andrew
   To His Coy Mistress: V5
Masefield, John
   Cargoes: V5
Milton, John
   [On His Blindness] Sonnet 16: V3
   On His Having Arrived at the Age of Twenty-Three: V17
Noyes, Alfred
   The Highwayman: V4
Owen, Wilfred
   Dulce et Decorum Est: V10
Pope, Alexander
   The Rape of the Lock: V12
Raine, Craig
   A Martian Sends a Postcard Home: V7
Raleigh, Walter, Sir
   The Nymph's Reply to the Shepherd: V14
Rossetti, Christina
   A Birthday: V10
   Remember: V14
Service, Robert W.
   The Cremation of Sam McGee: V10
Shakespeare, William
   Sonnet 18: V2
   Sonnet 19: V9
   Sonnet 30: V4
   Sonnet 29: V8
   Sonnet 55: V5
   Sonnet 116: V3
   Sonnet 130: V1
Shelley, Percy Bysshe
   Ode to the West Wind: V2
Smith, Stevie
   Not Waving but Drowning: V3
Tennyson, Alfred, Lord
   The Charge of the Light Brigade: V1
   The Eagle: V11
   The Lady of Shalott: V15
   Proem: V19
   Tears, Idle Tears: V4
   Ulysses: V2
Williams, William Carlos
   Queen-Ann's-Lace: V6
   The Red Wheelbarrow: V1
Wordsworth, William
   Lines Composed a Few Miles above Tintern Abbey: V2
Yeats, W. B.
   Easter 1916: V5
   An Irish Airman Forsees His Death: V1
   The Lake Isle of Innisfree: V15
   Leda and the Swan: V13
   Sailing to Byzantium: V2
   The Second Coming: V7

German

Blumenthal, Michael
   Inventors: V7
Erdrich, Louise
   Bidwell Ghost: V14
Mueller, Lisel
   Blood Oranges: V13
   The Exhibit: V9
Rilke, Rainer Maria
   Childhood: V19
Roethke, Theodore
   My Papa's Waltz: V3

Ghanaian

Du Bois, W. E. B.
   The Song of the Smoke: V13

Hispanic

Cruz, Victor Hernandez
   Business: V16
Espada, Martín
   Colibrí: V16

Indian

Shahid Ali, Agha
   Country Without a Post Office: V18
Tagore, Rabindranath
   60: V18

Indonesian

Lee, Li-Young
   Early in the Morning: V17
   For a New Citizen of These United States: V15
   The Weight of Sweetness: V11

Irish

Boland, Eavan
 Anorexic: V12
Hartnett, Michael
 A Farewell to English: V10
Heaney, Seamus
 Digging: V5
 A Drink of Water: V8
 Midnight: V2
 The Singer's House: V17
Muldoon, Paul
 Meeting the British: V7
Yeats, William Butler
 Easter 1916: V5
 An Irish Airman Foresees His Death: V1
 The Lake Isle of Innisfree: V15
 Leda and the Swan: V13
 Sailing to Byzantium: V2
 The Second Coming: V7

Jamaican

McKay, Claude
 The Tropics in New York: V4
Simpson, Louis
 In the Suburbs: V14

Japanese

Ai
 Reunions with a Ghost: V16
Bashō, Matsuo
 Falling Upon Earth: V2
 The Moon Glows the Same: V7
 Temple Bells Die Out: V18

Jewish

Blumenthal, Michael
 Inventors: V7
Espada, Martín
 Colibrí: V16
 We Live by What We See at Night: V13
Piercy, Marge
 Barbie Doll: V9
Shapiro, Karl
 Auto Wreck: V3

Kiowa

Momaday, N. Scott
 Angle of Geese: V2
 To a Child Running With Outstretched Arms in Canyon de Chelly: V11

Lithuanian

Milosz, Czeslaw
 Song of a Citizen: V16

Mexican

Paz, Octavio
 Duration: V18
Soto, Gary
 Small Town with One Road: V7

Native American

Ai
 Reunions with a Ghost: V16
Erdrich, Louise
 Bidwell Ghost: V14
Harjo, Joy
 Anniversary: V15
Momaday, N. Scott
 Angle of Geese: V2
 To a Child Running With Outstretched Arms in Canyon de Chelly: V11
Ortiz, Simon
 Hunger in New York City: V4
 My Father's Song: V16
Revard, Carter
 Birch Canoe: V5
Rose, Wendy
 For the White poets who would be Indian: V13
Silko, Leslie Marmon
 Four Mountain Wolves: V9
 Story from Bear Country: V16

Osage

Revard, Carter
 Birch Canoe: V5

Polish

Milosz, Czeslaw
 Song of a Citizen: V16
Szymborska, Wislawa
 Astonishment: V15

Russian

Akhmatova, Anna
 Midnight Verses: V18

Levertov, Denise
 In the Land of Shinar: V7
Merriam, Eve
 Onomatopoeia: V6
Shapiro, Karl
 Auto Wreck: V3

St. Lucian

Walcott, Derek
 A Far Cry from Africa: V6

Scottish

Burns, Robert
 A Red, Red Rose: V8
Byron, Lord
 The Destruction of Sennacherib: V1
MacBeth, George
 Bedtime Story: V8

Senegalese

Wheatley, Phillis
 To His Excellency General Washington: V13

Spanish

Williams, William Carlos
 The Red Wheelbarrow: V1

Swedish

Sandburg, Carl
 Chicago: V3

Vietnamese

Huong, Ho Xuan
 Spring-Watching Pavilion: V18

Welsh

Levertov, Denise
 In the Land of Shinar: V7
Thomas, Dylan
 Do Not Go Gentle into that Good Night: V1
 Fern Hill: V3
 The Force That Through the Green Fuse Drives the Flower: V8

Subject/Theme Index

***Boldface** denotes discussion in Themes section.

A

Abandonment
Childhood: 42, 46, 50
Ithaka: 124, 126
Proem: 217–218, 223
somewhere i have never travelled,gladly beyond: 277–279
True Night: 295, 297

Acceptance and Belonging
The City Limits: 80

Adultery
The Cinnamon Peeler: 64
Perfect Light: 192–193

Adulthood
Childhood: 30–33
His Speed and Strength: 95, 97, 99–100

Adventure and Exploration
Ithaka: 114, 117, 119–120, 124–125
On Location in the Loire Valley: 166–169

Africa
Ithaka: 115–116, 118
Once Again I Prove the Theory of Relativity: 131, 133

Alcoholism, Drugs, and Drug Addiction
Proem: 214, 216–217

Alliteration
On Location in the Loire Valley: 157–158
True Night: 286–287

Ambition
True Night: 297–299, 306

American Midwest
Once Again I Prove the Theory of Relativity: 143–146

American Northwest
True Night: 291–293, 295

American West
True Night: 291, 293–297

Anger
Perfect Light: 199, 203, 204

Anti-Semitism
The Boy: 17–18

Art
Childhood: 30

Arthurian Legend
Proem: 221

Asia
His Speed and Strength: 102–104
True Night: 291, 294, 298–301, 304

Atonement
Perfect Light: 196, 200, 203
Proem: 220, 223–224
somewhere i have never travelled,gladly beyond: 270

Authoritarianism
The Boy: 15, 18

B

Beauty
And What If I Spoke of Despair: 3, 5–8
Childhood: 38, 40, 42–46, 48, 50, 52
Once Again I Prove the Theory of Relativity: 129, 131–133

Proem: 214, 220–221, 223–224
somewhere i have never travelled,gladly beyond: 266–269

Birth and Motherhood
Seven Seeds: 240

The Brevity of Life
Perfect Light: 189

Buddhism
True Night: 283, 288, 294–297, 299–300, 302, 305–306

C

Chaos and Order
The Boy: 16

Childhood
And What If I Spoke of Despair: 7–8
The Boy: 22–24
Childhood: 28, 30–38, 40–41, 49–50
His Speed and Strength: 97–100
Once Again I Prove the Theory of Relativity: 139–142

Christianity
The City Limits: 86–87

City Life
Once Again I Prove the Theory of Relativity: 143, 145

Class
Ordinary Words: 174

Classicism
Perfect Light: 198–199
Seven Seeds: 246–247

Communism
His Speed and Strength: 100–101

345

Couplet
On Location in the Loire Valley: 154–160

Courage
Childhood: 42, 46

Creativity
Once Again I Prove the Theory of Relativity: 143–145

Cruelty
The Cinnamon Peeler: 69–70, 72
Once Again I Prove the Theory of Relativity: 139–140, 142

Curiosity
On Location in the Loire Valley: 165–168, 170
Ordinary Words: 181–182, 184

Cynicism
Ithaka: 125

D

Dance
Once Again I Prove the Theory of Relativity: 130, 132, 152
True Night: 302, 304–306

Death
The Boy: 17–18, 25–26
Childhood: 37, 40–50
The Cinnamon Peeler: 70–72, 74
On Location in the Loire Valley: 161–163, 165
Ordinary Words: 179–180, 182–184
Perfect Light: 189, 191–203
Proem: 205, 207–211, 214, 216–225, 227–236
Seven Seeds: 237–238, 240–241, 244–248
somewhere i have never travelled,gladly beyond: 266–270, 276–277, 279–280
True Night: 300–302, 304–305

Death In Life
On Location in the Loire Valley: 156

Depression and Melancholy
Perfect Light: 197–198, 202–203
Proem: 214, 216, 218, 220, 224

Description
The Cinnamon Peeler: 54, 56
The City Limits: 90–91
Perfect Light: 196, 199, 202–203
Proem: 225–226

Desire
Seven Seeds: 241

Despair
And What If I Spoke of Despair: 1–9, 11
Proem: 225, 228, 231

Disease
Childhood: 40, 43–44, 49, 52

Divorce
Ordinary Words: 178

Drama
Childhood: 39–40, 44, 48, 50

Dreams and Visions
Childhood: 30–32, 37–41, 43, 45
The City Limits: 88–91
True Night: 298–303, 305, 307–310

E

Ecology
And What If I Spoke of Despair: 1, 3–6
True Night: 287–288

Elegy
Proem: 217–219, 224, 226, 232–233

Emotions
And What If I Spoke of Despair: 3–4, 6–7, 9, 11
The Boy: 25
Childhood: 31–32, 34–35, 41, 43, 48–49
The Cinnamon Peeler: 58, 60, 65, 69–70, 74
The City Limits: 79–81
His Speed and Strength: 109
Ithaka: 115, 126–127
On Location in the Loire Valley: 165, 167–168
Once Again I Prove the Theory of Relativity: 129, 132–133, 135, 137, 144
Ordinary Words: 174–175, 177–178
Perfect Light: 186, 190, 193, 198, 201–202, 204
Proem: 211, 213, 215–219, 223, 225–232
Social Life: 256
somewhere i have never travelled,gladly beyond: 264, 266, 270, 274, 276–279, 281
True Night: 294, 301, 304

Environmental Destruction
And What If I Spoke of Despair: 4

Eternity
Perfect Light: 198, 201
Proem: 225, 228, 231
somewhere i have never travelled,gladly beyond: 272–275
True Night: 302, 304–305

Europe
The Boy: 17–18
Childhood: 32–33, 37–52
The Cinnamon Peeler: 68, 70, 72, 75
His Speed and Strength: 100–101
Ithaka: 114, 117–118
Perfect Light: 190–191
Proem: 205, 210–211, 214, 216–224

Evil
Perfect Light: 196, 199–200, 203
Proem: 218, 220

F

Faith
somewhere i have never travelled,gladly beyond: 268

Family Life
The Cinnamon Peeler: 64
His Speed and Strength: 105
Ordinary Words: 181
Proem: 229, 232

Farm and Rural Life
The Cinnamon Peeler: 55–56, 59–60

Fate and Chance
On Location in the Loire Valley: 168, 170
Once Again I Prove the Theory of Relativity: 146–149, 152
Perfect Light: 186, 188–190, 196–203
Proem: 215, 218–220, 223

Fear
The City Limits: 81

Fear and Terror
Childhood: 30–32, 41–44, 46–47, 49–50
The City Limits: 77, 80–81, 83, 85–86
Proem: 207–209, 217–219, 222, 224

Femininity
His Speed and Strength: 98–99, 102
somewhere i have never travelled, gladly beyond: 266–267

Feminism
The Boy: 17
His Speed and Strength: 104–106
Perfect Light: 197, 202–203

Film
The Cinnamon Peeler: 68, 70–71, 74–75
On Location in the Loire Valley: 153–156, 161–162

Folklore
The Cinnamon Peeler: 74
Ithaka: 115, 117
Once Again I Prove the Theory of Relativity: 150
Perfect Light: 197

Forgiveness
Perfect Light: 197–198, 204
Proem: 208–209, 212–213

Free Will
Proem: 208

Free Will vs. Determinism
Proem: 207–208, 210

Friendship
Proem: 215, 222

G

Gender
The Boy: 17
Gender Roles
The Boy: 17
Genetic Engineering
And What If I Spoke of Despair: 5
Ghost
Childhood: 43, 47, 49, 51
Once Again I Prove the Theory of Relativity: 147–148
Perfect Light: 198, 201
Proem: 220, 222, 224, 234
God
Childhood: 41, 45–46
The City Limits: 84–88
Perfect Light: 201–203
Proem: 206–213
Great Depression
somewhere i have never travelled, gladly beyond: 266, 269–270
Grief and Sorrow
And What If I Spoke of Despair: 3, 6, 7, 9
Childhood: 30–34
Ordinary Words: 172, 174–175, 182–185
Perfect Light: 192–194, 196–204
Proem: 205, 208–214, 217, 219–221, 233–236
Seven Seeds: 237, 240–241

H

Happiness and Gaiety
Ithaka: 120, 121, 124–125
Perfect Light: 201, 203
Hatred
Childhood: 38, 40–41, 45, 47
His Speed and Strength: 98–103
Ithaka: 126–127
Perfect Light: 198–199, 202–204
Heaven
Childhood: 45–46
On Location in the Loire Valley: 169
Hell
Seven Seeds: 237, 239, 243
Heroism
Childhood: 44, 46, 49–50
Proem: 218–220
True Night: 298, 300, 302
History
The Boy: 13, 16–17
The Cinnamon Peeler: 68, 74–75
His Speed and Strength: 95, 100
Ithaka: 117–119
Proem: 214–215, 220, 224
somewhere i have never travelled, gladly beyond: 269
True Night: 288, 292, 294, 296–297, 299, 306

Homosexuality
The Boy: 20–21
Ithaka: 122–123, 125–127
Honor
Childhood: 46
Proem: 222
True Night: 297
Hope
His Speed and Strength: 95, 98, 100, 102
Ithaka: 114–117
Once Again I Prove the Theory of Relativity: 144–146
Proem: 215, 217–218, 223, 235–236
Human Condition
Childhood: 37
Humility
Proem: 227, 231
Humor
The Cinnamon Peeler: 71–72, 74–75
His Speed and Strength: 97, 99
Ordinary Words: 181, 183–185
Proem: 214, 221, 225
Social Life: 252, 254
somewhere i have never travelled, gladly beyond: 279–280

I

Ignorance
somewhere i have never travelled, gladly beyond: 274
Imagery and Symbolism
And What If I Spoke of Despair: 5–8
Childhood: 30–32, 35, 37
The Cinnamon Peeler: 57, 59, 69–70
The City Limits: 79–80, 83, 88–91
His Speed and Strength: 98–99
Ithaka: 116–117, 119, 122, 124, 127
On Location in the Loire Valley: 166–167
Ordinary Words: 175, 177
Perfect Light: 186, 188, 192
Proem: 214, 216, 221, 223, 225–227, 229–232
Seven Seeds: 237–239, 241–242, 244–248
Social Life: 260
somewhere i have never travelled, gladly beyond: 268–269, 274–275
True Night: 298–301
Imagination
The Boy: 19–20
The Inability To Know
On Location in the Loire Valley: 156

Innocence Versus Knowledge
Perfect Light: 189
Insanity
The Cinnamon Peeler: 71–72, 74
Proem: 214, 217, 220
Irony
His Speed and Strength: 110–111
Ithaka: 125, 127
Perfect Light: 188, 190, 195–196
Social Life: 253–254, 261–262
somewhere i have never travelled, gladly beyond: 279–280
Isolation
Childhood: 31

J

Judaism
The Boy: 13, 15–18

K

Killers and Killing
The Cinnamon Peeler: 70, 72
Perfect Light: 189, 196–198, 203
Kindness
Childhood: 41–42, 45, 49–50, 52
Knowledge
And What If I Spoke of Despair: 11
On Location in the Loire Valley: 167–168
Perfect Light: 188–190, 195–196
Proem: 207–209, 211
True Night: 297, 300, 302, 305

L

Landscape
Childhood: 39–40, 46–47, 51–52
The Cinnamon Peeler: 69–70, 72, 74–75
The City Limits: 88–91
Ithaka: 114–115, 117–118
On Location in the Loire Valley: 167–169
Ordinary Words: 177–178
Proem: 216, 219–220, 223–224
Seven Seeds: 239–243
Social Life: 253–256
True Night: 291–306
Language
Ordinary Words: 174
Life As a Journey
Ithaka: 115
Limitations and Opportunities
The City Limits: 84–85, 88
Literary Criticism
The City Limits: 83
True Night: 293
Loneliness
Childhood: 28, 30–32, 43–44, 49–50

Loneliness (continued)
  Ithaka: 122, 125
  Proem: 216–218, 220–221
  somewhere i have never travelled,gladly beyond: 276, 281
  True Night: 292

Loss
  Ordinary Words: 174

Love
  The Cinnamon Peeler: 58
  somewhere i have never travelled,gladly beyond: 267

Love and Passion
  And What If I Spoke of Despair: 3–4
  The Boy: 25–26
  Childhood: 39–51
  The Cinnamon Peeler: 54–60, 63–65, 70–71, 73–75
  His Speed and Strength: 106, 109–111
  Ithaka: 124–127
  On Location in the Loire Valley: 160–161, 165–170
  Once Again I Prove the Theory of Relativity: 129–133, 135–138, 140–146
  Ordinary Words: 177–178, 181, 183–184
  Perfect Light: 193–194, 197, 199–200, 202, 204
  Proem: 213–215, 217–236
  Seven Seeds: 239, 241, 243
  Social Life: 261–262
  somewhere i have never travelled,gladly beyond: 264, 266–281
  True Night: 300, 302, 304, 306

Love As the Origin of Art
  Once Again I Prove the Theory of Relativity: 133

Lower Class
  Childhood: 39, 42, 45–46

Loyalty
  Childhood: 38–39, 43, 45–46, 48, 52
  Proem: 214–215
  True Night: 305–306

M

Marriage
  The Cinnamon Peeler: 56–61, 63–64
  Ordinary Words: 174–178
  Perfect Light: 196–202
  Proem: 215, 217, 219, 225, 229–232

Masculine Versus Feminine
  His Speed and Strength: 99

Masculinity
  His Speed and Strength: 96–97, 99

Memory
  Childhood: 31
  Ordinary Words: 174

Memory and Reminiscence
  Ithaka: 124–126
  Perfect Light: 196, 200–202

Mental and Physical Infirmity
  Proem: 214, 217, 219

Mental Instability
  Proem: 214

Middle East
  The Cinnamon Peeler: 54, 58–60, 68, 70, 74
  Once Again I Prove the Theory of Relativity: 131, 133

Monarchy
  Childhood: 40–41, 46–47, 49, 51
  Proem: 214, 216, 219–224

Money and Economics
  Childhood: 38, 40, 47, 51
  Proem: 214, 216–218

Morals and Morality
  Ithaka: 123–125, 127
  Perfect Light: 197, 204
  Proem: 214, 220–221, 224–225, 227, 231–232
  True Night: 301–302, 304

Motherhood
  His Speed and Strength: 96–97, 102, 104–108
  Seven Seeds: 237–238, 240, 242–243

Mourning
  Proem: 209

Music
  Childhood: 38, 40, 46, 49, 51–52
  The Cinnamon Peeler: 68, 70–74
  On Location in the Loire Valley: 168, 170
  Once Again I Prove the Theory of Relativity: 130–132
  Ordinary Words: 172, 174–175, 181–184
  Perfect Light: 198–202
  Proem: 228, 230–232
  Social Life: 252–254, 256
  somewhere i have never travelled,gladly beyond: 277–279, 281

Mystery and Intrigue
  somewhere i have never travelled,gladly beyond: 264, 266–269

Myths and Legends
  Childhood: 37, 40–42, 46, 50–51
  The Cinnamon Peeler: 65–72, 74
  His Speed and Strength: 95, 97, 102
  Ithaka: 113–121
  Once Again I Prove the Theory of Relativity: 150
  Perfect Light: 197–203
  Proem: 215, 217, 224
  Seven Seeds: 237–248
  Social Life: 260
  True Night: 293–296, 298–300, 303

N

Naivete
  Perfect Light: 186, 188–190, 194–196

Narration
  The Boy: 13, 15, 17–21
  Childhood: 37, 40, 43, 45–46, 50
  The Cinnamon Peeler: 65–68, 70–72, 75
  The City Limits: 88–90
  His Speed and Strength: 99, 105–106
  Ithaka: 113, 116, 119–121
  Once Again I Prove the Theory of Relativity: 141–145
  Perfect Light: 196, 198–200, 202
  Proem: 217–220, 222–223
  True Night: 292, 295

Nature
  And What If I Spoke of Despair: 3–9, 11
  Childhood: 46
  The Cinnamon Peeler: 71
  The City Limits: 77, 79–93
  His Speed and Strength: 97
  On Location in the Loire Valley: 153, 165–167, 169–170
  Ordinary Words: 177
  Perfect Light: 188, 197, 199, 201–202
  Proem: 214, 219, 223, 225, 227–230
  Social Life: 252–255, 257–259, 261
  somewhere i have never travelled,gladly beyond: 267–269, 276
  True Night: 283, 289–290, 292, 294, 296–299, 302–306, 308

Nature In Suburban America
  Social Life: 254

1950s
  Ordinary Words: 176, 178

1960s
  The City Limits: 82–83

1980s
  True Night: 287

North America
  The Cinnamon Peeler: 68, 71, 75
  His Speed and Strength: 100–104
  Once Again I Prove the Theory of Relativity: 131, 133–134, 143
  True Night: 300–306

Nuclear War
  And What If I Spoke of Despair: 4–5

Nurturance
  And What If I Spoke of Despair: 3, 6

O

The *Odyssey*
Ithaka: 116

P

Painting
Childhood: 30–32, 35–36, 39–41, 43, 47, 51
Once Again I Prove the Theory of Relativity: 130–131
Perfect Light: 194

Paradox
The City Limits: 80

Paranormal
Once Again I Prove the Theory of Relativity: 148

Perception
Childhood: 37–40, 42, 45, 48
True Night: 285–287, 289, 298, 302, 304–306

Permanence
The Cinnamon Peeler: 66
Perfect Light: 201–202
Proem: 229–230, 232

Persecution
Ithaka: 123, 125

Perseverance
Once Again I Prove the Theory of Relativity: 132–134

Personal Identity
The Boy: 13, 15–22
The Cinnamon Peeler: 65–67

Personification
And What If I Spoke of Despair: 6
The City Limits: 88, 90
Seven Seeds: 238, 240, 242
somewhere i have never travelled,gladly beyond: 266–267

Philosophical Ideas
On Location in the Loire Valley: 168–170
Proem: 219–220, 225, 231–232
somewhere i have never travelled,gladly beyond: 275, 279, 281

Plants
Social Life: 252–255, 259

Pleasure
Ithaka: 120–127

Poetry
And What If I Spoke of Despair: 1–11
The Boy: 13, 15–26
Childhood: 28, 30–39, 47–48, 51–52
The Cinnamon Peeler: 54–72, 74–75
The City Limits: 77, 79–93
His Speed and Strength: 95–111
Ithaka: 113–127
On Location in the Loire Valley: 153–170
Once Again I Prove the Theory of Relativity: 129, 131–140, 143–146, 149–150, 152
Ordinary Words: 172, 174–185
Perfect Light: 186–204
Proem: 205–236
Seven Seeds: 237–243, 246–248
Social Life: 250, 252, 254–256, 259–262
somewhere i have never travelled,gladly beyond: 264, 266–269, 271–281
True Night: 283–310

Point of View
The Boy: 21

Politicians
His Speed and Strength: 100–101

Politics
The Boy: 15–17
Childhood: 38, 40, 44, 52
The Cinnamon Peeler: 59–60
His Speed and Strength: 100–101
Perfect Light: 190–191
Proem: 216, 218, 222, 224
True Night: 297–298, 301–305

Poverty
Childhood: 41–42, 45–47

The Power of Scent
The Cinnamon Peeler: 58

Pride
Childhood: 38, 41, 46, 51–52

Prophecy
The City Limits: 88–91

Psychology and the Human Mind
The Boy: 16–17
Childhood: 31–33, 40–43
The Cinnamon Peeler: 68–69
Ithaka: 123–125
Perfect Light: 196, 202–203
Proem: 215, 219

R

Race
The Boy: 13, 16–17
His Speed and Strength: 95, 97–99, 101
Once Again I Prove the Theory of Relativity: 129, 133–134, 138–141, 143–146

Racial Conflict
His Speed and Strength: 99

Racism and Prejudice
The Boy: 20–21

Religion and Religious Thought
Childhood: 43, 45
The City Limits: 84–87
Once Again I Prove the Theory of Relativity: 147
Perfect Light: 201
Proem: 207–208, 211, 215–216, 219, 228–232
somewhere i have never travelled, gladly beyond: 280–281
True Night: 298, 302, 304

Religious Works
The City Limits: 86–88

Revenge
Perfect Light: 204

Reverence
Proem: 208

Romantic Love
Once Again I Prove the Theory of Relativity: 131

S

Saints
Childhood: 39, 41, 45–46, 49–50

Science and Technology
And What If I Spoke of Despair: 1, 3–7, 9–11
On Location in the Loire Valley: 165–168, 170
Ordinary Words: 181, 184
Proem: 207–208, 211

Sculpture
Childhood: 30, 32, 39, 46–48

Self-Absorption
Social Life: 254

Self-Discovery
The City Limits: 81

Sentimentality
Ithaka: 125, 127

Setting
The Cinnamon Peeler: 59
Perfect Light: 188, 190, 192
Social Life: 250, 253, 255, 257–258

Sex and Sexuality
The Boy: 15–18
Childhood: 39–45, 47, 51–52
The Cinnamon Peeler: 54–63, 70–74
Ithaka: 122–124, 126–127
Once Again I Prove the Theory of Relativity: 139–140, 142
Perfect Light: 196, 199, 202
somewhere i have never travelled,gladly beyond: 268–271, 275, 277, 279–280

Sexual Desire
The Cinnamon Peeler: 58

Shifts of Consciousness
True Night: 285

Sickness
Childhood: 38, 40–42, 44, 52
Proem: 217, 219, 222, 224

Sin
Perfect Light: 199
Proem: 208, 221–222

Social Order
The Cinnamon Peeler: 63–66

Sonnet
The Boy: 22, 24–25

Sonnet *(continued)*
    Proem: 226–227
Soul
    The City Limits: 90–91
    Proem: 234–236
Space Exploration and Study
    On Location in the Loire Valley: 165, 167–170
    Ordinary Words: 181–182, 184
Spirituality
    Childhood: 38, 40, 45–46
    Proem: 206–211, 228–232
    somewhere i have never travelled, gladly beyond: 268–269
Sports and the Sporting Life
    His Speed and Strength: 99–100, 105–106
Storms and Weather Conditions
    Childhood: 35–37, 39, 42–44, 51
    Perfect Light: 197, 201–202
    somewhere i have never travelled, gladly beyond: 266–268
    True Night: 285, 287, 291–292, 295–296
Strength
    His Speed and Strength: 95–97, 99–101, 105–106
Structure
    Childhood: 36–37
    The Cinnamon Peeler: 61–62, 71–72
    The City Limits: 86–87
    Proem: 210–211, 218–219, 221
    True Night: 299, 302, 306–307, 309
Suburban Life
    Social Life: 250, 252–258
Suicide
    Perfect Light: 186, 189–197, 199, 203

T

Time and Change
    Perfect Light: 198–199, 202
    Proem: 216, 219, 221–222, 225
    Seven Seeds: 238, 240, 242
    somewhere i have never travelled, gladly beyond: 274
    True Night: 300–301, 304
Tone
    Ithaka: 120–122, 126–127
    On Location in the Loire Valley: 155–156
Transcendentalism
    somewhere i have never travelled, gladly beyond: 281
Trust
    Proem: 229–231
    somewhere i have never travelled, gladly beyond: 276, 281

U

Uncertainty
    somewhere i have never travelled, gladly beyond: 273–275
Understanding
    Childhood: 42, 46
    True Night: 299
Utopianism
    Ithaka: 120–121
    Perfect Light: 195

V

Vietnam War
    His Speed and Strength: 102–103, 104

W

War, the Military, and Soldier Life
    And What If I Spoke of Despair: 3–4, 6, 8
    Childhood: 37–38, 40–45, 47, 49–51
    His Speed and Strength: 95–104
    Perfect Light: 188–191
    somewhere i have never travelled, gladly beyond: 270
    True Night: 302–305
Wildlife
    And What If I Spoke of Despair: 3–6, 9–11
    The Cinnamon Peeler: 69–73, 75
    The City Limits: 77, 79–80, 82, 87–88
    Ordinary Words: 172, 174
    Perfect Light: 197, 199–200
    somewhere i have never travelled, gladly beyond: 276, 280–281
    True Night: 289–290, 299–302, 304, 306, 309
World War II
    somewhere i have never travelled, gladly beyond: 270
Writing
    The Boy: 16

Cumulative Index of First Lines

A

A brackish reach of shoal off Madaket,— (The Quaker Graveyard in Nantucket) V6:158
"A cold coming we had of it (Journey of the Magi) V7:110
A few minutes ago, I stepped onto the deck (The Cobweb) V17:50
A gentle spring evening arrives (Spring-Watching Pavilion) V18:198
A line in long array where they wind betwixt green islands, (Cavalry Crossing a Ford) V13:50
A narrow Fellow in the grass (A Narrow Fellow in the Grass) V11:127
A pine box for me. I mean it. (Last Request) V14: 231
A poem should be palpable and mute (Ars Poetica) V5:2
A stone from the depths that has witnessed the seas drying up (Song of a Citizen) V16:125
A tourist came in from Orbitville, (Southbound on the Freeway) V16:158
A wind is ruffling the tawny pelt (A Far Cry from Africa) V6:60
a woman precedes me up the long rope, (Climbing) V14:113
About me the night moonless wimples the mountains (Vancouver Lights) V8:245
About suffering they were never wrong (Musée des Beaux Arts) V1:148
Across Roblin Lake, two shores away, (Wilderness Gothic) V12:241
After the party ends another party begins (Social Life) V19:251
After you finish your work (Ballad of Orange and Grape) V10:17
Again I've returned to this country (The Country Without a Post Office) V18:64
"Ah, are you digging on my grave (Ah, Are You Digging on My Grave?) V4:2
All Greece hates (Helen) V6:92
All night long the hockey pictures (To a Sad Daughter) V8:230
All winter your brute shoulders strained against collars, padding (Names of Horses) V8:141
Also Ulysses once—that other war. (Kilroy) V14:213
Anasazi (Anasazi) V9:2
And God stepped out on space (The Creation) V1:19
And what if I spoke of despair—who doesn't (And What If I Spoke of Despair) V19:2
Animal bones and some mossy tent rings (Lament for the Dorsets) V5:190
As I perceive (The Gold Lily) V5:127
As I walked out one evening (As I Walked Out One Evening) V4:15
As virtuous men pass mildly away (A Valediction: Forbidding Mourning) V11:201
As you set out for Ithaka (Ithaka) V19:114
At noon in the desert a panting lizard (At the Bomb Testing Site) V8:2
Ay, tear her tattered ensign down! (Old Ironsides) V9:172

B

Back then, before we came (On Freedom's Ground) V12:186
Bananas ripe and green, and ginger-root (The Tropics in New York) V4:255
Because I could not stop for Death— (Because I Could Not Stop for Death) V2:27
Before the indifferent beak could let her drop? (Leda and the Swan) V13:182
Bent double, like old beggars under slacks, (Dulce et Decorum Est) V10:109
Between my finger and my thumb (Digging) V5:70
Beware of ruins: they have a treacherous charm (Beware of Ruins) V8:43

Bright star! would I were steadfast as thou art— (Bright Star! Would I Were Steadfast as Thou Art) V9:44

By the rude bridge that arched the flood (Concord Hymn) V4:30

By way of a vanished bridge we cross this river (The Garden Shukkei-en) V18:107

C

Celestial choir! enthron'd in realms of light, (To His Excellency General Washington V13:212

Come with me into those things that have felt his despair for so long— (Come with Me) V6:31

Complacencies of the peignoir, and late (Sunday Morning) V16:189

Composed in the Tower, before his execution ("More Light! More Light!") V6:119

D

Darkened by time, the masters, like our memories, mix (Black Zodiac) V10:46

Death, be not proud, though some have called thee (Holy Sonnet 10) V2:103

Devouring Time, blunt thou the lion's paws (Sonnet 19) V9:210

Do not go gentle into that good night (Do Not Go Gentle into that Good Night) V1:51

Do not weep, maiden, for war is kind (War Is Kind) V9:252

Don Arturo says: (Business) V16:2

(Dumb, (A Grafted Tongue) V12:92

E

Each day the shadow swings (In the Land of Shinar) V7:83

Each night she waits by the road (Bidwell Ghost) V14:2

F

Falling upon earth (Falling Upon Earth) V2:64

Five years have past; five summers, with the length (Tintern Abbey) V2:249

Flesh is heretic. (Anorexic) V12:2

For three years, out of key with his time, (Hugh Selwyn Mauberley) V16:26

Forgive me for thinking I saw (For a New Citizen of These United States) V15:55

From my mother's sleep I fell into the State (The Death of the Ball Turret Gunner) V2:41

G

Gardener: Sir, I encountered Death (Incident in a Rose Garden) V14:190

Gather ye Rose-buds while ye may, (To the Virgins, to Make Much of Time) V13:226

Go down, Moses (Go Down, Moses) V11:42

Gray mist wolf (Four Mountain Wolves) V9:131

H

"Had he and I but met (The Man He Killed) V3:167

Had we but world enough, and time (To His Coy Mistress) V5:276

Half a league, half a league (The Charge of the Light Brigade) V1:2

Having a Coke with You (Having a Coke with You) V12:105

He clasps the crag with crooked hands (The Eagle) V11:30

He was found by the Bureau of Statistics to be (The Unknown Citizen) V3:302

Hear the sledges with the bells— (The Bells) V3:46

Her body is not so white as (Queen-Ann's-Lace) V6:179

Her eyes were coins of porter and her West (A Farewell to English) V10:126

Here they are. The soft eyes open (The Heaven of Animals) V6:75

His speed and strength, which is the strength of ten (His Speed and Strength) V19:96

Hog Butcher for the World (Chicago) V3:61

Hold fast to dreams (Dream Variations) V15:42

Hope is a tattered flag and a dream out of time. (Hope is a Tattered Flag) V12:120

"Hope" is the thing with feathers— (Hope Is the Thing with Feathers) V3:123

How do I love thee? Let me count the ways (Sonnet 43) V2:236

How shall we adorn (Angle of Geese) V2:2

How soon hath Time, the subtle thief of youth, (On His Having Arrived at the Age of Twenty-Three) V17:159

How would it be if you took yourself off (Landscape with Tractor) V10:182

Hunger crawls into you (Hunger in New York City) V4:79

I

I am not a painter, I am a poet (Why I Am Not a Painter) V8:258

I am the Smoke King (The Song of the Smoke) V13:196

I am silver and exact. I have no preconceptions (Mirror) V1:116

I am trying to pry open your casket (Dear Reader) V10:85

I became a creature of light (The Mystery) V15:137

I cannot love the Brothers Wright (Reactionary Essay on Applied Science) V9:199

I felt a Funeral, in my Brain, (I felt a Funeral in my Brain) V13:137

I have just come down from my father (The Hospital Window) V11:58

I have met them at close of day (Easter 1916) V5:91

I haven't the heart to say (To an Unknown Poet) V18:221

I hear America singing, the varied carols I hear (I Hear America Singing) V3:152

I heard a Fly buzz—when I died— (I Heard a Fly Buzz—When I Died—) V5:140

I know that I shall meet my fate (An Irish Airman Foresees His Death) V1:76

I leant upon a coppice gate (The Darkling Thrush) V18:74

I looked in my heart while the wild swans went over. (Wild Swans) V17:221

I prove a theorem and the house expands: (Geometry) V15:68

I see them standing at the formal gates of their colleges, (I go Back to May 1937) V17:112

I sit in the top of the wood, my eyes closed (Hawk Roosting) V4:55

I'm delighted to see you (The Constellation Orion) V8:53

I've known rivers; (The Negro Speaks of Rivers) V10:197

I was sitting in mcsorley's. outside it was New York and beautifully snowing. (i was sitting in mcsorley's) V13:151

I will arise and go now, and go to Innisfree, (The Lake Isle of Innisfree) V15:121

If all the world and love were young, (The Nymph's Reply to the Shepard) V14:241

If ever two were one, then surely we (To My Dear and Loving Husband) V6:228

If I should die, think only this of me (The Soldier) V7:218

"Imagine being the first to say: *surveillance*," (Inventors) V7:97

In 1936, a child (Blood Oranges) V13:34

In a while they rose and went out aimlessly riding, (Merlin Enthralled) V16:72

In China (Lost Sister) V5:216

In ethics class so many years ago (Ethics) V8:88

In Flanders fields the poppies blow (In Flanders Fields) V5:155

In India in their lives they happen (Ways to Live) V16:228

In May, when sea-winds pierced our solitudes, (The Rhodora) V17:191

In the groves of Africa from their natural wonder (An African Elegy) V13:3

In the Shreve High football stadium (Autumn Begins in Martins Ferry, Ohio) V8:17

In Xanadu did Kubla Khan (Kubla Khan) V5:172

Ink runs from the corners of my mouth (Eating Poetry) V9:60

Is it the boy in me who's looking out (The Boy) V19:14

It is a cold and snowy night. The main street is deserted. (Driving to Town Late to Mail a Letter) V17:63

It is an ancient Mariner (The Rime of the Ancient Mariner) V4:127

It is in the small things we see it. (Courage) V14:125

It little profits that an idle king (Ulysses) V2:278

It looked extremely rocky for the Mudville nine that day (Casey at the Bat) V5:57

It seems vainglorious and proud (The Conquerors) V13:67

It was in and about the Martinmas time (Barbara Allan) V7:10

It was many and many a year ago (Annabel Lee) V9:14

Its quick soft silver bell beating, beating (Auto Wreck) V3:31

J

Januaries, Nature greets our eyes (Brazil, January 1, 1502) V6:15

Just off the highway to Rochester, Minnesota (A Blessing) V7:24

just once (For the White poets who would be Indian) V13:112

L

l(a (l(a) V1:85

Let me not to the marriage of true minds (Sonnet 116) V3:288

Listen, my children, and you shall hear (Paul Revere's Ride) V2:178

Little Lamb, who made thee? (The Lamb) V12:134

Long long ago when the world was a wild place (Bedtime Story) V8:32

M

maggie and milly and molly and may (maggie & milly & molly & may) V12:149

Mary sat musing on the lamp-flame at the table (The Death of the Hired Man) V4:42

Men with picked voices chant the names (Overture to a Dance of Locomotives) V11:143

"Mother dear, may I go downtown (Ballad of Birmingham) V5:17

Much Madness is divinest Sense— (Much Madness is Divinest Sense) V16:86

My black face fades (Facing It) V5:109

My father stands in the warm evening (Starlight) V8:213

My heart aches, and a drowsy numbness pains (Ode to a Nightingale) V3:228

My heart is like a singing bird (A Birthday) V10:33

My life closed twice before its close— (My Life Closed Twice Before Its Close) V8:127

My mistress' eyes are nothing like the sun (Sonnet 130) V1:247

My uncle in East Germany (The Exhibit) V9:107

N

Nature's first green is gold (Nothing Gold Can Stay) V3:203

No easy thing to bear, the weight of sweetness (The Weight of Sweetness) V11:230

Nobody heard him, the dead man (Not Waving but Drowning) V3:216

Not marble nor the gilded monuments (Sonnet 55) V5:246

Not the memorized phone numbers. (What Belongs to Us) V15:196

Now as I was young and easy under the apple boughs (Fern Hill) V3:92

Now as I watch the progress of the plague (The Missing) V9:158

O

O Captain! my Captain, our fearful trip is done (O Captain! My Captain!) V2:146

O Lord our Lord, how excellent is thy name in all the earth! who hast set thy glory above the heavens (Psalm 8) V9:182

O my Luve's like a red, red rose (A Red, Red Rose) V8:152

O what can ail thee, knight-at-arms, (La Belle Dame sans Merci) V17:18

"O where ha' you been, Lord Randal, my son? (Lord Randal) V6:105

O wild West Wind, thou breath of Autumn's being (Ode to the West Wind) V2:163
Oh, but it is dirty! (Filling Station) V12:57
old age sticks (old age sticks) V3:246
On either side the river lie (The Lady of Shalott) V15:95
On the seashore of endless worlds children meet. The infinite (60) V18:3
Once upon a midnight dreary, while I pondered, weak and weary (The Raven) V1:200
Once some people were visiting Chekhov (Chocolates) V11:17
One day I'll lift the telephone (Elegy for My Father, Who Is Not Dead) V14:154
One foot down, then hop! It's hot (Harlem Hopscotch) V2:93
one shoe on the roadway presents (A Piéd) V3:16
Out of the hills of Habersham, (Song of the Chattahoochee) V14:283
Out walking in the frozen swamp one gray day (The Wood-Pile) V6:251
Oysters we ate (Oysters) V4:91

P

Pentagon code (Smart and Final Iris) V15:183
Poised between going on and back, pulled (The Base Stealer) V12:30

Q

Quinquireme of Nineveh from distant Ophir (Cargoes) V5:44

R

Red men embraced my body's whiteness (Birch Canoe) V5:31
Remember me when I am gone away (Remember) V14:255

S

Shall I compare thee to a Summer's day? (Sonnet 18) V2:222
She came every morning to draw water (A Drink of Water) V8:66
She sang beyond the genius of the sea. (The Idea of Order at Key West) V13:164
She walks in beauty, like the night (She Walks in Beauty) V14:268
Side by side, their faces blurred, (An Arundel Tomb) V12:17
Since the professional wars— (Midnight) V2:130
S'io credesse che mia risposta fosse (The Love Song of J. Alfred Prufrock) V1:97
Sky black (Duration) V18:93
Sleepless as Prospero back in his bedroom (Darwin in 1881) V13:83
so much depends (The Red Wheelbarrow) V1:219
So the man spread his blanket on the field (A Tall Man Executes a Jig) V12:228
So the sky wounded you, jagged at the heart, (Daylights) V13:101
Softly, in the dark, a woman is singing to me (Piano) V6:145
Some say it's in the reptilian dance (The Greatest Grandeur) V18:119
Some say the world will end in fire (Fire and Ice) V7:57
Something there is that doesn't love a wall (Mending Wall) V5:231
Sometimes walking late at night (Butcher Shop) V7:43
Sometimes, a lion with a prophet's beard (For An Assyrian Frieze) V9:120
Sometimes, in the middle of the lesson (Music Lessons) V8:117
somewhere i have never travelled,gladly beyond (somewhere i have never travelled,gladly beyond) V19:265
South of the bridge on Seventeenth (Fifteen) V2:78
Stop all the clocks, cut off the telephone, (Funeral Blues) V10:139
Strong Men, riding horses. In the West (Strong Men, Riding Horses) V4:209
Such places are too still for history, (Deep Woods) V14:138
Sundays too my father got up early (Those Winter Sundays) V1:300
Swing low sweet chariot (Swing Low Sweet Chariot) V1:283

T

Take heart, monsieur, four-fifths of this province (For Jean Vincent D'abbadie, Baron St.-Castin) V12:78
Tears, idle tears, I know not what they mean (Tears, Idle Tears) V4:220
Tell me not, in mournful numbers (A Psalm of Life) V7:165
Temple bells die out. (Temple Bells Die Out) V18:210
That is no country for old men. The young (Sailing to Byzantium) V2:207
That time of drought the embered air (Drought Year) V8:78
That's my last Duchess painted on the wall (My Last Duchess) V1:165
The apparition of these faces in the crowd (In a Station of the Metro) V2:116
The Assyrian came down like the wolf on the fold (The Destruction of Sennacherib) V1:38
The broken pillar of the wing jags from the clotted shoulder (Hurt Hawks) V3:138
The bud (Saint Francis and the Sow) V9:222
The Bustle in a House (The Bustle in a House) V10:62
The buzz saw snarled and rattled in the yard (Out, Out—) V10:212
The courage that my mother had (The Courage that My Mother Had) V3:79
The Curfew tolls the knell of parting day (Elegy Written in a Country Churchyard) V9:73
The force that through the green fuse drives the flower (The Force That Through the Green Fuse Drives the Flower) V8:101
The green lamp flares on the table (This Life) V1:293
The ills I sorrow at (Any Human to Another) V3:2
The instructor said (Theme for English B) V6:194
The king sits in Dumferling toune (Sir Patrick Spens) V4:177

The land was overmuch like scenery (Beowulf) V11:2
The last time I saw it was 1968. (The Hiding Place) V10:152
The Lord is my shepherd; I shall not want (Psalm 23) V4:103
The man who sold his lawn to standard oil (The War Against the Trees) V11:215
The moon glows the same (The Moon Glows the Same) V7:152
The old South Boston Aquarium stands (For the Union Dead) V7:67
The others bent their heads and started in ("Trouble with Math in a One-Room Country School") V9:238
The pale nuns of St. Joseph are here (Island of Three Marias) V11:79
The Phoenix comes of flame and dust (The Phoenix) V10:226
The rain set early in to-night: (Porphyria's Lover) V15:151
The river brought down (How We Heard the Name) V10:167
The rusty spigot (Onomatopoeia) V6:133
The sea is calm tonight (Dover Beach) V2:52
The sea sounds insincere (The Milkfish Gatherers) V11:111
The slow overture of rain, (Mind) V17:145
The Soul selects her own Society—(The Soul Selects Her Own Society) V1:259
The time you won your town race (To an Athlete Dying Young) V7:230
The way sorrow enters the bone (The Blue Rim of Memory) V17:38
The whiskey on your breath (My Papa's Waltz) V3:191
The wind was a torrent of darkness among the gusty trees (The Highwayman) V4:66
There are strange things done in the midnight sun (The Cremation of Sam McGee) V10:75
There have been rooms for such a short time (The Horizons of Rooms) V15:79
There is the one song everyone (Siren Song) V7:196
There's a Certain Slant of Light (There's a Certain Slant of Light) V6:211
There's no way out. (In the Suburbs) V14:201
There will come soft rains and the smell of the ground, (There Will Come Soft Rains) V14:301
There you are, in all your innocence, (Perfect Light) V19:187
These open years, the river (For Jennifer, 6, on the Teton) V17:86
They eat beans mostly, this old yellow pair (The Bean Eaters) V2:16
they were just meant as covers (My Mother Pieced Quilts) V12:169
They said, "Wait." Well, I waited. (Alabama Centennial) V10:2
This girlchild was: born as usual (Barbie Doll) V9:33
This is my letter to the World (This Is My Letter to the World) V4:233
This is the Arsenal. From floor to ceiling, (The Arsenal at Springfield) V17:2
This is the black sea-brute bulling through wave-wrack (Leviathan) V5:203
This poem is concerned with language on a very plain level (Paradoxes and Oxymorons) V11:162
This tale is true, and mine. It tells (The Seafarer) V8:177
Thou still unravish'd bride of quietness (Ode on a Grecian Urn) V1:179
Three times my life has opened. (Three Times My Life Has Opened) V16:213
Time in school drags along with so much worry, (Childhood) V19:29
to fold the clothes. No matter who lives (I Stop Writing the Poem) V16:58
Tonight I can write the saddest lines (Tonight I Can Write) V11:187
tonite, *thriller* was (Beware: Do Not Read This Poem) V6:3
Turning and turning in the widening gyre (The Second Coming) V7:179
'Twas brillig, and the slithy toves (Jabberwocky) V11:91
Two roads diverged in a yellow wood (The Road Not Taken) V2:195
Tyger! Tyger! burning bright (The Tyger) V2:263

W

wade (The Fish) V14:171
Wanting to say things, (My Father's Song) V16:102
We could be here. This is the valley (Small Town with One Road) V7:207
We met the British in the dead of winter (Meeting the British) V7:138
We real cool. We (We Real Cool) V6:242
Well, son, I'll tell you (Mother to Son) V3:178
What dire offense from amorous causes springs, (The Rape of the Lock) V12:202
What happens to a dream deferred? (Harlem) V1:63
What of the neighborhood homes awash (The Continuous Life) V18:51
What thoughts I have of you tonight, Walt Whitman, for I walked down the sidestreets under the trees with a headache self-conscious looking at the full moon (A Supermarket in California) V5:261
Whatever it is, it must have (American Poetry) V7:2
When Abraham Lincoln was shoveled into the tombs, he forgot the copperheads, and the assassin . . . in the dust, in the cool tombs (Cool Tombs) V6:45
When I consider how my light is spent ([On His Blindness] Sonnet 16) V3:262
When I have fears that I may cease to be (When I Have Fears that I May Cease to Be) V2:295
When I see a couple of kids (High Windows) V3:108
When I see birches bend to left and right (Birches) V13:14
When I was born, you waited (Having it Out with Melancholy) V17:98
When I was one-and-twenty (When I Was One-and-Twenty) V4:268
When I watch you (Miss Rosie) V1:133
When, in disgrace with Fortune and men's eyes (Sonnet 29) V8:198
When the mountains of Puerto Rico (We Live by What We See at Night) V13:240
When the world was created wasn't it like this? (Anniversary) V15:2

When they said *Carrickfergus* I could hear (The Singer's House) V17:205
When you consider the radiance, that it does not withhold (The City Limits) V19:78
Whenever Richard Cory went down town (Richard Cory) V4:116
While my hair was still cut straight across my forehead (The River-Merchant's Wife: A Letter) V8:164
While the long grain is softening (Early in the Morning) V17:75
While this America settles in the mould of its vulgarity, heavily thickening to empire (Shine, Perishing Republic) V4:161
While you are preparing for sleep, brushing your teeth, (The Afterlife) V18:39
Who has ever stopped to think of the divinity of Lamont Cranston? (In Memory of Radio) V9:144
Whose woods these are I think I know (Stopping by Woods on a Snowy Evening) V1:272
Why should I let the toad *work* (Toads) V4:244

Y

You are small and intense (To a Child Running With Outstretched Arms in Canyon de Chelly) V11:173
You do not have to be good. (Wild Geese) V15:207
You were never told, Mother, how old Illya was drunk (The Czar's Last Christmas Letter) V12:44

Cumulative Index of Last Lines

A

A heart whose love is innocent! (She Walks in Beauty) V14:268

a man then suddenly stops running (Island of Three Marias) V11:80

A perfect evening! (Temple Bells Die Out) V18:210

a space in the lives of their friends (Beware: Do Not Read This Poem) V6:3

A sudden blow: the great wings beating still (Leda and the Swan) V13:181

A terrible beauty is born (Easter 1916) V5:91

About my big, new, automatically defrosting refrigerator with the built-in electric eye (Reactionary Essay on Applied Science) V9:199

about the tall mounds of termites. (Song of a Citizen) V16:126

Across the expedient and wicked stones (Auto Wreck) V3:31

Ah, dear father, graybeard, lonely old courage-teacher, what America did you have when Charon quit poling his ferry and you got out on a smoking bank and stood watching the boat disappear on the black waters of Lethe? (A Supermarket in California) V5:261

All losses are restored and sorrows end (Sonnet 30) V4:192

Amen. Amen (The Creation) V1:20

Anasazi (Anasazi) V9:3

and all beyond saving by children (Ethics) V8:88

and all the richer for it. (Mind) V17:146

And all we need of hell (My Life Closed Twice Before Its Close) V8:127

and changed, back to the class ("Trouble with Math in a One-Room Country School") V9:238

And Death shall be no more: Death, thou shalt die (Holy Sonnet 10) V2:103

And drunk the milk of Paradise (Kubla Khan) V5:172

and fear lit by the breadth of such calmly turns to praise. (The City Limits) V19:78

And Finished knowing—then— (I Felt a Funeral in My Brain) V13:137

And gallop terribly against each other's bodies (Autumn Begins in Martins Ferry, Ohio) V8:17

and go back. (For the White poets who would be Indian) V13:112

And handled with a Chain—(Much Madness is Divinest Sense) V16:86

And has not begun to grow a manly smile. (Deep Woods) V14:139

And his own Word (The Phoenix) V10:226

And I am Nicholas. (The Czar's Last Christmas Letter) V12:45

And I was unaware. (The Darkling Thrush) V18:74

And in the suburbs Can't sat down and cried. (Kilroy) V14:213

And it's been years. (Anniversary) V15:3

And life for me ain't been no crystal stair (Mother to Son) V3:179

And like a thunderbolt he falls (The Eagle) V11:30

And makes me end where I begun (A Valediction: Forbidding Mourning) V11:202

And 'midst the stars inscribe Belinda's name. (The Rape of the Lock) V12:209

And miles to go before I sleep (Stopping by Woods on a Snowy Evening) V1:272

and my father saying things. (My Father's Song) V16:102

And no birds sing. (La Belle Dame sans Merci) V17:18

And not waving but drowning (Not Waving but Drowning) V3:216

And oh, 'tis true, 'tis true (When I Was One-and-Twenty) V4:268

And reach for your scalping knife. (For Jean Vincent D'abbadie, Baron St.-Castin) V12:78

and retreating, always retreating, behind it (Brazil, January 1, 1502) V6:16
And settled upon his eyes in a black soot ("More Light! More Light!") V6:120
And shuts his eyes. (Darwin in 1881) V13: 84
And so live ever—or else swoon to death (Bright Star! Would I Were Steadfast as Thou Art) V9:44
and strange and loud was the dingoes' cry (Drought Year) V8:78
and stride out. (Courage) V14:126
and sweat and fat and greed. (Anorexic) V12:3
And that has made all the difference (The Road Not Taken) V2:195
And the deep river ran on (As I Walked Out One Evening) V4:16
And the midnight message of Paul Revere (Paul Revere's Ride) V2:180
And the mome raths outgrabe (Jabberwocky) V11:91
And the Salvation Army singing God loves us. . . . (Hope is a Tattered Flag) V12:120
and these the last verses that I write for her (Tonight I Can Write) V11:187
And those roads in South Dakota that feel around in the darkness . . . (Come with Me) V6:31
and to know she will stay in the field till you die? (Landscape with Tractor) V10:183
and two blankets embroidered with smallpox (Meeting the British) V7:138
and waving, shouting, *Welcome back*. (Elegy for My Father, Who Is Not Dead) V14:154
And would suffice (Fire and Ice) V7:57
And yet God has not said a word! (Porphyria's Lover) V15:151
and you spread un the thin halo of night mist. (Ways to Live) V16:229
And Zero at the Bone— (A Narrow Fellow in the Grass) V11:127
(answer with a tower of birds) (Duration) V18:93
As any She belied with false compare (Sonnet 130) V1:248
As ever in my great Task-Master's eye. (On His Having Arrived at the Age of Twenty-Three) V17:160
As far as Cho-fu-Sa (The River-Merchant's Wife: A Letter) V8:165
As the contagion of those molten eyes (For An Assyrian Frieze) V9:120
As they lean over the beans in their rented back room that is full of beads and receipts and dolls and clothes, tobacco crumbs, vases and fringes (The Bean Eaters) V2:16
aspired to become lighter than air (Blood Oranges) V13:34
at home in the fish's fallen heaven (Birch Canoe) V5:31
away, pedaling hard, rocket and pilot. (His Speed and Strength) V19:96

B

Back to the play of constant give and change (The Missing) V9:158
Before it was quite unsheathed from reality (Hurt Hawks) V3:138
Black like me. (Dream Variations) V15:42
Bless me (Hunger in New York City) V4:79
But be (Ars Poetica) V5:3
but it works every time (Siren Song) V7:196
But there is no joy in Mudville—mighty Casey has "Struck Out." (Casey at the Bat) V5:58
But, baby, where are you?" (Ballad of Birmingham) V5:17
But we hold our course, and the wind is with us. (On Freedom's Ground) V12:187
by good fortune (The Horizons of Rooms) V15:80

C

Calls through the valleys of Hall. (Song of the Chattahoochee) V14:284
chickens (The Red Wheelbarrow) V1:219
clear water dashes (Onomatopoeia) V6:133
come to life and burn? (Bidwell Ghost) V14:2
Comin' for to carry me home (Swing Low Sweet Chariot) V1:284

D

Dare frame thy fearful symmetry? (The Tyger) V2:263
"Dead," was all he answered (The Death of the Hired Man) V4:44
deep in the deepest one, tributaries burn. (For Jennifer, 6, on the Teton) V17:86
Delicate, delicate, delicate, delicate—now! (The Base Stealer) V12:30
Die soon (We Real Cool) V6:242
Do what you are going to do, I will tell about it. (I go Back to May 1937) V17:113
Down in the flood of remembrance, I weep like a child for the past (Piano) V6:145
Downward to darkness, on extended wings. (Sunday Morning) V16:190
Driving around, I will waste more time. (Driving to Town Late to Mail a Letter) V17:63
dry wells that fill so easily now (The Exhibit) V9:107

E

endless worlds is the great meeting of children. (60) V18:3
Eternal, unchanging creator of earth. Amen (The Seafarer) V8:178
every branch traced with the ghost writing of snow. (The Afterlife) V18:39

F

fall upon us, the dwellers in shadow (In the Land of Shinar) V7:84
Fallen cold and dead (O Captain! My Captain!) V2:147
filled, never. (The Greatest Grandeur) V18:119
Firewood, iron-ware, and cheap tin trays (Cargoes) V5:44
Fled is that music:—Do I wake or sleep? (Ode to a Nightingale) V3:229
For I'm sick at the heart, and I fain wad lie down." (Lord Randal) V6:105
For nothing now can ever come to any good. (Funeral Blues) V10:139
forget me as fast as you can. (Last Request) V14:231

G

going where? Where? (Childhood) V19:29

H

Had anything been wrong, we should certainly have heard (The Unknown Citizen) V3:303
Had somewhere to get to and sailed calmly on (Mus,e des Beaux Arts) V1:148
half eaten by the moon. (Dear Reader) V10:85
hand over hungry hand. (Climbing) V14:113
Happen on a red tongue (Small Town with One Road) V7:207
Has no more need of, and I have (The Courage that My Mother Had) V3:80
Hath melted like snow in the glance of the Lord! (The Destruction of Sennacherib) V1:39
He rose the morrow morn (The Rime of the Ancient Mariner) V4:132
He says again, "Good fences make good neighbors." (Mending Wall) V5:232
He writes down something that he crosses out. (The Boy) V19:14
Has set me softly down beside you. The Poem is you (Paradoxes and Oxymorons) V11:162
How at my sheet goes the same crooked worm (The Force That Through the Green Fuse Drives the Flower) V8:101
How can I turn from Africa and live? (A Far Cry from Africa) V6:61
How sad then is even the marvelous! (An Africian Elegy) V13:4

I

I am black. (The Song of the Smoke) V13:197
I am going to keep things like this (Hawk Roosting) V4:55
I am not brave at all (Strong Men, Riding Horses) V4:209
I could not see to see— (I Heard a Fly Buzz—When I Died—) V5:140
I didn't want to put them down. (And What If I Spoke of Despair) V19:2
I have just come down from my father (The Hospital Window) V11:58
I cremated Sam McGee (The Cremation of Sam McGee) V10:76
I hear it in the deep heart's core. (The Lake Isle of Innisfree) V15:121
I never writ, nor no man ever loved (Sonnet 116) V3:288
I romp with joy in the bookish dark (Eating Poetry) V9:61
I see Mike's painting, called SARDINES (Why I Am Not a Painter) V8:259
I shall but love thee better after death (Sonnet 43) V2:236
I should be glad of another death (Journey of the Magi) V7:110
I stand up (Miss Rosie) V1:133
I stood there, fifteen (Fifteen) V2:78
I take it you are he? (Incident in a Rose Garden) V14:191
I turned aside and bowed my head and wept (The Tropics in New York) V4:255
I'll be gone from here. (The Cobweb) V17:51
I'll dig with it (Digging) V5:71

If Winter comes, can Spring be far behind? (Ode to the West Wind) V2:163
In a convulsive misery (The Milkfish Gatherers) V11:112
In balance with this life, this death (An Irish Airman Foresees His Death) V1:76
In Flanders fields (In Flanders Fields) V5:155
In ghostlier demarcations, keener sounds. (The Idea of Order at Key West) V13:164
In hearts at peace, under an English heaven (The Soldier) V7:218
In her tomb by the side of the sea (Annabel Lee) V9:14
in the family of things. (Wild Geese) V15:208
in the grit gray light of day. (Daylights) V13:102
In the rear-view mirrors of the passing cars (The War Against the Trees) V11:216
in this bastion of culture. (To an Unknown Poet) V18:221
iness (l(a) V1:85
Into blossom (A Blessing) V7:24
Is Come, my love is come to me. (A Birthday) V10:34
is still warm (Lament for the Dorsets) V5:191
It asked a crumb—of Me (Hope Is the Thing with Feathers) V3:123
it is the bell to awaken God that we've heard ringing. (The Garden Shukkei-en) V18:107
It rains as I write this. Mad heart, be brave. (The Country Without a Post Office) V18:64
It was your resting place." (Ah, Are You Digging on My Grave?) V4:2
it's always ourselves we find in the sea (maggie & milly & molly & may) V12:150
its bright, unequivocal eye. (Having it Out with Melancholy) V17:99
its youth. The sea grows old in it. (The Fish) V14:172

J

Judge tenderly—of Me (This Is My Letter to the World) V4:233
Just imagine it (Inventors) V7:97

L

Laughing the stormy, husky, brawling laughter of Youth, half-naked, sweating, proud to be Hog Butcher, Tool Maker, Stacker of Wheat, Player with Railroads and Freight Handler to the Nation (Chicago) V3:61
Learn to labor and to wait (A Psalm of Life) V7:165
Leashed in my throat (Midnight) V2:131
Let my people go (Go Down, Moses) V11:43
life, our life and its forgetting. (For a New Citizen of These United States) V15:55
Like Stone— (The Soul Selects Her Own Society) V1:259
Little Lamb, God bless thee. (The Lamb) V12:135

M

'Make a wish, Tom, make a wish.' (Drifters) V10: 98
make it seem to change (The Moon Glows the Same) V7:152
midnight-oiled in the metric laws? (A Farewell to English) V10:126

Monkey business (Business) V16:2
More dear, both for themselves and for thy sake! (Tintern Abbey) V2:250
My love shall in my verse ever live young (Sonnet 19) V9:211
My soul has grown deep like the rivers. (The Negro Speaks of Rivers) V10:198

N

never to waken in that world again (Starlight) V8:213
Nirvana is here, nine times out of ten. (Spring-Watching Pavilion) V18:198
No, she's brushing a boy's hair (Facing It) V5:110
no—tell them no— (The Hiding Place) V10:153
Noble six hundred! (The Charge of the Light Brigade) V1:3
nobody,not even the rain,has such small hands (somewhere i have never travelled,gladly beyond) V19:265
Not even the blisters. Look. (What Belongs to Us) V15:196
Nothing gold can stay (Nothing Gold Can Stay) V3:203
Nothing, and is nowhere, and is endless (High Windows) V3:108
Now! (Alabama Centennial) V10:2
nursing the tough skin of figs (This Life) V1:293

O

O Death in Life, the days that are no more! (Tears, Idle Tears) V4:220
O Lord our Lord, how excellent is thy name in all the earth! (Psalm 8) V9:182
O Roger, Mackerel, Riley, Ned, Nellie, Chester, Lady Ghost (Names of Horses) V8:142
of gentleness (To a Sad Daughter) V8:231
of love's austere and lonely offices? (Those Winter Sundays) V1:300
of peaches (The Weight of Sweetness) V11:230
Of the camellia (Falling Upon Earth) V2:64
Of the Creator. And he waits for the world to begin (Leviathan) V5:204
Of what is past, or passing, or to come (Sailing to Byzantium) V2:207
Old Ryan, not yours (The Constellation Orion) V8:53
On the dark distant flurry (Angle of Geese) V2:2
On the look of Death— (There's a Certain Slant of Light) V6:212
On your head like a crown (Any Human to Another) V3:2
One could do worse that be a swinger of birches. (Birches) V13:15
Or does it explode? (Harlem) V1:63
Or help to half-a-crown." (The Man He Killed) V3:167
or nothing (Queen-Ann's-Lace) V6:179
or the one red leaf the snow releases in March. (Three Times My Life Has Opened) V16:213
ORANGE forever. (Ballad of Orange and Grape) V10:18
outside. (it was New York and beautifully, snowing . . . (i was sitting in mcsorley's) V13:152
owing old (old age sticks) V3:246

P

Perhaps he will fall. (Wilderness Gothic) V12:242
Petals on a wet, black bough (In a Station of the Metro) V2:116
Plaiting a dark red love-knot into her long black hair (The Highwayman) V4:68
Pro patria mori. (Dulce et Decorum Est) V10:110

R

Rage, rage against the dying of the light (Do Not Go Gentle into that Good Night) V1:51
Raise it again, man. We still believe what we hear. (The Singer's House) V17:206
Remember the Giver fading off the lip (A Drink of Water) V8:66
Rises toward her day after day, like a terrible fish (Mirror) V1:116

S

Shall be lifted—nevermore! (The Raven) V1:202
Simply melted into the perfect light. (Perfect Light) V19:187
Singing of him what they could understand (Beowulf) V11:3
Singing with open mouths their strong melodious songs (I Hear America Singing) V3:152
slides by on grease (For the Union Dead) V7:67
Slouches towards Bethlehem to be born? (The Second Coming) V7:179
So long lives this, and this gives life to thee (Sonnet 18) V2:222
Somebody loves us all. (Filling Station) V12:57
Stand still, yet we will make him run (To His Coy Mistress) V5:277
startled into eternity (Four Mountain Wolves) V9:132
Still clinging to your shirt (My Papa's Waltz) V3:192
Stood up, coiled above his head, transforming all. (A Tall Man Executes a Jig) V12:229
Surely goodness and mercy shall follow me all the days of my life: and I will dwell in the house of the Lord for ever (Psalm 23) V4:103
syllables of an old order. (A Grafted Tongue) V12:93

T

Take any streetful of people buying clothes and groceries, cheering a hero or throwing confetti and blowing tin horns . . . tell me if the lovers are losers . . . tell me if any get more than the lovers . . . in the dust . . . in the cool tombs (Cool Tombs) V6:46
Than that you should remember and be sad. (Remember) V14:255
That then I scorn to change my state with Kings (Sonnet 29) V8:198
That when we live no more, we may live ever (To My Dear and Loving Husband) V6:228
That's the word. (Black Zodiac) V10:47
the bigger it gets. (Smart and Final Iris) V15:183
The bosom of his Father and his God (Elegy Written in a Country Churchyard) V9:74

The dance is sure (Overture to a Dance of Locomotives) V11:143
The eyes turn topaz. (Hugh Selwyn Mauberley) V16:30
The garland briefer than a girl's (To an Athlete Dying Young) V7:230
The guidon flags flutter gayly in the wind. (Cavalry Crossing a Ford) V13:50
The hands gripped hard on the desert (At the Bomb Testing Site) V8:3
The holy melodies of love arise. (The Arsenal at Springfield) V17:3
the knife at the throat, the death in the metronome (Music Lessons) V8:117
The Lady of Shalott." (The Lady of Shalott) V15:97
The lightning and the gale! (Old Ironsides) V9:172
the long, perfect loveliness of sow (Saint Francis and the Sow) V9:222
The Lord survives the rainbow of His will (The Quaker Graveyard in Nantucket) V6:159
The man I was when I was part of it (Beware of Ruins) V8:43
the quilts sing on (My Mother Pieced Quilts) V12:169
The red rose and the brier (Barbara Allan) V7:11
The self-same Power that brought me there brought you. (The Rhodora) V17:191
The shaft we raise to them and thee (Concord Hymn) V4:30
The sky became a still and woven blue. (Merlin Enthralled) V16:73
The spirit of this place (To a Child Running With Outstretched Arms in Canyon de Chelly) V11:173
The town again, trailing your legs and crying! (Wild Swans) V17:221
the unremitting space of your rebellion (Lost Sister) V5:217
The woman won (Oysters) V4:91
their guts or their brains? (Southbound on the Freeway) V16:158
There is the trap that catches noblest spiritts, that caught—they say—God, when he walked on earth (Shine, Perishing Republic) V4:162
there was light (Vancouver Lights) V8:246
They also serve who only stand and wait." ([On His Blindness] Sonnet 16) V3:262
They are going to some point true and unproven. (Geometry) V15:68
They rise, they walk again (The Heaven of Animals) V6:76
They think I lost. I think I won (Harlem Hopscotch) V2:93
This is my page for English B (Theme for English B) V6:194
This Love (In Memory of Radio) V9:145
Tho' it were ten thousand mile! (A Red, Red Rose) V8:152
Though I sang in my chains like the sea (Fern Hill) V3:92
Till human voices wake us, and we drown (The Love Song of J. Alfred Prufrock) V1:99
Till Love and Fame to nothingness do sink (When I Have Fears that I May Cease to Be) V2:295
To every woman a happy ending (Barbie Doll) V9:33
to glow at midnight. (The Blue Rim of Memory) V17:39
to its owner or what horror has befallen the other shoe (A Pièd) V3:16
To live with thee and be thy love. (The Nymph's Reply to the Shepherd) V14:241
To strive, to seek, to find, and not to yield (Ulysses) V2:279
To the moaning and the groaning of the bells (The Bells) V3:47
To the temple, singing. (In the Suburbs) V14:201

U

Undeniable selves, into your days, and beyond. (The Continuous Life) V18:51
Until Eternity. (The Bustle in a House) V10:62
unusual conservation (Chocolates) V11:17
Uttering cries that are almost human (American Poetry) V7:2

W

War is kind (War Is Kind) V9:253
watching to see how it's done. (I Stop Writing the Poem) V16:58
Went home and put a bullet through his head (Richard Cory) V4:117
Were not the one dead, turned to their affairs. (Out, Out—) V10:213
Were toward Eternity— (Because I Could Not Stop for Death) V2:27
What will survive of us is love. (An Arundel Tomb) V12:18
When I died they washed me out of the turret with a hose (The Death of the Ball Turret Gunner) V2:41
when they untie them in the evening. (Early in the Morning) V17:75
when you are at a party. (Social Life) V19:251
When you have both (Toads) V4:244
Where deep in the night I hear a voice (Butcher Shop) V7:43
Where ignorant armies clash by night (Dover Beach) V2:52
Which Claus of Innsbruck cast in bronze for me! (My Last Duchess) V1:166
which is not going to go wasted on me which is why I'm telling you about it (Having a Coke with You) V12:106
white ash amid funereal cypresses (Helen) V6:92
Who are you and what is your purpose? (The Mystery) V15:138
Wi' the Scots lords at his feit (Sir Patrick Spens) V4:177
Will hear of as a god." (How we Heard the Name) V10:167
Wind, like the dodo's (Bedtime Story) V8:33
With gold unfading, WASHINGTON! be thine. (To His Excellency General Washington) V13:213
with my eyes closed. (We Live by What We See at Night) V13:240
With the slow smokeless burning of decay (The Wood-Pile) V6:252
With what they had to go on. (The Conquerors) V13:67
Would scarcely know that we were gone. (There Will Come Soft Rains) V14:301

Y

Ye know on earth, and all ye need to know (Ode on a Grecian Urn) V1:180

You live in this, and dwell in lovers' eyes (Sonnet 55) V5:246

You may for ever tarry. (To the Virgins, to Make Much of Time) V13:226

you who raised me? (The Gold Lily) V5:127

you'll have understood by then what these Ithakas mean. (Ithaka) V19:114

Ref.
PN
1101
.P756

2004
v.19